A HANDBOOK OF MIDDLE ENGLISH

A HANDBOOK OF MIDDLE ENGLISH

BY

FERNAND MOSSÉ

TRANSLATED BY

JAMES A. WALKER

THE JOHNS HOPKINS UNIVERSITY PRESS
BALTIMORE AND LONDON

The Johns Hopkins University Press, Baltimore, Maryland 21218
The Johns Hopkins University Press Ltd., London

Library of Congress Catalog Card Number 68-17255
ISBN 0-8018-0478-7

Originally published, 1952
Second printing, 1961
Third printing, 1964
Fourth printing, 1966
Fifth printing, 1968
Sixth printing, 1975

FOREWORD

Professor Fernand Mossé of the Collège de France is at home in all the Germanic languages and literatures, but for many years he has paid particular attention to English. Since he is a medievalist he has interested himself first and foremost in the earlier periods, and since he is teacher as well as investigator he has long been concerned to smooth the path of students taking their first steps into a field far from our day and time. A few years ago this concern of his ripened into a work that won general recognition as soon as it came out: his *Manuel de l'Anglais du Moyen Age des Origines au XIVe Siècle.* In the *Manuel* the author's mastery of the material and talent for clear and orderly presentation are happily combined. In this work we have by far the best introduction to medieval English now available.

The present book is a translation of the second part of Mossé's *Manuel,* the part devoted to Middle English. It will be followed in due course, one hopes, by a translation of the Old English part. We of the English-speaking world are deeply indebted to French learning and to French civilization generally. This book adds to our debt, not least by lightening our labors. We welcome it the more because it bears witness to the lively interest that the French now take in our common medieval heritage, an interest that Professor Mossé himself has done so much to evoke.

KEMP MALONE

PREFACE

Design and Organization

This *Handbook* is designed for students of Middle English, and, as well, for those interested in English literature between 1100 and *ca.* 1400. Knowledge of Old English is desirable but not indispensable for using the book.

The aim here is to put into one book a complex of information usually available only in separate and scattered studies: a general grammar of Middle English; texts preceded by a literary introduction and a selected bibliography; MS data, a grammatical analysis and textual explication in the notes; and a glossary that lists all spelling variants except Orm's. Since the book is organized around only the texts that appear in it, the general grammar is drawn from them and presented in as simplified a form as possible without too much distorting the multiplicity of fact. But there should be no dissimulating the difficulties involved in such a procedure. The truth is that before the increasingly general adoption of one kind of London English as the common national literary, commercial, and administrative language from about 1300 on, there could be no grammar of Middle English. Until then we only have records of very local dialects, varying from town to town, and not even regional norms, let alone a national norm. And even for any one region changes were going on so rapidly that only the most striking features can be described. Further there is personal idiosyncrasy. Each author, and then each succeeding copyist, follows the tendencies peculiar to his own experience. A copyist from the North changes a Southern text to suit his own speech habits. An Anglo-Norman scribe does not hear some English phonemes (e. g. /hwič/ versus /wič/) and so deletes them or uses spelling conventions that do not fit English material. There were no contemporary grammarians or analysts of the language (except Orm), and there are few discernible traditions (except for the *St. Catherine* group and *Ancrene Wisse*). The grammati-

cal outline at the head of the notes for each text sketches the main
characteristics of the dialect recorded in that MS and interprets
the' spelling symbols. The larger grammar synthesizes these remarks, taking rather broad liberties with time and narrower
liberties with place. In this general grammar information is
purposely repeated, e. g. pronouns appear under their own heading
and again under syntax. The aim is convenience and reinforce-
ment in learning. Grateful acknowledgment is made to all the
larger works and special studies on which this part of the *Handbook* is based. A definitive grammar for Middle English by period
and place is the most serious lack in this field today.

Spelling and Sound: Symbol and Signal

The relation between the spelling symbols and the sound signals
of the spoken language presents another problem. For almost a
century the records of medieval languages have been treated as
dead and inert matter, and for years discussions have attributed
to the least graphic variant some subtle phonetic value. Applied
to Old and Middle English this myopia has resulted in absurdities
against which there must be some reaction even in an elementary
book. I do not pretend that there are not obscurities and un-
certainties, far from it, but I believe it is possible, in a large
measure, to get at the phonetic reality underlying the spelling
symbols and that this is worth doing for the 12th as well as for
the 14th century.

These spelling marks (called graphs) are Latin alphabetic
symbols standing for speech sounds. Such sounds are and were
signals to which members of the language community responded.
Such responses are the meaning of the signals. But the speech
signals have a surprising persistency. Individual phonemes have
changed very slowly, and the sequence of groups of the phonemes
(words and phrases), which is probably the primary signalling
device, has changed almost not at all. Responses to the signals,
the meanings of them, have changed much faster, reflecting all
social and psychological change. Thus language, or the speech
system, changes very little across time. Meaning, essentially a

psychological fact and not a language fact, changes a great deal. Our first aim is to get at the speech signals underlying the spelling. Our second is to get at the probable response elicited from members of the community when these signals reached them (mostly by ear, then, but also by eye). The latter is the meaning of the printed symbols which represent speech signals.

How to Read These Texts

Adults in our society have learned to by-pass the " alphabetical symbol(s)==a speech sound " relationship and have learned to respond directly to a complex of graphs mediated by the eye. This is a long learning process for many people and it produces a secondary result. First we respond in great strength to ortho-graphic variation. Second we all tend to think that marks on the page are the basic language and the sound system either secondary or nonexistent (this, of course is quite true for mathematical symbols and many Latin loans or new coinages). Alteration of the spelling disturbs us deeplee nd wee reegahrd such chanjz az chanjz in the langgwij. Spelling variations for the same speech vocable make us wallow in a graphic chaos because of these deeply learned responses to spelling variants (e. g. *bear/bare*). They are important to us. Insight into this behavior, so deeply learned as to be automatic, must be gained before these texts can be read.

a. Become as a little child again and read symbol for symbol aloud. Even giving the modern phonetic equivalent for the ME graphs will take the student a long way. But if the phonetic values listed in §§8-9 are put on a card and constantly referred to, the speech system of ME can be approximated. If you suppress your response to the eye patterns and listen to your vocalization, the strangest looking texts will begin to make surprising sense without a great reference to the glossary.

b. But there is another difficulty. The ME graph may be a homograph for a vocable still used in Modern English. The tendency here will be to make the immediate modern semantic response to this set of symbols, e. g. ME *make,* which unfor-

tunately should elicit the response we now make to *mate, wife*, etc.
If, however, that word had been read aloud as [mak(ə)], the
tendency to respond to the eye-pattern would have been sub-
stantially decreased.

   c. The phonetic resemblance to modern speech signals, especially
the constancy of the sequence of the sounds despite their individual distortion to modern ears, will enable the student to
identify what curious spelling ordinarily conceals. Once he has
made this crucial identification he is free to guess whether the
meaning of the vocable has changed between then and now. If
the guess works, very good, if not, there is the glossary (always
being on the lookout for the traps discussed under " b " above:
grant merci is not the equivalent of 'great mercy' or 'grant
mercy' but of 'many thanks').

The Glossary and the Problem of Meaning

   The glossary is as complete as possible, listing all variant
spellings of the same vocable. It is somewhat sketchy in supplying
modern equivalents of the ME graphs and vocables. It is expected,
indeed practically required, that the student continually consult
the great and monumental OED.[1] There he will find a wide range
of alternate responses and the contexts in which they appear. A
considerable effort has been made in listing the glossary forms to
facilitate this cross reference. The system is explained at the
head of the glossary. Only by such reference can the student
build up the sufficient reservoir of information that makes possible
a wide range of alternate responses, and then a very narrow range
of statistically most probable responses for any one line. The
other method of building up meaningful responses is to read widely
in the social and cultural history of the time—especially the

---

[1] *A New English Dictionary on Historical Principles* edited by James A. H.
MURRAY and others, Oxford, 1888 *et seq.* was reissued in 1933 with a new
title page reading *The Oxford English Dictionary.* This was unfortunate, but
so it remains. The proper abbreviation, today, is thus *OED*; older references
use *NED*.

religious—and some of the political. The literary history is, of course, assumed as basic to all these others. Failure to use the OED will not be fatal but will give the student a very wrong view of the depth and richness of the material he is reading. Remember that a deficiency in meaning most probably lies in you and by no means necessarily in the text.[2] Meaning does not lie in language but in people.

The Texts

The choice of texts was difficult. The compromise between literary interest and linguistic usefulness forced the exclusion of many worthwhile documents. The hope is that each text, with a few notable exceptions, serves both purposes. Thus there is a sample of all dialects, and at the same time, of all literary genres. Since translation and imitation for the ME period, as for the Elizabethan, was a major part of the creative activity in literature, sources for such translations, when known, have been added below the ME text for a fruitful comparison of how English literature was shaping its own course despite the originals. Successive translations of the same documents have also been included to show literary and linguistic development.

Each text follows some one MS faithfully except where the latter is clearly corrupt. Thus very few variants (of interest only to very advanced students) will be found. Punctuation and capitalization are also modern impositions. So is the use of *i, j, u* and *v*. These modernizations are graphic only, designed for easier modern reading, and do not distort the linguistic evidence. Medieval scribal conventions are a later study. Facsimiles of five MSS permit excursions into palaeography. Chronology (always open to question) was chosen as the base of the order of presentation. This is arbitrary, but so would be organization by dialect

---

[2] For a further discussion of reading older material for meaning see "Theory of Reading" (pp. 279-291) in Martin Joos and Frederick R. WHITE-SELL, *Middle High German Courtly Reader*, University of Wisconsin Press, 1951. For an insight into medieval rhetorical traditions and 'levels of meaning' see the first two chapters of the ROBERTSON-HUPPÉ book listed under the Piers Plowman selection (no. XXI).

area, and this last raises at least as many questions of fact as do
the dates.

Acknowledgments

This *Handbook* follows many like it, and I have profited from
the work of my predecessors. I acknowledge this large debt,
apparent to any specialist, to those who have worked in the great
field of Middle English. I owe many thanks to those who read
the French edition, to those who reviewed it and suggested many
of the improvements incorporated here. I thank equally Professor
Stefán Einarsson and Professor Kemp Malone who felt the book
worthy of an English edition. And last but not least, Professor
James A. Walker, who volunteered as a translator and has taken
the trouble to render the French as faithfully as possible, to read
the proof, and to suggest many welcome changes in detail.

FERNAND MOSSÉ

July 15, 1952
Paris, France

TABLE OF CONTENTS

II

TEXTS

PART ONE. 12th CENTURY

TABLE OF CONTENTS

FACSIMILES

ABBREVIATIONS, PRINTING SYMBOLS, REFERENCES TO SELECTIONS

A =	accusative or adjunct (syntax)	ModE	Modern English (1500 to present)
acc	accusative	ModGer	Modern German (current)
adj(s)	adjective(s)	MS(S)	manuscript(s)
adv(s)	adverb(s)	N	North
Archiv	see bibl.	N, nom	nominative
auxil	auxiliary	N, Nt, neut	neuter
bibl.	bibliography	*NED*	see *OED*
ca	circa	O	object (syntax)
cent	century	OE	Old English (600-1150)
CGmc	Common Germanic	*OED*	*Oxford English Dictionary*
comp(ar)	comparative	OF	Old French (mostly Anglo-Norman)
Cp.	compare		
D, dat	dative	OHG	Old High German
dem(on)	demonstrative	ON	Old Norse (mostly Old Icelandic)
E	East		
EME	early Middle English (1050-1200)	OSax	Old Saxon
		part	participle
EM, EMid(l)	East Midland(s)	pers	person, personal
eModE	Early Modern English (1450-1600)	pl	plural
		PMLA	see bibl.
EPNSoc	English Place Name Society (Publ. of)	PN	place name
		poss	possessive
F, fem	feminine	pp	past participle
F	French	p., pp.	page(s)
G, gen	genitive	pres (part)	present (participle)
Gmc	Germanic	pret, prt	preterit
Ger	German	pron	pronoun
HOE	*Handbook of Old English* Johns Hopkins Press	REM	REMARK
		RES	see bibl.
id.	*idem* 'the same'	S	subject (syntax)
IE	Indo-European	S	South
ind(ic)	indicative	SE	south-east
imp(er)	imperative	sg	singular
IPA	International Phonetic Association	str	strong
		subj	subjunctive
JEGP	see bibl.	super	superlative
lit.	literally	SW	south-west
l(l).	line(s)	v.	verse
M, masc	masculine	V, vb	verb (syntax), verb (part of speech)
ME	Middle English (1150-1500)		
		W	West
Mid(l)	Midland(s)	WGmc	West Germanic
MLN	see bibl.	wk	weak
MLR	see bibl.	Wo	Worcestershire

PRINTING SYMBOLS

[] 1. encloses IPA symbols, in roman type.
2. In texts, encloses dropped words or letters.
3. In translations in notes, often indicates the ME word repeated for orientation.

( ) In translations, words added to original for fuller explanation.

⟨ ⟩ In texts, words or letters added by editor-author.

>   appears later as, presumably "evolves into" or "becomes".

<   appears earlier as, presumably "develops from".

§ (§) = paragraph(s).

*   placed before a word or form indicates a form reconstructed by analogy; placed after a word indicates a non-attested form. Words added to the text by editor-author are post-starred in glossary.

+   followed by, added to.

·· 1. as a phonetic mark, indicates central vowel [ö], [ü] as opposed to front [e], [ɪ] or back [u].
2. as a metrical mark, indicates pronounced vowel.

—   macron over a single letter indicates a "long" vowel; over a digraph (two letters) indicates the digraph does not represent a diphthong and also indicates length of the vowel represented by the digraph. $\bar{a}, \bar{o}; \overline{ea}, \overline{ou}$ etc. vs $\breve{e}a, \breve{o}u$.

‿   breve placed over a letter indicates a "short" vowel: $\breve{e}, \breve{i}, \breve{y}$.

~   tilde placed over a letter indicates nasal quality, usually vowels: $\tilde{a}, \tilde{e}$ etc.

þ [þ] as in *thin*, also thus in texts except when intervocalic, then [ð].

ð [ð] as in *then*, except in texts where it interchanges with þ.

ʋ   bilabial voiced spirant, like *u* in South German *Qual*.

g   velar voiced spirant, like *g* in North German *Wagen*.

[x] as in German *ach*.

[ç] as in German *ich*.

ċ   in texts = [č] of *church*.

sċ in texts = [š] of *shirt*.

ċġ in texts = [ǧ] of *George*.

ǧ   in texts and glossary = [ǧ].

ġ   in texts and glossary = [j] of *yes*.

ḥ = non-etymological *h*.

[ŋ] IPA symbol for sound in *sing*.

[ʍ] (upside down *w*) = voiceless [w], initial of *white* in Northern Britain and Irish dialects and in some few American dialects.

ẹ = close *e* in contrast to following:

ẹ = open *e*.

ę   in verse, is silent in contrast to:

ë   in verse, which is to be pronounced [ə].

ọ   open *o*.

å   open *o* before a nasal.

ọ   close *o*.

x̣   unaccented syllable (in metrics).

x́   accented syllable (id.).

Λ   pause (id.).

ˈ   a thin vertical line indicates ˈstress on the following syllable. See Kenyon and Knott, *A Pronouncing Dictionary of American English*.

REFERENCE TO THE TEXTS

The Middle English selections are referred to in two ways:

1. When the whole selection is at issue, XX; or a complete part of a selection XX 2 (part 2 of no. XX).
2. When a single line is at issue, 20/71 (line 71 of no. XX) or 20₂/15 (line 15 of section 2 of no. XX).

BIBLIOGRAPHY

I. REFERENCE WORKS

The fundamental work is the following:

J. E. WELLS. *A Manual of the Writings in Middle English 1050-1400*, New Haven, Conn., 1916 (with nine supplements to 1945).

Good bibliographies will also be found in:

The Cambridge Bibliography of English Literature, edited by F. W. BATESON, Cambridge, 1940.

W. L. RENWICK and HAROLD ORTON. *The Beginnings of English Literature to Skelton 1509* (Introductions to English Literature, vol. I), 2nd ed., London, 1952 [pp. 253 ff. contain a reasonably selected but quite current bibliography for Middle English].

For all questions of language and grammar refer to:

A. G. KENNEDY. *A Bibliography of the Writings on the English Language from the Beginning of Printing to the End of 1922*, Cambridge (Mass.), 1927.

The preceding works should be supplemented by the following annual collections:

Modern Humanities Research Association. Annual Bibliography of the English Language and Literature, Cambridge, 1921 and ff.

The Year's Work in English Studies, edd. SIDNEY LEE, F. S. BOAS et alii, Oxford, 1919 and ff.

For the poetry see:

CARLETON BROWN and R. H. ROBBINS. *An Index of Middle English Verse*, New York, 1943.

Finally for history see:

CHARLES GROSS. *The Sources and Literature of English History from the earliest Times to about 1485*, rev. ed., New York, 1931 (in particular pp. 499 f.).

II. GRAMMAR

There is no complete and exhaustive grammar of Middle English. Several, which remain unfinished, are still important. These are:

LORENZ MORSBACH. *Mittelenglische Grammatik.* Erste Hälfte, Halle, 1896.

RICHARD JORDAN. *Handbuch der mittelenglischen Grammatik.* I. *Teil: Lautlehre*, 2nd ed. rev., Heidelberg, 1934.

and

K. LUICK. *Historische Grammatik der englischen Sprache*, Leipzig, 1913 and f. [unfinished; the published part is an extremely detailed study of the sound system and its development].

Some important information will be found in:

RENÉ HUCHON. *Histoire de la langue anglaise, Tome II, De la Conquête normande a l'introduction de l'Imprimerie*, Paris, 1930.

and in:

H. C. WYLD. *A Short History of English*, 3rd ed., London, 1927.
KARL BRUNNER. *Die englische Sprache, Ihre geschichtliche Entwicklung*, Halle, 1950-1951, 2 vols.

The only complete précis are:

MAX KALUZA. *Historische Grammatik der englischen Sprache. 2. Teil: Lautlehre Formenlehre des Mittel- und Neuenglischen*, 2nd ed., Berlin, 1907 (Middle English grammar, pp. 1-203).
JOSEPH and ELIZABETH WRIGHT. *An Elementary Middle English Grammar*, Oxford, 1928.
E. E. WARDALE. *An Introduction to Middle English*, London, 1937.
KARL BRUNNER. *Abriss der mittelenglischen Grammatik*, 2nd ed., Halle, 1948.
M. M. ROSEBOROUGH. *An Outline of Middle English Grammar*, New York, 1938.

For syntax there is no work that surveys the total problem for all of Middle English. Besides the historical grammars one may consult the following books:

LEON KELLNER. *Historical Outlines of English Syntax*, 2nd ed., London, 1905.
EUGEN EINENKEL. *Geschichte der englischen Sprache. II. Historische Syntax*, 3rd ed., Strasbourg, 1916.

III. DICTIONARIES

A complete dictionary of Middle English is in preparation under the auspices of the University of Michigan at Ann Arbor and under the direction of HANS KURATH and SHERMAN KUHN. Meanwhile the best dictionary remains:

A New English Dictionary on Historical Principles, edited by JAMES MURRAY and others, Oxford, 1888-1933 [*OED*].

See as well:

EDUARD MÄTZNER. *Altenglische Sprachproben nebst ein Wörterbuch. II. Wörterbuch*, Berlin, 1878 and f. [unfinished; contains vocabulary up to *misbileven*].
A. L. MAYHEW and W. W. SKEAT. *A Concise Dictionary of Middle English from A. D. 1150 to 1580*, Oxford, 1888.
F. H. STRATMANN. *A Middle-English Dictionary*, A new Edition, revised and enlarged by HENRY BRADLEY, Oxford, 1891 [antiquated].

IV. ETYMOLOGY

For all the older part of the vocabulary the *OED* is the best source of etymological information.

V. DIALECTOLOGY

J. MORSBACH. *Über den Ursprung der neuenglischen Schriftsprache*, Heilbronn, 1888.
B. A. MACKENZIE. *The Early London Dialect*, Oxford, 1928.
J. P. OAKDEN. *Alliterative Poetry in Middle English. Vol. I. The Dialectal and Metrical Survey*, Manchester, 1930.
R. W. CHAMBERS and M. DAUNT. *A Book of London English 1384-1425*, London, 1931.
S. MOORE, S. B. MEECH, and H. WHITEHALL. *Middle English Dialect Characteristics and Dialect Boundaries*, Ann Arbor, 1935.

For studies of dialect details, refer to:

H. R. PATCH and R. J. MENNER. 'A Bibliography of Middle English Dialects' in *Studies in Philology*, XX (1923), 479-95.

VI. LITERARY HISTORY

ALOIS BRANDL. *Mittelenglische Literatur 1150-1500* (in the 1st ed. of *Grundriss der germanischen Philologie of* H. PAUL, II, i, pp. 607-718).

The Cambridge History of English Literature, ed. by A. W. WARD and A. R. WALLER, Vol. I and II, Cambridge, 1907.

B. TEN BRINK. *History of English Literature*, Vol. I and II, London, 1883-1896.

J. J. JUSSERAND. *A Literary History of the English People*, London, 1905.

W. H. SCHOFIELD. *English Literature from the Norman Conquest to Chaucer*, London, 1906.

H. HECHT and L. L. SCHÜCKING. *Die englische Literatur im Mittelalter*, Potsdam, 1930.

W. P. KER. *English Literature, Mediaeval*, London, 1912 .[Small book published in the *Home University Library*. Rapid but excellent survey].

R. M. WILSON. *Early Middle English Literature*, London, 1939 [concise and quite up to date].

G. KANE. *Middle English Literature, A Critical Study of the Romances, the Religious Lyrics, Piers Plowman*, London, 1951.

L. A. HIBBARD. *Medieval Romance in England. A Study of the Sources and Analogues of the Non-Cyclic Metrical Romances*, New York, 1924.

J. P. OAKDEN. *Alliterative Poetry in Middle English. Vol. II: A Survey of the Traditions*, Manchester, 1935.

H. GLUNZ. *Die Literarästhetik des europäischen Mittelalters*, Bochum, 1937.

See as well J. E. WELLS' *Manual* mentioned above and also:

A. C. BAUGH. "Middle English Literature," in *A Literary History of England* by A. C. BAUGH, KEMP MALONE et al., New York, 1948.

G. K. ANDERSON. "Old and Middle English Literature from the Beginnings to 1485," in *A History of English Literature*, ed. HARDIN CRAIG, New York, 1950.

VII. HISTORIES

M. BATESON. *Medieval England*, 1066-1350, London, 1905.

H. W. C. DAVIS. *Medieval England*, Oxford, 1924.

C. G. CRUMP and E. F. JACOB. *The Legacy of the Middle Ages*, Oxford, 1927.

G. G. COULTON. *Medieval Panorama: The English Scene from Conquest to Reformation*, Cambridge, 1938.

A. L. POOLE. *From Domesday Book to Magna Carta 1087-1216*, Oxford, 1951.

J. J. JUSSERAND. *Wayfaring Life in the Middle Ages*, London, 1889 and later printings.

L. F. SALZMAN. *English Life in the Middle Ages*, London, 1926.

G. M. TREVELYAN. *England in the Age of Wycliffe*, London, 1899 and later printings.

G. R. OWST. *Preaching in Medieval England*, Cambridge, 1926. *Literature and Pulpit in Medieval England*, Cambridge, 1933.

Chaucer's World compiled by E. RICKERT, ed. by C. C. OLSON and M. M. CROW, New York, 1948 [rich collection of contemporary documents].

VIII. ANTHOLOGIES

R. MORRIS and W. W. SKEAT. *Specimens of Early English.* Part I, 1150-1300, Part II, 1298-1393, Oxford, 1898 [a trifle dated].

O. F. EMERSON. *A Middle English Reader.* New and Revised Edition, 1915 [with a good grammatical introduction].

A. S. COOK. *A Literary Middle English Reader*, Boston, 1915.

JOSEPH HALL. *Selections from Early Middle English*, 1130-1250. 2 vol. Oxford, 1920 [excellent].

BRUCE DICKINS and R. M. WILSON. *Early Middle English Texts*, Cambridge, 1951 [excellent].

K. SISAM. *Fourteenth Century Verse and Prose* (with a *Middle English Vocabulary* by J. R. TOLKIEN). Oxford, 1921 [excellent].

A. BRANDL and O. ZIPPEL. *Mittelenglische Sprach- und Literaturproben*, 2nd ed., Berlin, 1927.

R. W. CHAMBERS and M. DAUNT. *A Book of London English 1389-1425.* Oxford, 1931 [excellent].

G. GREGORY SMITH. *Specimens of Middle Scots*, Edinburgh, 1902.

W. E. FRENCH and C. B. HALE. *Middle English Metrical Romances*, New York, 1930.

IX. TRANSLATIONS

Besides those indicated in the headnotes a complete list of modern translations can be found in:

C. P. FARRAR and A. P. EVANS. *Bibliography of English Translations from Medieval Sources*, New York, 1946.

X. SOME PERIODICALS

ANGLIA, *Zeitschrift für englische Philologie*, Halle, 1877 and f.

ARCHIV FÜR DAS STUDIUM DER NEUEREN SPRACHEN AND LITERATUREN, Elberfeld, then Braunschweig, 1846 and f. [Archiv].

ENGLISCHE STUDIEN, *Organ für englische Philologie*, Heilbronn, then Leipzig, 1877-1943.

ENGLISH AND GERMANIC STUDIES, Birmingham, 1947 and f.

ENGLISH STUDIES, Amsterdam, 1919 and f.

JOURNAL OF ENGLISH AND GERMANIC PHILOLOGY, Bloomington, Evanston, then Urbana, 1897 and f. [JEGP].

LEEDS STUDIES IN ENGLISH AND KINDRED LANGUAGES, Leeds, 1932 and f.

LONDON MEDIAEVAL STUDIES, London, 1937 and f.

MEDIUM ÆVUM, Oxford, 1932 and f.

MODERN LANGUAGE NOTES, Baltimore, 1886 and f. [MLN].

THE MODERN LANGUAGE REVIEW, Cambridge, 1905 and f. [MLR].

PUBLICATIONS OF THE MODERN LANGUAGE ASSOCIATION OF AMERICA, Baltimore, Cambridge, Mass., then New York, 1884 and f. [PMLA].

THE REVIEW OF ENGLISH STUDIES, London, 1925 and f. [RES].

SPECULUM, *A Journal of Mediaeval Studies*, The Mediaeval Academy of America, Cambridge, Mass., 1926 and f.

INTRODUCTION

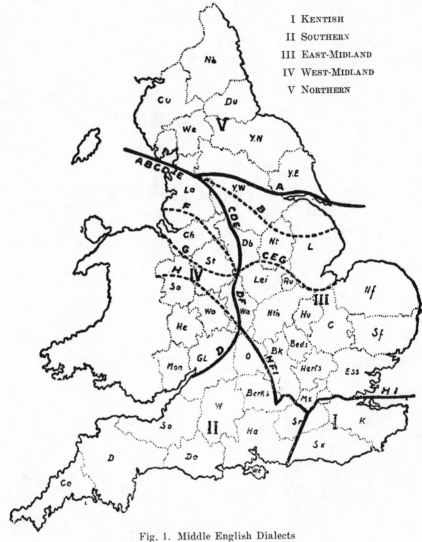

I Kentish
II Southern
III East-Midland
IV West-Midland
V Northern

Fig. 1. Middle English Dialects
(according to Moore-Meech-Whitehall)

INTRODUCTION

Middle English

§ 1. It is conventional to call " Middle English " the English spoken and written in Great Britain between about 1150 and 1500, that is, during the period intermediate between Old English (OE) and Modern English (ModE).

To be sure, these dates are only convenient reference points (cp. HOE § 1, REM. II) : under any normal development the evolution of a language knows no break in continuity. But, if one compares the totality of traits that characterize the texts written in the period called " Middle English " with those of the preceding period, one is struck by certain constant differences :

1. Finally and in inflectional endings the vowels (insofar as they survive) have been uniformly levelled to $e[\varepsilon/\partial]$ (cp. § 35) : OE *stānas*, ME *stǫnes* ' stones ', OE *nosu*, ME *nǫse* ' nose ', OE *drifon*, ME *driven* ' we (you, they) drove '.

2. This phonetic levelling brought about a profound alteration and a great simplification in inflection (cp. § 53).

3. From this there resulted a tendency (already begun in OE) to resort to analytic constructions and to make use of prepositions instead of case endings. Cp. for example, these two translations of Luke XV. 15 : " adhaesit uni civium regionis illius " :

Old English : [*hē*] *folgode ānum burg-sittendum menn ðæs rices* (HOE 1/48) ;

Wyclif : [*hē*] *clęvede* tō *ǫǫn* of *þe citizeins* of *þat còntrē* (24/8).

4. Finally, the vocabulary swarms with French words (a result of the Norman Conquest) and Scandinavian words (resulting from the colonization of the Danelaw). In a line of Chaucer such as :

> Tō *tāke the botel thēr the poyson was* ($27_{4B}/886$)

only the grammatical words (*tō, the, thēr, was*) are native, *tāke* is Scandinavian, *botel* and *poyson* are French.

REMARK. — There is no doubt that from before the Norman Conquest, spoken and colloquial Old English contained in embryo the sounds and forms that

1

are typical of Middle English. Cp. on this point Kemp MALONE, " When did Middle English begin? " *Curme Volume of Linguistic Studies* (Language Monographs, No. VII, 1930), 110-17, and F. P. MAGOUN, JR., " Colloquial Old and Middle English," *Harvard Studies and Notes in Philology and Literature,* 19 (1937), 167-73.

The Dialects

§ **2.** From a grammatical point of view what one is accustomed to call " Middle English " is only a convenient entity. In point of fact, it is only towards the end of the 14th century that we see the language of London—the language of the Chancery, of the court, and of great poets like Chaucer—assume throughout the country the form of a common written and literary language. Previously, only dialects existed, local speech-forms that changed from one town to the next. Since there was no norm, each writer, each copyist, employed spontaneously the speech of his own region without giving any thought to what might be said elsewhere (people travelled enough to be conscious of what Chaucer has called " the great diversity of English." cp. also what John of Trevisa says, 26/9 ff.). It is no exaggeration to say that " every writer was largely a law unto himself (H. C. Wyld)."

Roughly speaking, however, five varieties, five dialects of Middle English can be distinguished, geographically distributed as shown in Fig. 1:

In the South-East *Kentish* (I);

In the South-West *Southern* (II);

In the middle of the country, the Midlands, the *East-Midland dialect* (III) and *West-Midland dialect* (IV);

Finally the *Northern dialect* (V) which extends up into Scotland (*Scotch*).

REMARKS. — I. It is possible, in a strict sense, to distinguish three further subdivisions in the East-Midland dialect and four in the West-Midland (in Fig. 1, separated by dotted lines).

II. Note the position of London, the capital (South-East Midlands), at the boundary of Kentish and not far from that of the South-Western dialect.

III. If the student compares the boundaries of these dialects with those of Old English (HOE, Fig. 1), he will note that the dialectal areas do not coincide. The most important innovation is, considering the unity of Mercian, the subdivision into East and West-Midlands.

IV. One gets these dialect divisions by superimposing the approximate areas of extension of the most striking phonetic and morphological phenomena (taking account of the topography and the lessons of history), namely:

the phonetic treatment of OE *ā* (line A, fig. 3, cp. § 27), of OE *ǎ* (line D, fig. 2, cp. § 25), of OE *y* and *ēo* (line F, figs. 4 and 5, cp. §§ 29 and 30), and of OE *f-* (line I, fig. 6, cp. § 44.1).

the form of the verb *shall* (line C, cp. § 102 REM).

These dialectal areas are the ones established by S. MOORE, S. B. MEECH and H. WHITEHALL in their important "Middle English Dialect Characteristics and Dialect Boundaries," *University of Michigan Publications, Language and Literature,* 13 (1935), 1-60.

Another dialect map for Middle English with slightly different boundaries will be found in J. P. OAKDEN, *Alliterative Poetry in Middle English,* I. *The Dialectal and Metrical Survey* (Manchester, 1930).

It is impossible to insist too strongly on the approximate and provisional character of these areas, which have only an indicative value.

V. One should remember that in Great Britain in the west and north in the Middle Ages English ran up against the Celtic tongues more than in our own day: Gaelic in the north and west of Scotland, Welsh in Wales, and Cornish (today extinct) in Cornwall in the south-western part of the country.

§ 3. A grammatical survey of Middle English can then, apart from the common tendencies indicated in § 1, only be a juxtaposition of dialectal traits or of the grammar of authors. Taken as a basis for description, the language of Chaucer would give a very inexact idea of the variety—and even the uncertainty—of forms and sounds during a period of about three hundred and fifty years. The elements of grammar which follow have been made as succinct as possible. The introductions at the head of the notes dealing with each text will give the reader the necessary grammatical information for these texts. The student will see to what an extent, apart from a few exceptional cases, the localization of literary texts and the determination of dialects is still an imprecise and delicate matter.

§ 4. It is accordingly with reservations that we make the following dialectal division for the texts published in this *Handbook*:

Northern Dialect

XXII. J. BARBOUR, *The Bruce* (Scotch).

XVI. RICHARD ROLLE OF HAMPOLE; XVII. L. MINOT; XX. Alliterative *Morte Arthure* (original in North-West-Midlands); XXIX. *Towneley Mysteries*.

Midland Dialects

West-Midlands: III. *Ancrene Wisse* (Herefordshire?); IV. *Sawles Warde* (ibidem); V. LAWMAN, *The Brut*; XVIII. *Sir Gawain and the Green Knight* (Lancashire or Derby?); XIX. *The Pearl* (ibidem); XXI. W. LANGLAND, *Piers Plowman* (South-West, impure).

North-East-Midlands: I. *Peterborough Chronicle* (Northampton); VII. *Ormulum*; XII. *Havelok the Dane* (very impure); XIV. ROBERT MANNYNG OF BRUNNE (southern Lincolnshire).

South-East Midlands: XXIII. *Mandeville's Travels*; XXIV. WYCLIF.

London: XXV. *The Mercers' Petition* (Middlesex); XXVII. G. CHAUCER; XXVIII. J. GOWER (Kentish influences?).

Kentish

IX. *Kentish Sermons* (impure); XV. MICHEL OF NORTHGATE; *Aȝenbite of Inwyt* (The Prick of Conscience) (Canterbury).

Southern Dialects

VI. *The Owl and the Nightingale* (Surrey?); VIII. *King Horn* (ibidem?); XI. *Proclamation of Henry III* (with influences from the East-Midlands).

II. *Poema Morale*; X. *The Vox and the Wolf* (impure).

XIII. 2. TH. DE HALES, *Luve Ron*; XIII. 3. *Judas*; XXVI. JOHN OF TREVISA (impure).

GRAMMAR

PART ONE

THE SOUNDS

CHAPTER ONE

ALPHABET, PRONUNCIATION, ACCENTUATION

Handwriting

§ 5. Just as in OE, the handwriting of the texts in ME is based on that of the Latin manuscripts of the Middle Ages, carried into the Germanic countries by Christianity. But the insular writing of OE, introduced by Irish monks, was succeeded from about 1150 on by the Carolingian minuscule, at once more angular and in which thick strokes and thin strokes are more sharply contrasted (cp. the plates in this volume with those in HOE). It was only towards 1400 that the cursive minuscule called the *Chancery hand* appeared, which is the origin of modern handwriting.

Alphabet

§ 6. After the Norman Conquest the scribes continued at first to employ the alphabet previously in use:

a, æ, b, c, d, e, f, ȝ, h, i, k, l, m, n, o, p, r,
s, t, þ, ð, u, p, x, y.

But on the one hand, the phonetic value of a certain number of these letters changed, also that of digraphs and trigraphs; on the other, additions and modifications were being introduced.

By the end of the 14th century this alphabet had become:

a, b, c, d, e, f, g, (ȝ), h, i, k, l
m, n, o, p, q, r, s, t, (þ), u, v, w, x, y, z

from which ȝ and þ were about to disappear, replaced by *y* and *th*.

7

Spelling

§ 7. The spelling in ME manuscripts rests partly on OE traditions and partly on French or Latin habits introduced' by Anglo-Norman scribes. From this point of view the language is characterized by its lack of regularity; it was not until after the close of the 14th century that a norm tended to be established. During the greater part of this period the manuscripts were frequently copied by one or more scribes speaking a different dialect from that of the text they were copying, sometimes even by Anglo-Normans but little familiar with English. This explains the very great value of such autograph manuscripts as those of the *Ormulum* (VII, see pl. 2) or the *Aʒenbite of Inwyt* (XV, see pl. 4), or even certain very good MSS as that of *Ancrene Wisse* (III, see pl. 1) or of the Ellesmere MS of the *Canterbury Tales* (XXVII/4, see pl. 5), and finally, certain Public Records which have an air of authenticity, like the royal *Proclamation* of 1258 (XI) or the *Mercers' Petition* (XXV).

The special introduction to each text put in at the head of the notes for each selection provides detailed information. But the student will do well to read and re-read the general remarks which follow and to master this information if he is not to be put off by the inconsistent appearance of the texts.

§ 8. The letters æ, ð and ρ (*wynn*) gradually disappeared; æ was replaced by *ea, a* or *e*; þ was substituted for ð, with which, to all intents and purposes, it did double duty. ρ (called ' wynn ' or ' wen ') was replaced by *u, uu* and finally by *w* which came from the Continent. In its turn, towards 1400, þ gradually went out of use and *th* was normally written in its place. After the Norman Conquest a newcomer, the letter *g*, replaced in the alphabet the OE ʒ (called ' yogh ') but only as a stop, at least in native words: one wrote *gadering* ' gathering ' and not *ʒaderinʒ, god* ' good ' not *ʒod*, etc. In a slightly modified form (ʒ) this letter ' yogh ' continued to be used during a great part of the ME period as a velar and palatal spirant; for instance, the writing shows *ʒer* ' year ', *ʒare* ' ready ', *ʒong* ' young ', *riʒt* ' right ', *broʒte* ' brought ', *þurʒ* ' through '. But after 1300 this ' yogh ' was replaced initially by *y* (*yeer, yare, yong*), elsewhere by *gh* (*right, brought, þurgh*), *at first without modification of the phonetic value.*

REMARKS. — I. *th* instead of *þ* already appears in the *Peterborough Chronicle* (*thrǫte* 1/35, *thŭ* 1/45, *ōther* 1/55, etc.); but this digraph had no vogue until near the end of the 14th century, when it came in again because *þ* and *y* had assumed shapes that ran the risk of being confused with each other. To distinguish them it was necessary to overdot the *y* (with the value of *þ*).

II. The scribe of the *Peterborough Chronicle* everywhere replaces *ȝ* with *g*, but this is an exceptional fact. For the use of the letter *g*, the difference between Old and Middle English does not always appear in the printed texts because the OE *ȝ* of the MSS is generally transcribed *g*. For this feature examine reproductions of MSS.

III. The letter *g*, imported from the Continent by Anglo-Norman scribes, remained in French words like *gentil, message* with its value [*dž*]. By analogy it was used to write the same sound in native words, thus *segge* 'man' 21₂/160 (< OE *seċġ*) pronounced [scdžə]. This sound will be written *ǧ* in this book: *seǧǧe, heǧǧe,* [hɛdžə], *riǧǧe, ǧentil, enǧel.*

IV. In the North-West-Midland dialect (MS. of *Sir Gawain and the Green Knight*), the Northern dialect (*Morte Arthure*) and Scots (J. BARBOUR), the letter *ȝ* was equally used at the end of words with the value *z* or *s*. Thus, *cóntrayeȝ* 18/713, *he rydeȝ* 18/714 is written for *cóntrayes, hē rȳdes*. To avoid any confusion these are transcribed *cóntrayez, hē rȳdez*.

V. In Scots *ȝh* was frequently written instead of *ȝ*, for example *ȝhe* 'you' 22/441 and passim, *failȝhe* 'to fail' 22/231.

VI. In Scots (BARBOUR) the letter *β* was used indistinguishably in the manuscripts for final *s, ss: pryβ* 22/239, *rayβ* 22/414.

VII. Alongside *ght* the cluster *ht* was also used, survival of an OE tradition; thus *þohte* 6/940, *riht* 6/950 (alongside *riȝt* 6/969). In the north, *cht* was preferred (*thoucht* 22/426, *richt* 22/454), a spelling which has to a certain extent been carried into modern Scots.

VIII. *u* instead of *w* was not rare in the 12th and 13th centuries: *suikes* 'traitors' 1/11, *suoren* 'sworn' 1/14, *tuo* 'two' 10/73, *bituene* 'between' 13₄/33, etc. The Anglo-Norman scribes even wrote (and pronounced?) *v* for *w*, thus *vise* 6/961 for *wise*.

§ 9. The letter *k*, which was not unknown to the English scribes before the Conquest, became more frequent. It was fairly regularly used before letters like *i, e, n, l* where *c* would have produced in the writing a succession of downstrokes or 'minims' difficult to distinguish. One wrote *kepe* 'keep', *kille* 'kill', *kinde* 'kind' (but *care* 'care' rather than *kare, cou* 'cow' rather than *ku*), *kniht* (alongside *cniht*), *knave, kloke*. In a medial or final position we find currently *k, c, ck, kk*.

§ 10. To express certain vocalic sounds OE resorted to various groups of letters, in particular, *ea, eo* (cp. HOE §§ 12-13). These spellings persist in ME, only they no longer represent diphthongs but

simple sounds: *ĕa* indicates the sound *ę̄* (as in *deaƌ* 'death', *eadi*
'blessed') even when this *ę̄* does not derive from OE *ēa* (thus *eapple*
'apple', OE *æppel, eaver* 'ever' OE *æfre*); *eo* indicates the sound
[ö]: thus *eode* 'went', *leof* 'dear', *beon* 'to be'. It is also used for
the same sound [ö] derived from the *ue* of French words (*people,
preove* 'proof'). These are marked *ēa, ēo, dēaƌ, pēople*.

French Traditions

§ 11. Anglo-Norman scribes, when they copied English manuscripts, rapidly introduced into them certain of their practices.

For instance, they had the practice of using the letter *u* to write
the sound [ü] which OE scribes wrote with the letter *y*; they generalized this procedure. They wrote, then, *sunne* 'sin' (OE *synn*), *murþe*
'mirth' (OE *myrgƌ*). This is shown as *ü*: *sünne, mürþe*. In spite
of this the letter *y* was preserved and frequently used but only as a
variant of *i* to make the reading of MSS easier: *mynyster* was clearer
in the writing of the time than *minister* where the first four letters
would have formed an ambiguous series of minims; but there is no
difference in pronunciation between *paradys* and *paradis*, between
shyne and *shine*, between *y-falle* and *i-falle*, etc.

The letter *o* was used, from about 1250, to indicate the sound [u]
when in the vicinity of the downstroke letters *m, n, u, v, w*. They
wrote *comen* 'to come' as well as *cumen, sonne* 'sun' as well as
sunne, love 'love' as well as *luve*, but, to be sure, they continued to
pronounce [u]. Again this was one of the practices meant to make
MSS easier to read. This *o* is marked *ó*: *còmen, sònne, lòve*. A little
later the French spelling *ou, ow* was introduced for the sound [ū],
a device which became habitual in the 14th century when they wrote
hous 'house' instead of *hus, abouten* 'around' instead of *abuten*, etc.
I indicate this with *ōu*: *hōus, abōuten*.

REMARKS. — I. What precedes allows one to understand that the spelling of
certain texts presents great ambiguity since *sunne* is to be read [sunnə] if it
refer to 'sun' and [sünnə] if it refers to 'sin'. Students should be careful,
in reading ME, always to keep in mind, if possible, the etymology of the words.
When the letter *u* is found in a ME word that has in ModE an *i* (*sin*) or an
e (*merry*), it generally represents the ME sound [ü].

II. Another ambiguity, at least in 12th century texts, comes from the fact
that ceɪtain Anglo-Norman scribes used *o* with the value of [ö]. This is the
case for the *Poema Morale* (II) and *The Owl and the Nightingale* (VI), for
example, where we have spellings like *soƌƌen* 'since' 2/9, *hovene* 'heaven'

2/25, 6/897, *sovene* 'seven' 2/26, words in which one must pronounce an [ð].
I indicate this with *ö*: *löf* 'dear', *hörte* 'heart'.

It is to Anglo-Norman influence that must be attributed the introduction of *ie* to indicate [ē] as in *þief* alongside *þef* 'thief'. This
spelling, which was first met especially in words of French origin
(*chief, brief, fieble*), was not extended to native words (*field, hiere,*
etc.) until much later. It rests on the fact that in Anglo-Norman
the diphthong *ie* had become *ē*. I indicate this with *īe*: *þīef*.

§ 12. For the consonants, continental practice imposed the use of
the spelling *ch* for [tš], a sound that OE had in the 11th century but
which no one knew how to indicate in a clear fashion (cp. HOE § 14).
On the model of French words like *chaunge, cheef, charme* they wrote
child (OE *čild*), *cherle* (OE *čeorl*), *chirche* (OE *čiriče*). For the
use of *g* for [dž] cp. § 8 REM. III.

The same for the sound [š]: at first the Anglo-Norman scribes
used *s* (*srive*) or *ss* (*ssipe*), then *sch* (*schrive, schippe*); finally *sh*
(*shrive, shippe*) definitely established itself.

It is worthy of note in this connection that the cluster [sk] is scarcely
to be found in ME except in Scandinavian loans (like *skin, sky, skill*
"reason") and in French loans (like *scarce, escape*) and where this
cluster is the result of metathesis of [ks], cp. § 48. 2.

We have seen above that the letter *c* was only used, before the
Norman Conquest, for the sound [k] (and its palatalized form). The
Anglo-Norman scribes used it before *e, i* with the value of [ts]: *milce*
'mercy' 4/18 (OE *milts*) and later with the value [s]: *certayn, citee*.

These same scribes introduced the spelling *qu* in place of OE *cw*
(*quethen* 'to say' OE *cweðan, quyke* 'alive' OE *cwic*), as well as
the use of the letter *v* for the sound [v], although OE writing used
f for [f] as well as [v]. The letter *z* to indicate [z] is frequent
only in Kentish.

Innovations

§ 13. On the model of the spellings *ch, sh,* where the letter *h* has
only a diacritical value, we have seen that *gh* was introduced for the
palatal spirant [ç] (as in German *ich*) after *e, i* and the velar spirant
[x] (as in German *ach*) after *a, o, u*. This practice undoubtedly
favored the extension of *th* to replace *þ* and *ð*. *wh-* is also generalized

in place of OE *hw-* (*wher, why, what* instead of OE *hwer, hwy, hwæt,* etc.). In the North this sound was written *quh-, qu-* (*quhat, quat*).

REMARKS. — I. The spelling *hu-* for *hw-, wh-* is frequent in Kentish (see no. XV). Moreover, the Anglo-Norman scribes frequently reduced *hw-* to *w-*, thus in the *Owl and the Nightingale* we find *wat, wile,* etc., for *what, while* (but see § 52.3). The Scots spelling *quh-, qu-* indicates a strong pronunciation of the spirant [xw]- at least originally.

Finally, under the influence of Latin traditions, *i* was written for *j* and *u* for *v*; however, *v* was used for initial *u*. Thus the MSS have *ioie, iustise* for *joie, justise* and *loue, vuel, vnder* for *love, uvel, under.*

II. For the convenience of the beginner I have re-established everywhere the modern usage for *j, u,* and *v* and print *joie, uvel,* etc.

III. The personal pronoun, first singular, in its reduced form *i* and the prefix *i-* (<OE *ǧe-*) are sometimes written, especially in the MSS of the 15th century, with a *j* that resembles a capital *I*. In the selections in this Handbook I have normalized this character and—always for the sake of clarity— follow the modern practice for this pronoun (*I*, but *y, ich*). The prefix *i-, y-,* is always separated in the selections in this Handbook by a hyphen (*i-chosen, y-fere*).

Quantity

§ 14. The length of vowels was infrequently expressed, at least at the start of ME, by reduplication (*wiis* for *wīs*); then, from 1350 on, the procedure was, generalized, in particular at London and Oxford for *e* and *o*, and in a closed syllable, *feet, good* was written instead of *fet, god*. In an open syllable, as a consequence of lengthening (cp. § 19) it was the weak final *e* which ultimately indicated the length of the preceding vowel (*nāme* as opposed to *năm*). But this procedure had nothing regular about it, and there was some recourse to doubling consonants to show shortness of the preceding vowel (*mĕtte, mĕtt* as opposed to *mēte*). Orm uses the device quite systematically (see Notes, p. 355). This spelling device has its roots in the long (double) consonants of West-Germanic gemination (HOE § 31).

In the north the length of the vowel was indicated otherwise. In the second half of the 14th century the diphthongs *ai, oi, ui* were respectively reduced to *ā, ō, ū,* but the new sounds continued to be written *ai, oi, ui*. By analogy *i* was used as a sign of length for the vowel immediately preceding, and *guid, deid, raid* was written for *gūd, dēd, rād.*

Likewise in the South [ü̈] was often written *ui*: *fuir* ' fire ' (OE *fȳr*), *luitel* ' little ' 10/260, *builden* ' to build ' (which has remained in the modern spelling for *build*).

Pronunciation

§ **15.** The analytical description of the spelling that has just been given makes it unnecessary to explain in detail the pronunciation of Middle English. It will be sufficient to set up, for the convenience of the reader, a recapitulative table of this, at least for the vowels and the diphthongs.

Phonetic Value	Key Words	Middle English Examples
i	ModE *pit*	by, bidde, niȝt, chyldern
ī	ModE *sea*	binde, lyf, wiis, milde, child
e	ModE *men*	belle, helpen, peny, mery
ẹ̄	F *bête*	eten, speken, deað
ẹ̄	F *fée*	fet, feld, deed, fieble, þief (Scots deid)
a	F *gamme*	catte, catel, fast
ā	Ger *Vater*	name, fare, caas, table (Scots raid)
o	F *homme*	God, sorwe, body
ǭ	ModE *saw*	stoon, old, hond, nose, noble
ō	F *zone*	good, mone, fot
ö	F *œuf*	cheorl, eorðe, hoven
ȫ	Ger *schön*	beon, neode, bo, preove, people
ü	F *lu*	sunne, muchel
ǖ	Ger *grün*	fur, builden, vertu
u	ModE *put*	but, us, hunger, love, sone, comen
ū	Ger *gut*	hous, soun, grund, honowr, (Scots guid)
ai	ModE *I*	dai, saide, cayre
ei	ModE *day*	wei, wai, leide, preie, seint
oi	ModE *boy*	poysoun, joie
au	ModE *cow*	straw, sauȝ, saȝ, cause
eu	e+u	dew, fewe, blew, rewme, bewte
iu	i+u	triwe (trewe), reule
ou	ModE *go*	soule, fouȝten
ui	u+i	anoy, point

The greater part of the Middle English consonants were pronounced pretty much as in ModE. The reader's attention is invited only to the following sounds:

Phonetic Value	Key Words	Middle English Examples
[ç]	Ger *ich*	fiȝt, right, niht, heȝ, þurȝ
[x]	Ger *ach*	cauȝte, roȝe, thogh, doughter, laughter

For the texts of the 14th century, like those of *Mandeville*, John of Trevisa, Chaucer, and Gower, where the spelling approaches, to a great extent, modern spelling, the student should make an effort to avoid giving the letters the phonetic value they have in present day English. One must not forget, in particular, that " the great vowel shift " and the silencing of *-gh*(-) are later than the 14th century.

Accentuation

§ 16. In native or Germanic words (and consequently in Scandinavian loans) the accentuation in ME did not differ from that of OE (cp. HOE § 15) : the strongest stress falls on the root syllable of simple words; in long words and compounds the post-radical heavy syllable can take a secondary accent (but one less strong and less frequent than in OE).

REMARKS. — I. The single exception to this rule is the word *el'levene* ' eleven ' (OE *'endleofan*). But it is not rare that for the needs of rime and meter poets displace the accent and make it fall on a heavy final syllable like *-ing*. Thus *swoȝ'ning* to rime with *þing* (8/444) or *ly'vynge* to rime with *brynge* (27.ᴅ/847). This is only a poetic license very natural to an age when poets were trying to force the English language into the isosyllabism of French or Italian verse.

II. A certain number of prefixes (or of first elements of compounds functioning as such) are unaccented. Thus *a-* (*a'drede, a'quelle, a'rise*), *al-* (*al'myȝti, al'lone*), *at-* (*at'stonden*), *bi-* (*bi'foren, bi'hynden, bi'leve*), *for-* (*for'ȝete, for'lete*), *i-* (*i'knowe, y'wis*), *mis-* (*mis'dede, mis'like*), *þer-* (*þer'fore, þer'on, þer'of*), *un-* (*un'blyþe, un'binden*).

§ 17. Words borrowed from French during the ME period progressively adapted themselves to the type of accentuation inherited from OE—as the rhythm of the verse demonstrates. Since French words were accented on the final, this determined, at length, a profound modification of the type of accent (and also of the pronunciation itself) of these words. For the French element we witness in ME, therefore, a displacement of the accent away from the final towards the initial:

1. Type 'x(x). No change for disyllables ending in weak -*e*: thus we have *table*. For others we have, for example, *'glorie, 'storie, 'studie* with *i* pronounced like [j]), then *'glory, 'story, 'study*; but we have *'suffren* instead of OF *suf'frir*.

2. Type x'x. OF *ci'té* becomes in English *ci'tee, 'ci̦tee*, then *'city*. For a long time the accentuation of disyllables of this type was floating; the same word could be accented x'x or 'xx, cp. Chaucer's line

in 'divers art and in di'vers figures

Cant. Tales D 1486

3. Type x'x(x). OF *mi'racle* tended to be accented in ME *'miracle* 'xxx; but there was a great deal of vacillation. Chaucer still accents *pre'sence, ma'tere, no'blesse, e'terne, co'rage, ser'vice, ho'noure(n), go'verne(n)*, etc.

4. Type xx'x. This is the pattern of trisyllables of the OF class *parle'ment, gene'ral, glori'ous*. It evolves in ME towards 'xxx and often 'x(x)x by syncope of the *e* in pronunciation, thus *'gen(e)ral* (cp. § 39), or passage of *i* to [j], thus *'glorious*.

For further details see the article by Ed. ECKHARDT, "Der Übergang zur germanischen Betonung bei den Wörtern französischer Herkunft im Mittelenglischen," *Englische Studien*, 75 (1942), 9-66.

CHAPTER TWO

THE VOWELS

A. QUANTITATIVE CHANGES

First Phase of Lengthening

§ 18. In OE the quantity of an accented vowel was in principle independent of the nature of the syllable in which it was found. Aside from certain combinative changes, the quantity of the vowels inherited from Germanic remained stable. The stem vowels of OE *bĕran* 'to carry', *fæder* 'father', *lŭfu* 'love' were short as they had been in Germanic (cp. CGmc *bĕran-*, Gothic *fădar, lŭbo*). Those of OE *cēpte* 'he kept', *fīftēne* 'fifteen' remained long just like those of OE *cēpan* 'to keep', *fīf* 'five'.

However, before the end of the OE period short vowels lengthened before the consonant groups *mb, nd, ld, rd, rð*; instead of *lămb* 'lamb', *findan* 'to find', *cĭld* 'child', *wŏrd* 'word' we get *lāmb, findan, cīld, wōrd*, except when a third consonant immediately follows, as in the plurals *lămbru, chĭldru*, and also except in words that do not bear sentence stress like *ănd, ŭnder, wŏlde*.

REMARKS. — I. In Northern English there was no lengthening before *-nd, -mb*; we have the following with short vowels, *find(e), bĭnd(e), clĭm* 'climb' (and also *lănd, hănd*, which extend into the Midlands area).

II. According to the system of spelling invented towards the end of the 12th century by the monk Orm, in his dialect, lengthening occurred also before the groups *ng, rl, rn, rþ*, and *rz*, with hesitation before *nd, ng* (Orm writes *stund* 'time', but *stannden* 'stand', *ʒung* 'young', but *ganngenn* 'to go').

Towards the close of the 14th century lengthening was maintained only before *mb* (for *i* and *o*), *nd* (for *i* and *u*), and *ld* (for all vowels). In Chaucer, for example, we have *child, feeld, binden, bōunden, lōmb, clȳmben*, and exceptionally, *sǫǫnd* 'sand', *woord, sǫǫng*.

Second Phase of Lengthening

§ 19. In the course of the first half of the 13th century and already in the 12th in Northern English, it seems there intervened in English

16

an entirely new principle: the quantity of the vowel depends, thence-forward, on the nature of the syllable, whether it is open (i. e. termi-nated by a vowel) or closed (i. e. terminated by a consonant), and also on the accent and on the length of the word.

In disyllables, if the accented syllable was open, the short vowels *a*, *e*, *o* lengthened into *ā*, *ę̄*, *ǭ*: we have thus *fā-re*, *bę̄-ren*, *cǭ-te*. For the vowels *i* and *u*, lengthening took place later and was less general. In the 14th century it occurs in the Northern dialect. It was accom-panied by a qualitative change $i > ē$, $u > ō$, thus OE *wiku* > ME *wēke* 'week', OE *bitel* > ME *bētel* 'beetle', *mikel* > *mēkel* 'great', OE *duru* > ME *dōre* 'door', OE *wudu* > ME *wōde* 'wood'. This lengthening penetrated into the North-West Midlands (the dialect of *Sir Gawain*). Only later did it reach London, cp. the modern forms *evil* ($ī < ę̄ < i <$ OE *y*), *week*, *beetle*, etc.

REMARKS. — I. This second phase of lengthening taking place only in two-syllable words, double forms are produced in the middle of a declension of the same word, of one or two syllables. Generally analogy settled this in one or the other direction.

We have in ME *flesch* but *flēsches*, *wish* but *wīshes*, *yok* but *yōkes*, *staf* but *stāves* (an opposition still preserved in ModE for this last word), *path* but *pāthes*.

The same in disyllables. We should have regularly *āker* but *ăkeres*, *sādel* but *sădeles*, *crādel* but *crădeles*. Analogy generalized the long vowel in *āker*: *ākeres*, *crādel*: *crādeles* (cp. the modern forms *acre* [eikə], *cradle* [krɛidl]), the short in *sădel*: *sădeles* (ModE *saddle* [sædl]). This was facilitated by the fact that, in words of this kind, syncope of one of the two unaccented vowels could modify, in a different fashion, the nature of the radical syllable. It is possible that on one hand *āker(e)s*, *crādel(e)s*, won out and on the other *săd(e)les*.

II. Final -*ĭ* < OE -*iġ* generally prevents lengthening of the preceding vowel in an open syllable: we have *bŏdi* 'body', *măny* 'many'.

French Loan Words

§ 20. French loan words obey the same tendencies. In a final accented position short vowels lengthen (*pi'tę̄*, *ver'tü̆*), as well as in monosyllables ending in a simple consonant (*bę̄k*, *pür*, *cās*, *fōl*, *fīn*) and before *r* + consonant (*pǭrk*, *pōrt*). In the accentual types 'xx and x'xx, in an open syllable, the vowel is long: *blāme*, *escāpen*, *stōrię*, as well as before consonant + liquid (*tāble*), liquid + conso-nant (*pērle*, *scārce*), and sometimes also before the group *st* (*hāste*, *cǭste*, 'coast', but *cŏsten* 'to cost'). It happens that the penult vowel remains short in disyllables in -*i* (or -*é*), -*on*, -*oūn*: *cĭ'té*, *cĭty*, *prĭson*, *bărōun*.

In a closed syllable the vowel remains short: *sĭmple*, *defĕnden*, *dĕtte* (alongside *dēte*), *dobble* (alongside *dóuble*).

In the accentual type '×(×)×, the vowel of the accented syllable is generally short: '*ămorous*, '*mătere*, '*rĕgular*, '*pŭnisshen*; but before *i* we have a long vowel in open syllables '*pātient*, '*cūrious*.

Shortening

§ 21. In a general fashion long accented vowels shorten in closed syllables before consonant groups (except for the groups which caused the first phase of lengthening, § 18) regardless of the origin of the group; that is to say, the phenomenon took place whether the consonantal group was part of the root of the word, e. g., OE *sōfte* > ME *sŏfte* 'soft', or whether it was the result of inflection, e. g. the weak preterits *kĕpte* (infinitive *kēpen* 'to keep'), *lădde* (infinitive *lēden* 'to lead'), *mĕtte* (inf. *meeten* 'to dream') or by composition, e. g. *fĭftēne* as opposed to *fȳve*, *wĭmman* as opposed to *wīf* 'woman', *wĭsdom* as opposed to *wīs* 'wise'; Orm has *wissdom*.

This phenomenon is progressive; it is only noticeable from the beginning of the 13th century on, and it could be reversed by analogy: one finds *ēvre*, *ōþre* because of *ēver* 'ever', *ōþer* 'other'.

REMARK. — Probably this shortening did not take place before the group *st*: we find *gāst*, *gǭst* 'spirit', *prẹ̄st* 'priest', *blāst* 'blast', *lẹ̄st* 'least', *mǭst* 'most', *Crīst* 'Christ', *ẹ̄st* 'East', etc., but there is a good deal of hesitation.

Shortening took place before two unaccented syllables: alongside *hǭly* there is *hŏliday*, and *stĭrŏpes* alongside OE *stīrāpas* (< *stigrāpas*) 'stirrups'. A fortiori if the accented vowel was short, it did not lengthen in an open syllable.

§ 22. Long unaccented vowels shortened: OE *wĭsdōm* > ME *wĭsdŏm* (according to Eliason MLN 69, 137 from 9th or 10th century; see Jordan § 23); the same with *kinedŏm* 'kingdom', *wurðlĭche* 'noble', as opposed to OE -*līċ*; in disyllables OE *iġ* > *ī* then -*ĭ* (*hōlĭ*, *bŏdĭ*). The same for unaccented prefixes: OE *ā'rīsan* > ME *ă'rīsen* 'to arise'. Finally grammatical words like *ăn*, *ă* (alongside *ān*, *ā*), *mĭ(n)* *mȳ* (alongside *mīn*), *tŏ*, *tĕ* (alongside *tō*), *hăve* (alongside *hāve*) etc.

The same is true, after the displacement of accent (cp. § 17 above), for previously long vowels or diphthongs of French origin: they tended to shorten or to simplify: there is *pardon* instead of *par'dōun, 'honur* instead of *ho'nōur, 'aunter* instead of *aven'tūre, 'gramer* instead of *gram'maire, 'pales* instead of *pa'lais,* etc. But this was scarcely generalized before the end of the 14th century.

B. QUALITATIVE CHANGES

1. In Accented Syllables

Short Vowels

§ **23.** Aside from the quantitative changes indicated above, the OE short vowels, *i, e, a, o* and *u,* in closed syllables, remained without change in ME: OE *sinkan* > ME *sinke(n)* 'to sink', OE *willa* > ME *wille* 'desire'; OE *bedd* > ME *bedde* 'bed', OE *helpan* > ME *helpe(n)* 'to help'; OE *catt* > ME *catt(e)* 'cat', OE *lapian* > ME *lappe(n)* 'to lap up'; OE, ME *God;* OE, ME *full,* OE, ME *cuppe* 'cup'. For the treatment of OE *y* see § 29.

Treatment of Short æ

§ **24.** It must be remembered that in OE the short vowel æ arising from West Germanic *a* by palatalization, is only encountered in a closed syllable (HOE § 18), thus OE *bær* 'he carried', *sæt* 'he sat', and in open syllables before the front vowel *e,* thus OE *fæder* 'father', *æppel* 'apple', *wæter* 'water'.

REMARK. — In Mercian (or more exactly, in the West-Midland area) and in Kentish, from the OE period on, this vowel had already closed to *e: ber, set.* In the ME period West-Midland and Kentish keep *e: ber, set, wes* 'was', *þet* 'that', *fĕder* 'father'. In West-Midland we also find the spelling *ea* (thus *eappel* 'apple' 3/10) because in this dialect *ea* had become *ę.* Then in the 13th century in West-Midland and in the 14th in Kentish the quality *a* is generalized.

From about 1100 on the articulation of æ depalatalized and was retracted to *a*; we have therefore in ME *bar, sat, appel,* and with lengthening in an open syllable (§ 19) *fāder.* However, during the 12th century the spelling æ was still to be found.

Treatment of OE å

§ **25.** In OE å was the quality taken by WGmc *a* before a nasal consonant (HOE § 21. 4). In late OE *o* was the typical spelling for this sound in Anglian (*mon* 'man', *noma* 'name') while in West-Saxon they preferred to write *a* (*man, nama*).

In ME only West-Midland preserved the quality *o* (writing *mon, nom, on(d)sware* 'answer'). See Fig. 2.

REMARKS.—I. West-Midland also has ǫ before -*nd* thus *hǫnd* 'hand', *lỹnd* 'land', but since the other dialects of the Midlands and of the South participate in the move *ā* > *ǭ*, elsewhere, with the exception of the North and the North-East-Midland, ultimately was reached, by another way, the state *lǭnd, hǭnd* (Northern *land, hand*; North-East-Midland [Orm], *lānd, hānd*). *hānd*).

Little by little, however, short *a* became dominant in East-Midland. In the 14th century, in Robert Mannyng of Brunne, there was hesitation: alongside the rimes *fōnde* : *lōnde* (14/4095-6) we find -*stande* : *hande* (14/4047-8). The type *hand, land* penetrated London English and the common language in the 15th century.

II. Before -*ng* and -*mb*, *ǭ* maintained itself in the Midlands and in the South, e. g. *lǭng, sǫng, cǭmb, wǫmb*. Then towards 1400 the vowel shortened before -*ng* (whence *long, song*), while the long form was maintained before -*mb*. The exceptions are explained partly by analogy (*lamb, hang*) and partly by borrowing from the Northern dialect (*fang* 'fang').

Long Vowels

§ 26. Aside from the quantitative changes indicated in §§ 21 and 22, the OE long vowels *ī, ē̜, ō* and *ū* remained in ME: OE *wīn* > ME *wīne* 'wine', OE *bītan* > ME *bīte(n)* 'to bite'; OE *cwēn* > ME *quēne* 'queen', OE *cēpan* > ME *kēpe(n)* 'to keep', OE *fēt* > ME *fēt, feet* 'feet'; OE *scōh* > ME *schō* 'shoe', OE *gōd* > ME *good* 'good', OE *brōþer* > ME *brōþer* 'brother', OE *þū* > ME *þōu*. OE *nū* > ME *nōw* 'now', OE *hūs* > ME *hūs, hōus* 'house'. For the spelling *ōu, ōw,* cp. § 11.

Treatment of OE *ā*

§ 27. 1. OE *ā* remained in Northern English but was fronted and raised early in the 13th century, e. g. *wā* 'woe', *stān* 'stone', *bānys* 'bones', *nāne* 'none', *smāt* 'he smote' (OE *wā, stān, bānas, nān, smāt*). For spellings cf. § 19.

2. In the rest of England (Midlands and South) *ā* was rounded into open *ǭ*: *wǭ, stǭn* or *stǫǫn, bǭnes, nǭne, nǫǫn, smǭt,* see Fig. 3

REMARKS.—I. For the type *ald/ǭld* see further § 30, REM II. For the type *lānd/lǭnd* see above § 25, REM. I.

II. It has been justly remarked (H. C. WYLD, *History²*, § 156) that the

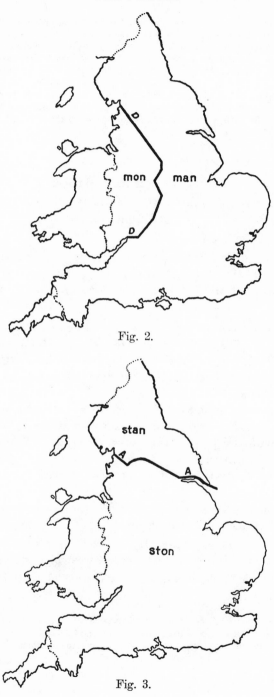

Fig. 2.

Fig. 3.

rounding of *ā* into *ǭ* must have started very early, otherwise we could not explain why OE *stān* became *stǭn* while the *ā* of French loan-words remained unchanged (*dāme, fāme* etc., cp. § 33). As early as the *Peterborough Chronicle*, indeed, we find sporadically a few words with *ǭ* (like *mǭre* < OE *māra* ' more '); the *Poema Morale*, the *Ancrene Wisse*, and the *Ormulum* have only *ā*; of the two MSS of the *Brut* by Lawman, the older (about 1205) occasionally has *ǭ*, the more recent (about 1250) generally has *o̧*. One can deduce from this that the movement towards the rounding of *ā* must have commenced well before the middle of the 12th century, but it is not shown in the spellings until after the first quarter of the 13th century.

Treatment of OE Long *ǣ*

§ 28. The evolution of OE *ǣ* is more complex.

One must recall that in OE the West-Saxon dialect—which is the literary dialect of the 9th and 10th centuries—merges in *ǣ* two sounds of different origin:

1. The sound that derives from the fronting of WGmc **ā*; thus OE *dǣd* ' deed ' (OSax *dād*, OHG *tāt*, ModGer *Tāt*), OE *strǣt* ' paved road ' (OSax *strāt*, OHG *strāz*, ModGer *Strāsse*). By convention this sound is called *ǣ₁*.

2. The sound which is the product of the *i* or *j*-mutation of OE *ā* (deriving from WGmc **ai*); thus OE *dǣl* ' part ' (WGmc **daili-*, OHG *teil*, ModGer *Teil*), OE *tǣċan* ' to teach ' (from WGmc **taik-ja-n*, cp. OE *tācn*, OHG *zeihhan*, ModGer *Zeichen* ' sign '). This sound is called *ǣ₂*.

On the contrary, from the OE period, in the Anglian dialects north of the Thames, these two sounds remain distinct: to *ǣ₁* there corresponds a close vowel [ẹ̄], written *e* (*dēd, strēt*), while *ǣ₂* remains the open vowel [ę̄], written *ǣ* (*dǣl, tǣcan*).

Finally in Kentish *ǣ₁* and *ǣ₂* are also merged but in a close vowel [ẹ̄].

In ME the dialects of the North and a great part of those of the Midlands continue to distinguish two vowels of different aperture:

1. close *ẹ̄* which continues OE *ǣ₁* (ME *dẹ̄d, strẹ̄te, hẹ̄r*). In general I indicate this simply by *ē* except in ambiguous cases.

2. open *ę̄* which continues OE *ǣ₂* and which I shall indicate *ę̄*: ME *dę̄l, sę̄, tę̄chen*.

REMARKS. — I. In ME south of the Thames, Kentish continues to merge *ǣ₁* and *ǣ₂* in close *ẹ̄*, while the dialects of the south-middle and south-east (which represent the descendants of West-Saxon) always merge them in open *ę̄*.

II. One will note that in ModE generally the spelling corresponding to ME ẹ̄ (OE ǣ₁) is *ee*: *deed, street*, that of ME ệ̄ (OE ǣ₂) being *ea*: *deal, teach*.

III. In London where the dialects of the Midlands and the South joined, there was doubtless a certain hesitation, and it appears likely that towards the end of the 15th century the open vowel tended to become close and to be identified with ẹ̄.

IV. In the 13th century in a region of the South-East-Midland near London (and comprising the countries of Essex, Hertford, Bedford, Huntington and a part of the county of Cambridge), OE ǣ became ā [*sā, tāche(n), strāt(e)*]. This phenomenon also pushed on into London where we often find *strāte* 'street' in the 13th century. It is exemplified in a good number of place-names in *Strāt-* (as opposed to others in *Strẹ̄t-*). In the current London dialect it progressively disappeared in the 14th century, replaced by ẹ̄.

V. Thus the sound ǣ̆ (low front slack), which had been such a typical feature of OE, completely disappeared from ME.

Treatment of OE y̆̄

§ 29. This sound in OE was the *i*-mutation of *u* (and had the value of F *u* in *pur* 'pure'); it was represented in ME according to dialect by *ü, i* or *e* (see Fig. 4).

1. It remained *ü*, short or long, in the southern and south-western third of England, i. e. West-Midland (except for almost the whole of Lancashire), and the South-West. It was written *u* and sometimes, when it was long, *ui* or *uy*.

2. In the dialects of the North and of the East-Midland, by unrounding it became *i*, written *i* or *y*.

3. In the dialects of the South-East, including Kentish of course, it became ẹ̆.

Thus we have:

OLD ENGLISH	MIDDLE ENGLISH		
	SW and W Mid 1.	E Mid and North 2.	SE 3.
cynn 'kin'	*kün*	*kin*	*ken*
synn 'sin'	*sünne*	*synne*	*senne, zenne*
pytt 'pit'	*pütte*	*pitte*	*pette*
myrige 'merry'	*mürie*	*myry*	*mery*
ćirće 'church'	*chürche*	*chirche*	*cherche*
*lyft 'left'	*lüft*	*lift*	*left*
fy̆r 'fire'	*für*	*fir*	*fẹ̄r, vẹ̄r*
mȳs 'mice' pl.	*müs*	*mis*	*mẹ̄s*

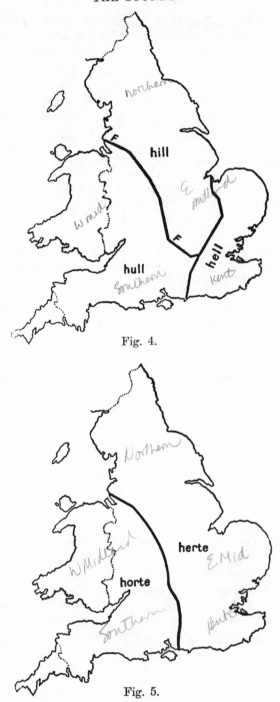

Fig. 4.

Fig. 5.

REMARKS. — I. Well before the Norman Conquest OE ȳ had become ę̄ in Kentish. Outside of Kent this tendency is encountered in Sussex, Surrey, and as far as the southern part of the East-Midlands (Essex, Suffolk, occasionally Norfolk) and finally in the dialect of the City of London about the middle of the 14th century.

II. In fact the London region remained for a long time a terrain of conflict between *ü/i/e*. The *Proclamation of Henry III* (1258) sometimes has *ü* (*küneriche* 11/7, *Kanterbüry* 11/28) sometimes *e* (*i-wersed* 11/18). The *Petition of the Mercers* (1386) still has *lüst* (25/43), but generally *i*. In the same MS (Ellesmere MS) of the *Canterbury Tales* we have for a single word (27₄ᴮ) separated by a few lines the forms *myrie* 963, *murye* 843 and *merie* (riming with *berie*) 884. W. HEUSER, *Alt-London* (Osnabrück, 1914) and B. A. MACKENZIE, *Contributions to the History of the Early London Dialect* (Oxford, 1927), have shown that in the dialect of the City of London, *e*, in the case that concerns us, comes from the influence of the neighboring Essex dialect and not from Kentish. The forms with *e* that are met in Chaucer and perhaps also those of Gower (*ken, senne, mery, berye* 'to bury', *pettes* 'pits', *dent* 'a blow') are therefore probably London City forms and not necessarily Kenticisms.

III. The difficulty presented by the interpretation of forms with *ē* outside of Kent comes from the fact that *i* (deriving from OE ȳ) could have spontaneously given rise to *ē* (cp. § 19). The presence of forms of this type (e. g. *ēvil*) in a dialect has no value as a criterion. Those words alone are convincing which had in OE ȳ in a closed syllable not subject to lengthening. If they yield *e*, without *i* under the same circumstances yielding it, this is proof that the *e*- forms indeed come from OE *y*- forms.

IV. It will be noticed that the modern written language has sometimes retained the spelling of one dialect (build, busy, bury) with the pronunciation of another [bɪld, bɪzɪ, berɪ].

V. Already in OE before palatalized consonants, *y > i* in the Southwest: one finds ME *drihten* 'lord', *riġġ* 'ridge', *briġġe* 'bridge', *biġġen* 'buy', *thinchen* 'to seem' (OE *dryhten, rycġ, byċġan, þynċan*).

VI. With reference to what is said above and what follows (§ 30), it should be noticed that during the ME period there existed in the eastern half of England a striking tendency to avoid front rounded vowels such as *ü* and *ö* and to replace them with unrounded ones, *i* and *e*. But this seems to have been a rather slow process.

Reduction of Diphthongs

§ **30.** From the 10th century OE had only two diphthongs: *ēa* and *ēo* (the former diphthong *īe* had already been simplified into *i* or *y*). In the course of the 11th century the OE diphthongs were reduced to simple vowels: *ēa* becomes *æ* and follows the course of *ǽ* (§24) and *ǣ* (§ 28), and its later evolution is merged with that of these vowels; *ēo* became *ȫ*, that is to say, only the first element (*e*) of this diphthong remained, but assumed the rounded articulation of the second element

(*o*) and the result was $\ddot{o}$ (the probable evolution being $\overline{eo} > \ddot{o}o > \ddot{o}$).
Then, in the course of the 12th century, $\ddot{o}$ was unrounded and pro-
gressively moved toward $\bar{\ell}$, except in the South and West-Midlands
where this unrounding is not encountered until much later, first for
the short vowel, then, in the 14th century, for the long.
We find for example:

10th cent.	11th cent.	12th cent.
dēad ' dead '	*dǣd*	*dę̄d*
hlēapan ' leap, run '	*lǣpen*	*lę̄pe(n)*
dēop ' deep '	*dȫp*	*dę̄p*
bēon ' to be '	*bȫn*	*bę̄n*

In a parallel fashion the OE " digraphs " *ea, eo* in which the second
element was an obscure glide or rather indicated a variety of quality
in the vowel or the preceding or following consonant (HOE § 12),
resulted respectively in ME *a* and *e* in the 12th century. This is much
rather a question of spelling than of phonetic evolution.

10th cent.	11th cent.	12th cent.
feallan ' fall '	*fællen*	*falle(n)*
healf ' half '	*hælf*	*half*
heard ' hard '	*hǣrd* (§ 18)	*hārd*
heorte ' heart '	*hörte*	*herte*
heofon ' heaven '	*höven*	*heven*
seolfor (< *siolfor*) ' silver '	*sölver*	*selver*

REMARKS. — I. Just as in OE (cp. HOE § 12 and § 13), the study of the
phonetic evolution of the diphthongs in ME is made very complex by the
uncertainty and the lack of precision of the spellings (cp. above § 10 and § 11
REM. II). One continued to employ the spellings *ea, eo* long after these
diphthongs had been reduced, and we encounter numerous other spelllings.

II. Before *ll* and *l*+consonant, Anglian no longer had " diphthongs "
(HOE § 22 REM. IX): *fallan, half*. Before *ld* the vowel lengthened; opposed
to West-Saxon *eald* ' old ', *ceald* ' cold ', *healdan* ' to hold ' there was Anglian
ald, cald, haldan which gave *āld, cāld, hāldan*, and this *ā* following the course
of OE *ā* (§ 27) yielded *ǭ* south of the Humber: *ǭld, cǭld, hǭlde(n)*.

III. The varieties of pronunciation which were produced in OE after a
palatal consonant (*ċ, sċ, ġ*) before *æ* and *e* long or short (HOE § 23) are
reflected in ME. Corresponding to OE *ġiefan, ġifan, ġefan* ' to give ', there
was ME *ʒeve(n), ʒive(n)* ; corresponding to OE *ċeaster, caster, ċester*, we find
ME place-names in *-chester* (*Manchester, Dorchester, Lanchester*) and *-caster*
(*Doncaster, Lancaster*) ; cp. also OE *sċeal, sċal*, with ME *shell, shall*.

IV. When in OE *ġi-, ġe-, sċe-* were notations for [j] or [š] before *o* or *a* (HOE § 23 REM. III), we find in ME only *ʒ, y,* or *s(c)h*, for ex. *ʒung, ʒong* (OE *ġeong*) 'young', *schort* (OE *sċeort*) 'short', *ʒōre, yōre* (OE *ġeāra*) 'in the past'.

V. In Kentish by displacement of accent, OE *ea* becomes *y'a* (*dy'ad* 'dead', *dy'ave* 'deaf', *y'alde* 'old'), OE *'eo* becomes *y'e* (*dy'evel* 'devil', *þy'ef* 'thief', *y-hy'erþ* 'he hears'.

VI. We know that in Anglian before [ç] and [x], written *c, g* and *h,* the diphthongs were simplified, *ēa, ēo > ē, īo > ī* (HOE § 20 REM.). On the further development in ME see below, § 31.

Appearance of New Diphthongs

§ 31. Whereas OE diphthongs (moreover rather unstable, cp. HOE § 13, REM. I) disappeared we witness in ME the creation of a great number of new diphthongs. To understand clearly the following processes, it should be remembered that one of the ways diphthongs are developed is by the shifting of the syllable boundary. In fact the boundary-sound between two syllables belongs to both of them but the boundary may be shifted and the speaker may tend to consider that boundary-sound as belonging entirely to either the first or the second syllable. In OE, words like *weġan,* 'to weigh', *glōwan* 'to glow' seem to have been divided *we-ġan, glō-wan*; then at the end of the OE period *weġ-e(n), glōw-e(n),* and later on when finals were weakened or dropped, *wei-e, glow-e,* which resulted in new diphthongs being evolved.

The new ME diphthongs may be classified under four heads:

1. Vocalization of palatal *ġ* after *æ, e, i.* Thus we have:

OE *æġ* > ME *ai*: OE *dæġ* 'day' > ME *dai, day*
OE *eġ* > ME *ei*: OE *weġ* 'way' > ME *wei, wey,* OE *leġde* 'laid' > ME *leide,* OE *weġan* 'to weigh' > ME *weie(n)*;
OE *ǣġ* > ME *ei*: OE *grǣ̆ġ* 'gray' > ME *grei.*

REMARKS — I. Rather early, *ei* was merged with *ai* [*æi*].

II. In the second half of the 14th century in the Northern dialects *ai > ā,* but continued to be written *ai,* and this *ai,* as we have seen (§ 14), was used in turn as a spelling for the earlier *ā* (e. g. *maid* 'he made').
OE *ēġ > ME ei* then *ai*: OE *hēġ* 'hay' > ME *hei, hai,* OE **dēġde* 'he died' > ME *deide, daide.*

III. Before a vowel this *ei* tends to simplify once more into *i*: OE *ēġe* 'eye' > ME *eie* then *īe,* OE *lēġan* 'to prevaricate' ME *leie(n)* then *līe(n)* alongside *lyʒen* 15/73.

This monophthonging occurred first in the South-West at the end of the 13th century then gradually became dominant in other regions.

IV. OE *īġ* did not yield a diphthong, but simply *ī*: OE *niġen* ' nine '>ME *nīn(e)*, OE *stīgan* ' to mount '>*stīgen* ME *stīe*.

According to the dialectal development of OE *ȳ̆* (§ 29), the group *ȳ̆ġ* yielded in ME *ī* in the North and East-Midlands, *üi* (which later reduces to *ü*) in the West-Midlands and finally *ei* in Kent and the South-East. Thus OE *byġeþ* ' he buys ' > ME *bīeþ* (whence the infinitive *bȳen*), *büieþ* (then *büeþ*, *büþ* 3/109), *beieþ* (whence the inf. *beye*).

2. Development of an obscure vowel before [x] and [ç]. A *u*-glide develops before the velar spirant [x], an *i*-glide before the palatal spirant [ç]. Thus we have the diphthongs *au, ou, ei*. For example:

OE [ax] > ME [aux]: OE *tæhte* ' he taught ' > *tăhte* > ME *taughte*, OE (Anglian) *sæh* ' he saw ' > *sah* > ME *saugh*;

OE [āx] > ME [oux] (except in the North where we have [a(u)x]): OE *dāh* ' dough ' > ME *dough* (North: *daugh*);

OE [ŏx] > ME [oux]: OE *dohtor* ' daughter ' > ME *douhter*, OE *bŏhte* ' he bought ' > *bŏhte* > ME *bouhte*, OE *plōh* ' plow ' > ME *plouʒ*, OE *ġenōh* ' enough ' > ME *y-nough*.

V. OE [ŏx] did not yield a diphthong in Northern English where we have *doghter, boghte, enogh, eneuch*.
Even south of the Humber it is probable that this diphthong *ou* was later smoothed to *ū*, hence *plūh, y-nōw*, etc., under the influence of inflected forms.

OE [eç] > ME [eiç]: OE *eahta* ' eight ' > *ehta* > ME *eiʒte*, eighte, OE *seah* ' he saw > *seh* > ME *seigh*, OE *feohtan* ' to fight ' > ME *feighte(n)*;

OE [ēç] > ME [eiç] > [īç]: OE *hēah* ' high ' > *hę̄h* > ME *heigh* (then *high* from 1350), OE *nēah* ' near ' > *nę̄h* > ME *neigh* (then *nīgh*).

VI. [ēç] did not yield diphthongization in the North (and to a certain extent in the North-West-Midlands) where we have *hēgh, nēgh*.

VIa. In late ME forms such as *high, nīgh*, the *ī* may be due to analogy with inflected forms.

3. Vocalization of velar *g* after *a, o, u* in the middle of a word.

Under these conditions the OE voiced velar spirant [g] vocalized to *u*, and formed a diphthong with the preceding vowel. Thus:

OE [ag] > ME [au] (written *aw* before a vowel) : OE *dragan* ' drag ' > ME *drawe(n)*, OE *haga* ' hedge ' > ME *hawe*;

OE [āg] > ME [ou] : OE *āgan* ' possess ' > ME *owen*;

OE [ōg] > ME [ou] : OE *boga* ' bow ' > ME *bowe*, OE *plōgas* ' plows ' > ME *plowes*.

VII. OE [ŭg] did not yield a diphthong, but simply *ū* (written *u, ou, ow*) in ME: OE *fugol* ' bird ' > ME *fōul, fōwl*, OE *būgan* ' bend ' > ME *bōwe(n)*.

4. Fusion of vowel with *w* in the same syllable. Thus we have:

a + *w* > *au*: OE *strawes* (genitive) ' straw ', whence ME (nominative) *straw*;

ā + *w* > *ou* (*au* in the North) ; OE *blāwan* ' to blow ' > ME *blowe* (North *blawe*), OE *cnāwan* ' to know ' > ME *knowe* (North *knawe*), OE *sāwol* ' soul ' > ME *soule* (North *saule, sawle*) ;

ō + *w* > *ow*: OE *glōwan* ' glow ' > ME *glowe*;

ǣ (*eā*) + *w* > *eu*: OE *lǣwed* ' lay, ignorant ' > ME *lew(e)d*, OE *sċēawian* ' to show ' > ME *schewe(n)* (but *sċēāwian* ' to show ' gives ME *schowe(n)*).

ēo + *w* > *öu* > *eu*: OE *nēowe* ' new ' > ME *neowe, newe*, OE *trēowþ* ' truth ' > ME *treuthe*.

VIII. OE *fēōwer* ' four ' > ME *fōur*, OE *ēōw* ' you ' > ME *ȝōū* by displacement of accent '*eo* > *e*'*o*.

IX. In the 14th century *eu* tended to become *iu* whence the spelling *niwe, triwthe*. The spelling *nwe* perhaps indicates a reduction of the diphthong to *u*.

ī + *w* > *iu* which in the 14th century merged with the preceding (see REM. IX above), whence the spellings *ew, w*: OE *stīġeweard* ' steward ' > *stīward* > ME *stiward, steward, stward* (cp. the family name *Stuart*), OE *tiwesdæġ* ' Tuesday ' > ME *tiwesdai, tewesday, tuesday*, OE *trīewe*, ' true ' > ME *trew(e), trwe*.

Vowels in Scandinavian Loan-Words

§ 32. Although the great majority of these words are not evidenced before ME, most of them came into English before the Norman Conquest.

Old Norse vowels, which were not very different from those of Old English from the point of view of quality and articulation, followed the same course as the latter and call for no further remark. This is the case for all the simple ON vowels ĭ, ĕ, ă, ŏ, ŭ, ў. Only the ON diphthongs *ai, au* and *ey* did not exist in OE.

ON *ai* (later *ei*) merged with the ME diphthongs *ai, ei*: ON *greiða* 'get ready' > ME *greiþe(n)*, ON *þeir* 'they' > ME *þei*, ON *nei* 'no' > ME *nay*, ON *veikr* 'weak' > ME *waik*, ON *freista* 'to ask' > ME *frayst*, ON *leika* 'to play' > ME *laike*.

ON *au* appeared in ME under the forms *au, ou, ō*: ON *gaukr* 'cuckoo' > ME *gauk, gouk, gōke*. In unstressed positions we have *o*: ON *vindauga* 'window' ME *windoʒe*. Before *h* ON *au* was reduced very early to *ō*, so that ON *þauh* 'although' > *þōh* > ME *þŏh, thogh, þough* (while OE *þeah* 'although' > *þẹ̄h* > ME *þēʒ, þeyʒ*.

ON *ey* (proceeding from the *i*-mutation of *au*) merged in ME with *ei, ai*: ON *treysta* 'trust' > ME *treiste(n), traiste(n)*.

Vowels in French Loan-Words

§ 33. It was by the intermediary of Norman that French loan-words entered English from 1100 to 1300. They appeared therefore under the form they had in Northern French and not under the form of Central French as was the case after 1300. To these were added, little by little, a good number of Latin words under a French form.

The vowels which were identical or very close in the two languages merged, for instance,

$$i, e, a, ö, u, ü$$

long or short, and the diphthongs

$$ai, eu, au, ui$$

and followed the course of the corresponding native sounds (*ö* > *e*, outside of West-Midlands, *eu* > *iu*).

Short *ü* (written *u* as in French) persisted in West-Midlands where the sound was normal, but it was not merged with *ü* < OE *y* (which was perhaps less tense). Elsewhere OF short *ü* was replaced by [u]: *jüst, jüdge*, became *just, judge*.

Long *ü* caused more difficulty; either [*ū*] or [*jū*] were rather quickly substituted for it: *süre, düke, refüsen, rüde*. This is at least what appears to result from the rimes (*nature: emperour*) or from the spellings (*vertew, deuke* with *ew, eu* which serve to indicate [*jū*]).

The Anglo-Norman nasal vowels disappeared, replaced by corresponding oral vowels. For Anglo-Norman *an* + dental, *am* + labial, *aun* and *aum* were substituted, thus *daunce, aunt, chaunge, chaumbre* (which perhaps represents an effort on the part of the cultivated classes to pronounce the French nasal vowel); but *an, am* are also to be found: *dance, chambre*, etc. (pronunciation of the lower classes?).

REMARKS. — I. *o* before a nasal + consonant became *u* in Anglo-Norman, whence ME *noūmbre, mōunt, cōunt, profōund* (also written *mūnt, profūnd*, etc.).

II. Before a consonant (in particular liquids, dentals and *s*) OF *ai* and *ei* often reduced to *ę̄*: OF *fraile* > ME *fręle*, OF *deis* 'table' > ME *dęs*, OF *saisir* 'seize' > ME *sęsen*; the same in unaccented positions: OF *raison* > ME *rę̄'soun*, OF *saison* > ME *sę̄'sun* 'season'.

III. Towards the end of the 13th century the French *u*- diphthongs simplified before labials and before *š* and *ž* (except in the North and North-West):

> *au* > *ā*: *saufe* > *sāfe*
> *eu* > *ę̄*: *rewme* 'realm' > *rę̄me*
> *ou* > *ǭ*: *soudier* 'soldier' > *sǭdier*

IV. OF *ie* had become *ę̄* in Anglo-Norman, but it often retained the older spelling in English and one finds *brief* alongside *bręf, breef, chief* alongside *chęf, cheef*, etc.

V. The OF diphthong *üi* had already become *ü* in Anglo-Norman (but continued to be written *ui*). In English it followed the course of French *ü* and became *iu* or *u*: *fruit, suite, constrewe*.

The diphthong *oi*, not native to English, was introduced into it without difficulty: *chois, noise, joie, joyn*.

The diphthong *ei* remained the same as in English: *moneie, feiþ* 'faith', *streit* 'narrow'.

The OF triphthong *eau* was reduced to *eu* and followed the course of that diphthong (*beu'té*, but the previous spelling was frequently retained *beau'té, 'beauty*).

In Anglo-Norman the palatalized consonants *l', n',* [ɲ], determine the formation of *i*- diphthongs which went over into ME: *batal'e* > ME *bataile, gan'e* > ME *gain, plen'* > ME *plein, plain*.

VI. Under a direct French influence the Scotch tried to keep the palatalized consonant *l'* and rendered it by *lʒ* (thus *assalʒe* 22/459 'to assail' instead of *assaile*).

Summary: Origin of Middle English Vowels (14th Century)

§ 33a.

I. SHORT VOWELS

i OE *ĭ* (§ 23), *ī* (§ 21), *y* (§ 29.2 and REM. V);
   ON *ĭ* (§ 32);
   OF *ĭ* (§ 20).

e OE *ĕ* (§ 23), *ē* (§ 21), *eo* (§ 30, by intermediary of *ö*);
   ON *ĕ* (§ 32);
   OF *ĕ* (§ 20).

a OE *ă* (§ 23), *ǽ* (§ 24), *ȧ* (§ 25), *ea* (§ 30), *ā* (§ 21);
   ON *ă* (§ 32);
   OF *ă* (§ 20).

o OE *ŏ* (§ 23), *ȧ* (§ 25), *ō* (§ 21);
   ON *ŏ* (§ 32);
   OF *ŏ* (§ 20).

u OE *ŭ* (§ 23);
   ON *ŭ* (§ 32);
   OF *ŭ* (§ 20), *ü* (§ 33).

ö OE *eo* (§ 30).

ü OE *y* (§ 29.1);
   ON *y* (§ 32);
   OF *ü* (§ 33).

II. LONG VOWELS

ī OE *ī* (§ 26), *ĭ* (§ 18), *ȳ* (§ 29.2), *ĭġ* (§ 31, REM. IV);
  EME *ēġ* (§ 31, REM. III), *ei* (< OE *e* before [ç], § 31.2);
   ON *ī,ȳ* (§ 32);
   OF *ĭ* (§ 20).

ẹ̄ OE *ē* (§ 26), *ĕ* (§§ 18, 19), *ī* (§ 19), *ǽ₁* (§ 28), *ǽ₂* (Kent,
     § 28, REM. I), *ēo* (by intermediary of *ȫ*, § 30);
   ON *ē* (§ 32);
   OF *ĕ* (§ 20);
   AN *ē* (§ 33, REM. IV).

ę̄ OE $\bar{æ}_2$ (§ 28), $\bar{æ}_1$ (South, § 28, Rem. I), $ĕ$ (§ 19), $\bar{e}a$ (§ 30);
    OF $ĕ$ (§ 20), *ai, ei* (§ 33, Rem. II), *eu* (§ 33, Rem. III).

ā   OE $ā$ (North, § 27), $ă$ (§§ 18, 19), $æ_1$, $æ_2$ (South-East-Mid-
             lands, § 28, Rem. IV);
    ON $ā$ (North, § 32);
    OF a (§ 20), *au* (§ 33, Rem. IV).

ǭ   OE $ā$ (§ 27), $ŏ$ (§§ 18, 19), $å$ (§ 25, Rem. I and II);
    OF $ŏ$ (§ 20), *ou* (§ 33, Rem. III), $ō$ (§ 33).

ọ̄   OE $ō$ (§ 26), $ŏ$ (§ 18), $ŭ$ (§ 19);
    ON $ō$ (§ 32), *au* (§ 32).

ū   OE $ū$ (§ 26), $ŭ$ (§ 18), $ŭg$ (§ 31, Rem. VII);
    ON $ū$ (§ 32);
    OF $ū$ (§ 33 and Rem. I), $ü$ (§ 33).

ȫ   OE $ēo$ (South, and West-Midland, § 30);
    OF   *ue* (§§ 10 and 33).

ǖ   OE $ȳ$ (West-Midlands, § 29.1);
    OF $ü$ (§ 20), $ü$ (§ 33).

III. DIPHTHONGS

iu   OE $īw$ (§ 31.4);
     OF   *eu* (§ 33).

ei   OE $ĕġ$, $\bar{æ}ġ$ (§ 31.1), $ĕ$ and $ẹ$ before [ç] (§ 31.2);
     ON   *ai, ei, ey* (§ 32);
     OF   *ai* (§ 33);
     AN   *ei* (§ 33), *a, e* before l', n' (§ 33).

au   OE   *a* before [x] (§ 31.2), *ag* (§ 31.3), *aw* (§ 31.4);
     ON   *au* (§ 32);
     OF   *au* (§ 33).

oi   OF   *oi* (§ 33).

ou   OE $ā$ and $ō$ before [x] (§ 31.2), $āg$, $ŏg$ (§ 31.3),
             $āw$, $ōw$ (§ 31.4).
     ON   *au* (§ 32);
     OF   *ou* (§ 33).

2. In Unaccented Syllables

General Tendencies

§ 34. As has been said at the beginning (§ 1) one of the out-standing traits which mark the contrast between Old and Middle English is the weakening of vowels in unaccented positions. A consequence of the dynamic stress which tends to throw into shadow everything that is not the accented syllable, this transformation, begun long since (in OE according to Jordan § 133), operates in two stages on the vowel in final position:

1. levelling of the different vowels to *e*;
2. total suppression of this vowel *e* (after passing through the intermediary stage of [ə]).

OE Short Vowels

§ 35. The Old English vowels *a, o, u* merged into *e* as finals and in flexional endings. Thus we have:

Old English	Middle English
sōna ' at once '	*sǫne*
dogga ' dog '	*dogge*
tūnas ' villages '	*tūnes*
tungan ' tongues '	*tungen*
helpan ' help '	*helpe(n)*
sċeadu ' shade '	*schāde*
talu ' story '	*tāle*
sunu ' son '	*sòne*
hēafod ' head '	*hęved*
mōdor ' mother '	*mǫder*
gladost ' gladdest '	*gladest*
macod ' made '	*māked*
tungum ' by tongues '	*tungen*
bundon ' (they) bound '	*bunden*

Thus the flexional endings or terminations *-a, -an, -as, -ast, -aþ, -ol, -on, -or, -ost, -u, -um, -un* became in ME: *-e, -en, -es, -est, -eþ, -er, -el.*

REMARK. — From the 13th century on, first in Northern English, then in the other dialects, we find *i* or *y* instead of *e* in final syllables before a consonant.

For example we have 3rd sg *walkys* 29/197, *giffis* 22/227, pl *freyndys* 29/566, *clerkis* 22/249, pp *merkyd* 29/586 and in the same way, *mēkill* 22/246, *lȳtyll* 29/577, *tǭkyn* 29/611.

Silencing of Final -*e*

§ 36. From the 12th century final -*e* became the obscure vowel [ǝ] then was dropped, little by little, in the pronunciation, although it continued to be written for a long time yet (and into the present epoch).

This began to appear first in unaccented grammatical words: *whanne* 'when' > *whan, þanne* 'then' > *þan, bute, bote* 'but' > *but, bôt, ʒese* 'yes' > *yes.* Then in the 13th century in the North, in the 14th century in the Midlands and South, -*e* was dropped in words of two or three syllables and first in disyllables with short radical vowel: *sóne* 'son' became *sòn* [sune > sunǝ > sun] in a period when *tāle* 'tale' was still pronounced in two syllables [ta·lǝ].

REMARKS — I. It must not be forgotten that scribes had taken up the habit of adding by simple analogy a non-etymological final -*e* to many words. Thus OE *col* 'coal', gen *cǫles* gives ME *cǫle*, and in the same way, ME *lǭre* < OE *lār* 'learning'.

II. Poetry, more conservative than prose, and the more so as it was refined, preserves right up to the end of the 14th century (cp. Chaucer, Gower) the possibility of counting (i. e. of pronouncing) or not the final -*e* according to the necessity of the meter and the harmony of the verse.

Silencing of *e* in Flexional Endings

§ 37. In a general manner, this phenomenon does not take place before the 15th century. Until that time, in the preterit and past participle of weak verbs in -*ed* (but not always), in comparatives in -*er* and superlatives in -*est,* the vowel was still pronounced.

However, syncope was possible:

1. for -*es* (pres ind 2-3rd sg and pl in the Northern dialect, gen and nom pl of substantives in the North, and northern part of the Midlands). This process, started at the beginning of the 14th century, was completed by about 1400. cp. Barbour:

> Frēdom(e) all solac(e) to man giff(i)s
> He lev(y)s at eß that frēly lev(y)s   22/227-8
> It merrys him, body and bān(y)s
> And dēd(e) anoyis him bot ān(y)s   22/271-2

2. for *-eþ* (3rd sg) in the Midlands and South, everywhere after a heavy radical syllable. Compare in the following lines of Gower the forms *gadreþ, pulleþ* on the one hand and *scherþ, berþ* on the other (here and in §§ 39 and 40 *ë* indicates a pronounced flexional vowel, *ę* on the contrary a silent one) :

> Sche fŏnd and gadrëþ herbës suŏtë
> Sche pullëþ up sŏm be þe rŏtë
> And manyę wiþ a knȳf sche scherþ
> And allę intŏ her char sche berþ   28/3999 ff.

Elision

§ 38. 1. In proclitic words, before a vowel, elision of *-e, -o*, or *-i* was possible; one pronounced (and sometimes wrote) *th'emperour* 27₁/368, *t'assay* 27₁/346 (for *to assay*), *t'unnderrstanndenn* 7/48, *t'eve* ' this evening ', *ȝe'tt* for *ȝe itt* 7/3367.

2. Just as in OE (HOE § 35.5) the negative *ne* elides its vowel before auxiliaries and the verb *wite(n)* ' to know ' : *nis = ne is, nęre = ne węre, nil = ne will, naveþ = ne haveþ, nǫt = ne wǫt,* etc.

Syncope of *e* in Trisyllables

§ 39. Old English already had syncope of the post-tonic vowel before liquids (*fugol* ' bird ' nom pl *fuglas, wundor* ' miracle ' gen sg *wundres*). The same phenomenon appears in ME in a much more extended fashion. Thus OE *þanone > þanene > þanne* (which, as we have seen above, ends up as *þan*). OE *fæderas* ' fathers ' > ME *fadres*, OE *munecas > ME mònkes, munkes* (on which a singular *mònk, munk* was reconstructed). This syncope is frequent in Orm who has *enngell* ' angel ' pl *enngless* or *heffness < OE heofones* ' of heaven ', *heffne < OE heofone* ' to heaven '. In the same way we have, as well, *evęrich* ' each ', *owęne* ' own ' (27₄ᴮ/704), *strogęlen* ' struggle '. It was extended to French loan-words: *unbokęle* ' to open ', *seurętee* ' surety ' and even to other vowels occasionally (at least in poetry), thus *suffisaunt* 27₄ᴮ/932, *paraventüre* 27₄ᴮ/935.

Development of a Glide

§ 40. This phenomenon is the inverse of the preceding. In disyllables a glide develops rather frequently in a medial position between a consonant and a nasal, liquid or *w* which follow, thus making tri-syllable like *dēvëles* alongside *dēvles* ' devils ', *ę̄vëre/ę̄vre* ' ever '. Be-tween a liquid and *ȝ* or *w* (product of a former g)˙ it assumes the quality *o*: we find *folowen/folwen* (< OE *folgian* ' to follow '), *halowen/halwen* ' to holler ', *morowe/morwe* ' tomorrow ' (< OE *morgen*).

REMARK. — This glide is very unstable. Poets always have the right to suppress it (or not to make it count) according to the needs of the meter. Cp. for example, Chaucer who writes *y-halowed* 27₁/379, *y-folowed* 27₁/390 (but *folwed* 27₁/397) *brētherẹn* 27₄ᴃ/777 when the verse demands the pronuncia-tions *halwed, folwed, brēthren.*

In a final syllable, between a consonant and nasal or liquid, there is the same development of a glide. Thus *tǭken* ' sign ' < OE *tācn*, *sweven* ' dream ' < OE *swefn*, *setel* ' seat ' < OE *setl*, *āker* ' field ' < OE *æcr*. Cp. also *þuruh* ' through ' alongside *þurh*.

Vowels in Unaccented Prefixes

§ 41. There is generally a reduction of these prefixes with a change of vowel: OE *ȝe-* > ME *i-, e-* (*enōgh, iwis*), OE *of-, on-, ond-* > ME *a-* (*aboute* < *onbūtan, adrēdan* < *ofdrǣdan, anōn* < *on ān*), OE *ymbe-* > ME *um(b)-* (*umstride* ' astride ', *umwhīle* ' now and then ').

§ 42. In French loan-words an unaccented initial vowel may be dropped: ME *mende(n)* < OF *amender*, ME *scāpe(n)* < OF *escaper*, it is even possible to have complete disappearance of the prefix: ME *fende(n)* < OF *defendre*.

Fig. 6.

CHAPTER THREE

THE CONSONANTS

Stability of the System

§ 43. Whereas the vowels went through profound modifications in their passage from OE to ME, what is striking is *the stability of the consonantal system.* Taken as a group, the consonants of OE maintain themselves as such in ME. In the case of French loan-words, their adaptation to the Germanic type of articulation was made without difficulty; and as for words derived from Scandinavian, the type of articulation remained practically the same.

The modifications are primarily pure spelling problems. They are numerous and important, and have been described above, § 8 ff. The treatments that follow deal almost entirely with points of detail, or with very particular facts for this or that dialect.

Voicing of Voiceless Spirants

§ 44. 1. Initially, before a voiced element, *f* and *s* become *v* and *z* south of the Thames. Thus there is *vader* 'father' (Midl. *fader*), *valle* 'fall' (Midl. *fallen*), *volk* 'folk' (Midl. *folk*), *vox* 'fox' (Midl. *fox*), see Figure 6; *zenne* 'sin' (Midl. *synne*), *ziğğe* 'say' (Midl. *seyen*), *zwȳn* 'swine' (Midl. *swin*), *zwǭ* 'so' (Midl. *swǭ*). This voicing is particularly obvious in Kentish texts; elsewhere the spellings do not always show it. (cp. § 12).

It is probable that under the same conditions and in the same dialects *þ* was voiced, but since the spellings everywhere show *þ, th* for the surd as well as for the voiced, and since *ð*, when it is used, is used indiscriminately, it is impossible to draw definite conclusions.

2. In the middle of a word, between two voiced elements, and in all dialects, *f, s, þ > v, z, ð*. This tendency was already at work in OE (HOE § 34); in ME the spellings only show this change for the pair *f/v*: OE *seofon* 'seven' > ME *seven,* OE *swefn* 'dream' > ME *sweven.* Cp. the declensional forms *wīf* 'woman' gen sg and pl *wīves,* the same in *thēf/thēves* 'thief', *turf/turves* 'turf' ; *calf* still had a dative *calve* (13₁ₐ/9) in the 13th century.

39

3. In a final position *-s* > *-z* in unaccented words or syllables, as indicated by some manuscripts which employ *ȝ* or *z* for this purpose.

Devoicing of Voiced Consonants

§ 45. 1. As finals in unaccented monosyllables, *-v, -z, -ð* devoice to *f, s, þ*, at least in the Northern dialect where we have *gif* ' to give ' (Midl. *ȝiven*), *luf* ' to love ' (Midl. *lóven*), *rīs* ' to rise ' (Midl. *rīsen*).

2. Final *-d* becomes *-t* after a voiceless consonant in trisyllabic past participles of weak verbs: we have *punischt* alongside *punisched*.

3. The same devoicing of *-d* into *-t* occurred in West Midlands after *l, r, n*: we have *lǫnt, wīnt, bẹrt, fẹlt* for *lǫnd* ' land ', *wīnd* ' wind ', *bẹrd* ' beard ', *fẹld* ' field '.

Vocalization of Consonants

§ 46. 1. The OE prefix *ǵe-* became *i-* (also written *y-*) by the intermediary *ǵi-* then *ī-*. It remains as an initial, but it is lost in the middle of compounds: OE *nēah-ǵebūr* ' neighbor ' > ME *neiȝbōre, nēȝbūr.*

2. From OE times on, an *i*-glide tended to develop between a liquid and *ǵ* plus vowel, thus OE *myriǵe* ' merry ' alongside *myrǵe, byriǵan* ' to bury ' alongside *byrǵan*. This *-iǵ-* yields *-i-* in ME; *myrie* (*mürie*), *berie* (*bürie*). In the same way, in the final position, the OE adjective suffix *-iǵ* (HOE § 143.8) gives ME *ī* then *ĭ*: OE *bisiǵ* > ME *bysy* ' busy ', OE *hāliǵ* > ME *hǫli* ' holy '.

3. *g* becomes *w* after the back vowels *a, o, u*, and the liquids *l, r* before 1200 (except in Kentish where the change does not appear until about 1400): OE *dragan* > ME *drawen* ' to drag ', OE *folgian* > ME *fol(o)wen* ' to follow ', OE *sorh*, gen *sorge* > ME *sorwe* ' sorrow ', cp. § 31.3.

Assimilation

§ 47. 1. Total or partial sandhi assimilation of dentals in unaccented words: *and þat* > *and tat, and þe* > *and te* 1/9, *at þe* > *atte*, OE *æt þǣm* > ME *atte(n), art þu* > *artu, wilt þu* > *wiltu*.

2. *fm* > *mm*: *lemman* ' lover ' alongside *lēfman, wimman* ' woman ' alongside *wīfman*.

3. $n > m$ before f and p: OF *confort* > ME *comfort*, OF *nonper* > ME *noūmpere* 'umpire'.

4. $pf > ff$: OE **cēapfaru* > ME *chaffāre* 'commerce'.

Metathesis

§ 48. 1. The most frequent is that of r: OE *beorht* > ME *briht*, *bright*, OE *þridda* > ME *third* (alongside *thridde*); in the same way we have in ME *frest* and *first* 'interval', *þruh, throgh* and *þurh* 'through', *brid* and *bird* 'bird'.

2. One must also note *ks* (written x) > *sk* in *aske* alongside *axe* 'to ask' (OE *āxian*). Normally OE *āscian* gives ME *ashien* (cp. 2nd sg *aisheit* 6/995). Cp. HOE § 35.2*b*.

Dropping of Consonants and Simplification of Consonant Groups

§ 49. 1. Post-consonantal w disappears before the back vowels *a, o, u*: OE *swā* 'thus, so, etc.', > ME *sǭ* (alongside *swǭ*), the same for OE *ealswā* > ME *alsǭ, alse, as* (alongside *alswǭ*). *sǭte* 'sweet' appears alongside *swǭte, suche* 'such' alongside *swuche* (cp. the modern pronunciation and the traditional spelling in *sword, answer*).

2. Before a vowel, initial *w*- or *h*- of certain verbal forms (especially auxiliaries) becomes silent after the negative *ne*, by contraction of the whole grouping, whence *nas, nille, nolde, nǫt, naveþ* for *ne was, ne wille, ne wōt*, etc. (cp. § 38.2 and HOE § 35.5).

3. In the Midlands and the South, l often drops before or after *ch*: we have OE *ǣlc* 'each' > ME *ęche*, OE *swylc* 'such' > ME *suche*, OE *hwylc* 'which' > ME *which*, OE *micel* 'much' > ME *myche* (alongside *michel*). The Northern dialect retains such forms as *ilk, swilk, quilk, mikel*.

4. The disappearance of inflectional final -*n* is slow but general: OE *steorran* gen and dat sg > ME *sterre* 'star', OE *sittan* inf > ME *sitten* then *sitte*, OE *sāwon* pret pl > ME *sāwen* then *sāwe* 'they saw', OE *hæfdon* pret pl > ME *hadden* then *hadde* 'they had'; see § 53, and David W. REED, *The History of Inflectional n in English Verbs before 1500*, University of California Publications in English, Volume 74, Berkeley and Los Angeles, 1950.

In short unaccented grammatical words before a consonant, -*n* likewise drops: *ān, ǫ̆n,* > *ă, ǫ̆* ' an, a, one ', *năn, nǫ̆n* > *nă, nǫ̆* ' none ', *mīn* > *mĭ* ' my ', *on* > *o* ' upon ', *in* > *i* ' in ', etc.

5. Before a consonant *-v-* drops: we have *hē̆d* ' head ' alongside *hē̆ved, lādy̆* ' lady ' and *lavedi, lǫrd* ' lord ' and *lǫverd*.

6. Before *st*, between *s* and *m* a *t* drops: we have *best* < *betst* ' better ', *last* ' last ' < *latst, latest, blosme* ' to blossom ' < OE *blōstmian*.

7. Before *s*, a *d* is also sometimes silenced: *answerie* ' answer ' < *andswerien, gospel* < *godspelle, gossip* 'co-parent-in-God ' < *godsib*.

8. Before *n, r* a *þ* (*ð*) drops in grammatical words: we have *wher* alongside *whether* ' if ', *sin* alongside *siþen* ' since '.

9. There is a loss of *k* in the preterit and past participle of *māke(n)* ' to make ': we have *mād(e)* alongside *mākede, māked*. In the same way there is the past participle *tān* ' taken ' alongside *tāken*.

10. In late ME, in unaccented words and syllables, a final *-ch* is lost. We have (and this rather early) *I* ' I ' alongside *ich*. The suffix *-lich* becomes *-lī, -ly*: *lǭth(e)ly* ' ugly ' alongside *lǭth(e)lich, lyghtly* ' easily ' and *lihtlǐche*.

11. Initial *h* becomes silent before *l, n, r*: thus *lē̆pe(n)* < OE *hlēāpan* ' leap, run ', *rynge(n)* ' sound out ' < OE *hringan, rayled* ' covered ' alongside OE *hræ̇gl* ' clothes ', *nute* ' nut ' < OE *hnutu; h* also becomes silent before a vowel in the personal pronoun *it* < *hit*. (That this was by no means general can be inferred from the preservation of *hit* in many ModE dialects in the United States.)

REMARK. — It is difficult to say to just what extent the numerous spellings where OE *hw, wh-* is reduced to *w-* (cp. § 13) represent a genuine silencing of *h-* in the South.

Development of Consonants

§ 50. 1. A *d* develops between *n* and *l, l* and *r*: OE *spinel* > ME *spindle* ' bobbin, spindle ', OE *ealra* gen pl ' of all those ' > ME *alder-* (*alderbeste* ' best of them all '), OE *þunor* ' thunder ' > ME *þunder*.

2. A *t* develops between *s* and *n* and after final *n* or *s*: *glistnen* inf ' to glisten ' alongside the pres part *glisnande* ' glistening ', *agayns* > *against, behē̆ste* ' to promise ' cp. OE *behǣs* ' a promise ', OF *ancien* > ME *auncient*, OF *fesan* > ME *fesaunt* ' pheasant ', OF *tiran* > ME *tyraunt*.

3. A *b* develops between *m* and *l* and after final *-m*: OE *brēmel* 'briar, bramble' gen *brēmles* > ME *brẹ̈mble,* OE *þȳmel* 'thumbstall, thimble' > ME *þimble,* cp. ME *slumber* 'slumber' with ME *slómerynge* 'slumbering'; OE *þūma* 'thumb' > ME *þŭmb(e).*

4. A *p* develops between *m* and *n* or *t*: OE *nemnan* 'to name' > ME *nempne,* OF *damnable* > ME *dampnable,* OE *ǣmtiġ* > ME *empty.*

Change of Articulation

§ 51. *þ* (*ð*) before *m, n, r, l,* becomes *d*: OE *fæðm* 'fathom' > *fadme,* OE *byrðen* 'burden' > ME *birden.*

Other Consonantal Changes

§ 52. 1. In the North and in Scotland, sometimes as well in parts of the East-Midlands, *w* becomes *v*: *vicht* 'vigorous' (*wight*), *vode* 'forest' (*wóde*), *viss* 'wise' (*wīs*).

2. Equally in the North the final *-is(c)h* becomes *-is*: *inglis* 'English', *punnys* instead of *punishe* 'to punish' etc.

3. In the South, or more exactly, among Anglo-Norman scribes (cp. § 12), *wh-* (new spelling for OE *hw-*) often became *w-* (See notes to selections VI, X, and XII for examples): there is *wīle* instead of *whīle* 'while', *wō* instead of *whō, wī* instead of *whȳ,* etc. This may come from a difficulty in articulating a breathed *h,* for we also have *ōure* for *hōure* 'hour' (but see above § 49.11 REM.). This may also indicate an early tendency to reduce [hw] to [w] such as developed later on.

REMARKS. — I. The same scribes by hypercorrection put *h* before words with an initial vowel: e. g., *hūle* for *ūle* 'owl'.

II. Whether or not to pronounce *h* in words written with *wh* troubles speech teachers in America to this day. Records of the standard dialect show only [w] in this position; hypercorrectness recommends [hw].

See Raven I. McDavid, Jr., "Some Social Differences in Pronunciation," *Lang. Learning* 4. 102–16 (1952-53), reprinted in Harold B. Allen, ed., *Readings in Applied Linguistics* (251–61, esp. 255), Appleton-Century-Crofts, U. S. A., 1964, and in the same volume, H. B. Allen, "The Linguistic Atlases: Our New Resource" (212–19, esp. 215). See also R. I. McDavid, Jr. and V. G. McDavid, "h before semi-vowels in Eastern United States," *Language* 28. 41–62 (1962).

PART TWO

THE FORMS

CHAPTER FOUR

GENERAL

Simplification of Forms

§ 53. While Old English is still a richly inflected speech, Middle English, by way of simplification, is a *speech poor in inflection*. The tendency was hastened by the social upheaval and the mixture of tongues that the Norman Conquest brought about, but it was already noticeable in Old English from the end of the 10th century.

Three elements played a determining role in this acceleration:

1. As we have seen above (§ 35), there was a confusion of the unaccented vowels *a, o, u* and *e*, in particular in the syllables that carried the inflection; these different qualities were rapidly levelled in *e*.

2. Analogical substitution from the 11th century of -*an* (then -*en*) for the OE declensional ending -*um*, then progressive loss of all final -*n*'s in inflections.

3. Progressive silencing in the current pronunciation (if not in the orthography) of -*e* final, or become such.

The morphological consequences of these phenomena were the following:

1. *Reduction of the number of case forms* in the declension of the noun, increasing indistinctness of person and mood in the verb. If we judge this by the mistakes made by the scribes, this tendency already operated strongly in the spoken language as early as the 10th century. One of the first modifications which was generalized in the 11th century was the substitution of -*on*, -*an*, then -*en* for the ending

44

-*um* of the dative plural (for substantives), and of the dative singular and plural (for adjectives). There was therefore a moment when *gumen* represented all the singular (except the nominative *gume* 'man') and all the plural (except the genitive *gumene*). But the acceleration is so rapid that, even from the time of one of the oldest Middle English texts, *The Peterborough Chronicle* (selection No. 1), written in 1154, the ending -(*e*)*s* tends to be generalized whatever may be the gender and the type of declension, first, in the singular for the genitive, secondly, in the plural for all cases; and, in many instances, the dative singular is often deprived of inflection; one reads in this text 1/19 *mid deoveles and yvele men* (where OE would have had *mid deoflum and yflum mannum*), 1/54 *biscopes land* (OE *biscopa land*), 1/63 *for ure sinnes* (OE *for urum synnum*), 1/34 *fæstned to an beom* (OE *to anum beame*). On the pattern of the first vocalic declension of OE (HOE § 44 ff.) of the type *tūn* 'village', pl *tūnas* (ME *tūnes*) we find a plural *weorces* 'works' (where OE had the plural *weorc*), *sónes* (OE *suna*) 'sons', *nadres* (OE *nædran*) 'serpents', *limes* (OE *leomu*) 'limbs'. In this same archaic text, the difference between the two declensions, strong and weak, of the adjective (HOE § 78 ff.) is suppressed, and already many of the adjectives have become invariable.

The same can be said about the simplification of forms in the verb. A single ME form like *hadde* corresponds to the 1st and 3rd singular (OE *hæfde*) as well as to the plural (OE *hæfdon*). In the Northern dialect, still more evolved, *had* corresponds, besides the preceding forms, to the preterit optative plural (OE *hæfden*). The Northern dialect extends by analogy the ending -*s* of 2nd singular to the 3rd and to the whole of the plural in the present indicative (*tākes, hēres, has*).

2. *Loss of grammatical gender.* — The endings of Old English made it very easy to distinguish grammatical gender, for the strong declensions, for example, the masculine plurals (*stānas* 'stones'), the neuters (*scipu* 'ships', *word* 'words', *wíf* 'women') or the feminines (*cwēna* 'queens', *hánda* 'hands', *sáwla* 'souls') were still quite distinct. The same for types of weak declensions (*ēagan* 'eyes', *ēaran* 'ears', *fæderas* 'fathers', *ǣgru* 'eggs', *béc* 'books'). From the moment when people said in the plural *schippes, wórdes* or *wíves* for neuters, *quēnes, hǫndes, soules,* for feminines as well as for masculines (*stǫnes*), and the same for the consonantal declensions (*eyes,*

ẹ̄res, fadres, egges, bōkes), nothing in the word any longer indicated its gender. Now at the same time the definite article was simplified and rapidly became invariable; there was therefore no longer either inflectional ending nor any mark of grammatical gender, and the latter disappeared, in its turn replaced as early as Middle English by "natural" gender in the manner of Modern English. Thus the 3rd person feminine pronoun agrees with the word *wīf* 'woman' a former neuter; thus further the monk Orm, as early as the last years of the 12th century, writes *þe whel* (7/3642) like ModE *the wheel,* whereas in OE the use of the article (*þæt hwēol*) would have clearly shown that the word was neuter. By association of ideas masculine abstract substantives tended to become feminine; *sònne* 'sun' is masculine, *mōne* 'moon', *sterre* 'star' are feminine; *dẹ̄eth* 'death' is personified under the traits of an old man (*an ǭld man*) in the *Pardoner's Tale* 27₄ᴮ/675 ff. For other words there was the influence of the gender in French or Latin.

REMARK. — South of the Thames, analogy often acted in Middle English in favor of plurals of the weak type in *-en,* cf. § 57.

3. *Simplification of types of conjugations.* — The difference which existed in Old English between diverse types of weak conjugations tended to become extinct: opposed to OE preterits *fremede* 'he did', *dēmde* 'he judged', *macode* 'he made', ME uniformly has *fremde, dēmde, māde.* Even though the Midlands and South still have two forms for the preterit of the strong verb, opposing the singular *bǭnd* to the plural *bōunde(n)* for the verb 'to bind' (and in the same way, Midl *saugh/sāwe(n)* for 'to see', *sat/sete(n)* for 'to sit') the Northern dialect already recognized no more than a single form for the whole tense: *band, sagh, sat.*

4. Finally, in all inflections, analogy exerted a powerful force in *reducing the number of anomalous forms.* Thus Old English still recognized, in certain cases (HOE § 89), different vocalic forms for the adjective and its degrees of comparison, having *grēat* 'large' but *grīetra* 'larger', *lǎng* 'long, tall' but *lengra* 'longer'. Middle English no longer possessed more than the pair *grēt/gretter* and often replaced *lĕnger* by *lǫ̆nger* because it was more "regular".

CHAPTER FIVE

THE SUBSTANTIVES

General Tendencies

§ 54. As early as Old English there are three poles of attraction for the inflection of substantives (HOE § 67):

1. The vocalic inflection of *a*-stems for masculines and neuters. The *i*-stems (of the type *ġiest* 'stranger') are declined like *stān*, the neuters (of the type *flǣsċ* 'flesh') like *word*. The declensional forms in -*es* of the genitive singular (*stānes*) and in -*as* of the nominative-accusative plural (*stānas*) become dominant over other types of masculines: more and more *fæder* 'father' was declined gen *fæderes*, nom pl *fæderas* or *frēond* 'friend' gen *frēondes*, nom pl *frēondas*.

2. The vocalic inflection of *ō*-stems for feminines: On the model of *ġiefu* 'gift' (pl *ġiefa* then *ġiefe*) are declined the feminine *i*-stems (*dǣd* 'deed') and *īn*-stems (*strengu* 'strength')

3. Finally the consonantal inflection of *an*-stems, called the weak declension (*nama* 'name' pl *naman*).

The Three Types of Inflection

§ 55. The tendencies analyzed in the preceding chapter combine to increase this force of attraction in such a way that at the start of Middle English one can still distinguish three types of inflection:

	I	II	III
Sg Nom-Acc	—	-e	-e
Gen	-(e)s	-es	-e
Dat	-e	-e	-e
Pl	-(e)s	-es	-en, gen -en(e)

For example:

	I			II		III	
Sg NA	stǭn	trē	wȳf	ēnde	soule	nāme	
G	stǭnes	trēs	wȳves	ēndes	soules	nāme	
D	stǭn(e)	trē	wȳve	ēnde	soule	nāme	
Pl	stǭnes	trēs	wȳves	ēndes	soules	nāmen	(gen nāmene)

stǭn 'stone', former masculine (*a*-stem); *trē* 'tree', *wȳf* 'woman', former neuters (*a*-stems); *ēnde* 'end', former masculine (*ja*-stem); *soule* 'soul', former feminine (*ō*-stem); *nāme* 'name', former consonantal *an*-stem.

Schematizing a good deal, one can say that at the start of **Middle English** the dialectal distribution of these three types is the following:

the Northern dialect only shows type I;
the Midlands dialects show types I and II;
south of the Thames types I, II, and III appear.

In the course of the Middle English period the evolution is the following:

1. Type III tends to disappear and merges with type II. The declension of *nāme* thus becomes:

Sg	NA	nāme
	G	nāmes
	D	nāme
PL		nāmes

2. Then type II merges with type I by the silencing of final *-e*, in such a way that by the end of the Middle English period there is no more, outside of a few exceptions, than a single type of declension:

Sg	NAD	stǭn
	G	stǭn(e)s
Pl		stǭn(e)s

which is to say that we have reached the state of the modern language.

REMARK. — To be sure, what has just been said applies to the actual forms of the spoken language. From the point of view of the spelling, final *-e* (silent) tends on the contrary to be extended, and scribes wrote *wȳfe* 'woman' and finally *stǭne* like *ēnde, soule, nāme,* etc.

The Cases in Detail: I. Singular

§ 56. 1. *Nominative.* — We see that between types I and II the substantives are distributed according to whether they end in final *-e* (type II *ēnde, soule*) or not (type I *stǭn, trē, wȳf*). In the Northern dialect, from the beginning, final *-e* became silent (*end, saul, luf* 'love').

2. *Accusative.* — It became practically identical with the nominative case where it was not already so in Old English.

3. *Genitive.* — The ending *-es* or *-s* of masculine-neuter *a*-stems was extended to all substantives and to all three genders. It was written *-is* or *-ys* in Northern texts, also at times there was the device

26/23 *a child hys brouch* 'a child's toy' (cp. § 109, REM.) where *child hys* is perhaps the phonetic equivalent of *childes, childis*.

A genitive in *-en* is only encountered in the oldest Southern texts. There were still a few *genitives with zero inflection*; in this case it may be a matter of former strong feminine *e*-genitives, as in 7/36 *sawle nēde* 'soul's need' or 7/3653 *sawle brǣd* 'soul's bread, spiritual nourishment', 20/708 *werlde ryche* 'world's realm', or it may be weak declension substantives (in *-an* > *-en* > *-e*) like 3/130 *ancre ahte* 'nun's possessions', 3/110 *heorte blōd*, 27₄ᵦ/902 *herte blood* 'heart's blood', 29/611 *ẹẹre-marke* 'ear('s)-mark (for sheep)' or finally old genitives already deprived of their endings in Old English, such as the names of relatives (cp. HOE § 63) as in 5/32 *his fāder saule* 'his father's soul', *hir doghter nāme* 'her daughter's name'. But since, as a general rule, the genitive complement of the noun had always been ante-posed (§ 167), it is sometimes difficult, in the case of *ẹẹre-marke* or of 5/13999 *his süster sune* to distinguish them from compound nouns (cp. OE *swuster sunu* 'sister's son').

We have to do with another type of genitive singular with zero ending in the words in *-s* or *-ch* or before a word starting with *s-*, for reasons of euphony: 3/141 *þe church vestemenz* 'the church's vestments', 27₁/372 *the forest sȳde*, 'the forest's edge', *hors feet* 'horse's hooves', but this has absolutely nothing regular about it, and we find 16/66 *man saule* 'man's soul' beside 16/48 *mens syghte* 'men's sight'.

4. *Dative.* — A dative in *-en* (for substantives of the older weak declension) is witnessed only in the oldest Southern texts. In so far as Middle English still had an inflection for the dative singular, it was *-e*; but from the beginning there was a great deal of hesitation in its use: for substantives whose nominative ends in a consonant, very early we find datives without inflectional endings: thus the datives *hūs* (1/29, 7/5, 27₄ᵦ/785), *ʒer* (7/32), *God* (2/49). The dative being essentially the case of the indirect object, the inflectional ending tends to be replaced by a preposition, compare 10/158 *Gode þonk* and its modern equivalent *thank(s) to God*. The Middle English that represents, in this respect, a transitional period, shows sometimes—especially in verse—the example of prepositions followed by a dative in *-e*: for ex:

> ¹Nou ich ¹am in ¹clenë ¹livë
> Ne ¹recchẹ ich of ¹childë ¹ne of ¹wivë   10/227-8

(opposed to the nominatives *lif, wif*, cp. § 44.2).

The Cases in Detail: II. Plural

§ 57. The normal inflectional ending is *-es* for all substantives, and, barring the few exceptions which will be treated later, this *nominative-accusative inflection* is extended into the genitive and dative so that there is a *common form* for all cases in the plural.

But this extension, realized at a very early moment in the Northern dialect and in a section of the Midlands, operated more slowly in the rest of England because it had to fight against the rivalry of the inflectional ending *-en*. The dialects of the South not only maintained but extended this ending by analogy to substantives which are not from former Old English *an*-stems. On the model of *eyen* 'eyes' < OE *eāgan* (27₄/684, cp. *ę̄hnen* 3/28, *eyne* 12/680, etc.), of *fān* 'foes' < OE *fān* (3/55, cp. *i-foan* 11/20), of *hȳnen* 'hinds, servants' < OE *hīwan* (24/12) and several others, were made plurals such as *shoon* 'shoes' 24/23 (OE *scōs*), *dēoflen* 'devils' 3/86 (OE *dēoflas*), *wōrden* 'words' 11/36 (OE *word*), *sünnen* 'sins' 10/177 (OE *synna*), *sǫnden* 'messengers' 3/58 (OE *sånda*), *hǫnden* 'hands' 3/74 (OE *hånda*), *brētheren* 'brothers' 27₄ᴮ/777 (OE *brōðor*), *dehtren* 'daughters' (OE *dohtor*), *children* 'children' (OE *ċildru*), *kȳn* 'cows' (OE *cȳ*), and even *plāten* 'pieces (of money)' 13₃/4 (OF *plates*) etc. It was not until the 14th century that the plural in *-es* definitely won out, but Modern English, current or archaic, has preserved a few of these *en*-plurals (*oxen, children, brethren, kine*).

REMARK. — The vowels of *dehtren, brētheren* are formed, it seems, on those of the dative singular inflection in Old English (*dehter, brēðer*, cp. HOE § 63). The adoption of the form *kȳn* perhaps was facilitated by the old genitive plural OE *cȳna*.

Umlaut Plurals

§ 58. Middle English preserved a certain number of umlaut plurals of the former radical consonant stems (HOE § 61): *fēt* 'feet', *men* 'men', *gees* 'geese', *tēþ* 'teeth', *kȳn* 'cows'. We find also, now and again, *gēt* 'goats' 10/167 and *hēnd* 'hands' (from ON *hendr*) 12/505, alongside the more current forms *gǫtes, hǫndes*.

REMARK. — The word *breech* 'trousers, pants' is the former OE plural *brēċ* from the singular *brōc*; but in Middle English the word is generally treated like a singular and a regular plural *brēches* is re-made from it.

r-Plurals

§ 59. Of this type of plural, already very much reduced in Old English (HOE § 65), there remained in Middle English only the three words *lǫmb* 'lamb' (pl *lǫmber*), *calf* 'calf' (pl *calvre*) and *child* 'child' (pl *childer*) which had as well the 'double plurals' in *-en*: *lǫmbren, calvren* (alongside *lambes, calves*) and *children*, the last alone having survived. For the name of 'egg' *ei*, Middle English knew only the double plural *ei-r-en* (the Northern dialect substituted a form of Scandinavian origin *egg*, pl *egges* which is the sole surviving form in the modern language).

Plurals without Inflectional Signals

§ 60. It is convenient to distinguish here several categories of substantives:

1. *Former neuter monosyllables* with long syllables which, in Old English, had a nominative-accusative plural with zero inflection (cp. HOE § 46.4). These words, which in Middle English normally had a plural in *-es*, are also found, especially in the 12th and 13th centuries, with a plural without inflectional ending: thus there is *wōrd* 'word(s)' 5/31, *þing* 'thing(s)' (3/16 *alle þe wa þing* 'all the bad things'), *lēaf* 'leaf(s)' 5/23 *ʒēr* 'year(s)' (see below).

In the same category fall the names of domestic animals, certain of which have preserved until today an invariable plural, thus in Middle English, *hors* 'horses' 12/701, *swȳn* 'pigs' 12/701, 21₃/19, 24/10, *shēp* 'sheep' 10/167, 12/700, 21₃/18 and still *dēr* 'wild animals', *neet* 'cattle'; some of these words are often used with a collective significance: 24/10 *tō kēpe swȳn* 'to raise hogs'.

2. Under the probable influence of the word *ʒēr* 'year(s)', which belongs to the preceding category, a certain number of terms of measure, of various formation, origin and gender are used in the plural without inflection after a numeral, especially at the end of a syntactic group. One wrote 3/30 *vōur þūsend ʒer* 'four thousand years', 14/72 *fȳve wyntyr* 'five winters', 14/64 *syxe mȳle* 'six miles' 27₁/422 *fourty or fifty fadme lengthe* 'forty or fifty fathom(s) length' (but they could also say 14/69 *tēn ʒēres* 'ten years') and the same with *niht* 'night(s)', *pōund* 'pound(s)', *mark* 'mark(s), i. e. about eight ounces', etc.

REMARK I. — In the preceding locutions *foot* or *fadme* could also very possibly represent former genitive plurals (OE *fōta, fæðma*) which we know were the rule after numerals (cp. HOE § 157 2*b*) in Old English.

3. In a sporadic fashion *former consonantal stems* (HOE § 60 ff.) like *süster* ' sisters ' 3/16, *bōc* ' books ', *feōnd* ' enemies ' 5/14059; cp. *foot, niht,* above.

4. *Words of romance origin ending in a sibilant.* —.For example, 20/808 *the seven scȳence* ' the seven (liberal) arts ', 21₄/317 *tweyne of his prentis* ' two of his apprentices ', 26/40 *meny caas* ' many cases ', 27₁/463 *tēn vers* ' ten verses '.

II.— In such cases as 27/376 *thre mot* ' three notes (on a hunting horn)' (riming with *hot*), 18/1316 *two . . . dame* ' two ladies ' (riming with *same*), it is more likely a matter of negligence on the part of the poet, for we find this just as much with a native word: 8/497 *his twelf y-fere* ' his twelve companions ' (riming with *lupere*).

Genitive Plural

§ 61. Although the extension of the nominative plural in *-es* to all substantives and all cases in the plural was a rapid phenomenon, we find, especially in the oldest texts, some survivals of genitive plurals like 1/41 *xix wintre* ' nineteen winters ' (cp. § 60 REM. I), 3/139 *ōðer monne þinges* ' other men's things ' (the same with *menne* 21₃/29 and 70), 5/13995 *richest alre kinge* ' most powerful of all kings ' (cp. the OE genitives *wintra, mănna, cyninga*). Similarly, especially in the South, we find genitive plurals in *-ene* which represent the older weak declension genitive plurals in *-ena* or their extension, as in 5/9 *englene lǫnde,* 11/37 *Englene loande* ' England (lit. land of the Angles)' and also *widewene* 10/201, *lollarene* 21₃/31, *knāvene* 21₃/54.

Inflection of Romance Loans

§ 62. The numerous French substantives which crowded into English from the 13th century on had no difficulty in inserting themselves into the new type of simplified inflection of Middle English, they may even have contributed to favoring its extension. Indeed, the declension of substantives in Old French was already reduced, for feminines and neuters, to the contrast singular/plural and we have *heure/heures* ' hour ', *joie/joies* ' joy '. The masculines, on the contrary, still distinguished in the singular as in the plural, two cases, the subject case and the object case, and we have, for example:

Sg Subject	*murs* ' wall '	*bers* ' baron '	*sire* ' lord '
Object	*mur*	*baron*	*seigneur*
Pl Subject	*mur*	*baron*	*seigneur*
Object	*murs*	*barons*	*seigneurs*

But, from the beginning of the 13th century, the feminine-neuter pattern was extended to the masculines because for the latter the object form came to be used for the subject.

In Middle English we have, thus, for the feminines and neuters *hōure/hōures* as well as *joie/joies*. For the masculines the words were borrowed in the singular under the object case form which did not require an inflectional signal: thus, it is not the subject *bers* but the object case *baron* which passes into Middle English (*barōun*). As for the plural, since it was almost always in -*s* (or sometimes in -*z*) in Old French, it was quite naturally identified with the plural in -(*e*)*s* which was being generalized for English words (OF *barons* > ME *barōuns*). The same inflectional signal in the genitive singular was used for these French words as for native words (*hōures*, *joies*, *barōuns*) which completed their acclimatization.

REMARKS. — I. Exceptionally, certain words were borrowed into English under the subject case form, for example *sire*, *povert*(*e*) (alongside the object case form *povertee*).

II. In Old French *z* was written for *ts* at the end of words: whence some plurals like *restemenz* 3/141. Following this, in English, *tz* was used, thus *emprisonementz* 25/19, *merchauntz*, etc.

III. On plurals of the type *vers*, cp. above § 60.4.

IV. Words borrowed from Latin enter English — at least up to 1400 — under their French garb.

CHAPTER SIX

THE PRONOUNS

Reduction of Case Forms

§ 63. Just like that of substantives, the inflection of the pronouns which, in Old English, was relatively rich (cp. HOE § 68), suffered an equally great simplification in Middle English, but this was only effected little by little. The end product of this gradual process is the *complete elimination of the accusative* to the profit of the dative which henceforth served as the object case opposed to the nominative, the subject case (such had commenced in Old English for a part of the personal pronouns). Besides, in the personal pronoun, the old genitive case ceased to be used as such in EME and assumed gradually the function of possessive pronoun (cp. § 66). To express the genitive, *of* followed by the object case was used. Alongside the possessive adjective, already in existence in Old English, we see appearing in the 14th century a distinct possessive pronoun, at least for the plural. The evolution of the demonstratives is more drastic: the article rapidly became invariable and the other demonstratives maintained, in the end, only the distinction of singular and plural, losing all inflection for case and all contrast for gender. In the other direction, it is in the course of Middle English that were created the relative pronouns which were lacking in Old English.

A. PERSONAL PRONOUNS

1. Personal Pronouns with Undifferentiated Gender

§ 64.	First Person		Second Person	
	Singular	Plural	Singular	Plural
Subject	ich, ic, ik, I, y	wē	þū, thou, tóu	ȝē, yē
Object	mḗ	ūs, óus	þē, thee, tē	eu, óu, ȝów, ȝóu, yóu

REMARKS. — I. *First person, singular, subject.* — *ich* is the stressed form of the South and the Midlands (also written *iĉ* up to 1200); *ic, ik* is the stressed form of the North. The latter form very early gave rise to an

54

unstressed form *y*, *I* (on the spelling cp. § 13, REM. III) which was used first, north of the Thames, before a word beginning with a consonant (1/39 *I ne can*, 2/5 *I lede*, 8/544 *I schal*); little by little this unstressed form became the general usage in the common language of the 14th century and even invaded the area south of the Thames, where, however, *ich* remained the usual form. Chaucer generally has *I* in all positions and only uses *ich* rarely (27₄ʙ/947 *sǭ thee'ch* 'as I hope to get along in the world'). *Mandeville*, Gower and Wyclif always have *I*. Note that in Middle English *I* is always short [ɪ]. It is only in the 15th century that the vowel was lengthened in a stressed position [ɪ>ɪ:>i/i·] to give rise to the Modern English diphthong [ei] then [ai]. But see Eliason *MLN* **69**, 137 who disputes Wyld's p. 228.

II. *First person, dual.* — Old English still possessed special forms for the dual, for the first two persons (cp. HOE § 68 f.). A few traces of these remained up to the start of the 13th century, at least for the first person; there was the subject case *wit* 'we two' (5/14039, 7/7) and the genitive (become possessive) *unker* (6/993 in *unker sīpe* 'in our case, i. e., for both of us').

III. *Second person, singular.* — Alongside *þŭ*, *þōu* there was an enclitic form *tŭ*, *tōw* (and even *te*) often attached to the verb (cp. § 47.1), for example *artōw* 'art thou', *hastōw* 'hast thou' (21₄/311), *wiltōw*, *woltōu* 'wilt thou' *wenest tŭ* 'thinkest thou' (3/25), *wilte* 'wilt thou' (12/528). In the same way, though rarer, the object case *þĕ* yielded after a final *-t* a form *tĕ*: 3/19 *went te awei* 'wend thee away'.

IV. *Second person, plural, object case.* — The oldest form is *eu*, *ōu* (<OE *ēow*); the current form, from the 13th century on, *ʒōw*, *ʒōu*, *yōu*, results either from a displacement of the accent ('*eow*>*e'ow*), or from a contamination of the subject case *ʒē* with *ōu*. On the use of the forms of the 2nd person plural, see § 118.

2. Third Person Pronouns

§ 65.   **Singular**

	M	Neut	F
Subject	hĕ, hee, hā, a	hit, it, a	1. hĕo, hue, hǭ, hĕ, ha, hĭ 2. ʒhō, chō, schō 3. schĕ, shĕ
Object	*Acc.* hine, hin *Dat.* him	hit, it him	} hire, hir, hure

Plural

	North	Midlands	South
	Scandinavian		Native	
Subj	þai, þay, thai	þei, þeʒ	hȳ, hĕo, hǭ, hĕ, ha, a	
Obj	þaim, thaim, thame	heom, hem	*Acc.* hī, hise, his, hes, hies, es *Dat.* heom, hem, hŏm, ham

REMARKS. — I. *Singular, masculine.* — The forms *ha, a* are naturally unstressed forms. The accusative forms *hine, hin* (<OE *hine, hiene*) are only met south of the Thames; they were supplanted everywhere else by the dative *him* which served as object.

II. *Singular, neuter.* — The form *it* results from the weakening of *h* in an unstressed position; it appeared as early as the 12th century; after the 14th century it definitely supplanted *hit* in the common literary language. In the object case Middle English always uses *hit* or *it* for the direct object, *him* for the indirect.

III. *Singular, feminine, subject.* — It is possible to gather the great diversity of forms into three principal types which correspond to a rather clear dialectal distribution (see Fig. 7):

1. The *hēo-* type which is that of the South and the West-Midlands. It was the form taken in Middle English by Old English *hēo* ' she ' and was at first written in the same way, even while being pronounced [hŏ]; some spellings like *ho* and *hue* perhaps correspond to the same pronunciation. Then [hŏ] was unrounded to [hē] written *he*; when the vowel closes it borders on [hī] written *hi, hy* which is the Kentish form. This form allows an unaccented form *ha* (for example in the *Ancrene Wisse*).

2. The *schǭ* type which is that of the Northern dialect and of Scots. It is perhaps the form taken in Middle English by the Old English feminine demonstrative *sēo*, then *sīo* with a displacement of accent (*s'io > si'o > sj'o*) which would have facilitated the palatization of *s* to *sh* [s to š]. But it must be remarked that the Old English feminine *hēo* could very well, by an analogous process (*h'io > hi'o > hj'o > hj'o*), arrive at the same palatization. Beside the spellings *shǭ, schǭ* we have *cho* (*Morte d'Arthur*, 20/715, etc.) and *ʒhō* in the *Ormulum* (a spelling which notes perhaps more precisely the stage [hjō]. This type, native of the North, was extended, however, to the North West Midlands (*Sir Gawain: scho* 18/1259 but normally *ho*) as well as the North East Midlands (*Ormulum, Havelok*).

3. The *schę̄, shę̄* type which is essentially that of the East-Midlands. It is found as early as the *Peterborough Chronicle* under the form *sćǣ*. This is the type which is met, to the exclusion of all others, in the common literary language, in the second half of the 14th century (*Mandeville*, Wyclif, Chaucer, Gower). The origin of the *schę̄* form is obscure and very controversial. It is not impossible that it goes back, just like the other two, but by a somewhat different process, to the Old English feminine 3rd person *hēo* (Cp. A. H. SMITH, RES, 1, 437 ff.). It is only necessary to remark that in certain dialectal areas of type 1 (*hēo/hō*) there was a homophony between the 3rd singular feminine pronoun and the 3rd plural (*hī, hī, hēo*) which resulted in a very great ambiguity.

IV. *Singular, feminine, object case.* — There existed, south of the Thames, an accusative form *hēo* in Lawman (5/21,14029), *hī* in the *Owl and the Nightingale*; but these forms of the accusative were eliminated from the end of the 13th century, and after that, in all dialects, it was the form inherited from the older dative which acted as object case. It was written, almost indiscriminately, *hir(e)* or *her(e)*.

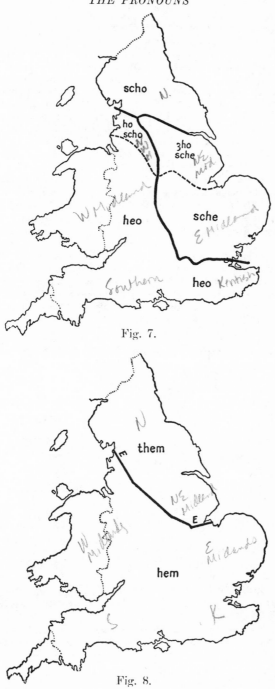

Fig. 7.

Fig. 8.

V. *Plural.* — The forms of the 3rd person plural pronoun for which the table above gives a rough distribution, are of three types:

1. *The native type*, represented in a pure state by the dialects of the South, agrees with the forms taken by Old English *hīe* (*hī*) and *him*, namely, Middle English *hȳ, hī* (subject), *hī* (accusative), *hem* (dative). On the spelling and the phonetic value of the diverse variants I would make the same observations as above (REM. III.1). Alongside *hī*, the accusative (which is scarcely met with except south of the Thames) has the curious forms *es* and (by a cross with *hī*) *his, hise, hes* whose equivalent we find not in Old English but on the Continent in Old Frisian, the West Germanic dialect closest to English. As for the other persons, the accusative was eliminated to the profit of the dative which became the sole object case.

2. *The Scandinavian type*, represented in a pure state by the Northern dialect and Scots and which agrees with the forms borrowed from Old Norse *þei-r* (subject), *þeim* (dative) whence Middle English *þai* and *þei, þaim*.

3. *The mixed type* which is that of the Midlands and which agrees with a subject form type 2 (Scandinavian) *þei, they* and an object form of type 1 (native) *hem* (written *'em* in the modern language). This type is that of the London dialect and the common language in the second half of the 14th century. As is well shown, and that very early, by the example of the *Ormulum* (where we find *þeȝ, hem* and *þeȝm*), it was the North that progressively contaminated the Midlands and London. An object form, *them*, was nevertheless unknown in the language of the capital before the 15th century.

For the geographic distribution of these various forms, see Fig. 8.

Possessive Pronouns (see also § 168)

§ **66.** 1st Pers.	2nd Pers.	3rd Pers.	
		Masc-Nt	Fem
Sg　mīn, mĭ	þīn, þĭ, thȳ̆	his, hise, hies hys, hüs	hire, here hir, her
Pl　ūr(e), ōur(e)	ȝūr(e), yōur(e), ōure	here, her, hör, heore, hare, hire, hüre; þeȝre, þayr, thair, thār.	

REMARKS. — I. The forms *mĭ, mȳ, þĭ, þȳ* are only found before consonants, but this is by no means obligatory. 27₄ᴮ/727 *mȳ lȳf* 'my life', 8/536 *þĭ wīf* 'thy wife', but 10/160 *mīne frēnd* 'my friends', 10/155 *þīne children* 'thy children'. Before a vowel (and before *h*) *mīn, þīn* are used: 27₄ᴮ/724 *mȳn āge* 'my age', 13₃/14 *þīn hę̄ved* 'your head'.

II. The possessives of the first and second persons are declined like adjectives (cp. § 74), that is, they take an *-e* in the plural when the singular does not end in that vowel: 3/24 *mīne lēove süstren* "my dear sisters," 12/620 *þīne cherles, þīne hīne* " your rustics, your servants." Besides, we meet in the 12th century traces of a more complete declension such as we have in Old English, for example, for the feminine genitive singular *þīre* (<OE *þīnre*; 5/14053 *þīre süster sune* 'the son of thy sister '), for the feminine dative singular *mīre, þīre* (<OE *mīnre, þīnre*; 5/14024 *mid mīre leoft hǫnde* 'with my left hand ', 6/915 *mid þīre stevene* 'with thy voice '); but this is only occasional and the same texts write 6/927 *mid mīne sǫnge* 'with my song '.

III. There existed in the 12th century forms of the dual for the 1st person (*unker* 6/993) and the second (*incer*).

IV. In the 3rd person singular *his* is naturally the common form for masculine and neuter. In the feminine the form most generally used up to 1400 is *hir(e)*. *Her* does not spread into the literary language until the 15th century and then rather slowly.

V. In the 3rd person plural the dialectal distribution of the types *her(e)* and *þeir(e)* is, on the whole, the same as that for the object case of the personal pronoun *hem* and *þaim*. The form *þeir(e)* is that of the Northern dialect and Scots, with the exception of the *Ormulum*, which, very early, employs the form *þeȝre*; no other East Midland text before the 15th century uses any other form except *her(e)*. In the North-West Midlands dialect the normal form is *hür(e)*, but after 1350 there is sometimes *þayr* (thus 18/1362). The Southern and Kentish forms are *heore* and *hare* (alongside *here, hire*).

The possessive forms just enumerated were used for a long time as adjectives and also as pronouns, for ex:

> Lǫverd, wē aren bǫþe þīne,
> þīne cherles, þīne hīne. 12/619-20

' Lord, we are both thine, thy rustics, thy servants '. However, in the course of Middle English, a differentiation occurred. The possessives in -*r(e)* had special forms for the pronoun in -*res*: *hires, heres* (3 sg f), *ōures* (1st pl), *ȝoures* (2nd pl), *heres, þeires, þaires* (3 pl). These new forms appeared first in the North and only reached the Midlands in the second half of the 14th century when they entered the literary language. Chaucer writes:

> But myghte this gōld be caried fro this plãce
> Hoom to mȳn hõus, or elles untō *yõures* —
> For wel wē wǫt þat al this gōld is *õures* — 27₄ᴮ/784-6

' But if this gold could be carried home from this place to my house or else to yours (for we know well that all this gold is ours)'. Cp. also 18/1387.

This form also begins to be used for the post-positional possessive adjective:

> He was, pardee an ǫld felawe *of yõures* 27₄ᴮ/672

' He was, pardee, an old friend of yours '.

VI. Orm, in East-Midland had already used the pronominal form *þeȝȝrs*.

VII. In the South and the Midlands, it was on the model of the forms in
-n (*min*, *þin*) that the possessive pronouns of the type *hisen*, *hiren*, *ōuren*,
jōuren, *heren*, *theiren* were made. These forms, which did not get into the
literary language, survive in the dialects of today — especially in the United
States.

B. DEMONSTRATIVE PRONOUNS

1. The Definite Article

§ 67. While in Old English the demonstrative-article was a grammatical word provided with a complete flexion with three grammatical
genders in the singular (cp. HOE § 72), the tendency in all dialects
in Middle English was towards simplification: first to be eliminated
were the nominative singular forms *sē* (masculine), *sēo* (feminine)
which were replaced by a new form *þe*, which tended to become from
a very early period the common invariable form of the article even in
the South (*Poema Morale, The Owl and the Nightingale*, John of
Trevisa) and in East-Midland (*Peterborough Chronicle, Ormulum*).
The Northern dialect recognizes only this indeclinable form. The
London region used it as early as the *Proclamation* of 1258.

However, concurrent with this invariable form, we still encounter
inflected forms in the 12th and 13th centuries in the dialects of the
South and of the West-Midland. Here are the examples which are
found in the texts of this *Handbook*:

		S W Midlands	S E (London)	Kent
Sg Masc	N			sē 9/23
	A	þene 3/52, 10/113, 126, 242	þane 11/24	þane 9/10
	G	þes 5/22		
	D	þan 5/10, þēne 5/29	**þan**	þā 9/16, þō 9/3, 5
Nt	NA	þet 3/113, þat 10/74 etc.	þæt 11/6	þet 9/13
	Instr	þe 3/53		
Fem	N			si 9/13
	A	þā 5/15		þō 9/12, tō 9/10
	D	þer 3/29, þāre 5/21	þǣre 11/37	þō 9/29
Pl	NA	þā 5/23	þō 11/36	þō 9/11, 28
	D		þan 11/9, 13	

In the East-Midland dialect, the *Peterborough Chronicle* as early as 1154 shows alongside the invariable form only one plural *þā* (1/19) ; the situation is the same in the *Ormulum*.

In the common literary language (Wyclif, Chaucer, Gower) the article has regularly become an indeclinable word. The plural *þō*, however, appeared still in the *Travels of Mandeville*, alongside *the*, and in Gower (with the value of a demonstrative).

REMARK. — The old instrumental masculine and neuter *þӯ* is no longer used after Middle English begins, except as an adverb, in particular before the comparative (cp. § 115.4) ; it has the form *þe* (which is confused with the article) or *þī* (6/860).

2. The Genuine Demonstratives

§ **68.** 1. The word *þat*, which ceased to be used as the grammatical neuter of the article, took on more and more the value of the singular demonstrative for all grammatical genders. As a plural first the forms of the article *þā*, *þō* (*þeo*) were used except in the North. Then this latter form was eliminated little by little in favor of *þās, þōs* (< OE *þās*).

REMARK. — In Orm, after a dental, *þat* becomes *tat* (cp. § 47.1).

2. The OE type of compound demonstrative masc *þĕs*, neut *þis*, fem *þēos*, pl *þās* still maintained itself with these forms differentiated for gender up to the end of the 12th century. Thus in *Ancrene Wisse* we find 3/85 *þes king* ' this king ', 3/95 *þis scheld* ' this shield ' (neut), 3/83 *þeos leafdi* ' this lady ', plural 4/34 *þeo* ' those '. There are even remnants of flexion : masc acc sg 5/14073 *þisne swikedom* ' this treason ', fem dat sg 3/85 *o þisse wīse* ' in this manner '.

Then *þis* (neut nom-acc sg) in the East-Midlands and the North, *þes* (masc nom sg) in the South were generalized without distinction and without flexion. On this singular was formed a new plural *þise*, *þēse*.

3. Other Demonstratives

§ **69.** Middle English shows the· demonstratives *self* (*seolf, sölf,* pl *selve, selven*) ' the same person ' and *ilk, ilch, ych* ' the same person or thing, that very one ' which serve to constitute re-enforcing forms (cp. § 121) for the personal pronoun and for the demonstratives; *ilk*(*e*) was also bound in with the definite article to give *thilke* ' this very one ' (for ex. 6/1038).

C. INTERROGATIVE PRONOUNS

§ 70. 1. The pronoun *whō* 'who?' neut *what* 'what?, which?' has the following forms:

	Masculine-Feminine	Neuter
N	whō (wō, huō)	⎧ what,
		⎨ (wat, hwat, hwet, quat)
A	whōm	⎩ what

G	whōs
D	whōm (wōm, whām, whaym)

2. The pronouns and adjectives *whether* (*weþer, whēr(e), huader, quhethir*) 'which?' and *which* (*hwucche, huyche, whylk, wylke*) 'who? what? which one?'

D. RELATIVE PRONOUNS

§ 71. The relative pronoun *par excellence* in Middle English is *þat, that* (*þet*) 'who, what, he who, etc., that which etc.'. It is met at the start combined with *sē* (*sē þet* 9/16), and, as well, up to 1250 we find *þe* (1/19, 4/34, 13₂/80) which may represent the relative particle of Old English (HOE § 181), but perhaps may also be a particular use of the new definite article (cp. A. McIntosh, *English and Germanic Studies*, 1 (1948), 73-87). Both are indeclinable.

In the 14th century began to be used as relatives the interrogative pronouns *which*, pl *whiche* 'who, that, which' (and, as an adjective 'the one, that '—e. g., *which book I took* = 'that book I took', equally *the which* 'this, that one') as well as the genitive *whōs* and the object case *whōm*.

REMARKS. —.I. It will be noted that the subject form *whō* is still *not yet used as a simple relative*, but only as an interrogative. One could say 10/122 *Wō haveþ þē in þe pütte i-brout?* 'Who has put you in the well?' It was impossible to say * *Criseyde whō felte*, but only 27₂/1198 *Criseyde which . . . felte* ' C. who felt . . .' This last example shows that *which* is widely used in Middle English with a person as antecedent.

II. In Scots we also find the relative particle *at* (of Scandinavian origin): 22₁/247-8 *do That at hys hart hym drawis to* ' do That which his heart urges him to do '.

§ 72. The principal adverbial relatives are *thēr, thēr that, whēr, whēr that* and *as, whēreas* ' where ' : 27₄ᵦ/886 *the botel thēr the poyson was* ' the bottle where the poison was ', 27₄ᵦ/749 *Ī moote gǭ thider as I have to gǭ* ' I must go there where I have to go ', 23/51 *a paradys whēre þat þey scholde see God* ' a paradise where they would see God '. There exist, besides, numerous composite relative adverbs like *whērmid* ' with which ', *whērof* ' from, of which ', *whēron* ' upon which ', *whērthourgh* ' by means of which ', etc.

what serves as a neuter conjunctive pronoun ' that which ' (alongside *þat*) and as the relative adjective ' which '.

E. INDEFINITE PRONOUNS

§ 73. The principal indefinite adjectives and pronouns are :

al ' all '

ani, any ' any '

auʒt, oght ' anything '

bǭth(e), bāþe ' both '

ēch, ich, alc (i-whilc) ' each ' *ēchǭn* ' each one '

ei ' all, some '

eyþer ' either '

elles ' something else '

everych ' each, each one, every,' *everychǭn* ' each one, everyone '

man, mon, men, me ' they ' (in ' they say '), ' one ' (in ' one says ')

manў̆, manў̆ ǭn ' many, many a one '

nǭn(e), nǭ, nān(e), nā ' none '

ǭn(e), ān(e) ' someone '

ōther ' other '

sòm(e), sum ' certain one(s), some '

swich, such, swilk ' such '

þelli, þülli ' such '

whǭ (for ex. 28/4111 *Bot whǭ þat wole of wondres hiere* ' but for anyone who wants to hear of marvels '), *whōsǭ* ' whoever '.

CHAPTER SEVEN

ADJECTIVES AND NUMERALS

Flexion of Adjectives

§ 74. 1. The only ones provided with flexions are monosyllabic adjectives terminated by a consonant. These adjectives distinguish the weak and strong flexion. Thus, for *gōd* 'good' and *leef* 'dear, beloved' there is:

	Strong Forms	Weak Forms
Sg	gōd, leef	gōde, leeve
Pl	gōde, leeve	gōde, leeve

The same for: *al* 'all', *brǭd* 'wide', *dēf* 'deaf', *hǭl* 'whole', *lǫng* 'tall, long', *smal* 'slender, small', *strǭng* 'strong', *swich* 'such', etc.; also the same for *fast* 'firm', *ful* 'full', *līch* 'like' used alone or as suffixes and *-les* 'devoid of'.

REMARKS. — I. Some disyllabic adjectives in *-el*, *-er*, *-en* or *-y* at times follow the strong flexion. These are: *mikel* 'large', *ēvel*, *ȳvel* 'evil', *litel* 'small', *biter* 'bitter', *ōper* 'other, second', *owen* 'own', *manȳ* 'many', *eni* 'any, no'.

II. In principle the monosyllabic adjectives of French origin terminated by a consonant follow the same rules, thus *saint/sainte* 'holy' *breef/brēve* 'short', *cleer/clēre* 'clear', *fresch/fresche* 'fresh', etc. In the same way a few dissyllables terminated by a consonant and accented on the final syllable like *di'vers/di'verse*. This disappears when the accent shifts to *'divers*.

III. There were still to be found, as a trace of the French system, some adjectives (of French origin) which had a plural in *-s* when the adjective was post-positional: *goodes temporeles*, *plāces delitables*, *pinges spirituels*, 25/4 *many wronges subtiles*; but this is exceptional (cp. the few traces which subsist in the modern language: *lords spirituals*, etc.).

2. All the other adjectives are invariable. One wrote, therefore, in all positions *grēne* 'green', *dēre* 'dear', *bysȳ* 'busy', *nēdȳ* 'needy', *hēpen* 'heathen', *ǭpen* 'open', *frē* 'generous, noble', etc.

IV. In the Northern dialect, consequent to the loss of final *-e*, all trace of adjective flexion tended to disappear.

V. The above indications are only valid for the best MSS; too often scribes used to add final *-e* indiscriminately.

VI. In the 12th century the Southern and Midlands dialects retained more important traces of adjectival flexion. For the strong forms we have:

Sg masc acc	-ne	alcnc 5/29, ænnc 7/3364
masc-neut gen	-es	ōðcrs 2/30, ūvclcs 3/83, āncs 4/30
fem gen-dat	-rc	āre 5/3, āʒere 5/14054
Pl gen	-re	alre 3/6, 5/13995

For the weak flexion there are some forms in -cn for all cases and genders outside the nominative singular (thus for the plural there is hālcchcn 'holy' 1/62, ōprcn 'other' 4ₐ/9). But even though the indefinite article ān still has some traces of flexion in the Ormulum (gen sg āncss 7/3337, masc acc ænne 7/3374 alongside 7/3366 inn ā cribbe 'in a crib'), on the other hand in the very oldest East-Midland text, the Peterborough Chronicle, it is already invariable (1/30 in ān čæstc 'in a chest', 1/45 al ā dæis fāre 'in a full day's journey', 1/56 tō ān tūn 'to a village', etc.).

One of the rare survivals found in the 14th century is aller (alder) genitive plural of al 'all'. Chaucer still writes he was ōure aller cōk 'he was the cock for (of) all of us'; and petrified formulas are also met like 12/720 alderbeste 'best of all', 15/32 alpervcrst 'the first all, first of all', etc.

Comparison of Adjectives

§ 75. 1. The comparative is formed by means of the suffix -re (then -er), the superlative by means of -est, with doubling of the final consonant and shortening of the radical vowel (if it is long) before -cr; and the extension into the superlative. We have, for ex:

glad 'glad'	gladdrc, gladdcr	gladdest
grcct 'large'	grcttcr	grcttest
lātc 'late'	latter	last (<lat lcst)

But often, by analogy, the long vowel is reintroduced into the comparative and superlative. (Cp. the modern competing forms latter/later.)

2. A few adjectives preserve, in the comparative degrees, an umlauted radical vowel as was the case in Old English for derived forms in *-iran- and *-ista- (HOE § 89.1). There are, for ex:

lǭng, lang 'long'	lcngcr	lcngest
strǭng, strang 'strong'	strcngcr	strcngcst
ǭld, ald 'old'	cldcr	cldest
niʒ, nɛ̄ʒ 'near'	nɛ̄rc, ncrrc	next

But we already find (besides the eliminated forms) some forms refashioned by analogy on the vowel of the positive, especially in the North (langcr, ālder, āldesl).

3. A small number of adjectives — the same as in Old English

(cp. HOE § 89.3) — use *suppletive forms* for the degrees of comparison — that is, forms drawn from a root different from that of the positive form. These are:

	Comp	Superl
gōd, 'good'	*bet(t)re, better, (bet)*	*best*
lītel 'little'	*lesse, lasse*	*lęste*
mikel 'large'	*mǫre māre (mǭ)*	*mǭst*
ēvel 'evil'	*werse, würse*	*werst, würst*

REMARK. — *mǫre, mǭst* are still adjectives: 27₁/465 the *mǫste pitee*, the *mǫste rōwthe* 'the greatest pity, the greatest compassion'; *mǭ* and *bet* are adverbial forms: 27₁/408 *moo floures* 'more flowers'.

4. On the process of the *periphrastic comparison* by means of the adverbs *mǭ (mā), mǫre* and *mǭst,* see § 115 2 *b.*

Numerals

§ **76.** 1. In principle *cardinal numbers are adjectives,* but outside the first three, which at the start retain remnants of flexion, they rapidly became invariable. Thus we have:

1. *ǫǫn, ǫǫ* (North: *ān, ā*). — 2. *twǭ, tǭ* (North *twā*) and, in the South, *tweye, tweyne* (genitive *tweire*) without distinction of gender. — 3. *þree, þreō, þrī,* with generalization of *þree* (the former feminine) without distinction of gender (*þrinne* 12/716). — 4. *fōur(e).* — 5. *fīf, fȳve.* — 6. *syxe, sex(e).* — 7. *sevyn, seve.* — 8. *e(i)ʒte* (North *aght*). — 9. *niʒen, nīne.* — 10. *tēn.* — 11. *enleven.* — 12. *twelf, twelve.* — 13. *þrettēne.* — 14. *fourtēne.* — 15. *fiftēne,* etc. — 20. *twentĭ̈.* — 21. *ǫǫn and twentỹ.* — 24. *fōure and twentỹ* (27₁/455), etc. — 30. *þrittĭ,* etc. — 100. *hundred, hundreth.* — 1000. *þōusent, þūsen.*

REMARK. — *scǭre* 'twenty' is used as in 26/31 *þe ʒēr of ōure Lord a þōusond þrē hondred fōure scǭre and fȳve* 'the year of our Lord 1385' (trace of a vigesimal system).

2. The *ordinal numbers* are:

1st. *first (e), ferst, fürst, fryst* and *forme* (3/35). — 2nd. *ōþer,* and later *secōunde* but only from 1350 on. — 3rd. *thridde, thyrde.* — 4th. *ferthe.* — 5th. *fifte.* — 6th. *sexte.* — 7th. *sevepe.* — 8th. *eʒtepe.* — 9th. *nente* (19/1012). — 10th. *tēʒþe, tiþe.* — 11th. *endlefte, ellefte.* — 12th. *twelfte,* etc. Note 42nd: *twō and fōwertiʒþe* (11/25).

3. *A few multiplicatives* in *-fǭld (-fald),* for example *seovevald* (4/1) 'sevenfold', *hundredfǒld* 'hundredfold'; *ǫnes* 'once', *twȳes* 'twice', *þrīes* 'thrice'.

CHAPTER EIGHT

THE VERBS

General

§ 77. In ME the verb had:

1. A single voice, *the active voice.* The passive was expressed by a perisphrastic construction composed of the verb " to be " and the past participle, cp. § 145.

2. Two simple tenses, the *present* and the *preterit.* The other tenses, perfect, pluperfect, future present and past were *compound* or *periphrastic tenses.*

3. Three moods, the *indicative* the *subjunctive-optative* (present and preterit) and the *imperative.* The subjunctive was often expressed by means of periphrases composed of a modal auxiliary and the infinitive; the same is true for the hortative using *lete.*

4. Two numbers, the *singular* and the *plural.*

5. Three persons in the singular and, just as in OE, a single form in the plural.

6. Four verbal nouns, the *infinitive,* present and past, the *verbal substantive* in *-ing,* the *present participle* and the *past participle.*

§ 78. Apart from the irregular verbs, every verb in ME had a *complete conjugation* with tenses, moods and verbal nouns. Within these conjugations the simple forms are divided into two systems:

1. The *present system*: indicative, subjunctive, infinitive, verbal substantive and participle:

2. The *preterit system*: indicative and subjunctive. The past participle is usually listed as a part of this system. Actually, however, it is an adjective built on a verbal base and forms a system all its own.

§ 79. There existed in ME, as in OE, three types of verbs:

1. The *strong verbs* whose preterits had no suffix. The contrast between the present, the preterit, and, to a certain extent, the past participle, was effected by a change of the root vowel: to the present *I drinke* was opposed the preterit *I drank* and the past participle

67

(*y-*)*drunke*(*n*). This change rested on *vowel gradation*, a heritage of older Germanic and Indo-European, for an explanation of which the reader is referred to HOE §§ 96-99. In ME the strong verbs were still rather numerous and very important because they comprised many of those most ordinarily used; but this type of verb had ceased to be productive—it was dead.

2. The *weak verbs* which formed their preterit and their past participle without change of radical vowel but by the addition of a *dental suffix*, ME *-de, -te, -(e)d*. Opposed to the present *I hēre* ' I hear ' there was the preterit *I her-de* and the past participle (*y-*)*her-d*. This type of verb was very much alive and quite productive; for this reason, save perhaps two or three exceptions due to analogy, all the verbs borrowed from French or built from French or Latin words follow the weak verb flexion. For example the verb *crȳe* borrowed from F *crier* had a preterit *I crȳed* and a past participle (*y-*)*crȳed*, and it was the same for thousands of verbs.

3. A few *irregular verbs*, survivors from quite ancient forms, to wit:

a) *perfect-present verbs* (also termed ' preterit-present verbs '), a type of strong verb whose perfect in Indo-European had taken on meanings of present time which it still retained in English: thus *I wọt* ' I know '. For these verbs, in Germanic, a new preterit grew up based on the weak flexion (*I wis-te* ' I knew ') and sometimes, but not always, an infinitive (*witen* ' to know '). On the whole, these verbs, generally without participles, present and past, had a *defective conjugation*. Very few in number, they are quite important, because this group contained all the modal auxiliaries and function words (Henry Sweet ' form words ') for periphrastic future tenses;

b) some verbs, equally few in number but of very high relative frequency, to wit, *bēn* ' to be ', *gọn* ' to go ', *dōn* ' to do ', *I wille* ' I want to ', remnants of a very archaic type, Indo-European verbs in *-mi*. The first two were formed from two or more roots: these are called *suppletive verbs*.

Strong Verb Classes

§ 80. These were seven in number as in OE. Taking account of the forces of analogy, phonetic evolution and the variations in dialectal forms, each of these classes continued the corresponding OE class.

§ 81. The essential difference between Old and Middle English in the matter of strong verbs consists in three points:

1. Reduction in number of these verbs, either by simple loss or by passing over into the weak group. Thus OE *lēōn* 'to lend, give', *hnīgan* 'to bow down' did not survive in ME; while *dwīnen* 'to melt' became weak. It very often happened that weak and strong forms of the same verb competed for many centuries. Thus for the verb *crēpe* 'to creep' alongside the strong preterit *crǭpe* there existed a weak form *crepte*, in the same way we find a preterit *rȳsed* 18/1313 instead of *rǭs* for the verb *rīse* 'to rise'.

2. Tendency to reduce the two vowel grades (1st and 3rd sg; 2nd sg, pl all persons) in the preterit to one or the other vowel. Already in OE the preterits of classes VI and VII and a part of those in class V had only one vowel grade for both numbers and all persons. This reduction of four vowel grades to three was equally favored by the similarity (in classes I and III) of the vowels of the preterit plural and the past participle. There was not yet any stability in ME concerning this: the differing forms multiplied. Sometimes it was the vowel of the pret sg, sometimes that of the pret pl or the past participle which tended to be generalized. The dialects differed: the Northern dialect had only one vowel for the preterit; those of the South (and London) had two; the Midlands vacillated.

3. Progressive elimination of consonant alternation (cp. HOE § 39): although the OE verb *ćēosan* 'to choose' had the forms pret sg *ćēas*, pret pl *curon*, pp *ġe-coren*, the corresponding ME verb *chēsen* had the pret pl *chǭsen* (alongside *curen*) and the pp *chǭse(n)* (alongside *y-cǭren, corn*). On this point as well, the evolution of the dialects was more or less rapid.

§ 82. *Class I* — Vowel series:

present *ī* — pret sg *ǭ* (North *ā*)— prt pl *i* — pp *i*.

Example *wrīten* " to write "

wrīte — wrǭt (wrāt)— writen — (y-)writen

And similarly *(a)bīde* 'to remain', *agrīse* 'to be frightened', *(a)rīse* 'to rise', *atwīte* 'to blame', *bistrīden* 'to bestride', *bȳten* 'to bite', *drȳven* 'to drive', *glīden* 'to glide', *līþen* 'to go', *rīden* 'to ride ', *rȳven* ' to split ', *schrīven* ' to confess ', *slȳde* ' to slide ', *smȳten* ' to smite ', *stīe* ' to climb ' (with a preterit *stȳh* by analogy with another class), *strȳken* ' to strike ', *umstrīde* ' to bestride ', *wrīen* ' to cover ' (pret *wrẹh, wreah* by analogy with class II), *wrīþe* ' to writhe '.

REMARKS. — I. By analogy the French loans *strīve* ' to strive ' (< OF *estriver*), *fȳne* ' to finish ' (< OF *finer*) were put into this class of strong verbs; *rȳven* was borrowed from Scandinavian.

II. *thee* ' to succeed, get along ' and *wrīen* are contracted verbs which already in OE belonged to this class.

§ 83. *Class II.* Vowel series:

Pres *ẹ̄, (ū)* — pret sg *ẹ̄* — pret pl *u* (then *ǭ*) — pp *ǭ*.

Example *chẹ̄se* ' to choose ' :

$$chẹ̄se — chẹ̄s — curen \text{ (then } chǭsen) — (y\text{-}) cǭren$$
$$\text{(then } (y\text{-}) chǭsen).$$

And similarly *bēde* ' to order ', *crēpe* ' to creep ', *flēten* ' to float ', *flēn* ' to flee ', *flēʒen* (*flȳe*) ' to fly ', *forbēde* ' to forbid ', *forlēse* ' to lose ', *frēse* ' to freeze ', *grēten* ' to weep ', *schēten* (*schōte, schūt*) ' to shoot ', *unlouke* ' to open '.

REMARKS. — I. *loūten* ' to bow ' is most often weak, *flēn* ' to flee ' had a weak preterit *fledde*, on the other hand the preterit of this verb began to be merged with that of *flēʒen* ' to fly ' ; *forlēse* had a weak preterit *forlost*. The verb *būʒen, bōʒen, boūwen* ' to bow ' had a pret sg *bey, bēʒ* (alongside weak forms *boūʒede, bōwede*).

II. Remnants of consonantal alternation: *forlǭren* pp of *forlēse* ' to lose ', *floūe* pret sg and *flugen* pret pl of *flȳe* ' to fly '.

III. The sound *ǭ* moved into the pret sg, thus *crǭpe* (from *crēpe*), *schǭt* (from *schēten*).

§ 84. *Class III.* — Three subdivisions:

a) before " nasal + consonant " the vowel series was:

pres *ĭ* — pret sg *ă(ǭ̆)* — pret pl *ŭ* — pp *ŭ*

with short vowels before -*nk,* -*ng,* -*mp* and long (§ 18) before -*nd,* -*mb.* Examples *drinken, finden*:

$$drinke — drank \ (drǫnk) — drunken —(y\text{-}) drunke(n)$$
$$finde — fǫnd, foūnd \text{ (North } fănd) — foūnden — (y\text{-}) foūnde(n)$$

On the model of *drinken* were conjugated: (*bi-*)*ginnen,* (*i-*)*limpen* 'happen', *ringen* 'to ring', *schrinken* 'to shrink (from)', *singen* 'to sing', *springen* 'to spring', *stinken* 'to stink', *swyngen* 'to swing', *swinken* 'to work', *wynne* 'to make money'.

On the model of *finden* were conjugated: *bīnden* 'to bind', *clīmben* 'to climb', *grīnden* 'to grind', *wīnden* 'to wind'.

REMARKS. — I. In the pret sg there was the type *drank* in the East and the type *drǫnk* in the West (cp. § 25).

II. Alongside *rinnen* 'to run' there was the form *rennen* (<ON *renna*).

III. Before *ng* (*singen, swyngen, springen*) the pret sg had a long vowel (*sāng, sǭng,* etc.).

b) before "liquid + consonant" the vowel series was:

pres *e* — pret sg *a*(*o*) — pret pl *o* — pp *o*

Example *helpen* 'to help' :

helpe — halp(holp) — holpen — (y-)holpe(n)

And similarly *berʒen* 'to protect', *bresten* (< *bersten*) 'to burst', *ʒēlden* (with lengthening of the vowel before *ld,* cp. § 18) 'to give', *sterven* 'to die', *werpen* 'to throw', *werþen* (but generally *worþe*(*n*), *wurþ*) 'to become', *welden* (*walden*) 'to rule'.

c) before *ʒt* the vowel series was:

pres *i* — pret sg *au* — pret pl *ou* — pp *ou.*

Example *fighten* 'to fight'

fighte — faught — foughten — (y-)foughte(n).

§ 85. *Class IV.* — In principle, the vowel series was:

pres *ę̄* — pret sg *a* — pret pl *ę̄* — pp *ǭ.*

For example *stę̄len* 'to steal' :

stę̄le — stal — stę̄len — (y-)stǭle(n)

And similarly *bę̄ren* 'to bear', *hę̄le* 'to conceal', *tę̄re* 'to tear', as well as a few verbs which were previously a part of class V, but whose pp in ME had the vowel sound *ǭ*, like *brę̄ken* 'to break', *drę̄pen* 'to kill', *spę̄ken* 'to speak', *trę̄den* 'to tread', *wrę̄ken* 'to avenge', *wę̄ven* 'to weave'.

REMARKS. — I. The verb *schēren* 'to shear' had a pret sg *schar*, pret pl *schāren* (*schǫren, schēren*), pp *schǫr*(*e*)*n*.

II. Two verbs with different root vowels are included in this class: *nimen* 'to take', pret sg *nam*(*nŏm*), pret pl *nōmen* (*nāmen*), pp (*y-*)*numen* and *cŏmen, cumen* 'to come', pret sg *cam* (*cŏm*), pret pl *cōmen*, pp (*y-*)*cŏme*(*n*), (*y-*)*cumen*.

III. In this class the vowel *ǭ* of the past participle tended to move into the pret pl, then into the sg.

IV. In this class and in the following, from as early as the *Peterborough Chronicle* we find, due to Scandinavian influence, a few forms in the pret pl with the sound *a*: *iafen* 'they gave' 1/10, *waren* 'they were' 1/18, 48, *namen* 'they took' 1/52, *drapen* 'they killed' 1/37, and *forbaren* 'they forbore' 1/51.

§ 86. *Class V.* — Vowel series:

pres *ē̦* — pret sg *a* — pret pl *ē̦* — pp *ē̦*.

For example *mē̦ten* 'to measure':

mē̦te — mat — mē̦ten —(*y-*)*mē̦ten*.

The same for *knē̦den* 'to knead', *wē̦ȝen* 'to weigh', *ē̦ten* 'to eat', (with pret sg *ē̦t*), *quē̦þen* 'to say' (with pret sg *quoþ, quod* alongside *quaþ*), *ȝeten* (and North *get*) 'to get', *forȝeten* 'to forget', *ȝeven*, *ȝive*(*n*) 'to give' (as well as the Northern form *gif*).

Verbs with the vowel *i*[ɪ] like *bidden* 'to ask' also belonged to this class, and *sitten* 'to sit', as well as *līen* (North *lig*, South *liǧǧen*) 'to lie' (pret sg *lay*, pret pl and pp *leyen*).

REMARK. — The old contracted verb *sēn* 'to see' also belonging to this class, had quite different forms according to the dialects. See the paradigms given in § 96.

§ 87. *Class VI.* — Vowel series:

pres *ā* — pret sg *ǭ* — pret pl *ǭ* — pp *ā*

Example *fāren* 'to go' :

fāre — fǭr — fǭren — (*y-*)*fāren*

The same for *forsāken, schāken* 'to shake', *schāpen* 'to make, create, shape', *tāken* 'to take' (loan from ON *taka*), *wāken* 'to waken', *waxen* 'grow, wax' (from class VII), as well as *drāȝen, drawen* 'to draw' (pret sg *drōȝ, drow*, pret pl *drōȝen, drowen*, pp *drāȝen drawen*) and *laughen* (*lōȝ, lough — lōȝen, louwen — laughen*). The verbs *hē̦ven* 'to lift' and *swē̦ren* 'to swear' had a present in *ē̦* which was the result of *j* — mutation (Gothic *haf-ja-n*) — preterits *hǭf — hǭven* and *swǫr — swǫren*. Still belonging to this class: *standen, stonden* ' to stand ' (*stōd —* pp (*y-*)*standen, stonden*) and the contracted verbs *flęn, flǫn* ' to flay ' and *slęn, slǫn* ' to slay ' (pret *slouh —* pp *slayn*).

§ 88. *Class VII.* — As in OE this class contained the old redupli- cated verbs (HOE § 107) whose vowel in the pret sg and pl was ME *ē* or *ęw* (< OE *ēōw*) while the vowel common to the present system and the past participle might be quite varied according to phonetic evolution.

Examples: *fallen* ' to fall ', *blowen* ' to blow '.

$$falle — fęl(fīl) — (y-)fallen$$
$$blowe — blęw — (y-)blowen$$

Those conjugated with a preterit in *ē* (or *ī*) are: *lēten* ' to let ', *hǫlden, halden* ' to hold ', *fǫn, fangen* ' to seize ', *hǫn, hangen, honge* ' to hang ', *lēpen* ' to leap ', *hǫten* ' to command, to call ' (pret *hyʒt, hęt*), *wēpen* ' to weep ', *drēden* ' to dread '. Those with a preterit in *ęw* are: *hewen* ' to hew ', *growen* ' to grow ', *knowen* ' to know ', *mowen* ' to mow ', *sowen* ' to sow ', *throwen* ' to throw '.

REMARK. — Many of these verbs had weak forms in ME: this is the case for *flowen* ' to flow ', *slēpen* ' to sleep ', *wēpen* ' to weep ', *drēden* ' to dread ') etc.

The Weak Verbs

§ 89. The weak verbs are divided into two categories according to whether their preterits ended in *-ed(e)* or in *-de, -te*, that is to say, according to whether the dental suffix was or was not preceded by the vowel *-e-*. But it must not be forgotten that in ME there was con- siderable interchange of forms between these divisions.

In principle the past participle ended in *-ed* for the first group, in *-d* or *-t* for the second.

§ 90. First Group — paradigm *hǫpen* ' to hope ' :

pret *hǫpede —* pp (*y-*)*hǫped*

This group contained:

a) OE weak verbs of class I with an originally short radical vowel, with the exception of those whose roots ended in *d* or *t* (type I *a*, cp. HOE § 122, REM. II), like *stēren* ' to stir ' (pret *stērede* pp (*y-*)*stēred),* *ęrien* ' to plow ', *węrien* ' to protect ', *dęren* ' to injure ', *hęrien* ' to praise ', etc.

b) most OE verbs of weak class II [in which *-ode* had become *-ed(e)*], for example *lĕrnen* 'to learn, to teach' (pret *lĕrnede,* pp *y-lĕrned*), *betăknen* 'to betoken, to symbolize', *clēpen* 'to call' (pret *clepte* alongside *clēpede*), *spellen* 'to explain, to tell', *tilen* 'to cultivate', *clensen* 'to cleanse', *folwen* 'to follow', *lŏve* 'to love', *þōlen* 'to suffer', *wunen* 'to inhabit', *wŏnder* 'to wonder', (pret *wŏndrede*), *hōpen* 'to hope', *lōken* 'to look', *pȳnen* 'to torture', *pleyen* 'to play', (pret *pleyde* alongside *pleyede*), *māken* 'to make' (pret *mākede* and *măd,* pp (*y-*)*māked* and (*y-*)*mād*), etc;

c) loan-words attracted to this group by phonetic analogy, for example, *chaunge* 'to change', (pret *chaungede,* pp *y-chaunged*), *travaile* 'to work', etc.

REMARK. — *crȳe* 'to cry', *ascrȳe* 'to exclaim', *espȳe* 'to spy', *preie* 'to pray' and similar F loans vacillated between pret *crȳede* and *crȳde,* pp *preied* and *preid*.

§ 91. Second group — paradigm *hĕren* 'to hear':

pret *herde* — pp (*y-*)*herd*

This group contained all the other weak verbs, and in particular:

a) OE weak verbs of class I with originally long radical (type I *b*) like *dēlen* 'to divide, to deal', *dēmen* 'to judge', *fēlen* 'to feel', *hēlen* 'to hide', *lēren* 'to teach', *sēmen* 'to seem', *wēnen* 'to hope, to expect', etc.;

b) some verbs from class I with short radical and stem ending in *-d* or *-t* like *letten* 'to let or hinder', *setten* 'to set' (pret *sette,* pp *y-set*) which already had this same form in OE: or like *leyen, lei* 'to lay' (pret *leide,* pp *y-leid*) and *deyen* 'to die' (< ON *deyja*), etc.

REMARKS. — I. When the vowel was long in the present system, it shortened in closed syllables in the preterit and past participle (cp. § 21), thus: *mēten* '1. to meet, 2. to dream' (pret *mĕtte*), *grēten* 'to greet' (pret *grĕtte*), and the same for *swēten* 'to sweat', *wēten* 'to wet', *hēren* 'to hear' (pret *hĕrde*).

II. However, we find the forms *sēmede, lērede, wēnede* and, by analogy, *sēmde, lērde, wēnde* with long vowels.

III. Verbs whose radical ended in consonant + *t* and a certain number of verbs ending in consonant + *d* had a preterit in *-te* and a past participle in *-t.* Thus *casten* 'to cast' (*caste — y-cast*), *resten* 'to rest', *lasten* 'to last', *listen* 'to please'; *plighten* 'to promise' (*plihte — y-plight*), *gilten* 'to sin' ; *henten* 'to catch' (*hente — y-hent*), *glenten* 'to glint', *stenten, stinten* 'to stop'.

renden 'to rend, to tear' (*rente* — *y-rent*), *senden* 'to send', *lenden* 'to land from a ship', *benden* 'to bend', *wenden* 'to go', (*went* and *wende* — *wend* and *y-went*), *blende* 'to mix, to blend'.

The same was true for a certain number of verbs with radicals in *-n, -p, -l,* or *-s,* like *mēnen* 'to mean' (*mente* — *y-ment*), *lẹnen* 'to lean', *kēpen* 'to keep' (*kepte* — *y-kept*) and the previously strong verbs *slēpen* 'to sleep', *wēpen* 'to weep', *lēpen* 'to leap', *crĕpen* 'to creep', *fēlen* 'to feel' (*felte*), *kissen* 'to kiss' (*kiste*).

IV. Under the same conditions *v* devoiced to *f* and *z* to *s*: *lẹven* 'to leave' (*lefte*), *bilẹven* 'to believe' (*bilefte*), *clẹven* 'to cleave to, to cling' (*clefte*), *lōsen* [*z*] 'to lose' (*lost*). Sometimes the *v* was completely lost: *bihōven* 'to behoove' (*byhōde* 18/717).

V. Verbs with long vowel + *d* in the present system shortened the vowel (and doubled the consonant in the preterit) in the past forms. There were, for example: *blĕden* 'to bleed' — pret *blĕdde* — pp *y-blĕd,* and the same for *fĕden* 'to feed', *hȳden* 'to hide', *spĕden* 'to succeed', *sprẹden* 'to spread', *nĕden* 'to need'.

VI. In ME verbs with an earlier OE *ǣ* as a radical vowel vacillated in the past between *a* and *e*: *lẹden* 'to lead' (pret *ladde* and *ledde*), *lẹven* 'to leave' (*lafte, lefte*), *sprẹden* 'to spread' (*y-sprad*), and the previously strong verbs *drēden* 'to dread' (*dradde, dred*), *rĕden* 'to read' (*radde*), *grēden* 'to cry out' (*gradde*), *schẹden* 'to fall' (*schadde*), *clẹthen* 'to clothe' (*cladde*), *to-snǣden* 'to cut to pieces' (*to-snadde*).

VII. *þ* + *d* yielded *dd*: *kīpen* 'to make known' pret *kidde* and cp. above *clẹthen* 'to clothe'.

VIII. *ll* + *d* yielded *ld*: *fillen* 'to fill' (*filde*), *callen* 'to call' (*calde*), *spillen* 'to despoil' (*y-spild*), *fellen* 'to fell' (*y-feld*).

IX. For radicals ending in [ndž], [ntš] there were sometimes past forms with [ɪnd] or rather [ɲd] (with [ɲ] spelled *in*?): *menǧe* 'to disturb' (pp *meynd* 28/4049, *i-mend* 6/870), *adrenchen* 'to drench, to drown' (pret *adreynten*).

c) OE weak verbs of class I with umlauted vowel in the present system (type I *c*). Thus in ME there was:

tellen 'to tell' — *tọlde* (*talde*) — *y-tọld*

and similarly *quellen, a-quellen* 'to kill', *sellen* 'to sell' ;

tẹchen 'to teach' — *taughte, taʒte* — *y-taught*

and similarly *rẹchen* 'to reach', *lacchen* 'to seize' (and by analogy with the latter, *ca*(*c*)*chen* 'to catch' from OF *cachier*) ;

sēchen, sēken 'to seek' — *soughte* — *y-sought*

and similarly *recchen* 'to reckon, to concern', *bȳen, büǧǧen* 'to buy', *abȳe* 'to expiate', *þinken* 'to seem', *þenchen* 'to think', *bringen* 'to bring' ; *werchen, wirken* 'to work' — *wroghte, wrahte* — *y-wrought.*

d) OE verbs of class III: *hăven* 'to have' (*hafde, hadde* — *y-hafd, y-had,* with many dialectal variants), *seyen, seǧǧe* 'to say' (*seide* —

y-seid). On the other hand *liven* 'to live' generally had the forms *livede, y-lived*.

e) French loans attracted into this group by phonetic analogy. Thus *agraunte* 'to promise' had the pp *agraunt* 14/4160, *depeynte* 'to paint' had the pp *depeynt*.

Verbs Borrowed From French

§ 92. With very few exceptions verbs borrowed from French became weak verbs in ME and were classed in one of the two preceding groups. Their form is usually to be traced to the French 3rd person plural of the present tense, thus *chaunge*(n) < F *change-nt*, *studie*(n) <F *estudie-nt*, *delivere*(n) <F *delivre-nt*, *florische*(n) <F *florisse-nt*, *perishe*(n) <F *perisse*(nt), *braundysche*(n) <F *brandisse-nt*, *persaven* < F *perceive-nt*, *joyn*< F *joigne-nt*, *pleyne*(n) < F *plaigne-nt*, *move*(n) < F *meuve-nt* etc. A few were remodeled on the basis of the adjectival past participle — *peinte*(n), *feinte*(n) — or on the infinitive (*obeien*).

Most of the verbs agreed with group I as defined above, others, especially those which ended in a vowel (*crye, preie*), with group II.

Verb Flexion   A. Present System

§ 93. While in OE the present systems of the strong verbs and weak verbs of class I contrasted with weak verbs of class II and both with weak verbs of class III, in ME the flexion became uniform in the present system regardless of the verb type, but this flexion was quite different in each of the dialects. Here are the endings:

		North	Midlands	South
Ind	sg 1	-(e)	-e	-e
	2	-es	-est,(-es)	-(e)st
	3	-es	-es, eþ	-eþ
	pl	-es, -is	-es, -e(n)	-eþ
Subj	sg	-(e)	-e	-e
	pl	-(en)	-e(n)	-e(n)
Imp	sg 2	—	—	—
	pl 2	-es	-eþ	-eþ
Infinitive		—	-(e)n	-e(n)
Participle		-and(e)	-and, -ende, -ing(e)	-inde, -ing(e)

For the dialectal areas of the principal endings see Fig. 9 (pres ind 3rd sg), 10 (pres ind pl) and 11 (pres participle -*nd*/-*ng*).

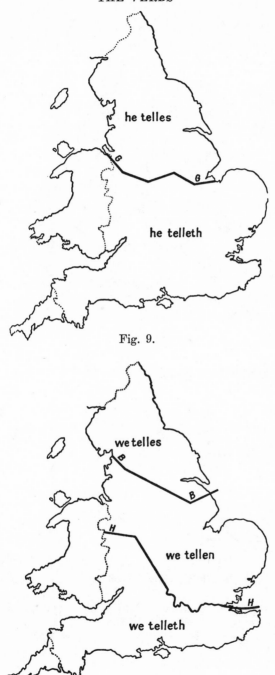

Fig. 9.

Fig. 10.

Fig. 11.

§ 94.   Thus, choosing the verb *hēre*(n) 'to hear' for our paradigm,
we have:

			North	Midlands	South
Ind	sg	1	hēr (e)	hēre	hēre
		2	hēres	hēres (t)	hēr (e) st
		3	hēres	hēres, hēreþ	hēreþ
	pl		hēres	hēres, hēre (n)	hēreþ
Subj	sg		hēr (e)	hēre	hēre
	pl		hēr (en)	hēre (n)	hēre (n)
Imp	sg	2	hēr	hēr	hēr
	pl	2	hēres	hēreþ	hēreþ
Infinitive			hēr (e)	hēre (n)	hēre (n)
Participle			hērand	hērand, hērende, hēring (e)	hērinde, hēring (e)

REMARKS. — I. In the Northern dialect a certain number of frequently
used verbs had apocopated forms: *lī* 'to lie', *tā* 'to take', *hā* 'to have', *sai*
'to say', *mā* 'to make'. These were conjugated, for example:

```
Ind   sg 1    tā        Imp 2 sg  tā
        2, 3   tās             2 pl  tās
        pl     tās        Inf       tā
     Subj      tā
```

Ia. In the Northern dialect the s- ending is gradually extended to the 1st person singular of the present indicative.

II. In the Northern dialect, in the present indicative (except for the 2nd sg), the verb had no ending when it was immediately preceded or followed by a personal pronoun, thus 16/47 *Swā þay* hāfe *undirstandynge and* fastes *and* wākes ' as long as they have understanding and fast and wake ', 29/513 *sǭ* say *wē*.

III. In the Midland dialects, and especially in the language of London in the 14th century *n-* endings were beginning to disappear. (See David W. REED, *The History of Inflectional* n *in English Verbs before 1500*, University of California Publications in English, Vol. 7, No. 4, pp. 157-328. Berkeley and Los Angeles, 1950.) Chaucer wrote *dauncę* and *pleyen* in the same line (in which the scansion shows the *e* was silent):

$$\overset{\times}{\text{They}}\ \overset{\times}{\text{dauncę}}\ \overset{\times}{\text{and}}\ \overset{\times}{\text{pleyen}}\ \overset{\times}{\text{at}}\ \overset{\times}{\text{dees}}\ \overset{\times}{\text{bothę}}\ \overset{\times}{\text{day}}\ \overset{\times}{\text{and}}\ \overset{\times}{\text{nyght}}$$

27/₄ᵦ467

IV. Syncopated forms were found in the Southern dialects in the 3rd sg present when the radical ended in a dental *d* or *t*; thus there was *hē bint* instead of *hē bindeþ*, and similarly *sent* 2/42, *send* 11/3 (for *sendeþ*), *scheot* 4/42 (for *scheoteþ*), *let* 15/32 (for *letteþ*), etc.

V. Certain Southern and South-western dialects maintained the endings in OE weak verbs of class II particularly well. The flexion of the verb *mākien* ' to make ' can serve as a paradigm:

```
Ind sg 1  mākie           subj sg    mākie
       2  mākest          pl         mākie(n)
       3  mākeþ
    pl    mākieþ          imp sg 2   māke
                          pl 2       mākieþ
```

But the dialect of the *Ancrene Wisse* (no. III) went even further and shows a very clear distinction between long and short stems. See the grammatical introduction to this text.

VI. The Southern dialects still had, in the 12th century, an inflected form of the infinitive (the so-called gerundive): 3/89 *tō dōnne*, 3/22 *tō ēotenne*, 5/14016 *tō hewene*, etc.

VII. Principally in those forms of the imperative where the plural pronoun followed the verb, the latter had no ending: 9/23 *grēde wē* ' let us cry out ', 9/26 *siǧǧe wē* ' let us say ', 3/139 *ne write ȝē* ' do not know '.

VIII. For details the reader must consult the grammatical introductions for each text.

Verb Flexion   B. Preterit System

§ 95. Just as in OE there was a clear distinction in this system between strong and weak verbs in the indicative as well as in the subjunctive and past participle. The dialectal differences were less pronounced than was the case for the present system and may be reduced to an opposition of the North to the rest of England. The North generally had a single form in all numbers and persons in the weak verb, and, in the strong verb, only the past participle had a different form. Thus there were the following endings:

		Strong Verbs		Weak verbs		
		North	South and Midl.	Group I	Group II	
Ind	sg 1	—	—	-ed(e)	-d(e)	-t(e)
	2	—	-(e)	-edest	-dest	-test
	3	—	—	-ed(e)	-d(e)	-t(e)
	pl	—	-e(n)	-ed(e)(n)	-d(e)(n)	-t(e)(n)
Subj	sg	—	-e	-ed(e)	-d(e)	-t(e)
	pl	—	-e(n)	-ed(e)(n)	-d(e)(n)	-t(e)(n)
Past part		-(e)n	-(e)n, -e(n)	-ed	-d	-t

REMARKS. — I. When the strong verb had two vowel grades in the preterit (which we have seen was the case in classes I to V), in principle the pattern was the following:

1st vowel grade: 1sg and 3sg
2nd vowel grade: 2sg, 1-3 pl ind, sg and pl subj.

But by analogy the 2nd sg either took on the vowel of the 1st and 3rd, or the vowel of the plural was extended into the 1st and 3rd sg.

II. In the Northern dialect the vowel of the 1st and 3rd sg was extended into all persons in the indicative and subjunctive.

III. The striking contrast in the endings of the 2nd sg pret between strong and weak verbs was well maintained up to the end of the 14th century. Chaucer wrote

Allas, dēth, what ayleth thē
That *thŏu noldest* have tāken mē
Whan *thŏu tŏke* my lādy swēte   27₁/481-3

In the North, however, the 2nd sg *est*-ending of the weak verb often disappeared.

IV. The past participle might be preceded by the pre-verb y-, i- (<OE ġe-). This particle was lacking in the North, North-West-Midland and East-Midland. In the literary language of London during the 14th century the forms were in free variation; Chaucer, for example, uses the particle, but not with any regularity. Gower, on the contrary, does not use it.

§ 96. Paradigms for the strong verbs *bīnden* 'to bind', *sēn* 'to see', *tāken* 'to take':

			North	Midl & South	North	Midl	South
Ind	sg	1	band	bǫnd	sagh	sauʒ	siʒ
		2	band	boūnde	sagh	sawe	sye
		3	band	bǫnd	sagh	sauʒ	siʒ
	pl		band	boūnde(n)	sagh	sāwe(n)	siʒe
Subj		1	band	boūnde	sagh	sūwe	siʒe
		2	band	boūnde(n)	sagh	sāwe(n)	siʒe
Past part			bunden	(y-)boūnde(n)	sēn	(y-)sēn(e)	i-seʒe

			North	Midl and South
Ind	sg	1	tōk	tōk
		2	tōk	tōke
		3	tōk	tōk
	pl		tōk	tōke(n)
Subj	sg		tōk	tōke
	pl		tōk	tōke(n)
past part			tāken, tān	(y-)tāke(n)

§ **97.** Paradigms for the weak verbs *hǫpen* ' to hope ', *hēre(n)* ' to hear ', *hăve(n)* ' to have ', *kisse(n)* ' to kiss ':

			North	Midl and South	North	Midl and South
Ind	sg	1	hǫped	hǫped(e)	herd	herde
		2	hǫped	hǫpedest	herd	herdest
		3	hǫped	hǫped(e)	herd	herde
	pl		hǫped	hǫped(e)(n)	herd	herde(n)
Subj	sg		hǫped	hǫped(e)	herd	herde
	pl		hǫped	hǫped(e)(n)	herd	herde(n)
Past p			hǫped	(i)hǫped	herd	(i-)herd

			North	Midl and South	North	Midl and South
Ind	sg	1	had	had(d)e	kist	kiste
		2	had	had(d)(e)st	kist	kistest
		3	had	had(d)e	kist	kiste
	pl		had	had(d)e(n)	kist	kiste(n)
Subj	sg		had	had(d)e	kist	kiste
	pl		had	had(d)e(n)	kist	kiste(n)
Past p			had	(i-)had	kist	(i-)kist

Perfect Present Verbs

§ 98. Most of these verbs maintained themselves in ME and show only phonetic changes when compared with their OE forms (HOE §§ 124-130). They are listed here according to the strong verb class to which they correspond.

Class I

§ 99. 1. *wǭt* ' I know '

Pres ind sg 1 and 3 *wǭt*, 2 *wǭst*, pl *wite(n)* ; subj *wite*; imp *wite*, inf *wite(n)* ; pres participle *witende, witinge*.

Pret *wiste* (*weste, wüste*) ; pp *wist* (alongside *i-wysse, y-wis* used as an adverb ' certainly, for sure ').

Negative forms: *nǭt*, pl *nute*, pret *niste*. Contracted form *ichot* ' I know '.

REMARKS. — I. The Northern dialect had a pres ind sg 1 and 3 *wāt*, 2 *wāst*, pl *wāt*; inf *wit(e)* ; pret *wist*.

2. *owe* ' I possess, I have '.

Pres ind sg 1 *owe*, 2 *owest*, 3 *owe(þ)*, pl *owe(n)* ; subj *owe, owe(n)* ; inf *owen, ōʒen*.

Pret *ahte* (*ōʒte, auhte, ouhte*).

II. The Northern dialect had pres ind *agh*, inf *agh*, pret *aght*. South-West-Midland had a 12th century present *āh*, pl *āhen*. The adjective *owen* (*āʒen, awen*) ' own ' was a verbal adj formed from this root in pre-Old English. It was not a past participle in ME, nor was it such in OE.

Class II

§ 100. *dowe* ' I am good for . . .'

Pres sg 1 and 3 *dowe*; inf *dugen*.

Pret *douhte*.

Class III

§ 101. 1. *can, con* ' I can ', ' I know how ', ' I am able '.

Pres ind sg 1 and 3 *can, con*, 2 *canst, const*, pl *cunnen* (*cunneþ*); subj *cunne, cònne*; inf *cunne(n)*.

Pret *cūþe, cōude*; pp *cūþ*.

REMARKS. — I. The Northern dialect had only *a* forms in the present: 2sg *canst*, 1st and 3rd, all pl *can*; no *con, conne*.

2. *þarf* ' I need '.

Pres ind sg 1 and 3 *þarf, þar, þerf,* 2 *þarf(t),* pl *þurve(n)* ; subj *þurve;* inf *þurven.*
Pret *þurfte, þórfte.*

3. *dar* ' I dare '.

Pres ind sg 1 and 3 *dar,* 2 *darst,* pl *dar;* subj *durre;* inf *durren.*
Pret *durste, dórste.*

II. *unnen* ' to wish, to grant ', which also belonged to this class, was still to be found in the 12th century.

Class IV

§ 102. 1. *món* ' I intend, shall, must ', used only in the Northern dialect.

Pres ind *món;* subj *mune.*
Pret *mónde, mōunde.*

2. *shal* ' I must, I have to '

Pres ind 1 and 3 *shal,* 2 *shalt,* pl *shul(l)e(n)* ; subj *shule.*
Pret *shólde, shulde.*

REMARK. — The Northern dialect shows only two forms: pres *sal,* pret *suld.* Kentish had the forms: pres ind 1 and 3 *ssell, ssoll,* 2 *sselt,* pl *ssolle;* pret *ssolde.*

Class VI

§ 103. *mōt* ' I can, I must '.
Pres ind sg 1 and 3 *mōt,* 2 *mŏst,* pl *mōte(n)* ; subj *mōte.*
Pret *mŏste.*

Unclassified

§ 104. *may, mei* ' I have the physical capacity to, . . . the possibility of '.

Pres ind sg 1 and 3 *mai,* 2 *miht* (*maht* 3/73), pl *mugen, mōwen* (*mahen* 4/24) ; subj *mōwe* (*mahe, muȝe*).

REMARK. — The Northern dialect showed only two forms: pres *mai,* pret *might* or *moght.*

Irregular Verbs

§ 105. Four verbs were quite irregular: these were *bēn* ' to be ', *wil(le)* ' I desire, I want to, I will ', *dō(n)* ' to do ', and *gǭ(n)* ' to go '.

1. The following were the forms of the verb $b\bar{e}(n)$ ' to be '.

		North	West-Midland	East-Midland	South	Kentish
Pres Ind sg	1	am, bē	am	am	am, ǽm, em,	em
	2	ert, es, bēs	art	art, (bēst)	art, bēst,	
	3	es, bēs	is, ys, bēōþ, būþ	is, ys (bēþ)	is, bēōþ, bēþ	bȳeþ
	pl	ār(e), ēr(e), es, bēs	arn	ār(e)n, bēōþ, beyn, bēn, bē(sinden)	bēōþ, bēþ, būþ	bȳeþ
Subj sg		bē	bē	bē(sī)	bē, bő (sie)	bȳ
	pl	bē	bēn	bēn	bēōn, bőn, (sien)	
Imp sg	2	bē	bē	bē	bēō, bő	
	pl 2	bēs	bēþ	bēþ	bēōþ	
Infinitive		bē	bēn	bēn, bē	bēōn, bőn, bő	bī, bīe(n)
Gerundive					tō bēōnne	
Participle		bēand(e)		bēing		
Prt Ind sg	1	was, wes	was	was	was	wes
	2	was, wes	wőre	wēre, wast	wēore	
	3	was, wes	was	was	was	
	pl	wēr, wār(e), wes	wőren	wēre(n)	wēore, wǽre	
Subj sg		wār(e)	wőre	wēre	wēre	
	pl	wār(e)	wőren	wēre(n)	wēre	
Past Part		bēn	bēn	(y-)bē(n)	i-bē	

REMARKS. — I. Negative forms *nam, nart, nis; nas, nes, nĕre* etc.

2. The following were the forms of *wil(le)* ' I want to, I will ' :

Pres ind sg 1 and 3 *wil, wille, wile*; South-West *wülle, wüle* (and with agglutinated pronoun *ich, chülle* 3/75) ; from the 14th century on, in the Midlands, *wol, wolle, wole*; 2nd sg *wilt, wült, wolt*; pl *wilen, woln, wol, wülleþ*; subj *wile, wole.*

Pret sg 1 and 3 *wolde* (*wilde, walde, wulde*), 2 *woldest*, pl *wolden* (*wilden, wild, wald*) ; past p *wold.*

II. The present tense form *wol* was very frequent in the common literary language. Chaucer and Gower used it more frequently than *wil*. It is an innovation made from the preterit *wol-de* and is the source of ModE *won't.*

III. The Northern dialect had the invariable forms pres *wil, wel*, pret *wald, weld.*

IV. Frequently used negative forms: pret sg 1 and 3 *nil, nül, nülle*, 2nd sg *neltōu, nültū* (with suffixed pronoun), pl *nülleþ* pret *nalde, nülde, naldest*, etc., etc.

3. The following were the forms of the verb *dō(n)* ' to do '.

		North	Midlands	South
Pres ind sg	1	dō	dō	dō
	2	dōs	dōst	dēst
	3	dōs	dōþ	dēþ
	pl	dōs	dō(n)	dōþ
Subj sg		dō	dō	dō
	pl	dō	dō(n)	dō(n)
Imp sg		dō	dō	dō
	pl	dō(s)	dōþ	dōþ
Inf		dō	dō(n)	dō(n)
Gerundive		—	—	tō dōn(n)e
Pres part		dō(a)nd(e)	dōinge	dōinde
Preterit		dide	dide	dēde, düde
Past part		dōn	(y-)dōn	i-dōn

4. The following were the forms of the verb gǭ(n) 'go'.

		North	Midlands	South
Pres ind sg	1	gā	gǭ	gǭ (Kent guo)
	2	gās	gǭst	gēst
	3	gās	gǭþ	gēþ
	pl	gās	gǭ(n)	gǭþ
Subj sg		gā	gǭ	gǭ
	pl	gā	gǭ(n)	gǭ(n)
Imp sg		gā	gǭ	gǭ
	pl	gā(s)	gǭþ	gǭþ
Infinitive		gā(n)	gǭ(n)	gǭ(n)
Pres part		[gangand]	gǭende, gǭinge	gǭinde
Preterit		went	ʒēde, ʒǭde, wente	ēode, ʒēde, ʒōde
Past part		gān(e)	(y-)gǭ(n)	i-gǭ

V. As in OE (HOE § 134) the verb gǭ(n) had no preterit based on the root used in the present system. In ME the South (and the Midlands in the 12th century) used the suppletive forms ēode and ʒēde, ʒǭde (from the OE suppletive ēode, ʒe-ēode) for the preterit. The North and the Midlands used a new suppletive form went(e) from the current verb wenden 'to go'. This form appeared first in the North and moved gradually through the Midlands to the South.

Alongside this defective verb gǭ(n) there was the class VII strong verb gangen, gongen 'to go' from which the North borrowed its present participle gangand.

PART THREE

THE SENTENCE

CHAPTER NINE

ELEMENTS OF THE SENTENCE

A. THE NOUN

Use of Cases

§ 106. The progressively fast loss of case endings, with the exception of the genitive, had two effects on the syntactical structure: the use of prepositions increased in importance; word order, and the order of word groups in the sentence tended towards fixed patterns and this order and these patterns began to take on structural significance. From this point of view, ME was in an intermediate position between OE and ModE: in the 12th century there were still very clear survivals of OE case forms used for the same syntactical purposes as in OE; in the 14th century all traces of the dative and the accusative had been lost; if certain idioms still remained they were only stereotypes or "petrified forms."

1. Accusative

§ 107. *The adverbial accusative expressing time* (HOE § 156.4) was still morphologically differentiated in the language of London in 1258: 11/24 *witnesse usselven æt Lundene,* **þane** *eʒtetenþe day on þe monthe of Octobre* 'witness ourselves at London **on the** 18th day of the month of October'. But at the end of the 14th century there was nothing to distinguish this from the common case: 27₄ᵦ/679 *He hath a thousand slayn this pestilence* 'he has slain a thousand **during** the pestilence'.

2. Dative

§ 108. Similarly, in OE the principal role of the dative was a *dative of attribution* or the indirect object of the predicate. So long

87

as traces of flexion remained for articles or adjectives it is possible to see that the dative still persisted, as in Lawman 5/21 *he heo ʒef þare æðelen Ælienor* 'he gave it **to** the noble Eleanor', 5/13997 *brohte tidinge Arðure þan kinge* 'brought tidings **to** Arthur, the king'; but already in Orm, it is the context alone that shows that *all follc* plays the role of a dative: 7/3352 *To kiþenn ʒuw þatt all follc iss Nu cumenn mikell blisse* 'to make known to you that **to** everybody there is now come a great joy', similarly 3/135-6 *ha chepeð hire sawle þe chapmon of helle* 'she sells her soul **to** the merchant of hell'. The modern solution of this ambiguity was already reached when the preposition *to* was used as in 24/21 *þe fadir seide to his servauntis* 'the father said to his servants'.

REMARK. — Naturally the preposition was not used when the indirect object was a personal pronoun placed immediately after the verb and before the direct object: 24/3 *þe fadir departide him his goodis* 'the father gave him his share of the property'.

§ 109. *The possessive dative*, (HOE § 158.2) also called dative of reference, was maintained in ME: 1/31-2 *him bræcon alle the limbs* 'broke all the limbs (with reference) to him' = 'broke all his limbs', 5/6 *hit com him on mode* 'it came into his mind', 8/564 *god him is the dubbing* 'his trappings are fine', 12/616 *fel him to þe fet* 'fell at his feet'.

REMARK. — There was possibly a possessive dative at issue in such cases as 5/14025 *Modred <h>is hafd* 'Modred's head' (lit. 'to Modred his head'), 26/23 *a child hys brouch* 'a child's plaything'; but it may equally have been a matter of false spelling of the genitive (*Modredis, childys*). It must be remarked, however, that this locution is found with feminine forms, thus *The wyf of Bathe hir tale* 'the Wife of Bath's tale' (and the same in the plural) where it could not be a question of the spelling of the genitive, but entirely one of analogical extension of the pattern of such a masculine as *the Millere his tale* 'the Miller's tale'; moreover this idiom is to be found independently in a number of Germanic dialects (cp. Germ. *meinem Vater sein Haus*).

3. Genitive

§ 110. Aside from the personal pronouns we have seen that only the genitive singular retained a clear cut case ending.

1. *The adverbial genitive* is still found now and then in the 12th century: 3/80 *lives* 'alive', 3/104 *willes* 'voluntarily', and also as a *temporal modifier*: 1/20 *be nihtes and be days* 'nights and days' (which is a petrified adverbial genitive in ModE). The numeral

forms *ones, anys* 'once', *twyes* 'twice', *þries* 'thrice' were better preserved and, again, survive in ModE.

2. *The adnominal genitive.* — For instance, 3/56 *a mihti kinges luve* 'a mighty king's love', 11/1 *þurh Godes fultume,* 'by means of God's help', 27₄ₐ/700 *pigges bones* 'pig's bones', 13₃/21 *nones cunnes eiȝte* 'no kind of property'. It will be noticed that in ModE this use of the genitive has been gradually restricted and replaced by the *of*-adjunct.

The survivals in the plural were rather rare: 10/201 *widewene kors* 'widows' curse', 14/80 *handlyng sinne* 'sins' handbook' = 'handbook of sins', 21₃/73 *lordene sones* 'lords' sons'.

It often happens, especially in the plural, that we have to do with a *genitive with zero ending.* Examples in the singular: 3/130 *ancre ahte* 'nun's possession', 27₁/372 *the forest syde* 'the forest's edge', 27₄ₐ/695 *Oure Lady veyl* 'Our Lady's veil'. Examples in the plural: 3/128 *heordemonne hure* 'shepherds' wages', 6/888 *tweire kunne salve* 'a two *kinds' salve', 12/499 *þe seli children blod* 'the innocent children's blood', 26/21 *gentilmen children* 'gentlemen's children' (Caxton writes *gentilmens children*).

It is not always certain in the preceding locutions whether we are dealing with the " genitive + substantive " group or with a compound noun (20/708 *werlde ryche* 'world's realm') or even with simple juxtaposition (28/3961 *mydnyht tyde* 'midnight hour').

REMARK. — I. For the order of these elements and their consequence, see further on § 167 REM.

3. *Partitive genitive.* — *a*) With adjectives and nouns of measure: 20/801 *ten fote large* 'ten foot's extent', ModE 'ten foot (Ø) long', 19/1030 *twelve forlonge space* 'twelve furlong's length/twelve furlong length' (these all show divided usage in ModE, with the standard spoken language tending toward a form with zero ending).

b) With numerals in the 12th century: 1/41 XIX *wintre* [for the OE genitive plural *wintra*] 'nineteen winters'.

c) With superlatives: 5/13995 *richest alre kinge* 'most powerful of all kings'.

II. On the phrases *a maner song, alle kynnez peere, a galoun ale,* see § 167 REM.

III. On the pseudo-partitive of the type *an olde felawe of youres* see § 168.

§ 111. *The* of-*adjunct.* — This periphrasis occurs in OE; but apparently due to the influence of Latin and French *de* the genitive with *of* appears more and more after 1066: 1/17 *men of þe land* 'men of the land', 2/18 *eie of monne* 'fear of man', 3/17 *delit of sunne* 'delight of sin', 3/103 *þe scheld of þi gode wil* 'the shield of thy good will', 27₁/326 *the story of Troye,* and similarly: 7/3369 *an off Godess enngless* 'one of God's angels', 1/58 *naht þarof* 'nothing thereof', 27₁/304 *some of hem* 'some of them'.

The former genitive complement of the adjective (*a*) or of the verb (*b*) especially, from the 12th century on, was expressed only by *of*-phrases:

a) 3/64 *of alle men feherest* 'fairest of all men'.

b) 1/48 *men sturven of hungær* 'men died of hunger', 3/21 *hwerof chalengest tu me* 'of what dost thou accuse me', 3/68 *talde hire of his kinedom* 'told her of his kingdom' (*narravit ei de suo regno*), 3/112 *þet leðer* [*wes*] *of Godes licome* 'the leather was (made) of God's body', 6/869 *mi song is of longinge* 'my song is of desire' = 'comes from desire'.

Traces of Adjective Flexion

§ 112. There was some use of both strong and weak flexion of adjectives, which was normal in Old English, till the beginning of the 13th century. This was very irregular, however, and what system there was has been outlined above, § 74.

The consonantal or weak flexion was used when the adjective was preceded by a demonstrative, a possessive, or the definite article: 5/29 *þene almihten Godd* 'the almighty God', 5/21 *þare æðelen Ælienor* 'to the noble Eleanor', 5/14001 *wið þene ȝeonge cniht* 'with the young knight', 3/24 *mine leove sustren* 'my dear sisters' ; or when the adjective was used substantively: 4/27 *his ahne* 'his own', 4/28 *alle þe oðre* 'all the others'.

The vocalic or strong flexion was used in all other cases, in particular when the adjective was not preceded by the article: 3/83 *uveles cunnes cunde* 'of a bad kind of nature', 3/94 *efter monies wene* 'according to the advice of many', 3/6 *on ealre erst* 'first of all', 7/3337 *Inn aness weress hewe* 'in a man's guise'.

REMARK. — Even in the earliest ME texts we find:

1. confusion in the use of these flexions: 3/115 *efter kene cnihtes deað* 'after a brave knight's death' (where we should expect to find the strong form *kenes*);

2. tendency towards invariable adj forms: 1/30 *in an ćæste* 'in a chest', 1/56 *to an tun* 'to a village', 7/3366 *inn a cribbe* 'in a crib'. It was this tendency that was not long in becoming dominant.

Adjective used Substantively

§ 113. In ME adjectives could be used substantively without any restriction and they remained, generally, invariable.

They could be applied to an individual (especially in poetry): *þat swete* 'that sweet (one, lady)', 29/644 *that fre* 'that noble (person)'; or to a group: 2/34 *þe fremede* 'the strangers', 16/54-5 *þe lufand and þe lufed* 'the loving and the loved', 12/543 *þe halte and þe doumbe* 'the halt and the dumb', 11/11 *ure treowe* 'our loyal (ones, servants)'; or to animals: 18/1162 *þe broun* 'the browns, the brown beasts, stags', or to things: 5/7 *þa æðelen* 'the noble (ones, i. e. deeds)', 20/761 *þe depe* 'the deep (sea)', and finally to abstractions, 13₂/78 *heore hot* 'their hot(ness)', 18/747 *þe cold* 'the cold'.

§ 114. After the indefinite article the use of the prop-words *one(s)*, *thing(s)* was not unknown from the middle of the 14th century. Chaucer had the Wife of Bath say *I was a lusty oon* 'I was a lusty one'; but on the whole the prop-word was still apparently superfluous: 12/604-5 *On hise riht shuldre a kynemerk, A swiþe briht, a swiþe fair* 'on his shoulder a king-mark, a very bright (one), a very fair (one)', 13₅/11-12 *Never ȝete y nuste non Lussomore in londe* 'never yet did I know a more gracious (one, girl) in the country', 23/7 *he had a full fair castell and a strong* 'he had a very handsome castle and a strong (one)'.

§ 114 a. We also find adjectives used substantively without any article: 2/36 *unholde* 'the enemies', 3/94 *efter monies wene* 'according to many's belief', 11/19 *oni oþer onie* 'one or several'.

Comparison of Adjectives

§ 115. 1. *The comparative of equality* was expressed with *as . . . as*: 14/4004 *as meke as byrd in cage* 'as meek as (a) bird in (a) cage', *so . . . as* 27₄ᴮ/843 *That sholde live so murye as I* 'who may live as happy as I ', *also . . . so*: 12/589 *Also briht so it were day* 'as bright as (if) it were day '.

2. *Comparative of superiority and superlative.*— ME had two processes:

a) use of the suffixes *-er, -est*; this traditional process was inherited from OE (cp. HOE § 162.2) ;

b) use of a periphrastic construction involving the adverbs *mo, more, most*. This innovation which arose in OE (used with participial adjectives) was possibly re-enforced by French influence. In any case from 1300 on it proliferated. It appeared as well with native adjectives as with those of French or Latin origin, and regardless of the number of syllables. We find just as many like 26/68 *more noble*, 25/1 *the moost noble*, 27₁/302 *the moste solempne* 'the most dignified', 26/68 *more profytable*, 25/67 *the moost profitable*, as like 27₂/1219 *more swete* 'sweeter', 28/4081 *more wylde* 'wilder', 14/4156 *more unkynde*, 25/2 *most ryghtful and wysest conseille* 'most just and wisest counsel ', 29/244 *more gracyus and rychere* 'more gracious and richer '.

The pleonastic or double comparison is not rare, especially in works of a popular nature: 23/59 *the most fairest damyselles*.

The comparative is normally followed by *than*: 2/1 *Ich em nu alder þene ich wes* 'I am now older than I was ', 27₁/407 *gayer than the heven*; in Northern English the conjunction *or* was used: 29/486 *I had lever be dede or she had any dysease* 'I would rather be dead than that she should have any discomfort '.

3. To express the *absolute superlative* 'very, quite', ME had a wide assortment of adverbs: *ful good* 'very/quite good', 27₁/324 *ful clere* 'very clear', 10/190 *swiþe sore*, 14/4103 *wundyrly sore* 'very severe(ly)', 27₁/454 *ryght yong* 'quite young', 27₄ᵦ/942 *he is moost envoluped in synne* 'he is most/quite enveloped in sin '.

4. " By that much more " was expressed by means of the previous instrumental (OE *þ̄ȳ*) which in even the earliest ME had become indistinguishable from the definite article *þe, the*, placed before the comparative: 10/202 *ich fare þe wors* 'I fare the worse', 21₁/31 *to cheeven þe bettre* 'to succeed the better', 27₄ₐ/714 *he songe the murierly and loude* 'he sang all the more merrily and loud '. Cp. also the adverbs *na-the-less, ne-þe-les, no-þe-les* 'nevertheless '.

Personal Pronoun

§ 116. 1. When the verb had no other subject the personal pronoun was generally used in ME and in that position it took on, more and more, the value of a " person indicator " which was necessary because of the loss of verb endings that formerly made it possible to distinguish persons when no subject was expressed.

2. When the subject was placed sufficiently far behind the verb, a tendency grew up to use a pronoun as anticipatory subject: 21$_3$/59 *it ben aires of hevene, alle þet ben crounede* ' they are heirs of heaven, all that are tonsured '. On the use of *ther* see § 174.

3. Reciprocally it happened, especially in poetry, that the subject was repeated by a personal pronoun directly before the verb: 21$_2$/175 *Alle þis route of ratones to þis reson þei assented* ' all this assembly of rats, to this argument they assented ', 18/1127 *Geste þat go wolde her gromez þay calden* ' guests that desired to go, their grooms they called '.

The same was true for the direct object: 18/1249-50 *þe prys and þe prowess þat plesez al oþer, If I hit lakked, oþer set at lyȝt, hit were littel daynté* ' the reputation and the prowess that pleases all others, if I demeaned it, or set (it) at little, that would be (an act of) little good breeding '.

§ 117. On the other hand the pronoun-subject was left unexpressed:

a) sometimes in rapid and familiar conversation: 29/235-6 *how farys sho? — Lyys walteryng, by the rode* ' How fares she? — Lies weltering, by the rood ! ' ;

b) sometimes also in poetry: 6/882 *þat boþ her, wo is hom þes* ' those that are here, shame it is for that ', 6/929-30 *Ich bidde hom þat heo i-swike, Þat heom selve ne biswike* ' I bid them that they should cease (from sin), that (they) should not deceive themselves ' ;

c) in co-ordinate or juxtaposed clauses in which the subject remains the same: 23/66 *þei assembled hem with force, and assayleden his castell, and slowen him and destroyeden alle the faire places and all the nobletees of þat paradys* ' they assembled in force and attacked his castle, and killed him and destroyed all the beautiful places and all the lovely things in that paradise ' ;

d) in impersonal constructions (which were quite numerous):

10/153 *ne beþ nout ʒet þre daies ago* '(it) is not yet three days ago ',
12/696 *betere us is of londe to fle* ' we had better flee the country ',
12/497 *began him for to rewe* '(he) began to repent ', 14/4071 *so
him byrde* ' as (it) might happen to him ', 18/717 *feʒt him byhode*
' to fight (it) behooved him ', 27₁/291 *me thoghte thus* '(it) seemed
to me thus ', 27₁/293 *me mette thus* '(I) dreamed thus ', 28/3959
as hir liste ' as (it) pleased her ', 18/1201 *hym wondered* '(it)
astonished him ', 18/1214 *me schal worþe at your wille* '(I) shall be at
your disposal '.

REMARK. — Concurrently there were constructions, though still rather infrequent, with a pronoun subject: 27₄B/671 *it was me toold* (instead of *me
was toold* ' it was said to me ', 18/1214 *þat me wel lykes* ' that is very pleasing
to me '.

Use of " Thou " and " You "

§ 118. There does not seem to have been any social or prestige
connotations attached to the use of *þū* ' thou ' and *ǧē* ' ye, you ' in OE
or EME. A distinction called a " plural of politeness " tended to
develop, however, from the end of the 13th century. Superiors were
addressed by *you*-forms and adolescents so addressed an adult: thus
27₄B/671 ff, the young boy uses *you* to the patrons of the inn. In
upper class society *you* was used among equals; in the lower ranks
thou was used as in OE (27₄B/944-50 and passim). But this use of
you-forms was still quite irregular. It was not unusual to go from
" thou " to " you " and from " you " to " thou " when speaking to
the same person and in the same sentence, thus 12/485-6 *Al Denemark
I wile you yeve To þat forward þu late me live* ' all Denmark will I
give you in return for the agreement (that) thou lettest me live '.
In the *Second Shepherds' Play*, sometimes the other shepherds use
" thou " to Mak (29/199, 222, 224, 235, etc.) and sometimes " you "
(29/208, 209, 217, 218, 220, etc.). In the extremely refined and
courtly atmosphere of *Gawaine and the Green Knight* " you " is
regularly used in conversations involving Gawain, the Lady and the
Lord of the castle. But the Lady uses " thou " to Gawaine when the
situation suggests that her tone has become more intimate. On the
other hand, Gawain uses *thou* when addressing God, and in the
Pardoner's Tale the " old man " uses " you " in speaking to his mother,
Earth (27₄B/734).

The Royal " We "

§ 119. This use of the plural was an inheritance from antiquity. It was used in OE and the use continued into ME. Examples are found in the *Proclamation of Henry III* (11/passim).

The Reflexive

§ 120. A true reflexive pronoun, identifiable by morphology, did not exist in ME. As in OE (HOE § 163.7) the personal pronoun served this function: 3/89 *dude him i turneiment* ' put himself in a tournament ', 5/14057 *þu mihtest þe awreken* ' you might avenge yourself ', 17/18 *to confort him with grapes* ' to comfort himself with grapes ', $21_1/20$ *summe putten hem to þe plouз* ' some set themselves to plowing ', 24/25 *ete we and fede us* ' let us eat and feed ourselves ', 29/520 *she lade hir* ' she laid herself down '.

The personal pronoun was also used for the *pseudo-reflexive*: 5/14036 *gun hire зeongen* '(she) began to go ', $13_3/25$ *him com ur Lord gon* '(there) came Our Lord walking ', $13_3/36$ *ar þe coc him crowe* ' before the cock crows '. It may be noted here that pronominal verbs were quite numerous in ME.

Re-enforcing Pronominal Forms

§ 121. Re-enforcing forms were made with *self, owen* and *ilk* ' same '.

1. The word *self* (*seolf, solf, sulf*) ' self ' (pl *selve, selven*) could be used either as an adjective or as a substantive. In the first case it was added to the personal pronoun: *me self* (7/43), *þe self, himself* (8/490) *him selve* (alongside *hine self* $4_A/11$), *hem selve(n)* ; in the second case to the possessive forms (but in ME only to the first two persons) *mi self* (5/14030) *þy self, our selve(n), your selve(n)*. A few examples will show clearly that on the whole this was still a matter of re-enforcing forms and not of reflexives: 5/14030 *mi seolf, ich gon atstonden uppen ane wolden* ' myself, I did take a defensive position in a forest ', 8/489-90 *And alle his feren twelf He schal kniзten himself* ' and all his twelve companions he, himself, shall knight ', 18/1267 *Hit is þe worchyp of your self* ' it is your own generosity ', $27_1/463-4$ *He made of rym ten vers or twelve Of a compleynte to hymselve* ' He composed ten or twelve verses in rime in the form of a complaint upon his person '.

2. To re-enforce the idea of possession (and not just the person) *owen* ' own ' was used: 5/14054 *an his aȝere hond* ' in his own hand ', in particular when the possessive was post-positional and received sentence stress: 20/709 *a knyghte of thyn awen* ' a knight of thine own ', 24/49 *he hadde no house of his owene* ' he had no house of his own ', 18/1384 *ȝe crave hit as your awen* ' you may claim it as your own '.

3. Re-enforcing forms of the demonstrative were made with *ilke,* *ilche* ' same ': 18/1256 *þat ilk lorde* ' that very lord ', 14/4015 *þis yche abbot* ' that same abbot ', 27₂/1193 *thise ilke tweye* ' those two '. *self* could be used under the same conditions: 18/751 *þat self niȝt* ' that same night '.

The Articles

§ 122. The use of the definite and indefinite articles was much more extensive than in OE (HOE § 166 and 167), but this use developed only gradually, and was still very free, especially in poetic language where it depended on the necessities of the verse.

§ 123. *The definite article.* — 1. Attention should be paid to its absence, before the 14th century, in cases like the following: 3/32 *biginnunge ant rot of al þis ilke reowðe,* '(the) beginning and (the) root of all this same evil ' which should be compared with the French phrase *commencement et racine de tout cest mal,* 5/25 *feþeren he nom mid fingren and on bocfelle fiede* ' he took (the) pen in his fingers and wrote on (the) parchment ' (or ' a pen ' and ' a parchment '), 6/957 *ich fleo bihinde bure* ' I flee behind (the) house ', 21₄/367 *til sonne ȝede to reste* ' until (the) sun went down ', 27₄ᴮ/703 *to lyve and dye ech of hem for oother* ' to live and die, each of them for (the) other '.

2. On the other hand the article was used before a title followed by a proper name: 1/1 *þe king Stephne* ' king Stephen ', 6/942 *þe king Alfred* ' king Alfred ', 1/8 *þe biscop Roger* ' bishop Roger ', (but 1/4 *Henri king* ' king Henry ', 8/532 *Aþulf kniȝt* ' Knight Athulf ').

3. In East-Midland (perhaps due to Scandinavian influence), in the 12th century, the article was used instead of a possessive: 1/2-3 *ðat he sċulde ben alsuiċ alse the eom wes* ' that he would be just as

his uncle was ', 1/25 *me henged bi the þumbes other bi the hefed* ' they hung (people) by **their/the** thumbs or by **their/the** head(s)'.

4. From the moment when it became invariable it was superfluous to repeat it in cases like: 19/1056 *bryȝter þen boþe þe sunne and mone* ' brighter than the sun and moon '.

§ **124.** *The indefinite article.* — 1. Attention should be paid to its absence in such cases 8/475 *þu shalt bere crune* ' thou shalt wear **a** crown ', 8/482 *god kniȝt he schal ȝelde* ' he will make **a** good knight ' (but cp. 8/503-4 *He smot him a litel wiȝt And bed him beon a god kniȝt* ' he hit him a little tap and bade him be a good knight '), 18/1244 *I am wyȝe unworþy* ' I am **an** unworthy man ', 28/4105 *sche semeþ faie and no womman* ' she seems to be **a** fairy and no woman '; after comparisons the presence or absence of the indefinite article depends very often on demands of meter, cp. 14/4004 *as 'meke as 'bryd in 'kage* ' as meek as (a) bird in (a) cage ' and *A 'voys he 'haddę as 'smal as 'hath a 'goot* ' a voice he had as thin and high as a goat has '.

2. The article was equally lacking in verbal locutions composed of "verb + substantive," thus 27₄ʙ/469 *doon sacrifise* ' to make a sacrifice ', 27₄ʙ/744 *yeve reed* ' give counsel ', (but 27₄ʙ/691 *Er that he dide a man a dishonour* ' before he did a man a harmful thing ').

3. Notice the use of the definite article before an expression of measure in the plural where the words are thought of as a unit: 27₄ʙ/771 *an eighte busshels.*

B. The Verb

1. Simple Forms

The Tenses

§ **125.** Just as in OE the verb, from a morphological point of view, had only two tenses, the present and the preterit.

1. The morphological present still expressed future time and the preterit expressed perfected future time:

a) 12/672 *eteth he nevre more bred* ' he will nevermore eat bread ', 15/22 *Þe cherche nys non hare, hy abyt me wel* ' the church is not a hare, it will [or ' can '] wait for me all right ', 27₄ʙ/752 *Nay, olde cherl, by God, thou shalt not so. . . Thou partest nat so lightly, by Seint John!* ' nay, you old joker, by God, you will not (do) so . . . you [don't] will not get away so easy, by St. John! ' ;

b) 3/19-20 *hwa-se hefde i-seid to Eve . . . hwat hefde ha i-ondsweret?* ' whoever might have said (such) to Eve . . . what would she have answered? 10/134-5 *ȝif ich þine come hevede i-wend Ich hedde so i-bede for þe þat* . . . ' If I had expected your coming I would have so prayed for you that . . .' 13₂/109-11. *If þu him woldest luve beode . . . He broughte þe to suche wede þat* ' If you willingly offered him (your) love . . . he would give you such clothes that . . .'.

2. The use of the historical present, practically unknown in OE, became frequent in ME, especially in the 14th century — probably under French influence: 10/168 *Þe wolf haveth hounger swiþe gret For he nedde ȝare i-ete* ' The wolf is very hungry for he had not eaten for a long time ', 21₄/304 ff. *Now bigynneþ Glotoun for to go to schrifte And kaires hym to-kirke-ward his coupe to schewe, Ac Beton þe brewestere bad hym good morwe, And axed of hym with þat whider-ward he wolde* ' Now Glutton gets ready to go to confession and takes his way churchward to tell his sins, but Beton, the brewer, bade him good morning and asked him at the same time where he wanted (to go)', 28/3999 ff. *Sche fond and gadreþ herbes suote; Sche pulleþ up some be þe rote, And manye wiþ a knyf sche scherþ, And alle into hir char sche berþ. Thus whan sche haþ þe hulles sought, The flodes þer forȝat sche nought* . . . ' She found and gathers sweet herbs; some she pulls up by the root and many she cuts with a knife, and all she carries into her car. Thus when she has sought (such things in) the hills, she did not forget the streams '.

REMARK. — Particular attention is called to a lack of " sequence of tenses " found here in the best ME usage. Such a stylistic trait still persists in ModE and provides frequent opportunities for teachers to " correct " this fault.

Modality

§ 126. In simple sentences or in a main clause the subjunctive is frequently found under the following circumstances:

a) to express a realisable wish (with the present). In this sense it may be called an optative: 5/2 *liðe him beo Drihten* ' may God be merciful to him ', 5/14075 *Min hafved beo to wedde* ' may my head be pledged as security ', 10/96 *wo worþe . . . lust and wille* ' may evil befall desire ', 18/1263 *Mary yow ȝelde* ' may the Virgin Mary repay you ', 27₄ʙ/766 *God save you.* This type of sentence was often preceded by *as, so* : 29/523 *as have I ceyll* ' as I hope to have happiness ', 10/130 *so God þe rede* ' may God so counsel you '.

b) to express an unrealisable wish (with the preterit) : 13₃/8 *Judas, þou were wurþe me stende wid ston* ' Judas you would deserve that people stoned you '.

c) as the equivalent of an imperative, particularly in the 3rd person : 7/110 *þatt wite he wel* ' let him know well ', 29/200 *ylkon take hede* ' let each one take heed ', 11/4 *þæt witen ȝe wel alle* ' let all of you know well '.

d) followed by a hypothetical subordinate clause : 18/1245 *Bi God, I were glad and yow god þoȝt* ' by God I would be glad if it seemed good to you ', 27₂/1210-11 *Ne hadde I er now . . . Ben ȝold, i-wys, I were now nought heere* ' if I had not, before now, (already) given in, certainly, I would not be here now ', 27₄ʙ/690 *To ben avysed greet wysdom it were* ' it would be extremely wise to be aware '.

On the use of the subjunctive in subordinate clauses, see below §§ 152 ff.

§ 127. The imperative was very often re-enforced by an accompanying pronoun subject; this pronoun could be placed either before or after the imperative form : 8/472-3 *Kyng, he sede, þu leste A tale mid þe beste* ' king, he said, do listen to one of the best stories ', 10/121 *ne gabbe þou me nout* " don't you mock at me ', 27₃/254 *hyde ye youre beautes* ' hide your beauty '.

Nominal Forms of the Verb

§ 128. The nominal forms of the verb found in ME are the infinitive and the verbal *-ing* substantive, on the one hand, the present and past participles on the other hand.

§ 129. Normally the infinitive plays the role of an adjunct to a verb, a substantive, an adjective or an adverb.

1. The infinitive as an adjunct to a verb had two forms :

a) either the plain infinitive which was the case after temporal auxiliaries (*shall, will*) or modal auxiliaries (*may, can, dar, mot, lete,* etc.), and, just as in OE, after a certain number of verbs such as *go, hear, think*. We find, for example: 29/643 *go se* 'go see', 10/170 *he herde speken* 'he heard spoken' 21₂/164 *as I here telle* 'as I hear said', 28/3956 *I thenke tellen* 'I think to tell (a story)= I think I will tell'. It is also used in the so-called accusative-with-infinitive construction. 21₂/160-1 *I have y-sein segges . . . beren biʒes* 'I have seen men wear collars', 27₁/451 *Then found I sitte even upryght* 'then I found (him) sitting right up straight', 28/4060 *sche bad alle oþre go* 'she bade all the others go', 14/4120 *Why wuld þey nat suffre hym lyve* 'why would they not let him live', 28/4167 *sche ʒaf him drink a drauhte* 'she gave him a draft to drink';

> Note as well cases in which verbs of motion are followed by a second verb of motion in the plain infinitive form to make the meaning more precise. This is a frequent construction in the 12th and 13th centuries with *come*, for example: 5/13996 *þa com þer . . . an oht mon riden* 'then a brave man came riding there', 5/14033 *þa com an guldene leo liðen* 'then a golden lion came travelling', 10/108 *þer com a wolf gon* 'a wolf came along', 13₃/35, *In him com ur Lord gon* 'In came Our Lord'.

b) or the infinitive was used with *to* or with *for to* (and in Northern English and Scots, *for till*): 4/45 *makie to cwakien heovene* 'make heaven quake', 4/17 *hwet ha ahen his deorewurðe milce to ʒelden* 'what they ought to pay back for his precious mercy', 5/13994 *Arður wende to aʒein al Rome* 'Arthur planned to rule all Rome', 7/8 *takenn . . . to follʒhenn* 'taken to follow', 7/48 *hellpenn . . . to sen* 'help to see', 23/44 *þanne wolde he maken hem to drynken* 'then he wanted to make them drink'.

> REMARK. — This construction corresponds exactly to the use of the gerundive or inflected infinitive in OE (HOE § 172), and, in the 12th century, this inflected form had not entirely disappeared, cp. above § 94, REM. VI.

for to was first used with an idea of purpose in the sense of " in order to," " for the purpose of," cp. the following examples and the corresponding Old French: 3/78 *for te ofgan* ' pur deservir '/' in order to obtain ', 3/107 *for te bineomen* ' pur tolir '/' in order to deprive ' 3/110 *for te ofdrahen* ' pur fortraire '/' in order to attract ' ; but from the beginning of that period and in the same text *to* is found with this same semantic force: 3/120 *to schawin* ' pur lui moustrer '/' in order to show him ', 3/122 *to ofdrahen* ' pur fortraire '/' in order to draw away '. From the end of the 13th century, there was no longer any difference of meaning between *to* and *for to*, and by way of reciprocity, just as *to* was used for purpose, *for to* was used where no purpose was involved. The forms were at that point in free variation: 21₂/172 *ʒif him list for to laike* ' if it pleases him to play ', 21₄/304 *bigynneth . . . for to go* ' begins . . . to go ', 27₁/416 *Hyt ys no nede eke for to axe* ' there is no need, also, to ask '. It is not unusual to find *to* and *for to* in the same sentence: 21₃/61-2 *Hit bycomeþ for clerkus Crist for to serven And knaves uncrouned to cart and to worche* ' it is fitting for clerks to serve Christ and for untonsured laymen to cart and work ', 27₁/345 ff. *Me thoght I herde an hunte blowe T'assay his horn and for to knowe Whether . . .* ' it seemed to me I heard a hunter blow to try out his horn and to find out whether . . .'.

II. A possible origin of this use of *for + to* may lie in the construction *for + object + to + infinitive* (called the accusative-with-infinitive construction), cp. 6/1017-8 *For hom to lere gode þewes And for to leten hor unþewes* ' for them to learn good moral habits and to abandon their bad habits '.

III. Exceptionally, in the 13th century, *for* without *to* is found before infinitives: 2/53 *for habben Godes are* ' to have God's mercy ' (MS L; MSS TE: *for to*).

Thus a verb used as adjunct to another verb in ME might be:

1st, the plain infinitive: *I thinke tellen* ' I mean to tell ', 23/54 *þei wolde go sle* ' they wanted to go and kill ' ;

2nd, the infinitive preceded by *to*: 28/4026 *sche þoghte to beginne* ' she thought to begin ' ;

3rd, the infinitive preceded by *for to*: 23/61 *wenten . . . for to sle* ' they went to kill ' ;

4th, the verbal noun in *-ing*: 27₁/348 *I herde goynge* ' I heard go ' (or ' going ' in ModE).

2. *An infinitive used as an adjunct to an adjective or an adverb* was preceded by *to*: 3/64 *feherest to bihalden* ' fairest to behold ', 2/17 *erʒe to done god* ' slow to do good ', 13₅/14 *face feir to fonde* ' a face beautiful to see ' ; 1/33-4 *thre men hadden onoh to bæron onne* ' three men had enough (to do) to carry one '. This was a direct continuation of the OE inflected infinitive.

§ **130.** *The infinitive as subject* was still rather unusual in ME. It grew up from the interchange of position between the subject and the verbal part of the predicate in phrases with the verb *to be,* or with impersonal verbs. We find at first, for instance, 4/7 *þet is eche lif to seon and cnawen soð God* ' it is eternal life to see and to know (the) true God '. 8/480 *Hit nere noȝt forloren For te kniȝti Child Horn* ' it would not be a loss to knight Child Horn ' and, by permutation we proceed to 27₄ᵦ/690 *To been avysed greet wisdom it were* ' to be aware would be extremely wise ', 27₁/325 *to byholde hyt was gret joye* ' to behold it was (a) great joy '.

§ 131. The *verbal substantive* in *-ung,* then *-ing* never stopped gaining importance during the ME period.

It was in free variation with the infinitive as adjunct to another verb, cp. above § 129 and also 27₂/1235-6 *When that she hereth any herde tale Or in the hegges any wyght styringe* ' when she hears any shepherd talk or in the hedges anybody stirring '.

It could function with verb force: 4ₐ/26 *non vallynge doun* ' no falling down ' (i. e. ' no lessening ') or as a substantive: 26/15 *þis apeyrynge of þe burþ-tonge* ' this deteriorating/deterioration of the native tongue ' ; it could also be both at once: 25/40 *bi puttyng forth of whom so it were* ' by putting forward whoever it might be '.

It might be reduced to a simple substantive: 3/95 *þet þis scheld naveð siden is for bitacnunge þet . . .* ' that this shield has no sides is for (the) betokening that . . .' ; but almost always it retains something of the activity-idea of a verb, thus *huntynge* in the following examples 27₁/350 *al men speken of huntyng* ' all men talk about hunting ', 27₁/373-4 *Every man dide ryght anoon As to huntynge fil to doon* ' every man did right away what was proper to do for hunting ', 27₁/355 *they wolde on huntynge goon* ' they wanted to go hunting '.

The fact that the verbal substantive was very early merged in form with the new present participle contributed greatly to its retaining verb characteristics.

§ 132. The syntactical problems raised by *participles* are mostly concentrated in their use in periphrastic verbal phrases and these can be inspected now.

2. Verbal Periphrases

The Aspects

§ **133.** The periphrastic locution with *to be* and the present participle was not unknown in OE (HOE § 169.1) and continued to be used to emphasize an idea of duration (*durative aspect*). Little by little its use was extended and its area of meaning became more precise, but before the 15th century this periphrasis was hardly to be found except in the preterit and the present and it was limited to a few verbs like *go, come, dwell, live, fight, do* and *consent*, among others: 23/4 *þere was dwellinge sometyme a riche man* ' once upon a time a rich man was living there ', 16/17-8 *Arestotill sais þat þe bees are feghtande agaynes hym þat will drawe þaire hony fra thaym* ' Aristotle says that bees fight against them that want to take their honey from them ', 14/4127-8 *Above þe erthe þey were stynking þat to þe beres deþ were consentyng* ' above the earth (i. e. while still alive and not buried) they (the bodies of those) were stinking who had consented to the bear's death '. The true development of this periphrasis belongs to the modern era.

§ **134.** To express the idea of a " beginning " action (*inchoative aspect*) ME normally used the verb *gin(ne)*, especially its preterit forms *gan (gon, can, con)* followed by the plain infinitive or preceded by *to*; *gin(ne)* was simply the equivalent, by the loss of the first syllable, of *agin(ne)* ' begin ' (< OE *onginnan*) ; in any case we often find *agin* and *begin* alongside *gin* in this periphrasis (see examples below). This construction is found in OE, but now increases.

The true inchoative aspect of this periphrasis is well illustrated in cases like the following 5/14 *Laȝamon gon liðen* ' Lawman began to travel ', 5/14016 *he bigon to hewene* ' he began to hew ', 5/14031 *ich þer wondrien agon* ' I began to wander there ', 8/495 *þe day bigan to springe* ' the day began to dawn ', 10/239 *þe wolf gon sinke, þe vox arise* ' the wolf began to sink, the fox to rise ', 27₁/312 *al my chambre gan to rynge* ' my whole chamber began to ring '.

But very early the sense of *gan* faded and poets usually yielded to the temptation to use it as a semantically empty function word which did not add anything to the meaning of the verb which it preceded, but did serve as a time indicator, almost a tense flexion: 10/83 *he gon him biþenche* ' he considered ', 14/72 *Fyve wyntyr wyþ hym gan y wone* ' I lived with him five winters ', 14/4014 *in here tyme þe abbot gan deye* ' in their time the abbot died ', 18/1174-5 *þe lorde . . . con launce and lyȝt* ' the lord . . . started ahead and (then) dismounted ', 18/1206 *ful lufly con ho lete* ' she acted very graciously ', 27₂/1232 *gan eche of hem in armes other wynde* ' each of them wound their arms about the other '.

REMARK. — In the 12th Century the verb *fang* was used in an analogous periphrasis: 3/11 *Eve . . . feng to delitin i þe bihaldunge* ' Eve began to delight in the beholding '.

§ 135. The use of the periphrasis with *wil* (*wold*) was established early in ME to express the idea of an action which is done (or was done) habitually (*frequentative aspect*), thus 6/895-6 *Þu draȝst men to fleses luste Þat willeþ þine songes luste* ' you draw to desires of the flesh men who listen (habitually) to your song ', 23/33-4 *whan þat ony god knyght . . . cam to see this rialtee, he wolde lede him into his paradys* ' when any good knight . . . came to see this realm, he would (always) lead him into his paradise ', 29/592 *kynde will crepe where it may not go* ' (human) nature will creep where it cannot walk '.

§ 136. A *causative aspect* was generally expressed by means of a periphrasis with *do* and sometimes *make*, and, in the North by *ger*: 10/251 *þi soule-cnul ich wile do ringe* ' I will have your death-knell rung ', 12/658 *Grim dede maken a ful fayr bed* ' Grim caused to be made a very beautiful bed ', 25/26 *he did cary grete quantitee of Armure* ' he had a great quantity of armor carried ', 27₂/1242 *sodeynly rescous doth hym escapen* ' suddenly rescue causes him to escape '.

12/542 *Jesu Crist þat makede to go þe halte* ' Jesus Christ who made the lame walk ', 17/80 *Þe prince . . . gert nakers strike and trumpes blaw* ' the prince . . . had kettledrums struck and trumpets blown '.

The Tenses

§ 137. The verbal periphrases expressing ideas of time were of two types according to whether the auxiliary combined with a past participle or with an infinitive.

§ 138. In the first case we have to deal with the *compound tenses* that had already begun to appear in OE (HOE § 170.3*a*) and whose use was considerably extended during the ME period.

To form compound tenses dealing with past time *to have* (for transitive verbs) and *to be* (for intransitive) continued to be used: 7/11 *icc hafe don* ' I have done ', 1/4-5 *hade . . . gadered* '(he) had gathered ', etc;

24/31 *þi broþir is comen* ' your brother has come ', 28/3959 *sche was vanysshyt* ' she had disappeared ', etc.

From a very early time then, English was endowed not only with a perfect and a pluperfect but also with a future perfect (*shal/wil* + auxil. verb + past participle) and with a future pluperfect (*sholde/ wolde* + auxil. verb + past participle, in hypothetical statements): 3/23 [*Eve*] *walde . . . habben i-ondsweret* ' Eve would have answered '. Starting in this period are found forms which can be classed as past infinitives (which freely combined with modal auxiliaries, for ex. 3/106 *ne mahte he . . . habben arud us?* ' could he not have saved us? ') and past imperatives: 29/663 *Hold youre tonges, have done!* ' Hold your tongues, have done '.

REMARK. — Note the narrative use of the perfect as equivalent to the preterit: 22/451-2 *And quhen the kyngis hounde has seyn/Thai men assale his mastir swa,/He lap till ane* ' And when the king's hound has seen (= saw) the men assail his master so, he leapt at one '.

§ **139.**   Wherever we have an auxiliary combined with an infinitive (either present or past), by definition we are dealing with *periphrastic tenses*. This is especially true for the future and its past which used the auxiliaries *shal* and *wil*, a process already under way in OE (HOE § 170.3*b*).

REMARKS. — I. The verb *worþe* ' to become ' was still used as the future of *to be*: 8/459-60 *Wiþ selver and wiþ golde Hit wurþ him wel i-ȝolde* ' with silver and with gold will he be well repaid ' (impersonal constr. in ME), 10/191 *ich wot to-niȝt ich worþe ded* ' I know (that) tonight I shall be dead ', 10/248 *þi biȝete worþ wel smal* ' your profit will be quite small '.

II. In the North the future auxiliary was *mon*, thus 20/813 *I mon swelte as-swyth ore ȝe tell me my swefen* ' I will die this moment unless you interpret me my dream '.

The use of these auxiliaries showed free variation for *shal* or *wil* in all persons; at the most it may be possible to discern a tendency to use *wil* (in all persons) when volition is included and *shal* when obligation is included.

Thus in *Havelok the Dane* when the hero is making all sorts of promises to the usurper Godred in order to save his life, he says, 12/485 ff. *Al Denemark I wile you yeve, To þat forward þu late me live; Here I wile on boke swere, Þat nevre more ne shal I bere Ayen þe, loverd, sheld ne spere . . . Loverd, have merci of me!* *To-day I wile fro Denemark fle, Ne nevere more comen ageyn; Sweren y wole þat Bircabein Nevere yete me ne gat* ' I will give you all Denmark, on condition that you let me live; here I will swear on the Bible, that never more, lord, will I bear against you shield or spear . . . Lord, have mercy on me. Today I will flee from Denmark, and never more come back again; I will swear that Bircabein (the last king) never begot me '. And in the same poem when a supernatural occurrence has revealed to his foster-father Grim that the child entrusted to him is the son of the king, he peremptorily affirms 12/606 ff. *þis ure eir þat shal be loverd of Denemark, He shal ben king strong and stark; He shal haven in his hand Al Denemark and Engeland,* etc. ' This is our heir that shall be lord of Denmark; he shall be a king strong and powerful; he shall have in his hand all Denmark and England '.

But examples like these do not represent the general usage, which varies from one text to another; thus in the poem *Judas,* Jesus says to Peter, 13₃/36 *þou wolt fursake me þrien ar þe coc him crowe,* compare the King James version, Mark 14.30, "before the cock crow twice thou shalt deny me thrice " on the other hand Wyclif has the prodigal son say 24/13 *y shal rise and go to my fadir* where the King James version has, Luke 15.18 " I will arise and go to my father." But even in the modern literary language usage is still unsettled, despite the rules established by prescriptive grammarians of the 18th century and repeated uncritically in present day textbooks. All that can be said is that in ME *shal* could be used in all persons and that *wil* was being so introduced more and more.

The completion of this process can be seen in Charles Fries' study, *American English Grammar* (1940), pp. 164-6 where *will* was found to be the generalized form for simple futurity; *shall* has been eliminated except in questions, where it remains in the first person. When *shall* does appear in declarative statements in the first person " intention " and " determination " seem also to be present, and not simple futurity alone.

III. What has just been said is equally valid for the past as for the present future: 27₄ᴮ/712 *they wolde han troden* ' they would have trod ', 29/509 *som shuld have boght it full sore* ' some would have paid very dear for it '.

IV. Note the locutions with ideas of a future obligation involving " to be " and " to have " + " to " + infinitive (and cp. Fries, *Amer. Engl. Gr.*, pp. 167-70): 11/13 *þo i-setnesses þæt beon i-makede and beon to makien* ' those establishments that have been made and are to be made ', 27₄ᴮ/749 *I moote go thider as I have to go* ' I must go there where I have to go '.

§ 140. Finally, the existence in ME (rather rare) of a dominant ModE periphrasis should be noted: *do* in present and preterit form + infinitive: 2/56 *ʒive for Godes luve, þenne deþ hes wel i-halden* ' (let a man) give his (possessions) for God's love, then does (he) truly keep his (possessions)', 12/523 *þer anon he dede sende after a fishere* ' thereupon he did send after a fisherman ', 17/62 *when he did fell his grete okes* ' when he did fell his great oaks '. Most of the time *do* in such cases is already found used as a semantically empty function word, often an expletive for metrical purposes.

REMARK. — This use may have arisen from the quite frequent use of *do* to avoid repetition of a verb (called the " vicarious " *do*) as in 2/2 *ich welde mare þene ich dede* ' I know more than I did ', 27₄ᴀ/676 *But smothe it heeng as dooth a strike of flex* ' But smooth it (his hair) hung as does a hank of flax ', 28/3967 *sche glod forþ as an addre doþ* ' she glided onward as an adder does '.

Modality

§ 141. The verbal periphrases which express modality are made up of modal auxiliaries such as *dar* ' dare ', *may, can, moot* ' must ', *shal* ' be obliged, must ', *ouhte* ' ought ', *wil* ' want to ' + plain infinitive (except sometimes after *ouhte*). The conditions under which these were used are sufficiently like those in ModE as to make details superfluous. It should be noticed, in particular, that *shal* and *wil* retained their original OE meanings except in those cases where they are obviously semantically empty function words used as " future auxiliaries." This is especially the case with *wil* which in ME is very often used to express volition where ModE prefers *want, wish*, etc. and, in the negative, *refuse*, for ex. 13₂/109 *if þu him woldest luve beode* ' if you would (wished to, desired to) offer him (your) love ', 27₄ᴮ/727 *Ne Deeth, allas! ne wol nat han my lyf* ' Even death, alas, refuses to take my life ', 13₃/20-1 *wolte sulle þi Loverd? — I nul* *sulle my Loverd* ' do you want to sell your lord? — I don't want to sell my Lord ', 24/33 *þis eldre sone hadde dedeyn and wolde not come in* ' this elder son was annoyed and refused to (didn't want to) come in ', 29/255 *I am cold and nakyd and wold have a fyere* ' I am cold and naked and would like to have a fire '.

The Moods

§ **142.** The *hortative mood,* which was used from the 13th century on for the first and third person to fill out the imperative, was a periphrasis formed by means of *let, lat* + object pronoun (or substantive) + plain infinitive: 8/515 *let him us alle kniʒte* ' let him knight us all ', 29/655 *Let us seke hym there* ' let us seek him there ', 29/595 *Lett bren this bawde* ' let this procuress be burned '.

§ **143.** The *conditional* was often expressed by means of the " modal " preterits of the auxiliaries *shuld, myght (maht), wold*: 1/45 *þu myhtes faren all a dæis fare, sćuldest thu nevre finden man in tune sittende* ' you could travel a full day's journey, (and) you would not find a man remaining in (a) village ', 2/13 *ich mihte habbe bet i-don* ' I could have done better/I might have done better ', 2/14 *Nu ich walde, ah ich ne mei* ' now I would like to, but I don't have the physical capacity ', 21₂/185 *Thouʒ we culled þe catte ʒut sholde þer come anoþer* ' though we killed the cat, yet would there come another '.

REMARK. — Although formed with preterits (which, originally, were in reality preterit subjunctives) these conditional periphrases expressed only mood and not time relations.

§ **144.** The subjunctive as well came to be expressed by means of periphrasis involving a modal auxiliary:

1. *may (might)* in subordinate object clauses (cp. § 154): 27₁/467-9 *Hit was gret wonder that Nature Myght suffre any creature To have such sorwe* ' it was a great wonder that Nature might permit any creature to have such sorrow ', or in subordinate clauses of purpose (cp. § 154.1) 12/675 *þat y mowe riche be* ' so that I may be rich '.

2. *shuld* (and sometimes *wold*) in subordinate object clauses: 27₄ᴮ/845 *the feend . . . Putte in his thought þat he sholde poyson beye* ' the devil put (it) in his mind that he should buy poison ', 28/3948-9 *preiþ hire þat . . . Sche wolde make* ' asked her that she make ', 29/665

To Bedlem he bad that we shuld gang 'To Bethlehem he bade that we should go', 14/4104 *he pleyned . . . þat hys solas shulde be no more* ' he grievously complained . . . that he should nevermore know comfort ', or in subordinate clauses of condition (cp. § 158) : 21₄/340 *In cove-naunte þat Clement shulde þe cuppe fille* ' on condition that Clement should fill the cup ', or, as well, in hypothetical clauses : 12/513-4 *yf he were brouht of live And mine children wolden þrive* ' if he were put to death my children might prosper '.

The Passive

§ 145. ME, like OE previously, had recourse to periphrasis for the passive, which had no morphological expression (as is true for many other languages). The locution was " to be " (*ben*) or " to become " (*worþe*)+ the past participle : 1/2 [*he*] *wes underfangen* ' he was received ', 7/3654 *Iesu Crist iss borenn þær* ' Jesus Christ was born there ', 10/103 *Ich am i-kaut* ' I am caught ', 7/3343 *þeȝȝ wurrdenn swiþe offdredde* ' they were very much afraid ', 8/460 *hit wurþ him wel i-ȝolde* ' it was well repaid him ' ; *worþe* is found in use into the 14th century but less frequently than *ben*.

CHAPTER TEN

STRUCTURE OF THE SENTENCE

Concord

§ 146. *In principle* concord was normal in ME for number, gender, and case, just as there was sequence of tense.

1. *Concord of appositives.* — An appositive was regularly put in the same case as the word with which it was in apposition: 5/22 *Ælienor þe wes Henries quene, þes heȝes kinges* ' Eleanor who was Henry's, the sovereign king's, queen ' ; but lack of concord was already beginning to appear 21₄/341 *Hikkes hode hostellere* [instead of *hostelleres*] ' Hick the tavern-keeper's hood '.

There was a similar appositive concord with adjective *sum* (instead of a genitive) : 8/498 *Sume hi were luþere* ' some (of) them were wicked '. The same for *echon* which might refer to a plural subject: 27₁/335 *My windowes were shette echon* ' Every one of my windows were shut '.

2. *Concord with collectives.* — It was not unusual to have a collective subject, morphologically singular, agreeing with a plural verb form: 1/56 *al þe tunsċipe flugæn* ' the whole village fled (pl)', 25/3 *compleynen . . . the folk of the Mercerye* ' the Mercer group complain ', 27₄B/464 *yonge folk that haunteden folye* ' young folk that spent (pl) their time in idle folly '. The same was true of concord in the pronoun : — morphologically sg forms were referred to by morphologically pl pronouns: 25/24 *noman sholde come to chese her Mair* ' no one was allowed to come to choose his mayor '.

§ 147. A general lack of concord, however, was quite frequent in ME.

1. Often, with a compound subject (undoubtedly thought of as forming a unit) the verb remained in the singular: 13₄/3 *Lef ant gras ant blosmes springes* ' leaf and grass and blossoms spring up ', 20/793

110

Hys brest and his brayell was blodye all over ' his breast and his belly were bloody all over ', 27₁/427-8 *And many an hert and many an hynde Was both before me and behynde* ' and many a hart and many a doe were both before me and behind '.

2. This was frequent when the subject was placed after the verb: 13₂/65 *Hwer is Paris and Heleyne* ' Where are Paris and Helen ', or where the verb came between elements of a compound subject: 1/61-2 *hi sæden ðat Crist slep and his halechen* ' they said that Christ and his saints slept (sg)'.

3. In the following case the verb agrees with the predicate (considered as psychological subject) : 18/1251 *hit ar ladyes innoʒe* ' there are a great many ladies ', 21₃/59 *it ben aires of hevene all þat ben crounede* ' they are heirs of heaven, all who are tonsured '.

4. Conforming to OE usage, *many* could be used before a singular word: 21₂/197 *many mannus malt* ' many (a) man's malt ' ; very early, however, this construction became *many a* as in ModE, but this new form was also used before plurals: 23/17 *many a diverse thinges* ' many various things ', which indicates a hesitation about which construction and what kind of concord to adopt.

§ 148. *Sequence of tenses* was often lacking. The use of the historical present which was discussed above (§ 125.2) is not sufficient to explain the abrupt transition from present to preterit and vice-versa, even in the same sentence, as, for example, in 27₄ᴮ/851 *And forth he gooth, no longer wolde he tarie, Into the toun, unto a pothecarie* ' and on he goes/went, no longer did he desire to delay, into the village to an apothecary ('s shop)', 27₄ᴮ/813 *if I kan shape it so That it departed were among us two Hadde I not doon a freendes torn to thee* ' if I can/could plan it so that it (the treasure) were divided among us two, had I not done a friend's service for you ', 28/3948-9 *Jason . . . preiþ hire þat his fader ʒoupe Sche wolde make aʒeinward newe* ' Jason asks/asked her if she would make his father's youth new again '. It might be remarked that a lack of sequence of tenses is a dominant stylistic trait in languages in which we have recorded oral narratives as in Old Icelandic, but is infrequent in Old English (written monkish prose). (See § 125 REM.)

Negation

§ **149.**   For negation ME had the following devices at its disposal:

1. For word-negation there was the prefix *un-*, the suffix *-les*, the prepositions *bote* and *withoute(n)*, the adjective *nā, nō.*

Furthermore, there were the indefinite negative pronouns, *nān, noon, noman.*

2. For sentence-negation there was the adverb *ne, na* which might agglutinate with certain verbs (*nil, nam, nōt, nabbe,* etc.) or other adverbs (*nevere*) or conjunctions (*nawþer, neythir, nepeles,* etc.). From an original re-enforcing element, OE *wiht* ' someone, something, thing ', added to *nā, nō* was derived the adverb *noht* (*naʒt*), *not* (*nat*).

3. Normal negation of verbs was produced by *ne, na* placed before the verb; but to re-enforce this negative *noght, not* was added after the verb: 17/36 *he ne held it noght* ' he did not hold it '. But from the middle of the 14th century *not* alone, and after the verb, began to be used: 29/519 *my wyfe rose nott* ' my wife did not get up ', 29/539 *cry not so* ' don't cry so ', and especially it was placed after auxiliary verbs: 23/71 *it is not longes gon* ' it is not long ago ', 23/55 *þat þei scholde not drede to don it* ' that they should not fear to do it ', 24/33 *wolde not come in* ' would not come in '.

4. Double and even triple negatives were common in ME: 1/23 *ne wæren nævre nan martyrs swa pined* ' no martyrs were ever so tortured ', 3/131 f. *loki þet hit namon ne eili, ne ne hearmi, ne þet hire þoht ne beo nawiht þron i-festenet* ' see to it that it injures no one, nor harms, nor that their thought be in any way fixed thereon '.

Ellipsis

§ **150.**   The infinitive of verbs of motion, of the verb *to be* and *to make* could be left unexpressed after an auxiliary: 1/36 *ðat he ne myhte nowiderwardes* ' that he wasn't able (to turn or go) anywhere ', 10/244-6 *Weder wolt þow? — Weder ich wille, þo vox sede, ich wille oup* ' Where (do) you want (to go) ? — Where (do) I want (to go) ?, said the fox, I want (to go) up ', 10/85 *adoun he moste* ' down he had (to go) ', 15/21 *þe wombe zayþ: þo ne sselt* ' the belly says: thou shalt not (do so) ', 6/1025 *wat sold ich þar mid mine songe* ' what would I (do) there with my song? '.

CHAPTER ELEVEN

THE COMPOUND SENTENCE

A. COORDINATION

§ 151. The principal coordinating conjunctions were:

1. *Copulative coordinate.* — *and* (*ant, ent*), *ac* 'and'.

2. *Disjunctive coordinate.* — *oþer, or* 'or', *eyþer* (*ayþer*) . . . *oþer* (*or*) 'either . . . or', *wheþer* 'whether', *ne, nor* 'nor', *neyþer* (*noþer*) . . . *nor* (*ne*) 'neither . . . nor'.

3. *Adversative coordinate.* — *ac, bote* 'but', *naþeles* (*neþeles, noþeles*) 'nevertheless'.

4. *Consecutive coordinate.* — *þan*(*ne*), *þen*(*ne*) 'then', *forþi* 'for this reason', *for why* 'for', *ȝete, ȝit* 'yet, however, still', *right as . . . right so* 'even as . . . even so'.

B. SUBORDINATION

Relative Clauses

§ 152. 1. *Attributive clauses.* — Up to the beginning of the 13th century, the invariable relative particle *þe* (*þa*) was used as a subordinating relative, either by itself or combined with a demonstrative: 1/19 *þa men þe hi wenden ðat ani god hefden* 'the men that they thought had any money', 1/48 *sume ieden on ælmes þe waren sum wile riċe men* 'some went begging who a little while (before) were rich men', 4/34 *For-þi seide ure Laverd to þeo þe him hefden i-cwemet* 'For this reason our Lord said to those who had pleased him . . .'.

But from the 12th century on, the most frequently used relative was the indeclinable *þat* which appears for all cases and genders, in the sg as well as the pl; 1/30 *an ċæste þat was sċort* 'a chest that was short', 27₄ᵦ/859 ff. *And thou shalt have A thyng that, also God my soule save, In al this world ther is no creature That eten or dronken hath of this confiture Noght but the montance of a corn of whete That he ne shal his lif anon forlete* 'And you shall have a thing (such) that, as God may save my soul, in all this world there is no creature that has

113

eaten or drunk of this mixture nothing but the amount of a grain of wheat that will not lose his life '.

In turn *þat* was used by itself, as in the preceding examples, or coupled with a demonstrative: 9/16 *se þet sucurede hem ine þa peril* ' he who aided them in that danger ', or with a personal pronoun 27₁/403 *They two that make floures growe* ' those two (divinities) that make the flowers grow '.

2. *Predicative clauses.* — Just as in OE (cp. HOE § 181 REM. IV) *þat* was used as a conjunctive neuter pronoun to introduce predicative clauses: 2/20 *repen þet ho er sowen* ' to reap what they previously sowed ', 8/518 *Do nu þat þi wille is* ' Do now what(ever) your desire is ', 14/4044 *God hadde herd þat he besoght* ' God had heard what he asked for ', 28/4025 *tok out ferst þat was þerinne* ' took out first what was in there '.

REMARKS. — I. On the displacement of the preposition with the relative *þat* see below § 169.3.

II. Just as in OE (HOE § 181 REM. I) we frequently find in ME a subordinate with a zero relative often by simple contact between the antecedent and the verb of the sub-clause. 5/20 *þa makede a Frenchis clerc, Wace wes i-hoten* ' which a French clerk made, (who) was named Wace ', 10/71 *one putte, wes water inne* ' one well in (which) (there) was water ', 21₄/362-3 *Is non so hungri hounde in Hertfordshire, Durst lape of the levynges* ' (there) is no hound so hungry in Hertfordshire (that) would dare lap up any of the leavings ', 22₁/273 *is nane, can tell* ' (there) is none (who) can tell ', 27₄ᴮ/675 *Ther cam a privee theef, men clepeth Deeth* ' there came a secret thief men call Death ', 27₁/365 *I asked oon, ladde a lymere* ' I asked one (who) led (on a leash) a stag-hound ', 29/195 *who is that, pypys so poore* ' who is he (who) pipes so poor? '.

In indirect questions it was naturally the interrogative pronoun which filled out the role of the relative: 29/515-6 *then may ye se Who had hir* ' then you can see who had her ', 28/3953-4 *Bot what sche did in þat matiere, It is a wonder þing to hiere* ' but what she did in that matter, it is a wondrous thing to hear '.

§ **153.** As the preceding examples demonstrate the *indicative* mood was used in relative subordination. Sometimes the *subjunctive* is found:

a) after verbs of commanding, asking and wishing: 5/28-30 *Nu biddeð Laʒamon Alcne æðele mon ... þet þeos boc rede and leornia þeos runan* ' Now Lawman asks each noble man who may read this book and learn these secrets ' ;

b) with an idea of possibility: 3/117-8 *i swuche stude þer me hit sonest seo* ' in such a place where a person might soonest see it ', 11/18 *wherþurʒ this besiʒte murʒe beon i-let* ' through which this provision might be hindered ' ;

c) after a negative main clause: 4/5 *wiðuten euch þing þet mahe hearmin oðer eilin* ' without anything that may harm or injure ', 15/68 *he ne heþ vot þet him moʒe sosteyni* ' he doesn't have a foot that may sustain him '.

d) in certain indirect questions, cf. § 160.2.

REMARK. — In the above paragraph as in those that follow, I have only chosen convincing examples where the morphological distinction between indicative and subjunctive was still clear. The great number of cases in which, from the beginning of ME, the difference between the moods was not formally discernible had the consequence of a progressive and rapid decay of the role of the subjunctive in subordinate clauses. What is said here concerning such use, then, is only a probable approximation of the facts.

Object Clauses

§ **154.** The subordinating conjunction is *þat* ' that, in order that, so that '.

I. It was followed by the subjunctive:

1. In purpose clauses: 5/34 *þat hire þe selre beo* ' that things may be the better for her ', 6/925-6 *And warni men . . . Þat þi dweole-song heo ne forlere* ' And I warn men . . . so that your deceitful song may not mislead them '. 10/197-8 *Tel þine sunnen on and on Þat þer bileve never on* ' Confess your sins every one so that never a one be left ', 12/522 *þat he ne flete in the flod* ' so that he may not float on the water '.

2. After verbs of wishing (commanding, compelling) and asking: 3/80 *biseche ich þe . . . þet tu luvie me* ' I beseech you that you love me ', 11/9 *we willen . . . þæt þæt ure rædesmen . . . habbeþ i-don . . . beo stedefæst* ' we desire that what our counsellors have done be permanent ', 12/504 *he wolde þat he ded wore* ' he wished that he were dead ', 7/97 *himm bidde icc þatt he't write rihht* ' I order him to write it correctly '.

3. After verbs of doubting, uncertainty or estimation: 5/14072 *no weneð heo navere to soðe þat þu cumen aʒain from Rome* ' she never expects, indeed, that you will come back from Rome ', 10/217-8 *Ich*

wende . . . þat ich i-seie were soþ ' I supposed (that) what I saw was
true ', 13₃/18 *Þe Jewes . . . awenden he were wode* ' the Jews thought
he was crazy ', 27₄ᴃ/681 *me thynketh that it were necessarie* ' it seems
to me that it would be necessary ', 27₄ᴃ/689 *I trowe his habitacioun
be there* ' I believe his habitation is there ', 6/860 *Ich rede þi þat
men bo ȝare* ' I advise you that men should be ready '.

4. In comparative statements: 3/41 *þe forme . . . makeþ him . . .
ȝet betere þen he beo* ' the first makes him still better than he is ',
6/876 *Ich wepe bet þane þu singe* ' I cry better than you sing ', 6/931-2
For betere is þat heo wepen here þan elles-hwar beon deovlene fere
' for it is better that they should weep here than elsewhere be devils'
companions '.

REMARK. — Exact comparatives (*right*) *as . . .* (*right*) *so*, '(even) as ' . . .
'(even) so ' always took the indicative.

II. On the other hand whenever it was a matter of facts, of verifi-
cation, of reality, the indicative was used: 27₄ᴃ/937-8 *Looke whiche
a seuretee it is to you alle That I am in youre felaweshipe y-falle* ' See
what a surety it is for you all that I have fallen in with your group '.

Adverbial Clauses of Time

§ 155. The subordinating words and phrases are: *þat time þat*
' when ', *þe while þat* ' as far as ', *ar, er* ' before ', *to time, til þat*
' until ', *when* ' when '.

I. The mood in a sub-clause of time is normally the indicative:
7/3610-1 *þatt time þatt his moderr wass I þewwdom unnderr Laferrd*
' at the time when his mother was in the Lord's service ', 27₂/1234
whan she bygynneth to synge ' when she starts to sing ', 12/663 *Sone
so it was liht of day* ' as soon as it was daylight '.

II. Nevertheless the subjunctive is found:

1. Frequently after *er, ar* ' before ' : 13₃/36 *ar þe coc him crowe*
' before the cock crows ', 27₄ᴃ/700-1 *he shal be slayn . . . er it be nyght*
' he will be killed before it is night '.

2. When the statement is hypothetical or indefinite: 2/21 *þe hwile
þet he bo alive* ' while he may be alive ', 12/621-2 *Loverd, we sholen
þe wel fede Til þet þu conne riden on stede* ' lord, we will feed you
well until the time that you can ride a horse ', 17/6 *Ordanis he still*

for to dwell To time he think to fight ' he orders (them) to remain still until the time he thinks (appropriate) to fight '.

Adverbial Clauses of Cause or Reason

§ 156. Subordinating words or phrases: *for-þy* ' for, for this reason ', *resun why þat, for þat* ' reason why, because, for the reason that '.

These were always followed by the indicative: 14/4129-31 *seynt Gregory Tellyþ þys tale, resun why Þat envye is a cursed synne* ' Saint Gregory tells this tale (concerning) the reason why envy is a cursed sin '.

Adverbial Clauses of Concession

§ 157. Subordinating words: *þeჳ, þogh, though that* ' though, although ', *how . . . so* ' however . . .'.

These were followed by the subjunctive: 6/879 *þeჳ sume men bo þurჳut gode* ' although some men are completely good ', 13₂/81 *þeyh he were so riche mon As Henry* ' although he was as rich a man as Henry ', 14/4159 *þogh every day a man hyt haunte* ' though a man practice it every day ', 25/55 *how lawful so it were* ' however lawful it might be '.

Adverbial Clauses of Condition

§ 158. Subordinating words: *ჳef, yf* ' if ', *swulċ, swa sum, als, als if, al so* ' as if ', *bute, bute ჳef* ' but, unless, except that ', *to þat forward (þat)* ' on the condition that '.

These were normally followed by the subjunctive: 5/14052 *ჳif hit weore i-lumpe* ' if it should happen ', 12/513 *yf he were brouht of live* ' if he was put to death/if he should be put to death ', 25/3 *if it lyke to yow* ' if it please(s) you ', 5/14005 *swulċ he weore swiðe seoc* ' as if he were very sick ', 7/3655 *swa summ itt wære off moderr* ' as if it was/were of (a) mother ', 12/508 *starinde als he were wod* ' staring as if he were crazy ', 2/24 *bute him God bo milde* ' unless God be/is merciful to him ', 27₄ᵦ/741 *but he trespasse in word* ' unless he trespass(es) in word ', 12/486 *to þat forward þu late me live* ' on condition that you let me live '.

Similarly conditional inversion, that is to say, a conditional clause with question word-order and zero subordinant, was always followed by the subjunctive: 12/694 *wite he him live* '(if) he knows him (to be) alive ', 25/40 *were it never so unprevable* ' were it never so unprovable '.

Adverbial Clauses of Purpose

§ 159. Subordinating word: *þat* ' so that, in order that '.

This was frequently followed by the subjunctive: 5/14060 *And slæn heom alle clane þet þer no bilaven nane* ' and slay them all completely (so) that there be none left ', 6/866 *þat him bo sur þat er was swete* '(so) that it be sour to him (what) previously was sweet ', 6/871 *þat mon bi me hine biþenche* ' so that (a) man by means of me may reflect on his misdeeds '.

Predicative Clauses

§ 160. 1. *Completive sub-clauses* often followed an imperative with a zero subordinant, or with *to þan þat* ' so that ' and required the subjunctive: 8/452 *se he holde foreward* ' see (that) he keep(s) his agreement ', 27₄ᵦ/830 *looke thou do the same* ' see (to it that) you do the same ', 15/43 *huyche bysinesse hi doþ to þan þet hare metes by wel agrayþed* ' this care they take so that their food be/is well prepared '.

REMARK. — On the infinitive in completive clauses, cp. above § 129.1.

2. Indirect questions used the same subordinants as direct questions. The mood of the sub-clause was generally the subjunctive: 4/14-5 *witen of al þet is ant wes ant eaver schal i-wurðen, hwet hit beo, hwi ant hwerto ant hwerof hit bigunne* ' to know about all that is and was and ever shall be, what it may be, why and from what it began ', 6/1010 *hi nute elles wat hi do* ' they don't know at all what they are doing ', 6/1006 *hi ne reccheþ hu hi libbe* ' they don't care how they live ', 27₁/346-7 *for to knowe Whether hyt were clere or hors of soun* ' in order to know whether it was clear or raucous in sound '.

Final Remarks on Subordinants

§ 161. Relative or conjunctive subordinants were often re-enforced by *þat* or *as*: *how that, whan that, which that, which as, where as, þer as, whaym þat, if that, though þat, sith þat, after þat, bycause þat, also soone as þat,* etc.

2. Conversely the element *þat* might be missing and the result is a zero conjunctive subordinant as in 6/957 *þu seist* ⟨ ⟩*ich fleo bihinde bure* 'you say (that) I fly behind (a) dwelling', 17/61 *It semid*⟨ ⟩*he was ferd* 'it seemed he was afraid', 29/503 *I wold*⟨ ⟩ *ye dynyd* 'I would you dined', or a conjunctive locution without *þat* as in 21₂/193 *þe while*⟨ ⟩*he caccheþ conynges* 'while he catches coneys'.

C. CORRELATION

§ 162. We still encounter in ME examples of a type of correlative construction such as was to be found in OE (HOE §§ 191 ff.) and which consisted in using an anticipatory subordinant in the main clause which was thus repeated twice in the sentence to clearly show the linking of the two propositions; but this process is much less frequent than in OE. Nevertheless, here are a few cases:

þa . . . þa: 1/12-3 *þa þe suikes undergæton ðat he milde man was . . . þa diden hi alle wunder* 'when the traitors perceived that he was a mild (sort of) man, then did they all sorts of horrible deeds'.

þat . . . þat: 7/3608-13 *And tatt te Laferrd Jesu Crist Was borenn her to manne Þatt time þatt hiss moderr was I þewwdom unnderr laferrd Þatt dide he forr to shæwenn swa Unnseȝȝenliȝ mecnesse* 'And that the Lord Jesus Christ was born as a man here below at the time that his mother was in the service of the Lord, that he did to show an ineffable meekness', 11/4 *þæt witen ȝe wel alle þæt* 'know all of you that . . .'.

so . . . so: 9/3 *And* so *hi were in þo ssipe*, so *aros a great tempeste of winde* 'and when they were in that ship, there arose a great storm of wind'.

hit . . . þat: 18/1257 *I haf* hit *holly in my honde þat al desyrez* 'I have it wholly in my hand, that (which) all desire'.

that . . . how that: 27₁/354-5 *whan I herde* that, How that *they wolde on huntynge goon* 'when I heard that they wanted to go hunting'.

REMARKS. — I. When the sentence was long, it was not unusual that a preceding element was taken up again by means of a pronoun: 21₂/175 *Alle þis route of ratones to þis reson þei assented* 'all this assembly of rats agreed to this reasoning', cp. § 116.3.

II. Sometimes the antecedent of a relative might be a possessive: 21₃/48 *ich synge for hure soules of suche as me helpen* 'I sing for the souls of such as help me' (*hure . . . suche as*).

III. It often happened in long periodic sentences that the connection between the clauses was not well made and that there were very abrupt changes of construction, called anacolutha: 25/38 ff. *So that what man, pryvé or apert in special, that he myght wyte, grocchyng, pleyned or helde ayeins any of his wronges, or bi puttyng forth of whom so it were, were it never so unprevable, were apeched and it were displesyng to him Nichol, anon was emprisoned,* following this literally we have ' so that whatever man, either secretly or openly, that he [Nicholas] might find out about [*wite*], grouching, or complained or held (an opinion) against his [Nicholas'] wrongs, or by the testimony of anybody at all, were it ever so unprovable, were accused if it (the reported opinion) was displeasing to him, Nicholas, instantly was imprisoned '.

D. THE PERIOD

§ 163. Writers in ME were not unaware of the periodic sentence in which subordinate clauses are piled up behind a single main clause. Here are two examples, the first in epic style (5/14052-60), the second in lyric (27₂/1233-9). The sub-clauses are marked off into substantive, adjective and adverb clauses.

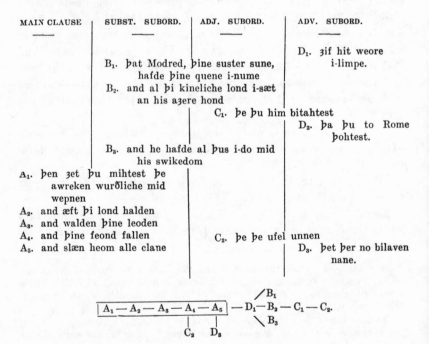

MAIN CLAUSE	SUBST. SUBORD.	ADJ. SUBORD.	ADV. SUBORD.
			D₁. ȝif hit weore i-limpe.
	B₁. þat Modred, þine suster sune, hafde þine quene i-nume		
	B₂. and al þi kineliche lond i-sæt an his aȝere hond		
		C₁. þe þu him bitahtest	
			D₂. þa þu to Rome þohtest.
	B₃. and he hafde al þus i-do mid his swikedom		
A₁. þen ȝet þu mihtest þe awreken wurðliche mid wepnen			
A₂. and æft þi lond halden			
A₃. and walden þine leoden			
A₄. and þine feond fallen		C₂. þe þe ufel unnen	
A₅. and slæn heom alle clane			D₃. þet þer no bilaven nane.

(D₁) If it had happened (B₁) that Modred, your sister's son, had taken your queen (B₂) and put all your kingly realms into his own hand (C₁) that you entrusted to him (D₂) when you intended (to go) to Rome, (B₃) and that he had done all this by his treachery (A₁) then indeed you might avenge yourself worthily by means of arms (A₂) and again hold your realm (A₃) and rule your people (A₄) and fell your enemies (C₂) who offered you (this) evil (A₅) and kill them all completely (D₃) (so) that not one were left (alive).[1]

MAIN CLAUSE	SUBST. SUBORD.	ADJ. SUBORD.	ADV. SUBORD.
			D₁. And as the newe abaysed nyghtyngale . . .
		C₁. that stynteth first	D₂. whan she bygynneth to synge
			D₃. whan that she hereth
	B₁. any herde tale		
	B₂. or in the hegges any wyght stirynge		
			D₁. . . . and [1] after, siker, doth hire vois outrynge
A₁. right so Criseyde . . . . . . opned hire herte			D₄. whan hire drede stente
A₂. and tolde hym hire entente			

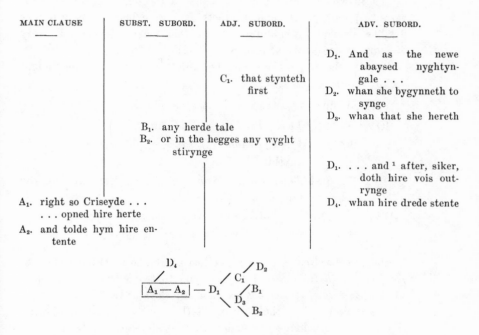

D₁ . . .) And as the just frightened nightingale (C₁) that stops at first (D₂) when she begins to sing —(D₃) when she hears (B₁) any shepherd speak (B₂) or in the hedges any person stirring —(D₁) and [2] afterward, secure, rings out her voice (D₂) when her fright has stopped, (A₁) even so Cressida opened her heart (A₂) and told him her intent.

---

[1] The exclamative clause *swa nulle hit ure Drihten*! 'may God not wish it so' (line 14052) has been left out intentionally.

[2] Here *and* is anacoluthic.

CHAPTER TWELVE

POSITION OF ELEMENTS IN THE SENTENCE

Freedom of these Positions

§ 164. Despite the progressive impoverishment of flexion the order in ME in which the principal elements of the sentence, subject (S), verb (V), object (O) and adjuncts (A) were placed was still very flexible — a trait, it might be added, that makes ME initially very difficult for speakers and readers of ModE.

The six relative positions that the subject, verb, and its object might occupy were as follows:

SVO 20_1/693 *he takez hys leve* ' he takes his leave '.

SOV 27_1/397 *I hym folwed* ' I followed him '.

VSO 29/571 *gaf ye the chyld any thyng?* ' did you give the child anything? '

VOS 27_{4B}/684 *Thus taughte me my dame* ' thus my mother taught me '.

OSV 10/207 *al þou most sugge* ' you must tell everything '.

OVS 27_{4A}/680 *but hood wered he noon* ' but he wore no hood '.

And in subordinates there might just as well be SVO 3/80 (*biseche ich þe) þet tu luvie me* ' I beseech you that you love me ' as SOV 11/11 (*þe treowþe) þæt heo us oȝen* ' the loyalty that they owe us '. In the same sentence the position of the same elements could vary, thus 5/28-30 *Nu biddeð Laȝamon Alcne æðele mon . . . þet þeos boc rede* (OV) *and leornia þeos runan* (VO) ' Now Lawman bids each noble man that reads this book and masters this learning '. But in a general way even if the order of the elements was free, their positions were not always a matter of indifference. There were tendencies, not strict rules, and it must not be forgotten that a great part of surviving ME texts are poetry where rhythm commands everything. It will be noticed that in 14th century prose (*Mandeville*, Wyclif, John of Trevisa) the order of the elements is a great deal more " regular " and already conforms to modern usage.

Noun Group

§ **165.** *Position of the article.* — The article is always placed before the substantive or the attribute adjective. However, the article followed the adjectives *all, both, each, half, many, such, which*: 27₄B/874 *al the nyght* ' all (during) the night ', 18/742 *on uche a halve* ' on each side ', 28/4095 *many an oþer þing* ' many an other thing ', 23/54 *such a lord*, 27₄B/937 *whiche a seuretee* ' which surety '. With *how, so, too* the article was carried over to a position behind the adjective: 27₁/307 *so swete a steven* ' so sweet a voice '.

§ **166.** *Position of attributive adjective.* — Its normal position was before the substantive. This was the usage in 14th century prose: thus texts XXIII, XXIV and XXV do not show any post-positive adjectives. In poetry the situation was different; for reasons of rime, rhythm or alliteration the poets frequently availed themselves of the right to put the attributive adjective after its substantive. The model of French, constructions borrowed from that language or imitations based on it, certainly facilitated this post-position which presents the following varieties:

a) simple post-positive adjective (this was by far the most frequent case) : 18/713 *in contrayez straunge* ' in strange countries ', 27₄B/661 *thise riotoures thre* ' these three roisterers ', 28/3947 *of arte magique* ' of magic art ' ;

b) two or more post-positive adjectives: 18/1207 *wyth lyppez smal laȝande* ' with small laughing lips ', 27₄B/839 *thise floryns newe and brighte* ' these bright and new florins ' ; this type was rather rare.

c) a pre-positive and a post-positive adjective: 27₃/249 *thy gilte tresses clere* ' your clear golden tresses ', 21₁/16 *with deop dich and derk* ' with a deep and dark ditch ', 23/10 *a strong wall and a fair* ' a strong and beautiful wall ' ; this type was slightly more current.

REMARK. — The order " adjective + article (demonstrative, possessive) + substantive " that is still encountered in Lawman was undoubtedly a survival from OE (cp. HOE § 196.2): 5/3 *at æðelen are chirechen*, lit. ' at noble a church ', 5/14026 *mid deore mine sweorde* ' with dear my sword ', 5/14079 *mid sele þan kinge* ' with good the king '. Cp. the last survival of this in Shakespearian " dear my lord."

§ **167.** *Position of the noun adjunct.* — When the noun adjunct was a genitive it was generally pre-positive: 14/4128 *þe beres deþ* 'the bear's death', $27_{4A}/700$ *pigges bones* 'pig's bones', $21_3/73$ *lordene sones* 'lords' sons', $27_2/1200$ *an aspes leef* 'an aspen's leaf'.

Prepositional noun adjuncts (usually with *of*) were generally postpositive: *a gobet of the seyl* 'a hunk of the sail', $27_1/360$-1 *a gret route of huntes* 'a large group of hunters', $10/140$ *þe blisse of paradiis* 'the bliss of paradise'.

An inverse order was not, however, uncommon either for the genitive: $13_2/1$ *a mayde Cristes* 'a virgin of Christ', $14/80$ *handlyng synne* 'handbook of sins', or for the prepositional adjunct: $27_1/295$ *with smale foules a gret hep* 'a great number of little birds', $27_1/422$ *of fourty or fifty fadme lengthe* 'a length of forty or fifty fathoms', $27_1/440$ *of every thing the noumbre* 'the number of everything', $26/2$ *of so meny people longages and tongues* 'languages and tongues of so many people'.

REMARK. — Notice the transformation under the pressure of word order, of locutions containing the words *kin* (*ken, cunne*) and *maner* 'kind, sort, manner'.

First there were locutions with pre-positive genitives: $19/1028$ *alle kynnez perre* 'gems of all kind', $13_3/21$ *for nones cunnes eizte* 'for a property of any sort', $21_3/20$ *eny oþer kyns craft* 'an occupation of any other kind'. But quite frequently occurred a pre-positive genitive with zero ending as in $6/888$ *tweire kunne salve* 'a salve of two kinds', $22_2/413$ *na kyn thyng* 'a thing of no kind', and it was interpreted as if the second element was the adjunct of the first: 'all kind(s) of gems', 'any sort of property', 'any other kind of occupation', etc.; with *maner* we come across locutions of the type $23/13$ *all maner vertuous herbes* 'all manner of beneficent herbs', $26/30$ *þat maner techyng* 'that manner of teaching', $27_1/471$ *a maner song* 'a kind of song'. Therefore, as early as the second half of the 14th century, there was a tendency, so to speak, to "re-introduce" the mark of the prepositional post-positive adjunct, namely *of*, and to write $23/12$ *all maner of frutes*, $21_1/18$ *alle maner of men*, thus bringing this locution into its modern syntactical pattern. [It should be noted, interestingly enough, that in Modern American spoken English the locution *all kinds books* is reappearing. But this is probably due to the *of* dropping phonetically to [ə] and thence to an almost indistinguishable breath sound.]

§ 168. *Position of the possessive.* — It was in the course of ME, as we have seen (§ 66) that the distinction between possessive adjective and possessive pronoun was established, a distinction which, for a long time, was purely semantic for certain persons. In principle they could be distinguished by stress, the pronoun always bore the stress, the adjective — at least when it was pre-positive — might be un-stressed, cp. for example

x x́ x x x́ x x́ x x́
þi stevene is wop and min skentinge 6/986

'your voice is (a) screech and mine delight'. But the position of the possessive was not fixed, and when post-positive it was always accented whether adjective or pronoun: 7/1 *Nu broþerr Wallterr, broþerr "min* 'Now brother Walter, brother mine' [a petrified form in this position still surviving in ModE], 8/539 *Nu þu hast wille "þine* 'now you have your desire'. The post-positive possessive pronoun could be re-enforced by *owen*: 18/1384 *ʒe crave hit as your awen* 'you demand it as your own'; it was often preceded by *of*: 24/25 *þis sone of myn* 'this son of mine', 24/49 *he hadde no house of his own*. The new forms *hers, ours, youres, thaires* were always post-positive: 18/1386-7 *þat I haf worthyly wonnen . . . hit worþez to ʒourez* 'what I have fittingly won, it becomes yours', and finally the locution is reached 27₄ʙ/672 *an olde felawe of youres* 'an old friend of yours'. (see § 66 Rem. VII.)

Position of Prepositions

§ 169. The preposition was normally placed before the word which it governed. But it frequently was found behind such words (and it is then what is called, more exactly, a *postposition*):

1. in a general way, when it governed a personal pronoun. This was often a problem of rhythm, and is scarcely found except in poetry: 5/14035 *þa leo me orn foren to* 'this lion ran towards me', 7/3340 *þatt enngell comm annd stod hemm bi* 'that angel came and stood by them', 8/532 *and Aþulf kniʒt þe biforn* 'and the knight Athulf before you', 12/526 *he seyde him to* 'he said to him', 14/4083 *hem betwene* 'between them';

2. similarly in poetry when the preposition governs a substantive: 18/1386 *þis wonez wythinne* 'within this dwelling', 18/1388 *his armez wythinne* 'in his arms', 28/4079 *The fyri auters al aboute* 'all around the fiery altars'.

3. This displacement was the rule in relative sub-clauses introduced by *þat* (as in OE with the relative particle *þe*, cp. HOE § 197.3): 3/22 *þe eappel þet ich loki on* 'the apple that I look at', 8/535 *do nu þat þu er of spake* 'do now what you previously spoke of', 15/1-2 *þet is*

a vice þet þe dyvel is moche myde y-payed 'that is a vice that the devil is very satisfied with', 17/75 *þe felde* . . . *þat king Edward was in* 'the field that king Edward was in', 20/815 *the dragon þat þow dremyde of* 'the dragon that you dreamed of'.

Subject-Predicate Group

§ 170. The order "subject-predicate" was the most usual. It is found in independent or main clauses: 25/58 *we ben openlich dis-claundred* 'we are openly slandered', 20/793 *his brayell was blodye* 'his belly was bloody', 28/3962 *the world was stille* 'the world was still', 28/4105 *sche semeþ faie* 'she seems (to be) a fairy'. Similarly in sub-clauses: 11/9 *we willen . . . þæt þæt ure rædesmen . . . habbeþ i-don . . . beo stedefæst* 'we desire that what our councilors have done be permanent', 13₃/18 *þe Jewes . . . awenden he were wode* 'the Jews thought he was crazy', 27₄ᵦ/704 *as though he were his brother* 'as though he was/were his brother'. Again, in sub-clauses it is not infrequent to find the verb *to be* placed after the predicative adjective: 12/504 *he wolde þat he ded wore* 'he wished that he were dead', 5/34 *þat hire þe selre beo* 'so that (things) might be better for her'.

§ 171. Inverse order (which was not unknown in sub-clauses) is principally found in independent or main clauses when the predicate is emphasized (cp. § 182: 3/130 *ladlich þing is hit, wat Crist, hwen . . .* 'an ugly thing it is, Christ knows, when', 4/39 *eadi beoð þeo . . . þe . . .* 'blessed are those who', 27₁/340 *blew, bryght, clere was the ayr* 'blue, bright, clear was the air', 29/607 *a pratty child is he* 'a pretty child is he'.

Subject-Verb Group[1]

§ 172. The order "subject-verb-(object)" is, so to speak, the commonplace word-order: 24/1 *a man hadde two sones* 'a man had two sons'. This order was maintained when the subject was an inter-rogative pronoun: 10/122 *wo haveþ þe in þe putte i-brout?* 'who has put you in the well?', 27₁/366 *who shal hunte here?* 'who is to hunt here?'.

§ 173. The inverse order "verb-subject" was quite frequent in ME. Here are the principal situations in which it is found:

---

[1] In what follows only the finite verb is taken into consideration.

1. *Direct questions*: 29/571 *Gaf ye the chyld any thyng?* ' Did you give the child anything? ', 29/656 *hard ye not?* ' didn't you hear? ', similarly when the sentence began with an interrogative object: 10/181-2 *to wom shuld ich . . . ben i-knowe of mine misdede?* ' to whom should I confess my misdeeds? '.

2. *Partial questions* introduced by an interrogative adverb: 3/21 *hwerof chalengest tu me?* ' Of what do you accuse me? ', 18/1379 *how payez yow þis play?* ' how does this play please you? ', 20/703 *why ne myghte I dye in ʒour armes?* ' why might I not die in your arms? '.

3. Often when an object was placed at the head of the sentence either for emphasis: 27₄ₐ/680 *but hood, for jolitee, wered he noon* ' but hood, to put on gay front, he wore none ', or in pompous official style: 25/1-2 *To the moost noble and worthiest Lordes . . . compleinen . . . the folk of the Mercerye of London* ' The Mercers of London complain to the most noble and worthiest lords '.

REMARK. — There was nothing obligatory about this stylistic feature: 1/29 *sume hi diden in cruċethus* ' some they put in torture boxes ', 10/207 *al þou most sugge* ' you must tell all ', 14/88 *and as y wote ʒow shew y wyle* ' and what I know I will show you '.

4. When an adverbial adjunct was put at the head of the sentence: 27₁/322-3 *and with glas Were al the wyndowes wel y-glased* ' and with glass were all the windows splendidly glazed ', 27₁/438-9 *for by tho figures mowe al ken . . . rekene* ' for by means of those figures all can count '.

5. Frequently after an adverb of time (*þo, then, now*), of place (*ther*) or of connection (*thus, then,* etc.): 9/9 *þo aros up ure Lord* ' then rose up Our Lord ', 3/79 *nu þenne biseche ich þe* ' now, then, I beseech you ', 23/53 *and þan wolde he schewe hem his entent* ' and then he would show them his intention ', 29/249 *now wyll ye se what I profer* ' now you will see what I offer ', 23/4 *þere was dwellynge somtyme a riche man* ' Once there lived a rich man ', (but 24/5 *and þer he wastide his goodis* ' and there he wasted his property '), 23/50-1 *and after þat ʒit scholde he putten hem in a fayrere paradys* ' and yet after that he would put them in a more beautiful paradise ', 3/14 *þus eode sunne bivoren* ' thus went sin in front ', 17/13 *þus in Braband has he bene* ' thus he has been in Braband ', 25/36 *and thus yet hiderward hath the Mairaltee ben holden* ' and thus up to now has the

mayoralty been held . . .', (but 23/63-4 *and þus oftentyme he was revenged of his enemyes* 'and thus often he was revenged on his enemies' with a pronoun subject), 4/33-4 *for-þi seide ure laverde to þeo þe . . .* 'for that reason Our Lord said to those who . . .'.

6. In *comparative* clauses: 3/89 *as weren sumhwile cnihtes i-wunet to donne* 'as sometimes knights were wont to do', 28/4172-4 *and lich unto þe freisshe Maii . . . Riht so recovereþ he his floures* 'and like the fresh month of May, even so he recovers his flowers'.

7. After a conjunctive sub-clause placed at the head: 9/3 *and so hi were in þo ssipe, so aros a great tempeste* 'and when they were on board ship, then arose a great storm', 7/3608-13 *Annd tatt te Laferrd Jesu Crist Wass borenn her to manne . . . Þat dide he forr to shæwenn swa Unnseӡӡendliӡ mecnesse* 'And that the Lord Jesus Christ was born as a man here below, that he did to show an ineffable meekness'.

8. In optative or imperative sentences like 27₂/1224 *take every womman heede* 'let every women take heed . . .'.

§ 174. The "verb-subject" order is also encountered in declarative sentences of the type 27₁/307 *was never herd so swete a steven* '(there) was never heard so sweet a voice', 22/273-4 *is nane can tell The halle condicioun of a threll* '(there) is none (who) can tell the whole condition of a slave'.

But quite early the verb tended to be preceded by the characteristically ModE pseudo-subject *there*: 14/4001-2 *þer were twey men of holy wyl Þat levyd togedyr* 'there were two men of holy desires that lived together', 24/7 *þer fel a gret hungre in þat lond* 'a great famine befell that country', 27₁/388-9 *ther cam by mee A whelp* 'a pup came up to me', 28/4149 *anon þer sprong up flour and gras* 'instantly there sprang up flower(s) and grass'.

REMARK. — Alongside *ther*, the neuter pronoun (*h*)*it* was also used with the same force up to the 13th century: 12/591 *of hise mouth it stod a stem* 'from his mouth there came a ray'.

§ 175. The order "verb-subject" was also found in a *conditional inversion*: (cf. § 158) 6/1026-7 *Ne sunge ich hom never so longe, Mi songe were i-spild ech del* 'even if I sang to them ever so long, my song would be entirely lost (on them)', 12/681 *wiltu ben erl, go hom swiþe* 'if you will be an earl, go home quickly', 25/40 *were it never so unprevable* 'no matter how unprovable it was', 27₂/1210-1 *Ne hedde*

I er now . . . Ben ʒold . . . I were now nought heere ' if I had not given (myself to you) before now I would not be here now '.

Verb-Object Group

§ 176. The usual order puts the object after the verb: 26/7-8 *þe Flemmynges . . . habbeþ y-left here strange speche* ' the Flemings have given up their strange speech ', the indirect object generally preceding the direct object: 26/41-2 *gentilmen habbeþ now moche y-left for to teche here children Frensch* ' gentlemen have now, on the whole, left off teaching their children French ', 24/3 *þe fadir departide him his goodis* ' the father dealt him his (share of the) property '.

§ 177. This order was equally prevalent in sub-clauses: 10/191-2 *ich worþe ded Bote þou do me soume reed* ' I will die unless you do me some good ', 3/79 *for þe luve þet ich cuðe þe* ' for the love that I show you ', 4ₐ/4 *þet hy knawe þe zoþe God* ' that they may know the true God '.

§ 178. However, the object might well appear before the verb:

1. When it was a pronoun or a demonstrative: 27₁/397 *I hym folwed* ' I followed him ', 27₂/1201 *whan she hym felte hire in his armes folde* ' when she felt him fold her in his arms ', 15/68 *he ne heþ vot þet him moʒe sosteyni* ' he doesn't have (a) foot that can hold him up ', 3/141 *bute neode hit makie* ' unless need forces it '.

2. Quite as well when the object was a substantive: 3/76 *arudde þe of ham þe þi deað secheð* ' get rid of them who seek your death ', 20/699 *the wye thatt this were movede* ' the man that started this war '.

§ 179. With impersonal verbs the order " (indirect) object-verb " was normal: 10/94 *him þoute* ' it seemed to him ', 13₄/14 *me reweþ* ' I regret ', 14/4071 *so hym byrde* ' thus it happened to him ', 19/1044 *hem nedde* ' it was needful to them ', 21₂/174 *ʒif him wrattheth* ' if he gets angry ', 27₁/293 *me mette* ' I dreamed ', 20/760 *hym dremed* ' he dreamed ' (cp. other examples in § 117 *d*.).

§ 180. In the compound and periphrastic tenses the object or the adjunct was generally found between the inflected auxiliary verb and the participle or infinitive:

1. Pronominal object: 14/4029 *pryed God he wulde hym ʒeve* ' prayed God that He would give him ', 27₁/392 *ryght as hyt hadde*

me y-knowe 'just as if it (a pup) had known me', 27₄ᴮ/920-2 *relikes
... Whiche were me yeven by the popes hond* ' relics which were given
to me by the pope's hand '.

2. Nominal object: 5/14044 *ich habbe al niht of mine swevene
swiðe i-þoht* ' I have very much thought all (during) the night (about)
my dream ', 27₁/383-4 *the houndes . . . were on a defaute y-falle* ' the
dogs had fallen on a false scent ', 27₄ᴮ/679 *he hath a thousand slayn*
' he has killed a thousand '.

§ 181. In poetry these compound and periphrastic tenses frequently
show the order " participle (or infinitive)-auxiliary verb," particularly
in sub-clauses: 12/520 *I wile þat he drenched be* ' I want him to be
drowned ', 14/4046 *þanked hym . . . Þat he hym sent hadde swyche
solace* ' thanked him that he had sent such solace ', 27₁/378 *the hert
y-founde ys* (riming with *houndes*) ' the stag is found ', 27₁/405-7
hit was . . . As thogh the erthe envye wolde To be gayer than the heven
' it was as though the earth (were) envious (and) wanted to be fairer
than the heavens ', 28/4150 *Where as þe drope falle was* ' where the
drop had fallen ', 28/4034 *Of which an alter mad ther was* ' of which
an altar was made there '.

Emphatic Position

§ 182. As has been mentioned above with reference to predicates
(§ 171), an element was frequently displaced or put at the head of
the sentence for emphasis. This explains the " inversions " of the
following types: 11/4 *þæt witen ȝe wel alle* ' Let it be well known to
you all ', 23/32 *and þat place he clept paradys* ' and that place he
named paradise ', 28/4114 *such merveille herde nevere man* ' such
(a) marvel a person never heard of ', 27₄ᴮ/865 *ye, sterve he shal* ' yes,
die he must '.

§ 183. This was still the case for adverbs of motion when they were
placed before the verb: 5/14022 *adun veol þa halle* ' down fell the
hall ', 12/565-6 *Hwan dame Leve herde þat, Up she stirte* ' when lady
Leve heard that, up she jumped ', 28/3988 *Doun fro þe sky þer cam
a char The whiche dragouns aboute drowe And þo sche gan hir hed
doun bowe And up sche styh* ' down from the sky there came a chariot,
which dragons drew around, and then she began to bow her head,
and up she climbed '.

TEXTS

I

RULES FOLLOWED IN ESTABLISHMENT OF TEXTS

Each extract is based on a single manuscript whose text was verified and then deferred to. In the case of an obvious error or evident corruption the corrections that have been made are noted by *italics* when there is substitution of letters or words, by caret brackets ⟨⟩ when there is addition of words. The readings of the original manuscript chosen as a base are reproduced in footnotes at the bottom of the page. It is therefore always easy to restore the actual manuscript text. All critical apparatus has been purposely omitted.

On the other hand, in order to facilitate the reading of these texts, the following rules were adopted:

1. Punctuation, use of capitals and minuscule and the division of words have been entirely modernized.

2. Normal medieval MS contractions and abbreviations have been expanded without any printed indications of this.

3. Modern usage has been followed for *i* and *j*, *u* and *v*; *F* instead of *ff*, *w* instead of *þ* (*wynn*).

4. On the other hand, the use of *þ* and *ð* has been retained instead of the modern *th*, and also "yoch" (ʒ) except where the latter represented a sibilant. This is especially true for *Sir Gawain*, *The Pearl* and the *Morte d'Arthur* where sibilant ʒ is transcribed as *z*. The *ß* of the *Bruce* has also been retained.

5. Final -*e* developed from OF -*é*(*e*) or -*ie* and from OE -*iġ* is printed *é* to distinguish it from weakened or silent final *e*.

6. Diacritical marks have only been used for texts from the 12th century. Where *sc* represents [š] and where *c* represents [č] they have been printed, respectively, *sċ* and *ċ* as is done in the first part of this *Handbook* for Old English texts.

7. Finally the Latin quotations have been recast in a normalized spelling.

For the rest, the grammatical introduction, which precedes the explanatory notes of each selection, attempts to furnish all information about the spelling of the manuscripts.

II

APPROXIMATE ORDER OF DIFFICULTY OF THE TEXTS

Easy texts: VII, XIV, XXIII, XXIV, XXVI, XXVII, XXVIII.

Moderately difficult texts: III, IV, V, VIII, IX, X, XI, XII, XIII, XV, XVI, XVII, XX, XXI, XXII, XXV.

Difficult texts: I, II, VI, XVIII, XIX, XXIX.

PART ONE

THE TWELFTH CENTURY

I

THE PETERBOROUGH CHRONICLE

A few of the *Chronicles* (more properly, *Annals*) in the vernacular language started under King Alfred (see HOE nos. III and XIII) were continued after the Conquest, thus demonstrating the continued vitality of English. But only *The Peterborough Chronicle* goes beyond the 11th century and so beyond the Old English period. The last part of this *Chronicle*, the part that covers the years 1132 to 1154, was put into writing a little after this latter date. At this period the older literary and orthographic traditions were still known, but they no longer had the same force. The scribe tried to reproduce as faithfully as possible the language spoken in his time and in his region. Thus he writes an early Middle English of the central north-east, but the syntax is confused, and the notation of the forms and the sounds, which seems to follow no method, is rather uncertain.

Editions:

B. THORPE. *The Anglo-Saxon Chronicle*. London, 1861 (Rolls Series).

C. PLUMMER. *Two of the Saxon Chronicles Parallel*. Oxford, 1892-1899.

Translation:

The Peterborough Chronicle, translated with an Introduction by Harry A. ROSITZKE, New York, 1951.

Consult also:

R. M. WILSON. *Early Middle English Literature*, pp. 96-101.

J. E. WELLS. *Manual*, pp. 190 ff. (bibliography, p. 792).

Anarchy in the Time of King Stephen

1137. Ðis gære for þe King Stephne ofer sæ to Normandi and ther wes underfangen, forþi ðat hi wenden ðat he sculde ben alsuic alse the eom wes, and for he hadde get his tresor; ac he todeld it and scatered sotlice. Micel hadde Henri King

133

5 gadered gold and sylver, and na god ne dide me for his saule
tharof.

Þa þe King Stephne to Englalande com, þa macod he his
gadering æt Oxeneford and þar he nam þe biscop Roger of
Sereberi, and Alexander Biscop of Lincol and te Canceler
10 Roger, hise neves, and dide ælle in prisun til hi iafen up
here castles.   Þa the suikes undergæton ðat he milde man
was and softe and god, and na justise ne dide, þa diden hi
alle wunder.   Hi hadden him manred maked and athes
suoren, ac hi nan treuthe ne heolden; alle hi wæron
15 forsworen and here treothes forloren, for ævric rice man his
castles makede and agænes him heolden, and fylden þe land
ful of castles.   Hi suencten suyðe þe wrecce men of þe land
mid castelweorces.   Þa þe castles waren maked, þa fylden hi
mid deovles and yvele men.   Þa namen hi þa men þe hi
20 wenden ðat ani god hefden, bathe be nihtes and be dæies,
carlmen and wimmen, and diden heom in prisun efter gold
and sylver, and pined heom untellendlice pining.   For ne
wæren nævre nan martyrs swa pined alse hi wæron; me
henged up bi the fet and smoked heom mid ful smoke; me
25 henged bi the þumbes other bi the hefed, and hengen bryniges
on her fet; me dide cnotted strenges abuton here hæved and
wrythen to ðat it gæde to þe hærnes.   Hi diden heom in
quarterne þar nadres and snakes and pades wæron inne, and
drapen heom swa.   Sume hi diden in crucet-hus, ðat is in
30 an cæste þat was scort and nareu and undep, and dide scærpe
stanes þerinne and þrengde þe man þærinne ðat him bræcon
alle þe limes.   In mani of þe castles wæron lof and grin, ðat
wæron rachenteges ðat twa oþer thre men hadden onoh to
bæron onne; þat was swa maced, ðat is, fæstned to an beom,
35 and diden an scærp iren abuton þe mannes throte and his
hals, ðat he ne myhte nowiderwardes, ne sitten ne lien ne
slepen, oc bæron al ðat iren.   Mani þusen hi drapen mid
hungær.

14 hi wæron] he *MS* — 35 þe] þa *MS*.

I ne can ne I ne mai tellen alle þe wunder, ne alle þe pines
ðat hi diden wrecče men on þis land; and ðat lastede þa xix 40
wintre wile Stephne was king, and ævre it was werse and
werse. Hi læiden ġældes on the tunes ævre umwile and
clepeden it tenserie. Þa þe wrecče men ne hadden nan more
to ġyven, þa ræveden hi and brendon alle the tunes ðat wel
þu myhtes faren all a dæis fare, sčuldest thu nevre finden 45
man in tune sittende ne land tiled. Þa was corn dære and
fle⟨s⟩č and čæse and butere, for nan ne was o þe land. Wrecče
men sturven of hungær; sume ieden on ælmes þe waren sum
wile riče men; sume flugen ut of lande. Wes nævre ġæt
mare wrecčehed on land, ne nævre hethen men werse ne 50
diden þan hi diden; |for oversithon ne forbaren hi nouther
čirče ne čyrče-iærd, oc namen al þe god ðat þarinne was and
brenden sythen þe čyrče and al tegædere. Ne hi ne forbaren
bisčopes land ne abbotes ne preostes, ac ræveden munekes
and clerekes and ævrič man other þe ower myhte. Ġif twa 55
men oþer .iii. coman ridend to an tun, al þe tunsčipe flugæn
for heom; wenden ðat hi wæron ræveres. Þe bisčopes and
leredmen heom cursede ævre, oc was heom naht þarof for
hi weron al forcursæd and forsuoren and forloren. Warsæ
me tilede, þe erthe ne bar nan corn, for þe land was al fordon 60
mid suilče dædes and hi sæden openliče ðat Crist slep and
his halechen. Suilč and mare þanne we cunnen sæin we
þoleden .xix. wintre for ure sinnes.

42 gældes] gæildes *MS.* — 55 ower] ouer *MS.* — 63 þoleden] þolenden
MS.

II

THE "POEMA MORALE"

The selection below belongs to a literary type much in vogue in the Middle
Ages. Meditating on the flight of time and the vanity of human wishes, the
author — one scarcely dares call him "the poet" — gives us a short course
in Christian morals: avoid sin, practice virtue, get ready for Judgment Day,
keep the tortures of hell in mind, in order to attain celestial bliss. The author

is a wise old man who wishes others to profit from his experience. One gets from this piece, where the personal element is noticeable, an impression of sincerity and moderation which is in striking contrast to other ME texts in the same genre. The popularity of this piece, written about 1150 in septenary rimed couplets, is witnessed by the seven MSS by which it has been preserved. What follows is a reproduction of the oldest, which dates from the end of the 12th century, and which contains a total of 270 lines (other MSS run to as high as 400 lines).

Editions:

MSS L and E are reproduced in *EETS*, 29, 159, (MORRIS, *Old English Homilies*) and by J. HALL. *Early Middle English*, pp. 30-46.

H. MARCUS. *Das frühmittelenglische " Poema Morale " kritisch herausgegeben*, Leipzig, 1934 (*Palaestra* 194) [critical edition based on Digby MS A. 4].

Consult also:

R. M. WILSON. *Early Middle English Literature*, pp. 178-9.
J. E. WELLS. *Manual*, p. 385 (bibliography, p. 823).

Ich em nu alder þene ich wes, a wintre ent a lare,
Ich welde mare þene ich dede, mi wit ahte bon mare.
Wel longe ich habbe child i-bon a worde ent a dede,
Þah ich bo a wintre ald, to ȝung ich em on rede.
5 Unnet lif ich habbe i-led ent ȝet, me þingþ, I lede;
Þenne ich me biþenche wel, ful sare ich me adrede.
Mest al þet ich habbe i-don bifealt to childhade;
Wel late ich ⟨h⟩abbe me biþocht, bute God me nu rede!
Fole idel word ich habbe i-queðen, soððen ich speke kuðe,
10 Fole ȝunge dede i-don, þe me ofþinchet nuðe.
Mest al þet me likede er, nu hit me mislikeð;
Þa muchel fulieð his wil, hinesolf he biswikeð.
Ich mihte habbe bet i-don, hefde ich þe⟨n⟩ i-selðe;
Nu ich walde, ah ich ne mei, for elde ent for unhelðe.
15 Elde me is bistolen on, er ich hit wiste;
Ne michte ich seon bifore me for smike ne for miste.
Erȝe we beoð to done god, ent to ufele al to þriste;
Mare eie stondeð men of monne þanne hom do of Criste.
Þe wel ne doð, þe hwile þe ho muȝen, wel oft hit schal rowen,
20 Þenne *ho* mawen sculen ent repen þet ho er sowen.

8 habbe *E*] abbe *L*. — 20 ho] ȝe *L*.

Do he to Gode þet he muȝe, þe hwile þet he bo alive.
Ne lipnie namon to muchel to childe ne to wive;
Þe himsolve forȝet for wive ne for childe,
He sċal cumen in uvel stude, bute him God bo milde.
Sendeð sum god biforen eow, þe hw⟨i⟩le þet ȝe muȝen, to hovene, 25
For betere is an elmesse biforen þenne boð efter sovene.
Al to lome ich habbe i-gult a werke ent o worde,
Al to muchel ich habbe i-spent, to litel i-hud in horde.
Ne beo þe lovre þene þesolf ne þin mei ne þin maȝe:
Sot is þet is oðers monnes frond betre þen his aȝen.   30
Ne lipnie wif to hire were, ne were to his wive;
Bo for himsolve ech mon, þe hwile þet he bo alive.
Wis is þe to himsolve þench, þe hwile þe ⟨he⟩ mot libben,
For sone wule hine forȝeten þe fremede ent þe sibbe.
Þe wel ne deð, þe hwile he mai, ne sċal, wenne he walde;   35
Monies monnes sare i-swinc habbeð oft unholde.
Ne sċal namon don a first ne slawen wel to done,
For moni mon bihateð wel, þe hit forȝeteð sone.
Þe mon þe wule siker bon to habben Godes blisse,   [i-wisse.
Do wel himsolf, hwile þet he mai, þenne haveð he his mid   40
    Þes riche men weneð bon siker þurh walle ent þurh diche:
Þe deð his echte on sikere stude, he hit sent to heveneriche.
For þer ne þerf he bon ofdred of fure ne of þove,
Þer ne *mei hit* him binimen þe laðe ne þe love,
Þer ne þerf he habben kare of ȝeve ne of ȝelde: 45
Þider he sent ent solf bereð to lutel ent to selde.
Þider we sċulen draȝen ent don, wel ofte ent i-lome;
For þer ne sċal me us naut binimen mid wrangwise dome.
Þider ȝe sċulen ȝorne draȝen, walde ȝe God i-leve,
For ne mei þer hit ou binimen king ne reve.   50
Al þet beste þet we hefden, þider we hit solde senden,
For þer we hit michte finden eft ent habben buten ende.
Þo þe ⟨h⟩er doð eni god for habben Godes are,

25 hwile *E* [hwle *L.* — 30 sot *E* [soht *L.* — 44 mei hit *T*] þerf he *L.*
— 50 þer] þet *L.*

Al he hit séal finden eft þer ent hundredfald mare.
55 Þe þet echte wile halden wel, hwile þe he muȝe es welden,
Ȝive hies for Godes luve, þenne deþ hes wel i-halden.

III

ANCRENE WISSE

James Morton was the first to publish this material and he entitled it *Ancren Riwle* (nowadays we say, more correctly, *Ancrene Riwle*), that is to say "Rule for Nuns." The better manuscript, from which these extracts are taken, calls it *Ancrene Wisse* "Guide for Nuns." It is one of the most important works in the history of English prose. Its style suggests many analogies with the "St. Catherine Group" (see farther on, no. IV) and constitutes the link between Ælfric's and Wulfstan's Old English literary prose (see HOE nos. IX-XII) and the great religious prose of the 16th century. Stylistic traditions from Old English, maintained apparently without interruption by the Conquest or its aftermath are here carried to a point of perfection: the author of this *Guide for Nuns* is recognized, today, as an incontestable artist who writes from a profound knowledge of human life, who knows how to draw portraits worthy of the best essayists and who treats with good sense and moderation, sometimes even with a grain of humor, problems of the ascetic and mystical life.

He tells us in his introduction that he was given the responsibility to set up a way of life (but *not* a monastic rule) for three well-born sisters who had decided to renounce the world and to lead the life of devoted recluses in the vicinity of some church. In the eight parts of his work, the author furnishes them abundant instructions on the inner life as well as on practical everyday living, following the teachings of the Church.

The *Ancrene Wisse* poses a great many problems almost none of which has been definitely resolved. All research designed to ferret out some actual person as the author has been vain, in spite of a great many ingenious hypotheses. Having apparently once enjoyed a tremendous popularity, the *Guide for Nuns* is found in Latin and in French as well as in English, and it has long been a question as to which of these three languages was that of the original. One is almost led to believe, today, that it waꜱ written in English, in the last third of the 12th century, even though the MSS that we have do not date earlier than 1230-1250.

Editions:

The Ancren Riwle, A Treatise on the Rules and Duties of Monastic Life, edited and translated by James MORTON, London, 1853 (*Camden Society* no. LVII).
The Latin of the Ancrene Riwle, ed. by C. D'EVELYN, Oxford, 1944 (*EETS*, no. 216).
The French Text of the Ancrene Riwle, ed. by J. A. HERBERT, Oxford, 1944 (*EETS*. no. 219).
Ancrene Wisse, ed. by J. R. R. TOLKIEN, Oxford, 1962 (*EETS*, No. 249).

Consult also:

R. W. CHAMBERS. *On the Continuity of English Prose from Alfred to More and his School,* Oxford, 1932.

R. M. WILSON. *Early Middle English Literature,* pp. 128-48.

J. E. WELLS. *Manual,* pp. 361-5 (bibliography, p. 820).

1. The Temptation of Eve

Nim nu ȝeme hwet uvel beo i-cumen of totunge; nawt an uvel ne twa, ah al þe wa þet nu is ant eaver ȝete wes ant eaver schal i-wurðen, al com of sihðe. Þet hit beo soð, lo her preove: Lucifer þurh þet he seh ant biheold on himseolf his ahne feiernesse leop into prude, ant bicom of engel 5 eatelich deovel. Of Eve ure alde moder is i-writen on alre earst in hire sunne inȝong of hire ehsihðe, *vidit igitur mulier quod bonum esset lignum ad vescendum, et pulchrum oculis, aspectuque delectabile, et tulit de fructu eius et comedit deditque viro suo:* þet is, Eve biheold o þe forboden eappel 10 ant seh hine feier ant feng to delitin i þe bihaldunge ant toc hire lust þertoward, ant nom ant et þrof ant ȝef hire laverd. Low hu hali writ spekeð, ant hu inwardliche hit teleð hu sunne bigon: þus eode sunne bivoren ant makede

---

Pernez ore garde quel mal est avenu de aboutier; ne pas un mal ne dous, mes to⟨ut⟩[...] tivetee qe ore est, et touz jours fust et touz jours serra, tout veint de vewe. Qe ceo soit voirs, veez-ci la pruve: Lucifer pur ceo q'il et regarda en soi meismes sa bealtee [...] dangre [...]Et d'Eve mere est escrit, tout al com⟨en⟩cement en l'entree de son pecchee de sa vewe, *Vidit enim mulier lignum* etc... Ceo est: ' Eve regarda la pome defendue et la vit bele et comenca sey deliter et la regardeure et talent li prist vers la pome et la prist et le manga et dona a son seignour.' Esgardez coment seinte escripture parle et come parfitement ele counte

---

Attende igitur quantum malum ex incauto aspectu processit, nedum unum malum aut duo sed omne malum quod fuit, est aut erit; cuius probatio hec est. Lucifer in se videns suam formositatem, prosiliit in superbiam et factus est ex angelo diabolus terribilis. De Eva matre omnium scriptum est quomodo peccatum in eam ingressum habuit per aspectum. Genesis iij: *Vidit igitur mulier quod bonum esset lignum ad vescendum et pulchrum oculis aspectuque delectabile et tulit de fructu eius et comedit deditque viro suo.* Ecce quomodo ex aspectu sequebatur affectus et ex affectu effectus damnabilis toti posteritati. Hoc

15 wei to uvel lust: ant com þe dede þrefter þet al moncun
i-feleð. Þes eappel, leove suster, bitacneð alle þe wa þing þet
lust falleð to ant delit of sunne. Hwen þu bihaldest te mon
þu art in Eve point: þu lokest o þe eappel. Hwa-se hefde i-seid
to Eve þa ha weorp earst hire ehe þron: 'A! Eve, went te
20 awei; þu warpest ehe o þi deað', hwet hefde ha i-ondsweret?
'Me, leove sire, þu havest woh. Hwerof chalengest tu me?
Þe eappel þet ich loki on is forbode me to eotene ant nawt to
bihalden.' Þus walde Eve i-noh reaðe habben i-ondsweret.
O mine leove sustren, as Eve haveð monie dehtren þe folhið
25 hare moder, þe ondswerieð o þisse wise: 'Me, wenest tu,'
seið sum, 'þet ich wulle leapen on him, þah ich loki on
him?' Godd wat, leove suster, mare wunder i-lomp. Eve, þi
moder, leop efter hire ehnen; from þe ehe to þe eappel, from
þe eappel i parais dun to þer eorðe, from þe eorðe to helle,
30 þer ha lei i prisun fowr þusent ȝer ant mare, heo ant hire

---

coment pecchee comenca. Issi ala vewe devant et fist voie a desir et a
malvois delit, et vint le fet apres lequel sent toute humeyne creature.
Ceste pome, chere soer, signifie toutes celes choses la ou chiet desir et
delit de pecchee. Kant vous regardez l'omme vous estes en le point de
Eve: vous regardez la pome. Qiqe eust dit a Eve quant ele jetta primes
son oil sure: 'A! Eve, tournez-vous en voie vous jettez vostre oil sure
vostre mort,' quei eust-ele respondue? 'Mi, chier sire, vous avez tort. De
qai me chalengiez-vous? La pome qe jeo regard mai est defendue de
mangier et nient a regarder.' Issi vodreit Eve par aventure aver respondue. O mes cheres soeres, come Eve ad mult des filles qe siwent.
[...] mes qe jeo le reg⟨arde⟩. ⟨Di⟩eu le siet, chere soere, greindre
merveille eschiet. Eve, vostre mere, sailli apres ses oilz; del oil desqa la
pome, de la pome en paradis aval a la terre, de la terre en enfern. La jut
ele en prisone quatre mil anz et plus, ele et touz les seons et juga toute

---

pomum significat omne delectabile in quo est peccatum. Si quis Eve
dixisset cum primo pomum respexit, 'O Eva, averte oculum quia mortem
tuam respicis', quid respondisset ipsa? 'Domine, iniuste me reprehendis
quia, licet inhibitum sit ne pomum comedam, non tamen ut illud aspiciam.' 21 Moralium [2]. c: *Semel species formae cordi alligata per
oculos, et caetera;* et post: *Intueri non debet quod non licet concupisci.*
O quot filias sui sequaces habet haec mater quae dicunt, 'Numquid
prosiliam in eum, licet eum aspiciam?'! Certe maius mirum accidit.
Cor Eve prosiliit ad oculum, ab oculo ad pomum, a pomo in paradiso
deorsum in mundum, a mundo in infernum. Ibi detenti sunt in carcere

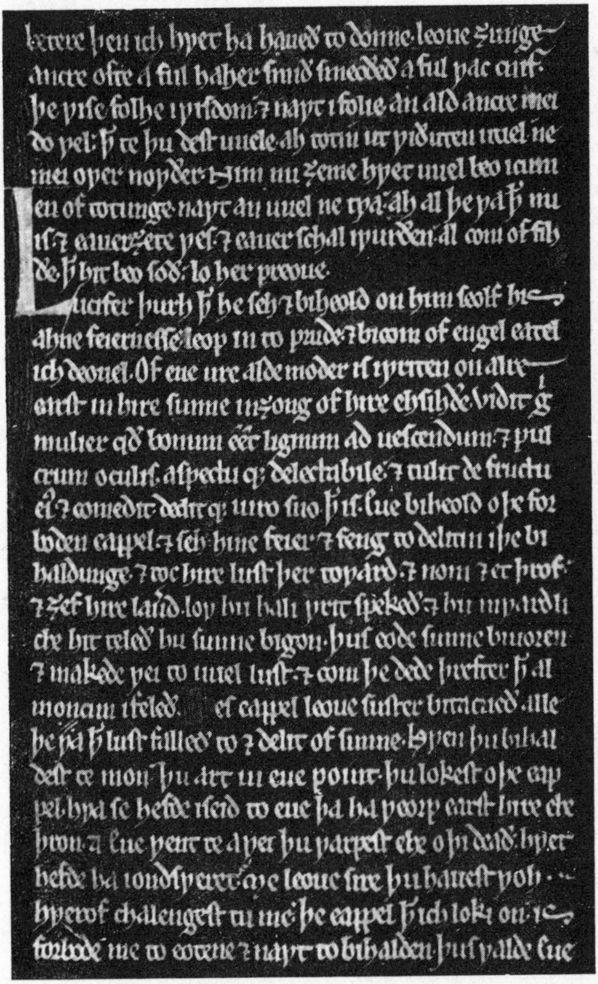

PLATE I

Ancrene Wisse

Ms. 402 Corpus Christi College, Cambridge
folio 13 *b* (lines 1–23 of text).

were ba, ant demde al hire ofsprung to leapen al efter hire
to deað wiðuten ende. Beginnunge ant rote of al þis ilke
reowðe wes a liht sihðe. Þus, ofte, as me seið, 'of lutel
muchel waxeð.'

2. The Flatterers

Fikeleres beoð þreo cunnes. Þe forme beoð uvele inoh; þe 35
oþre þah beoð wurse; þe þridde þah beoð wurst. *Vae illis qui*
ponunt pulvillos, etc. Vae illis qui dant bonum malum et
malum bonum, ponentes lucem tenebras et tenebras lucem; hoc
scilicet detractatoribus et adulatoribus pervenit. Þe forme,
ȝef a mon is god, preiseð him bivoren himseolf ant makeð 40
him, inoh reaðe, ȝet betere þen he beo: ant ȝef he seið wel
oðer deð wel, heveð hit to hehe up wið overherunge. Þe
oðer, ȝef a mon is uvel ant seið ant deð se muche mis þet
hit beo se open sunne þet he hit ne mahe nanes-weis allunge
wiðseggen, he þah, bivore þe mon seolf makeð his uvel 45
leasse. 'Nis hit nawt nu', he seið, 'se over uvel as me hit

---

sa progenie de saillir touz apres lui a mort sanz fin. Comencement et
racine de tout cest mal fut une legiere regardure. Issi sovent, sicome
l'en dit, de petit crest mult.

Losengours sunt en trois manieres. Les primers sunt assez malvois;
les altres sunt unquore pejors; li tiers sunt unquore plus malvois. Li
premers, si un homme soit bon, le preisent devant li-meismes, et le funt,
paraventure, meillour q'il ne soit; et s'il dit bien ou bien fet, le lievent
sus trop haut par trop preisir. L'altres, si un homme est malvois et
trespasse tant en dit ou en fet qe ceo soit si overte pecché q'il ne puisse
en nule maniere dedire, nepurquant devant l'omme meismes fet son
pecché meindre. 'Ceo n'est pas ore,' dit-il, 'si tres mal come hom le

---

iiij milibus annis et amplius, ipsa et vir eius et tota posteritas eius; sic
prosilierunt in mortem. Initium et radix totius mali fuit levis aspectus.
Sic ex modico crevit multum.

Adulatorum tria sunt genera. Primi mali, secundi peiores, tertii
pessimi. *Vae illis, etc.* Primum genus adulationis est, cum bonus in sui
praesentia laudatur, et si bene quid dixerit vel egerit, plus debito extolli-
tur. Secundum genus est quandocumque peccator sic egerit aut dixerit
quod certum sit eum errasse, adulator tamen in praesentia peccatoris
diminuere peccatum vel anullare nititur dicens: 'Non est tantum

makeð.   Nart tu nawt te ane i þis þing, þe forme ne þe leaste.
Þu havest monie feren.   Let i-wurðe, god mon.   Ne geast tu
nawt te ane.   Moni deð muche wurse.'   Þe þridde cunne of
50 fikelere is wurst, as ich seide, for he preiseð þe uvele ant his
uvele dede, as þe þe seið to þe cniht þe robbeð his povre
men, 'A! sire, as þu dest wel!   For eaver me schal þene cheorl
peolkin ant pilien, for he is as þe wiðin þe spruteð ut þe
betere þet me hine croppeð ofte.'

W. Midl.

3. The Love of Christ

55 A leafdi wes mid hire *fan* biset al abuten, hire lond al
destruet ant heo al povre, inwið an eorðene castel.   A mihti
kinges luve wes þah biturnd upon hire, swa unimete swiðe
þet he for wohlech sende hire his sonden, an efter oðer, ofte
somet monie, sende hire beawbelex baðe feole ant feire,

---

fet. Vous n'estes pas, en ceste chose, le primers, ne le derain ne serrez.
Vous avez mult des compaignons. Ne vous chalt, prodhom. Vous n'alez
pas sol. Plusours le funt mult novauz.' La tierce maniere de losengors
est pejoure qe nule des altres, sicome jeo dis avant, kar il preise le
malvois et son malvois fet, sicome celui qi dit al chivaler qe derobbe ses
povres gentz, 'A! sire, come vous fetes bien! Kar l'en deit touz jours le
vilein plumer et pelier, kar il est auxi come le sauz ke plus tret en
branches come plus so⟨vent⟩ . . . [*lacuna in the MS*].

Une dame fut de ses enimis assise tout environ, sa terre t⟨ou⟩te
destruite, et elle tout povre dedenz un chastel de terre. L'amour nepurquant d'un poestif roi fust vers lui si tres a demesure donee q'il pur
dauneure lui envea ses messages, un apres altre, sovent plusours en-

---

malum quantum dicitur. Non es tu primus qui sic egit nec eris ultimus.
Plures habes socios. Non cures, bone homo, non vadis solus. Multi
multo peius faciunt.' Tertium genus est pessimum, cum laudatur peccator
eo quod peccat, sicut aliquotiens dicitur impio militi rusticum quasi
excorianti: 'A! domine, benefacitis, quia oportet rusticos deplumare,
quia ita est de rustico sicut de salice qui eo magis crescit quanto
summitas eius abscinditur.'

Domina quaedam a suis inimicis undique fuit obsessa, terra ipsius
destructa et ipsa paupercula in terreo castello. Amor tamen potentis
Regis ad ipsam ita in immensum conversus erat quod pro suo amore
habendo misit ad eam nuntios, quosdam post alios, postmodum simul

sucurs of liveneð, help of his hehe hird to halden hire castel. 60
Heo underfeng al as on unrecheles ant swa wes heard
i-heortet þet hire luve ne mahte he neaver beo þe neorre.
Hwet wult tu mare? He com himseolf on ende, schawde
hire his feire neb, as þe þe wes of alle men feherest to bihalden, spec se swiðe swoteliche ant wordes se murie þet ha 65
mahten deade arearen to live, wrahte feole wundres ant dude
muchele meistries bivoren hire ehsihðe, schawde hire his
mihte, talde hire of his kinedom, bead to makien hire cwen
of al þet he ahte. Al þis ne heold nawt. Nes þis hoker
wunder? For heo nes neaver wurðe for te beon his þuften. 70
Ah swa, þurh his deboneirté, luve hefde overcumen him þet
he seide on ende: 'Dame, þu art i-weorret, ant þine van
beoð se stronge þet tu ne maht nanes-weis, wiðute mi sucurs
edfleon hare honden, þet ha ne don þe to scheome deað efter

---

semble, lui envea beaubelez beauz et plusours soucours de vitaille, aide de
ses genz pur tenir son chastel. Et ele receust tout ausi come rien ne
lui fust et issi fust dure de queor qe de s'amour ne poeit-il estre ja
le plus pres. Qe volez-vous plus? Il vint meismes a la fin, lui monstra
sa bele face sicome cil qe fut de touz homes le plus beel a regarder,
parla si tres doucement et paroles si deliciouses qe les porreient morz
resusciter, ovra mult des merveilles et fist grant mestrie devant ses oilz,
lui mostra son poer, li cunta de son reigne, li offri de faire reine de tout
ceo q'il avoit. Tout ceo rien ne valut. Ne fut-ceo escharnissable merveille? Qar ele ne fut unqe digne de estre sa baisse. Mes issi par sa
deboneireté amour le aveit venqu q'il dit a derein: 'Dame, vous estes
guerre de voz enimis qe sunt so forz qe vous ne poez en nule maniere

---

multos, misit ei donaria multa et pulchra, succursum victualium, auxilium
sui excercitus ad castellum ipsius tenendum. Ipsa admisit omnia quasi
non curans et sic erat dura corde quod ipsius amori nullatenus approxi-
mare potuit. Quid plura? Ipsemet tandem venit, faciem suam decoram
ostendit, tanquam ille qui fuit speciosus forma prae filiis hominum.
Sic suaviter locutus est et verba tam amena quod mortuos resuscitare
potuerunt ad vitam. Fecit multa mirabilia et prodigia in conspectu eius,
ostendit ei suam potentiam, narravit ei de suo regno, obtulit ut eam
faceret reginam omnium quae possedit. De hoc toto non curavit. Nonne
fuit hoc derisibile mirandum? Quia ipsa nunquam digna fuit ut esset
eius ancilla. Sed per suam benignitatem amor eum ita vicerat quod in
fine dixit: 'Domina, impugnaris et hostes tui ita fortes sunt quod non
potes aliquo modo absque meo adiutorio eorum manus effugere, quin post

75 al þi weane. Ich chulle, for þe luve of þe, neome þet feht upo
me, ant arudde þe of ham þe þi deað secheð. Ich wat þah
to soðe þet ich schal bituhen ham neomen deaðes wunde:
ant ich hit wulle heorteliche for te ofgan þin heorte. Nu
þenne, biseche ich þe, for þe luve þet ich cuðe þe, þet tu
80 luvie me lanhure efter þe ilke deað, hwen þu naldest lives!
Þes king dude al þus, arudde hire of alle hire van, ant wes
himseolf to wundre i-tuket, ant i-slein on ende. Þurh miracle
aras þah from deaðe to live. Nere þeos ilke leafdi of uveles
cunnes cunde, ȝef ha over alle þing ne luvede him herefter?
85 Þes king is Jesu, Godes sune, þet al o þisse wise wohede
ure sawle þe deoflen hefden biset. Ant he, as noble wohere
efter monie messagers ant feole god deden, com to pruvien
his luve, and schawde þurh cnihtschipe þet he wes luve-

79 *MS.* deað] dede dead.

---

sanz mon soucours eschaper hors de lour mains q'il ne vous mettent a
hountouse mort. Jeo voil pur l'amour de vous enprendre ceste bataille
sur mei et vous rescoure de ceaux qe vostre mort querreient. Je sai
nepurquant de voir que jeo entre eus recevrai morte plaie et icele voil
volentiers de queor pur deservir vostre queor. Ore dunqe vous requer-jeo
pur l'amour qe jeo vous moustre qe vous m'amez apres cel fet mort quant
vous ne volez vif! ' Cist roi fist tout ausi, la resceut de touz ses enimis
et il meismes fut vileinement defolee et oscis al derein. Par miracle
nepurquant releva de mort. Ne serreit cele dame de malvoise nature
estrete si ele sur toute rien apres ceo ne li amast?
Cist rois est Jhesu, le fiz Dieu, que tout en ceste maniere daunea nostre
alme qe diables avoient assise et il sicome noble dauneour apres plusours
messagiers et plusours bienfez ⟨v⟩int pur prover s'amour et moustra par

---

totam tuam aerumnam ad mortem contemptibilem te perducant. Volo
pro tuo amore pugnam inire ab illis te liberare qui mortem tuam
quaerunt. Scio tamen pro vero quod inter eos mortalia vulnera recipiam
et corditer hoc volo, ut cor tuum adquiram. Nunc ergo rogo te, pro
amore quem ostendo tibi, quod tu me diligas saltem post talis facti
mortem, ex quo noluisti dum viverem.' Rex iste sic fecit; ipsam ab
hostibus eruit omnibus et fuit ipsemet graviter vulneratus et tandem
occisus. Per miraculum tamen a mortuis resurrexit. Nonne foret ista
domina nimis ingrata si post haec ipsum super omnia non amaret?
Rex iste est Jesus Christus, Dei Filius, qui isto modo voluit animas
nostras ad suum inclinare amorem, quas daemones obsederant; et ipse
tanquam nobilis procus post multos nuntios et multa bona opera venit ad
suum probandum amorem et per militiam ostendit quod fuit dignus

wurðe, as weren sumhwile cnihtes i-wunet to donne, dude
him i turneiment ant hefde for his leoves luve his scheld i 90
feht, as kene cniht, on euche half i-þurlet. His scheld þe
wreah his Goddhead wes his leove licome þet wes i-spread o
rode, brad as scheld buven in his i-strahte earmes, nearow
bineoðen, as þe an fot, efter monies wene, set upo þe oðer.
Þet þis scheld naveð siden is for bitacnunge þet his deciples, 95
þe schulden stonden bi him ant habben i-beon his siden,
fluhen alle from him ant leafden him as fremede as þe
godspel seið: *Relicto eo, omnes fugerunt.* Þis scheld is
i-ȝeven us aȝein alle temptatiuns, as Jeremie witneð: *Dabis* _contracted form_
scutum cordis laborem tuum. Nawt ane þis scheld ne schilt 100
us from alle uveles ah deð ȝet mare, cruneð us in heovene:
Scuto bonae voluntatis. 'Laverd,' he seið, Davið, 'wið þe

---

chivalerie q'il fust digne d'amour, sicome chivalers ascune foiz soloient
faire, se mist en tournement et aveit pur l'amur de s'amie son escu en
bataille, sicome pruz chivaler de toutes parz percé. Son escu coveri sa
deité: ceo fu son cher corps qe fut estendu en croiz, large sicome escu
par desus en ses braz estenduz, estreit par desouz sicome l'un pie,
solum la quidance de plusours, sist par desus l'altre. Qe cest escu
n'avoit point des costees est pur signifiance qe ses disciples qe duissent
estre pres de lui et aver esté ses costez s'enfuirent touz de lui et li
lesserent ausi come estrange sicome la evangele dit: *Relicto eo omnes
fugerunt.* Cest escu nous est donee encontre toutes temptacions, sicome
Jeremie testmoigne: *Dabis scutum cordis laborem tuum.* Psalmista:
Scuto bonae voluntatis tuae coronasti nos. Nient soulement nous defend
cest escu de touz mals me fet enqore plus, nous corune en ciel: *Scuto*

---

amore, sicut solent quandoque milites facere. In torneamento se posuit
et habuit pro amore suae dilectae tanquam probus miles suum scutum
undique perforatum. Hoc scutum, quod suam deitatem cooperuit, fuit
eius pretiosum corpus extensum in cruce, latum sicut scutum superius
in brachiis suis extensis, strictum inferius tanquam uno pede, sicut
putant homines, posito super alium. Quod scutum istud non habet latera
est ad significandum quod sui discipuli, qui stetisse debuerunt iuxta eum
et fuisse ipsius latera, fugerunt omnes. Matthei xxvi: *Relicto eo omnes
fugerunt.* Hoc scutum nobis datum est contra omnes temptationes,
sicut Ieremias testatur, Threnorum iij: *Dabis scutum cordis laborem
tuum.* Nec solum hoc scutum nos protegit a cunctis malis sed nos
coronat in caelo. Psalmista: *Scuto bonae voluntatis tuae coronasti nos.*
Scuto, inquit, bonae voluntatis, quia voluntarie passus est quicquid

scheld of þi gode wil þu havest us i-crunet.' Scheld, he seið,
of god wil; for willes he þolede al þet he þolede. Ysaias:
105 *Oblatus est quia voluit.* 'Me, Laverd,' þu seist, 'hwerto? Ne
mahte he wið leasse gref habben arud us?' 3eoi, i-wiss, ful-
lihtliche; ah he nalde. For-hwi? For te bineomen us euch
bitellunge a3ein him of ure luve, þet he se deore bohte. Me
buð lihtliche þing þet me luveð lutel. He bohte us wið his
110 heorte blod, deorre pris nes neaver, for te ofdrahen of us ure
luve toward him þet costnede him se sare. I scheld beoð
þreo þinges, þe treo ant te leðer ant te litunge. Alswa wes i
þis scheld þe treo of þe rode, þet leðer of Godes licome, þe
litunge of þe reade blod þet heowede hire se feire. Eft, þe
115 þridde reisun: Efter kene cnihtes deað, me hongeð hehe i
chirche his scheld on his mungunge. Alswa is þis scheld, þet
is þe crucifix, i chirche i-set i swuch stude þer me hit sonest

---

bonae voluntatis tuae coronasti nos. Sire, ceo dit David, od l'escu de
vostre bone volunté vous nous avez coronez. Escu, ceo dit, de bone
volunté qe par sa volunté soffri-il tout ceo q'il soffri. *Ysaye: Oblatus est
quia voluit ipse.* Mes, sire, ceo me dites-vous, pur quei? Ne poieit-il od
meindre gref nous aver rescous? Oil, certes, mult legierement; mes il
ne voleit. Pur quei? Pur tolir nous chescune de⟨fense⟩ et surdit encontre
li de n⟨ostre amour⟩ q'il si cher nous achata. L'en achate legierement
chose qe l'en po eime. Il nous achata del sang de son queor plus cher pris
ne fu unqe pur fortraire de nous nostre amour vers lui qe si cher lui
cousta. En escu sunt trois choses, la fust et le cuir et la peinture. Ausi
avoit en cest escu le fust de la croiz, le quir del corps Nostre Seignour,
la peinture del sang vermeil qe si bel li coloura. Dereschief la tierce
reison apres la mort de pr⟨uz⟩ chivaler l'e⟨n⟩ pent en haut son escu en
remenbrance de lui. Ausi est cest escu, c'est le crucifix en le mouster

---

patiebatur. Isaias liij: *Oblatus est quia voluit.* Ad haec forte dices: 'Ut
quid hoc Deus? Numquid non potuit nos cum minori gravamine rede-
misse?' Immo certe, valde faciliter! Sed noluit. Quare? ut auferret nobis
omnem excusationem amoris nostri erga eum, quos tam care redemit.
Faciliter emitur quod parum diligitur. Ipse nos emit suo sanguine
pretioso. Carius pretium numquam extitit ad nostrum amorem attrahendum ad se, quem tam care emit. In scuto tria sunt, — lignum, corium
et color. Sic erat in isto scuto, — lignum crucis, corium corporis Christi,
color sanguinis rubicundi. Post mortem proborum militum suspenduntur
scuta eorum in alto in ecclesiis ad eorum memoriam. Sic scutum istud,
imago videlicet crucifixi, in eminenti loco ecclesiae ponitur ubi citius

seo, for te þenchen þerbi o Jesu Cristes cnihtschipe þet he
dude o rode.   His leofmon bihalde þron hu he bohte hire
luve, lette þurlin his scheld, openin his side, to schawin hire 120
his heorte, to schawin hire openliche hu inwardliche he
luvede hire ant to ofdrahen hire heorte.

4. Renunciation of the Goods of this World

Ʒe, mines leove sustren, bute ʒef neod ow drive ant ower
meistre hit reade, ne schulen habbe na beast bute cat ane.
Ancre þe haveð ahte þuncheð bet husewif, ase Marthe wes; 125
ne lihtliche ne mei ha nawt beo Marie, Marthe suster, wið
griðfullnesse of heorte.   For þenne mot ha þenchen of þe
kues foddre, of heordemonne hure, olhnin þe heiward, wearien
hwen he punt hire, ant ʒelden, þah, þe hearmes.   Ladlich
þing is hit, ʀat Crist, hwen me makeð i tune man of ancre 130
ahte.   Nu þenne, ʒef eani mot nedlunge habben hit, loki þet
hit namon ne eili, ne ne hearmi, ne þet hire þoht ne beo

---

assis en tiel lieu ou l'en puit plus tost veer pur pensir par ceo de la chivalerie Jhesu Crist q'il fist en la croiz. S'amie reg⟨ar⟩de en ceo coment il
achata s'amour, lessa percer son escu, overir son costé, pur lui moustrer
sou queor, pur lui moustrer overtement come parfundement il l'ama et
pur fortraire son queor a lui.

Vous, mes tres cheres soeres, ne duissez nule beste aver fors soul chat.
Recluse q'ad aumaille resemble housewif sicome fu Martha; ne en nule
manere puit-elle estre Marie od tout le queor vers Dieu. Kar dunqe lui
covendra penser del forage la vache, del louer le pastour, de querre la
grace de messer, maudir le quant il les enparke et nepurquant rendre les
dampnages. Lede chose est, Dieu le siet, quant l'en fait en ville pleinte
des bestes la recluse. Me nepurquant si il le vous covient bosoignable-

---

videatur ad memoriam militiae Jesu Christi quam exercuit in cruce, ut
dilecti illum respiciant qualiter eorum emit amorem. Patiebatur scutum
perforari, suum latus aperiri, ad cor suum ostendendum ut dilectis suis
intimaret quam intime eos dilexit et ad cor eorum attrahendum.

Carissimae sorores, nullum animal penes vos retineatis nisi summa
necessitate urgente et hoc de consilio Magistri vestri. Murilego dum
taxat excepto. Absur⟨d⟩um est novit Deus quod Anachoreta circa
huiusmodi occupetur. Verumtamen si necessarie ipsam animalia habere
opo⟨r⟩tet videat summopere ne cui noceant, et ne in his nimis mentem

nawiht þron i-festnet. Ancre ne ah to habben na þing þet
utward drahe hire heorte. Na chaffere ne drive ȝe. Ancre
135 þet is chepilt, þet is, buð for te sullen efter biȝete, ha chepeð
hire sawle þe chapmon of helle. Þing þah þet ha wurcheð,
ha mei þurh hire meistres read, for hire neode, sullen; hali
men sumhwile liveden bi hare honden.

Nawt, deore dehtren, ne wite ȝe in ower hus of oðer monne
140 þinges, ne ahte, ne claðes, ne boistes, ne chartres, scoren, ne
cyrograffes, ne þe chirch vestemenz, ne þe calices bute neode
oðer strengðe hit makie, oðer muchel eie: Of swuch witunge
is muchel uvel i-lumpen oftesiðen.

ment ascun aver, gardez q'il a nul hom ne nuyse ne face dampnage ne que
vostre pensee ne seit en ceo afermee. Recluse ne duist rien aver que hors
trahie son queor. De nule marchandise ne vous entremettez. Recluse qest
marchande ele bargaigne s'alme al marchand d'enfer.

Rien ne gardez en vostre maisone d'altrui choses, ne aver, ne draps,
nient les vestemenz de mouster, ne le chaliz si force ne le face, ou grand
doute: De tel gardier est sovent mal avenu.

opponat. Canens cum psalmista d⟨i⟩cente: *Nolite cor apponere.* Negotia-
tiones nulla⟨s⟩ excerceatis quia Anachor⟨e⟩ta emens emens quicquam ut car ⟨?⟩
vendat animam suam commercatori infernali. Si quid tamen man⟨ibus⟩
[. . . . .] ali[. . . . .]m ⟨custod ?⟩ iatis [. . .] gente necessitate vel[. . .] tante dominio rerum earum [. . .] utpote animalium
vestium. Ca⟨licum?⟩ seu alterius rei cuiuscumque. De huiusmodi enim
custodiis male suspiciones frequenter oriuntur.

IV

SAWLES WARDE

The continuity of religious literary prose inherited from Old English is
displayed in the 12th century, outside of the *Ancrene Wisse*, in a group of
texts, associated in three MSS, called the "St. Catherine Group." This
comprises really the legends of St. Catherine, St. Margaret, and St. Juliana,
a treatise on virginity (*Hali Meiðhad*), and, finally, an allegorical homily in
prose — *Sawles Warde* or "Soul's Guardian" from which this short extract
is taken.

Sawles Warde is a rather free adaptation, in very sure and close-knit style,
of some chapters (book IV, ch. 13-15) of Hugo of St. Victor's treatise *De
Anima*. The same passage was also translated independently, but in a much

more literal way, by Dan Michel of Northgate as an appendix to his *Aȝenbite of Inwyt* (see no. XV).

Edition:
Sawles Warde, An Early English Homily, ed. by R. M. WILSON, Leeds, 1938.

Consult also:
R. M. WILSON. *Early Middle English Literature*, pp. 117 and f.
J. E. WELLS. *Manual*, pp. 272-4 (bibliography, p. 803).

The Happiness of the Elect

Ha livieð á in a wlite, þet is brihtre seovevald ant schenre þen þe sunne ant eaver in a strengðe to don buten euch swinc al þet ha wulleð ant eavermare in a steal in al þet eaver god is, wiðute wonunge, wiðuten euch þing þet mahe hearmin oðer eilen, in al þet eaver is softe oðer swote. Ant 5 hare lif is Godes sihðe, ant Godes cnawlechunge, as ure laverd seide: 'Þet is, quoð he, eche lif to seon ant cnawen soð Godd, ant him þet he sende, Jhesu Crist, ure laverd, to ure alesnesse'; ant beoð for-þi i-lich him i þe ilke wlite þet he is; for ha seoð him, as he is, nebbe to nebbe. Ha beoð se 10 wise þet ha witen alle Godes reades, his runes ant his domes, þe derne beoð ant deopre þen eni sea dingle. Ha seoð i Godd alle þing ant witen of al þet is ant wes ant eaver schal i-wurðen, hwet hit beo, hwi ant hwerto ant hwerof hit bigunne. 15

A: AYENBITE OF INWYT: Hy lybbeþ be lyve wyþoute ende, wyþoute enye tyene, wy⟨þ⟩oute enye lessinge, wyþoute enye wyþstondynge. Hyre lyf is þe zyȝþe and þe knaulechynge of þe holy trinyté, ase zayþ oure lhord Jesus: 'Þis is þet lyf wyþoute ende, þet hy knawe þe zoþe God, and huam þe zentest, Jesu Crist;' and þervore y-lyche hy byeþ vor hy y-zyeþ ase 5 he is. Hy smackeþ þe redes and þe domes of God. Hy smackeþ þe kendes and þe causes and þe begynny⟨n⟩ges of alle þynges. Hy lovyeþ God

---

HUGO OF SAINT-VICTOR: Vivunt vita sine fine, sine molestia, sine diminutione, sine omni adversitate. Vita eorum visio et cognitio beatae trinitatis, sicut Dominus ait: 'Haec est vita aeterna, ut cognoscant te Deum verum, et quem misisti Iesum Christum.' Sapiunt consilia atque iudicia Dei, quae sunt abyssus multa. Sapiunt causas, et naturas, et origines omnium rerum. Amant Deum incomparabiliter, quia sciunt unde

Ha luvieð God wiðute met, for þet ha understondeð hu he
haveð bi ham i-don þurh his muchele godlec ant hwet ha
ahen his deorewurðe milce to ȝelden ant euchan luveð oðer
ase muchel as himseolven.

20 Se gleade ha beoð of Godd, þet al is hare blisse se muchel
þet ne mei hit munne na muð ne spealie ⟨na speche⟩; for-þi
þet euchan luveð oðer as himseolven. ⟨Euchan ha⟩veð of
oðres god ase muche murhðe as of his ahne. Bi þis ȝe
mahen seon ant witen þet euchan h⟨aveð su⟩nderlepes ase
25 feole gleadschipes as ha beoð monie alle; ant euch of þe ilke
gleadschipes is to eaver euchan ase muche gleadunge as his
ahne sunderliche; ȝet over al þis, hwen euchan luveð Godd
mare þen himseolven ant þen alle þe oðre, mare he gleadeð
of Godd wiðuten ei etlunge þen of his ahne gleadunge ant of
30 alle þe oðres. Neomeð nu þenne ȝeme, ȝef neaver anes
heorte ne mei in hire ⟨unde⟩rvon hire ahne gleadunge sunderliche, ⟨se unim⟩ete muchel is þe anlepi blisse, þet ha
nimeð in hi⟨re⟩ þus monie ant þus muchele. For-þi seide ure
laverd to þeo þe him hefden i-cwemet, *Intra in gaudium et*

A: wyþoute enye comparisoun, vor þet hy wyteþ huerto God his heþ y-broȝt
vorþ. Hy lovyeþ ech oþren ase hamzelve. Hy byeþ glede of God onzyginde.
10 Hy byeþ glede of zuo moche of hare oȝene holynesse, and vor þet ech
loveþ oþren ase himzelve, ase moche blisse heþ ech of oþres guode ase of
his oȝene. Þervore by zyker vor evrych heþ ase vele blyssen ase he heþ
velaȝes, and ase vele blissen to echen ase his oȝene of alle. And þervore
evreich more loveþ wyþoute comparisoun God, þet hym and oþre made,
15 þanne himzelve and alle oþre. More hy byeþ glede wyþoute gessynge o
Godes holynesse þanne of his oȝene and of alle oþre myd hym. Yef
þanne on onneaþe nymþ al his blisse, hou ssel he nyme zuo vele and zuo

---

et ad quid eos Deus provexit. Amant singuli singulos sicut seipsos. Gaudent
de Deo ineffabiliter, gaudent de tanta sua beatitudine. Et quia unusquisque
unumquemque diligit sicut seipsum, tantum gaudium quisque habet de
bono singulorum quantum de suo, quoniam bonum, quod non habet in
seipso, possidet in altero. Constat igitur quod singuli tot gaudia habent
quot socios, et singula gaudia tanta sunt singulis, quantum proprium
singulorum. Cum autem quisque plus amet Deum quam seipsum, et
omnes alios secum, plus gaudet de Dei felicitate quam de sua et omnium
aliorum secum. Si ergo cor uniuscuiusque vix capit suum gaudium,

caetera. ' Ga, quoð he, into þi laverdes blisse ' ; þu most al gan 35
þrin ant al beon bigotten þrin for in þe ne mei hit nanes-weis
neomen in.   Herof ha herieð Godd ant singeð á unwerget eaver
i-liche lusti in þis loftsonges, as hit i-writen is : *Beati qui*
habitant, et caetera.   ' Eadi beoð þeo, laverd, þe i þin hus
wunieð; ha schulen herien þe from ⟨worlde into wor⟩lde.' 40
Ha beoð alle ase lih⟨te ant as swifte as þe sunne⟩gleam, þe
sch⟨eot from est into west, ase þin ehe⟩lid tuneð ant openeð;
for hwerseeaver þe gast wule þe bodi is ananriht wiðute
lettunge, for ne mei ham na þing aȝeines etstonden.   For euchan
is almihti to don al þet he wule, ȝe, makie to cwakien heovene 45
ba ant eorðe wið his an finger.   Sikere ha beoð of al þis, of
þulli lif, of þulli wit, of þulli luve ant gleadunge þrof ant of
þulli blisse þet hit ne mei neaver mare lutlin ne wursin, ne
neome nan ende.

---

manye blyssen? And þervore hit is y-zed : ' guo into þe blysse of þyne
lhorde ' ; naȝt þe blisse of þine lhorde guo into þe, vor hy ne may.
Þerefter hy herieþ God wyþoute ende, wyþoute werynesse, ase hyt is 20
y-wryte : ' Lhord y-blyssed by þo þet wonyeþ ine þyne house, in wordles
of wordles ssolle herye þe '. Zuyfte hy byeþ, vor huer þet þe gost wyle
by, vor zoþe þer is þet body. Alle hy byeþ my⟨ȝ⟩tvolle. Zykere hy byeþ
of zuyche lyve, of zuo moche wysdome, of zuo moche love, of zuo moche
blysse, of zuyche heryinge, of zuyche holynesse þet non ende, non 25
lessynge, non vallynge doun ssole habbe.

---

quomodo capit tot et tanta gaudia? Ideo dicitur : ' Intra in gaudium
Domini tui '; non intret gaudium Domini tui in te, quia capi non posset.
Inde laudant Deum, sine fine, sine fastidio, sicut scriptum est : ' Beati,
qui habitant in domo tua, Domine, in saecula saeculorum laudabunt te.'
Veloces sunt, quia ubicunque esse vult spiritus, ibi est etiam corpus.
Omnes securi sunt. Securi sunt de tali vita, de tanta sapientia, de tanto
amore, de tanto gaudio, de tali laude, de tali velocitate, quod nullum
finem, nullam diminutionem, nullum detrimentum habebunt.

V

LAWMAN: THE BRUT

Modern critics have given the name of *Brut* to a vast chronicle in alliterative verse (16,120 long lines in its most extended version) which relates the history of Britain from the time of the Trojan ancestors of Brutus, its mythical founder, up to 689, a date when, under Cadwallader, the Britons were definitively pushed back into the mountains of Wales.

All that we know about the author comes from the few autobiographical lines that he put at the head of his work and which are to be found below in the first extract. He says he is named *Laȝamon* (*Laweman* in MS B: it is more natural to call him *Lawman* in ModE in spite of the traditional form, *Layamon*). He tells us that he was born in the north of Worcestershire. He was a priest and a cultivated man who was quite familiar with the older, pre-Conquest, English literature. To compose his chronicle he probably made use of Bede's *Ecclesiastical History* and he certainly used the *Roman de Brut* — a poem in Anglo-Norman by the trouvère Wace; also, undoubtedly, an Anglo-Norman translation of Geoffrey of Monmouth's *Historia Regum Britanniae*, thus incorporating all the extant Welsh and Breton legends in his chronicle, about a third of which is devoted to the life and exploits of King Arthur.

A narrator full of life, a vigorous and fecund writer, Lawman has a feeling for the picturesque. His vocabulary, almost exclusively Germanic, is rich and full of nuance. The *Brut* is one of the great works in English literature in the Middle Ages. Certain allusions to historical facts place the time of the composition of this work towards the end of the 12th century, undoubtedly between 1189 and 1205.

Editions:

Laȝamons Brut, or Chronicle of England, now first published by Sir Frederick MADDEN, London, 1847. [The only complete edition of the two MSS; also with a ModE transl.]

Layamon's Brut, Selections edited with Introduction, Notes and Glossary by Joseph HALL, Oxford, 1924. [Selections, in a critical text.]

Consult also:

R. M. WILSON. *Early Middle English Literature,* pp. 205-13.

J. E. WELLS. *Manual,* pp. 32-5, 191-5 (bibliography, pp. 792-4).

J. S. P. TATLOCK. *The Legendary History of Britain,* Berkeley, 1950.

1. Introduction

An preost wes on leoden,   Laȝamon wes i-hoten;
He wes Leovenaðes sone;   liðe him beo Drihten!
He wonede at Ernleȝe,   at æðelen are chirechen,

Uppen Sevarne staþe   (sel þar him þuhte)
Onfest Radestone;   þer he bock radde.   5
Hit com him on mode   and on his mern þonke
Þet he wolde of Engle   þa æðelæn tellen;
Wat heo i-hoten weoren   and wonene heo comen
Þa Englene londe   ærest ahten,
Æfter þan flode   þe from Drihtene com   10
Þe al her a-quelde   quic þat he funde,
Buten Noe and Sem,   Japhet and Cham,
And heore four wives   þe mid heom weren on archen.
Laȝamon gon liðen   wide ȝond þas leode;
And biwon þa æðela boc   þa he to bisne nom.   15
He nom þa Englisċa boc   þa makede seint Beda.
An oþer he nom on Latin,   þe makede seinte Albin
And þe feire Austin   þe fulluht brou⟨h⟩te hider in.
Boc he nom þe þridde,   leide þer amidden,
Þa makede a Frenchis clerc   Wace wes i-hoten,   20
Þa wel couþe writen,   and he heo ȝef þare æðelen
Ælienor þe wes Henries quene,   þes heȝes kinges.
Laȝamon þeos boc leide   and þa leaf wende;
He heom leofliche biheold;   liþe him beo Drihten!
Feþeren he nom mid fingren   and on bocfelle fiede   25
And þa soþe word   sette togadere
And þa þre boc   þrumde to are.
Nu b-iddeð Laȝamon
Alcne æðele mon   for þene alṁi⟨h⟩ten Godd
Þet þeos boc rede   and leornia þeos runan   30
Þat he þeos soðfeste word   segge tosumne
For his fader saule   þa hine forð brouhte,
And for his moder saule   þa hine to monne i-ber,
And for his awene saule   þat hire þe selre beo. Amen.

---

21 heo] hoe *MS.* — 23 þeos boc leide] leide þeos boc *MS.* — 25 on bocfelle fiede] fiede on bocfelle *MS.* — 28 biddeð] bidded *MS.* — 32 forð] ford *MS.*

2. Arthur's Dream

13995 Þa Arður wende to soðe   to aȝein al Rome,
And wunede inne Burguine,   richest alre kinge.
Þa com þer in are tiden   an oht mon riden
And brohte tidinge   Arðure þan kinge
From Moddrede his suster sune;   Arðure he wes wilcume,
14000 For he wende þat he brohte   boden swiðe gode.
Arður lai alle longe niht   and spac wið þene ȝeonge cniht;
Swa naver nulde he him sugge   soð hu hit ferde.
Þa hit wes dæi a marȝen   and duȝeðe gon sturien,
Arður þa up aras   and strehte his ærmes;
14005 He aras up and adun sat   swulċ he weore swiðe seoc;
Þa axede hine an væir cniht: 'Laverd, hu havest þu i-varen
Arður þa andswarede,   a mode him wes uneðe: [to-niht?'
'To-niht a mine slepe,   ðer ich læi on bure,
Me i-mætte a sweven;   ðervore ich ful sari æm.
14010 Me i-mette ðat mon me hof   uppen are halle;
Þa halle ich gon bistriden   swulċ ich wolde riden;
Alle þa lond þa ich ah,   alle ich þer oversah,
And Walwain sat bivoren me,   mi sweord he bar an honde.
Þa com Moddred faren þere   mid unimete volke;
14015 He bar an his honde   ane wi-ax stronge;
He bigon to hewene   hardliche swiðe,
And ða postes forheou alle   þa heolden up þa halle.
Þer ich i-seh Wenhever eke,   wimmonnen leofvest me.
Al þere muche halle-rof   mid hire honden heo todroh.
14020 Þa halle gon to hælden,   and ich hæld to grunden
Þat mi riht ærm tobrac;   þo seide Modred: 'Have þat!'
Adun veol ða halle   and Walwain gon to valle
And feol a þere eorðe;   his ærmes breken beine.
And ich i-grap mi sweord leofe   mid mire leoft honde
14025 And smæt of Modred ⟨h⟩is hafd   þat hit wond a þene veld.

14023 breken] brekeen *MS.* — 14024 sweorde] sweorede *MS.*

And þa quene ich al tosna*d*de   mid deore mine sweorde;

And seoðen ich heo adu*n* sette   in ane swarte putte;

And al mi volc riche   sette to fleme

Þat nuste ich under Criste   whar heo bicumen weoren.

Buten mi seolf ich gon atstonden   uppen ane wolden,   14030

And ich þer wondrien agon   wide ȝeond þan moren;

Þer ich i-sah gripes   and grisliche fuȝeles.

Þa com an guldene leo   liðen over dune,

Deoren swiðe hende   þa ure Drihten make⟨de⟩.

Þa leo me orn foren to   and i-veng me bi þan midle,   14035

And forð gun hire ȝeongen   and to þere sæ wende.

And ich i-sæh þ*a* uðen   i þere sæ driven,

And þe leo i þan vlode   i-wende wið me seolve.

Þa wit i sæ comen,   þa uðen me hire binomen;

Com þer an fisc liðe   and fereden me to londe.   14040

Þa wes ich al wet   and weri of sorȝen and seoc.

Þa gon ich i-wakien,   swiðe ich gon to quakien;

Þa gon ich to bivien   swulc ich al fur burne,

And swa ich habbe al niht   of mine swevene swiðe i-þoht.

For ich wat to i-wisse: Agan is al mi blisse!   14045

For a to mine live   sorȝen ich mot driȝe.

Wale, þat ich nabbe here   Wenhaver, mine quene!'

    Þa andswarede þe cniht: 'Laverd, þu havest unriht;

Ne sculde me navere sweven   mid sorȝen arecchen.

Þu ært þe riccheste mon   þa rixleoð on londen,   14050

And þe alrewiseste   þe wuneð under weolcne.

Ȝif hit weore i-limpe, —swa nulle hit ure Drihte!—

Þat Modred, þire suster sune,   hafde þine quene i-nume,

And al þi kineliche lond   i-sæt an his aȝere hond

Þe þu him bitahtest   þa þu to Rome þohtest,   14055

And he hafde al þus i-do   mid his swikedome,

Þe⟨n⟩ ȝet þu mihtest þe awreken   wurðliche mid wepnen,

14026 tosnadde] tosnaðde *MS.* — 14027 seoðð en] seoðð en *MS*; adun]
adum *MS.* — 14030 gon] gond *MS.* — 14037 þa] þæ *MS.* — 14044
swevene] swevenene *MS.* — 14045 wat] what *MS.*

And æft þi lond halden   and walden þine leoden,
And þine feond fallen   þe þe ufel unnen,
14060 And slæn heom alle clane   þet þer no bilaven nane!'
     Arður þa andswarede,   aðelest alre kinge:
'Longe bið ævere,   þat no wene ich navere,
Þat ævere Moddred,   mi mæi,
Wolde me biswiken   for alle mine richen,
14065 No Wenhaver, mi quene,   wakien on þonke;
Nulleþ hit biginne   for nane weorldmonne.'
Æfne þan worde forðriht   þa andswarede þe cniht:
'Ich sugge þe soð, leofe king,   for ich æm þin underling:
Þus hafeð Modred i-don;   þine quene he hafeð i-fon,
14070 And þi wunliche lond   i-sæt an his aȝere hond.
He is king and heo is que⟨ne⟩;   of þine kume nis na wene;
For no weneð heo navere to soðe   þat þu cumen aȝain from
Ich æm þin aȝen mon,   and i-seh þisne swikedom,   [Rome.
And ich æm i-cumen to þe seolven   soð þe to suggen.
14075 Min hafved beo to wedde   þat i-sæid ich þe habbe
Soð buten lese   of leofen þire quene
And of Modrede, þire suster sune,   hu he hafveð Brutlond
    Þa sæt hit al stille   in Arðures halle;   [þe binume!'
Þa wes þer særinæsse   mid sele þan kinge.
14080 Þa weoren Bruttisċe men   swiðe unbalde vor-þæn.

VI

THE OWL AND THE NIGHTINGALE

This exquisite poem borrows a form which had been familiar in the Middle Ages since Carolingian times, that of the 'debate' or quarrel in verse between two (or more) personages each of whom presents his own point of view, refutes his adversary's argument, and then, usually, the parties involved refer the argument to some third party who plays the role of arbiter to establish the winner. First in Latin, then from the end of the 12th century in the vernacular languages, we find such debates between the Body and the Soul, Summer and Winter, Water and Wind, the Violet and the Rose, the Scholar and the Knight, etc. Here the debate takes place between an Owl and a Nightingale. This animal element, borrowed from the fable, a genre much appreciated in this period, adds a great deal of zest to the narrative by the use of minute and concrete details. But the birds are nonetheless allegorical figures. The Owl undoubtedly represents religious didactic poetry, marked by seriousness; the Nightingale, on the other hand, stands for the new lyric and amorous poetry.

The scene takes place on a June night in some valley in the South of England, and lasts until daybreak. In the morning, after this oratorical tournament, the Thrush, the Wren, and the other diurnal birds declare the Nightingale the winner. But the latter does not want the argument to be decided by anyone except the judge that both had agreed on, namely, Master Nicholas of Guildford, and all the birds fly towards Portesham, his home in Dorset.

All the critics are fond of praising this poem in which we find so many innovations: it is the first — and the best — specimen of the 'debate' in the English language, the first to use, and already with a great deal of ease, the octosyllabic couplet imported from France. The French influence is still quite noticeable in the poem, in the vocabulary as well as in the inspiration. It is also the first example of that familiar style in which Chaucer was to excel. The frame of the poem, and the arguments follow exactly the procedure of contemporary law-courts. The whole poem, indeed, breathes that spirit of free discussion which flows in the literature of this first Renaissance that appeared in the 12th century.

The author, who must have had a strong personality, remains unknown in spite of research. The date of composition remains uncertain. Taking account of certain historical allusions, it can be placed approximately between the death of Henry II (1189) and the accession of Henry III (1216).

Editions:

The Owl and the Nightingale, ed. by J. E. WELLS, Boston and London, 1907 (revised edition, 1909).

Das mittelenglische Streitgedicht Eule und Nachtigall hrsg. von W. GADOW, Berlin, 1909 (*Palaestra* LXV) [critical text].

The Owl and the Nightingale, ed. by J. W. ATKINS, Cambridge, 1922 [with a very detailed introduction and a translation].

The Owl and the Nightingale, ed. by J. H. G. GRATTAN and G. F. H. SYKES, Oxford, 1935 (EETS, 119) [diplomatic edition].

Consult also:

R. M. WILSON. *Early Middle English Literature,* ch. vii, pp. 149-69.

J. E. WELLS. *Manual,* pp. 418-21 (bibliography p. 831).

B. SUNDBY. *The Dialect and Provenance of the ME Poem 'The Owl and the Nightingale '*(*Lund Studies in English,* XVIII), Lund, 1950.

> 'Ich rede þi þat men bo ȝare   860
> And more wepe þane singe,
> Þat fundeþ to þan hoven-kinge,
> Vor nis no man wiþute sunne.
> Vor-þi he mot, ar he wende honne,
> Mid teres and mid wope þete,   865
> Þat him bo sur þat er was swete.
> Þarto ich helpe, God hit wot,
> Ne singe ih hom no foliot;

861 and] an *C* (*similarly throughout*). — 863 wiþute] witute *C*, wiþuten *O*.

For al mi song is of longinge
870   And i-mend sumdel mid woninge,
Þat mon bi me hine biþenche,
Þat he groni for his unwrenche;
Mid mine songe ich hine pulte,
Þat he groni for his gulte.
875   Ʒif þu gest herof to sputinge,
Ich wepe bet þane þu singe;
Ʒif riʒt goþ forþ and abak wrong,
Betere is mi wop þane þi song,
Þeʒ sume men bo þurʒut gode
880   And þurʒut clene on hore mode,
Hom longeþ honne noþeles.
Þat boþ her, wo is hom þes,
Vor þeʒ hi bon hom solve i-borʒe,
Hi ne soþ her nowiʒt bote sorwe;
885   Vor oþer men hi wepeþ sore
And for hom biddeþ Cristes ore.
Ich helpe monne on eiþer halve,
Mi muþ haveþ tweire kunne salve:
Þan gode ich fulste to longinge,
890   Vor hwanne hin longeþ, ich hin singe;
And þan sunfulle ich helpe alswo,
Vor ich him teche ware is wo.
Ʒet ich þe ʒene in oþer wise;
Vor wane þu sittest on þine rise,
895   Þu draʒst men to fleses luste,
Þat w⟨i⟩lleþ þine songes luste.
Al þu forlost þe murʒþe of hovene,
For þarto nevestu none stevene;
Al þat þu singst is of golnesse,
900   For nis on þe non holinesse;
Ne weneð na man for þi pipinge,

---

869 mi] me *C*, my *O*. — 875 sputinge] disputinge *CO*. — 881 hom] hon *C*,
heom *O*. — 890 hwanne] þan *C*, hwenne *O*.

Þat eni preost in chir*ch*e singe.
ʒet I þe wulle an oðer segge,
ʒif þu hit const ariht bilegge.
Wi nultu singe an oðer þeode, 905
Þar hit is muchele more neode?
Þu neaver ne singst in Irlonde,
Ne þu ne cumest noʒt in Scotlonde;
Hwi nultu fare to Noreweie,
And singin men of Galeweie? 910
Þar beoð men þat lutel kunne
Of songe þat is bineoðe þe sunne.
Wi nultu þare preoste singe
And teche of þire writelinge,
And wisi hom mid þire stevene 915
Hu engeles singeð ine heovene?
Þu farest so doð an ydel wel,
Þa*t* springeþ bi burne þa*t* is snel,
And let fordrue þe dune
And floþ on idel þar adune. 920
Ac ich fare boþe norþ and su*þ*,
In eavereuch londe ich am cuuþ;
East and west, feor and neor,
I do wel faire mi meoster,
And warni men mid mine bere, 925
Þat þi dweole-song heo ne forlere.
Ich wisse men mid mine songe,
Þat hi ne sunegi nowiht longe;
I bidde hom þat heo i-swike,
Þat heom seolve ne biswike; 930
For betere is þat heo wepen here,
Þan elles-hwar beon deovlene fere?'

901 weneð] wened *C*, weneþ *O*. — 902 chirche *O*] chircce *C*. —903, 905
oðer] oder *C*, oþer *O*. — 914 writelinge *O*] þritelinge *C*. — 918 þat *O*] þar
C. — 920 floþ] floh *C*, flohþ] *O*. — 921 suþ] soþ *C*, souþ *O*. — 932 beon] to
beon *C*, beo *O*.

Þe niȝtingale was i-gramed,
And ek heo was sumdel of⟨s⟩chamed,
935 For þe ule hire atwiten hadde
In hwucche stude he sat and gradde,
Bihinde þe bure, among þe wede,
Þar men goð to here neode;
And sat sumdel and heo biþohte,
940 And wiste wel on hire þohte
Þe wraþþe binimeþ monnes red.
For hit seide þe king Alfred:
'Se⟨l⟩de ⟨gr⟩endeð wel þe loþe
And selde plaideð wel þe wroþe.'
945 For wraþþe meinþ þe horte blod,
Þat hit floweþ so wilde flod
And al þe heorte overgeþ,
Þat heo naveþ noþing bute breþ,
And so forleost al hire liht,
950 Þat heo ne siþ soð ne riht.
Þe niȝtingale hi understod
And overgan lette hire mod;
He mihte bet speken a sele,
Þan mid wraþþe wordes deale.
955   Þ'ule, heo seide: 'Lust nu hider!
Þu schalt falle, þe wei is slider.
Þu seist ich fleo bihinde bure;
Hit is riht, þe bur is ure.
Þar laverd liggeþ and lavedi,
960 Ich schal heom singe and sitte bi.
Wenstu þat wise men forlete
For fule venne þe riȝtte strete?
Ne sunne þe later shine,

---

933 igramed] igremet *C*, agromed *O*. — 934 ofschamed] ofchamed *C*,
ofschomed *O*. — 935 ule *O*] hule *C*. — 936 hwucche]hþucche *C*. — 943
selde *O*] sele *C*; grendeð] endeð *CO*. — 946 floweþ *O*] floþeþ *C*. — 961 wise
O] vise *C*.

Þeȝ hit beo ful ine nest⟨e⟩ þine?

Sholde ich for one hole brede   965

Forlete mine riȝte stede,

Þat ich ne singe bi þe bedde,

Þar loverd haveþ his love i bedde?

Hit is mi riȝt, hit is mi laȝe,

Þat to þe hexst⟨e⟩ ich me draȝe.   970

Ac ȝet þu ȝelpst of þine songe,

Þat þu canst ȝolle wroþe and stronge,

And seist þu *w*isest mankunne,

Þat hi biwepen hore sunne.

Solde euch mon wonie and grede,   975

Riȝt suich hi weren unlede,

Solde hi ȝollen also þu dest,

Hi miȝte oferen here *p*rost.

Man schal bo stille and noȝt grede;

He mot biwepe his misdede,   980

Ac þar is Cristes heriinge,

Þar me schal grede and lude singe.

Nis noþer to lud ne to long

At riȝte time chirche-song.

Þu ȝolst and wones⟨t⟩, and ich singe: 985

Þi stevene is wop and min skentinge.

Ever mote þu ȝolle and wepen

Þat þu þi lif mote forleten,

And ȝollen mote þu so heȝe

Þat ut berste bo þin eȝe.   990

Weþer is betere of twere twom,

Þat mon bo bliþe oþer grom?

So bo hit ever in unker siþe,

Þat þu bo sori and ich bliþe.

Ȝut þu aisheist, wi ich ne fare   995

---

964 neste *O*] nest *C.* — 970 þat *O*] þar *C*; hexste *O*] herst C. — 973 wisest *O*] visest *C.* — 978 prost] brost *C*, preost *O.* — 985 wonest *O*] wones *C.*

Into oþer londe and singe þare?
No! wat sholde ich among hom do,
Þar never blisse ne com to?
Þat lond nis god, ne hit nis este,
1000   Ac wildernisse hit is and weste;
Knarres and cludes hoven⟨e⟩-tinge,
Snou and haȝel hom is genge;
Þat lond is grislich and unvele,
Þe men boþ wilde and unisele;
1005   Hi nabbeþ noþer griþ ne sibbe,
Hi ne reccheþ hu hi libbe;
Hi eteþ fihs and flehs unsode,
Suich wulves hit hadde tobrode;
Hi drinkeþ milc and wei þarto,
1010   Hi nute elles wat hi do;
Hi nabbeþ noþ⟨er⟩ win ne bor,
Ac libbeþ also wilde dor;
Hi goþ bitiȝt mid ruȝe velle,
Riȝt suich hi comen ut of helle.
1015   Þeȝ eni god man to hom come, —
So wile dude sum from Rome,
For hom to lere gode þewes
And for to leten hore unþewes, —
He miȝte bet sitte stille,
1020   Vor al his wile he sholde spille.
He miȝte bet teche ane bore
To weȝe boþe sheld and spere,
Þan me þat wilde folc i-bringe,
Þat hi me wolde i-here singe.
1025   Wat sol⟨d⟩ ich þar mid mine songe?
Ne sunge ich hom never so longe,
Mi song were i-spild ech del;
For hom ne mai halter ne bridel

1001 hovene- *O*] hoven *C.* — 1024 me wolde *O*] me segge wolde *C.* —
1025 sold] sol *C*, schold *O.*

Bringe vrom hore wode wise,
Ne mon mid stele ne mid ise;   1030
Ac war lond is boþe este and god,
And þar men habbeþ milde mod,
Ich noti mid hom mine þrote,
Vor ich mai do þar gode note,
And bringe hom love tiþinge,   1035
Vor ich of chirche-songe singe.
Hit was i-seid in olde laȝe,
(And ȝet i-last þilke soþ-saȝe)
Þat man shal erien and sowe,
Þar he wenþ after sum god mowe;   1040
For he is wod þat soweþ his sed,
Þar never gras ne sprin⟨g⟩þ ne bled.'

1029 wode *O*] wude *C.* — 1030 ise] ire *CO.* — 1031 lond *O*] long *C.* —
1038 þilke *O*] wilce *C.* — 1042 springþ *O*] sprinþ *C.*

VII

THE ORMULUM

About the author of the *Ormulum* and his work we know nothing except what
this book tells us:

Þiss boc iss nemmned Orrmulum
Forrþi þatt Orrm itt wrohhte,

the beginning of the preface states.

Orm is a Scandinavian name (ON *ormr* 'serpent', OE *wyrm*) which was **fairly**
common in the North of England.

A 'dedication' of 342 verses, which precedes the body of the work, furnishes
us with some indirect information:

Nu, broþerr Wallterr, broþerr min
  Affterr þe flæshess kinde;
Annd broþerr min i Crisstenndom
  Þurrh fulluhht annd þurrh trowwþe
Annd broþerr min i Godess hus,   5
  ȝet o þe þridde wise,
Þurrh þatt witt hafenn tåkenn ba
  An reȝhellboc to follȝhenn,
Unnderr kanunnkess had annd lif,
  Swa-summ Sannt Awwsten sette;   10

from which we gather that the author was a canon in an Augustinian monastery
It was on the advice of his brother Walter that Orm composed his book:

> Icc hafe don swa-summ þu badd
> Annd forþedd te þin wille,
> Icc hafe wennd inntill Ennglissh
> Goddspelless hallȝhe láre,
> 15   Affterr þatt little witt þatt me
> Min Drihhtin hafeþþ lenedd.

A little later on Orm defines his objective:

> Icc hafe sammnedd o þiss boc
> 30   Þa goddspelless neh alle,
> Þatt sinndenn o þe messeboc
> Inn all þe ȝer att messe
> Annd aȝȝ affterr þe goddspell stannt
> Þatt tatt te goddspell meneþþ,
> 35   Þatt mann birrþ spellenn to þe follc
> Off þeȝȝre sawle nede.

This unfinished work, of which fragments survive totalling some 20,000 lines
was thus a sort of allegorical life of Christ following through each gospel fo
the day of the liturgical year in the Missal, put in chronological order an
accompanied by long commentaries, founded on a 'glossed or explained Bible
of the time and on a profound acquaintance with the exegetical literature o
his age.

The author excuses himself for having added to the text of the Gospel, whicl
he was obliged to do because of the meter he had chosen, and in order to be mor
complete and more explicit:

> 41   Icc hafe sett her o þiss boc
> Amang goddspelless wordess
> All þurrh mesellfenn, maniȝ word
> Þe ríme swa to fillenn;

but he thinks that, according to the rules of rhetoric of his time, greater clarit
will thus result. He is applying in this the rhetorical doctrine of "amplification
which all contemporary handbooks on the art of poetry recommend. (cp. Ed
FARAL, *Arts poétiques du XIIe et du XIIIe siècle*, pp. 61 f.)

> 45   Acc þu shallt findenn þatt min word,
> Eȝȝwhær þær itt iss ekedd,
> Maȝȝ hellpenn þa þatt redenn itt
> To sen annd t'unnderrstandenn
> All þess te bettre, hu þeȝȝm birrþ
> 50   Þe goddspell unnderrstanndenn . . .
> 55   Forr wha-se mot to læwedd follc
> Larspell off goddspell tellenn
> He mot wel ekenn maniȝ word
> Amang goddspelless wordess.

Orm was hardly a great artist, and his verse certainly has the monotony he wished for. He sought to edify, not to distract his reader; but there is one quality that cannot be denied him, namely, clarity.

The real interest aroused by *The Ormulum* comes from the system of spelling invented by the author and methodically used by him throughout this book, which we are fortunate to have a holograph manuscript of. For this reason *The Ormulum* is precious for the linguist. Orm attached the greatest importance to this orthographic system. This is demonstrated by the recommendations to eventual copyists that he put in his ' dedication ' :

> Annd wha-se wilenn shall þiss boc   95
> Eftt oþerr siþe writenn,
>
> Himm bidde icc þat he't write rihht,
>   Swa-summ þiss boc himm tæcheþþ
>
> All þwerrt-út affterr þatt itt iss
>   Uppo þiss firrste bisne,   100
> Wiþþ all swille ríme alls her iss sett,
>   Wiþþ all þe fele wordess;
> Annd tatt he loke wel þatt he
>   An bocstaff write twi33ess,
> E33whær þær itt uppo þiss boc   105
>   Iss writenn o þatt wise.
>
> Loke he wel þatt he't write swa,
>   Forr he ne ma33 nohht elless
> Onn Ennglissh writenn rihht te word,
>   Þatt wite he wel to soþe.   110

The following extracts will give an idea of the way Orm tells the gospel story and then explains it.

Edition:

The Ormulum, with Notes and Glossary of Dr. R. M. White, edited by Rev. Robert HOLT, Oxford, 1878, 2 vol. [a mediocre edition completed by the following].

Sigurd HOLM. *Corrections and Additions in the Ormulum Manuscript*, Upsal, 1922.

Consult also:

H. Ch. MATTHES. *Die Einheitlichkeit des Orrmulum*. Heidelberg, 1933.

H. H. GLUNZ. *Die Literarästhetik des europäischen Mittelalters*. Bochum-Langendreer, 1937 [especially pp. 311 ff. anl pp. 576 ff.].

R. M. WILSON. *Early Middle English Literature*, pp. 173-8.

J. E. WELLS. *Manual*, pp. 282-3 (bibliography, p. 804).

1. THE NARRATOR

Annunciation to the Shepherds

An enngell comm off heffness ærd,
    Inn aness weress hewe,
Till hirdess þær þær þeȝȝ þatt nihht
    Biwokenn þeȝȝre faldess.
3340   Þatt enngell com⟨m⟩ annd stod hemm bi
    Wiþþ heffness lihht annd leme.
Annd forrþrihht summ þeȝȝ sæȝhenn himm
    Þeȝȝ wurrdenn swiþe offdredde;
Annd Godess enngell hemm bigann
3345   To frofrenn annd to beldenn,
Annd seȝȝde hemm þuss o Godess hallf
    Wiþþ swiþe milde spæche:
' Ne be ȝe nohht forrdredde off me,
    Acc be ȝe swiþe bliþe,
3350   Forr icc amm sennd off heffness ærd
    To kiþenn Godess wille,
To kiþenn ȝuw þatt all follc iss
    Nu cumenn mikell blisse,
Forr ȝuw iss borenn nu to-daȝȝ
3355   Hælennde off ȝure sinness,
An wennchell þatt iss Jesu Crist;
    Þatt wĭte ȝe to soþe.
Annd her onnfasst he borenn iss
    I Daviþþ kingess chesstre,
3360   Þatt iss ȝe-hatenn Beþþleæm
    I þiss Judisskenn birde.
Annd her icc wile shæwenn ȝuw
    Summ þing to witerr tákenn:

Luc II. (8) Et pastores erant in regione eadem vigilantes, et custodientes vigilias noctis super gregem suum. (9) Et ecce angelus Domini stetit iuxta illos et claritas Dei circumfulsit illos, et timuerunt timore magno. (10) Et dixit illis angelus: Nolite timere; ecce enim evangelizo vobis gaudium magnum, quod erit omni populo: (11) Quia natus est vobis hodie

ȝe shulenn findenn ænne child
    I winndeclutess wundenn, 3365
Annd itt iss inn a cribbe leȝȝd,
    Annd tær ȝé't muȝhenn findenn.'
Annd sone anan se þiss wass seȝȝd
    Þurrh an off Godess enngless,
A mikell here off enngleþed 3370
    Wass cumenn üt off heffne,
Annd all þatt hirdeflocc hemm sahh
    Annd herrde whatt teȝȝ sungenn.
Þeȝȝ alle sungenn ænne sang
    Drihhtin to lofe annd wurrþe, 3375
Annd tuss þeȝȝ sungenn alle i-mæn,
    Swa-summ þe goddspell kiþeþþ:
' Si Drihhtin upp inn heffness ærd
    Wurrþminnt annd loff annd wullderr,
Annd upponn erþe griþþ annd friþþ, 3380
    Þurrh Godess mildherrtnesse,
Till i-whillc mann þatt habbenn shall
    God herrte annd aȝȝ god wille.'

Salvator, quis est Christus Dominus in civitate David. (12) Et hoc vobis signum: invenietis infantem pannis involutum, et positum in praesepio. (13) Et subito facta est cum angelo multitudo militiae caelestis laudantium Deum et dicentes: (14) Gloria in altissimis Deo et in terra pax hominibus bonae voluntatis.

2. THE EXEGETE

Why Jesus was Born in Bethlehem

Annd tatt te Laferrd Jesu Crist
    Wass borenn her to manne
Þatt time þatt hiss moderr wass 3610
    I þewwdom unnderr laferrd,
Þatt dide he forr to shæwenn swa
    Unnseȝȝenndliȝ mecnesse,

To tæchenn þurrh himmsellfenn swa

3615   Annd þurrh hiss hallȝhe bisne

Þatt ȝuw birrþ berenn bliþeliȝ

  Þewwdom off ȝure Laferrd;

Annd ec forr þatt he wollde swa

  Þurrh hiss þewwdom ūtlesenn

3620 Off defless þewwdom alle þa

  Þatt wel himm sholldenn follȝhenn.

Annd tatt te laffdiȝ Marȝe warrþ

  I Nazaræþ wiþþ childe,

Annd tatt ȝho comm off Galilew

3625   Till Beþþleæmess chesstre

Þatt time þatt ȝho Jesu Crist

  To manne shollde childenn,

Þatt iss nu filledd illke daȝȝ

  Þurrh Jesu Cristess þewwes.

3630 Forr Nazaræþ onn Ennglissh iss

  Alls iff þu nemmne 'blosstme',

Annd Galilew bitacneþþ 'whel',

  Swa-summ soþ boc uss kiþeþþ,

Annd Beþþleæm tacneþþ 'þatt hus

3635   Þatt lifess bræd iss inne',

Annd Godess þewwess blomenn aȝȝ

  Inn alle gode þæwess,

Her i þiss middellærdess lif

  Þatt þurrh þe whel iss tacnedd.

3640 Forr all þiss middellærdess þing

  Aȝȝ turrneþþ her annd wharrfeþþ

Nu upp, nu dun, swa-summ þe whel,

  Annd nohht ne stannt itt stille.

Annd Cristess þewwess aȝȝ occ aȝȝ

3645   Forrhoȝhenn annd forrwerrpenn

All werelldshipess fule lusst

  Annd alle fule þæwess,

Annd cumenn ūt off Galilew

  Gastlike o swillke wise,

PLATE II

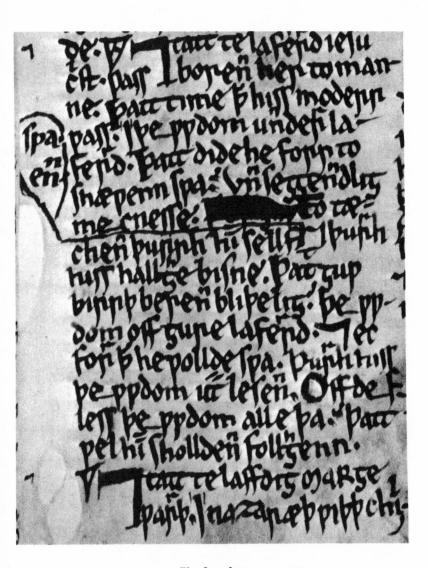

The Ormulum

Ms. Junius I, col. 89 (ll. 3608-3623)

Annd cumenn inntill Beþþleæm,   3650
    Þatt tacneþþ Cristess kirrke
Þatt Cristess flæsh annd Cristess blod
    Þe sawle bræd iss inne.
Annd Jesu Crist iss borenn þær
    Swa-summ itt wære off moderr,   3655
Þurrh þatt tatt hise þewwess þær
    Wiþþ spell off Godess lare
Don læwedd follc to sen summ del
    Annd don hemm t'unnderrstanndenn
Þatt Crist iss Godd, annd Crist iss mann,   3660
    An had off twinne kinde.

PART TWO

THE THIRTEENTH CENTURY

VIII

KING HORN

This poem is the oldest known specimen of the romances in English. It is based, possibly, on an old British tradition going back to the time when the Celts were trying to contain the westward advance of the invading Saxons. Later the same theme was used to express the same feelings the English felt when faced with the Scandinavian Viking penetrations. Finally, in its present form, it was attached to the popular literary current which marked the renaissance of the English spirit after the Norman Conquest.

It is the story of Prince Horn, son of Murry, King of Suddenne (?), who, abandoned to the waves with his companions by conquering Saracens, arrives at the country of Westernesse, where Rymenhild, the daughter of King Aylmar, falls in love with him. The lovers are discovered, Horn is banished and takes refuge in Ireland. There, faithful to Rymenhild, he refuses the hand of the local princess. Warned by Rymenhild, he returns just in time to prevent her marriage with Modi, King of Rennes. Horn kills his rival Modi, marries Rymenhild then and there, but leaves her again at once to recover Suddenne from the Saracens. This accomplished he returns to Westernesse again just in time to save Rymenhild once more, this time from a deceitful follower (Fikenhild). He sets Arnoldin on the deceased Aylmar's throne in Westernesse, Aþelbrus on Modi's throne in Rennes; returns to Ireland and marries off his closest companion Athulf to the local princess and then at last takes Rymenhild to Suddenne where they live happily ever after.

In the form we now have it the poem was perhaps designed to be recited to a popular audience. The style is characterized by a poverty of diction, a lack of any attempt at elegance and a lack of description of any kind. But the onward sweep of the story, direct, vigorous and concise, never slows down. The author is concerned with incidents, combat and adventure, much more than with love; there are still no courtly elements in the poem.

It is composed in a meter that marks the transition, still rather uncertain, between the former alliterative verse and the rimed verse developed under French influence. The isosyllabism is not yet regular.

This story was very popular in the Middle Ages. Besides the present poem, it gave rise to *Horn Child and Maiden Rimnild*, an English poem of the 14th century, to the Scots ballad *Hind Horn* (no. 17 in F. J. CHILD's collection), and to the 12th century Anglo-Norman *Horn et Rimel* as well as to Scandinavian and German versions.

170

The following extract comes at the moment when Rymenhild, King Aylmar of Westernesse's agressive daughter, has just declared her love to Horn and offered to marry him. Protesting that he is unworthy of such an honor because of his supposedly base birth, Horn refuses and Rymenhild swoons. Touched by her distress, Horn proposes that King Aylmar dub Horn knight; thus he will be in a proper position to carry out her wishes.

Editions:

Das Lied von King Horn, kritisch herausgegeben von Th. WISSMANN, Strassburg, 1881 (*Quellen und Forschungen*, 45).

King Horn, A Middle English Romance, ed. by Joseph HALL, Oxford, 1901.

Consult also:

W. H. FRENCH. *Essays on King Horn*, Ithaca, 1940 (*Cornell Studies in English* No. 30).

R. M. WILSON. *Early Middle English Literature*, pp. 218-21.

J. E. WELLS. *Manual*, pp. 8-10 (bibliography, pp. 762-3).

Rymenhild, þat swete þing,
Wakede of hire swoȝning.
'Horn,' quaþ heo, 'wel sone   445
Þat schal beon i-done:
Þu schalt beo dubbed kniȝt,
Are come seve niȝt.
Have her þis cuppe
And þis ring þer-uppe   450
To Aylbrus þe stuard,
And se he holde foreward:
Seie, ihc him biseche
Wiþ loveliche speche,
Þat he adun falle   455
Bifore þe king in halle,
And bidde þe king ariȝte
Dubbe þe to kniȝte.
Wiþ selver and wiþ golde

445 wel] uel *MS.* — 451 þe *L*] & *C.*

460 Hit wurþ him wel i-ʒolde.
Crist him lene spede
Þin erende to bede.'
    Horn tok his leve;
For hit was neʒ eve.

465 Aþelbrus he soʒte
And ʒaf him þat he broʒte;
And tolde him ful ʒare,
Hu he hadde i-fare;
And sede him his nede
470 And bihet him his mede.
    Aþelbrus also swiþe
Wente to halle blive
' Kyng,' he sede, ' þu leste
A tale mid þe beste;
475 Þu schalt bere crune
To-moreʒe in þis tune;
To-moreʒe is þi feste:
Þer bihoveþ geste.
Hit nere noʒt forloren
480 For to kniʒti Child Horn,
Þine armes for to welde,
God kniʒt he schal ʒelde.'
    Þe king sede sone:
' Þat is wel i-done.
485 Horn me wel i-quemeþ,
God kniʒt him bisemeþ.
He schal have mi dubbing
And afterward ⟨be⟩ mi derling.
And alle his feren twelf
490 He schal kniʒten himself:
Alle he schal hem kniʒte
Bifore me þis niʒte.'
    Til þe liʒt of day sprang,
Ailmar him þuʒte lang.

Þe day bigan to springe, 495
Horn com bivore þe kinge,
Mid his twelf y-fere,
Sume hi were luþere;
Horn he dubbede to kniȝte
Wiþ swerd and spures briȝte; 500
He sette him on a stede whit:
Þer nas no kniȝt hym i-lik.
He smot him a litel wiȝt
And bed him beon a god kniȝt.
Aþulf fel a-knes þar 505
Bivore the king Aylmar.
'King,' he sede, 'so kene
Grante me a bene:
Nu is kniȝ⟨t⟩ sire Horn
Þat in Suddenne was i-boren: 510
Lord he is of londe
Over us þat bi him stonde;
Þin armes he haþ and scheld
To fiȝte wiþ upon þe feld:
Let him us alle kniȝte, 515
For þat is ure riȝte.'
Aylmar sede sone y-wis:
'Do nu þat þi wille is.'
Horn adun liȝte
And makede hem alle kniȝtes. 520
Murie was þe feste
Al of faire gestes:
Ac Rymenhild nas noȝt þer
And þat hire þuȝte seve ȝer.
After Horn heo sente 525
And he to bure wente,
Nolde he noȝt go one,
Aþulf was his mone.
Rymenhild on flore stod,

530   (Hornes come hire þuȝte god)
     And sede: 'Welcome, sire Horn
     And Aþulf kniȝt þe biforn.
     Kniȝt, nu is þi time
     For to sitte bi me;
535   Do nu þat þu er of spake:
     To þi wif þu me take!
     Ef þu art trewe of dedes,
     Do nu ase þu sedes!
     Nu þu hast wille þine,
540   Unbind me of my pine.'
      'Rymenhild', quaþ he, 'beo stille:
     Ihc wulle don al þi wille.
     Also hit mot bitide
     Mid spere I schal furst ride,
545   And mi kniȝthod prove,
     Ar ihc þe ginne to woȝe.
     We beþ kniȝtes ȝonge
     Of o dai al i-sprunge,
     And of ure mestere
550   So is þe manere,
     Wiþ sume oþere kniȝte
     Wel for his lemman fiȝte,
     Or he eni wif take:
     For-þi me stondeþ þe more rape.
555   To-day, so Crist me blesse,
     Ihc wulle do pruesse,
     For þi luve, in þe felde
     Mid spere and mid schelde.
     If ihc come to lyve
560   Ihc schal þe take to wyve.'
      'Kniȝt', quaþ heo, 'trewe,
     Ihc wene, ihc mai þe leve:

Tak nu her þis gold-ring,
God him is þe dubbing;
Þer is upon þe ringe   565
I-grave Rymenhild þe ȝynge:
Þer nis non betere anonder sunne,
Þat eni man of telle cunne;
For my luve þu hit were
And on þi finger þu hit bere: 570
Þe stones beoþ of suche grace,
Þat þu ne schalt in none place
Of none duntes beon ofdrad,
Ne on bataille beon amad,
Ef þu loke þeran   575
And þenke upon þi lemman.
And sire Aþulf, þi broþer,
He schal have anoþer.
Crist, ihc þe biteche,
Wiþ loveliche speche,   580
Crist ȝeve god erndinge
Þe aȝen to bringe.'
     Þe kniȝt hire gan kesse,
And heo him to blesse,
Leve at hire he nam,   585
And into halle cam.

566 ȝynge *L*] ȝonge *C.* — 570 hit *L*] him *C.* — 579 Crist *L*] Horn *C*; biteche *L*] biseche *C.*

IX

KENTISH SERMONS

Laud MS 471 in the Bodleian Library at Oxford preserves the text of five sermons, in the Kentish dialect, which date from about 1250. They are not original sermons. They are translated from French versions of Latin homilies for Sundays and Feast Days written by Maurice de Sully, who was Bishop of Paris from 1160 to 1196.

For us the sole interest in these sermons, the fourth of which is printed here, rests in the dialectal forms which they contain and in the appearance of French loans.

Editions:

Richard MORRIS. *An Old English Miscellany*, London, 1872 (*EETS OS* 49), p. 26 and f.

Joseph HALL. *Selections from Early Middle English*, Oxford, 1920.

Bibliography:

J. HALL, above, pp. 657-8.
J. E. WELLS, *Manual* p. 1114.

Jesus Calms the Storm

Ascendente Iesu in naviculam, secuti sunt eum discipuli eius. Et ecce motus factus est magnus in mari, ita ut navicula operiretur fluctibus. Erat, autem illis ventus contrarius.

We redeth i þe holi godspelle of to-dai, þat ure lord Jhesu
Crist yede one time into ane ssipe and ⟨h⟩ise deciples mid
him into þe séé. And so hi were in þo ssipe, so aros a great
tempeste of winde. And ure lord was i-leid him don to slepe
5 ine þo ssipe, er þane þis tempeste aróós. Hise deciples hedde
gret drede of þise tempeste: so awakede hine and seiden to
him: 'Lord, save us, for we perisset.' And ha wiste wel
þet hi ne hadde nocht gode beleave ine him. Þo seide to
hem: 'Wat dret yw, folk of litle beliave?' Þo aros up ure
10 lord and tok þane wynd and to séé, and also raþe hit was
stille. And alse þo men, þet weren in þo ssipe, hedde i-seghe
þo miracle, so awondrede hem michel.
Þis is si vaire miracle, þet þet godspel of te-day us telþ.

Nos *lisons* en saint evangile d'ui ke N. S. Dex entra une fiez en une nef et si disciple le sivirent. Et si cum il furent en la mier, si leva un grant torment et Nostre Sire se esteit cochiez dormir en la nief, devant ceo ke li tormenz comencast. Et si disciple eurent grant pour del torment: si esveillerent et si li distrent: 'Sire, sauve nos *kar* nos perisons'. Et il estoit chose de ce k'il n'avoent *bone fiance* en lui. Et il lor dist: 'Que cremez vus, gent de petite fei?' Si leva sus, si chosa delivrement les venz et la mer sempres se furent appeisie. Et cum li hom qui erent en la *nef* eurent veu le miracle, si s'esmerveillerent mout.
Ceo est li *beaus* miracles ke l'evangille d'ui nus reconte. Si en duit estre

Þerefore sal ure beliaye bie þe betere astrengþed ine swiche
lorde þet siche miracle mai do and doþ, wanne he wile.   Ac 15
hit is us nyede þet se þet sucurede hem ine þa peril, þet us
sucuri ine ure niedes, þet we clepie to him, þet ha us helpe;
and he hit wille do bleþeliche, yef we him bisecheth merci
mid good i-wille, also himselven seith bi þe holi writes: *Salus
populi ego sum et caetera.*   'Hic am,' ha seiþ, 'helere of þe 20
folke; wanne hi to me clepieþ ine hire sorghen and ine hire
niedes, hic hi sucuri and beheme hem al here evel withute
ende.'   Grede we to him merci sikerliche, yef se devel us
wille acumbri þurch senne, þurch prede oþer þurch anvie
oþer þurch wreþe oþer þurch oþer manere of diadliche senne, 25
grede we to him merci and sigge we him: 'Lord, saúve us
þet we ne perissi', and þet he us delivri of alle eveles and
þet ha yef us swiche werkes to done in þise wordle, þet þo
saulen of us mote bien i-sauved a domesdai and gon to þo
blisce of hevene.   *Quod ipse praestare dignetur.*   30

affermé nostre creance. Car bien deit l'en creire en celui seignor qui tel
miracle pot fere et fet quant il veut. Or nus besoigne que cil qui securut
ses desciples en icel peril, qu'il nus sucurre en noz perilz; et il le fra
volontiers se nus l'en crion merci par bone volentié, si cum il meisme dist
par la sainte escripture: 'Je sui ', fet-il 'la salvetié del pople quant il
m'apeleront en lor besoigne et en lur angoises, jo les orroi et serrai lur
Deu pardurables '. Prion lui donc merci seurement se diable nus vout
enconbrer par peché, par orgoil et par envie o per ire ... crions li merci
et si li disons: 'Sire, salvez nos ke nus ne perisons '...et que il nus
delivre de tuz malz et qu'il nus doinst tot bien et nus dont tels ovres a
faere en cest siecle que les almes et les cors ⟨de nus⟩ poisent estre
sauvié al jor del joise.

X

THE FOX AND THE WOLF

Reynard the Fox, printed by Caxton in 1481, Chaucer's *Nun's Priest's Tale*
and this 'beast-tale' are the only remaining evidence, in the popular language,
that the extensive *Roman de Renart* was translated and re-worked in English.

Fables in Latin verse by Odo of Cheriton about 1220 (cp. HERVIEUX, *Les fabulistes Latins*, Vol. IV, Paris, 1896) furnish other proof, however, that the beast epic and *fabliaux* concerned with Renart and Ysengrin were then popular in England.

There is some confusion about terminology when dealing with these stories. *Fable* is the familiar short moral tale involving animal actors, as in *Æsop's Fables*. A *fabliau*, on the other hand, is a not quite so short humorous tale in verse dealing with the lower classes and sometimes so realistic as to be obscene; the *Roman de Renart* uses animals to represent people and its episodes are sometimes *fabliaux* (as are *Dame Siriz*, *The Miller's Tale* and *The Reeve's Tale*). This particular short story involving animals, though it hints at indecency, does not emphasize it, nor is that the prime purpose of the teller. This, and Chaucer's *Nun's Priest's Tale*, have been called 'beast-epics' to distinguish them from the *fabliaux*.

This adventure of 'Ysengrin in the Well' is evidently based on a French original; it comes very close to the version preserved in branch IV of the French *Roman de Renart*, which is printed for convenience below the English text. It will be noticed, in comparing the two, that the English author has treated the subject with independence and a certain originality. The story is told by him with a good deal of gusto and vigor.

Editions:

Middle English Humorous Tales in Verse, ed. by G. McKNIGHT, Boston and London, 1913 [with a good introduction and bibliography].
Le Roman de Renart publié par E. MARTIN, Strasbourg et Paris, 1882 [French text].

Consult also:

R. M. WILSON. *Early Middle English Literature*, pp. 246 and f.
J. E. WELLS. *Manual*, pp. 183 and f. (bibliography, p. 791).
L. SUDRE. *Les sources du roman de Renard*, Paris, 1893.
L. FOULET. *Le roman de Renard*, Paris, 1914 [in particular ch. XIV].

70   On aventure his wiit him brohute
           To one putte wes water inne,
           Þat wes i-maked mid grete ginne.
           Tuo boketes þer he founde,
           Þat oþer wende to þe grounde,

R. DE RENART, IV:

    Or a Renart le puis trouvé:
150 Moult par le vit parfont et lé.

Seigneurs, or escoutez merveilles!
En ce puis si avoit deus seilles:
Quant l'une vient, et l'autre vait.
Et Renars qui tant a mal fait,

Þat wen me shulde þat on opwinde,   75
Þat oþer wolde adoun winde.
He ne hounderstod nout of þe ginne,
He nom þat boket and lep þerinne;
For he hopede i-nou to drinke.
Þis boket beginneþ to sinke.   80
To late þe vox wes biþout,
Þo he wes in þe ginne i-brout:
I-nou he gon him biþenche,
Ac hit ne halp mid none wrenche;
Adoun he moste, he wes þerinne;   85
I-kaut he wes mid swikele ginne.
Hit miȝte han i-ben wel his wille
To lete þat boket hongi stille:
Wat mid serewe and mid drede
Al his þurst him overhede.   90
Al þus he com to þe grounde,
And water i-nou þer he founde.
Þo he fond water, ȝerne he dronk,
Him þoute þat water þere stonk,
For hit wes toȝeines his wille: 95
'Wo worþe,' quaþ þe vox, 'lust and wille
Þat ne can meþ to his mete!

---

155 Dessur le puis s'est acoutez
Grainz et marris et trespensez.
Dedens commence a regarder
Et son ombre a aboeter:
Cuida que ce fust Hermeline
160 Sa famme qu'aime d'amor fine,
Qui herbergie fust leens.
Renars fu pensis et dolens:
Il li demande par vertu:
'Di moi, la-dedens, que fais-tu?'
165 La vois du puis vint contremont:
Renars l'oï, drece le front.
Il la rapelle une autre fois:
Contremont resorti la vois.

Renars l'oï, moult se merveille:
Si met ses piez en une seille,   170
Onc n'en sot mot, quant il avale.
Ja i aura encontre male.
Quant il fu en l'eve cheüs,
Si sot bien qu'il fu deceüs.
     Or est Renart en male frape, 175
Maufez l'ont mis en celle trape.
Acoutez s'est a une pierre,
Bien vousist estre mors en biere,
Li chaitis sueffre grant hachiee:
Moult a souvent la pel moilliee. 180
Or est a aise de peschier.
Nulz nel pourroit esleeschier;

Ʒef ich nevede to muchel i-ete,

Þis ilke shome neddi nouþe,

100   Nedde lust i-ben of mine mouþe.

Him is wo in euche londe,

Þat is þef mid his honde.

Ich am i-kaut mid swikele ginne,

Oþer soum devel me broute herinne;

105   I was woned to ben wiis,

Ac nou of me i-don hit ḥiis!

     Þe vox wep and reuliche bigan;

Þer com a wolf gon after þan

Out of þe depe wode blive,

110   For he wes afingret swiþe.

Noþing he ne found in al þe niʒte

Wer-mide his honger aquenche miʒtte.

He com to þe putte, þene vox i-herde;

He him kneu wel bi his rerde,

115   For hit wes his neiʒebore

Ne prise deus boutons son sens.
  Seigneurs, il avint en cel tens,
185 En celle nuit et en celle heure,
Que Ysengrins tout sanz demeure
S'en est issus d'une grant lande,
Que querre li couvint viande,
Que la fain le grieve forment.
190 Tournez s'en est ireement
Devant la meson aus rendus,
Les granz galos i est venuz.
Le païs trouva moult gasté.
'Ci conversent,' dit-il, 'malfé,
195 Qant l'en n'i puet trouver viande
Ne rien de ce que on demande.'
Tournez s'en est tout le passet.
Courant s'en vint vers le guichet:
Par devant la rendation
200 S'en est venuz le grant troton.
Le puis trouva enmi sa voie
Ou Renars le rous s'esbanoie.

Dessur le puis s'est aclinez
Grainz et marriz et trespensez.
Dedens conmence a regarder   205
Et son umbre a aboeter.
Con plus i vit, plus esgarda,
Tout ensi con Renars ouvra:
Cuida que fust dame Hersens
Qui herbergiee fust leens   210
Et que Renars fust avec li.
Sachiez pas ne li embeli,
Et dist moult par sui maubailliz,
De ma fame vilz et honniz
Que Renars li rous m'a fortraite 215
Et ceens avec soi a traite.
Moult est ore traître lere.
Quant il decoit si sa conmere.
Si ne me puis de lui garder.
Mes se jel pooie atraper,   220
Si faitement m'en vengeroie.
Que james crieme n'en auroie.

And his gossip, of children bore.
Adoun bi þe putte he sat.
Quod þe wolf: 'Wat may ben þat,
Þat ich in þe putte i-here?
Hertou Cristine oþer mi fere?   120
Say me soþ, ne gabbe þou me nout,
Wo haveþ þe in þe putte i-brout?'
Þe vox hine i-kneu wel for his kun,
And þo eroust kom wiit to him;
For he þoute mid soumme ginne   125
Himself houp bringe, þene wolf þerinne.
Quod þe vox: 'Wo is nou þere?
Ich wene hit is Sigrim þat ich here.'
'Þat is soþ,' þe wolf sede,
'Ac wat art þou, so God þe rede?'   130
     'A,' quod þe vox, 'ich wille þe telle,
On alpi word ich lie nelle:
Ich am Reneuard, þi frend,
And ȝif ich þine come hevede i-wend,

Puis a uslé par grant vertu:
A son umbre dist: 'Qui es-tu?
225 Pute orde vilz, pute prouvee,
Qant o Renart t'ai ci trovee!'
Si a ullé une autre foiz,
Contremont resorti la voiz.
     Que qu'Isengrins se dementoit
230 Et Renars trestoz coiz estoit,
Et le laissa assez usler,
Puis si le prist a apeler.
'Qui est-ce, Diex, qui m'aparole?
Ja tiens ge ca dedenz m'escole'.
235 'Qui es-tu, va?' dist Ysengrin.
'Ja sui-je vostre bon voisin
Qui fui jadiz vostre compere,
Plus m'amiez que vostre frere.
Mais l'en m'apelle feu Renart
240 Qui tant savoit d'engin et d'art.'
Dist Ysengrins: 'C'est mes confors:

Des quant es-tu, Renart, donc mors?'
Et il li respont: 'Des l'autrier.
Nulz hons ne s'en doit merveiller,
Se je suis mors: aussi mourront 245
Tretuit cil qui en vie sont.
Parmi la mort les convendra
Passer au jor que Diex plaira.
Or atent m'ame nostre sire
Qui m'a geté de cest martire.   250
Je vos pri, biau compere dous,
Que me pardonnez les courrous
Que l'autrier eüstes vers moi.'
Dist Ysengrins: 'Et je l'otroi.
Or vous soient tout pardoné,   255
Compere, ci et devant Dé.
Mes de vostre mort sui dolens.'
Dist Renars: 'Et j'en suis joians.'
'Joians en es?' 'Voire, par foi.'
'Biau compere, di-moi pourquoi?' 260

135   Ich hedde so i-bede for þe,
     Þat þou sholdest comen to me.'
     'Mid þe?' quod þe wolf, 'war-to?
     Wat shulde ich ine þe putte do?'
     Quod þe vox: 'Þou art ounwiis,
140   Her is þe blisse of paradiis;
     Her ich mai evere wel fare
     Wiþouten pine, wiþouten kare:
     Her is mete, her is drinke,
     Her is blisse wiþouten swinke;
145   Her nis hounger never mo
     Ne non oþer kunnes wo;
     Of alle gode her is i-nou.'
     Mid þilke wordes þe wolf lou.
      'Art þou ded, so God þe rede,
150   Oþer of þe worlde?' þe wolf sede.
     Quod þe wolf: 'Wenne storve þou,
     And wat dest þou þere nou?
     Ne beþ nout ȝet þre daies ago,
     Þat þou and þi wif also
155   And þine children, smale and grete,
     Alle togedere mid me hete.'
     'Þat is soþ,' quod þe vox,
     'Gode þonk, nou hit is þus,
     Þat ⟨seþ⟩ ihc am to Criste wend,
160   Not hit non of mine frend.
     I nolde, for al þe worldes goed,

148 wolf] volf *MS.* — 159 wend] vend *MS.*

'Que li miens corps gist en la biere
Chiez Hermeline en la tesniere,
Et m'ame est en paradis mise,
Devant les piez Jhesu assise:
265 Comperes j'ai quanque je veil.
Je n'oi onques cure d'orgueil.
Se tu es ou regne terrestre,

Je sui en paradis celestre.
Ceens sont les gaaigneries,
Les bois, les plains, les praieries: 270
Ceens a riche pecunaille,
Ceens puez veoir mainte aumaille
Et mainte oeille et mainte chievre,
Ceens puez-tu veoir maint lievre

Ben ine þe worlde, þer ich hem fond.

Wat schuld ich ine þe worlde go,

Þer nis bote kare and wo,

And livie in fulþe and in sunne? 165

Ac her beþ joies fele cunne:

Her beþ boþe shep and get.'

Þe wolf haveþ hounger swiþe gret,

For he nedde ʒare i-ete;

And þo he herde speken of mete, 170

He wolde bleþeliche ben þare:

'A,' quod þe wolf, 'gode i-fere,

Moni goed mel þou havest me binome;

Let me adoun to þe kome,

And al ich wole þe forʒeve.' 175

'ʒe,' quod þe vox, 'were þou i-srive

And sunnen hevedest al forsake

And to klene lif i-take,

Ich wolde so bidde for þe,

Þat þou sholdest comen to me.' 180

'To wom shuld ich,' þe wolf seide,

'Ben i-knowe of mine misdede?

Her nis noþing alive

---

275 Et bues et vaches et moutons,
Espreviers, ostors et faucons.'
Ysengrins jure saint Sevestre
Que il voudroit la-dedens estre.
Dist Renars: 'Lessiez ce ester,
280 Ceens ne poez vous entrer:
Paradis est celestiaus,
Mais n'est mie a touz conmunaus.
Moult as esté touz jors trichierres,
Fel et traïtres et boisierres.
285 De ta famme m'as mescreü:
Par Dieu et par sa grant vertu,
Onc ne li fis desconvenue,
N'onques par moi ne fu foutue.

Tu dis que tes filz avoutrai,
Onques certes nel me pensai. 290
Par cel seigneur qui me fist né,
Or t'en ai dit la verité.'
Dist Ysengrins: 'Je vous en croi,
Jel vos pardoing en bonne foi.
Mais faites-moi leens entrer.' 295
Ce dist Renars: 'Lessiez ester.
N'avons cure ceens de noise,
La poez veoir celle poise.'
Seigneur, or escoutez merveille!
A son doi li moustre la seille. 300
Renars set bien son sens espandre:
Que pour voir li a fet estendre,

Þat me kouþe her nou srive.

185 Þou havest ben ofte min i-fere,
Woltou nou mi srift i-here,
And al mi liif I shal þe telle?'
'Nay,' quod þe vox, 'I nelle.'
'Neltou?' quod þe wolf, 'þin ore,

190 Ich am afingret swiþe sore;
Ich wot to-niȝt ich worþe ded,
Bote þou do me so*ume* reed.
For Cristes love, be mi prest.'
Þe wolf bey adoun his brest

195 And gon to siken harde and stronge.
'Woltou,' quod þe vox, 'srift ounderfonge,
Tel þine sunnen on and on,
Þat þer bileve never on.'
      'Sone,' quod þe wolf, 'wel i-fa*ie*.

200 Ich habbe ben qued al mi lifdaie;
Ich habbe widewene kors,
Þerfore ich fare þe wors.
A þousent shep ich habbe abiten
And mo, ȝef hy weren i-writen.

205 Ac hit me ofþinkeþ sore.
Maister, shal I tellen more?'
'Ȝe,' quod þe vox, 'al þou most sugge,
Oþer elleswer þou most abugge':
'Gossip,' quod þe wolf, 'forȝef hit me,

210 Ich habbe ofte sehid qued bi þe.
Men seide þat þou on þine live
Misferdest mid mine wive;
Ich þe aperseivede one stounde

192 soume] somne *MS.* — 199 i-faie] I fare *MS.*

Poises sont de bien et de mal.
'Par Dieu le pere esperital,
305 Diex si par est ainsi poissanz,
Que quant li biens est si pesanz,
Si s'en devale ca de jus,
Et touz li maus remaint lassus,

And in bedde togedere ou founde.
Ich wes ofte ou ful ney   215
And in bedde togedere ou sey;
Ich wende, al-so oþre doþ,
Þat ich i-seie were soþ,
And þerfore þou were me loþ;
Gode gossip, ne be þou nohut wroþ.'   220
'Wolf,' quod þe vox him þo,
'Al þat þou havest herbifore i-do,
In þohut, in speche and in dede,
In euche oþeres kunnes quede,
Ich þe forȝeve at þisse nede.'   225
'Crist þe forȝelde!' þe wolf seide.
'Nou ich am in clene live,
Ne recche ich of childe ne of wive.
Ac sei me wat I shal do,
And ou ich may comen þe to.'   230
'Do?' quod þe vox, 'ich will þe lere,
I-siist þou a boket hongi þere?
Þer is a bruche of hevene blisse,

216 sey] ley *MS.* — 221 wolf] vuolf *MS.*

Mais hons, s'il n'a confesse prise,   Son cul tourna vers orient   325
Ne pourroit ja en nule guise   Et sa teste vers occident,
Ci avaler, je le te di.   Et commenca a orguener
As tu tes peschiez regehi?'   Et tres durement a usler.
'Oïl,' fait-il, 'a un viel levre   Renars qui fait mainte merveille,
Et a dame H⟨aouis⟩ la chievre   Estoit aval en l'autre seille   330
Moult bien et moult tres saintement.   Qui ou puis estoit avalee.
Compere, plus hastivement   Ce fu par pute destinee
Me faites la dedens entrer!'   Que Renars s'est dedens couchiez.
Renars commence a regarder: Par temps iert Ysengrins iriez.
'Or vous estuet dont Dieu proier   Dist Ysengrins: 'J'ai Dieu proié.' 335
Et moult saintement gracier   'Et je,' dist Renars, 'gracié.
Que il vous face vrai pardon   Ysengrin, vois-tu ces merveilles,
De vos pechiez remission;   Que devant moi ardent chandeilles?
Ainsi i pourries entrer.'   Jhesu te fera vrai pardon
Ysengrins n'i volt plus ester;   Et moult gente remission.'   340

Lep þerinne, mid i-wisse,

235 And þou shalt comen to me sone.

Quod þe wolf: 'Þat is liȝt to done.'

He lep in and way sumdel;

Þat weste þe vox ful wel.

Þe wolf gon sinke, þe vox arise;

240 Þo gon þe wolf sore agrise.

Þo he com amidde þe putte,

Þe wolf þene vox opward mette.

'Gossip,' quod þe wolf, 'wat nou?

Wat havest þou i-munt, weder wolt þou?'

245 'Weder ich wille?' þe vox sede,

'Ich wille oup, so God me rede!

And nou go doun wiþ þi meel,

Þi biȝete worþ wel smal.

Ac ich am þerof glad and bliþe,

250 Þat þou art nomen in clene live.

Þi soule-cnul ich wile do ringe

And masse for þine soule singe.'

Þe wrecche bineþe noþing ne vind

Bote cold water, and hounger him bind;

255 To colde gistninge he wes i-bede,

*V*roggen haveþ his dou i-knede.

Þe wolf in þe putte stod,

256 vroggen] wroggen *MS.*

Ysengrins l'ot: adont estrive
Au seel abatre de rive,
Il joint les piez, si sailli ens.
Ysengrins fu li plus pesans,
345 Si s'en avale contreval.
Or escoutez le bautestal!
Ou puis se sont entre encontré,
Ysengrins l'a araisonné:
'Compere, pourquoi t'en viens-tu?'
350 Et Renars li a respondu:
'N'en faites ja chiere ne frume,
Bien vous en dirai la coustume:
Quant li uns va, li autres vient,
C'est la coustume qui avient,
Je vais en paradis la-sus,   355
Et tu vas en enfer la-jus.
Du diable sui eschapez
Et tu t'en revas as maufez.
Moult es en granz viltes cheois
Et j'en sui hors, bien le sachois. 360
Par Dieu le pere esperitable,
La-jus conversent li diable.'

Afingret so þat he *w*es wod;
I-nou he cursede þat þider him broute;
Þe vox þerof luitel route. 260

258 wes] ves *MS.*

Des que Renars vint a la terre,
Moult s'esbaudi de faire guerre.
365 Ysengrins est en male trape;

Se il fust pris devant Halape,
Ne fust-il pas si adoulez,
Que quant ou puis fu avalez.

XI

London dialect – Southern extremity of E

PROCLAMATION OF HENRY III

Midland – ancestor of Mod English

This text is doubly interesting. It is the first example of the official use of the English language since William the Conqueror, and as it is dated (18 October 1258), it presents a good specimen of the speech of the London region in the middle of the 13th century.

Many and many a time Henry III had sworn to observe Magna Carta (1215); he never kept his word. The barons organized themselves, and, led by Simon de Montfort, they forced from the King the Provisions of Oxford, which confirmed Magna Carta and stipulated that three parliaments should meet every year. A proclamation signed by the King, by which he undertook to respect the new reforms, was sent into all the counties of England, and in order to reach everybody, it was issued not only in Latin and French, but also — and this was the innovation — in English. It is to be noted, however, that the English text was undoubtedly only a translation of the French, as can be seen by comparing it with the French version that is printed here for that purpose. Only two copies of the English text survive. The one reproduced was sent into the county of Huntingdon, the other into Oxford.

Consult: *translation of a formal document*

J. E. WELLS. *Manual,* p. 442 (bibliography, p. 836).
H. C. WYLD. *A History of Modern Colloquial English,* 3rd edition, Oxford, 1936, pp. 50-51.

OE hlāf > O

Henri, þurʒ Godes fultume King on Engleneloande, Lhoa-verd on Yrloande, Duk on Normandi, on Aquitaine, and Eorl on Anjow, send i-gretinge to alle hise holde, i-lærde and i-lea-wede on Huntendoneschire. Þæt witen ʒe wel alle þæt we wil-

modE loaf

construe it   *possessions*   *ignorant*

PATENT ROLLS, 42 HENRY III m. I, n. I. — Henri, par le grace Deu, Rey de Engleterre, sire de Irlande, duc de Normandie, de Aquitien, et cunte de Angou, a tuz ses feaus clers et lays saluz.

Sachez ke nus volons et otrions ke se ke nostre conseil, u la greignure

5 len and unnen þæt þæt ure rædesmen, alle oþer þe moare dæl
of heom þæt beoþ i-chosen þur3 us and þur3 þæt loandes folk
on ure kuneriche, habbeþ i-don and schullen don in þe worþ-
nesse of Gode and on ure treowþe, for þe freme of þe loande,
þur3 þe besi3te of þan toforen i-seide redesmen, beo stedefæst
10 and i-lestinde in alle þinge abuten ænde. And we hoaten alle
ure treowe, in þe treowþe þæt heo us o3en, þæt heo stede-
fæstliche healden and swerien to healden and to werien þo
i-setnesses þæt beon i-makede and beon to makien þur3 þan
toforen i-seide rædesmen oþer þur3 þe moare dæl of heom,
15 alswo alse it is biforen i-seid; and þæt æhc oþer helpe þæt
for to done bi þan ilche oþe a3enes alle men, ri3t for to done
and to foangen, and noan ne nime of loande ne of e3te, wher-
þur3 þis besi3te mu3e beon i-let oþer i-wersed on onie wise.
And 3if oni oþer onie cumen her on3enes, we willen and
20 hoaten þæt alle ure treowe heom healden deadliche i-foan,
and for þæt we willen þæt þis beo stedefæst and lestinde, we
senden 3ew þis writ open i-seined wiþ ure seel, to halden
amanges 3ew ine hord.

Witnesse usselven æt Lundene, þane e3tetenþe day on þe
25 monþe of Octobre in þe two and fowerti3þe 3eare of ure
cruninge.

---

partie de eus ki est esluz par nus et par le commun de nostre reaume, a
fet, u fera, al honur de Deu et nostre fei, et pur le profit de notre reaume
sicum il ordenera seit ferm et estable en tuttes choses a tuz jurz; et
comandons et enjoinons a tuz noz feaus et leaus, en la fei k'il nus deivent,
k'il fermement teignent, et jurgent a tenir et a maintenir les establisse-
menz ke sunt fet, u sunt a fere, par l'avant dit cunseil, u la greignure
partie de eus, en la maniere k'il est dit desuz; et k'il s'entre-eident a ce
fere par meismes tel serment cuntre tutte genz dreit fesant et prenant;
et ke nul ne preigne de terre ne de moeble par quei ceste purveaunce
puisse estre disturbee u empiree en nule manere; et se nul u nus viegnent
encuntre ceste chose, nus volons et comandons ke tuz nos ⟨f⟩eaus et
leaus le teignent a enemi mortel; e pur ce ke nus volons ke ceste chose
seit ferme et estable, nos enveons nos lettres overtes seelees de nostre seel
en chescun cunté, a demorer la en tresor.

Tesmoin meimeismes a Londres le disutime jur de Octobre, l'an de
nostre regne quaraunte secund.

And þis wes i-don ætforen ure i-sworene redesmen: Boneface
Archebischop on Kante-buri. Walter of Cantelow, Bischop
on Wirechestre. Simon of Muntfort, Eorl on Leirchestre.
Richard of Clare, Eorl on Glowchestre and on Hurtford. 30
Roger Bigod, Eorl on Northfolke and Marescal on Enȝlene-
loande. Perres of Savveye. Willelm of Fort, Eorl on
Aubemarle. Johan of Plesseiz, Eorl on Warewik. Johan,
Geffrees sune. Perres of Muntfort. Richard of Grey. Roger
of Mortemer. James of Aldithel, and ætforen oþre i-noȝe. 35
And al on þo ilche worden is i-send into ævrihce oþre shcire
over al þære kuneriche on Engleneloande and ek intel
Irelonde.

Et ceste chose fu fete devant:
Boneface arceveske de Cantreburi, Gauter de Cantelou eveske de Wyre-
cestre, Simon de Montfort cunte de Leycestre, Richard de Clare cunte
de Gloucestre et de Hertford, Roger le Bigod cunte de Norfolke, et
mareschal de Engleterre, Humfrey de Bohun cunte de Hereford, Piere
de Saveye, Guilame de Forz cunte de Aubemarle, Johan de Plesseiz cunte
de Warrewyk, Roger de Quency cunte de Wyncestre. Johan le fiz
Geffrey, Piere de Muntfort, Richard de Grey, Roger de Mortemer, James
de Audithel, et Hugue le Despenser.

XII

HAVELOK THE DANE

NE Midland dialect

Just like *King Horn* (which is found in the same manuscript) *Havelok
the Dane* is an unpretentious romance aimed at an audience not concerned
with courtly refinement. It dates about 1270 and must have been composed
in the region of Lincoln and Grimsby. At least the tale is linked with a
legend which makes Grim, the adoptive father of Havelok, the eponymous
hero who founded the town of Grimsby.
The adventures of Havelok were told for the first time by the Anglo-
Norman *trouvère* Geffrei Gaimar in his *Estorie des Engles* composed about
1150; another OF poem of the end of the 12th century, the *Lai of Haveloc* is
entirely devoted to this hero. These versions, as well as the English poem
which concerns us here, go back to an independently used common source; but
between this source and our poem there must have been other English versions
that have been lost. In the 14th and 15th centuries, the legend was retold
by various chroniclers, among others Robert Mannyng of Brunne (cp. no. XIII)
towards 1338, and Caxton ca. 1480. At Grimsby itself the tradition has been
maintained and the town still has a seal on which Grim and Havelok are
represented.

Although the legend of Havelok brings up names of known Scandinavian historicity, it is improbable that it has an historical basis. As so often happens, it is a fabric woven out of elements borrowed from folklore; one element can be found as far back as the legend of Servius Tullius (the flame that appears on the hero's face, or which, as with Havelok, comes out of his mouth), others are common to the Hamlet legend. At some one moment these popular traditions got associated with known historical names.

As for the name of the hero, Havelok, it seems fairly certain that it is a Celtic anthroponym (Welsh *Abloec*, Old Irish *Amhlaibh*). Its similarity to the Scandinavian name *Ōlāfr* (or *Anleifr* from Common Norse * *Anulaiƀaʀ*) caused its adoption as the Celtic equivalent of the Norse name by the Celts of Great Britain. For instance, Amhlaibh is the form under which, in Irish chronicles, we find the name of *Anlaf Cuaran*, son of Sigtryggr, the Viking chief who founded the (petty) kingdom of Dublin in 888.

Anlaf's actual life was quite full of adventure (it was his army that was wiped out at the celebrated battle around Bruna's stronghold, *Brunanburh*, A.D. 937), and the legends about him that formed after his death attracted other current folk-legends. Anlaf was surnamed *cuaran* 'leather-stocking', an epithet which is also found in Gaimar's story and our poem. The name *Bircabein*, actual father of Havelok, is a well known Scandinavian nickname.

It is probable that the legend, transmitted from North Wales into Northumbria, passed from there to the Danes in Lincolnshire where it was fixed into its present form about the time of Canute (1016-1035).

The story is as follows:

On his death bed the King of England, Athelwold, entrusts his only daughter Goldeboru to Godrich, Earl of Cornwall, to raise and to marry her to the handsomest, strongest and best man in England. At this same time, across the seas in Denmark, King Bircabein similarly entrusts his son Havelok and his two daughters to Earl Godard. The latter cuts the throats of the two girls (before Havelok's eyes) and gives Havelok to a poor fisherman named Grim to drown. But during the night Grim sees the royal flame come from Havelok's mouth and recognizes him by this, and the king-mark (apparently a shining gold cross) on his shoulder, as the future king of Denmark. With the child and his own family he flees Denmark and lands by chance at the mouth of the Humber River in England; there he founds the town of Grimsby. Havelok grows up, becomes the cook's servant knave in Godrich's household and gets a great reputation for strength and physical appearance by his work and by his performance in putting the stock at a local track meet. Godrich thus hears of him, declares that he fits the dying king's requirements and forces Goldeboru to marry Havelok, by which he hopes to demean the princess and get all England for himself. The young couple go back to Grimsby. Grim is dead but his children treat Havelok as a lord. Goldeboru, however, is not exactly reconciled to her new life but fortunately she sees the marvelous flame as she lies awake regretting her present unpleasant circumstances (*sory and sorwful was she ay*). She also sees *on hise shuldre, of gold red, . . . a swithe noble croiz*. An angel appears and confirms her vague hopes by telling her Havelok is of royal birth and the two of them will rule Denmark and England. This makes her very happy and she kisses Havelok who doesn't wake up even at this. They go to Denmark, with Grim's three sons as loyal aides, and there come under the protection of the powerful Count Ubbe. Together they capture and hang the usurper Godard, and Havelok becomes king. Then he comes back to England (landing again at Grimsby with a Danish army). Godrich rallies the English against these foreigners who 'burn churches, and bind priests, and strangle monks and nuns both' (l. 2882 f.). The poem interestingly calls Havelok's forces the *ferd* (2622) and not *here*. Also common people are named by name as, afoot, they destroy Godrich's mounted *erls*. Goldeboru appears on the scene and the English nobility yield to her legal claim. Godrich is fittingly burned alive. One of Grim's daughters is nobly married to the Count of Chester; Bertram the cook, Havelok's former master, is rewarded for his previous good treatment of Havelok with the earldom of Cornwall and a second daughter of Grim. Havelok and Goldeboru live happily ever after, producing fifteen children.

The following passage comes just after Godard has cut the throats of Havelok's sisters.

Editions:

The Lay of Havelok the Dane, ed. by W. W. SKEAT and revised by K. SISAM, Oxford, 1915.
Havelok hrsg. von F. HOLTHAUSEN, 3. Aufl., Heidelberg, 1928.

Consult also:

R. M. WILSON. *Early Middle English Literature*, pp. 221-5.
J. E. WELLS. *Manual*, pp. 13-15 (bibliography, pp. 763-4).
M. DEUTSCHBEIN. *Studien zur Sagengeschichte Englands*. I. Teil: *Die Vikinger-sagen*, Cöthen, 1906.

NE Midland Dialect

> Þer was sorwe, ⟨h⟩wo-so it sawe!
> Hwan þe children bi þ⟨e⟩ wawe
> Leyen and sprauleden in þe blod,   475
> Havelok it saw, and þe⟨r⟩bi stod.
> Ful sori was þat seli knave,
> Mikel dred he mou*h*te have,
> For at hise herte he saw a knif,   *borrowed fr Scand.*
> For to reven him hise lyf.   480
> But þe k⟨n⟩ave þat litel was
> He knelede bifor þat Judas
> And seyde: 'Loverd, merci nou!
> Manrede, loverd, bidd' I you!

478 mouhte] mouthe *MS.* — (*similarly the MS often has* th *for* ht).

485   Al Denemark I wile you ȝeve,

To þat forward þu late me live;

Here I wile on boke swere,

Þat nevre more ne shal I bere

Aȝen þe, loverd, shel⟨d⟩ ne spere,

490   Ne oþer wepne, that may you dere.

Loverd, have merci of me!

To-day I wile fro Denemark fle,

Ne nevere more comen ageyn;

Sweren y wole þat Bircabein

495   Nevere yete me ne gat.'

    Hwan þe devel he⟨r⟩de þat,

Sumdel bigan him for to rewe;

Withdrow þe knif, þat was lewe

Of þe seli children blod;

500   Þer was miracle fair and god,

Þat he þe knave nouht ne slou

But fo⟨r⟩ rewnesse him wit⟨h⟩drow.

Of ⟨H⟩avelok rewede him ful sore,

And þouhte he wolde þat he ded wore,

505   But on þat he wit⟨h⟩ his hend

Ne drop him nouht, þat fule fend!

    Þouhte he, als he him bi stod,

Starinde als he were wod:

'Yif y late him lives go,

510   He mihte me wirchen michel wo,

Grith ne get y nevere mo,

He may ⟨me⟩ waiten for to slo;

And yf he were brouht of live,

And mine children wolden þrive,

515   Loverdinges after me

Of al Denemark mihten he be.

---

487 I] hi *MS.* — 490 wepne] wepne bere *MS.* — 504 þouhte] þoucte *MS.*
(*Similarly the MS often has* ct *or* cht *for* ht). — 505 he with] he nouth wit
MS. — 506 drop] drepe *MS.*

God it wite, he shal ben ded,
Wile I taken non oþer red;
I shal do casten him in þe se,
Þer I wile þat he drench⟨ed⟩ be,   520
Abouten his hals an anker god,
Þat he ne flete in the flod.'
    Þer anon he dede sende
After a fishere þat he wende,
Þat wolde al his wille do,   525
And sone anon he seyde him to:
'Grim, þou wost þu art my þral,
Wilte don mi wille al
Þat I wile bidden þe,
To-morwen shal ⟨I⟩ maken þe fre,   530
And auhte þe yeven, and riche make,
With-þan þu wilt þis *knave* take,
And leden him with þe to-niht,
Þan þou sest *þe* mone-liht,
Into þe se, and don him þerinne;   535
Al wile ⟨I⟩ taken on me þe sinne.'
    Grim tok þe child and bond him faste,
Hwil þe bondes mihte laste
Þat weren of ful strong line:
Þo was Havelok in ful strong pine;   540
Wiste he nevere er ⟨h⟩wat was wo:
Jesu Crist, þat makede to go
Þe halte, and þe doumbe speke,
Havelok, þe of Godard wreke!

522 þat] þad *MS.* — 532 knave] child *MS.* — 534 þan] þai *MS*; þe] se
MS. — 541 er] her *MS.* — 543 speke] speken *MS.* — 544 wreke] wreken *MS.*

After 544 the fragment of the Cambridge MS. adds:
a   And þat he do him al quic flo
         Wyt⟨h⟩ schame and pine and mekel wo!
         For he it servede on fele manere
         Als ye schuln forwar⟨d⟩ here.

545   Hwan Grim him havede faste bounden,
      And siþen in an old cloth w⟨ou⟩nden,

      . . . .

      A kevel of clutes, ful unwraste,
      Þat he ⟨ne⟩ mou*h*te speke ne fnaste,
      Hwere he wolde him bere or lede;
550   Hwan he havede don þat dede,
      As þe swike him *bad*, he yede,
      Þat he shulde him forth ⟨lede⟩,
      And him drinchen in þe se;
      ⟨For⟩ þat forwarde makeden he.
555   In a poke, ful and blac,
      Sone he caste him on his bac,
      Ant bar him hom to hise cleve,
      And bitau*h*te him dame Leve,
      And seyde: ' Wite þou þis knave,
560   Also thou wi*lt* mi lif have ⟨save⟩;
      I shal dreinchen him in þe se,
      For him shole we ben maked fre,
      Gold haven y-nou and oþer fe;
      Þat havet⟨h⟩ mi loverd bihoten me.'
565   Hwan dame ⟨Leve⟩ herde þat,
      Up she stirte, and nou*h*t ne sat,

   He was traitur in mani a kas   *e*
   And he it abou⟨h⟩te þat he swilc was.
   He brou⟨h⟩te þe child in mechel sorwen,
   Yet wurth ⟨h⟩is soule nevere borwen.
   He bad Grim don ⟨h⟩is comaundeme⟨n⟩t
   And þerfore was he ate þe last schent. *j*

546 old] eld *MS.* —

After 546 the fragment of the Cambridge MS adds:

   He þriste in his muth wel faste
After 549 :
   For Godard hadde comaund him so

 551 As] hwan *MS*; bad] hauede *MS.* — 560 wilt] with *MS.* — 567 so
harde adoune] adoun so harde *MS.*

And caste þe knave so harde adoun⟨e⟩,
Þat he crakede þer hise croune
Ageyn a gret ston, þer it lay.
Þo Havelok mihte sei: 'Weilawei! 570
Þat evere was I kinges bern!'
Þat him ne havede grip or ern,
Leoun or w⟨u⟩lf, w⟨u⟩lvine or bere,
Or oþer best, þat wolde him dere.

So lay þat child to middelniht, 575
Þat Grim bad Leve bringen liht,
For to don⟨e⟩ on his cloþes:
'Ne þenkeste now⟨h⟩t of mine oþes *a so change had taken place*
Þat ich have mi loverd sworen?
Ne wile I nouht be ⟨nou⟩ forloren. 580
I shal him beren to þe se,
(Þou wost þat ⟨it bi⟩hoves me)
And I shal drenchen him þerinne;
Ris up swiþe, an⟨d⟩ go þu binne,
And blou þe fir, and liht a kandel.' 585
Als she shulde hise cloþes handel
On for to don, and blawe þe fir,
She saw þerinne a liht ful shir,
Also briht so it were day,
Aboute þe knave þer he lay. 590
Of hise mouth it stod a stem,
Als it were a sunnebem;
Also liht was it þerinne,
So þer brenden cerges ⟨b⟩inne:
'Jhesu Crist!' ⟨q⟩wat⟨h⟩ dame Leve, 595
'Hwat is þat liht in ure cleve!
Ris up Grim, loke ⟨h⟩wat it menes,
Hwat is þe liht, as þou wenes?'
He stirten boþe up to þe knave,

568 þat he crakede þer hise croune] þat hise croune he þer crakede *MS.*
— 581 him beren] beren him *MS.* — 597 Ris] Sir *MS*; loke] and loke *MS.*

600 (For man shal god wille have)
 Unkeveleden him, and swiþe unbounden;
 And sone anon ⟨upon⟩ him funden,
 Als he tirveden of his serk,
 On hise ri*ht* shuldre a kynemerk,
605 A swiþe bri*ht*, a swiþe fair:
  ' Goddot! ' quath Grim, ' þis ure eir
 Þat shal ⟨ben⟩ loverd of Denemark,
 He shal ben king strong and stark;
 He shal haven in his hand
610 A⟨l⟩ Denemark and Engeland;
 He shal do Godard ful ⟨gret⟩ wo,
 He shal him hangen or quik flo;
 Or he shal him al quic ⟨do⟩ grave,
 Of him shal he no merci have.'
615 Þus seide Grim, and sore gret,
 And sone fel him to þe fet,
 And seide: ' Loverd, have merci
 Of me, and Leve, that is me bi!
 Loverd, we aren boþe þine,
620 Þine cherles, þine hine.
 Loverd, we sholen þe wel fede,
 Til þat þu con⟨n⟩e riden on stede,
 Til þat þu con⟨n⟩e ful wel bere
 Helm on heved, sheld and spere.
625 He ne shal nevere, sikerlike,
 Godard, ⟨wite,⟩ þat fule swike.
 Þoru oþer man, þan þoru þe,
 S⟨h⟩al I nevere freman be.
 Þou shalt me, loverd, fre maken,
630 For I shal yemen þe and waken;
 Þoru þe wile I fredom have.'
  Þo was Haveloc a bliþe knave.

---

621 Loverd] Lowerd *MS.* — 625 nevere [neuere wite *MS.* — 627 man, þan] man louerd þan *MS.*

He sat him up, and cravede bred,
And seide: 'Ich am ⟨wel⟩ney ded,
Hwat for hunger, ⟨h⟩wat for bondes   635
Þat þu leidest on min hondes;
And for ⟨þe⟩ kevel at þe laste
Þat in mi mouth was þrist ⟨so⟩ faste.
Y was þe⟨r⟩with so harde prangled,
Þat I was þe⟨r⟩with ney strangled.'   640
   'Wel is me, þat þu may*ht* ete!
Goddot!' quath Leve, 'y shal þe fete
Bred an⟨d⟩ chese, butere and milk,
Pastees and flaunes, al with *s*wilk
Shole we sone þe wel fede,   645
Loverd, in þis mikel nede.
Soth it is, þat men seyt⟨h⟩ and *s*wereth:
Þer God wile helpen, nou*ht* ne dereth.'
   Þanne sho havede brou*ht* þe mete,
Haveloc anon bigan to ete   650
Grundlike, and was ful bliþe;
Couþe he nou*ht* his hunger miþe.
A lof he et, y wot, and more,
For him hungrede swiþe sore.
Þre dayes þerbiforn, I wene,   655
Et he no mete, þat was wel sene.
   Hwan he havede eten and was fed,
Grim dede maken a ful fayr bed;
Uncloþede him, and dede him þerinne,
And seyde: 'Slep, sone, with michel winne   660
Slep wel faste, and dred þe nou*ht*,
Fro sorwe to joie art þu brou*ht*.'
   Sone so it was li*ht* of day,
Grim it undertok þe wey
To þe wicke traitour Godard,   665

Þat was ⟨of⟩ Denema⟨r⟩k a stiward,
And seyde: 'Loverd, don ich have
Þat þou me bede of þe knave;
He is drenched in þe flod,
670   Abouten his hals an anker god;
He is witerlike ded,
Eteth he nevre more bred;
He liþ drenched in þe se!
Yif me gold ⟨and⟩ oþer fe,
675   Þat y mowe riche be,
And with þi chartre make ⟨me⟩ fre,
For þu ful wel bihete 't me,
Þanne I last spak with þe.'
   Godard stod, and lokede on him
680   Þoruhlike, with eyne grim,
And seyde: '⟨Grim⟩, wiltu ben erl?
Metathesis   Go hom swiþe, fule drit-cherl;   *two consonants rl*
Go heþen, and be evere more
Þral and cherl, als þou er wore!
685   Shal⟨tu⟩ have non oþer mede,
For litel ⟨shal⟩ I do þe lede
To þe galwes, so God me rede!
For þou haves don a wicke dede:
Þou mai⟨h⟩t stonden her to longe,
690   Bute þou swiþe ⟨h⟩eþen gonge.'
   Grim þouhte to late þat he ran
Fro þat traytour, þa⟨t⟩ wicke man;
And þouhte: '⟨H⟩wat shal me to raþe?
Wite he him live, he wile ⟨us⟩ baþe
695   Heye hangen on galwe-tre:
Betere us is of londe to fle,
And berwen boþen ure lives,
And mine children, and mine wives.'

680 þoruhlike] þoruthlike *MS.* — 687 galwes] galues *MS.* — 693 raþe]
rede *MS.* — 694 live] on liue *MS*; baþe] beþe *MS.*

Grim solde sone al his corn,
Shep wit⟨h⟩ wolle, net wit⟨h⟩ horn,   700
Hors, and swin ⟨and get⟩ wit⟨h⟩ berd,
Þe gees, þe hennes of þe yerd;
Al he solde, þat ou*ht* dou*ht*e,
Þat he evre selle mou*ht*e,
And al he to þe peni drou: 705
Hise ship he greyþede wel i-now,
He dede it tere, an⟨d⟩ ful wel pike,
Þat it ne doutede sond ne krike;
Þerinne dide a ful god mast,
Stronge kables, and ful fast.   710
Ores gode, an⟨d⟩ ful god seyl,
Þerinne wantede nou*ht* a nayl,
Þat evere he sholde þerinne do:
   Hwan he havede 't greyþed so,
Havelok þe yunge he dede þerinne,   715
Him and his wif, hise sones þrinne,
And hise two dou⟨h⟩tres, þat faire wore,
And sone he ley*de* in an ore,
And drou him to þe heye se,
Þere he mi*ht* alþer-best⟨e⟩ fle.   720
   Fro londe woren he bote a mile,
Ne were ⟨it⟩ nevere but ane hwile,
Þat it ne gan a wind to rise
Out of þe north, men calleth 'bise',
And drof hem intil Engelond,   725
Þat al was siþen in his hond,
His, þat Havelok was the name;
But or, he havede michel shame,
Michel sorwe and michel tene.
And þeih he gat it al bidene,   730
Als ye shulen nou forthwar⟨d⟩ lere

Instability of lang.

718 he leyde] dede he leyn *MS.* — 720 miht alþer-beste] alþerbest mith *MS.* — 723 gan] bigan *MS.* — 730 þeih] þrie *MS.* — 731 lere] here *MS.*

Yf that ye wilen þerto here.
    In Humber Grim bigan to lende,
In Lindeseye, at þe north-ende,
735   Þer sat ⟨h⟩is ship upon þe ṣonḍ,
But Grim it drou up to þe lọnḍ.
And þere he made a litel cote,
To him and ⟨ek⟩ to hise flote.
Bigan he þere for to erde
740   A litel hus to maken of ẹrþe.
So þat he wel þanne were
Of here herboru herborwed þere,
And for þat Grim þat place au⟨h⟩te,
Þe stede of Grim þe name lau⟨h⟩te,
745   So þat Grimesbi ⟨it⟩ calle
Þat þeroffe speken alle,
And so shulen men callen it ay,
Bitwene þis and domesday.

734 at] rith at *MS.* — 739 erde] erþe *MS.* — 741 þanne] þore *MS.* —
745 it calle] calleth alle *MS.*

XIII

LYRIC POETRY

(13th — 14th cent.)

The marriage of Eleanor of Aquitaine to Henry II (1152, see *Eleanor of Aquitaine and the Four Kings*, the admirable life of this admirable, one might say indomitable woman by A. KELLY, Harvard University Press, Cambridge, 1950) marked the beginning of the influence of the Provençal *troubadours* in England. Eleanor was the grand-daughter of William IX, count of Poitiers, the first of those *troubadours* who invented the art of interlacing complicated rime-schemes in stanzaic form. Other celebrated *troubadours* like Bernart de Ventadour and Bertran de Born lived at times at the court of Henry II, as a number of their poems indicate, and interested themselves rather a good deal in English affairs. But it was mainly by way of the *trouvères* of the North of France that the lyricism of the *langue d'oc* really reached England. To this influence must be added that of those wandering clerics, the *goliards*, and that of liturgical hymns in rimed Latin.

Thus a deep current of lyric poetry sprung up in England which was to run in new channels. But if, in England, they imitated the meters and the stanzaic forms of the troubadours, if they sang, like them, of love and springtime, they did not imitate the affectation and sentimental refinement of the *midi*. English poetry was indebted to the French for these forms, but it was far from a servile copy of the work of the troubadours; it infused into their airy stanzas more seriousness and melancholy. Finally it applied the same techniques to works of a religious nature.

From what must undoubtedly have been a fairly abundant production there remains only what has been preserved in a few manuscripts, about two hundred poems, of which the extracts below are a representative sample.

Editions:

E. K. CHAMBERS and SIDGWICK. *Early English Lyrics*, London, 1907.
Carleton BROWN. *Religious Lyrics of the XIVth Century*, Oxford, 1924.
Carleton BROWN. *English Lyrics of the XIIIth Century*, Oxford, 1932 [an excellent collection in which all the following texts are to be found].

Consult also:

H. J. CHAYTOR. *The Troubadours and England*, Cambridge, 1923.
J. AUDIAU. *Les troubadours et l'Angleterre*, 1927.
R. M. WILSON. *Early Middle English Literature*, ch. xi, *Lyric Poetry*, pp. 250-74
G. KANE. *Middle English Literature*, London, 1951.
A. K. MOORE. *The Secular Lyric in Middle English*, Lexington, 1951.
J. E. WELLS. *Manual*, pp. 485-538.

1 a. Sing, Cuckoo

This little poem, full of the freshness of spring, is the oldest known lyric poem; it dates from about 1230-40 according to some, from about 1300-1310 according to Baugh or Bukofzer. A monk in Reading Abbey copied it into his notebook with its music, and thus saved for us the first example of a rondeau with its musical notation, a perfect canon, in England. The theme is that of awakening of Spring or *reverdie* that French poets had brought into fashion.

Edition:
Sumer is icumen in, by J. B. HURRY, 2nd ed., London, 1914.

Consult also:
M. BUKOFZER. *Sumer Is Icumen in: A Revision*, Berkeley, 1944.
On its importance from the point of view of music, see GROVE, *Dictionary of Music*, 3rd ed. (1908), iv, pp. 747-54; 4th ed. (1940), v, 191-2.

> *Sing, cuccu, nu! Sing, cuccu!*
> *Sing, cuccu! Sing, cuccu, nu!*
>
> Sumer is i-cumen in;
>   Lhude sing, cuccu!
> Groweþ sed, and bloweþ med,   5
>   And springþ þe w⟨u⟩de nu.
>   Sing cuccu!

PLATE III

Sing, Cuckoo

(MS Harley 978)

Awe bleteþ after lomb,
Lhouþ after calve cu;
10   Bulluc sterteþ, bucke verteþ;
Murie sing, cuccu!
Cuccu! cuccu!
Wel singes þu, cuccu;
Ne swik þu naver nu.

1 b. Sunset on Calvary

Edmund Rich, archbishop of Canterbury, composed, before his death in 1240 at the abbey of Pontigny a work entitled *Le merure de Seint Eglise* or *Speculum Ecclesiae*. This work is known in many French, Latin and English MSS, but it seems that the original was written in Anglo-Norman.

After describing the grief of the Virgin at the moment of the Crucifixion when the Savior entrusted her to St. John (cp. John 19.25-27), the author adds: " E pur ceo dit un Engleis en teu manere de pite ", and he cites the following quatrain (fragment of a traditional ballad?), which, in its simplicity, is one of the most perfect and one of the most moving lyric poems in medieval English.

The " Engleis " in question was perhaps the author himself, St. Edmund of Pontigny.

Edition:

Carleton BROWN. *A Register of Middle English Religious and Didactic Verse*, Part I, Oxford, 1916 [which publishes the text of a good number of the manuscripts].

Carleton BROWN. *English Lyrics of the 13th Century*, Oxford, 1932.

Consult also:

J. E. WELLS. *Manual*, p. 988.

Nou goth sonne under wode;
Me rewes, Marie, þi faire rode.
Nou goth sonne under tre;
Me rewes, Marie, þi sone and þe.

2. Thomas de Hales, *Love Song*

This poem of which seven of the twenty-five stanzas are printed here is attributed, in the manuscript where it is entitled *a luve ron* 'love song', to Thomas de Hales, a Minorite; he seems to have written it, towards the middle of the 13th century, at the request of a young nun:

A mayde Cristes me bit yorne
Þat ich hire wurche a luve ron.

The author preaches in it, in characteristic fashion, the vanity of human wishes and the love of the Lord, the true King.

In lines 65-80 he develops, with a great deal of charm, the theme *ubi sunt qui ante nos fuerunt*, a universal theme, no doubt, but which was certainly a favorite one in the Middle Ages ever since Boethius (book II, meter 7):

> Ubi nunc fidelis ossa Fabricii manent,
> Quid Brutus aut rigidus Cato?

down to Villon's *Ballade des dames du temps jadis*. This melancholy motif exercised a great attraction for the English soul. It was already found in an Old English poem, *The Wanderer* (see HOE no. XVI. 2); in Middle English it appears frequently, and Lydgate still echoes it in *Like a Midsummer Rose*. One of the most successful of these poems is that in the Digby MS No. 86 in the Bodleian which begins thus:

> Were beþ þey ⟨þat⟩ beforen us weren
> Houndes ladden and hawekes beren
> And hadden feld and wode?
> Þe riche levedies in hoere bour
> Þat wereden gold in hoere tressour,
> Wiþ hoere briȝtte rode?

Just like Boethius and Villon, Thomas de Hales, it will be noticed, uses the prestigious and evocative names of historical and legendary heroes.

Edition:

R. Morris. *An Old English Miscellany*, London, 1872, pp. 93-9.

> Hwer is Paris and Heleyne,   65
>   Þat weren so bryht and feyre on bleo?
> Amadas, Tristram, and Ideyne,
>   Yseude, and alle þeo?
> Ector, wiþ his scharpe meyne,
>   And Cesar, riche of wor⟨l⟩des feo?   70
> Heo beoþ i-glyden ut of þe reyne,
>   So þe schef is of þe cleo.
>
> Hit is of heom al so hit nere.
>   Of heom me haveþ wunder i-told —
> Nere hit reuþe for to here —   75
>   Hw hi were wiþ pyne aquold,
> And hwat hi þoleden alyve here?
>   Al is heore hot i-turnd to cold.

67-8 Amadas & dideyne. tristram yseude *MS*. — 75 here] heren *MS*.

Þus is þes world of false fere;
80   Fol he is þe on hire is bold.

Þeyh he were so riche mon
    As Henry, ure ⟨noble⟩ kyng,
And also veyr as Absalon,
    Þat nevede on eorþe non evenyng,
85 Al were sone his prute agon,
    Hit nere on ende w⟨u⟩rþ on heryng.
Mayde, if þu wilnest after leofmon,
    Ich teche þe enne treowe King.

A! swete, if þu i-knowe
90   Þe gode þewes of þisse Childe!
He is feyr, and bryht on heowe,
    Of glede chere, of mode mylde,
Of lufsum lost, of truste treowe,
    Freo of heorte, of wisdom wilde;
95 Ne þurfte þe never rewe,
    Myhtestu do þe in his ⟨h⟩ylde.

He is ricchest mon of londe,
    So wide so mon spekeþ wiþ muþ;
Alle heo beoþ to his honde,
100   Est and west, norþ and suþ.
Henri, King of Engelonde,
    Of hym he halt, and to hym buhþ.
Mayde, to þe he send his sonde,
    And wilneþ for to beo þe cuþ.

105 Ne byt he wiþ þe lond ne leode,
    Vouh, ne gray, ne rencyan.
Naveþ he þerto none neode;
    He is riche and weli man.
If þu him woldest luve beode

95 þurfte] þurhte *MS.* — 103 sonde] schonde *MS.*

And bycumen his leovemon, 110
He brouhte þe to suche wede
Þat naveþ king ne kayser non.

Hwat spekestu of eny bolde
Þat wrouhte þe wise Salomon?
Of jaspe, of saphir, of merede golde, 115
And of mony on oþer ston?
Hit is feyrure of feolevolde
More þan ich eu telle con;
Þis bold, mayde, þe is bihote,
If þat þu bist his leovemon. 120

3. Judas

This short poem which dates from about 1300 is the oldest known example
of the traditional ballad in England. It already shows the specific traits of
the genre: rapid and dramatic movement, elliptical conciseness, absence of
transitions. Here, besides, the presence of a sister of Judas and the motive
alleged for his betrayal (to recover the thirty pieces of silver that Jesus had
entrusted to him and which he was robbed of while sleeping) are two popular
traits unknown in the gospels or apocryphal tradition.

Editions:
J. F. CHILD. *The English and Scottish Popular Ballads*, Boston, 1882-98,
Vol. I, p. 242 and f., V, p. 288 and f.
K. SISAM. *Fourteenth Century Verse and Prose*, Oxford, 1921, etc., pp. 168-69.

Consult also:
G. H. GEROULD. *The Ballad of Tradition*, Oxford, 1932.

Hit wes upon a Scere Þorsday þat ure Loverd aros;
Ful milde were þe wordes he spec to Judas:

' Judas, þou most to Jurselem, oure mete for to bugge;
Þritti platen of selver þou bere upo þi rugge.

Þou comest fer i þe brode stret, fer i þe brode strete; 5
Summe of þin cunesmen þer þou meiȝt i-mete.

I-mette wid ⟨h⟩.s soster, þe swikele wimon.
' Judas, þou were w⟨u⟩rþe me stende þe wid ston;

6 meiȝt] meist *MS* (*similarly the MS has s for ȝ in lines 19, 21, 22, 28, 31-4.*

⟨Judas, þou were w⟨u⟩rþe me stende þe wid ston,⟩
10　For þe false prophete þat tou bilevest upon.'

'Be stille, leve soster, þin herte þe tobreke!
Wiste min Loverd Crist, ful wel he wolde be wreke.'

'Judas, go þou on þe roc, heie upon þe ston;
Lei þin heved i my barm, slep þou þe anon.'

15　Sone so Judas of slepe was awake,
Þritte platen of selver from hym weren i-take.

He drou hymselve bi þe top, þat al ⟨h⟩it lavede a blode;
Þe Jewes out of Jurselem awenden he were wode.

Foret hym com þe riche Jeu þat heiȝte Pilatus.
20　'Wolte sulle þi Loverd þat heite Jesus?'

'I nul sulle my Loverd for nones cunnes eiȝte,
Bote hit be for þe þritti platen þat he me bitaiȝte.'

'Wolte sulle þi Lord Crist, for enes cunnes golde?'
'Nay, bote hit be for þe platen þat he habben wolde.'

25　In him com ur Lord gon, as ⟨h⟩is postles seten at mete:
'Wou sitte ye, postles, ant wi nule ye ete?

⟨Wou sitte ye, postles, ant wi nule ye ete?⟩
Ic am abouȝt ant i-sold to-day for oure mete.'

Up stod him Judas: 'Lord, am I þat?
30　I nas never o þe stude þer me þe evel spec.'

Up him stod Peter, ant spec wid al ⟨h⟩is miȝte:
'Þau Pilatus him come wid ten hundred cniȝtes,

⟨Þau Pilatus him come wid ten hundred cniȝtes,⟩
Yet ic wolde, Loverd, for þi love fiȝte.'

35　'Still þou be, Peter, wel I þe i-cnowe;
Þou wolt fursake me þrien ar þe coc him crowe.'

4. When the Nightingale Sings

This is a typical love poem. The evocation of spring is a convenient excuse for the poet to express the pain of a lover who supplicates his *suete lemmon* to grant him at least a kiss. It is not quite certain that the last line does not sound a Cavalier note.

Edition:

G. L. Brook. *The Lyrics in Harley 2253*, Manchester University Press, 1948.

> When þe nyhtegale singes,
>   Þe wodes waxen grene;
> Lef ant gras ant blosme springes
>   In Averyl, y wene;
> Ant love is to myn herte gon   5
>   Wiþ one spere so kene,
> Nyht ant day my blod hit drynkes,
>   Myn herte deþ me tene.
>
> Ich have loved al þis ӡer,
>   Þat y may love na more;   10
> Ich have siked moni syk,
>   Lemmon, for þin ore;
> Me nis love never þe ner,
>   Ant þat me reweþ sore;
> Suete lemmon; þench on me,   15
>   Ich have loved þe ӡore.
>
> Suete lemmon, y preye þe
>   Of love one speche;
> Whil y lyve in world so wyde
>   Oþer nulle y seche.   20
> Wiþ þy love, my suete leof,
>   My blis þou mihtes eche;
> A suete cos of þy mouþ
>   Mihte be my leche.
>
> Suete lemmon, y preӡe þe   25
>   Of a love-bene:

ʒef þou me lovest, ase men says,
　　Lemmon, as y wene,
Ant ʒef hit þi wille be,
30　　　Þou loke þat hit be sene;
So muchel y þenke upon þe
　　Þat al y waxe grene.

Bituene Lyncolne ant Lyndeseye,
　　Norhamptoun ant Loundè,
35　　Ne wot y non so fayr a may,
　　As y go fore y-bounde.
Suete lemmon, y preʒe þe
　　Þou lovie me a stounde;
Y wole mone my song
40　　　On wham þat hit ys on y-long.

5. Blow, Northern Wind

Another love poem. The poet enumerates in detail the charms of the one that he loves and expresses his own torment. This poem is much closer to the conventions of courtly poetry. The refrain from a popular carol had become associated with the formal poem with which its naive simplicity makes a fine contrast.

Edition:

G. L. BROOK. *The Lyrics in Harley 7753*, Manchester University Press, 1948.
Leo SPITZER. *Archivum Linguisticum*, III (1951), 1-22 and 164 (a detailed literary commentary).

Blow, northerne wynd,
Sent þou me my suetyng!
Blow, norþerne wynd,
　Blou! blou! blou!

5　　Ichot a burde in boure bryht,
Þat fully semly is on syht,
Menskful maiden of myht,
　Feir and fre to fonde;
In al þis wurhliche won,
10　A burde of blod ant of bon
Never ʒete y nuste non
　Lussomore in londe.

Wiþ lokkes lefliche and longe,
Wiþ frount ant face feir to fonde,
Wiþ murþes monie mote heo monge,   15
    Þat brid so breme in boure;
Wiþ lossom eye, grete ant gode,
Wiþ browen blysfol under hode;
He þat reste him on þe rode
    Þat leflich lyf honoure!   20

Hire lure lumes liht
Ase a launterne a nyht,
Hire bleo blykyeþ so bryht;
    So feyr heo is ant fyn!
A suetly suyre heo haþ to holde,   25
Wiþ armes, shuldre, ase mon wolde,
Ant fyngres feyre for te folde;
    God wolde hue were myn!

Middel heo haþ menksful smal;
Hire loveliche chere as cristal;   30
Þeȝes, legges, fet, ant al,
    Y-wraht *is* of þe beste.
A lussum ledy lasteles
Þat sweting is, ant ever wes;
A betere burde never nes   35
    Y-heryed wiþ þe heste.

Heo is dereworþe in day,
Graciouse, stout, ant gay,
Gentil, jolyf so þe jay,
    Worhliche when heo wakeþ.   40
Maiden murgest of mouþ;
Bi est, bi west, by norþ ant souþ,
Þer nis fi⟨þ⟩ele ne crouþ
    Þat such murþes makeþ.

32 is] wes *MS*.   44 þat] sat *MS*.

45   Heo is coral of godnesse,
      Heo is rubie of ryhtfulnesse,
      Heo is cristal of clannesse,
          Ant baner of bealté;
      Heo is lilie of largesse,
50   Heo is parvenke of prouesse,
      Heo is solsecle of suetnesse,
          Ant ledy of lealté. . .

      For hire love y carke ant care,
80   For hire love y droupne ant dare,
      For hire love my blisse is bare,
          Ant al ich waxe won;
      For hire love in slep y slake,
      For hire love al nyht ich wake,
85   For hire love mournyng y make
          More þen eny mon.

PART THREE
THE FOURTEENTH CENTURY

XIV

ROBERT MANNYNG OF BRUNNE

HANDLYNG SYNNE

All that we know of the author of the *Handlyng Synne* or *Sins' Handbook* is what he tells us at the beginning of his work, which will be found reproduced below. Native of the village of Bourn, in Lincolnshire, he belonged to the strict order of Gilbertines whose parent house was at Sempringham. Similarly, in the introduction to his other work, the *Chronicle*, he says:

> Of Brunne I am; if any me blame,
> Robert Mannyng is my name;
> Blissed be he of God of hevene
> Þat me Robert with gude wille nevene!
> In the third Edwardes tyme was I,
> When I wrote alle þis story,
> In the hous of Sixille I was a throwe;
> Danz Robert of Malton, þat ʒe know,
> Did it wryte for felawes sake
> When þai wild solace make.

We know that he wrote this verse *Chronicle* in 1338 when he was staying at Sixhill priory. It is made up of two parts. The first, in octosyllabics, which goes from the flood up to 689, is based, just as Lawman's poem was (see no. V), on Wace's Anglo-Norman *Brut*; the second part, in alexandrines, runs from 689 to the death of Edward I and rests on the Anglo-Norman *Chronique* by Pierre de Langtoft. From the 12th to the 14th century it was fashionable to write history in verse, and we must wait for John Capgrave (1393-1464) to find prose once more used for this purpose.

The *Handlyng Synne*, begun in 1303, is an extremely interesting work. It is a rather free translation of a practical handbook for the laity to use at confession, the *Manuel de Pechiez* redacted in Anglo-Norman verse about 1250 and for a long while attributed to William de Wadington. From this

211

book Robert of Brunne has kept, above all, the *exempla*, concrete examples in the form of vivid stories that the Friars had made fashionable in the 13th century the better to hold the interest of the common people (cp. the Pardoner's remarks on this in his Prologue), to fix their attention and instruct them while entertaining them. Thus we find in this *Handlyng Synne* a collection of tales, just like the *Confessio Amantis* of Gower (see no. XXVIII). Sometimes, as in the story of the Hermit and his bear — which illustrates the sin of envy (*invidia*) — we have a free translation of the original; sometimes Robert Mannyng adds as *exempla* stories of his own invention. He is an agreeable narrator, full of good-nature, charm and simplicity. One must not look for high literary qualities in him; he had a horror of obscurity and affectation:

> Haf I alle in myn Inglis layd
> In symple speche as I couthe
> Þat is lightest in mannes mouthe.
> 75 I mad noght for no disours,
> Ne for no seggers, no harpours,
> But for the luf of symple men
> Þat strange Inglis can not ken;
> For many it ere þat strange Inglis
> 80 In ryme wate never what it is,
> And bot þai wist what it mente,
> Ellis me thoght it were alle schente

(*Chronicle.*)

His tales are full of variety and interest, and he intermingles in them remarks and observations that are now very precious for giving us a knowledge of English customs in his day.

Edition:

Robert of Brunne's 'Handlyng Synne' ed. by F. J. FURNIVALL, London, 1901 (*EETS OS*, 119 and 123).

Consult also:

E. J. ARNOULD. *Le Manuel des Péchés, Étude de littérature religieuse anglo-normande.* Paris, 1940 [especially ch. VII].

J. E. WELLS. *Manual*, pp. 199-202, 342-44 (bibliography, pp. 794 and 816).

1. Prologue

To alle crystyn men undir sunne,   *pronounced as son*
And to gode men of Brunne,
Borne

expect i "e" is Kentish influence

And speciali, alle <u>be</u> name,

Þe felaushepe of Symprynghame,　　　　　　60

Roberd of Brunne grete<u>þ</u> ȝow　　　þ = usual ending
　　　　　　　　　　　　　　　　　　　in norther dialect "s"
In al godenesse þat may to prow.　　W. Midland before d or t
　　　　　　　　　　　　　　　　　　þ is assimilated
　Of Brunnewake yn Kestevene,　　　into t "gret"

Syxe myle besyde Sympryngham evene,

Y dwelled yn þe pryorye　　　　　　65

Fyftene ȝere yn cumpanye,

In þe tyme of gode dane Jone

Of Camelton, þat now ys <u>gone</u>:

In hys tyme was y þere ten ȝeres,

And knewe and herd of hys maneres;　　　70

Syþyn with dane Jone of Clyntone,

Fyve wyntyr wyþ hym gan y wone;

Dane Felyp was mayster þat tyme

Þat y began þys Englyssh <u>ryme</u>.　　*y is alternate for i*

Þe ȝeres of grace fyl þan to be　　　75

A þousynd and þre hundred and þre.

　In þat tyme turnede y þys

On Englyssh tunge out of Frankys,

Of a boke as y fonde ynne;

Men clepyn þe boke 'handlyng synne.'　　　80

　In Fren<u>sh</u>e þer a clerk hyt sees,

He clepyþ hyt 'manuel de pecches.'

'Manuel' ys 'handlyng with ho<u>nde</u>';

'Pecches' ys 'synne', y undyrsto<u>nde</u>.

Þese twey wurdys þat beyn otwynne,　　　85

Do hem togedyr, ys 'handlyng synne'.

And weyl ys clepyd, for þys skyle;

And as y wote, ȝow shew y wyle.

2. The Hermit and His Bear

Þer were twey men of holy wyl

Þat levyd togedyr, withouten yl,

Alone yn an ermytage,

And as meke as bryd yn kage;

4005   Þe toon, men calle Eutycyus,

Þe touþer hyght Florentyus.

A gode clerk was þe toon,

He turned to þe feyþ many on.

Eutycyus was þe clerk

4010   Þat taght þe folk of Goddys werk.

Florens was nat so moche yn lore,

Yn preyours he was evermore.

    Þer besyde was an abbey,

And yn here tyme þe abbot gan deye;

4015   Whan þys yche abbot was dede,

Alle þe munkes toke hem to rede,

And chese hem syre Eutycyus

To be abbot of here hous.

On alle manere fyl so here lot,

4020   Eutycyus þey made here abbot.

    Aftyr Eutycyus, Florens gan dwelle

And woned alone yn hys celle.

WILLIAM DE WADINGTON [?], *Manuel de Pechiez.*

E dit, qe jadis douz homes furent

Qe ensemble seinte vie eslurent;

Li uns fut apelé Euticius,

3930   L'autre out nun Florencius;

Ensemble maneient ambedou

En un hermitage qe il urent eslu.

L'un converti mult de gent,

Eutice, par sun document;

Florencius fut meins lettré,   3935

Sa vie en oreisun ad mené.

Près de euz une abbeie i aveit

Dunt li abbez morz esteit,

As moignes est ensi covenu

Qe Euticius fu eslu.   3940

Sa celle a Florence lessa,

Qe apres Eutice i habita,

Florens made ⟨þarfore⟩ grete mone
For þat he shuld dwel alone;
And had grete sorowe, and was drery,　　4025
As many be þat lese gode cumpany.
On a day, he bad hys orysun,
And was yn grete afflyccyon,
And pryed God he wulde hym ȝeve
Sum gode cumforte withal to leve.　　4030
Þus preyd Florens yn hys bede
Þat Gode shuld sende hym sum felaurede.
　　Whan he ros up of his orysown,
He ȝede yn hys celle up and down,
And opened hys ȝate, and loked oute,　　4035
And sagh a bere wylde and stoute.
Þys yche bere come to þe gate ~Old Norse road~
To Florens þat stode yn þe ȝate; ~OE gate~
But when þe bere come at hym nere,
Þe bere to hym loutede, and made feyre chere　　4040
(Feyre chere as a bere myght make)
And was so meke þat he myȝt hym take.
Þys yche Florens hym beþoght
Þat God hadde herd þat he besoght,
And þanked hym of hys swete grace,　　4045
Þat he hym sent hadde swyche solace.
For a myracle, ȝe may hyt undyrstande,
Þat a wylde bere was tame to hande.

4023 made þarfore *O*] made *H*.

Qe mult mari esteit
Qe sul meindre li coveneit.
3945　En seint oreisun se est mis,
Si ad Deu mut requis,
' Qe solaz & confort li fut duné
Pus qe sun frere i fut alé
Hors a la porte ou il ala

Un urs tut savage trova,　　3950
Qe nule fierté luy mustra,
Car sa teste a val enclina.
Par tant ad Florence entendu,
Qe de Deu a luy enveié fu.
Mult ad Deu regracié　　3955
Qe oir vout qe aveit prié.

Þys gode man hadde syxe shepe,
4050   And noun hyrde hem for to kepe;
He badde þe bere þat he shulde go
And dryve hys shepe to and fro,
And kepe hem weyl þat noun hem dere,
' And þou shalt be my gode bere.'
4055   Þe bere hym louted with semblant glad,
For to do as Florens hym badde;
To þe bere, he seyde hys avys:
' Every day whan y ete twyys,
Come þou home at hygh undurne,
4060   And no lenger yn þe felde sojurne;
And every day, when y faste,
Come at þe noun, home, at þe laste.'
So dyd þe bere ⟨þan⟩, every day,
One oure passed hym never away
4065   Þat he ne come home, þe yche cele,
And boþe tymes he knew hem wele.
      Þys Florens hadde cumforte and game
At hys bere, þat hyt was so tame,
And loved hyt moche withoute fayle
4070   For þe myracle and þe grete mervayle:
For soþe ⟨to seye⟩ so hym byrde,
For he was a merveylus hyrde.
A bere þurgh kynde shulde ete shepe;

4063 þe bere þan *O*] þe bere *H.* — 4071 soþe to seye *O*] soþe *H.*

Berbiz aveit, cinc ou sis,
Mes de pastur fu mult enquis:
Al urs les comanda garder,
3960   Semblant fist le urs otrier.
Assez fut pastur mervillus;
Car berbiz manger soleit l'urs.
Le jur qe Florence douz fé manga,
Al hostel venir, le comanda,

Le urs & les berbiz qe il mena 3965
A tierce; mes quant il juna,
Qe al hostel a none venist;
E l'urs chescun jur ensi fist,
Un seul jur n'ad trespassé
Utre ceo qe li fu comandé.   3970
Le seint esteit mult solacé;
Plusurs del miracle unt parlé.

And here as an hyrde he ȝafe to hem kepe.

Þyt yche merveyle myȝt nat be hyd,   4075
But yn alle þe cuntré hyt was weyl kyde
Þat Florens had a tame bere,
And was an hyrde, shepe to were.

Þe abbot þat hyghte Eutycyus
Had foure dyscyplys ful envyus,   4080
Þat alle day of þys bere spakk
With grete envye, gretely to lakk;
And seyd, alle foure hem betwene
Wyþ grete envye, scorne, and tene,
'More merveyl doþe Florencyus   4085
Þan doþe oure mayster Eutycyus.'
Þey seyde: 'hyt shal nat so go;'
And made forward, þat bere to slo,
As þey seyd, þey dyd þat woghte;
Þe whyche dede ful soure þey boghte.   4090
At þe tyme, þe bere, o day come noghte;
Florens had þerof grete þoghte;
He ros and ȝede ynto þe felde,
And aftyr hys bere faste behelde.
At þe laste, hys bere he fonde,   4095
Besyde hys shepe, slayn on a londe.
As-swyþe hymself gan to rede
Who hadde do þat yche dede;
Ȝyt pleyned he more þe myschaunce

Qatre desciples Euticius,
Pur lur peché malaventurus,
3975 Envie aveint mult grant
Qe lem de Florence parle tant,
Qe lur mestre Euticius
Miracles feseit nuls.
Pur ceo, l'urs unt geyté,
3980 E par envie l'unt tué.
Dehez eyent li maluré!

Si averunt, qe apres ert prové.
Le urs ne revint cum il soleit;
Florence de ceo mult doleit.
As chanz, en un jur est alé,   3985
Sun urs i ad mort trové.
Le seint home tost saveit
Qe sun urs tué aveit.
Lur peché pleint mult plus
D'assez qe ne fet l'urs;   3990

4100
    Þat þer shulde falle on hem venjaunce,
    Þan he pleyned hys owne dere
    Þat þey had slayn his gode bere.
    Noþeles he pleyned wundyrly sore
    Þat hys solas shulde be no more.

4105
       Eutycyus þe abbot, his felawe,
    Herd sey hys bere was do adawe;
    And come to hym on hys dysport,
    To make Florens gode cumfort.
    Florens seyd Eutycyus unto:

4110
    'Yn God truly y tryst so,
    Þat venjaunce shal on hem take
    Yn þys lyfe for my sake.
    Of Jhesu Cryst þey hade no drede,
    To sle þat hylpe me yn my nede,

4115
    Felunlyche, as for envey,
    And he ded no man folye;
    He was me sent, þurgh Goddys grace,
    To be myn helpe and my solace;
    Þat God wulde hym me ȝeve,

4120
    Why wuld þey nat suffre hym lyve?
    God almyȝty shal do hys wyl
    Wyþ hem, and mo, þat do so yl.'
       As he seyde, so gan hyt falle;
    Gode toke venjaunce on hem alle;

4125
    Meseles þey waxe þan to pyne,
    Here lemes roted before here yne;

Longtens nepurquant doleit
Qe sun solaz perdu aveit.
Sun cumpainun l'ad mandé,
E, al meuz qe il pout, solacé.
3995 Mes Florence li respundi:
'En Deu de ciel tant me afi
Qe en ceste vie, veant la gent,
De ceus prendra vengement;
Car il ne duterent Jhesu Crist

Qe mun urs, qe nul mal lur fist, 4000
Cruelement ⟨ils⟩ unt tué.
Certes, il feseient grant peché,
Kar joe estait mut solacé par ly,
E il ne lur feseit mal ne ennui.'
Issi avint cum il dist, 4005
Car vengeance grant Jhesu prist
Des qatre qe oscirent sun urs;
Tost apres devindrent leprus;

Above þe erþe þey were stynkyng,
Þat to þe beres deþ were consentyng.

    Þarfore þe pope seynt Gregory
Tellyþ þys tale, resun why   4130
Þat envye ys a cursed synne,
Any man to falle þer-ynne.
    Moche are they wurþy to suffre shame
Þat for envye brynge a man yn blame,
Or make hym lese hys wurldly aght,   4135
Or frendys also to be unsaght.
Who-so þat doþ, he may hym drede,
No þyng but peyne shal be hys mede.
    Syn þys wurlde fryst bygan,
Envye haþ be ever yn man;   4140
Lucyfer had fyrst envye
Þat man was made to state so hye;
Yn paradys he made hym falle,
And seþen of hys ofspryng alle;
So that envye haþ reyned ay   4145
Yn alle mankynde unto þys day;
And, Englys men namely
Are þurgh kynde of herte hy:
A forbyseyn ys tolde þys,
Seyd on Frenshe men and on Englys: 4150
'Þat Frenshe men synne yn lecherye,

Les membres, devant lur mort, pur-
          [rirent,
4010 De ceus que l'urs Florence oscirent.
Seint Gregoire nus ad par tan mustré
Cum envie est mauveis peché,
Pus qe si grant venjance prist
De cest peché, Jhesu Crist,
4015 En ceste vie, veant la gent,
Sauve del alme le turment
Pur si grant mesprisium

Cun fu de un urs occisiun.
Si ne deit estre ublié
Le peché qe tuz jurs ad duré 4020
Pus qe le mund fu comencé,
Ceo est tresun le maluré.
En parais, li maufé
Par sa grant iniquité
Decevait humene ligné 4025
Par cest tres maveis pechié;
Envie aveit le cheitif grant,

And Englys men yn envye.'
Lecherye ys flesshly synne;
Envye cumþ of þe soule wyþynne;
4155   Lechery ys þe lesse, we fynde,
And envye ys þe more unkynde;
For y se noun yn hys lyve
Þat of envye kan hym shryve;
Þogh every day a man hyt haunte,
4160   ȝyt wyl no man be hyt agraunte.
Telle to any þat he haþ envye,
He seyþ aȝen: 'hyt ys a lye.'
How mow þey þan shryve þat synne
Þat seyn þey have no gylt þerinne?
4165   We Englys men þeron shulde þynke
Þat envye us nat blynk⟨e⟩.

4166 blynke *O*] blynk *H*.

Qe Deus ama home tant,
Qe la joie de ciel deveit aver,
4030 Dunt le traitre chai premer.
En furme se mist de un serpent
Quant fist cel enchantement.
Par unt Eve trahi privement
Pus Adam; allaz, a tute gent!

XV

DAN MICHEL OF NORTHGATE
AYENBITE OF INWYT

An Augustinian monk at Canterbury translated into his Kentish dialect in 1340 the *Somme des Vices et des Vertues* by Friar Lorens of Orléans. The new title was *Aȝenbite of Inwyt*, which is ' The Remorse ' or more exactly ' The Prick of Conscience '. The original *Somme*, compiled in 1279 at the request of Philip the Bold, King of France, (cp. 'La somme le Roi ' in Ch. V. LANGLOIS, *La vie en France au moyen âge*, IV: *La vie spirituelle*, Paris, 1928, pp. 123-198) was a very popular work until the 15th century and frequently translated. It was long supposed to be the source for Chaucer's *Parson's Tale*; Germaine DEMPSTER (pp. 723-760 in *Sources and Analogues of the Canterbury Tales*, Chicago, 1941) finds two other *Summa vitiorum* to be this source. There is a Midland prose treatment, *þe boc of vices and vertues* (about 1400) and Caxton translated the *somme* into English under the title *The Ryall Book*.

By good fortune we have the unique holograph manuscript which is precisely localized and dated (a note indicates that it was finished 27 October 1340). This text is of great linguistic interest, for it is possible, thanks to it, to have some precise evidence about the dialect spoken in Kent at that time. The literary interest is null, the translation bad and full of errors; the work does not appear to have had any contemporary success despite the good intentions formulated by the author in a few poor verses at the end of his manuscript:

> Nou ich wille þet ye y-wyte
> Hou hit is y-went
> Þet þis boc is y-write
> Mid Engliss of Kent.
> Þis boc is y-mad vor lewede men,
> Vor vader and vor moder, and vor oþer ken,
> Ham vor to berȝe vram alle manyere zen,
> Þet ine hare inwytte ne bleve no voul wen.

Following the *Somme* of Friar Lorens, the author has translated from Hugo of St. Victor the same passage from *De Anima* which is found in *Sawles Warde*. An extract from this translation by Dan Michel will be found printed under *Sawles Warde* (no. IV).

Edition:

The Ayenbite of Inwyt ed. by R. MORRIS, London, 1866 (*EETS OS* 23).

Consult also:

J. E. WELLS. *Manual*, pp. 345-6 (bibliography, p. 817).
J. K. WALLENBERG. *The Vocabulary of Dan Michel's Ayenbite of Inwyt*. Uppsala, 1923.

Gluttony

Verst zigge we of þe zenne of glotounye þet is a vice þet þe
dyevel is muche myde y-payd and moche onpayþ God. Be
zuych zenne heþ þe dyevel wel grat miȝte in manne. Huerof
we redeþ ine þe godspelle þet God yaf y-leave þe dyevlen to
5 guo into þe zuyn; and þo hi weren ine ham, hise adreynten
ine þe ze, ine tokninge þet þe glotouns ledeþ lif of zuyn and
þe dyevel heþ y-leave to guo in ham and hise adrenche ine
þe ze of helle and ham to do ete zuo moche þet hi tocleve an
zuo moche drinke þet hy ham adrencheþ.
10 Huanne þe kempe heþ his velaȝe y-veld and him halt be

*Pres participles
beginning wi -ing*

la
lat. sing

acc.

contraction

should be þ

Þe boc of vices and vertues. —	W. CAXTON, *The Ryall Book.* —
First wole we speke of þe synne	And fyrst we shal saye of the synne
of glotonye, for þat is a defaute	of glotonye / whiche is a vyce that
and an yvel þat wondre moche	moche pleaseth the devyl, and dys-
likeþ þe devel and myche mys-	pleaseth to god. By this synne
lykeþ God, for þurgh þat synne	hathe the devyl grete power in man
haþ þe devel gret power in man	wherof we rede in the gospel that
and womman, as clerkes redeþ in	god gaf lycence to devylles for to
þe gospelle þat God ȝaf leve to	entre in to swyn, and whan they
þe develes to gon in-to swyn, &	were entred they drowned them in 5
whan þei were wiþ-ynne þe swyn,	the see. Thys sygnefyeth that the
5 þei made hem alle renne in-to þe	glotons that lede the lyf of hogges
see hevedlynge and drenche hem-	and of swyn the devyls have leve
self. In tokenynge þat glotouns	to entre in to them & to drowne
þat leden here lif in glotonye as	them in the see of helle. And
swyn, þe devel haþ power to entre	maketh them to ete so moche that
wiþ-ynne hem and drenche hem in	they breste / & drynke so moche
þe see, þat is to seye in helle, and	that they be drowned. whan the
to make hem so moche to ete þat	champyon hath owerthrowen his 10
þei bresteþ, and so moche to	
drynke þat þei drencheþ. Whan	
10 a chaumpioun haþ sconfited and	

Premierement dirons du pecchié de glotonie qui est uns vices qui
plaist mout au diable e mout desplaist a Dieu. Par tel pecchié a li
diables mout grant pooir en home. Dont nous lisons en l'euvangile que
Dieu dona congié as diables d'entrer en porciaus; e quant il i furent
entré, il les noierent en la mer, en signifiance que es glotons qui mainent
vie de porciaus, a li diables congié d'entrer e de eus noier en la mer
d'infer e de eus tant faire menger que il crevent, e tant boivre q'il se
noient.

PLATE IV

Ayenbite of Inwyt

MS. Arundel 57, folio 14 *b* (lines 5-35 of text).

þe þrote, wel onneaþe he arist. Alsuo hit is of þan þet þe
dyevel halt be þa zenne; and þervore bleþeliche he yernþ to
þe þrote ase þe wolf to þe ssepe him vor to astrangli, ase he
dede to Even and to Adam in paradys terestre. Þet is þe vissere
of helle þet nymþ þane viss bi þe þrote and by þe chinne. Þis 15
zenne moche mispayþ God. Vor þe glotoun makeþ to grat
ssame huanne he makeþ his god of ane zeche vol of dong, þet
is, of his wombe þet he loveþ more þanne God, and ine him
y-lefth and him serveþ. God him hat veste; þe wombe zayþ:
'Þou ne sselt, ac et longe and atrayt.' God him hat be þe 20

---

cast doun his enemy, he takeþ
hym bi þe þrote and suffreþ not
hym, his þankes, arise; & riȝt so
is it of hym þat þe devel haþ
cauȝt in þat synne, and þerfore
he takeþ hym bleþelikest bi þe
þrote, riȝt as a wolf doþ a schep
for to strangle hym. And as he
dide to Eve and to Adam in erþely
paradis. Þis is þe fischere of helle
þat fischeþ and takeþ þe fesch bi
15 þe mouþ and bi þe þrote. Þis
vice dispeseþ moche God, for a
glotoun doþ gret schame to God
whan he makeþ his god of a sakful
of dong, þat is to fille his wombe,
þat he loveþ more þan God and
douteþ, and þerfore he serveþ here
of al here askynge. God biddeþ
hym fast; his wombe biddeþ hym
fast not, ' but ete þy mete al in
ese, and sitte þer-at longe y-now,
and þou schalt ete þe betere and
20 þe more.' God biddeþ hym ryse

felowe, he holdeth hym by the
gorge by cause he shold not
relyeve. Ryght so is hyt of hym
that the devyl holdeth by hys
synne in his mete the devyl renneth to hys gorge lyke as the wolf
dooth to the sheep for to strangle
hym. lyke as he dyd to Adam &
Eve in paradys terestre. Thys is
the fysshar of helle whiche taketh
the fysshes wyth the grynnes by
the throte / This vyce dyspleseth 15
moche / for the gloton doeth to
hym grete shame whan he maketh
his god of a sacke ful of dunge.
That is his bely whyche he loveth
more than god and doubteth &
serveth it. God commaundeth that
he shold faste. The bely sayth nay.
thou sha⟨l⟩t not / but thou shalte
eete longe and by leyzer /God com- 20

Quant li champions a son compaignon abatu e il le tient par la gorge, 10
a envis se relieve. Ausi est de celui que li diables tient par cest vice; e por
ce volentiers li court a la goule come li lous a la berbiz por li estrangler,
come il fist a Eve e a Adam en paradis terestre. C'est li peeschierres
d'enfer qui prent les poissons par la goule a le emecon. Cest vice desplait 15
mout a Dieu. Car li glotons si fait trop grant honte, quant il fait son
dieu d'un sac plain de fiens, c'est de son ventre q'il aime plus que Dieu,
e le crient e le sert. Dieu li commande a jeuner; li ventre dist: 'Non
feras, ainz mangerez longuement e atrait.' Dieu li comande de matin 20

morȝen arise; þe wombe zayþ: 'Þo ne sselt; ich am' to vol;
me behoveþ to slepe. Þe cherche nys non hare, hy abyt me
wel.' And huanne he arist, he begynþ his matyns and his
benes and his oreysones and zayþ: 'A, God huet ssole we
25　ete to-day? Huader me ssolle eny þing vynde þet by worþ?'
Efter þise matynes comeþ þe laudes; and zayþ: 'A, God,
huet we hedde guod wyn yesteneven and guode metes!' And
efterþan he bewepþ his zennes and zayþ: 'Allas!' he zayþ,
'ich habbe y-by nyeȝ dyad to-niȝt; to strang wes þet wyn
30　t'eve, þet heaved me akþ. Ich ne ssel by an eyse alhuet ich
habbe y-dronke.' Þous to þe kueade zayþ.

---

herly; his wombe biddeþ hym lye
stille, for he is to ful to rise so
herly. 'I mote slepe, for þe
chirche is noon hare; he wole abide
me wel.' And whan he schal rise,
he bigynneþ his beedes and seiþ,
'A, lord God, what schule we ete
to-day? Where schule we fynde
25　any þing þat ouȝt is?' And after
þes mateynes, þan comeþ þe
laudes: 'A, lord God, we drunken
good wyn ȝister-even and ete good
mete.' Þan schal he bigynne to
wepe for his synnes, and seiþ,
'Alas, I have be almost ded to-
nyȝt; þe wyn was to strong of
ȝister-even; myn heved akeþ.' þis
30　man haþ an yvel god. þis god
and þis vice bryngeþ a man to

mandeth to ryse erly. his god his
bely sayth thou shalte not. I am
over ful me lyst to slepe. The
chirche is none hare he wyl not
flee awaye. and it is not yet open.
It shal wel abyde and tary for me:
And whan the gloton aryseth he
begynneth his matyns and his
prayers and sayth. O god what
shal we ete this day. shal we not
fynde that is ony thynge worthe / 25
After these matyns comen the
Lawdes & sayth / A Lord god
how wel dranke we yester evyn
the good wyn. and how good mete
ete we. Thenne after this bywepeth
the gloton his synnes and sayth.
Alas sayth he I wende wel thys
nyght to have deyed. The wyne
yesterevyn was over stronge / myn
heed aketh. I shal not be eased tyl
I have dronken. This god of the　30
wombe of glotonye is over evyl for

---

lever; son dieu dist: 'Non feras; je sui trop plains; dormir m'estuet.
Li moustiers n'est pas lievres, il m'atendra bien.' Et quant il se lieve,
si commence ses matines e ses oreisons e prieres, e dist: 'Dieu, que
25　mangerons hui? Trovera l'en chose que vaille?' Aprés ces matines
vienent les laudes; e dist: 'Dieu, come nous eumes bon vin ersoir e bones
viandes.' Aprés si plore ses pecchiés e dist: 'Las, dist-il, j'ai esté anuit
30　mors; trop fu fort le vin d'ersoir; la teste me duelt; je ne serai a aise,
si aurai beu.' Ci a malvais dit.

Þis zenne let man to ssame. Vor, alþerverst, he becomþ
tavernyer; þanne he playþ ate des; þanne he zelþ his
oȝen; þanne he becomþ ribaud, holyer and þyef; and þanne
me hine anhongeþ. Þis is þet scot þet me ofte payþ.   35

*
* *

Þe vifte boȝ is þe bysihede of glotuns þet ne zecheþ bote to
þe delit of hare zuelȝ. Þise byeþ propreliche lechurs þet ne
zecheþ bote þet lost of hare zuelȝ. Ine þri þinges nameliche
liþ þe zenne of zuyche volke. Verst ine þe greate bysihede þet
hy habbeþ to porchaci and to agraiþi. Efterward mid grat lost 40
þet hy habbep ine þe us.   Efterward ine þe blisse þet

---

schame, for first he bigynneþ to
be a taverne-goer and an aale-
goere, and after he is a dees-pleiere,
and after he silleþ his heritage
and al þat he haþ, and after þat
he bicomeþ an harlot, holour, and
þef; and so comeþ he to be honged,
and þis is scot þat he paieþ
35 comuly.

Þe fifþe braunche, to delyte in
queynte and deyntevous metes, as
þes glotouns doþ þat deliten hem
and biþenkeþ what manere mete
savoureþ hem best. Þilke beþ
propurly glotouns of mouþ, for
þei þenkeþ on no þing so moche
as on þe delyt and to fille here
þrotes. In foure þinges namely
is þe synne of suche men. First
in þe grete bisynesse þat þei have
to purveye it and diȝte it. And
40 after in gret likynge þat þei have
to usen it. And after in þe grete
joye þat þei have to speke þer-of

fyrst he bycome a tavern gooar / &
frequenteth tavernes. after he
playeth at the dyce. & after he
selleth his good awaye / after he
bycometh a rybaulde / an holyer
and letchour and at the laste he
hangeth on the galowes. This is the
salarye and the scotte that is ofte
payed for the synne of glotonye. 35

The V braunche of glotonye is
the curiosite of glotons / whiche
thynke on none other thynge but
for to delyte them in metes, they
ben proprelye lychorous which
seche not sauf onely the delytes
of theyr throte & mouth. In iii
thynges namely lyeth the synne
of suche peple / Fyrst in the grete
charge that they have in pour-
chasyng & in arayeng their metes /
After in the glorye & in the grete 40
playsyr that they have in seyng
& beholdyng them / & that they

Cel vice maine home a honte. Car premierement il devient tavernier;
puis jue as dez; puis vent le sien; puis devient ribaus, houlers e lerres;
e puis le pent on. Ce est l'escot qu'il en paie sovent.   35
    La quinte branche ⟨est⟩ la curieuseté des glotons qui ne quierent fors
a lor palais deliter. Cil sont proprement leccheor qui ne quierent fors les
deliz de lour goule. En iij choses nomeement gist li pecchiéz de tieus
genz. Premierement en la grant cure qu'il ont en porchacier e appareillier. 40

hi habbeþ ine þe recordinge. And huo þet miȝte telle
huyche bysinesse hi doþ to þan þet hare metes by wel agrayþed
and ech to his oȝene smac and hou hy moȝe maki of one mete
45 vele mes desgysed vor hare voule lost. And huanne þe mes
byeþ y-come on efter þe oþer, þanne byeþ þe burdes and þe
trufles vor entremes. And ine þise manere geþ þe tyme; þe
wreche him voryet, þe scele slepþ. Þe maȝe gret and zayþ:
'Dame Zuelȝ, þo me slast, ich am zuo vol þet ich tocleve.'
50 Ac þe tonge þe lyckestre him ansuereþ and zayþ: 'Þaȝ þou
ssoldest tocleve, ich nelle naȝt lete askapie þis mes.' Efter þe
lecherie þet is ine etinge comþ þe blisse þet is ine þe recorder.

---

and reherse it; and þat þei mowe
speke þe more þer-of, he doþ al
his powere to diȝte it wel and
nobley and biþenke what saus is
best þerfore, and every mete bi
hymself have alle his riȝttes. And
also how þey mow make of o þing
many manere servyses, and al for
to savoure wel in þe palet of þe
45 mouþ. And whan þe mes comen
and beþ brouȝt, eche after oþere,
þan bigynneþ bourdes and trefles
in stede of an enter-mes, and þus
goþ þe tyme. þe wrecche forȝet
hymself, and resoun slepeþ. þe
stomake crieþ and seiþ, 'A, dame
þrote, þou sleest me! I am so ful
þat I breste!' but þan answereþ
50 þe glotouns tonge and seiþ, 'þeiȝ
þou breste, þis good mossel schal
be ete.' And after þe glotonye of

may recounte what dylygence they
put to that, & that the metes
been wel arayed, & that everyche
have his right & propre sawce, &
how they may of one thynge make
dyvers messes dysguysed for the
delycyousnesse of the mouthe / &
whan the messys or the metes   45
comen in one after another,
thenne besayd the bourdes for
entremesses & thus goeth the tyme,
& the caytyfs forgete them self &
reason slepeth and thynketh no
thynge of the deth, ne on the
synnes that they do, their stomack
cryeth and sayth, Dame throte ye
slee me / I am so ful that I am
lyke to breke. Thenne the lychorous
tongue answereth though thou   50
sholdest to-brest I shal not suffre
this licorous mete escape me, after

Aprés ou grant delit qu'il ont en user. Aprés en la gloire qu'il ont en
recorder. E qui porroit raconter quele curiosité il mettent a ce que lor
viandes soient bien appareillées e chascune a sa propre savour, e coment
45 il puissent faire d'une viande divers mes desguiséz por lor palais deliter?
Et quant li mes sont venuz l'un aprés l'autre, lors sont les bordes e les
truffes por entremes. E ensi li tens s'en vait; li chaitis s'oublie; la
raison dort. L'estomac crie e dist: 'Dame geule, vous me tués; je sui
50 si plains que je crieve.' Mais la langue la lecheresse li respont e dist:
'Se tu devoies crever, ne lairai-je pas ce mes eschaper.' Aprés la lecherie

Efterward hi wesseþ þet hi hedden nykken of crane and
wombe of cou, vor þet þe mosseles blefte lenger in þe þrote
and more miʒten vorzuelʒe.　　　　　　　　　　　　　　　　　55

Nou þou hest y-hyerd þe zennes þet comeþ of glotounye
and of lecherie. And þervore þet zuyche zennes arizeþ
communliche ine taverne, þet is welle of zenne, þervore ich
wylle a lite take of þe zennes þet byeþ y-do ine þe taverne.
Þe taverne ys þe scole of þe dyevle huere his deciples studieþ　60
and his oʒene chapele þer huer me deþ his servese and þer
huer he makeþ his miracles zuiche ase behoveþ to þe dyevle.
At cherche kan God His virtues sseawy and do His miracles:

57 and ¹] adn *MS.* — 62 behoveþ] bohoveþ *MS.*

---

etynge, þan comeþ þe joye to telle
þer-of, and woschen þat þey hadde
þrotes as cranes and wombe as a
kow þat þe goode swete mosseles
myʒt dwelle lengere in þe þrote,
and to devoure more mete and to
55　store wel þe wombe.

Now ʒe have herde þe synnes of
glotonye and lecherie, and for
suche synnes begynneþ most at þe
taverne, þer is þe welle of synne.
þerfore wole we touche of synnes
þat ar don at þe taverne. þe
taverne is þe develes scole hous,
60　for þere studieþ his disciples, and
þere lerneþ his scolers, and þere
is his owne chapel, þere men and
wommen redeþ and syngeþ and
serveþ hym, and þere he doþ his
myracles as longeþ þe devel to do.

the lycorousnes of mete cometh
vaynglory that is to remembre it.
Thenne desyre and wesshe they
that they had as longe a necke
as a crane / & as grete a bely as a
cowe that they myght yet devoure
& swalowe more mete / Now hast　55
thou herde the synnes that comen
of glotonye & of lycourousnesse.
and by cause that these synnes
sourden and comen ofte in the
taverne whiche is fontayne of
synne. Therfore I wyl a lytel
touche the synnes that ben made
and done in the taverne. The
taverne is the scole of the devyl
where as his dyscyples studye, and　60
his propre chapel where as his
servyce is doon. and that is the
place where he sheweth & doeth
his myracles both day and nyght.
suche as apperteynen the devyl for

---

qui est en mengier vient la gloire qi est en recorder. Aprés si souhaident
qu'il eussent col de grue e ventre de vaiche por ce que li morsiaus lor
demorast plus en la gorge e plus eussent devorer.　　　　　　　　55
　Ore as tu oi les pecchiéz qui vienent de glotonie e de lecherie. E por
ce que tiex pecchiéz sordent communalment en la taverne qi est fontaine
de pecchié, por ce voel je un poi toucher des pecchiéz qui sont fait en la
taverne. La taverne est l'escole au diable ou ses deciples s'estudient e　60
sa propre chapele la ou l'en fait son servise e la ou il fait ses miracles

þe blynde to liȝte, þe crokede to riȝte, yelde þe wyttes of þe
65 wode, þe speche to þe dombe, þe hierþe to þe dyave. Ac þe
dyevel deþ al ayenward ine þe taverne. Vor huanne þe glotoun
geþ into þe taverne, ha geþ opriȝt; huanne he comþ ayen he
ne heþ vot þet him moȝe sostyeni ne bere. Huanne he þerin
geþ he y-zycþ and y-herþ and specþ wel and onderstant; huan
70 he comþ ayen he heþ al þis vorlore ase þe ilke þet ne heþ wyt
ne scele ne onderstondinge. Zuyche byeþ þe miracles þet þe
dyevel makeþ. And huet lessouns þer he ret. Alle velþe

72 lessouns] lessonus *MS.*

In holy chirche is God ywoned
to do myracles and schewe his
vertues: þe blynde to seen, þe
croked to gon riȝt, brynge wode
men in-to here riȝt wytte, doumbe
men to speke, deve men here
65 herynge. But þe devel doþ þe
contrarie of al þis in þe taverne.
For whan a glotoun goþ to þe
taverne he goþ riȝt ynow, and
whan he comeþ out he ne haþ
no fot þat may bere hym; and
whan he goþ þidre he hereþ and
seeþ and spekeþ and understondeþ,
and whan he comeþ þannes-ward
alle þes ben y-lost, as he þat haþ
70 no witt ne resoun ne under-
stondynge. þes ben þe miracles

to do. Atte chyrche our Lord god
hath a custome to shewe his vertues
& to make his myracles lyke as
ye may see in many places, the
blind for to see, the lame and
croked to be redressyd, to mad men
their wytte, to dombe men speche /
& to deef men theyr heryng / But 65
the devyl in the tavern doth al the
contrarye. for the taverne is his
chapel as is afore sayd where men
dooth to hym servyce. for whan
the man goeth to taverne he goeth
alle ryght. and whan he retorneth
he hath neyther fote ne honde by
whyche he may hym self bere ne
susteyne. and whan he goeth
thyder he speketh wel, hereth and
understondeth. and whan he retorneth he hath loste alle thys /
lyke as he that hath neyther wytte 70
ne reason ne memorye in hym self.
Suche been the myracles that the

---

teles comme il afiert au diable. Au moustier set Dieus ses vertus
65 moustrer e ses miracles faire: les avoegles enluminer, le contrait
redrescer, rendre le sens as forsenez, la parole as mues, l'oie as sours.
Mais li diables fait tout le contraire en la taverne. Car quant li glous
va en la taverne, il va touz dreis; quant il revient, il n'a pié qui le
puisse soustenir ne porter. Quant il i va, il voit e oit e parle bien e
70 entent; quant il revient, il a tout ce perdu comme cil qi n'a sens ne
raison ne memoire. Tieus sont les miracles que li diables fait. E quex

he tekþ þer, glotounye, lecherie, zuerie, vorzuerie, lyeʒe miszigge, reneye God, evele telle, contacky and to vele oþre manyeres of zennes. Þer ariseþ þe cheastes, þe strifs, þe man- 75 slaʒþes; þer me tekþ to stele and to hongi. Þe taverne is a dich to þieves and þe dyevles castel vor to werri God an His halʒen.

þat þe devel doþ, and ʒit he techeþ a lessoun of al foulenesse: þere he techeþ hem glotonye, lecherie, swere and forswere, to lye and mysseyn, to reneye God and his halewen, and evele reken-ynge, gile, and many oþere manere synnes. þere arisen contekkes and
75 debates and manslawʒtres. þe taverne is a þeves dich and þe develes stronge castel or hous for to werre wiþ God and alle þe halewen.

devyl maketh in the taverne. & what lesson is redd in the taverne I shal say to you. Ther is redde lerned herde & seen all fylthe and ordure of synne, that is to wete glotonye lecherye sweryng for-sweryng lyeng myssayeng renyeng god & his sayntes, mysherkenyng brawlyng & many other synnes. Thenne sourden & comen stryves homycides or manslaughter, there 75 is lernyd to stele and to hange / the tavern is a fosse & a pytte of thevys, and also it is the fortresse of the devyl for to warre ayenst god & his sayntes

---

leçons i list il? Toute ordure i aprent on: glotonie, lecherie, jurer, parjurer, mentir, mesdire, renoier Dieu, mesconter, bareter e trop d'autres manieres de pecchiés. La sordent les tençons, les mellees, les 75 omicides. La aprent on a embler e a pendre. La taverne est une fosse a larrons e forteresce au diable por guerroier Dieu e ses sains.

XVI

RICHARD ROLLE OF HAMPOLE

Richard Rolle is the greatest mystic and writer of mystical devotions of 14th century England. During his lifetime, and especially after his death, he exercised a very wide influence which the considerable number of manuscripts of his works bears witness to. He had such disciples as Walter Hilton, William Nassyngton and Juliana Lampit of Norwich. But he was not only a mystic, he was also a master of English prose.

He was born about 1300 at Thornton Dale near Pickering in Yorkshire and studied at Oxford. Discouraged by scholasticism he did not take holy orders, but became a hermit and lived a life of prayer and meditation in solitude on the estate of Sir John Dalton. There he began to write in Latin and English. Then he established himself in the county of Richmond not far from Ainderby where one of his disciples, Margaret Kirkby, was living as a recluse. It was for her that he wrote *The Form of Living* (from which extract no. 2 is taken) and *Ego dormio et cor meum vigilat*. When he was nearing fifty he retired to Hampole, near Doncaster in the south of Yorkshire. There he died in September 1349. He was considered a saint by his devotees; they wrote an office for him, they vaunted his miracles; but the Church has never seen fit to canonize him.

Even if he did indeed write a lot, he could never have done all the work attributed to him; such can only have been done by his followers or his school. One of these doubtful works is *The Pricke of Conscience*, a long, dull, didactic poem which enjoyed a very great success. On the other hand it is not exactly easy to determine just which are his authentic works. They comprise, we feel certain, *Commentary on the Psalter, Meditations on the Passion*, the *Commandement* and other shorter pieces like the *Bee and the Stork* (below, no. 1) as well as lyric poetry with such modern titles as *A Song of Love-longing to Jesus*, and others.

Richard Rolle was a mystic devoted to divine love. He appeals much more to the heart than to the mind. Lost in the ecstasy of his contemplation, he ignored the world that he had renounced in his youth, and the difficulties of his age escaped him. His prose, very strongly rhythmical, very melodious, puts him in the long line of great religious writers.

Edition:

English Writings of Richard Rolle Hermit of Hampole ed. Hope Emily ALLEN, Oxford, 1931.

Consult also:

H. E. ALLEN. *Writings Ascribed to Richard Rolle, Hermit of Hampole, and Materials for his Biography*, New York and London, 1927.
J. E. WELLS. *Manual*, pp. 444-51 (bibliography, p. 837).

1. The Bee and the Stork

The bee has thre kyndis. Ane es, þat scho es never ydill and scho es noghte with thaym þat will noghte wyrke, bot castys thaym owte and puttes thaym awaye. Anothire es, þat, when scho flyes, scho takes erthe in hyr fette, þat scho be noghte lyghtly overheghede in the ayere of wynde. The thyrde es, þat scho kepes clene and bryghte hire wyngez. Thus ryghtwyse men þat lufes God are never in ydyllnes; for owthyre þay ere in travayle, prayand or thynkande or redande or othere gude doande or withtakand ydill mene and schewand thaym worthy to be put fra þe ryste of heven, for þay will noghte travayle. Here þay take erthe, þat es, þay halde þamselfe vile and erthely, that thay be noghte blawen with þe wynde of vanyté and of pryde. Thay kepe thaire wynges clene, that es, þe twa commandementes of charyté þay fulfill in gud concyens; and thay hafe othyre vertus unblendyde with þe fylthe of syne and unclene luste.

Arestotill sais þat þe bees are feghtande agaynes hym þat will drawe þaire hony fra thaym. Swa sulde we do agaynes devells þat afforces tham to reve fra us þe hony of poure lyfe and of grace. For many are þat never kane halde þe ordyre of lufe ynence þaire frendys, sybbe or fremmede; bot outhire þay lufe þaym over mekill, settand thaire thoghte unryghtwysely on thaym, or þay luf thaym over lyttill, yf þay doo noghte all as þey wolde till þam. Swylke kane noghte fyghte for thaire hony, forthy þe develle turnes it to wormode, and makes þeire saules oftesythes full bitter in angwys and tene and besynes of vayne thoghtes and oþer wrechidnes; for thay are so hevy in erthely frenchype, þat þay may noghte flee intill þe lufe of Jhesu Criste, in þe wylke þay moghte wele forgaa þe lufe of all creaturs lyfande in erthe.

Wharefore accordandly Arystotill sais þat some fowheles are of gude flyghyng, þat passes fra a lande to anothire;

21 ynence] ynesche *MS.* — 22 *After* mekill *the MS adds* or thay lufe þam over lyttill. — 26 wormode *MS Durham*] wormes *MS Thornton.*

some are of ill flyghynge, for hevynes of body, and for þaire
neste es noghte ferre fra þe erthe. Thus es it of thaym þat
35 turnes þam to Godes servys; some are of gude flyeghynge,
for thay flye fra erthe to heven and rystes thayme thare in
thoghte and are fedde in delite of Goddes lufe, and has
thoghte of na lufe of þe worlde; some are þat kan noghte
flyghe fra þis lande, bot in þe waye late theyre herte ryste
40 and delyttes þaym in sere lufes of men and women als þay
come and gaa, nowe ane and nowe anothire, and in Jhesu
Criste þay kan fynde na swettnes; or if þay any tyme fele
oghte, it es swa lyttill and swa schorte, for othire thoghtes þat
are in thaym, þat it brynges thaym till na stabylnes; ⟨f⟩or
45 þay are lyke till a fowle, þat es callede strucyo or storke, þat
has wenges and it may noghte flye for charge of body. Swa
þay hafe undirstandynge and fastes and wakes and semes
haly to mens syghte; bot thay may noghte flye to lufe and
contemplacyone of God, þay are so chargede wyth othyre
50 affeccyons and othire vanytés.

2. The Love of God

Luf es a byrnand ȝernyng in God, with a wonderfull delyte
and sykernes. God es lyght and byrnyng. Lyght clarifies
oure skyll; byrnyng kyndels oure covayties þat we desyre
noght bot hym. Lufe es a lyf, copuland togedyr þe lufand
55 and þe lufed. For mekenes makes us swete to God; pureté
joynes us tyll God; lufe makes us ane with God. Luf es
fayrhede of al vertues. Luf es thyng thurgh þe whilk God
lufes us, and we God, and ilk ane of us other. Lufe es
desyre of þe hert, ay thynkand til þat þat it lufes; and when
60 it hase þat it lufes, þan it joyes, and na thyng may make it
sary. Lufe es a st⟨i⟩ryng of þe saule, for to luf God for
hymself, and all other thyng for God; þe whilk lufe, when it
es ordaynde in God, it dose away all inordinate lufe in
any thyng þat es noght gude. Bot al dedely syn es inordynate
65 lufe in a thyng þat es noght; þan lufe puttes out al dedely

syn. Luf es a vertu, þat es rightest affeccion of man saule. Trowth may be withowten lufe, bot it may noght helpe withouten it. Lufe es perfeccion of letters, vertu of prophecy, frute of trowth, help of sacramentes, stablyng of witt and conyng, rytches of pure men, lyfe of dyand men. Se how 70 gude lufe es. If we suffer to be slayne, if we gyf al þat we have til beggar-staf, if we kan als mykel als al men kan in erth, til al þis, withouten lufe, es noght bot sorow ordande and torment. If þou will aske how gode es he or scho, ask how mykel lufes he or scho; and þat kan na man tel, for I 75 hald it bot foly to deme a mans hert þat nane knawes bot God. Lufe es a ryghtwis turnyng fra al ertly thynges, and es joynd til God withouten departyng, and kyndelde with þe fire of þe Haly Gaste, fer fra fylyng, fer fra corrupcion, oblyst till na vice of þis lyfe, hegh aboven all fleschely lustes, ay 80 redy and gredy til contemplacion of God, in all thynges noght overcomen, þe sowme of al gude affeccyons, hele of gude maners, ende of comawndementes of God, dede of synnes, lyf of vertues, vertu whils feghtyng lastes, crowne of over-comers, mirynes til haly thoghtes. Withouten þat, na man 85 may pay God; with þat, na man synnes. For if we luf God in al oure hert, þar es na thyng in us thurgh þe whilk we serve to syn. Verray luf clenses þe saule, and delyvers it fra þe pyne of hell, and of þe foule servys of syn, and of þe ugly felyschip of þe devels; and of þe fendes sonn makes God 90 sonn, and parcenel of þe heritage of heven. We sall afforce at cleth us in lufe, als þe yren or þe cole dose in þe fyre, als þe ayer dose in þe sonn, als þe woll dose in þe hewe. Þe cole swa clethes it in þe fyre þat al es fyre; ⟨þe ayre swa clethes it in þe son þat al es ligʰt;⟩ and þe woll swa substan- 95 cialy takes þe hewe þat it es lik it. In þis maner sall a trewe lufar of Jhesu Criste do: his hert sal swa byrne in lufe þat it sal be turned intil fyre of lufe, and be, als it war, al fire, and he sal sa schyne in vertues þat in na parte of hym he be myrke in vices. 100

94-5 þe ayre... ligth *MS R.*

northern dialect w/
midland
influences

XVII

LAURENCE MINOT

Laurence Minot is known because he mentions himself twice in the eleven political poems on the wars of Edward III that we have by him, but we know nothing about him personally or about his life except that his poetry shows him to be the kind of hack writer that would have been quite at home in the 18th century. Since these occasional poems seem to have been written very shortly after the events that he celebrates, we suppose that they were written between 1333 and 1352. In a very brisk and packed style, though not entirely lacking in tags like 'trewly to tell' and inanities like 'whare he before was seldom sene', he sings the victories of Edward III over the Scots and the French, and treats no other theme except southern English chauvinism. There is some further interest in the effusiveness of Minot's works when it is considered that Edward III's continual wars were not always entirely popular. They also reflect on Edward's literary taste, cp. Chaucer's *Rime of Sir Thopas*.

The following poem bears on the first invasion of France. Edward III and Philip were about to engage in battle. Edward had established his troops near the Flamengerie and awaited the arrival of Philip on Saturday 23 October 1339. Instead of attacking, Philip withdrew his battle-line several miles to St. Quentin, abandoning behind him a thousand horse in a swamp.

Edition:

The Poems of Laurence Minot, ed. by Joseph HALL, Oxford, 3rd ed., 1915.

Consult also:

J. E. WELLS. *Manual*, pp. 215-7 (bibliography, p. 797).

Song of Edward

<blockquote>

Edward, oure cumly king,
In Braband has his woning,
  With mani cumly knight;
And in þat land, trewly to tell,
5 Ordanis he still for to dwell
  To time he think to fight.

Now God, þat es of mightes maste,
Grant him grace of þe Haly Gaste,
  His heritage to win!
10 And Mari moder, of mercy fre,
Save oure king and his menȝé
  Fro sorow and schame and syn!

</blockquote>

Þus in Braband has he bene,
Whare he bifore was seldom sene,
   For to prove þaire japes;   15
Now no langer wil he spare,
Bot unto Fraunce fast will he fare,
   To confort him with grapes.

Furth he ferd into France;
God save him fro mischance   20
   And all his cumpany!
Þe nobill duc of Braband
With him went into þat land,
   Redy to lif or dy.

Þan þe riche floure-de-lice   25
Wan þare ful litill prise,
   Fast he fled for ferde;
Þe right aire of þat cuntré
Es cumen, with all his knyghtes fre,
   To schac him by þe berd.   30

Sir Philip þe Valayse,
Wit his men in þo dayes,
   To batale had he thoght;
He bad his men þam purvay
Withowten lenger delay,   35
   Bot he ne held it noght.

He broght folk ful grete wone,
Ay sevyn oganis one,
   Þat ful wele wapnid were;
Bot sone whe⟨n⟩ he herd ascry   40
Þat king Edward was nere þarby,
   Þan durst he noght cum nere.

19 Furth] ffurth *MS.* — 37 broght] bcoght *MS.*

In þat morni⟨n⟩g fell a myst,
And when oure I⟨n⟩gliss men it wist,
45   It changed al þaire chere;
Oure king unto God made his bone,
And God sent him gude confort sone,
    Þe weder wex ful clere.

Oure king and his men held þe felde
50   Stalwortly, with spere and schelde,
    And thoght to win his right,
With lordes, and with knightes kene
And oþer doghty men bydene
    Þat war ful frek to fight.

55   When sir Philip of France herd tell
Þat king Edward in feld walld dwell,
    Þan gayned him no gle;
He traisted of no better bote,
Bot both on hors and on fote
60   He hasted him to fle.

It semid he was ferd for strokes,
When he did fell his grete okes
    Obout his pavilyoune;
Abated was þan all his pride,
65   For langer þare durst he noght bide,
    His bost was broght all doune.

Þe king of Beme had cares colde,
Þat was ful hardy and bolde
    A stede to umstride,
70   ⟨He and⟩ þe king als of Naverne
War fain ⟨for⟩ ferd in þe ferene,
    Þaire heviddes for to hide.

45 changed] shanged *MS.* — 68 ful] fur *MS.* — 71 fain for ferd] faire feld *MS.*

And leves wele — it es no lye —
Þe felde hat *F*lemangrye
    Þat king Edward was in,   75
With princes þat war stif ande bolde,
And dukes þat war doghty tolde
    In batayle to bigin.

Þe princes þat war riche on raw
Gert nakers strike and trumpes blaw,   80
    And made mirth at þaire might;
Both alblast and many a bow
War redy railed opon a row,
    And ful frek for to fight.

Gladly þai gaf mete and drink   85
So þat þai suld þe better swink,
    Þe wight men þat þar ware.
Sir Philip of Fraunce fled for dout,
And hied him hame with all his rout;
    Coward, God giff him care !   90

For þare þan had þe lely flowre
Lorn all halely his honowre,
    Þat so-gat fled for ferd;
Bot oure king Edward come ful still,
When þat he trowed no harm him till,   95
    And keped him in þe berde.

74 Flemangrye] fflemangrye *MS*.

XVIII

SIR GAWAIN AND THE GREEN KNIGHT

    A manuscript dating from somewhere near the end of the 14th century, today in the British Museum (Cotton Nero A 10) contains in the same small angular script and in an ink now faded, four poems of the same period to which have been given the names *The Pearl, Patience, Cleanness,* and *Sir Gawain and the Green Knight.* They are all in alliterative verse. *Patience* and *Cleanness* are two homilies, the first on the story of Jonah, the second which contrasts the purity of Christ and of His Virgin Mother with the impurity of all creatures from the fallen angels and the Fall of Man down to Nebuchadnezzar and Belshazzar. On the problems posed by the mystical *Pearl* see below, no. XIX. These four poems are probably by the same author: same language, same vocabulary, same stylistic traits; and even though the subjects are different, the moral pre-occupations of the author remain noticeably the same. As for *Sir Gawain and the Green Knight*, it is the master-piece of ME alliterative poetry in which Gawain, the perfect knight, faithful devotee of Our Lady, resists the test instigated by Morgan la Fée and preserves his purity intact.

Here is the argument of the poem:

On New Year's Day at the court of King Arthur, a knight of huge stature rides his horse into the hall and stops the festivities. Clad all in green, with green hair, he rides a horse equally green. He challenges all the knights present to give him a stroke with the great axe he carries on the condition that they later receive the same favor from him. After some dismay Gawain asks Arthur leave to be the champion, swears to observe the pact, seizes the axe and lops off the head of the Green Knight. The monster picks up his head, mounts his horse, tells Gawain to meet him a year hence at the Green Chapel, and departs. The year fleets by. After difficult and strange wandering (extract no. 1) Gawain reaches a magnificent castle on Christmas day, is told that the Green Chapel is nearby and agrees to be a guest till his time. For three successive days the master of the castle is to go hunting, during this time Gawain is to take his ease, and both agree to exchange each night what the fortunes of the day may bring to each of them.

Early the next morning the lady of the castle visits Gawain still a-bed, and engages him in double-entendre badinage. This scene is repeated during the three days on which the master of the castle hunts first the hart, then the boar and then the fox (handled with detailed description of the niceties of each chase) and these scenes mark three degrees in Gawain's temptation. The first day the conversation is, though pointed, still chaste and courteous; the second allows the lady to be more obvious; and on the third Gawain's full courtesy is required to refuse without acknowledging the dilemma. In exchange for the spoils of the chase, Gawain first gives the master what he had received (one kiss, then two); but the third day he conceals from the lord the lady's last gift, a magic belt that makes the wearer proof against all blows.

On New Year's Day Gawain goes to the Green Chapel and prepares to receive from the Green Knight the blow of the axe. Twice Gawain flinches and is reproached by the Green One. He holds still for the third but is cut only skin deep. Gawain gets up to fight back but holds off his blow when he hears that the Knight is lord of the castle. He was sent to King Arthur by Morgan la Fée. It was he who had put his wife up to making proof of Gawain's virtue. He would have done Gawain no harm had not Gawain concealed the magic belt. Gawain goes back to King Arthur's court and recounts this awesome adventure. The whole court decides hereafter to wear green belts in honor of Gawain.

Gaston Paris considered *Sir Gawain* the jewel of Middle English literature. By its variety, the beauty of its descriptions, the balance of the composition, its well worked out dramatic progress, the richness and precision of the diction, the intricate delicacy of the dialogue, it is the work of a consummate artist. In matters of the hunt or in the conversations with the lady the author excels in almost physically creating atmosphere. Once the supernatural elements are admitted, the subject is treated with all the introspective psychology of a modern novel.

The first extract which shows Gawain in search of the Green Chapel will give some idea of the deep feeling for nature that animated the poet. The second, which gives the first day of the temptation and the details of the stag-hunt, will admirably show all the author's qualities.

Editions:

Sir Gawain and the Green Knight, ed. by J. R. R. TOLKIEN and E. V. GORDON, Oxford, 1925.

Sir Gawain and the Green Knight, re-edited by Sir Israel GOLLANCZ with introductory Essays by M. DAY and M. S. SERJEANTSON, London, 1940.

Consult also:

G. L. KITTREDGE. *A Study of Gawain and the Green Knight*, Cambridge, Mass., 1916.

J. E. WELLS. *Manual*, pp. 54-7 (bibliography, p. 770).

1. Gawain's Journey

Mony klyf he overclambe	in contrayez straunge,	
Fer floten fro his frendez	fremedly he rydez;	
At uche warþe oþer water	þer þe wyȝe passed,	715
He fonde a foo hym byfore,	bot ferly hit were,	
And þat so foule and so felle	þat feȝt hym byhode;	
So mony mervayl bi mount	þer þe mon fyndez,	
Hit were to tore for to telle	of þe tenþe dole.	
Sumwhyle wyth wormez he werrez,	and with wolves als,	720
Sumwhyle wyth wodwos	þat woned in þe knarrez,	
Boþe wyth bullez and berez,	and borez oþerquyle,	
And etaynez þat hym anelede,	of þe heȝe felle;	
Nade he ben duȝty and dryȝe,	and Dryȝtyn had served,	
Douteles he hade ben ded,	and dreped ful ofte.	725
For werre wrathed hym not so much	þat wynter was wors,	
When þe colde cler water	fro þe cloudez schadde,	
And fres er hit falle myȝt	to þe fale erþe;	
Ner slayn wyth þe slete	he sleped in his yrnes,	
Mo nyȝtez þen innoghe	in naked rokkez,	730

718 so] fo *MS.* — 727 schadde] schadden *MS.*

Þer as claterande fro þe crest　　þę colde borne rennez,
And henged heȝe over his hede　　in hard ysse-ikkles.
Þus in peryl, and payne　　and plytes ful harde,
Bi contray cayrez þis knyȝt,　　tyl Krystmasse even,
735　　　　　　　　al one;
　　　　Þe knyȝt wel þat tyde
　　　　To Mary made his mone
　　　　Þat ho hym red to ryde,
　　　　And wysse hym to sum wone.

740　Bi a mounte on þe morne　　meryly he rydes,
　　Into a forest ful dep　　þat ferly watz wylde,
　　Hiȝe hillez on uche a halve,　　and holtwodez under,
　　Of hore okez ful hoge　　a hundreth togeder;
　　Þe hasel and þe haȝþorne　　were harled al samen,
745　With roȝe raged mosse　　rayled aywhere,
　　With mony bryddez unblyþe　　upon bare twyges,
　　Þat pitosly þer piped　　for pyne of þe colde.
　　Þe gome upon Gryngolet　　glydez hem under,
　　Þurȝ mony misy and myre,　　mon al hym one,
750　Carande for his costes,　　lest he ne kever schulde,
　　To se þe servy⟨se⟩ of þat Syre　　þat on þat self nyȝt
　　Of a burde watz borne　　oure baret to quelle;
　　And þerfore sykyng he sayde:　'I beseche þe, Lorde,
　　And Mary þat is myldest　　moder so dere,
755　Of sum herber þer heȝly　　I myȝt here masse,
　　Ande þy matynez to-morne,　　mekely I ask,
　　And þerto prestly I pray　　my pater and ave,
　　　　　　　　and crede.'
　　　　He rode in his prayere,
760　　　　And cryed for his mysdede,
　　　　He sayned hym in syþes sere,
　　　　And sayde 'Cros Kryst me spede!'

734 cayrez] caryeȝ *MS.*

2. The Stag-Hunt and Gawain's First Temptation

Ful erly bifore þe day þe folk uprysen,
Gestes þat go wolde, hor gromez þay calden,
And þay busken up bilyve, blonkkez to sadel,
Tyffen he⟨r⟩ takles, trussen her males,
Richen hem þe rychest, to ryde alle arayde, 1130
Lepen up lyȝtly, lachen her brydeles,
Uche wyȝe on his way, þer hym wel lyked.
Þe leve lorde of þe londe watz not þe last,
Arayed for þe rydyng, with renkkez ful mony;
Ete a sop hastyly, when he hade herde masse, 1135
With bugle to bent-felde he buskez bylyve;
By þat any day-lyȝt lemed upon erþe,
He with his haþeles on hyȝe horsses weren.
Þenne þise cacheres þat couþe, cowpled hor houndez,
Unclosed þe kenel-dore and calde hem þeroute, 1140
Blwe bygly in buglez þre bare mote;
Braches bayed þerfore, and breme noyse maked,
And þay chastysed, and charred, on chasyng þat went;
A hundreth of hunteres, as I haf herde telle,
      of þe best; 1145
      To trystors vewters ȝod,
      Couples huntes ofkest;
      Þer ros for blastez gode,
      Gret rurd in þat forest.

At þe fyrst quethe of þe quest quaked þe wylde; 1150
Der drof in þe dale, doted for drede,
Hiȝed to þe hyȝe, bot heterly þay were
Restayed with þe stablye þat stoutly ascryed.
Þay let þe herttez haf þe gate, with þe hyȝe hedes,
Þe breme bukkez also, with hor brode paumez; 1155
For þe fre lorde hade defende, in fermysoun tyme,
Þat þer schulde no mon meve to þe male dere.

1137 þat] þat þat *MS.*

Þe hindez were halden in,   with hay and war,
Þe does dryven with gret dyn   to þe depe sladez;
1160 Þer myȝt mon se, as þay slypte,   slentyng of arwes,
At uche wende under wande   wapped a flone
Þat bigly bote on þe broun,   with ful brode hedez.
What! þay brayen, and bleden,   bi bonkkez þay deȝen,
And ay rachches in a res   radly hem folȝes,
1165 Hunterez wyth hyȝe horne   hasted hem after,
Wyth such a crakkande kry   as klyffes haden brusten.
What wylde so atwaped   wyȝes þat schotten
Watz al toraced and rent   at þe resayt,
Bi þay were tened at þe hyȝe,   and taysed to þe wattrez;
1170 Þe ledez were so lerned   at þe loȝe trysteres,
And þe gre-houndez so grete   þat geten hem bylyve,
And hem tofylched, as fast   as frekez myȝt loke,
       þer ryȝt.
    Þe lorde for blys abloy
1175   Ful oft con launce and lyȝt,
    And drof þat day wyth joy,
    Thus to þe derk nyȝt.

Þus laykez þis lorde   by lynde-wodez evez,
And G⟨awayn⟩, þe god mon,   in gay bed lygez,
1180 Lurkkez quyl þe day-lyȝt   lemed on þe wowes,
Under covertour ful clere,   cortyned aboute;
And as in slomeryng he slode,   sleȝly he herde
A littel dyn at his dor,   and derfly upon;
And he hevez up his hed   out of þe cloþes,
1185 A corner of þe cortyn   he caȝt up a lyttel,
And waytez warly þiderwarde,   quat hit be myȝt.
Hit watz þe ladi,   loflyest to beholde,
Þat droȝ þe dor after hir   ful dernly and stylle,
And boȝed towarde þe bed;   and þe burne schamed,
1190 And layde hym doun lystyly,   and let as he slepte.
And ho stepped stilly,   and stel to his bedde,
Kest up þe cortyn,   and creped withinne,

And set hir ful softly   on þe bed-syde,
And lenged þere selly longe,   to loke quen he wakened.
Þe lede lay lurked   a ful longe quyle,   1195
Compast in his concience   to quat þat cace
Myȝt meve oþer amount,   to mervayle hym þoȝt;
Bot ȝet he sayde in hymself: 'More semly hit were
To aspye with my spelle   ⟨in⟩ space quat ho wolde.'
Þen he wakenede, and wroth,   and to-hir-warde torned,   1200
And unlouked his yȝe-lyddez,   and let as hym wondered,
And sayned hym, as bi his saȝe   þe saver to worthe,
          with hande.
     Wyth chynne and cheke ful swete,
     Boþe quit and red in blande,   1205
     Ful lufly con ho lete,
     Wyth lyppez smal laȝande.

'God moroun, Sir Gawayn,'   sayde þat gay lady,
'Ȝe ar a sleper unslyȝe,   þat mon may slyde hider;
Now ar ȝe tan as-tyt!   Bot true uus may schape,   1210
I schal bynde yow in your bedde,   þat be ȝe trayst.'
Al laȝande þe lady   lanced þo bourdez.
'Goud moroun, g⟨ay⟩,'   quoþ Gawayn þe blyþe,
'Me schal worþe at your wille,   and þat me wel lykez,
For I ȝelde me ȝederly,   and ȝeȝe after grace,   1215
And þat is þe best, be my dome,   for me byhovez nede;'
And þus he bourded aȝayn   with mony a blyþe laȝter.
'Bot wolde ȝe, lady lovely,   þen leve me grante,
And deprece your prysoun,   and pray hym to ryse,
I wolde boȝe of þis bed,   and busk me better,   1220
I schulde kever þe more comfort   to karp yow wyth.'
'Nay, for soþe, beau sir,'   sayd þat swete,
'Ȝe schal not rise of your bedde,   I rych yow better,
I schal happe you here   þat oþer half als,
And syþen karp wyth my knyȝt   þat I kaȝt have;   1225
For I wene wel, i-wysse,   Sir Wowen ȝe are,

1208 gay]fayr *MS.*

Þat alle þe worlde worchipez,   quere-so ȝe ride;
Your honour, your hendelayk   is hendely praysed
With lordez, wyth ladyes,   with alle þat lyf bere.

1230 And now ȝe ar here, i-wysse,   and we bot oure one;
My lorde and his ledez   ar on lenþe faren,
Oþer burnez in her bedde,   and my burdez als,
Þe dor drawen, and dit   with a derf haspe;
And syþen I have in þis hous   hym þat al lykez,

1235 I schal ware my whyle wel,   quyl hit lastez,
      with tale.
      ȝe ar welcum to my cors,
      Yowre awen won to wale,
      Me behovez of fyne force

1240   Your servaunt be, and schale.'

'In god fayth', quoþ Gawayn,   'gayn hit me þynkkez,
Þaȝ I be not now he   þat ȝe of speken;
To reche to such reverence   as ȝe reherce here
I am wyȝe unworþy,   I wot wel myselven;

1245 Bi God, I were glad,   and yow god þoȝt,
At saȝe oþer at servyce,   þat I sette myȝt
To þe plesaunce of your prys;   hit were a pure joye.'
'In god fayth, Sir Gawayn,'   quoþ þe gay lady,
'Þe prys and þe prowes   þat plesez al oþer,

1250 If I hit lakked, oþer set at lyȝt,   hit were littel daynté;
Bot hir ar ladyes innoȝe   þat lever wer nowþe
Haf þe, hende, in hor holde,   as I þe habbe here,
To daly with derely   your daynté wordez,
Kever hem comfort,   and colen her carez,

1255 Þen much of þe garysoun   oþer golde þat þay haven.
Bot I louve þat ilk lorde   þat þe lyfte haldez,
I haf hit holly in my honde   þat al desyres,
      þurȝe grace.'
      Scho made hym so gret chere,

1260   Þat watz so fayr of face;

1255 þat] þat þat *MS.*

Þe knyȝt with speches skere,
A⟨n⟩swared to uche a cace.

'Madame,' quoþ þe myry mon,   'Mary yow ȝelde,
For I haf founden, in god fayth,   yowre fraunchis nobele;
And oþer ful much of oþer folk   fongen hor dedez,   1265
Bot þe daynté þat þay delen   for my disert nysen;
Hit is þe worchyp of your self   þat noȝt bot wel connez.'
'Bi Mary,' quoþ þe menskful,   'me þynk hit an oþer;
For were I worth al þe wone   of wymmen alyve,
And al þe wele of þe worlde   were in my honde,   1270
And I schulde chepen and chose   to cheve me a lorde,
For þe costes þat I haf knowen   upon þe, knyȝt, here,
Of bewté, and debonerté,   and blyþe semblaunt,
And þat I haf er herkkened,   and halde hit here trwee,
Þer schulde no freke upon folde   bifore yow be chosen.'   1275
'I-wysse, worþy,' quoþ þe wyȝe,   'ȝe haf waled wel better,
Bot I am proude of þe prys   þat ȝe put on me,
And soberly your servaunt   my soverayn I holde yow,
And yowre knyȝt I becom,   and Kryst yow forȝelde.'
Þus þay meled of muchquat,   til mydmorn paste,   1280
And ay þe lady let lyk,   a⟨s⟩ hym loved mych;
Þe freke ferde with defence,   and feted ful fayre.
Þaȝ *ho* were burde bryȝtest,   þe bur*n*e in mynde hade
Þe lasse luf in his lode,   for lur þat he soȝt
                    boute hone,   1285
         Þe dunte þat sc*h*ulde hym deve,
         And nedez hit most be done.
         Þe lady þenn spek of leve,
         He granted hir ful sone.

Þenne ho gef hym god day,   and wyth a glent laȝed,   1290
And as ho stod, ho stonyed hym   wyth ful stor wordez:
'Now he þat spedez uche spech   þis disport ȝelde yow!

1283 ho] I *MS*; burne] burde *MS*. — 1286 schulde] sclulde *MS*.

Bot þat ӡe be Gawan,　hit gotz ⟨not⟩ in mynde.'
'Querfore?' quoþ þe freke,　and freschly he askez,
1295 Ferde lest he hade fayled　in fourme of his costes.
Bot þe burde hym blessed,　and bi þis skyl sayde:
'So god as Gawayn　gaynly is halden,
And cortaysye is closed　so clene in hymselven,
Couth not lyӡtly haf lenged　so long wyth a lady,
1300 Bot he had craved a cosse,　bi his courtaysye,
Bi sum towch of summe tryfle,　at sum talez ende.'
Þen quoþ Wowen: 'I-wysse,　worþe as yow lykez,
I schal kysse at your comaundement,　as a knyӡt fallez,
Þat fere⟨s⟩ lest he displese yow,　so plede hit no more.'
1305 Ho comes nerre with þat,　and cachez hym in armez,
Loutez luflych adoun,　and þe leude kyssez;
Þay comly bykennen　to Kryst ayþer oþer.
Ho dos hir forth at þe dore,　withouten dyn more,
And he ryches hym to ryse,　and rapes hym sone,
1310 Clepes to his chamberlayn,　choses his wede,
Boӡez forth, quen he watz boun,　blyþely to masse,
And þenne he meved to his mete,　þat menskly hym keped,
And made myry al day　til þe mone rysed,
　　　　　with game.
1315　　　W*atz* never freke fayrer fonge,
　　　　Bitwene two so dyngne dame,
　　　　Þe alder and þe ӡonge,
　　　　Much solace set þay same.

And ay þe lorde of þe londe　is lent on his gamnez,
1320 To hunt in holtez and heþe,　at hyndez barayne;
Such a sowme he þer slowe　bi þat þe sunne heldet,
Of dos and of oþer dere,　to deme were wonder.
Þenne fersly þay flokked　in folk at þe laste,
And quykly of þe quelled dere　a querré þay maked.

. . . .

1295 costes] castes *MS.* — 1304 þat feres] & fire *MS*; so] fo *MS.* —
1315 watz] with *MS.*

Baldely þay blw prys,   bayed þayr rachchez,
Syþen fonge þay her flesche,   folden to home,
Strakande ful stoutly   mony stif motez
Bi þat þe day-lyȝt watz done   þe douthe watz al wonen   1365
Into þe comly castel, ˙þer þe knyȝt bidez
ful stille,
Wyth blys and bryȝt fyr bette,
Þe lord is comen þertylle,
When Gawayn wyth hym mette,   1370
Þer watz bot wele at wylle.

Thenne comaunded þe lorde in þat sale   to samen alle þe meny,
Boþe þe ladyes on loghe   to lyȝt with her burdes
Bifore alle þe folk on þe flette,   frekez he beddez
Verayly his venysoun   to fech hym byforne;   1375
And al godly in gomen   Gaway⟨n⟩ he called,
Techez hym to þe tayles   of ful tayt bestes,
Schewez hym þe schyree grece   schorne upon rybbes.
'How payez yow þis play?   Haf I prys wonnen?
Have I þryvandely þonk   þurȝ my craft served?'   1380
'Ȝe, i-wysse,' quoþ oþer wyȝe,   'here is wayth fayrest
Þat I seȝ þis seven ȝere   in sesoun of wynter.'
'And al I gif yow, Gawayn,'   quoþ þe gome þenne,
'For by acorde of covenaunt   ȝe crave hit as your awen.'
'Þis is soth,' quoþ þe segge,   'I say yow þat ilke;   1385
Þat I haf worthyly ⟨wonnen⟩   þis wonez wythinne,
I-wysse with as god wylle   hit worþez to ȝourez.'
He hasppez his fayre hals   his armez wythinne,
And kysses hym as comlyly   as h*e* couþe awyse:
'Tas yow þere my chevicaunce,   I cheved no more,   1390
I wowche hit saf fynly,   þaȝ feler hit were.'
'Hit is god,' quoþ þe god mon,   'grant mercy þerfore,
Hit may be such, hit is þe better,   and ȝe me breve wolde
Where ȝe wan þis ilk wele,   bi wytte of ȝorselven.'

1386 þat] & *MS.* — 1389 he] ho *MS.* — 1394 ȝorselven] horselven *MS.*

1395 'Þat watz not forward,' quoþ he,   'frayst me no more,
　　For ȝe haf tan þat yow tydez,   trawe ȝe non oþer
　　　　　　　ȝe mowe.'
　　　　　　Þay laȝed, and made hem blyþe,
　　　　　　Wyth lotez þat were to lowe;
1400　　　　To soper þay ȝede as-swyþe,
　　　　　　Wyth dayntés nwe innowe.

XIX

THE PEARL

　　It was said, at the head of the preceding text, that *The Pearl* is probably by the same author as *Sir Gawain and the Green Knight*. But while *Sir Gawain and the Green Knight* is a work of the poet's youth, we may well consider *The Pearl* to be the product of his maturity. Completely master of an art that would bring considerable earthly renown, still he seems to have a mind only turned towards heaven.

　　The Pearl is a lyric poem in one hundred and one stanzas of twelve verses each, of a character at once elegiac, mystical and allegorical, cast in a very refined and complicated artistic mold. All the resources of alliteration, rime, refrain, chain-linked stanzas, and a rich and varied vocabulary are at the disposal of powerful and bevisioned imagination infused with a deep and sincere passion. This jewel, a unique masterpiece in its genre is, like all subtle and refined works of art, a difficult poem.

　　The competence of the poet is so great that we do not know whether we are reading an artistically elaborated personal experience from the poet's own life (the loss of a child a little less than two years old) or whether we are dealing with a simple allegory like those in the *Roman de la Rose*, on a different level, but with that work as the model; in other words whether the 'pearl' is a symbol of personified purity and the poem a hymn to chastity, — or whether it is an idealized evocation, reticent and modest, of some lost Margaret for whom the father remains inconsolable. Indeed all these elements are intricately blended by the poet in the very woof and warp of an iridescent tapestry, and each reader is at liberty to give it the interpretation which corresponds with his own temperment.

　　In the month of August, on a feast day — probably the Feast of the Assumption — the poet falls asleep on the grave of the child he has lost, the pearl without price that fell into the grass. In a dream he finds himself transported to the middle of a marvelous countryside. On the other side of a river he sees, clothed in white, a young girl in whom he recognizes his child. A dialogue full of a mystical tenderness now takes place. The daughter tries to console her father; she explains to him that she is not lost; eternally beautiful, she is only, because of that, less accessible to human beings: the river which separates her from her father and which he would like to cross to meet her in Paradise, cannot, since the sin of Adam, be crossed except by the way of death. Espoused to the mystical Lamb, she is now one of those brides that St. John saw in his Apocalypse adorned for their wedding in the new Jerusalem. By special grace the father is allowed to see from afar the City of God: he sees unroll there the procession of the virgin brides of Christ, each one bearing on her breast the pearl of perfect happiness, and among them, his child. No longer able to restrain himself, the father rushes towards her and — wakes up in the garden where he went to sleep, but calm and resigned; now that he knows his child enjoys celestial bliss, he will submit himself to the will of God.

Edition:

The Pearl, ed. by Ch. G. Osgood Jr, Boston and London, 1906.
Pearl, ed. with a modern rendering by Sir Israel Gollancz, London, 1921.
The Pearl, ed. by E. V. Gordon, Oxford, 1953.

Consult also:

J. E. Wells. *Manual*, pp. 579-83 (bibliography, p. 864).

The New Jerusalem

As John þe apostel hit syȝ wyth syȝt,   985
I syȝe þat cyty of gret renoun,
Jerusalem so nwe and ryally dyȝt,
As hit watz lyȝt fro þe heven adoun.
Þe borȝ watz al of brende golde bryȝt,
As glemande glas burnist broun,   990
Wyth gentyl gemmez anunder pyȝt;
Wyth bantelez twelve on basyng boun,
Þe foundementez twelve of riche tenoun;
Uch tabelment watz a serlypez ston;
As derely devysez þis ilk toun   995
In Apocalyppez þe apostel John.

As ⟨John⟩ þise stonez in writ con nemme,
I knew þe name after his tale:
Jasper hyȝt þe fyrst gemme
Þat I on þe fyrst basse con wale;   1000
He glente grene in þe lowest hemme;
Saffer helde þe secounde stale;
Þe calsydoyne þenne wythouten wemme
In þe þryd table con purly pale;
Þe emerade þe furþe so grene of scale;   1005
Þe sardonyse þe fyfþe ston;

Þe sexte þe rybé he con hit wale
In þe Apocalyppce þe apostel John.

Ʒet joyned John þe crysolyt,
1010 Þe sevenþe gemme in fundament;
Þe aʒtþe þe beryl cler and quyt;
Þe topasye twynne-how þe nente endent.
Þe crysopase þe tenþe is tyʒt;
Þe jacyngh þe enlevenþe gent;
1015 Þe twelfþe, þe gentyleste in uch a plyt,
Þe amatyst purpre wyth ynde blente;
Þe wal abof þe bantels bent
O *jas*porye, as glas þat glysnande schon;
I knew hit by his devysement
1020 In þe Apocalyppez, þe apostel John.

As John devysed ʒet saʒ I þare.
Þise twelve degrés wern brode and stayre;
Þe cyté stod abof ful sware,
As longe as brode as hyʒe ful fayre —
1025 Þe stretez of golde as glasse al bare,
Þe wal of jasper þat glent as glayre;
Þe wonez wythinne enurned ware
Wyth alle kynnez perre þat moʒt repayre.
Þenne helde uch sware of þis manayre,
1030 Twelve forlonge space er ever hit fon,
Of heʒt, of brede, of lenþe, to cayre,
For meten hit syʒ þe apostel John.

As John hym wrytez ʒet more I syʒe:
Uch pane of þat place had þre ʒatez,
1035 So twelve in pourseut I con asspye,
Þe portalez pyked of rych platez,
And uch ʒate of a margyrye,
A parfyt perle þat never fatez.

1018 jasporye] masporye *MS.*

Uchon in scrypture a name con plye
O Israel barnez, folewande her datez;   1040
Þat is to say, as her byrþ-whatez,
Þe aldest ay fyrst þeron watz done.
Such lyȝt þer lemed in alle þe stratez
Hem nedde nawþer sunne ne mone.

    Of sunne ne mone had þay no nede;   1045
Þe self God watz her lompe-lyȝt,
Þe Lombe her lantyrne wythoüten drede;
Þurȝ hym blysned þe borȝ al bryȝt.
Þurȝ woȝe and won my lokyng ȝede,
For sotyle cler noȝt lette no lyȝt.   1050
Þe hyȝe trone þer moȝt ȝe hede
Wyth alle þe apparaylmente umbepyȝte,
As John þe appostel in termez tyȝte;
Þe hyȝe Godez self hit set upone.
A rever of þe trone þer ran outryȝte   1055
Watz bryȝter þen boþe þe sunne and mone.

    Sunne ne mone schon never so swete
A⟨s⟩ þat foysoun flode out of þat flet;
Swyþe hit swange þurȝ uch a strete
Wythouten fylþe oþer galle oþer glet.   1060
Kyrk þerinne watz non ȝete,
Chapel ne temple þat ever watz set;
Þe Almyȝty watz her mynyster mete,
Þe Lombe þe sakerfyse þer-to refet.
Þe ȝatez stoken watz never ȝet,   1065
Bot evermore upen at uche a lone;
Þer entrez non to take reset
Þat berez any spot anunder mone.

    The mone may þerof acroche no myȝte;
To spotty ho is, of body to grym;   1070

1046 lompelyȝt] lombelyȝt *MS.* — 1064 refet] reget *MS.* — 1068 anunder] an vndeȝ *MS.*

And also þer ne is never ny3t.

What schulde þe mone þer compas clym,

And to-even wyth þat worþly ly3t

Þat schynez upon þe brokez brym?

1075　　Þe planetez arn in to pover a ply3t,

And þe self sunne ful fer to dym.

Aboute þat water arn tres ful schym,

Þat twelve frytez of lyf con bere ful sone;

Twelve syþez on 3er þay beren ful frym,

1080　　And renowlez nwe in uche a mone.

    Anunder mone so gret merwayle

No fleschly hert ne my3t endeure,

As quen I blusched upon þat ba⟨y⟩ly,

So ferly þerof watz þe fasure.

1085　　I stod as stylle as dased quayle

For ferly of þat freuch fygure,

Þat felde I nawþer reste ne travayle,

So watz I ravyste wyth glymme pure.

For I dar say wyth conciens sure,

1090　　Hade bodyly burne abiden þat bone,

Þa3 alle clerkez hym hade in cure,

His lyf wer loste anunder mone.

XX

ALLITERATIVE MORTE ARTHURE

This fine poem in alliterative verse, from the second half of the 14th century, has sometimes been attributed to Huchown of the Awle Ryale. Following many others that he uses for inspiration (drawing particularly on Geoffrey of Monmouth and Lawman [cp. above no. V]), he takes up part of the Arthur legend, which he treats in an epic style, and to which he adds a great many original developments, like the grief of Guenevere at Arthur's departure (extract no. 1), or the elaboration of Arthur's dream (extract no. 2).

This poem was used as a source by Sir Thomas Malory for book V of his

Morte Darthur: by the corresponding text printed as a note, it will be seen
that Malory's imitation sometimes goes far afield.

The two episodes that are reproduced here take place at the moment when
Arthur has decided to cross the Channel and go on to the continent to fight
the emperor Lucius Iberius and to conquer Rome.

Editions:

by Ed. BROCK (London, 1871), Mary M. BANKS (London, 1900) and E.
.BJÖRKMAN (Heidleberg, 1915).

Consult also:

J. E. WELLS. *Manual*, pp. 36-8 (bibliography, pp. 767-8).

1. Arthur's Farewell to Guenevere

Nowe he takez hys leve   (and lengez no langere)
At lordez, at lege-men   þat leves hym byhynden.
And seyne þat worthilyche wy   went unto chambyre   695
For to comfurthe þe qwene   þat in care lenges;
Waynour waykly   wepande hym kyssiz,
Talkez to hym tenderly   with teres y-newe:
'I may wery the wye   thatt this werre movede,
That warnes me wyrchippe   of my wedde lorde;   700
All my lykynge of lyfe   owt of lande wendez,
And I in langour am lefte,   leve ȝe, for evere!
Why ne myghte I, dere lufe,   dye in ȝour armes,
Are I þis destanye of dule   sulde drye by myne one?'
'Grefe þe noghte, Gaynour,   fore Goddes lufe of hewen, 705
Ne gruche noghte my ganggynge: it sall to gude turne.
Thy wonrydez and thy wepynge   woundez myn herte,
I may noghte wit of þis woo,   for all þis werlde ryche;
I have made a kepare,   a knyghte of thyn awen,
Overlynge of Ynglande   undyre thyselven,   710
And that es sir Mordrede   þat þow has mekyll praysede,
Sall be thy dictour, my dere,   to doo whatt the lykes.'
Thane he takes hys leve   at ladys in chambyre,
Kysside them kyndlyche   and to Criste beteches,   [aschede,
And then cho swounes full swythe,   whe⟨n⟩ he hys swerde 715

*S*weye*s* in a swounyng,   swelte as cho walde.
He pressed to his palfray   in presance of lordes,
Prekys of the palez   with his prys knyghtes,
Wyth a reall rowte   of þe rounde table,
720 Soughte towarde Sandwyche: cho sees hym no more!

2. Arthur's Dream: The Dragon and the Bear

The kynge was in a gret cogge   with knyghtez full many,
In a cabane enclosede,   clenlyche arayede,
Within on a ryche bedde   rystys a littyll,
And with þe swoghe of þe see   he fell in swefnynge.
760   Hym dremyd of a dragon,   dredfull to beholde,
Come dryfande over þe depe   to drenchen hys pople,
Ewen walkande owte   of the weste landez,
Wanderande unworthyly   overe the wale ythez;
Bothe his hede and hys hals   ware halely all over
765 Oundyde of azure,   enamelde full faire:
His sc⟨h⟩oulders ware schalyde   all in *schire* sylvere,
Schreede over all þe schrympe   with schrinkande poyntez;
Hys wombe and hys wenges   of wondyrfull hewes,
In mervaylous maylys   he mountede full hye;
770 Whaym þat he towchede,   he was tynt for ever.

716 Sweyes] twys *MS.* — 759 he fell in swefnynge] in swefnynge he
fell *MS.* — 766 schire] clene *MS.*

GEOFFREY OF MONMOUTH, *Historia regum Britanniae,* cap. 164. — Dum
autem innumeris navibus circumseptus prospero cursu et cum gaudio
altum secaret, quasi media hora noctis instante, gravissimus somnus eum

---

A: Sir Thomas MALORY, *Works,* èd. E. Vinaver, I, pp. 196-198. — As the
kynge was in his cog and lay in his caban, he felle in a slumberyng and
dremed how a dredfull dragon dud drenche muche of his peple and com
fleyng one wynge oute of the weste partyes. And his hede, hym semed, was
enamyled with asure, and his shuldyrs shone as the golde, and his wombe
was lyke mayles of a merveylous hew, *and his tayle was fulle of tatyrs,*

Hys feete ware floreschede   all in fyne sabyll
And syche a vennymous flayre   flowe fro his lyppez
That the flode of þe flawez   all on fyre semyde.
    Thane come of þe Oryente   ewyn hym agaynez
A blake bustous bere   abwen in the clowdes   775
With yche a pawe as a poste   and paumes full huge,
With pykes full perilous,   all plyande þam semyde;
Lothen and lothely,   lokkes and oþer,
All with lutterde legges,   lokerde unfaire,
Filtyrde unfrely,   wyth fomaunde lyppez,   780
The foulleste of fegure   that fourmede wɪs ever.
He baltyrde, he bleryde,   he braundyschte þerafter;
To bataile he bounnez hym   with bustous clowez:
He romede, he rarede,   that roggede all þe erthe,
So ruydly he rappyd   to ryot hymselven.   785
    Thane the dragon on dreghe   dressede hym aȝaynez,
And with hys d⟨i⟩nttez hym drafe   on dreghe by þe walkyn:
He fares as a fawcon,   frekly he strykez;
Bothe with feete and with fyre   he feghttys at ones.
The bere in the bataile   þe bygger hym semyde   790
And byttes hym boldlye   wyth balefull tuskez;
Syche buffetez he hym rechez   with hys brode klokes,

785 rappyd to] rappyd at to *MS*.

intercepit. Sopitus etiam per somnum vidit ursum quemdam in áere
volantem, cuius murmure tota litora intremebant; terribilem quoque
draconem ab occidente advolare, qui splendore oculorum suorum patriam
illuminabat; alterum vero alteri occurrentem miram pugnam committere;

A: and his feete were florysshed as hit were fyne sable. *And his clawys
were lyke clene golde,* ⟨and⟩ an hydeouse flame of fyre there flowe oute
of his mowth, lyke as the londe and the watir had flawmed all on fyre.
Than hym semed there com oute of the Oryent a grymly beare, all blak,
in a clowde, and his pawys were as byg as a poste. *He was all to-
rongeled with lugerande* lokys, and he was the fowlyst beste that ever
ony man sye. He romed and rored so rudely that merveyle hit were
to telle. Than the dredfull dragon dressyd hym ayenste hym and come

Hys brest and his brayell   was blodye all over.

He rawmpyde so ruydly   that all þe erthe ryfez,

795 Rynnande on reede blode   as rayne of the heven.

He hade weryede the worme   by wyghtnesse *and* strenghe,

Ne ware it fore þe wylde fyre   þat he hym wyth defendez.

  Thane wandyrs þe worme   awaye to hys heghttez,

Commes glydande fro þe clowddez   and cowpez full even,

800 Towchez hym wyth his talounez   and terez hys rigge

Betwyx þe taile and the toppe   ten fote large.

Thus he brittenyd the bere   and broghte hym o lyfe,

Lette hym fall in the flode,   fleete whare hym lykes!

So they brynge þe bolde kyng   bynne þe schippe-burde,

805 Þat nere he bristez for bale   on bede, whare he lyggez.

  Than waknez þe wyese kynge,   wery foretravaillede,

Takes hym two phylozophirs   that folowede hym ever,

In the sevyn scyence   the suteleste fonden,

The cony⟨n⟩geste of clergye   undyre Criste knowen;

810 He tolde þem of hys tourmente,   þat tym þat he slepede,

Drechede with a dragon,   'and syche a derfe beste,

Has mad me full wery;   as wysse me oure Lo⟨ve⟩rd,

I mon swelte as-swythe,   ore ȝe tell me my swefen!'

796 and strenghe] of strenghte *MS.* — 812-3 as wysse . . . my swefen]
ȝe tell me my sweven ore I mon swelte as swythe as wysse me oure lorde
MS.

sed praefatum draconem, ursum saepius irruentem, ignito anhelitu com-
burere combustumque in terram prosternere. Expergefactus ergo Arturus

A: in the wynde lyke a faucon, and freyshely strykis the beare. And agayne
the gresly beare kuttis with his grysly tuskes, that his breste and his
bray⟨l⟩e was bloodé, and ⟨the reed blood⟩ rayled all over the see. Than
the worme wyndis away and fleis uppon hyght and com downe *with such
a sowghe,* and towched the beare on the rydge that fro the toppe to the
tayle was ten foote large. And so he rentyth the beare *and brennys hym
up clene that all felle on pouder, both the fleysh and the bonys,* and so hit
flotered abrode on the sea. Anone the kynge waked ⟨and was sore
abasshed⟩ of his dreme, and in all haste he sente for a philozopher and
charged hym to telle what sygnyfyed his dreme.

'Sir,' saide þey son thane,   thies sagge philosopherse,
'The dragon þat þow dremyde of,   so dredfull to schewe, 815
That come dryfande over þe deepe,   to drynchen thy pople,
Sothely and certayne   thyselven it ⟨betakn⟩es,
That thus saillez over þe see   with thy sekyre knyghtez.
The colurez, þat ware castyn   appon his clere wengez,
May be thy kyngrykez all   that thow has ryghte wonnyn; 820
And the ta*tte*rede taile   with tonges so huge
Betakyns þis faire folke   that in thy fleet wendez.
The bere, that bryttenede was   abowen in þe clowdez,
Betakyns the tyrauntez   þat tourmentez thy pople;
Or ells with somme gyaunt   some journee sall happyn   825
In syngulere batell   by ȝoureselfe⟨n⟩ one,
And þow sall hafe þe victorye   thurghe *vertu* of oure Lorde,
As þow in thy visione   was *veray*ly schewede.
Of this dredfull dreme   ne drede the no more,
Ne kare noghte, sir conquerour,   bot comforth thy selven, 830
And thise þat saillez over þe see   with thy sekyre knyghtez.'

821 tatterede] tachesesede *MS.* — 827 vertu] helpe *MS.* — 828
verayly] opynly *MS.*

---

astantibus quod somniaverat indicavit. Qui exponentes dicebant draconem significare eum, ursum vero aliquem gigantem qui cum ipso
congrederetur; pugnam autem eorum portendere bellum, quod inter ipsos
futurum erat; victoriam vero draconis illam quae ei proveniret.

A: 'Sir,' seyde the phylozopher, 'the dragon thou dremyste of betokyns
thyne owne persone that thus here sayles with thy syker knyghtes; and
the coloure of his wyngys is thy kyngdomes that thou haste with thy
knyghtes wonne. And his tayle that was all to-tatered sygnyfyed your
noble knyghtes of the Rounde Table. And the beare that the dragon
slowe above in the clowdis betokyns som tyraunte that turmentis thy
peple, other thou art lyke to fyght with som gyaunt boldely in batayle
be thyself alone. Therefore of this dredfull dreme drede the but a lytyll,
and care nat now, sir conquerroure, but comfort⟨h⟩ thyself.

XXI

WILLIAM LANGLAND
PIERS PLOWMAN

To a great extent medieval literature is addressed to an upper class that the author wants to instruct or amuse. In such works there is rarely any concern with common people, their life, their suffering, their hopes. The most remarkable exception to this is a vast alliterative poem called by W. W. Skeat *The Vision of William concerning Piers the Plowman*. That this was a work very much read in the 14th and 15th centuries may be gathered from the fact that no less than fifty manuscripts survive. Skeat, who was the first to classify them, noted that these manuscripts divide themselves quite naturally into three groups corresponding to three successive stages of revision which are called versions A, B, and C. Version A, the shortest (2,567 lines), seems to date 1362-3. Version B is almost three times as long (7,242 lines): according to certain additions like the parable of belling the cat (see extract no. 2), an evident allusion to the political crisis of 1376-7, its composition is thought to be somewhere near this date. Finally version C, a revision of B, is very little longer (7,357 lines) because additions are compensated for by omissions, but it differs sharply from the other two, and its date of composition is put in the last years of the 14th century.

In spite of rather impassioned controversy, especially for academic circles, and since the death of J. M. Manly, it is possible to agree that the three versions are the work of the same author who would have, himself, developed and changed, and would have reworked his essentially topical poem in the course of these changes in his life and times. Basing our assumptions on the colophons (inscriptions at the end of many manuscripts), and on later allusions, it would appear that the author was named William Langland. There is practical agreement that the verse

> ' I have lived in *londe*,' quod I, ' my name is *Longe Wille* '

is an anagram in which the author names himself. Besides, a 15th century manuscript affirms that he was born in Shropshire not far from Malvern (where the first vision is placed) and that he was the son, undoubtedly illegitimate, of a Stacy (or Eustace) of Rokayle who stemmed from the Despencer family that lived at Shipton-under-Wychwood in Oxfordshire. Finally, from a few apocryphal lines added by a certain John But, it would seem that William Langland died in 1399. There has been a great deal of discussion about these more or less facts, but the discussion does not get us very far, for the life of W. Langland remains unknown to us.

Few medieval works have a tone as personal as *Piers Plowman*; to read it is sufficient to get a psychological biography of its author (see, for example, extract no. 3 which is a straight confession). If William Langland was not precisely a ' man of the people ', his temperament and the vicissitudes of life brought him, closer than any other, to understanding and expressing the ideas of the common people. Above all, he is a powerful writer, at once a mystic and a realist, sometimes a see-er of visions, sometimes a merciless critic of the social injustice of his time, the spokesman for the humble and the masses, tireless defender of constitutional liberty; a man profoundly sincere and religious, he aspires to a reform of society, the Church, religion, but not to a revolution; by his instinctive need to think in allegories, he is in direct line with John Bunyan. Not so great as Dante, more truly English than Chaucer, he is the most attractive literary figure of the 14th century in his country.

It was formerly considered that *Piers Plowman* was made up of a series of badly connected visions without any preconceived plan. The structure of the vast work and its architecture now appear more clearly as the role of its main personage, Piers Plowman, and his character have been elucidated by the studies of H. W. WELLS, N. K. COGHILL and others. Nevertheless, it would be hard to give a concise summary of its contents.

As appears from the more complete B-Text the whole work is to be divided into four sections: The *Visio de Petro Plowman* (Prologue and Passus I to VII), the *Vita de Dowel* (Passus VIII to XV) the *Vita de Dobet* (Passus XVI to XVIII), and the *Vita de Dobest* (Passus XIX to the end). The general theme of the poem being the Salvation of Man.

Only the first section, from which our extracts are taken, will be considered here. It is a study of human life in the Active World as it existed in Langland's time and it serves as a sort of introduction to the three other sections. It opens with a first vision. The poet goes to sleep on a May morning, listening to the sound of a brook, on a Malvern Hill (extract no. 1); he sees a great field full of folk, all humanity, represented by examples from each class and condition. A woman appears who is Holy Church; she explains the country-side and the vision, tells how humanity ought to live, instructs kings and nobles in their duty towards Truth; she goes on to say that faith without works is vain, and that the road to heaven passes through Love. Then there comes a great lady, magnificently dressed, who has the equivocal name of Lady Meed (meaning both 'legitimate reward' and 'corrupt bribery', 'bribe', 'ill-gotten gains'). She is to marry Falsehood but Theology objects to the marriage. The king proposes that she should marry Conscience, but Conscience refuses and exposes her faults. At this moment Peace enters with a complaint against Wrong. Wrong, knowing the complaint to be true, wins over Wit and Wisdom by Meed's help and buys off Peace with a present. Reason, however, advises the king that Wrong should still be punished and that kings should act justly. The king agrees, appoints Reason counsellor and all go to church. The sleeper wakes for a moment but drops off into a second dream while saying his prayers, and now sees Conscience (A-text, Reason B and C) preaching to the field full of folk who begin to repent their sins. Each sin is personified and the seven deadly sins file by one by one and confess, which gives us a matchless series of genre portraits in almost more than modern realistic detail, like Glutton (extract no. 4). All agree to seek Truth, but nobody knows the way. At last Piers the Plowman, a mystical figure some-times representing the man of good-will and sometimes Christ himself, appears and agrees to lead them to Truth. They are to go through Meekness and come to Conscience and then past the personified ten commandments. Piers instructs each person in his particular duty towards work; with the aid of Hunger he forces the lazy and wasteful to work. The trip to Truth never gets started. After Hunger discourses, Truth hears of all this and sends Piers a pardon: whoever in this world lives according to the Gospel and works, may win Salvation. Such a life is to " Do-well ". (See R. W. FRANK, " The Pardon Scene in *Piers Plowman," Speculum* XXVI (1951), pp. 317-336).

This provides the transition to the other sections of the poem which consider in turn the three degrees of Mystic life, the life of layman in Active Life (*Dowel*), the Contemplative or Clerkly life (*Dobet*) and the superior active life, that of the Spiritual authorities or Bishops (*Dobest*); three degrees of spiritual life — the good life, the better life, the perfect life. The symbolic figure of Piers Plowman appears in each of these ways of life and makes the allegorical unity of the whole poem.

The only complete editions, at this moment, are those of W. W. SKEAT, one for the EETS (London, 1867-84), the other in two volumes (Oxford, 1886). The most recent edition of a single version is that of Thomas A. KNOTT and David C. FOWLER: *Piers the Plowman, A Critical Text of the A-version*, Baltimore, 1952. A critical edition of the three versions is being prepared at the University of London under the supervision of A. H. SMITH and the A-text edited by G. KANE is ready and will be published in the near future. There are some editions of parts of the B-text by W. W. SKEAT (10th ed., Oxford, 1924) and J. F. DAVIS (London, 1896), also translations into Modern English by K. M. WARREN (London, 1895), W. W. SKEAT (London, 1905), H. W. WELLS (London, 1935, the best), and N. COGHILL (London, 1949).

Consult also:

J. J. JUSSERAND. *Piers Plowman: a Contribution to the History of English Mysticism*, London, 1894

D. CHADWICK. *Social Life in the Days of Piers Plowman*, Cambridge, 1922.

A. H. BRIGHT. *New Light on ' Piers Plowman '*, Oxford, 1928.

H. W. WELLS. " The Construction of Piers Plowman," *PMLA*, XLIV (1929) 123-140.

N. K. COGHILL. " The Character of Piers Plowman considered from the B-text ", *Medium Aevum* II (1933) 108-135.

N. K. COGHILL. " The Pardon of Piers Plowman," *Proceedings of the British Academy*, Oxford, 1945.

R. W. CHAMBERS. " Piers Plowman: A Comparative Study," in *Man's Unconquerable Mind*, London, 1939, pp. 88-171.

E. T. DONALDSON. *Piers Plowman, The C-Text and Its Poet* (Yale Studies in English, 113), New Haven, 1949.

D. W. ROBERTSON, Jr. and B. F. HUPPÉ. *Piers Plowman and Scriptural Tradition*, Princeton, 1951.

G. KANE. *Middle English Literature*, London, 1951, pp. 182-248.

M. W. BLOOMFIELD. " Present State of ' Piers Plowman Studies ' " in *Speculum* XIV (1939), pp. 215-32 (cp. also J. R. HULBERT, *Modern Philology* XLV [1948] 215-25).

J. E. WELLS. *Manual*, pp. 244-68 (bibliography, pp. 800-2).

1. The First Vision (Version A, Prologue)

In a somer sesun,   whon softe was þe sonne,

I schop me into a schroud,   a scheep as I were.

In habite of an hermite   unholy of werkes,

Wende I wydene in þis world   wondres to here.

Bote in a mayes morwnynge   on Malverne Hulles   5

Me bifel a ferly,   a feyrie, me þouhte.

I was weori of wandringe   and wente me to reste

Undur a brod banke   bi a bourne syde,

And as I lay and leonede   and lokede on þe watres,

I slumberde in a slepyng;   hit sownede so murie.   10

   Þenne gon I meeten   a mervelous swevene,

Þat I was in a wildernesse,   wuste I never where;

And as I beoheold into þe est   anheiȝ to þe sonne,

I sauh a tour on a toft   triȝely i-maket;

A deop dale bineoþe   a dungun þerinne,

With deop dich and derk   and dredful of siht.

   A feir feld ful of folk   fond I þer bitwene,

Of alle maner of men   þe mene and þe riche,

Worchinge and wondringe,   as þe world askeþ.

Summe putten hem to þe plouȝ   and pleiden hem ful seldene 20

In eringe and in sowynge   swonken ful harde,

Þat monie of þeos wasturs   in glotonye distruen.

   And summe putten hem to pruide,   apparaylden hem

In cuntinaunce of cloþinge   queinteliche degyset; [þerafter,

To preyere and to penaunce   putten heom monye,   25

For love of ur lord   liveden ful harde,

In hope for to have   Heveneriche blisse;

As ancres and hermytes   þat holdeþ hem in heore celles;

Coveyte not in cuntré   to cairen aboute,

For non likerous lyflode,   heore licam to plese.   30

   And summe chosen chaffare,   to cheeven þe bettre,

As hit semeþ to ure siht   þat suche men scholden;

And summe murþhes to maken,   as munstrals cunne

⟨And gete gold wiþ here gle,   giltles, I trowe.⟩

   Bote japers and jangelers,   Judas children,   35

Founden hem fantasyes   and fooles hem maaden,

14 triȝely *I*] wonderliche *V.* — 29 cairen] cairen *V.* — 34 *this line,*
borrowed from MS I is lacking in V.

And habbeþ wit at heor wille   to worchen, ȝif hem luste. *ü*
Þat Poul precheþ of hem,   I dar not preoven heere;
Qui loquitur turpiloquium,   hee is Luciferes hyne.
40   Bidders and beggers   faste aboute eoden, *went archaic*
Til heor bagges and heore balies   weren bratful i-crommet; *past pple*
Feyneden hem for heore foode,   fouȝten atte alle; *could be spel*
In glotonye, God wot,   gon heo to bedde, *gh or ƚ*
And ryseth up wiþ ribaudye,   þis Roberdes knaves;
45 Sleep and sleuȝþe   suweþ hem evere.
    Pilgrimes and palmers   plihten hem togederes
For to seche Seint Jeme   and seintes at Roome;
Wenten forþ in heore wey   with mony wyse tales
And hedden leve to lyȝen   al heore lyf-tyme.
50 ⟨Ermytes on an hep   wiþ hokide staves,
Wenten to Walsyngham   and here wenchis after.⟩
    Grete lobres and longe,   þat loþ weore to swynke,
Cloþeden hem in copes,   to beo knowen for breþeren;
And summe schopen *hem* to hermytes,   heore ese to have.
55   I font þere freres,   all þe foure ordres,
Prechinge þe peple   for profyt of heore wombes,
Glosynge þe gospel,   as hem good likeþ,
For covetyse of copes   construeþ hit ille;
For monye of þis maistres   mowen cloþen hem at lyking,
60 For moneye and heore marchaundie   meeten ofte togedere.
Seþþe Charité haþ be chapmon   *and* cheef to schriven lordes,
Mony ferlyes han bifalle   in a fewe ȝeres.
But holychirche biginne   holde bet togedere,
Þe moste mischeef on molde   mounteþ up faste.

2. Council of Rats and Mice
(Version B, Prologue.)

Wiþ þat ran þere a route   of ratones at ones,
And smale mys with hem,   mo þen a þousande,

41 bratful *T*] faste *V.* — 50-1 *Line omitted in MS V and taken from*
T. — 54 schopen hem *T*] schopen *V.* — 61 and cheef *T*] cheef *V.* —

And comen to a conseille,   for here comune profit;
For a cat of a courte   cam whan hym lyked,
And overlepe hem ly3tlich,   and lau3te hem at his wille,   150
And pleyde wiþ hem perilouslych   and possed *hem* aboute.
'For doute of dyverse dredes   we dar nou3te wel loke;
And 3if we grucche of his gamen   he wil greve us alle,
Cracche us, or clowe us   and in his cloches holde,
That us lotheth þe lyf   or he lete us passe.   155
My3te we wiþ any witte   his wille withstonde,
We my3te be lordes aloft   and lyven at owre ese!'
    A raton of renon   most renable of tonge,
Seide for a sovereygne   help to hymselve:
'I have y-sein segges,' quod he,   'in þe Cité of London,   160
Beren bi3es ful bri3te   abouten here nekkes,
And some colers of crafty werk;   uncoupled þei wenden
Boþe in wareine and in waste   where hem leve lyketh;
And otherwhile þei aren elleswhere   as I here telle.
Were þere a belle on here bei3   bi Jhesu, as me thynketh,   165
Men my3te wite where þei went   and awei renne!
And ri3t so,' quod þat ratoun,   'reson me sheweth,
To bugge a belle of brasse   or of bri3te sylver,
And knitten on a colere   for owre comune profit,
And hangen it upon þe cattes hals;   þanne here we mowen   170
Where he ritt or rest   or renneth to playe.
And 3if him list for to laike   þenne loke we mowen,
And peren in his presence   þer-while hym plaie liketh,
And 3if him wrattheth, be y-war   and his weye shonye.'
    Alle þis route of ratones   to þis reson þei assented.   175
Ac þo þe belle was y-bou3t   and on þe bei3e hanged,
Þere ne was ratoun in alle þe route,   for alle þe rewme of Fraunce,
Þat dorst have y-bounden þe belle   aboute þe cattis nekke,
Ne hangen *it* aboute þe cattes hals   al Engelonde to wynne;
And helden hem unhardy   and here conseille feble,   180
And leten here laboure lost   and alle here longe studye.

151 possed hem *C*] possed *L.* — 179 hangen it *C*] hangen *L.*

A mous þat moche good   couthe, as. me thouȝte,
Stroke forth sternly   and stode biforn hem alle,
And to þe route of ratones   reherced þese wordes:
185 'Thouȝ we culled þe catte,   ȝut sholde þer come another,
To cracchy us and al owre kynde,   þouȝ we crope under benches,
For-þi I conseille alle þe comune   to lat þe catte worthe,
And be we never so bolde   þe belle hym to shewe;
For I herde my sire seyn,   is sevene ȝere y-passed,
190 Þere þe catte is a kitoun   þe courte is ful elyng;
Þat witnisseth holiwrite,   who-so wil it rede,
            Vae terrae ubi puer rex est, etc.
For may no renke þere rest have   for ratones bi nyȝte;
Þe while he caccheþ conynges   he coveiteth nouȝt owre caroyne,
But fet hym al with venesoun,   defame we hym nevere.
195 For better is a litel losse   þan a longe sorwe,
Þe mase amonge us alle,   þouȝ we mysse a schrewe.
For many mannus malt   we, mys, wolde destruye,
And also ȝe, route of ratones,   rende mennes clothes,
Nere þat cat of þat courte   þat can ȝow overlepe;   [selve.
200 For had ȝe, rattes, ȝowre wille   ȝe couthe nouȝt reule ȝowre-
I sey for me,' quod þe mous,   'I se so mykel after,
Shall never þe cat ne þe kitoun   bi my conseille be greved,
Ne carpyng of þis coler   þat costed me nevre.
And þouȝ it had coste me catel,   biknowen it I nolde,
205 But suffre as hymself wolde   to do as hym liketh,
Coupled and uncoupled   to cacche what thei mowe.
For-þi uche a wise wiȝte I warne   wite wel his owne.'
    What þis meteles bemeneth,   ȝe, men þat be merye,
Devine ȝe, for I ne dar,   bi dere God in hevene!

3. The Author and His Life (Version C, Passus VI)

Thus ich awaked, God wot,   w⟨h⟩anne ich wonede on Corne-
Kytte and ich in a cote,   cloþed as a lollere,   [hulle,

---

186 crope *R*] croupe *L*. — 1 God wot] wot god *P*.

And lytel *y*-let⟨e⟩ by,   leyve me for soþe,
Among lollares of London   and lewede heremytes;
For ich made of þo men   as reson me tauhte.   5
For as ich cam by Conscience,   wit⟨h⟩ Reson ich mette
In an hote hervest,   w⟨h⟩enne ich hadde myn hele,
And lymes to labore with   and lovede wel fare,
And no dede to do,   bote drynke and to slepe.
In hele and in unité   on me aposede;   10
Romynge in remembraunce,   thus Reson me aratede.
  'Canstow serven,' he seide,   'oþer syngen in a churche,
Oþer coke for my cokers,   oþer to þe cart picche,
Mowe oþer mowen,   oþer make bond to sheves,
Repe oþer be a repereyve,   and aryse erliche,   [nyghtes, 15
Oþer have an horne and be haywarde,   and liggen oute a
And kepe my corn in my croft   fro pykers and þeeves?
Oþer shappe shon, oþer cloþes,   oþer shep, oþer kyn kepe,
⟨H⟩eggen oþer harwen,   oþer swyn oþer gees dryve,
⟨Oþer⟩ eny oþer kyns craft   þat to þe comune nedeþ,   20
Hem þat bedreden be,   bylyve to fynde?'
  'Certes,' ich seyde,   'and so me God helpe,
Ich am to waik to worche   with sykel oþer with sythe,
And to long, leyf me,   lowe for to stoupe,
To worchen as a workeman,   eny w⟨h⟩yle to dure.'   25
  'Thenne havest þow londes to lyve by,'   quath Reson,
                              ['oþer lynage riche
That finden þe þy fode?   for an ydel man thow semest,
A spendour þat spende mot,   oþer a spille-tyme,
Oþer beggest þy bylyve   aboute at menne hacches,
Oþer faitest upon Frydays,   oþer feste-dayes in churches, 30
The w⟨h⟩iche is lollarene lyf   þat lytel ys preysed,
Þer ryghtfulnesse rewardeþ,   ryght as men deserveþ,
          Reddit unicuique iuxta opera sua.
Oþer þow art broke, so may be,   in body oþer in membre,

3 lytel] a lytel *P*; y-lete *I*] ich let *P*. — 20 eny oþer *M*] eny *P*; nedeþ
M] nudeþ *P*. — 27 ydel] hydel *P*. — 29 at] ate *P*. — 33 art] ert *P*.

Oþer y-maymed þrow som mys-hap,　　w⟨h⟩er-by þow myȝt
　　　　　　　　　　　　　　　　　　[be excused?

35　'W⟨h⟩anne ich ȝong was,' quath ich,　'meny ȝer hennes,
My fader and my frendes　　founden me to scole,
Tyl ich wiste wyterliche　　w⟨h⟩at holy wryt menede,
And w⟨h⟩at is best for þe body,　　as þe bok telleþ,
And sykerest for þe soule,　　by so ich wolle continue.
40　And ȝut fond ich nevere in faith,　　sytthen my frendes deyden,
Lyf þat me lyked,　　bote in þes longe clothes.
Yf ich by laboure sholde lyve　　and lyflode deserven,
That labour þat ich lerned best　　þer-with lyve ich sholde;
　　　　In eadem vocatione in qua vocati estis, manete.
And ich lyve in Londone,　　and on Londone bothe,
45　The lomes þat ich laboure with　　and lyflode deserve
Ys *pater-noster* and my prymer　　*placebo* and *dirige*,
And my sauter somtyme,　　and my sevene psalmes,
Thus ich synge for hure soules　　of suche as me helpen,
And þo þat fynden me my fode　　vouchen saf, ich trowe,
50　To be welcome w⟨h⟩anne ich come　　oþer-w⟨h⟩yle in a monthe,
Now with hym and now with hure　　and þus-gate ich begge,
Withoute bagge oþer botel,　　bote my wombe one.
And also moreover　　me þynkeþ, syre Reson,
Men sholde constreyne no clerke　　to knavene werkes;
55　For by lawe of *Levitici*　　þat oure Lord ordeynede,
Clerkes, þat aren crouned　　of kynde understondyng,
Sholde noþer swynke ne swete　　ne swere at enquestes,
Ne fyghte in no vauntwarde　　ne hus fo greve;
　　　　Non reddas malum pro malo.
For it ben aires of hevene　　alle þat ben crounede,
60　And in queer and in *kirkes*　　Cristes owene mynestres,

---

42 Yf] Hyf *P.* — 43 þer-with] þerwhit *P*; in eadem . . . manete *M*]
omitted *P.* — 44 Londone *M*] londene *P.* — 49 vouchen] vochen *P.* —
50 welcome] wolcome *P.*— 59 alle] and alle *P.* — 60 kirkes *I*] churches
P.

Dominus pars hereditatis meae; & alibi: clementia non constringit.

Hit bycomeþ for clerkus   Crist for to serven,
And knaves uncrouned   to cart and to worche,
For shold no clerk be crouned   bote yf he y-come were
Of franklens and free men,   and of folke y-weddede.
Bondmen and bastardes   and beggers children,   65
Thuse bylongeþ to labour   and lordes *kyn to* serven
Bothe God and good men   as here degree askeþ;
Some to synge masses,   oþer sitten and wryte,
Rede and receyve   þat reson ouhte spende;
Ac sith bondemenne barnes   han be mad bisshopes,   70
And barnes bastardes   han ben archidekenes,
And sopers and here sones   for selver han be knyghtes,
And lordene sones here laborers   and leid here rentes to wedde,
For þe ryght of *þis* reame   ryden aȝens oure enemys,
In confort of þe comune   and þe kynges worshep,   75
And monkes and moniales,   þat mendinauns sholden fynde,
Han mad here kyn knyghtes   and knyght-fees purchase⟨d⟩,
Popes and patrones   poure gentil blod refuseþ,
And taken Symondes sone   seyntewarie to kepe.
Lyf-holynesse and love   han ben longe hennes,   80
And wole, til hit be wered out,   or oþerwise y-chaunged.
For-þy rebuke me ryght nouht,   Reson, ich ȝow praye;
For in my conscience ich knowe   what Crist wolde þat ich
Preyers of ⟨a⟩ parfyt man   and penaunce discret   [wrouhte.
Ys þe leveste labour   þat oure lord pleseþ.   85
Non de solo,' ich seide,   'for soþe *vivit homo,*
Nec in pane & pabulo   þe *pater-noster* witnesseþ;
Fiat voluntas tua   fynt ous alle þynges.'
    Quath Conscience: 'By Crist,   ich can nat see this lyeþ;
Ac it semeth nouht parfytnesse   in cytees for to begge,   90
Bote he be obediencer   to pryour oþer to mynstre.'

66 kyn to *M*] children sholde *P.* — 70 Ac *M*] And *P.* — 74 þis *M*] þes *P.*

'That ys soth,' ich seide,   'and so ich byknowe,
That ich have tynt tyme   and tyme mysspended;
And ȝut, ich hope, as he   that ofte haveþ chaffared,
95 Þat ay hath lost and lost,   and atte laste hym happed
He bouhte suche a bargayn   he was þe bet evere,
And sette hus lost at a lef,   at þe laste ende,
Suche a wynnynge hym warth   þorw wordes of Hus grace;
  Simile est regnum caelorum thesauro abscondito in agro,
  Mulier quae invenit dragmam unam, et caetera;   [*& caetera:*
So hope ich to have,   of Hym þat is almighty,
100 A gobet of Hus grace   and bygynne a tyme,
Þat alle tymes of my tyme   to profit shal turne.'
  'Ich rede þe,' quath Reson þo,   'rape þe to bygynne
Þe lyf þat ys lowable   and leel to the soule'—   [wente.
'Ȝe, and continue;' quath Conscience,   and to þe *kirke* ich
105   And to þe *kirke* gan ich go   God to honourie,
Byfor þe crois, on my knees,   knocked ich my brest,
Sykinge for my synnes   seggynge my *pater-noster,*
Wepyng and wailinge   tyl ich was a slepe.

4. Glutton at the Tavern (Version B, Passus V)

Now bigynneth Glotoun   for to go to schrifte,
305 And kaires hym to-kirke-ward   his coupe to schewe.
  Ac Beton þe brewestere   bad hym good morwe,
And axed of hym with þat   whiderward he wolde.
  'To holi cherche,' quod he,   'for to here masse,
And sithen I wil be shryven   and synne namore.'
310   'I have gode ale, gossib,' quod she,   'Glotown, wiltow
'Hastow auȝte in þi purs   any hote spices?'   [assaye?
'I have peper and piones,' quod ⟨s⟩he,   'and a pounde of
A ferthyng-worth of fenel-seed   for fastyng-dayes.'   [garlike,
Þanne goth Glotoun in   and Grete-Othes after;

---

95 atte laste *I*] at þe latiste *P.* — 98 wordes] wyrdes *P.* — 99 is]
his *P.* — 104, 105 kirke *I*] churche *P.* — 107 synnes] sennes *P.* — 312
she *W*] he *L.*

Cesse þe souteresse   sat on þe benche,   315
Watte þe warner   and hys wyf bothe,
Tymme þe tynkere   and tweyne of his prentis,
Hikke þe hakeneyman   and Hughe þe nedeler,
Clarice of Cokkes-lane   and þe clerke of þe cherche,
Dawe þe dykere   and a dozeine other;   320
Sire Piers of Pridie   and Peronelle of Flaundres,
A ribibour, a ratonere,   a rakyer of Chepe,
A ropere, a redyngkyng   and Rose þe dissheres,
Godfrey of Garleke-hithe   and Gryfin þe walshe,
And upholderes an hepe,   erly bi þe morwe   325
Geven Glotoun with glad chere   good ale to hansel.
   Clement þe cobelere   cast of his cloke,
And atte New Faire   he nempned it to selle;
Hikke þe hakeneyman   hitte his hood after,
And badde Bette þe bochere   ben on his side.   330
Þere were chapmen y-chose   þis chaffare to preise;
Who-so haveth þe hood   shuld have amendes of þe cloke.
   Two risen up in rape   and rouned togideres,
And preised þese penyworthes   apart bi hemselve;
Þei couth nouȝte bi her conscience   acorden in treuthe,   335
Tyl Robyn þe ropere   arose bi þe southe,
And nempned hym for a noumpere   þat no debate nere,
⟨For to trye þis chaffare   bitwixen hem þre.⟩
   Hikke þe hostellere   hadde þe cloke,
In covenaunte þat Clement   shulde þe cuppe fille,   340
And have Hikkes hode hostellere   and holde hym y-served;
And who-so repented rathest   shulde arise after
And grete sire Glotoun   with a galoun ale.
   Þere was laughyng and louryng   and 'let go þe cuppe,'
And seten so til evensonge   and songen umwhile,   345
Tyl Glotoun had y-globbed   a galoun an a jille.
His guttis gunne to go*the*ly   as two gredy sowes;

---

338 *line omitted by L. and taken from MS O.* — 347 gothely *C*]
godly *L.*

  He pissed a potel in a *pater-noster*-while,
  And blew his rounde ruwet at his rigge-bon ende,
350 That alle þat herde þat horne held her nose after,
  And wissheden it had be wexed with a wispe of firses.
  He myȝte neither steppe ne stonde er he his staffe hadde;
  And þanne gan he go liche a glewmannes bicche,
  Somme tyme aside and somme tyme arrere,
355 As who-so leyth lynes for to lacche foules.
   And whan he drowgh to þe dore þanne dymmed his eighen,
  He *stu*mbled on þe thresshewolde an⟨d⟩ threwe to þe erthe.
  Clement þe cobelere cauȝte hym bi þe myddel,
  For to lifte hym alofte and leyde him on his knowes;
360 Ac Glotoun was a gret cherle and a grym in þe liftynge,
  And coughed up a caudel in Clementis lappe;
  Is non so hungri hounde in Hertfordschire
  Durst lape of the levynges so unlovely þei smauȝte.
  With al þe wo of þis worlde his wyf and his wenche
365 Baren hym home to his bedde and brouȝte hym þerinne.
  And after al þis excesse he had an accidie,
  Þat he slepe Saterday and Sonday til sonne ȝede to reste.
  Þanne wakede he of his wynkyng and wiped his eyghen;
  Þe fyrste worde þat he warpe was: 'where is þe bolle?'

357 stumbled *C*] trembled *L*.

XXII

JOHN BARBOUR

THE BRUCE

The *Bruce,* which its author dates 1375, marks the beginning of Scots literature — a political and not a linguistic animal (cp. Rolle's dialect with this). A chronicler named Wyntoun (1350?-1420?) tells us it was composed by John Barbour (1320-1395) who was archdeacon of Aberdeen, studied at Oxford (thanks to safe-conducts granted him by Edward III) and travelled in France (1365 and 1368). Wyntoun also attributes to him the composition of a *Brut* and a *Genealogy of the Stuarts,* both lost.

The *Bruce* is a long narrative poem of 13,549 lines in octosyllabic rimed couplets, divided into twenty books. It recounts the life and exploits of Robert Bruce (1274-1329), nationalist champion of Scotland, hero of Bannockburn. Events previous to 1304 are summarized in the prologue and the work begins with the moment when Robert finds himself offered the crown.

The author admits that the *Bruce* is an historical romance, but he seems to follow facts rather faithfully. The story is brisk, the characters very life-like. If the patriotism which breaks out on every page carries him now and then a little far from the truth, still it contributes to the episodes that Barbour narrates an irresistable animation and excitement.

The two extracts which are found below are typical of his style. The first is a veritable hymn to independence in the face of English threats, the second a tale worthy of Walter Scott.

Editions:

The *Bruce* was published by W. W. SKEAT in the EETS (London, 1870-88) and in the Scottish Text Society (Edinburgh, 1894).

Consult also:

Fr. BRIE. *Die nationale Literatur Schottlands von den Anfängen bis zur Renaissance,* Halle, 1937 (pp. 33-123).

J. E. WELLS. *Manual,* pp. 202-4 (bibliography, p. 795).

1. Freedom (Book I)

A! fredome is a noble thing!   225
Fredome mayβ man to haiff liking;
Fredome all solace to man giffis:
He levys at eβ that frely levys!
A noble hart may haiff nane eβ
Na ellys nocht that may him pleβ,   230
Gyff fredome failȝhe; for fre liking

Is ȝharnyt our all othir thing.
Na he, that ay haβ levyt fre,
May nacht knaw weill the propyrte,
235   The angyr, na the wrechyt dome
That is cowplyt to foule thyrldome.
Bot gyff he had assayit it,
Than all perquer he suld it wyt;
And suld think fredome mar to pryβ
240   Than all the gold in warld that is
Thus contrar thingis evirmar,
Discoweryngis off the tothir ar.
And he that thryll is has nocht his,
All that he haβ enbandownyt is
245   Till hys lord, quhat evir he be.
Yheit has he nocht sa mekill fre
As fre *liking* to leyve, or do
That at hys hart hym drawis to.
Than mayβ clerkis questioun,
250   Quhen thai fall in disputacioun,
That gyff man bad his thryll owcht do,
And in the samyn tym come him to
His wyff, and askyt hym hyr det,
Quhethir he his lordis neid sul let,
255   And pay fryst that he awcht, and syne
Do furth his lordis commandyne;
Or leve onpayit his wyff, and do
It that commaundyt is him to?
I leve all the solucioun
260   Till thaim that ar off mar renoun.
Bot sen thai mak sic comperyng
Betwix the dettis off wedding
And lordis bidding till his threll,
ȝe may weile se, thoucht nane ȝow tell,
265   How hard a thing that threldome is,

246 liking *H A*] wyll *E.* — 258 It *H*] Thai thingis *E.*

For men may weile se, that ar wyβ,
That wedding is the hardest band
That ony man may tak on hand.
And thryldome is weil wer than deid;
For quhill a thryll his lyff may leid,　　　　　　270
It merrys him, body and banys,
And dede anoyis him bot anys.
Schortly to say, is nane can tell
The halle condicioun off a threll.

2. The King and the Three Traitors (Book VII)

Swa hapnyt it that on a day,　　　　　　　　400
He vent till hwnt, for till assay
Quhat gammyn wes in that cuntré;
And sa hapnyt *that* day that he
By a vode-syde to sett is gane,
Vith his twa hundis hym allane;　　　　　　405
Bot he his swerd ay vith hym bare.
He had bot schort quhill syttyn thare,
Quhen he saw fra the vode cumand
Thre men vith bowis in thar hand,
That toward hym com spedely,　　　　　　　410
And he persavit that in hy,
Be thair effeir and thair havyng,
That thai lufit hym na kyn thyng.
He raiβ and his leysche till him drew he,
And leit his houndis gang all fre.　　　　　415
God help the kyng now for his mycht!
For, bot he now be viβ and vicht,
He sall be set in mekill preβ.
For thai thre men, vithouten leβ,
War his fayis all utrely,　　　　　　　　420
And had vachit so besaly,

403 that *E H*] a *C*.

To se quhen thai vengeans mycht tak
Of the kyng for Johne Cwmynys sak,
That thai thoucht than thai laser had;
425 And sen he hym allane wes stad,
In hy thai thoucht thai suld him sla,
And gif that thai mycht cheviß swa,
Fra that thai the kyng had slayn,
That thai mycht vyn the vode agayn,
430 His men, thai thoucht, thai suld nocht dreid.
In hy towart the kyng thai ȝeid,
And bend thair bowis quhen thai var neir;
And he, that dred in gret maneir
Thair arowis, for he nakit was,
435 In hy ane spekyng to thame mais,
And said: 'ȝhe aucht to shame, perdé,
Syn I am ane and ȝhe ar thre,
For to schut at me on fer!
Bot haf ȝhe hardyment, cum ner
440 Vith ȝour swerdis, me till assay;
Wyn me on sic viß, gif ȝhe may;
ȝhe sall weill mair all prisit be.'
'Perfay,' quod ane than of the thre,
'Sall no man say we drede the swa,
445 That we vith arrowis sall the sla.'
With that thair bowis avay thai kest,
And com on *fast* but langar *frest*.
The kyng thame met full hardely,
And smat the first so rigorusly,
450 That he fell ded doun on the greyn.
And quhen the kyngis hounde has seyn
Thai men assale his mastir swa,
He lap till ane and can hym ta
Richt be the nek full felonly,
455 Till top our taill he gert hym ly.

447 fast *E H*] than *C*; frest *E*] lest *C*.

And the kyng, that his swerd up had,
Saw he so fair succour hym maid,
Or he that fall*yn* wes mycht ryβ,
Had hym assalʒeit on sic wiβ
That he the bak strak evyn in twa. 460
The thrid that saw his fallowis swa
Forouten recoveryng be slayne,
Tuk till the vod his vay agane.
Bot the kyng followit spedely;
And als the hound that wes hym by 465
Quhen he the man saw gang hym fra,
Schot till hym soyn, and can hym ta
Richt be the nek, and till hym dreuch;
And the kyng that ves neir e-neuch,
In his risyng sic rowt hym gaf, 470
That stane-ded till the erd he draf.
The kyngis menʒe that war neir,
Quhen at thai saw on sic maneir
The kyng assalit sa suddandly,
Thai sped thame toward hym in hy, 475
And askit how that caβ befell.
And he all haly can thaim tell,
How thai assalʒeit hym all thre.
'Perfay,' quod thai, 'we may weill se
That it is hard till undirtak 480
Sic mellyng vith ʒow for to mak,
That so smertly has slayn thir thre
Forouten hurt:?—'Perfay,' said he,
'I slew bot ane forouten ma,
God and my hound has slane the twa. 485
Thair tresoune cumrit thame perfay
For richt vicht men alle thre var thai.'

458 fallyn *E*] fallit *C.*

XXIII

THE TRAVELS OF SIR JOHN MANDEVILLE

There has seldom been a travel book as popular as the *Travels* of Sir John Mandeville: we still have more than three hundred manuscripts, and before 1500, it is found translated into most of the western languages. The first part of these *Travels* is a pilgrim's guide to the Holy Land, the second is a description of the East. They are written in a clear and fluent prose and with a tone of sincerity that imposed on everyone for a very long time. For these travel stories are a great fraud. Sir John Mandeville, who in his preface says he is an Englishman and a native of St. Albans, probably never existed. The actual author of these pretended travels was undoubtedly a Liège physician Jehan de Bourgogne. He wrote them in French about 1356-7, without ever having left his native town. He cleverly used authentic accounts like those of Guillaume de Boldensele (1336) for the first part and Odoric de Pordenone (1330) for the second. His imagination supplied the rest. And he adopted the pseudonym of Sir John Mandeville as an extra precaution to mislead the reader.

The English text, therefore, is only a translation. The translator, whose personality remains unknown, was someone who had a deep and sure instinct for the English language and for sentence rhythm. On the other hand he did not always understand the French text too well (and thus translates *montaignes* 'mountains' as *þe hille of Aygnes* or *signes du ciel* as *swannes of hevene!* mistaking 'signes' for 'cygnes'). For a long time this talented translator was considered the 'father of English prose'. But this would ignore the current of religious and mystical prose which from *Sawles Warde* and the *Ancrene Wisse* up to Richard Rolle had maintained the older traditions nearly without interruption. Nevertheless, in the domain of secular prose these voyages are one of the first and best examples of a simple and clear style.

Edition:

Mandeville's Travels translated from the French of Jean d'Outremeuse, ed. by P. HAMELIUS, London, 1919 (*EETS OS* 153-4).

Consult also:

Malcom LETTS. *Sir John Mandeville: the Man and his Book.* London, 1949.
J. E. WELLS. *Manual*, pp. 433-7 (bibliography, pp. 834-5).

The Paradise of the Old Man of the Mountain

Besyde the yle of Pentexoire, þat is the lond of Prestre John, is a gret yle long and brode þat men clepen Milstorak; and it is in the lordschipe of Prestre John. In þat yle is gret plentee

JEHAN DE BOURGOGNE: Delez l'isle de Pentexoire, qi est au Prestre Johan, y a une grant isle longe et lee, qe homme appelle Milstorak; et est en la seignurie de Prestre Johan. En celle isle ad molt grant plenté des

of godes. Þere was dwellynge somtyme a riche man, and it
is not longe sithe, and men clept him Gatholonabes, and he 5
was full of cauteles and of sotyll disceytes. And he hadde a
full fair castell and a strong in a mountayne, so strong and
so noble þat noman cowde devise a fairere ne a strengere.
And he had let muren all the mountayne aboute with a strong
wall and a fair, and withinne þo walles he had the fairest 10
gardyn þat ony man myghte beholde, and þerein were trees
berynge all maner of frutes þat ony man cowde devyse. And
þerein were also all maner vertuous herbes of gode smell and
all oþer herbes also þat beren faire floures. And he had also
in þat gardyn many faire welles and, beside þo welles, he had 15
lete make faire halles and faire chambres depeynted all with
gold and azure. And þere weren in þat place many a dyverse
thinges and manye dyverse storyes. And of bestes and of
bryddes þat songen full delectabely and meveden be craft,
þat it semede þat þei weren quyke. And he had also in his 20
gardyn all maner of foules and of bestes þat ony man myghte
thenke on for to have pley or desport to beholde hem. And
he had also in þat place the faireste damyseles þat myghte
ben founde under the age of .xv. ȝeer and the faireste ȝonge
striplynges þat men myghte gete of þat same age; and all þei 25
weren clothed in clothes of gold full richely, and he seyde

---

biens. La soloit avoir un riche homme, il n'ad mye long temps, qe homme
appelloit Gachalonabes, q'estoit molt riches et molt cautelous. Et avoit
un molt beal chastell en une mountaigne si fort, si noble, come nul
homme purroit deviser. Et toute la mountaigne il avoit fait *emmurer*
de moltz beaux mures. Et dedeinz ces mures il avoit la plus beau gardyn
qe l'em poet voer, ou il avoit des arbres portantz toutz les maneres fruitz
si beals come homme poiat diviser ou veer. Et si avoit planter toutz
les herbes bien odorauntz et toutez herbes auxi qi portent bealx floures.
Et si avoit, et unqore y ad, moltz des bealx fountaignes. Et avoit fait
faire delez cellez fountaignez beals sales et beals chambres, toutez peintes
d'or et d'azure, et avoit fait faire molt de diverse chose et de diverses
museries des histoires et de diverses bestes et des oiseaux, qi chauntoient
et tourneient par engine si come ils fussent toutz vifs. Et si avoit mis
en ceo gardin toutes maneres des oysealx q'il poet trover et toutes les
bestes en quoy l'em poait prendre desduit ou solace a regarder. Et si
avoit mis les plus beals dameseyles souz l'age de xv. aunz qu'il poait
trover et les plus beaux jovenceaux de autiel age; et toutz estoient

þat þo weren aungeles. And he had also let make .III. welles
faire and noble and all envyround with ston of jaspre, of
cristall, dyapred with gold and sett with precious stones and
30 grete orient perles. And he had made a conduyt under erthe
so þat the .III. welles at his list, on scholde renne mylk,
anoþer wyn and anoþer hony; and þat place he clept paradys.
And whan þat ony gode knyght þat was hardy and noble
cam to see this rialtee, he wolde lede him into his paradys
35 and schewen him þeise wonderfull thinges to his desport and
the merveyllous and delicious song of dyverse briddes and
the faire damyseles and the faire welles of mylk, of wyn and
of hony plentevous rennynge. And he wolde let make
dyverse instrumentes of musik to sownen in an high tour, so
40 merily þat is was joye for to here and noman sholde see the
craft þereof. And þo, he seyde, weren aungeles of God and
þat place was paradys þat God had behight to his frendes,
seyenge: *Dabo vobis terram fluentem lacte et melle.* And
þanne wolde he maken hem to drynken of a certeyn drynk
45 whereof anon þei sholden be dronken, and þanne wolde hem
thinken gretter delyt þan þei hadden before. And þan wolde
he seye to hem þat, ȝif they wolde dyen for him and for his
love, þat after hire deth þei scholde come to his paradys, and
þei scholden ben of the age of þo damyselles, and þei scholde

---

vestus des draps d'or. Et disoit qe ceo estoient aungeles. Et si avoit
faire iii. fountaignes, bealx et nobles, et toutez environes de piere de
jaspe et de cristalle et ourles d'or et des piers preciouses et des perles.
Et avoit fait faire conduit par dessouz terre, si qe ces iii. fountaignez,
quant il voloit, il fesoit l'un currer de lait, l'autre de vin, et l'autre de
meel. Et cel lieu appelloit il Paradis. Et, quant ascun bon bachiler qi
estoit pruz et hardis le venoit veer, il le menoit en soun Paradys et le
mounstroit les diverses choses et le desduit et les diverses chantz
d'oiseaux et les bealx damesels et les bealx fountaignes de lait et de vin
et de meel. Et fesoit soner de divers instrumentz de musike en un haut
tour, saunz veer les menistriers. Et dissoit que ces estoient angels de
Dieu, et qe ceo estoit li paradys qe Dieu avoit promis a ses ames, en
disant, *Dabo vobis terram fluentem lac et mel.* Et puis il lour fesoit
boire un beverage, dount ils estoient tantost yvres; et puis il lour
sembloit uncore plus grand delit qe devaunt. Et adonqes disoit qe, s'ils
voillent morir pur l'amour de ly, q'ils viendroient apres la mort en ceo
Paradys et serroient al age de celles demoiselles et jeweroient ovesqes

pleyen with hem and ȝit ben maydenes. And after þat ȝit, 50
scholde he putten hem in a fayrere paradys where þat þei
scholde see God of nature visibely in his magestee and in his
blisse. And þan wolde he schewe hem his entent and seye
hem þat, ȝif þei wolde go sle such a lord or such a man þat
was his enemye or contrarious to his list, þat þei scholde not 55
drede to don it and for to be slayn þer fore hemself, for after
hire deth he wolde putten hem into anoþer paradys, þat was
an .c. fold fairere þan ony of the tothere; and þere scholde
þei dwellen with the most fairest damyselles þat myghte be,
and pley with hem everemore. And þus wenten many 60
dyverse lusty bacheleres for to sle grete lordes in dyverse
contrees þat weren his enemyes, and made hemself to ben
slayn in hope to have þat paradys. And þus oftentyme he
was revenged of his enemyes be his sotyll disceytes and false
cawteles. And whan the worthi men of the contree hadden 65
perceyved this sotyll falshod of this Gatholonabes, þei assembled hem with force, and assayleden his castell, and slowen
him and destroyeden all the faire places and all the nobletees
of þat paradys. The place of the welles and of the walles
and of many oþer thinges ben ȝit apertly sene, but the 70
ricchesse is voyded clene; and it is not longes gon sith þat
place was destroyed.

---

elles et toutdis demoeroient pucels, et apres il les mettroit uncqore en un
plus beal Paradys assez, ou ils verroient visiblement Dieu de nature en
sa majesté et en sa glorie. Et lors ly presentoient affaire toute sa
volunté. Et puis il lour disoit q'ils alassent occire tiel seignour q'estoit
ses contraires et q'ils n'en ussent mie paour a eux faire tuer pur
l'amour de ly, qar il les metteroit apres la mort en un autre Paradis
cent temps plus beal, et la demoroient ovesque plus beals damoyselles
a toutdis mais. Et ensy alerount ly bachelers occire des grantz seignours
du pais; et fesoyent eux mesmes tuer en esperance d'aler en ceo Paradys.
Et ensy cils homme se revengeoit de ses adversaires par ses grantz
seduccions. Et, quant ly riches hommes de pais eurent aparceu la
cautele et la malice de cesti Gathalonabez, ils assemblerount et alerount
assailler soun chastel et l'occirent et destruyoient toutz les beaux lieux
et toutz les noblesses qi estoient en ceste Paradys. Ly lieu est uncqore des
fountaignes et des ascuns autres choses et les murailles, mes les richesses
ne sount mie demoeres. Et si *n'a gaires lonc temps* que ly lieu fust
destruit.

XXIV

JOHN WYCLIF

Born into a good family of Yorkshire, about 1328, John Wyclif studied at Oxford, where he distinguished himself, and was made Master of Balliol College in 1360. Appointed curate of Fillingham (1361) then of Ludgershall (1368) he obtained his doctorate in theology in 1372 and entered the king's service. In 1374, after a diplomatic mission, he received as a reward the living of Lutterworth which he held until his death (1384). He divided his time between the duties of his livings, his studies, his teaching at Oxford, and London, where he preached a certain number of sermons.

This is not the place to review his position in so far as he was a reformer in theology, apostle of a religious communal state, nor is it the place to recall the tremendous role he played as precursor of the Reformation, nor to discuss his resounding polemics. It is as a writer of English prose that he interests us here. For Wyclif, who, like all the theologians of his time, had at first written a great deal in Latin, realized the necessity of reaching a larger audience so that he could influence them. Therefore he used English. With Nicolas of Hereford he undertook a complete translation of the Bible, a very heavy task for that period and one which was finished after his death by John Purvey. The one hundred and fifty manuscripts that survive despite papal orders for their destruction, are a sufficient testimony to the need which this enterprise filled. Still it is a mechanical, heavy and awkward translation. There is much more clarity and movement in his sermons where he often follows the sacred text very closely but with the rhetorical freedom of the preacher. Moreover, to drive home his ideas, he often found admirably incisive phrases.

Editions:

Select English Works of John Wyclif, ed. by Th. ARNOLD, Oxford, 1869-71.
The English Works of Wyclif hitherto unprinted, ed. by F. D. MATTHEW, London, 1880 (*EETS* 74).
Wyclif, Select English Writings, ed. by H. E. WINN, Oxford, 1929.

Consult also:

H. B. WORKMAN. *John Wyclif, A Study of the English Medieval Church*, Oxford, 1926.
J. E. WELLS. *Manual*, pp. 465-77 (bibliography, pp. 841-2).

1. The Prodigal Son

A man hadde two sones; and þe ȝonger of hem seide unto
his fadir: 'Fadir, ȝyve me a porcioun of þe substance þat falliþ
me.' And þe fadir departide him his goodis.   And soone
aftir, þis ȝonge sone gederide al þat fel to him, and wente forþ
5 in pilgrimage in to a fer contré; and þer he wastide his goodis,
lyvynge in lecherie.   And after þat he hadde endid alle his

goodis, þer fel a gret hungre in þat lond, and he bigan to be
nedy. And he wente oute, and clevede to oon of þe citizeins
of þat contré, and þis citisein sente him into his toun, to kepe
swyn. And þis sone coveitide to fille his beli wiþ pese-holes 10
þat þe hogges eten, and no man ȝaf him. And he, turninge
aȝen, seide: 'How many hynen in my fadirs hous ben ful of
loves, and y perishe here for hungre. Y shal rise, and go to
my fadir, and seie to him: "Fadir, I have synned in heven,
and bifore þee; now y am not worþi to be clepid þi sone, 15
make me as oon of þin hynen."' And he roos, and cam to
his fadir. And ȝit whanne he was fer, his fadir sawe him,
and was moved bi mercy, and renning aȝens his sone, fel on
his nekke, and kiste him. And þe sone seide to him: 'Fadir,
y have synned in hevene, and bifore þee; now I am not 20
worþi to be clepid þi sone.' And þe fadir seide to his servauntis anoon: 'Bringe ȝe forþ þe firste stoole, and cloþe ȝe
him, and ȝyve ȝe a ryng in his hond, and shoon upon his
feet. And bringe ȝe a fat calf, and sle him, and ete we, and
fede us; for þis sone of myn was deed, and is quykened aȝen, 25
and he was parishid, and is foundun.' And þei bigunne to
feede hem. And his eldere sone was in þe feeld; and whanne
he cam, and was nyȝ þe hous, he herde a symphonie and
oþer noise of mynystralcye. And þis eldere sone clepide oon
of þe servauntis, and axide what weren þes þingis. And he 30
seide to him: 'Þi broþir is comen, and þi fadir haþ slayn a fat
calf, for he haþ resceyved him saaf.' But þis eldere sone
hadde dedeyn, and wolde not come in; þerfore his fadir
wente out, and bigan to preie him. And he answeride, and
seide to his fadir: 'Lo, so many ȝeeris y serve to þee, y passide 35
nevere þi mandement; and þou ȝavest me nevere a kide, for
to fede me wiþ my frendis. But after þat he, þis þi sone, þat
murþeride his goodis wiþ hooris, is come, þou hast killid to
him a fat calf.' And þe fadir seide to him: 'Sone, þou art ever
more wiþ me, and alle my goodis ben þine. But it was nede 40
to ete and to make mery, for he, þis þi broþir, was deed, and
lyvede aȝen; he was perishid, and is founden.'

2. Christ's Poverty

In þe lif of Crist and His gospel, þat is His testament, wiþ
lif and techyng of His postlis, oure clerkis schullen not fynde
45 but povert, mekenesse, gostly traveile, and dispisyng of
worldly men for reprovyng of here synnes, and grete reward
in Hevene for here goode lif and trewe techyng, and wilful
sofforyng of deþ. Þerfore Jesus Crist was pore in His lif,
þat He hadde no house of His owene bi worldly title to reste
50 His heed þerinne, as He Hymself seiþ in þe gospel. And
Seynt Petir was so pore þat he hadde neiþer silver ne gold to
ȝeve a pore crokid man, as Petir witnesseþ in þe bok of
Apostlis Dedis. Seynt Poul was so pore of wordly goodis
þat he traveilede wiþ his hondis for his liflode and his felowis,
55 and suffride moche persecucion, and wakyng of gret þouȝt
for alle chirches in Cristendom, as he hymself witnessiþ in
many placis of holy writt. And Seynt Bernard writiþ to þe
pope, þat in ·þis worldly aray, and plenté of londis and gold
and silver, he is successour of Constantyn þe emperour, and
60 not of Jesus Crist and His disciplis. And Jesus confermyng
þis testament seide to His apostlis after His risyng fro deþ to
life, 'My Fadir sente me and I sende ȝow,'—þat is, to traveile,
persecucion, and povert and hunger and martirdom in þis
world, and not to worldly ⟨pompe⟩ as clerkis usen now. Bi
65 þis it semeþ, þat alle þes worldly clerkis havyng seculer
lordischipe, wiþ aray of worldly vanyté, ben hugely cursed
of God and man, for þei doun aȝenst þe riȝtful testament of
Crist and His postlis.

XXV

THE MERCERS' PETITION TO PARLIAMENT
(1386)

The interest in this text is primarily linguistic. It is the second known
document of its type in which the English language was used (the first, in
1344, was from Gloucestershire). Leafing through the *Rotuli Parliamentorum*,
a person will find nothing but Latin and Anglo-Norman until, suddenly, in

1386 he runs onto this petition in English, drawn up by the Mercers. The petition of the Cordwainers, which follows this, is in Anglo-Norman. It is necessary to wait until the beginning of the 15th century to see the use of English extended into these official acts.

The text gives us a specimen of London English, of middle-class usage, for the date indicated. Only the first part of the petition is printed here.

Editions:

L. MORSBACH. *Über den Ursprung der neuenglischen Schriftsprache*, Heilbronn, 1888 (pp. 171-7).

R. W. CHAMBERS and M. DAUNT. *A Book of London English 1384-1425*, Oxford, 1931 (pp. 33-7).

⟨T⟩o the moost noble and Worthiest Lordes, moost ryghtful and wysest conseille to owre lige Lorde the Kyng, compleynen, if it lyke to yow, the folk of the Mercerye of London ⟨as⟩ a membre of the same citee, of many wronges subtiles and also open oppressions, y-do to hem by longe tyme here 5 bifore passed.

Of which oon was, where the eleccion of Mairaltee is to be to the fre men of the Citee bi gode and paisible avys of the wysest and trewest at o day in the yere frelich, — there, noughtwithstondyng the same fredam or fraunchise, Nichol 10 Brembre wyth his upberers purposed hym, the yere next after John Northampton, Mair of the same Citee with stronge honde, as it is ful knowen, and thourgh debate and strenger partye ayeins the pees bifore purveyde was chosen Mair, in destruccion of many ryght.   15

For in the same yere, the forsaid Nichol, withouten nede, ayein the pees made dyverse enarmynges bi day and eke bi nyght, and destruyd the kynges trewe lyges, som with open slaughtre, somme bi false emprisonementz; and some fledde the Citee for feere, as it is openlich knowen.   20

And so ferthermore, for to susteyne thise wronges and many othere, the next yere after, the same Nichol, ayeins the forsaide fredam and trewe comunes, did crye openlich that noman sholde come to chese her Mair but such as were sompned; and tho that were sompned were of his ordynaunce and after 25 his avys. And in the nyght next after folwynge he did carye

grete quantitee of Armure to the Guyldehalle, with which as
wel straungers of the contree as othere of withinne were
armed on the morwe, ayeins his owne proclamacion that was
30 such that noman shulde be armed; and certein busshmentz
were laide that, when free men of the Citee come to chese her
Mair, breken up armed, crynge with loude voice 'sle! sle!'
folwing hem; wherthourgh the peple for feere fledde to houses
and other ⟨hidy⟩nges as in londe of werre, adradde to be ded
35 in comune.

*pres pple
-ing*

And thus yet hiderward hath the Mairaltee ben holden, as it
were of conquest or maistrye, and many othere offices als.
So that what man, pryvé or apert in special, that he myght
wyte, grocchyng, pleyned or helde ayeins any of his wronges,
40 or bi puttyng forth of whom so it were, were it never so
unprevable, were apeched and it were displesyng to hym
Nichol, anon was emprisoned. And, though it were ayeins
falshede of the leest officer that hym lust meynteigne, was
holden untrewe lige man to owre kyng; for who reproved
45 such an officer, maynteigned bi hym, of wronge or elles, he
forfaited ayeins hym, Nichol, and he, unworthy as he saide,
represented the kynges estat. Also if anyman, bi cause of
servyce or other leveful comaundement, approched a lorde,
to which lorde he, Nichol, dradde his falshede to be knowe
50 to, anon was apeched that he was false to the conseille of the
Citee and so to the kyng.

And yif in general his falsenesse were ayeinsaide, as of us
togydre of the Mercerye or othere craftes, or ony conseille
wolde have taken to ayeinstande it, or, as ⟨tyme⟩ out of mynde
55 hath be used, wolden companye togydre, how lawful so it
were for owre nede or profite, were anon apeched for arrysers
ayeins the pees, and falsly many of us, that yet stonden endited.
And we ben openlich disclaundred, holden untrewe and trai-
tours to owre Kyng. For the same Nichol sayd bifor Mair,
60 Aldermen and owre craft, bifor hem gadred in place of
recorde, that xx or xxx of us were worthy to be drawen and

hanged, the which thyng lyke to yowre worthy lordship by
an even Juge to be proved or disproved, the whether that
trowthe may shewe; for trouthe amonges us of fewe or elles
noman many day dorst be shewed. And nought oonlich 65
unshewed or hidde it hath be by man now, but also of bifore
tyme the moost profitable poyntes of trewe governaunce of
the Citee, compiled togidre bi longe labour of discrete and
wyse men, wythout conseille of trewe men (for thei sholde
nought be knowen ne contynued) in the tyme of Nichol Exton, 70
Mair, outerliche were brent.

XXVI

JOHN OF TREVISA

Ranulph Higden (died 1364) a Benedictine monk at St. Werburgh abbey,
Chester, composed under the title *Polychronicon* an historical compilation in
Latin which goes from the Creation to 1327. The work was such a success
in its time (more than a hundred manuscripts survive) that it was twice
translated into English. One of these, by John of Trevisa, was finished in
1387 and printed a century later by Caxton (1482) in a slightly modernized
form.

The translator, John of Trevisa, was born at Carados in Cornwall; he was
a Fellow of Exeter College from 1362 to 1369, then become a curate at Berkeley.
It was at the request of Sir Thomas Berkeley that he undertook the translation
of Higden's *Polychronicon*.

He translated as literally as possible, but not without errors. At times
he added pieces of his own invention. Among these are his observations on the
reforms in instruction at Oxford which are extremely valuable remarks for
historians of the development of English. His translation has the further
merit of being ranked among the earliest endeavors in English prose of the
14th century.

Higden's Latin text, which is reproduced here, allows the reader to see
what John of Trevisa added to that text. The corresponding passage from
Caxton will give the reader a useful point of comparison by which to measure
the changes in the language in about a century.

Edition:

*Polychronicon Ranulphi Higden together with the English Translations of John
Trevisa and of an unknown Writer of the XVth Century* ed. by Ch.
BABINGTON [then J. R. LUMBY], London, 1865-86.

Consult also:

J. E. WELLS. *Manual*, pp. 204-6 (bibliography, p. 795).
J. SWART. ' Polychronica ', *Neophilologus*, XXXIII (1949), pp. 227-233.

SW dialect w/ west Midland features

y > ü > u

The English Language in 1385

W Midland influence

As hyt ys y-knowe houȝ meny maner people buþ in þis ylond, þer buþ also of so meny people (longages) and tonges; noþeles Walschmen and Scottes, þat buþ noȝt y-melled wiþ oþer nacions, holdeþ wel nyȝ here furste longage and speche,

5 bote ȝef Scottes, þat were som tyme confederat and wonede wiþ þe Pictes, drawe somwhat after here speche. Bote þe Flemmynges, þat woneþ in þe west syde of Wales, habbeþ y-left here strange speche and spekeþ Saxonlych y-now. Also Englischmen, þeyȝ hy hadde fram þe bygynnyng þre maner

10 speche, Souþeron, Norþeron, and Myddel speche (in þe myddel of þe lond), as hy come of þre maner people of Germania, noþeles, by commyxstion and mellyng furst wiþ Danes and afterward wiþ Normans, in menye þe contray longage ys apeyred, and som useþ strange wlaffyng, chyter-

15 yng, harryng and garryng, grisbittyng. Þis apeyryng of þe

POLYCHRONICON RANULPHI HIGDEN, Lib. I, Cap. LIX: *De incolarum linguis.*

Ut patet ad sensum, quot in hac insula sunt gentes, tot gentium sunt linguae; Scoti tamen et Wallani, utpote cum aliis nationibus impermixti, ad purum paene pristinum retinent idioma; nisi forsan Scoti ex convictu Pictorum, cum quibus olim confoederati cohabitabant, quippiam contraverint in sermone. Flandrenses vero, qui occidua Walliae incolunt, dimissa iam barbarie, Saxonice satis proloquuntur. Angli quoque, quamquam ab initio tripartitam sortirentur linguam, austrinam scilicet, mediterraneam, et borealem, veluti ex tribus Germaniae populis procedentes, ex commixtione tamen primo cum Danis, deinde cum Normannis, corrupta in multis patria lingua peregrinos iam captant boatus et

---

A: *Text printed by* W. CAXTON *in 1482:* As it is knowen how many maner peple ben in this Ilond ther ben also many langages and tonges. Netheles walshmen and scottes that ben not medled with other nacions kepe neygh yet theyr first langage and speche/But yet tho scottes that were somtyme confederate and dwellyd with pyctes drawe somwhat after theyr speche/ But the Flemynges that dwelle in the westside of wales have lefte her straunge speche & speken lyke to saxons/also englysshmen though they had fro the begynnyng thre maner speches Southern northern and myddel speche in the middel of the londe as they come of thre maner of people of

10 Germania. Netheles by commyxtion and medlyng first with dan⟨e⟩s and afterward with normans In many thynges the countreye langage is appayred/ffor somme use straunge wlaffyng/chyteryng harryng garryng

þurþ-tonge ys bycause of twey þinges. On ys, for chyldern
in scole, aȝenes þe usage and manere of al oþer nacions, buþ
compelled for to leve here oune longage, and for to construe
here lessons and here þinges a Freynsch, and habbeþ, suþthe
þe Normans come furst into Engelond. Also, gentilmen 20
children buþ y-tauȝt for to speke Freynsch fram tyme þat ⓐ *(One, they)*
buþ y-rokked in here cradel, and conneþ speke and playe wiþ
a child hys brouch; and oplondysch men wol lykne hamsylf
to gentilmen, and fondeþ wiþ gret bysynes for to speke
Freynsch for to be more y-told of.   25

  Þys manere was moche y-used to-fore þe furste moreyn and
ys seþthe somdel y-chaunged. For Johan Cornwal, a mayster
of gramere, chayngede þe lore in gramer-scole, and construc-
cion of Freynsch into Englysch; and Richard Pencrych
lurnede þat manere techyng of hym, and oþer men of 30
Pencrych; so þat now, þe ȝer of oure Lord a þousond þre
hondred foure score and fyve, of þe secunde kyng Richard
after þe conquest nyne, in al þe gramer-scoles of Engelond
childern leveþ Frensch and construeþ and lurneþ an Englysch,

---

garritus. Haec quidem nativae linguae corruptio provenit hodie multum
ex duobus; quod videlicet pueri in scholis contra morem caeterarum
nationum a primo Normannorum adventu, derelicto proprio vulgari,
construere Gallice compelluntur; item quod filii nobilium ab ipsis
cunabulorum crepundiis ad Gallicum idioma informantur. Quibus pro-
fecto rurales homines assimilari volentes, ut per hoc spectabiliores

---

A: and grisbytyng/this appayryng of the langage cometh of two thynges/
One is by cause that children that gon to scole lerne to speke first
englysshe/& than ben compellid to construewe her lessons in Frenssh and 15
that have ben used syn the normans come in to Englond/Also gentilmens
childeren ben lerned and taught from theyr yongthe to speke frenssh.
  And uplondyssh men will counterfete and likene hem self to gentilmen
and arn besy to speke frensshe for to be more sette by. Wherfor it is sayd
by a comyn proverbe· Jack wold be a gentilman if he coude speke frensshe. 20
This maner was moche used to fore the grete deth· But syth it is somdele
chaunged For sir Johan cornuayl a mayster of gramer chaunged the
techyng in gramer scole and construction of Frenssh in to englysshe. and
other Scoolmaysters use the same way now in the yere of oure lord/M·iij/
C.lx.v. the /IX yere of kyng Rychard the secund and leve all frenssh in 25
scoles and use al construction in englissh. wherin they have avantage one

35 and habbeþ þerby avauntage in on syde and desavauntage yn
anoþer; here avauntage ys þat a lurneþ here gramer yn lasse
tyme þan childern wer y-woned to do; disavauntage ys þat
now childern of gramer-scole conneþ no more Frensch þan
can here lift heele, and þat ys harm for ham, and a scholle
40 passe þe se and travayle in strange londes, and in meny caas
also. Also gentilmen habbeþ now moche y-left for to teche
here childern Frensch. Hyt semeþ a gret wondur hou3
Englysch, þat ys þe burþ-tonge of Englyschmen and here
oune longage and tonge, ys so dyvers of soun in þis ylond;
45 and þe longage of Normandy ys comlyng of anoþer lond, and
haþ on maner soun among al men þat spekeþ hyt ary3t in
Engelond. Noþeles, þer ys as meny dyvers maner Frensch
yn þe rem of Fraunce as ys dyvers manere Englysch in þe
rem of Engelond.
50 Also, of þe forseyde Saxon tonge, þat ys deled a þre, and
ys abyde scarslysch wiþ feaw uplondysch men, *hyt* ys gret
wondur; for men of þe est wiþ men of þe west, as hyt were
undur þe same party of hevene, acordeþ more in sounyng of

44, 46 soun *H*] soon *C*. — 52 hyt] and MSS.

videantur, francigenare satagunt omni nisu. Ubi nempe mirandum
videtur, quomodo nativa et propria Anglorum lingua, in unica insula
coartata, pronunciatione ipsa sit tam diversa; cum tamen Normannica
lingua, quae adventitia est, univoca maneat penes cunctos.

De praedicta quoque lingua Saxonica tripartita, quae in paucis adhuc
agrestibus vix remansit, orientales cum occiduis tamquam sub eodem

A: way· that is that they lerne the sonner theyr gramer And in another
disavauntage/For nowe they lerne no ffrenssh ne can none/whiche is hurte
for them that shal passe the see/And also gentilmen have moche lefte to
30 teche theyr children to speke frenssh Hit semeth a grete wonder that
Englyssmen have so grete dyversyte in theyr owne langage in sowne and
in spekyng of it/whiche isall in one ylond. And the langage of Normandye
is comen oute of another lond/and hath one maner soune among al men
that speketh it in englond For a man of Kente Southern/western and nor-
35 thern men speken Frensshe al lyke in sowne & speche. But they can not
speke theyr englyssh so Netheles ther is as many dyverse manere of
Frensshe in the Royamme of Fraunce as is dyverse englysshe in the
Royamme of Englond Also of the forsayd tong whiche is departed in thre
is grete wonder/For men of the este with the men of the west acorde bett*er*

speche þan men of the norþ wiþ men of þe souþ; þerfore hyt
ys þat Mercii, þat buþ men of myddel Engelond, as hyt were 55
parteners of þe endes, undurstondeþ betre þe syde longages,
Norþeron and Souþeron, þan Norþeron and Souþeron undurstondeþ eyþer oþer.

Al þe longage of þe Norþhumbres, and specialych at Ӡork,
ys so scharp, slyttyng and frotyng, and unschape, þat we 60
Souþeron men may þat longage unneþe undurstonde. Y trowe
þat þat ys bycause þat a buþ nyӡ to strange men and aliens
þat spekeþ strangelych, and also bycause þat þe kynges of Engelond woneþ alwey fer fram þat contray: For a buþ more
y-turnd to þe souþ contray; and Ӡef a goþ to þe norþ contray, 65
a goþ wiþ gret help and strengthe. Þe cause why a buþ more
in þe souþ contray þan in þe norþ may be betre cornlond,
more people, more noble cytes, and more profytable havenes.

---

coeli climati lineati plus consonant in sermone quam boreales cum
austrinis. Inde est quod Mercii sive Mediterranei Angli, tanquam parti-
cipantes naturam extremorum, collaterales linguas arcticam et antarcti-
cam melius intelligant quam ad invicem se intelligunt iam extremi.
   Tota lingua Northimbrorum, maxime in Eboraco, ita stridet incondita,
quod nos australes eam vix intelligere possumus; quod puto propter
viciniam barbarorum contigisse, et etiam proper iugem remotionem regum
Anglorum ab illis partibus, qui magis ad austrum diversati, si quando
boreales partes adeunt, non nisi magno auxiliatorum manu pergunt.
Frequentioris autem morae in austrinis partibus quam in borealibus
causa potest esse gleba feracior, plebs numerosior, urbes insigniores,
portus accommodatiores.

A: in sownyng of theyr speche than men of the north with men of the south/ 40
   Therfor it is that men of mercij that ben of myddel englond as it were
partyners with the endes understande better the side langages northern
& sothern than northern & southern understande eyther other· Alle the
langages of the northumbres & specially at york is so sharp slytyng frotyng
and unshape that we sothern men may unneth understande that langage I 45
suppose the cause be that they be nygh to the alyens that speke straungely.
   And also by cause that the kynges of englond abyde and dwelle more
in the south countreye than in the north countrey.
   The cause why they abyde more in the south countrey than in the north
countrey. is by cause that ther is better corne londe more peple moo noble 50
cytees. & moo prouffytable havenes in the south contrey than in the north.

XXVII

GEOFFREY CHAUCER

No anthology of Middle English literature would be complete without Chaucer, certainly the greatest writer produced during that period; but it is extremely difficult to do justice to the author of the *Canterbury Tales* in a few pages: he deserves to be studied separately and in detail. The extracts which follow have the very simple aim of giving a summary idea of his principal works.

He was born in London about 1340 of a family of ample means (his father was a wine-merchant); in 1357 he became a page in the household of Lionel, son of Edward III; when he was about twenty he campaigned with the royal army in France where he remained for a time as a prisoner. He is found back at court (1367) first as a personal attendant to the king (*dialectus vallectus noster*), then as one of the Esquires of the Royal Household. Charged with diplomatic missions to France (1368-78), Flanders (1377) and Italy (1372-3 and 1378), he became a rather important person and occupied remunerative posts. Since he tied his fortune to that of John of Gaunt he suffered a temporary eclipse, along with his patron, between 1386 and 1389, and during the final years of his life was frequently in debt. He died about 1400 and was buried in Westminster Abbey. A diplomat, a man of affairs and a courtier, he had a cultivated mind and a passion for wide reading; he was interested in all the sciences of his time, and was an excellent observer and a profound student of human nature. An incomparable poet, he lived in or at Court and wrote for the Court. He was famous as a writer in his own day, and even more celebrated after his death — so much so that many works were attributed to him that he did not write; the philologists of the 19th century worked at separating out his authentic works — themselves numerous enough — from the apocryphal material.

It is possible to distinguish, roughly, four periods in Chaucer's literary career. He starts under French influence — which always remained strong — and undoubtedly tried to translate *Le Roman de la Rose*; he wrote short lyric poems and 'complaints' and composed *The Book of the Duchess* (1369-70). In a second period, which runs from 1372 to 1380, he wrote *The House of Fame*, versified the legend of St. Cecilia and composed some of the 'tragedies' later brought together in the *Monk's Tale*. Then he discovered the Italian poets who exercised on him a very powerful attraction (1380-86); it is in this period that we place the *Parliament of Fowls*, the first version of the *Knight's Tale*, the translation of Boethius and the *Legend of Good Women*, without counting a few short poems. The following period (1387-92) was even more productive: it was at this time that Chaucer undoubtedly conceived the idea of a collection of tales; he wrote the general prologue for them, and, to the tales already composed, added many others that he grouped together and attached by means of those 'links' or commentaries which are so delightful. The last years of his life were most likely given over to perfecting the *Canterbury Tales*; but death surprised him too soon and his *opus magnum* remained uncompleted. It was also in these last years that Chaucer wrote a few short pieces like *Lenvoy de Chaucer a Scogan* and *Lenvoy a Bukton*.

Viewed against the total background of English literature in the Middle Ages Chaucer by his virtues and defects, even by his genius, appears much more a Latin and French spirit — sometimes even Gallic — than English. With his irony and wit, his good humor, his horror at everything morose and sombre, his taste for limpidity, order, measure in all things, Chaucer is French. It is Chaucer who made fashionable — and how very fashionable — the French decasyllabic verse; he frequently employs French stanzaic forms, in particular the *ballade* (cp. nos. 2 and 3); he uses only an isosyllabic rimed verse like French writers. Like many of his cultured contemporaries he draws an innumerable number of his words from the vocabularies of French and Latin. Thanks to his genius he occupies without opposition one of the highest ranks in English literature and it is not idly that Spenser was able to call him

Dan Chaucer, well of Englishe undefyled.

However, the light that shines from his work must not blind the reader: the true English spirit is elsewhere: in Langland, Richard Rolle, the *Pearl* poet and the *Gawain* poet. Chaucer is an exception, and great as he is, he has his limitations: the tragic, the sublime, he never achieved; scarcely even the pathetic. As between Dante and Boccaccio, it is from the second that he draws his inspiration. In a century of ardent mysticism, in an epoch full of social strife, he proceeds, happy, smiling and bantering. He is the perfect teller of tales; but nothing more should be asked of him. That alone is sufficient for his glory.

Editions:

The principal editions of his complete works are those of W. W. SKEAT, (Oxford, 1894, 6 vol.) and of F. N. ROBINSON (Cambridge, Mass., 1933).

Consult also:

T. R. LOUNSBURY. *Studies in Chaucer*, New York, 1892.
E. LEGOUIS. *G. Chaucer*, London and New York, 1913.
G. L. KITTREDGE. *Chaucer and his Poetry*, Cambridge, Mass., 1915.
R. K. ROOT. *The Poetry of Chaucer*, rev. ed., Boston, 1922.
J. M. MANLY. *Some New Light on Chaucer*, New York, 1926.
J. L. LOWES. *Geoffrey Chaucer*, Oxford, 1934.
W. CLEMEN. *Der junge Chaucer, Bochum-Langendreer*, 1938.
H. R. PATCH. *On Rereading Chaucer*, Cambridge, Mass., 1939.
H. S. BENNETT. *Chaucer and the Fifteenth Century*, Oxford, 1947.
R. D. FRENCH. *A Chaucer Handbook*, 2nd ed., New York, 1947.
N. COGHILL. *The Poet Chaucer*, Oxford, 1949.
J. P. TATLOCK. *The Mind and Art of Chaucer*, Syracuse, 1950.
K. MALONE. *Chapters on Chaucer*, Baltimore, 1951.
B. TEN BRINK. *Chaucers Sprache und Verskunst*, Leipzig, 1899.
F. WILD. *Die sprachlichen Eigentümlichkeiten der wichtigeren Chaucer-Handschriften und die Sprache Chaucers*, Vienna, 1915.
J. E. WELLS. *Manual*, pp. 599-747 (bibliography, pp. 866-81).
E. P. HAMMOND. *Chaucer, A Bibliographical Manual*, New York, 1908 [to which must be added the supplements by D. D. GRIFFITH (Seattle, 1926) and by W. E. MARTIN, JR. (Durham, 1935)].
A. C. BAUGH. " Fifty Years of Chaucer Scholarship," *Speculum*, XXVI (1951), pp. 659-672.

1. The Book of the Duchess: *The Dream*

This poem, from Chaucer's youth, was composed in memory of the Duchess
Blanche, wife of his patron, John of Gaunt, a little after her death (12
September 1369). It is a rather artificial work, but full of charming passages
in which the author draws on what must have been rather recent reading:
the *Roman de la Rose*, Guillaume de Machault, Froissart, Ovid. From them,
he borrows both the framework and the details of his story.

After speaking of his melancholy as a rejected lover, the poet, who has tried
in vain to sleep, is reading one evening in Ovid the story of Ceyx and Alcyone;
he invokes Morpheus and finally falls asleep. This is the dream he dreams.

> Me thoghte thus: that hyt was May,
> And in the dawenynge I lay
> (Me mette thus) in my bed al naked,
> And loked forth, for I was waked
> 295　　With smale foules a gret hep
> That had affrayed me out of my slep,
> Thorgh noyse and swetnesse of her song.
> And, as me mette, they sate among
> Upon my chambre-roof wythoute,
> 300　　Upon the tyles, overal aboute,
> And songen, everych in hys wyse,
> The moste solempne servise
> By noote, that ever man, y trowe,
> Had herd; for som of hem song lowe,
> 305　　Som high, and al of oon acord.
> To telle shortly, att oo word,
> Was never herd so swete a steven, —
> But hyt had be a thyng of heven, —
> So mery a soun, so swete entewnes,
> 310　　That certes, for the toun of Tewnes,
> I nolde but I had herd hem synge;
> For al my chambre gan to rynge
> Thurgh syngynge of her armonye.
> For instrument nor melodye
> 315　　Was nowhere herd yet half so swete,
> Nor of acorde half so mete;

For ther was noon of hem that feyned
To synge, for ech of hem hym peyned
To fynde out mery crafty notes.
They ne spared not her throtes.   320
And sooth to seyn, my chambre was
Ful wel depeynted, and with glas
Were al the wyndowes wel y-glased,
Ful clere, and nat an hoole y-crased,
That to beholde hyt was gret joye.   325
For holly al the story of Troye
Was in the glasynge y-wroght thus,
Of Ector and of kyng Priamus,
Of Achilles and Lamedon,
And eke of Medea and of Jason,   330
Of Paris, Eleyne, and of Lavyne.
And alle the walles with colours fyne
Were peynted, bothe text and glose,
Of al the Romaunce of the Rose.
My windowes were shette echon,   335
And throgh the glas the sonne shon
Upon my bed with bryghte bemes,
With many glade gilde stremes;
And eke the welken was so fair, —
Blew, bryght, clere was the ayr,   340
And ful attempre, for sothe, hyt was;
For nother to cold nor hoot yt nas,
Ne in al the welken was no clowde.
    And as I lay thus, wonder lowde
Me thoght I herde an hunte blowe   345
T'assay hys horn, and for to knowe
Whether hyt were clere or hors of soun.
And I herde goynge, bothe up and doun,
Men, hors, houndes, and other thyng;

334 Of] And MSS.

350 And al men speken of huntyng,
How they wolde slee the hert with strengthe,
And how the hert had, upon lengthe,
So moche embosed, y not now what.
Anoon ryght, whan I herde that,
355 How that they wolde on huntynge goon,
I was ryght glad, and up anoon
Took my hors, and forth I wente
Out of my chambre forth I wente
I took my hors and never stente
360 Til I com to the feld withoute.
Of huntes and eke of foresteres,
With many relayes and lymeres,
And hyed hem to the forest faste
And I with hem. So at the laste
365 I asked oon, ladde a lymere:
'Say, felowe, who shal hunte here?'
Quod I, and he answered ageyn,
'Syr, th' emperour Octovyen,'
Quod he, 'and ys here faste by.'
370 'A Goddes half, in good tyme!' quod I,
'Go we faste!' and gan to ryde.
Whan we came to the forest syde,
Every man dide ryght anoon
As to huntynge fil to doon.
375 The mayster-hunte anoon, fot-hot,
With a gret horn blew thre mot
At the uncoupylynge of hys houndes.
Withynne a while the hert y-founde ys,
Y-halowed, and rechased faste
380 Longe tyme; and so at the laste
This hert rused, and staal away
Fro alle the houndes a privy way.
The houndes had overshette hym alle,
And were on a defaute y-falle.

Therwyth the hunte wonder faste 385
Blew a forloyn at the laste.
  I was go walked fro my tree,
And as I wente, ther cam by mee
A whelp, that fauned me as I stood,
That hadde y-folowed, and koude no good. 390
Hyt com and crepte to me as lowe
Ryght as hyt hadde me y-knowe,
Helde doun hys hed and joyned hys eres,
And leyde al smothe doun hys heres.
I wolde have kaught hyt, and anoon 395
Hyt fledde, and was fro me goon;
And I hym folwed, and hyt forth wente
Doun by a floury grene wente
Ful thikke of gras, ful softe and swete,
With floures fele, faire under fete, 400
And litel used, hyt semed thus;
For both Flora and Zephirus,
They two that make floures growe,
Had mad her dwellynge ther, I trowe;
For hit was, on to beholde, 405
As thogh the erthe envye wolde
To be gayer than the heven,
To have moo floures, swiche seven
As in the welken sterres bee.
Hyt had forgete the povertee 410
That wynter, thorgh hys colde morwes,
Had mad hyt suffre, and his sorwes,
All was forgeten, and that was sene.
For al the woode was waxen grene;
Swetnesse of dew had mad hyt waxe. 415
  Hyt ys no nede eke for to axe
Wher there were many grene greves,
Or thikke of trees, so ful of leves;
And every tree stood by hymselve

420   Fro other wel ten foot or twelve.
       So grete trees, so huge of strengthe,
       Of fourty or fifty fadme lengthe,
       Clene withoute bowgh or stikke,
       With croppes brode, and eke as thikke —
425   They were nat an ynche asonder —
       That hit was shadewe overal under.
       And many an hert and many an hynde
       Was both before me and behynde.
       Of founes, sowres, bukkes, does
430   Was ful the woode, and many roes,
       And many sqwirelles, that sete
       Ful high upon the trees and ete,
       And in hir maner made festes.
       Shortly, hyt was so ful of bestes,
435   That thogh Argus, the noble countour,
       Sete to rekene in hys countour,
       And rekene⟨d⟩ with his figures ten —
       For by tho figures mowe al ken,
       Yf they be crafty, rekene and noumbre,
440   And telle of every thing the noumbre —
       Yet shoulde he fayle to rekene even
       The wondres me mette in my sweven.
           But forth they romed ryght wonder faste
       Doun the woode; so at the laste
445   I was war of a man in blak,
       That sat and had y-turned his bak
       To an ook, an huge tree.
       'Lord,' thoght I, 'who may that be?
       What ayleth hym to sitten her?
450   Anoon ryght I wente ner;
       Than found I sitte even upryght
       A woonder wel-farynge knyght —
       By the maner me thoghte so —
       Of good mochel, and ryght yong therto,

Of the age of foure and twenty yer,　　　　455
Upon hys berd but lytel her,
And he was clothed al in blak.
I stalked even unto hys bak,
And there I stood as stille as ought,
That, soth to saye, he saw me nought;　　　460
For-why he heng hys hed adoun,
And with a dedly sorwful soun
He made of rym ten vers or twelve
Of a compleynte to hymselve,
The moste pitee, the moste rowthe,　　　　465
That ever I herde; for, by my trowthe,
Hit was gret wonder that Nature
Myght suffre any creature
To have such sorwe, and be not ded.
Ful pitous pale, and nothyng red,　　　　470
He sayd a lay, a maner song,
Withoute noote, withoute song;
And was thys, for ful wel I kan
Reherse hyt; ryght thus hyt began:
　‘I have of sorwe so gret won　　　　　475
That joye gete I never non,
Now that I see my lady bryght,
Which I have loved with al my myght
Is fro me ded and ys agoon.　　　　　479

　　Allas, deth, what ayleth the　　　　481
That thou noldest have taken me,
Whan thou toke my lady swete
That was so fair, so fresh, so fre,
So good, that men may wel y-se　　　　485
Of al goodnesse she had no mete!’

2. Troilus and Criseyde. *First Night of Love*

This is the only full length work that Chaucer ever finished. This story, first developed by Benoît de Sainte-Maure in his *Roman de Troie*, was re-told by Boccaccio in his *Filostrato* where the Italian poet transforms an insipidly sentimental story into a realistic and cynical picture of passion and sensuality. It is he who transforms Pandaro, a relative of Chryseis, into a striking figure and the principal person in the story next to the two lovers. In turn Boccaccio served as a model for Chaucer, but Chaucer transforms the story into a masterpiece of dialogue and psychological analysis.

The following passage, an extract from Book III, describes the celebrated scene in which, thanks to the help of a stormy night, Pandarus manages to arrange for the two lovers the meeting so longed for by Troilus. For Cressida's ideas see ll. 1210-11.

Editions:

The Book of Troïlus and Criseyde, ed. by R. K. Root, Princeton, 1926.
Extracts have been published by R. C. Goffin (Oxford, 1935) and G. Bonnard (Berne, 1943).

Consult also:

R. K. Gordon. *The Story of Troilus, as told by Benoit de Sainte-Maure, Giovanni Boccaccio, Geoffrey Chaucer and Robert Henryson*, London, 1934.
Th. A. Kirby. *Chaucer's 'Troilus', A Study in Courtly Love*, Louisiana State University, 1940.

> This Troilus, with blisse of that supprised,
> 1185   Putte al in Goddes hand, as he that mente
> Nothyng but wele; and sodeynly avysed,
> He hire in armes faste to hym hente.
> And Pandarus, with a ful good entente,
> Leyde hym to slepe, and seyde: 'If ȝe be wise,
> 1190   Swouneth nought now, lest more folk arise!'
>
> What myghte or may the sely larke seye,
> Whan that the sperhauk hath hym in his foot?
> I kan namore, ⟨but⟩ of thise ilke tweye,—
> To whom this tale sucre be or soot,—
> 1195   Though that I tarie a ȝer, somtyme I moot,
> After myn autour, tellen hire gladnesse,
> As wel as I have told hire hevynesse.

1193 but *J, omitted by Cp.*

Criseyde, which that felte hire thus i-take,
    As writen clerkes in hire bokes olde,
Right as an aspes leef she gan to quake,   1200
    Whan she hym felte hire in his armes folde.
    But Troilus, al hool of cares colde,
Gan thanken tho the blisful goddes sevene.
Thus sondry peynes bryngen folk in hevene.

This Troilus in armes gan hire streyne,   1205
    And seyde: 'O swete, as evere mot I gon,
Now be ȝe kaught, now is ther but we tweyne!
    Now ȝeldeth ȝow, for other bote is non!'
    To that Criseyde answerde thus anon:
'Ne hadde I er now, my swete herte deere,   1210
Ben ȝold, i-wys, I were now nought heere!'

O, sooth is seyde, that helede for to be
    As of a fevre, or other gret siknesse,
Men moste drynke, as men may ofte se,
    Ful bittre drynke; and for to han gladnesse,   1215
    Men drynken oft⟨e⟩ peyne and gret distresse;
I mene it here, as for this aventure,
That thorugh a peyne hath founden al his cure.

And now swetnesse semeth more swete,
    That bitternesse was assaied byforn;   1220
For out of wo in blisse now they flete;
    Non swich they felten syn they were born.
    Now is this bet than bothe two be lorn.
For love of God, take every womman heede
To werken thus, if it comth to the neede.   1225

Criseyde, al quyt from every drede and tene,
    As she that juste cause hadde hym to triste,
⟨Made hym swich feste, it joye was to seene,⟩

1211 i-wys *J*] I was *Cp*. — 1212 seyd] seyde *Cp J*. — 1216 ofte *J*]
oft *Cp*; gret *J*] grete *Cp*. — 1228 *line omitted in MS. Cp and taken
from J.*

When she his trouthe and clene entente wiste;
1230   And as aboute a tree, with many a twiste,
Bytrent and writhe the swote wodebynde,
Gan eche of hem in armes other wynde.

And as the newe abaysed nyghtyngale,
That stynteth first whan she bygynneth to synge,
1235   Whan that she hereth any herde tale,
Or in the hegges any wyght stirynge,
And after, siker, doth hire vois outrynge,
Right so Criseyde, whan hire drede stente,
Opned hire herte, and tolde hym hire entente.

1240   And right as he that seth his deth y-shapen,
And dyen mot, in ought that he may gesse,
And sodeynly rescous doth hym escapen,
And from his deth is brought in sykernesse,
For al this world, in swych present gladnesse
1245   Was Troilus, and hath his lady swete.
With worse happe God lat us nevere mete!

3. The Legend of Good Women

Ballade of Good Women

Another poem that Chaucer left unfinished and for which he is very much
indebted, in its conception, to the influence of his preferred French poets,
Machault, Deschamps and Froissart. It is made up of a prologue, of which there
are two different redactions, and of the legends of nine women faithful in love
from Cleopatra to Hypermnestra, passing through Lucrece, Dido and others.
The most attractive part remains the prologue in which this exquisite *ballade*
is found embedded.

Hyd, Absolon, thy gilte tresses clere;
250   Ester, ley thou thy meknesse al adown;
Hyd, Jonathas, al thy frendly manere;
Penalopee and Marcia Catoun,
Make of youre wifhod no comparysoun;
Hyde ye youre beautés, Ysoude and Eleyne:
255   My lady cometh, that al this may disteyne.

Thy faire body, lat yt nat appere,
  Lavyne! and thou, Lucresse of Rome toun,
And Polixene, that boghten love so dere,
  And Cleopatre, with al thy passyoun,
  Hyde ye your trouthe of love and your renoun; 260
And thou, Tisbé, that hast for love swich peyne:
My lady cometh, that al this may disteyne.

Herro, Dido, Laudomia, alle y-fere,
  And Phillis, hangyng for thy Demophoun,
And Canacé, espied by thy chere, 265
  Ysiphilé, betrayed with Jasoun,
  Maketh of your trouthe neythir boost ne soun;
Nor Ypermystre or Adriane, ye tweyne:
My lady cometh, that al this may dysteyne.

Readings of MS G: 251 thy *F*] thyn *G.* — 255 my lady cometh, that al
this *F*] Alceste is here, that al that *G* (*similarly 262, 269*). — 258 boghten
F] broughte *G.* — 259 And *F*] Ek *G.* — 260 of *F*] in *G.* — 263 y-fere
F] in-fere *G.* — 264 And *F*] Ek *G.* — 267 Maketh *F*] Mak *G*; neythir
F] in love no *G.* — 268 ye tweyne *F*] ne pleyne *G.*

4. The Canterbury Tales

For this collection of tales — which, as well, was never finished — Chaucer
is still celebrated above all. The *General Prologue* gives the plan — a pilgrimage
to St. Thomas à Becket of Canterbury. During the journey each of the thirty
pilgrims who have met by chance at the Tabard Inn, in Southwark, near
London, are to tell four stories to while away the time, two on the way to
Canterbury and two on the way home. Actually only twenty-four stories
survive, three of which are incomplete. The *Prologue* is also the occasion for
sketching the portrait of each of the pilgrims and this gallery is very justly
famous.

The story that Chaucer puts in the mouth of the Pardoner (or seller of
indulgences and relics), a very ambiguous person, is, like a certain number
of the tales, preceded by a prologue of its own in which the Pardoner, under
the pretext of explaining to his companions along the way why he always
preaches on avarice (*radix malorum est cupiditas*), gives a striking analysis
of his own character. The story that he tells is very much the type of those
exempla with which the preachers of the day liked to ornament their sermons.
It is also a folk-tale that is found in many literatures. Boccaccio, in his
Decameron, and the author of the *Cento Novelle Antiche* had already used it
as a source.

This tale is undoubtedly one of the last written by Chaucer; it is one of the
most successful.

Editions:

Geoffrey Chaucer's Canterbury Tales, nach dem Ellesmere Manuscript, hrsg.
von John KOCH, Heidelberg, 1915.
J. M. MANLY and E. RICKERT. *The Text of the Canterbury Tales, studied on
the Basis of all known Mss.*, Chicago, 1940, 8 vol.
The Pardoner's Tale, ed. by Carleton BROWN, Oxford, 1935.

Selections:

*Canterbury Tales by Geoffrey Chaucer, with an Introduction, Notes and a
Glossary* by J. M. MANLY, New York, 1928 [school edition of the principal
tales].

Consult also:

Chaucer's World, compiled by E. RICKERT. New York, 1948.
M. BOWDEN. *A Commentary on the General Prologue to the Canterbury Tales*,
New York, 1948.
J. A. WALKER. *Translation of Chaucer's Prologue with Running Commentary*,
Iowa City, 1950.
W. W. LAWRENCE. *Chaucer and the Canterbury Tales*, New York, 1950.
G. R. OWST. *Preaching in Medieval England*, Cambridge, 1926 [especially
pp. 99-110].
R. M. LUMIANSKY. " The Pardoner," *Tulane Studies in English*, I (1949).

A. *Portrait of the Pardoner*

(From the General Prologue)

With hym ther was a gentil Pardoner
670   Of Rouncivale, his freend and his compeer,
That streight was comen fro the court of Rome.
Ful loude he soong ' Com hider, love, to me!'
This Somonour bar to hym a stif burdoun,
Was nevere trompe of half so greet a soun.
675   This Pardoner hadde heer as yelow as wex,
But smothe it heeng as dooth a strike of flex;
By ounces henge hise lokkes þat he hadde,
And therwith he hise shuldres overspradde;
But thynne it lay, by colpons oon and oon.
680   But hood, for jolitee, wered he noon,
For it was trussed up in his walet.
Hym thoughte he rood al of the newe jet;
Dischevelee, save his cappe, he rood al bare.
Swiche glarynge eyen hadde he as an hare.

A vernycle hadde he sowed upon his cappe. 685
His walet ⟨lay⟩ biforn hym in his lappe,
Bretful of pardoun, comen from Rome al hoot.
A voys he hadde as smal as hath a goot.
No berd hadde he, ne nevere sholde have;
As smothe it was as it were late shave. 690
I trowe he were a geldyng or a mare.
But of his craft, fro Berwyk into Ware,
Ne was ther swich another Pardoner.
For in his male he hadde a pilwe-beer,
Which þat he seyde was Oure Lady veyl: 695
He seyde he hadde a gobet of the seyl
That seint Peter hadde, whan þat he wente
Upon the see, til Jhesu Crist hym hente.
He hadde a croys of latoun ful of stones,
And in a glas he hadde pigges bones. 700
But with thise relikes, whan þat he fond
A povre person dwellynge upon lond,
Upon a day he gat hym moore moneye
Than þat the person gat in monthes tweye;
And thus, with feyned flaterye and japes, 705
He made the person and the peple his apes.
But trewely to tellen atte laste,
He was in chirche a noble ecclesiaste.
Wel koude he rede a lessoun or a storie,
But alderbest he song an offertorie, 710
For wel he wiste, whan þat song was songe,
He moste preche and wel affile his tonge
To wynne silver, as he ful wel koude;
Therfore he song the murierly and loude.

686 lay *He] omitted El.*

B. *The Pardoner's Tale*

In Flaundres whilom was a compaignye
Of yonge folk that haunteden folye,
465 As riot, hasard, stywes, and tavernes,
Where as with harpes, lutes, and gyternes,
They daunce and pleyen at dees bothe day and nyght,
And eten also and drynken over hir myght,
Thurgh which they doon the devel sacrifise
470 Withinne that develes temple, in cursed wise,
By superfluytee abhomynable.
Hir othes been so grete and so dampnable
That it is grisly for to heere hem swere.
Oure blissed Lordes body they totere, —
475 Hem thoughte þat Jewes rente hym noght y-nough;
And ech of hem at otheres synne lough.

. . . .

661 Thise riotour⟨e⟩s thre of whiche I telle,
Longe erst er prime rong of any belle,
Were set hem in a taverne to drynke,
And as they sat, they herde a belle clynke
665 Biforn a cors, was caried to his grave.
That oon of hem gan callen to his knave:
'Go bet,' quod he, 'and axe redily
What cors is this þat passeth heer forby;
And looke þat thou reporte his name weel.'
670 'Sire,' quod this boy, 'it nedeth never-a-deel;
It was me toold er ye cam heer two houres.
He was, pardee, an old felawe of youres;
And sodeynly he was y-slayn to-nyght,
Fordronke, as he sat on his bench upright.
675 Ther cam a privee theef, men clepeth Deeth,
That in this contree al the peple sleeth,
And with his spere he smoot his herte atwo,

661 riotoures *Cp Ld*] riotours *El.*

PLATE V

The Pardoner's Tale
V. 463-488 (MS Ellesmere, fº 142)

And wente his wey withouten wordes mo.
He hath a thousand slayn this pestilence.
And, maister, er ye come in his presence, 680
Me thynketh that it were necessarie
For to be war of swich an adversarie.
Beth redy for to meete hym everemoore;
Thus taughte me my dame; I sey namoore.'
'By seinte Marie!' seyde this taverner, 685
'The child seith sooth, for he hath slayn this yeer,
Henne over a mile, withinne a greet village,
Bothe man and womman, child, and hyne, and page;
I trowe his habitacioun be there.
To been avysed greet wysdom it were, 690
Er that he dide a man a dishonour.'
  'Ye, Goddes armes!' quod this riotour,
'Is it swich peril with hym for to meete?
I shal hym seke by wey and eek by strete,
I make avow to Goddes digne bones! 695
Herkneth, felawes, we thre been al ones;
Lat ech of us holde up his hand til oother,
And ech of us bicomen otheres brother,
And we wol sleen this false traytour Deeth.
He shal be slayn, which þat so manye sleeth, 700
By Goddes dignitee, er it be nyght!'
  Togidres han thise thre hir trouthes plight
To lyve and dyen ech of hem for oother,
As though he were his owene y-bore brother
And up they stirte, *al* dronken in this rage, 705
And forth they goon towardes that village
Of which the taverner hadde spoke biforn.
And many a grisly ooth thanne han they sworn,
And Cristes blessed body they torente —
Deeth shal be deed, if that they may hym hente! 710
  Whan they han goon nat fully half a mile,

704 y-bore *He*] yborn *El.* — 705 al *He Cp Ld*] and *El.*

Right as they wolde han troden over a stile,
An oold man and a povre with hem mette.
This olde man ful mekely hem grette,
715   And seyde thus: 'Now, lordes, God yow see!'
The proudeste of thise riotour⟨e⟩s three
Answerde agayn: 'What, carl, with sory grace!
Why artow al forwrapped save thy face!
Why lyvestow so longe in so greet age?'
720   This olde man gan looke in his visage,
And seyde thus: 'For I ne kan nat fynde
A man, though þat I walked into Ynde,
Neither in citee nor in no village,
That wolde chaunge his youthe for myn age;
725   And therfore moot I han myn age stille.
As longe tyme as it is Goddes wille.
Ne Deeth, allas! ne wol nat han my lyf.
Thus walke I, lyk a restelees kaityf,
And on the ground, which is my moodres gate,
730   I knokke with my staf, bothe erly and late,
And seye: 'Leeve mooder, leet me in!
Lo, how I vanysshe, flessh, and blood, and skyn!
Allas! whan shul my bones been at reste?
Mooder, with yow wolde I chaunge my cheste
735   That in my chambre longe tyme hath be,
Ye, for an heyre-clowt to wrappe me!'
But yet to me she wol nat do that grace,
For which ful pale and welked is my face.
But, sires, to yow it is no curteisye
740   To speken to an old man vileynye,
But he trespasse in word, or elles in dede.
In Hooly Writ ye may yourself wel rede:
'Agayns an oold man, hoor upon his heed,
Ye sholde arise;' wherfore I yeve yow reed,
745   Ne dooth unto an oold man noon harm now,

716 riotoures (ryatourys *Ca*, ryettoures *Cp*, ryetoures *Ld*)] riotours
El.

Namoore than þat ye wolde men did to yow
In age, if that ye so longe abyde.
And God be with yow, where ye go or ryde!
I moote go thider as I have to go.'
   'Nay, olde cherl, by God, thou shalt nat so,'   750
Seyde this oother hasardour anon;
'Thou partest nat so lightly, by seint John!
Thou spak right now of thilke traytour Deeth,
That in this contree alle oure freendes sleeth.
Have heer my trouthe, as thou art his espye,   755
Telle where he is, or thou shalt it abye,
By God, and by the hooly sacrement!
For soothly thou art oon of his assent
To sleen us yonge folk, thou false theef!'
   'Now, sires,' quod he, 'if þat ye be so leef   760
To fynde Deeth, turne up this croked wey,
For in that grove I lafte hym, by my fey,
Under a tree, and there he wole abyde;
Noght for youre boost he wole him nothyng hyde.
Se ye that ook? Right ther ye shal hym fynde.   765
God save yow, þat boghte agayn mankynde,
And yow amende!' Thus seyde this olde man;
And everich of thise riotours ran
Til he cam to that tree, and ther they founde,
Of floryns fyne of gold y-coyned rounde,   770
Wel ny an .viij. busshels, as hem thoughte.
No lenger thanne after Deeth they soughte,
But ech of hem so glad was of that sighte,
For þat the floryns been so faire and bright⟨e⟩,
That doun they sette hem by this precious hoord.   775
The worste of hem, he spak the firste word.
   'Bretheren,' quod he, 'taak kepe what I seye;
My wit is greet, though þat I bourde and pleye.
This tresor hath Fortune unto us yeven,

774 brighte *He*] bright *El.*

780 In myrthe and joliftee oure lyf to lyven,
And lightly as it comth, so wol we spende.
Ey! Goddes precious dignitee! who wende
To-day that we sholde han so fair a grace?
But myghte this gold be caried fro this place
785 Hoom to myn hous, or elles unto youres —
For wel ye woot þat al this gold is oures —
Thanne were we in heigh felicitee.
But trewely, by daye it may nat bee.
Men wolde seyn that we were theves stronge,
790 And for oure owene tresor doon us honge.
This tresor moste y-caried be by nyghte
As wisely and as slyly as it myghte.
Wherfore I rede þat cut among us alle
Be drawe, and lat se wher the cut wol falle;
795 And he þat hath the cut with herte blithe
Shal renne to ⟨the⟩ towne, and that ful swithe,
And brynge us breed and wyn ful prively.
And two of us shul kepen subtilly
This tresor wel; and if he wol nat tarie,
800 Whan it is nyght, we wol this tresor carie,
By oon assent, where as us thynketh best.'
That oon of hem the cut broghte in his fest,
And bad hem drawe, and looke where it wol falle;
And it fil on the yongeste of hem alle,
805 And forth toward the toun he wente anon.
And also soone as that he was gon,
That oon ⟨of hem⟩ spak thus unto that oother:
'Thou knowest wel thou art my swor⟨e⟩n brother;
Thy profit wol I telle thee anon.
810 Thou woost wel that oure felawe is agon,
And heere is gold, and that ful greet plentee,
That shal departed been among us thre.

796 to the *He Ld*] to *El.* — 803 hem *He*] hym *El.* — 807 oon of hem
He] oon *El.*

But nathelees, if I kan shape it so
That it departed were among us two,
Hadde I nat doon a freendes torn to thee?' 815
   That oother answerde: 'I noot hou that may be.
He woot how that the gold is with us tweye;
Wh*at sh*al we doon? What shal we to hym seye?'
   'Shal it be conseil?' seyde the firste shrewe,
'And I shal tellen in a wordes fewe 820
What we shal doon, and bryngen it wel aboute.'
   'I graunte,' quod that oother, 'out of doute,
That, by my trouthe, I shal thee nat biwreye.'
   'Now,' quod the firste, 'thou woost wel we be tweye,
And two of us shul strenger be than oon. 825
Looke whan þat he is set, that right anoon
Arys as though thou woldest with hym pleye,
And I shal ryve hym thurgh the sydes tweye
Whil that thou strogelest with hym as in game,
And with thy daggere looke thou do the same; 830
And thanne shal al this gold departed be,
My deere freend, bitwixen me and thee.
Thanne may we bothe oure lustes all fulfille,
And pleye at dees right at oure owene wille.'
And thus acorded been thise shrewes tweye 835
To sleen the thridde, as ye han herd me seye.
   This yongeste, which þat wente unto the toun,
Ful ofte in herte he rolleth up and doun
The beautee of thise floryns newe and brighte.
'O Lord!' quod he, 'if so were þat I myghte 840
Have al this tresor to myself allone,
Ther is no man þat lyveth under the trone
Of God that sholde lyve so murye as I!'
And atte laste the feend, oure enemy,
Putte in his thought þat he sholde poyson beye, 845
With which he myghte sleen hise felawes tweye;

818 what shal] whal *El.*

For-why the feend foond hym in swich lyvynge
That he hadde leve hym to sorwe brynge.
For this was outrely his fulle entente,
850   To sleen hem bothe, and nevere to repente.
And forth he gooth, no lenger wolde he tarie,
Into the toun, unto a pothecarie,
And preyde hym þat he hym wolde selle
Som poyson, þat he myghte hise rattes quelle;
855   And eek ther was a polcat in his hawe,
That, as he seyde, hise capouns hadde y-slawe,
And fayn he wolde wreke hym, if he myghte,
On vermyn þat destroyed hym by nyghte.
    The pothecarie answerde : ' And thou shalt have
860   A thyng that, also God my soule save,
In al this world ther is no creature,
That eten or dronken hath of this confiture
Noght but the montance of a corn of whete,
That he ne shal his lif anon forlete;
865   Ye, sterve he shal, and that in lasse while
Than thou wolt goon a paas nat but a mile,
This poysoun is so strong and violent.'
    This cursed man hath in his hond y-hent
This poysoun in a box, and sith he ran
870   Into the nexte strete unto a man,
And borwed hym large botel⟨le⟩s thre;
And in the two his poyson poured he;
The thridde he kepte clene for his owene drynke.
For al the nyght he shoope hym for to swynke
875   In cariynge of the gold out of that place.
And whan this riotour, with sory grace,
Hadde filled with wyn hise grete botels thre,
To hise felawes agayn repaireth he.
    What nedeth it to sermone of it moore?
880   For right as they hadde cast his deeth bifoore,

---

848 hym *He*] hem *El.* — 871 botelles *Cp*] botels *El.* — 880 right
He] right so *El*

Right so they han hym slayn, and that anon.
And whan þat this was doon, thus spak that oon:
'Now lat us sitte and drynke, and make us merie,
And afterward we wol his body berie.'
And with that word it happed hym, par cas,   885
To take the botel ther the poyson was,
And drank, and yaf his felawe drynke also,
For which anon they storven bothe two.

But certes, I suppose that Avycen
Wroot nevere in no canon, ne in no fen,   890
Mo wonder signes of empoisonyng
Than hadde thise wrecches two, er hir endyng.
Thus ended been thise homycides two,
And eek the false empoysonere also.

O cursed synne of alle cursednesse!   895
O traytours homycide, O wikkednesse!
O glotonye, luxurie and hasardrye!
Thou blasphemour of Crist with vileynye
And othes grete, of usage and of pride!
Allas! mankynde, how may it bitide   900
That to thy creatour, which þat the wroghte,
And with his precious herte-blood thee boghte,
Thou art so fals and so unkynde, allas?

Now, goode men, God foryeve yow youre trespas,
And ware yow fro the synne of avarice!   905
Myn hooly pardoun may yow alle warice,
So þat ye offre nobles or sterylynges,
Or elles silver broches, spoones, rynges.
Boweth youre heed under this hooly bulle!
Com up, ye wyves, offreth of youre wolle!   910
Youre names I entre heer in my rolle anon;
Into the blisse of hevene shul ye gon.
I yow assoille, by myn heigh power,
Yow þat wol offre, as clene and eek as cleer
As ye were born. — And lo, sires, thus I preche.   915

And Jhesu Crist, that is oure soules leche,
So graunte yow his pardoun to receyve,
For that is best; I wol yow nat deceyve.

But, sires, o word forgat I in my tale:
I have relikes and pardoun in my male,
As faire as any man in Engelond,
Whiche were me yeven by the popes hond.
If any of yow wole, of devocioun,
Offren, and han myn absolucioun,
Com forth anon, and kneleth heere adoun,
And mekely receyveth my pardoun;
Or elles taketh pardoun as ye wende,
Al newe and fressh at every miles ende,
So þat ye offren, alwey newe and newe,
Nobles or pens, whiche þat be goode and trewe.
It is an honour to everich that is heer
That ye mowe have a suffisant pardoneer
T'assoille yow, in contree as ye ryde,
For aventures whiche þat may bityde.
Paraventure ther may fallen oon or two
Doun of his hors, and breke his nekke atwo.
Looke which a seuretee is it to yow alle
That I am in youre felaweshipe y-falle,
That may assoille yow, bothe moore and lasse,
Whan þat the soule shal fro the body passe.
I rede þat oure Hoost heere shal bigynne,
For he is moost envoluped in synne.
Com forth, sire Hoost, and offre first anon,
And thou shalt kisse my relikes everychon,
Ye, for a grote! Unbokele anon thy purs.'
'Nay, nay!' quod he, 'thanne have I Cristes curs!
Lat be,' quod he, 'it shal nat be, so thee'ch!
Thou woldest make me kisse thyn olde breech,
And swere it were a relyk of a seint,
Though it were with thy fundement depeint!

But, by the croys that Seint Eleyne fond,
I wolde I hadde thy coillons in myn hond
In stide of relikes or of seintuarie.
Lat kutte hem of, I wol thee helpe carie;
They shul be shryned in an hogges toord!'   955
  This Pardoner answerde nat a word;
So wrooth he was, no word ne wolde he seye.
  ' Now,' quod oure Hoost, ' I wol no lenger pleye
With thee, ne with noon oother angry man.'
But right anon the worthy Knyght bigan,   960
Whan þat he saugh þat al the peple lough,
' Namoore of this, for it is right y-nough!
Sire Pardoner, be glad and myrie of cheere;
And ye, sir Hoost, þat been to me so deere,
I prey yow þat ye kisse the Pardoner.   965
And Pardoner, I prey thee, drawe thee neer,
And, as we diden, lat us laughe and pleye.'
Anon they kiste, and ryden forth hir weye.

XXVIII

JOHN GOWER

CONFESSIO AMANTIS

  John Gower was born in Kent about 1330 and died in 1408. The little that we know of his life indicates that he must have been a man of at least some means. He appears in his writings like a sincerely religious person, convinced of the faults of the Church of his time, desirous both of doing well as a writer and courtier, and of doing good:· ' moral Gower ' his friend Chaucer called him in dedicating *Troilus and Criseyde* to him.

  He has the signal distinction of being one of those very rare men who successfully wrote poems in three languages: Latin, Anglo-French, and English. But his present literary reputation rests exclusively on his English works, and especially on the most important of them, the *Confessio Amantis* (about 1390) in some 34,000 octosyllabic rimed couplets. Following a method revived from the *Roman de la Rose*, he has a lover who confesses his sins to Genius, a priest of Venus. To enlighten the lover, the confessor instructs him in the nature of all the sins. These are at once the seven deadly sins of Christianity (and their ramifications) as well as sins a lover might commit that would make him fail in courtly love, all intermingled in a curious fashion — not to mention a hodge-podge of lectures on Sorcery, Marriage, Incest and other matters. The two conflicting strains — problems of sensual love and Christian sin — are pulled together at the end by a farewell to Earthly Love and a commendation to Heavenly Love (plus, again, considerable miscellanea). Each variety of sin explained by Genius is the occasion for him to give several *exempla*, or illustrative stories, and these tales are the heart of the work.

Thus in book V, the study of Avarice and its servants, Covetousness, False Witness and Perjury leads him to tell a story of perjury in love, the story of Jason and Medea (according to Benoît de Sainte-Maure's and Ovid's version), from which this extract is taken.

One must certainly not ask of Gower the qualities found in Chaucer. Between them there is the difference between talent and genius. But, as the following passage will show, Gower could tell a tale with charm and interest.

He has, he says,

undirtok
In Englesch for to make a book
Which stant betwene ernest and game.

(*C. A.*, VIII, 3107-9).

He manages his octosyllabics with sure mastery and his verse often has a lovely melody. His style is always clear and gracious, his diction always right. His reputation, which once was very great, has suffered unjustly in the modern period by comparison with the author of *Troilus*. In reality Chaucer and Gower share equally in the merit of having brought into English the best in French poetry. But, in contrast to Chaucer, Gower had no knowledge of the Italian poets.

He had the honor of being the first English poet to be translated into another modern language: we have a Spanish version of the *Confessio Amantis*, and this version supposes a Portuguese translation made in Gower's own lifetime.

Edition:

The Complete Works of Gower, ed. by G. C. MACAULAY, Oxford, 1899-1902, 4 vol.

Consult also:

W. P. KER. *Essays on Medieval Literature*, London, 1905 (pp. 101-34).
J. E. WELLS. *Manual*, pp. 585-98 (bibliography, pp. 865-6).

Medea Restores Eson's Youth

3945   Jason, which sih his fader old,
            Upon Medea made him bold

OVID, *Metam.*, L. VII.

. . . isto

175   Quod petis experiar maius dare munus, Iason.
           Arte mea soceri longum temptabimus aevum,

Of arte magique, which sche couþe,
And preiþ hire, þat his fader ȝouþe
Sche wolde make aȝeinward newe.
And sche, þat was toward him trewe,   3950
Behihte him þat sche wolde it do,
Whan þat sche time sawh þerto.
Bot what sche dede in þat matiere
It is a wonder þing to hiere;
Bo⟨t⟩ ȝit, for þe novellerie,   3955
I þenke tellen a partie.
   Thus it befell upon a nyght,
Whan þer was noght bot sterre-liht.
Sche was vanyssht riht as hir liste,
That no wyht bot hirself it wiste;   3960
And þat was at⟨t⟩e mydnyht tyde;
The world was stille on every side.
Wiþ open hed) and fot al bare,
Hir her tosprad, sche gan to fare;
Upon hir cloþes gert sche was,   3965
Al specheles, and on þe gras
Sche glod forþ as an addre doþ.
Non oþerwise sche ne goþ,
Til sche cam to þe freisshe flod,
And þere a while sche wiþstod.   3970

Non annis renovare tuis, modo diva triformis
Adiuvet et prasens ingentibus annuat ausis. »
   Tres aberant noctes ut cornua tota coirent
Efficerentque orbem; postquam plenissima fulsit   180
Et solida terras spectavit imagine luna,
Egreditur tectis vestes induta recinctas,
Nuda pedem, nudos umeris infusa capillos,
Fertque vagos mediae per muta silentia noctis
Incomitata gradus; homines volucresque ferasque   185
Solverat alta quies; [nullo cum murmure serpit
Sopitae similis;] nullo cum murmure saepes
Immotaeque silent frondes, silet umidus aer;
Sidera sola micant; ad quae sua bracchia tendens,

Thries sche torned hire aboute,
And thries ek sche gan doun loute;
And in þe flod sche wette hir her,
And þries on þe water þer

3975   Sche gaspeþ wiþ a drecchinge onde,
And þo sche tok hir speche on honde.
Ferst sche began to clepe and calle
Upward unto þe sterres alle;
To wynd, to air, to see, to lond

3980   Sche preide, and ek hield up hir hond
To Echates — and gan to crie —,
Which is goddesse of sorcerie;
Sche seide: 'Helpeþ at þis nede,
And as ȝe maden me to spede

3985   Whan Jason cam þe Flees to seche,
So helpe me nou, I ȝou beseche.'
Wiþ þat sche lokeþ, and was war,
Doun fro þe sky þer cam a char,
The which dragouns aboute drowe.

3990   And þo sche gan hir hed doun bowe,
And up sche styh, and faire and wel
Sche drof forþ boþe char and whel
Above in þ'air among þe skyes.

---

190   Ter se convertit, ter sumptis flumine crinem
Inroravit aquis ternisque ululatibus ora
Solvit et in dura summisso poplite terra:
« Nox, » ait, « arcanis fidissima, quaeque diurnis
Aurea cum luna succeditis ignibus astra,

195   Tuque triceps Hecate, quae coeptis conscia nostris
Adiutrixque venis cantusque artisque magorum,
Quaeque magos, Tellus, pollentibus instruis herbis,
Auraeque et venti montesque amnesque lacusque,
Dique omnes nemorum, dique omnes noctis, adeste. »
. . . .
         aderat demissus ab aethere currus.

220   Quo simul ascendit frenataque colla draconum
Permulsit manibusque levis agitavit habenas,
Sublimis rapitur subiectaque Thessala Tempe

The lond of Crete and þo parties
Sche soughte, and faste gan hire hye,   3995
And þere, upon þe hulles hyhe
Of Othrin and Olimpe also,
And ek of oþre hulles mo,
Sche fond and gadreþ herbes suote;
Sche pulleþ up som be þe rote,   4000
And manye wiþ a knyf sche scherþ,
And alle into hir char sche berþ.
Thus whan sche haþ þe hulles sought,
The flodes þer forȝat sche nought,
Eridian and Amphrisos,   4005
Peneie and ek Spercheidos;
To hem sche wente, and þer sche nom
Boþe of þe water and þe fom,
The sond and ek þe smale stones,
Whiche as sche ches out for þe nones,   4010
And of þe Rede See a part,
That was behovelich to hire art,
Sche tok; and after þat, aboute
Sche soughte sondri sedes oute
In feldes and in many greves,   4015
And ek a part sche tok of leves;
Bot þing, which mihte hire most availe,
Sche fond in Crete and in Thessaile.

Despicit et certis [*var.* Cretis] regionibus applicat angues;
Et quas Ossa tulit, quas altus Pelion herbas,
Quas Othrys Pindusque et Pindo maior Olympus,   225
Perspicit et placitas partim radice revellit,
Partim succidit curvamine falcis aenae.
Multa quoque Eridani placuerunt gramina ripis,
Multa quoque Amphrysi; neque eras immunis, Enipeu;
Nec non Peneos, nec non Spercheides undae   230
Contribuere aliquid iuncosaque litora Boebes.
. . . .

In daies and in nyhtes nyne,
4020   Wiþ gret travaile and wiþ gret pyne,
Sche was pourveid of every piece,
And torneþ homward into Grece.
Before þe gates of Eson
Hir char sche let awey to gon,
4025   And tok out ferst þat was þerinne;
For þo sche þoghte to beginne
Suche þing as semeþ impossible,
And made hirselven invisible,
As sche þat was wiþ air enclosed
4030   And mihte of noman be desclosed.
Sche tok up turves of þe lond
Wiþoute helpe of mannes hond,
Al heled wiþ þe grene gras,
Of which an alter made þer was
4035   Unto Echates, þe goddesse
Of art magique and þe maistresse,
And eft an oþer to Juvente,
As sche whiche dede hir hole entente.
Tho tok sche fieldwode and verveyne,
4040   Of herbes be noght betre tueyne,

4020 pyne] peyne *MS.*

Et iam nona dies curru pennisque draconum
235   Nonaque nox omnes lustrantem viderat agros,
Cum rediit; neque erant tacti nisi odore dracones,
Et tamen annosae pellem posuere senectae.
Constitit adveniens citra limenque foresque
Et tantum caelo tegitur refugitque viriles
240   Contactus; statuitque aras e caespite binas,
Dexteriore Hecates, ast laeva parte Iuventae,
Has ubi verbenis silvaque incinxit agresti,
Haud procul egesta scrobibus tellure duabus
Sacra facit cultrosque in guttura velleris atri
245   Conicit et patulas perfundit sanguine fossas.
Tum super invergens liquidi carchesia vini
Alteraque invergens tepidi carchesia lactis,

Of which anon wiþoute let
These alters ben aboute set.
Tuo sondry puttes faste by
Sche made, and wiþ þat hastely
A wether, which was blak, sche slouh,   4045
And out þerof þe blod sche drouh,
And dede into þe pettes tuo;
Warm melk sche putte also þerto
Wiþ hony meynd, and in such wise   *pastpple*
Sche gan to make hir sacrifise,   4050
And cried and preide forþ wiþal
To Pluto þe god infernal,
And to þe queene Proserpine.
And so sche soghte out al þe line
Of hem, þat longen to þat craft,   4055
Behinde was no name laft,
And preide hem alle, as sche wel couþe,
To grante Eson his ferste ȝouþe.
    This olde Eson broght forþ was þo,
Awei sche bad alle oþre go   4060
Upon peril þat mihte falle,
And wiþ þat word þei wenten alle,
And leften þere hem tuo alone.
And þo sche gan to gaspe and gone,
And made signes many on,   4065
And seide hir wordes þerupon;
So þat wiþ spellinge of hir charmes
Sche tok Eson in boþe hire armes,

Verba simul fundit terrenaque numina lenit
Vmbrarumque rogat rapta cum coniuge regem,
Ne properent artus anima fraudare senili.   250
Quos ubi placavit precibusque et murmure longo,
Aesonis effetum proferri corpus ad auras
Iussit et in plenos resolutum carmine somnos
Exanimi similem stratis porrexit in herbis.
Hinc procul Aesoniden, procul hinc iubet ire ministros 255

And made him for to slepe faste,
4070   And him upon hire herbes caste.
The blake wether tho sche tok,
And hiewh þe fleissh, as doþ a cok;
On eiþer alter part sche leide,
And wiþ þe charmes þat sche seide
4075   A fyr doun fro þe sky alyhte,
And made it for to brenne lyhte.
Bot whan Medea sawh it brenne,
Anon sche gan to sterte and renne
The fyri auters al aboute.
4080   Ther was no beste which goþ oute
More wylde, þan sche semeþ þer.
Aboute hir schuldres hyng hir her,
As þogh sche were out of hir mynde
And torned in an oþer kinde.
4085   Tho lay þer certein wode cleft,
Of which þe pieces nou and eft
Sche made hem in þe pettes wete,
And putte hem in þe fyri hete,
And tok þe brond wiþ al þe blase,
4090   And þries sche began to rase
Aboute Eson, þer as he slepte.
And eft wiþ water, which sche kepte,
Sche made a cercle aboute him þries,
And eft wiþ fyr of sulphre twyes;
4095   Ful many an oþer þing sche dede,
Which is noght writen in þis stede.

Et monet arcanis oculos removere profanos.
Diffugiunt iussi; passis Medea capillis
Bacchantum ritu flagrantis circuit aras
Multifidasque faces in fossa sanguinis atra
260   Tinguit et intinctas geminis accendit in aris
Terque senem flamma, ter aqua, ter sulphure lustrat.
Interea validum posito medicamen aeno
Fervet et exsultat spumisque tumentibus albet.

Bot þo sche ran so up and doun,
Sche made many a wonder soun;
Somtime lich unto þe cock,   Mode like
Somtime unto þe laverock,   4100
Somtime kacleþ as an hen,
Somtime spekeþ as don þe men.
And riht so as hir jargoun strangeþ,
In sondri wise hir forme changeþ,
S⟨ch⟩e semeþ faie and no womman.   4105
For wiþ þe craftes þat sche can
Sche was, as who seiþ, a goddesse;
And what hir liste, more or lesse,
Sche dede, in þe bokes as we finde,
That passeþ over mannes kinde;   4110
Bot who þat wole of wondres hiere,
What þing sche wroghte in þis matiere,
To make an ende of þat sche gan,
Such merveile herde nevere man.
   Apointed in þe newe mone,   4115
Whan it was time for to done,
Sche sette a caldron on þe fyr,
In which was al þe hole atir,
Wheron þe medicine stod,
Of jus, of water, and of blod,   4120
And let it buile in such a plit,
Til þat sche sawh þe spume whyt;
And þo sche caste in rynde and rote,
And sed and flour þat was for bote,

Illic Haemonia radices valle resectas
Seminaque floresque et sucos incoquit atros.   265
Adicit extremo lapides oriente petitos
Et quas Oceani refluum mare lavit harenas;
Addit et exceptas luna pernocte pruinas
Et strigis infames ipsis cum carnibus alas
Inque virum soliti vultus mutare ferinos   270

4125 Wiþ many an herbe and many a ston,
Wherof sche haþ þer many on.
And ek Cimpheius, þe serpent,
To hire haþ alle his scales lent;
Chelidre hire ȝaf his addres skin,
4130 And sche to builen caste hem in;
A part ek of þe horned oule,
The which men hiere on nyhtes houle;
And of a raven, which was told
Of nyne hundred wynter old,
4135 Sche tok þe hed wiþ al þe bile;
And as þe medicine it wile,
Sche tok þerafter þe bouele
Of þe seewolf, and for þe hele
Of Eson, wiþ a þousand mo
4140 Of þinges, þat sche hadde þo,
In þat caldron togedre, as blyve,
Sche putte, and tok þanne of olyve
A drie branche hem wiþ to stere,
The which anon gan floure and bere,
4145 And waxe al freissh and grene aȝein.
Whan sche þis vertu hadde sein,
Sche let þe leste drope of alle

Ambigui prosecta lupi; nec defuit illis
Squamea Cinyphii tenuis membrana chelydri
Vivacisque iecur cervi, quibus insuper addit
Ora caputque novem cornicis saecula passae.
275 His et mille aliis postquam sine nomine rebus
Propositum instruxit mortali barbara maius,
Arenti ramo iampridem mitis olivae.
Omnia confudit summisque inmiscuit ima.
Ecce vetus calido versatus stipes aeno
280 Fit viridis primo, nec longo tempore frondes
Induit et subito gravidis oneratur olivis.
At quacumque cavo spumas eiecit aeno
Ignis et in terram guttae cecidere calentes,
Vernat humus floresque et mollia pabula surgunt.

Upon þe bar⟨e⟩ flor doun falle;
Anon þer sprong up flour and gras
Where as þe drope falle was,   4150
And wox anon al medwe-grene,
So þat it mihte wel be sene.
Medea þanne knewe and wiste
Hir medicine is for to triste,
And goþ to Eson þer he lay,   4155
And tok a swerd, was of assay,
Wiþ which a wounde upon his side
Sche made, þat þerout mai slyde
The blod wiþinne, which was olde,
And sek, and trouble, and fieble, and cold.   4160
And þo sche tok unto his us
Of herbes al þe beste jus,
And poured it into his wounde,   *normal sf*
That made his veynes fulle and sounde.
And þo sche made his wounde clos,   4165
And tok his hand, and up he ros.
And þo sche ȝaf him drink a drauhte,
Of which his ȝouþe aȝein he cauhte,
His hed, his herte, and his visage
Lich unto twenty wynter age.   4170
Hise hore heres were away
And lich unto þe freisshe Maii,
Whan passed ben þe colde schoures,
Riht so recovereþ he his floures.

Quae simul ac vidit, stricto Medea recludit   285
Ense senis iugulum veteremque exire cruorem
Passa, replet sucis; quos postquam conbibit Aeson
Aut ore acceptos aut vulnere, barba comaeque
Canitie posita nigrum rapuere colorem;
Pulsa fugit macies, abeunt pallorque situsque   290
Adiectoque cavae supplentur corpore rugae
Membraque luxuriant; Aeson miratur et olim
Ante quater denos hunc se reminiscitur annos.

XXIX

THE TOWNELEY PLAYS

Middle-English literature has a great many 'mystery plays', or 'craft-gild plays', pieces cast in a popular mode that retell the stories of the Old and New Testaments. These were performed by the various merchandizing and manufacturing gilds during the great liturgical feast days. The extract that follows is taken from one of the most celebrated cycles, the series called the *Towneley Plays*, preserved in a unique manuscript and comprising thirty-two plays. Although the manuscript dates from the second half of the 15th century, it is presumed that the cycle was composed towards the end of the 14th century, and that some of these pieces, if not all of them, were played at Wakefield.

The *Second Shepherds' Play* is number 13 in this cycle that runs from the creation to the hanging of Judas. It is the first example of a stage comedy in the English language, and it recalls the French *Pathelin* in its humor and rapid movement.

Scene I: It is night-time, out in the country, in Yorkshire, near Horbury, probably. Three shepherds, Coll, Gib and Daw are talking. Enter Mak, one of their companions with an unsavory reputation in general and for sheep stealing in particular. He makes up a sack with them and goes to sleep. But Mak then gets up quietly, lifts a sheep, and goes off home to his wife, Gill.

Scene VI: The shepherds notice the loss, suspect Mak, go directly to his house where they find Gill still moaning because she has just that minute given birth. They are appeased and want to give the baby a present, upon which they discover it has an unconscionably long nose and looks very much like a sheep. They seize Mak, take him outside and toss him in a canvas.

Scene VII: Now avenged and the sheep recovered, they start to settle down to sleep again when an angel appears who announces the birth of the Savior; the shepherds then set off for Bethlehem.

Editions:

The Towneley Plays, ed. by G. ENGLAND and A. W. POLLARD, London, 1897 (*EETS ES* no. 71).

J. M. MANLY. *Specimens of Pre-Shakespearian Drama*, Boston, 1897 (vol. I, pp. 94-119).

A. S. COOK. *A Literary Middle English Reader*, Boston, 1915, pp. 525-54.

Consult also:

E. K. CHAMBERS. *The Mediæval Stage*, Oxford, 1903.
J. E. WELLS. *Manual*, pp. 555-60 (bibliography, pp. 860-1).

The Second Shepherds' Play

Scene I: The moors near Horbury, in the West Riding of Yorkshire.
Tunc intrat Mak, in clamide se super togam vestitus.

⌊starnes
190 *Mak.* Now Lord, for thy naymes vii,   that made both moyn and

Well mo then I can neven, thi will, Lorde, of me tharnys;
I am all uneven, that moves oft my harnes.
Now wold God I were in heven, for the⟨re⟩ wepe no barnes
    So styll.
  I Pastor. Who is that, pypys so poore?   195
  Mak. Wold God ye wyst how I foore!
  ⟨*I Pastor.*⟩ Lo, a man that walkys on the moore,
   And has not all his wyll.

II Pastor. Mak, where has thou gon? Tell us tythyng.
III Pastor. Is he commen? Then ylkon take hede to his thyng. 200
       [*et accipit clamidem ab ipso.*
Mak. What! ich be a yoman, I tell you, of the king;
      [*Pretending not to know them.*
The self and the same sond from a greatt lordyng,
    And sich.
   Fy on you! goyth hence
   Out of my presence!   205
   I must have reverence;
    Why, who be ich?

I Pastor. Why make ye it so qwaynt, Mak? ye do wrang.
II Pastor. Bot, Mak, lyst ye saynt? I trow that ye lang. [hang!
III Pastor. I trow the shrew can paynt, the dewyll myght hym 210
Mak. Ich shall make complaynt and make you all to thwang
    At a worde,
   And tell evyn how ye doth.
  I Pastor. Bot, Mak, is that sothe?
  Now take outt that sothren tothe   215
   And sett in a torde!

II Pastor. Mak, the dewill in youre ee! A stroke wold I leyne you.
III Pastor. Mak, know ye not me? By God, I couthe teyn you.
Mak. God looke you all thre! Me thoght I had sene you,
      [*As if recognizing them.*
Ye ar a fare compané.
I Pastor.   Can ye now mene you?   220
   II Pastor. Shrew, jape!

199 gon] gom *MS.* — 218 teyn] teyle *MS* (le *added by a later scribe*).

Thus late as thou goys,
What wyll men suppos?
And thou has an yll noys
225   Of stelyng of shepe.

Mak. And I am trew as steyll,   all men waytt!
Bot a sekenes I feyll   that haldys me full haytt:
My belly farys not weyll,   it is out of astate.
III Pastor. 'Seldom lyvs the dewyll   dede by the gate'.
230   *Mak.* Therfor
Full sore am I and yll,
If I stande stone-styll;
I ete not an nedyll
Thys moneth and more.

235 *I Pastor.* How farys thi wyff? By my hoode,   how farys sho?
Mak. Lyys walteryng, by the roode,   by the fyere, lo!
And a howse full of brude,   she drynkys well, to;
Yll spede othere good   that she wyll do!
            Bot s⟨h⟩o
240   Etys as fast as she can,
And ilk yere that commys to man
She bryngys furth a lakan,
And som yeres two.

Bot were I not more gracyus   and rychere be far,
245 I were eten outt of howse   and of harbar;
Yit is she a fowll dowse,   if ye com nar:
Ther is none that trowse   nor knowys a war,
            Then ken I.
Now wyll ye se what I profer? —
250   To gyf all in my cofer,
To-morne at next to offer
Hyr hed-maspenny
II Pastor. I wote so forwakyd   is none in this shyre:
I wold slepe if I takyd   les to my hyere.
255 *III Pastor.* I am cold and nakyd   and wold have a fyere.
I Pastor. I am wery, forrakyd   and run in the myre.
            Wake thou!
    II Pastor. Nay, I wyll lyg downe by,

For I must slepe truly.
III Pastor. As good a mans son was I   260
  As any of you

Bot, Mak, com heder! betwene   shall thou lyg downe.
Mak. Then myght I lett you bedene   of that ye wold rowne,
        No drede.   *[He says his prayers.*
  Fro my top to my too,   265
  Manus tuas commendo,
  Pontio Pilato
    Cryst-crosse me spede!
    [Tunc surgit, pastoribus dormientibus, et dicit:

Now were tyme for a man,   that lakkys what he wold,
To stalk prevely than   unto a fold,   270
And neemly to wyrk than   and be not to bold,
For he might aby the bargan,   if it were told
        At the endyng.
  Now were tyme for to reyll;
  Bot he nedys good counsell   275
  That fayn wold fare weyll
    And has bot lytyll spendyng.   *[He works a spell.*

Bot abowte you a serkyll   as rownde as a moyn,
To I have done that I wyll,   tyll that it be noyn,
That ye lyg stone-styll,   to that I have doyne,   280
And I shall say thertyll   of good wordys a foyne.
        On hight
  Over youre heydys my hand I lyft:
  'Outt go youre een, fordo your syght!'
  Bot yit I must make better shyft,   285
    And it be right.

Lord! what thay slepe hard!   that may ye all here:
Was I never a shepard,   bot now wyll I lere.
If the flok be skard,   yit shall I nyp nere.
How! drawes hederward!   Now mendys oure chere   290
        From sorow:
  A fatt shepe, I dar say;

291 From] ffron *MS.*

A good flese dar I lay,
Eftwhyte when I may,
295   Bot this will I borow.   [*Exit with the sheep.*

*
*   *

Scene VI: Mak's cottage. Mak singing within, and Gill his wife groaning.

475 *III Pastor.* Will ye here how thay hak?   Oure syre, lyst, croyne.
I Pastor. Hard I never none crak   so clere out of toyne;
Call on hym!
II Pastor.   Mak!   Undo youre doore soyne!
Mak. Who is that, spak   as it were noyne
480   On loft?
Who is that, I say?
III Pastor. Goode felowse, were it day —
Mak. As far as ye may,
Good, spekys soft

485 Over a seke womans heede   that is at maylleasse;
I had lever be dede   or she had any dyseasse.
Uxor. Go to an othere stede,   I may not well qweasse.
Ich fote that ye trede   goys thorow my nese.
So hee!
490   *I Pastor.* Tell us, Mak, if ye may,
How fare ye, I say?
Mak. Bot ar ye in this towne to-day?
Now how fare ye?

Ye have ryn in the myre   and ar weytt yit:
495 I shall make you a fyre,   if ye will syt.
A nores wold I hyre,   thynk ye on yit?
Well qwytt is my hyre,   — my dreme this is itt —
A seson.
I have barnes, if ye knew,
500   Well mo then e-newe,
Bot ' we must drynk as we brew ',
And that is bot reson.

I wold ye dynyd or ye yode,   me thynk that ye swette.
II Pastor. Nay, nawther mendys oure mode,   drynke nor mette.
Mak. Why, sir, alys you oght bot goode?

III Pastor.   Yee, oure shepe that we gett, 505
Ar stollyn as thay yode;   oure los is grette.
                Mak. Syrs, drynkys!
     Had I bene thore,
     Som shuld have boght it full sore.
     I Pastor. Mary, some men trowes that ye wore,   510
     And that us forthynkys.

II Pastor. Mak, some men trowys   that it shuld be ye.
III Pastor. Ayther ye or youre spouse   so say we.
Mak. Now if ye have suspowse   to Gill or to me,
Com and rype oure howse,   and then may ye se   515
                Who had hir,
     If I any shepe fott,
     Aythor cow or stott;
     And Gyll, my wyfe, rose nott
         Here syn she lade hir.   520

As I am true and lele,   to God here I pray,
That this be the fyrst mele   that I shall ete this day.
I Pastor. Mak, as have I ceyll,   avyse the, I say;
' He lernyd tymely to steyll   that couth not say nay '.
                Uxor. I swelt!   525
     Outt, thefys, fro my wonys!
     Ye com to rob us for the nonys!
     Mak. Here ye not how she gronys?
         Youre hartys shuld melt.

Uxor. Outt, thefys, fro my barne!   Negh hym not thor.   530
Mak. Wyst ye how she had farne,   youre hartys wold be sore.
Ye do wrang, I you warne,   that thus commys before
To a woman that has farne   bot I say no more.
                Uxor. A! my medyll!
     I pray to God so mylde,   535
     If ever I you begyld,
     That I ete this chylde
         That lygys in this credyll.

Mak. Peasse, woman, for Godys payn,   and cry not so:
Thou spyllys the brane   and makys me full wo.   540

II Pastor. I trow oure shepe be slayn,   what finde ye two?
III Pastor. All wyrk we in vayn.   As well may we go.
                    Bot hatters!
            I can finde no flesh,
545   Hard nor nesh,
            Salt nor fresh,
                Bot two tome platers.

Whik catell bot this,   tame nor wylde,
None, as have I blys,   as lowde as he smylde.
550 *Uxor.* No, so God me blys,   and gyf me joy of my chylde!
I Pastor. We have merkyd amys,   I hold us begyld.
                    II Pastor. Syr, don,
                Syr, Oure Lady hym save!
                Is youre chyld a knave?
555   *Mak.* Any lord myght hym have,
                This chyld, to his son.

. When he wakyns he kyppys,   that joy is to se.
III Pastor. In good tyme to hys hyppys   and in celé.
Bot who was his gossyppys,   so sone redé?
Mak. So fare fall thare lyppys —   [*Aside.*
560   *I Pastor.* Hark now, a le!
                    Mak. So God thaym thank,
            Parkyn and Gybon Waller, I say,
            And gentill John Horne, in good fay,
            He made all the garray,
565   With the greatt shank.

II Pastor. Mak, freyndys will we be,   for we ar all oone.
Mak. We? now I hald for me,   for mendys gett I none!
Fare well all thre,   all glad were ye gone.
                        [*The Shepherds leave the house.*

III Pastor. Fare wordys may ther be,   bot luf is ther none
570   This yere.
        I Pastor. Gaf ye the chyld any thyng?
        II Pastor. I trow not oone farthyng.
        III Pastor. Fast agane will I flyng.
            Abyde ye me here.   [*Goes back to the house.*

574 here] there *MS.*

Mak, take it to no grefe   if I com to thi barne.   575
Mak. Nay, thou dos me greatt reprefe,   and fowll has thou farne.
III Pastor. The child will it not grefe,   that lytyll day-starne.
Mak, with youre leyfe,   let me gyf youre barne
    Bot VI pence.
        [He approaches the cradle.
   Mak. Nay, do way: he slepys.   580
   III Pastor. Me thynk he pepys.
   Mak. When he wakyns, he wepys.
   I pray you go hence.
     [First and Second Shepherd return.

III Pastor. Gyf me lefe hym to kys   and lyft up the clowtt.
         [He sees the sheep. 585
What the dewill is this?   He has a long snowte.
I Pastor. He is merkyd amys;   we wate ill abowte.
II Pastor. 'Ill-spon weft,' i-wys,   'ay commys foull owte'.
   Ay, so!
   He is lyke to oure shepe!
III Pastor. How, Gyb! may I pepe?   590
   I Pastor. I trow, 'kynde will crepe
   Where it may not go'.

II Pastor. This was a qwantt gawde   and a far cast.
It was a hee frawde.
III Pastor.   Yee, syrs, was't?
Lett bren this bawde   and bynd hir fast.   595
'A fals skawde   hang⟨s⟩ at the last';
   So shall thou.
   Wyll ye se how thay swedyll
   His foure feytt in the medyll?
   Sagh I never in a credyll   600
   A hornyd lad or now.

Mak. Peasse byd I! what,   lett be youre fare!
I am he that hym gatt,   and yond woman hym bare.
I Pastor. What dewill shall be hatt,   Mak? Lo, God, Makys ayre!
II Pastor. Lett be all that,   now God gyf hym care,   605
   I sagh.
   Uxor. A pratty child is he
   As syttys on a womans kne;
   A dyllydowne, perdé,
   To gar a man laghe.   610

609 womans] wamans *MS.*

III Pastor. I know hym by the eere-marke,   that is a good tokyn.
Mak. I tell you, syrs, hark!   Hys noyse was brokyn.
Sythen told me a clerk   that he was forspokyn.
I Pastor. This is a fals wark,   I wold fayn be wrokyn;
615   Gett wepyn.
        Uxor. He was takyn with an elfe,
        I saw it my self.
        When the clok stroke twelf
        Was he forshapyn.

620 *II Pastor.* Ye two ar well feft   sam in a stede.
III Pastor. Syn thay manteyn thare theft,   let do thaym to dede.
Mak. If I trespas eft,   gyrd of my heede.
With you will I be left
I Pastor.   Syrs, do my reede.
          For this trespas,
625   We will nawther ban ne flyte,
        Fyght nor chyte,
        Bot have done as tyte
        And cast hym in canvas.
             [*They go outside and toss Mak in a sheet.*

                     *
                *   *

Scene VII: A field near Mak's cottage. Enter the three Shepherds.

I Pastor. Lord! what I am sore,   in poynt for to bryst.
630 In fayth I may no more,   therfor wyll I ryst.
II Pastor. As a shepe of vii skore   he weyd in my fyst.
For to slepe aywhore   me thynk that I lyst.
                III Pastor. Now I pray you,
          Lyg downe on this grene.
635   *I Pastor.* On these thefys yit I mene.
        III Pastor. Wherto shuld ye tene?
        Do as I say you.

      Angelus cantat ' gloria in excelsis '; postea dicat:

Angelus. Ryse, hyrdmen heynd!   For now is he borne
That shall take fro the feynd   that Adam had lorne;
640 That warloo to sheynd,   this nyght is he borne.

     637 Do] So *MS.*

God is made youre freynd   now at this morne.
     He behestys
   At Bedlem go se,
   Ther lygys that fre
   In a cryb full poorely   645
    Betwyx two bestys.
                [*Exit.*

I Pastor. This was a qwant stevyn   *as* ever yit I hard.
It is a mervell to nevyn   thus to be skard.
II Pastor. Of Godys son of hevyn   he spak upward.
All the wod on a levyn   me thoght that he gard   650
     Appere.
   III Pastor. He spake of a barne
   In Bedlem, I you warne.
   I Pastor. That betokyns yond starne.
          [*Pointing to the sky.*
   Let us seke hym there.   655

II Pastor. Say, what was his song?   Hard ye not how he crakyd
Thre brefes to a long.   [it?
III Pastor.   Yee, Mary, he hakt it.
Was no crochett wrong,   nor nothyng that lakt it.
I Pastor. For to syng us emong   right as he knakt it,
     I can.   660
   II Pastor. Let se how ye croyne.
   Can ye bark at the mone?
   III Pastor. Hold youre tonges, have done!
    I Pastor. Hark after, than.   [*They sing.*

II Pastor. To Bedlem he bad   that we shuld gang;   665
I am full fard   that we tary to lang.
III Pastor. Be mery and not sad,   of myrth is oure sang,
Everlastyng glad   to mede may we fang
     Without noyse.
   I Pastor. Hy we theder for-thy;   670
   If we be wete and wery,
   To that chyld and that lady
    We have it not to lose.

647 as] that *MS.*

CLASSIFICATION OF TEXTS BY GENRE AND SUBJECT

1. Verse romances.

VII. *King Horn*; XII. *Havelok the Dane*; XXVII / 2. CHAUCER, *Troilus and Criseyde*. Arthurian legend: V/2 Lawman, *The Brut*; XVIII. *Sir Gawain and the Green Knight*; XX. *Morte Arthure*.

2. Fabliaux, animal fables and tales.

X. *The Fox and the Wolf*; XIV / 2. *The Hermit and his Bear*; XXI / 2. W. LANGLAND, *The Council of Rats and Mice;* XXII / 2. J. BARBOUR, *The King and the Three Traitors*; XXVII / 4. CHAUCER, *The Pardoner's Tale*; XXVIII. J. GOWER, *Jason and Medea*.

3. Chronicles and historical documents.

I. *Peterborough Chronicle*; XI. *Proclamation of Henry III*; XXV. *Mercers' Petition*; XXVI. JOHN OF TREVISA.

4. Moral and religious works.

II. *Poema Morale*; III. *Ancrene Wisse*; IV. *Sawles Warde*; VII. *Ormulum*; IX. *Kentish Sermons*; XVI. Richard ROLLE OF HAMPOLE; XXIV. John WYCLIF.

5. Confessional handbooks and analogous works.

XIV. Robert MANNYNG, *Handlyng Synne*; XV. MICHEL OF NORTHGATE, *Aȝenbite of Inwyt*; XXVIII. J. GOWER, *Confessio Amantis*.

6. Mystical visions.

XIX. *The Pearl*; XXI / 1. W. LANGLAND, *Piers Plowman: the first vision*.

7. Travels and exoticism.

XXIII. *Travels of Sir John Mandeville*.

8. Dreams.

V / 2. LAWMAN, *Arthur's Dream*; XX / 2. *Arthur's Dream*; XXVII /1. CHAUCER, *The Book of the Duchess: the dream*.

9. Lyricism.

XIII. *Lyric poems*; XXVII / 3. CHAUCER, *Ballade of the 'Good Women'*.

10. **Autobiography.**

V / 1. LAWMAN, VII / Introd.; ORM, XIV / Introd. and 1; ROBERT MANNYNG OF BRUNNE; XXI / 3. WILLIAM LANGLAND.

11. **Debates.**

VI. *The Owl and the Nightingale.*

12. **Dramatic works.**

XXIX. *The Second Shepherds' Play.*

13. **Allusions to contemporary events.**

XVII. L. MINOT; XXI. W. LANGLAND.

14. **Genre portraits.**

III / 2. *The Flatterers*; XV. *Gluttony*; XXI / 4. *Glutton at the Tavern*; XXVII / 4ₐ. *Portrait of the Pardoner.*

NOTES

I

Text from Bodleian MS Laud Misc. 636 (ca. 1155).
Dialect of the North-east Midlands (Northampton).

Spelling. A mixture of traditional spellings inherited from OE and innovations no doubt due to the fact that this text had been taken down from dictation by a monk of the abbey of Peterborough accustomed to French methods.

I. *Old English traditions.* — Use of *g, c, sc* to note the sounds [j], [č], [š]. As in part I of this *Handbook*, to distinguish these from the stops [g] and [k], they are marked *ġ, ċ, sċ*. Thus *ġære* 1, *ġet* 3; *alsuiċ* 3, *riċe* 15, *ċirċe* 52; *sċulde* 2, *bisċop* 8, *sċort* 30, etc.

II. *French innovations.* — *th* used for *þ* (*ther* 2, *tharof* 6, *athes* 13), *w* for *hw* or *wh* (*wile* 41, 49, *ower* 55, *warsæ* 59), *ch* for [k] (*rachenteġes* 33, *halechen* 62), *qu* for *cw* (*quarterne* 28), *c = s* in *justice* 12.

III. *Other spelling features.* — Use of *u* for *w* after *s* (*suikes* 11, *suoren* 14, 59, *suenċten*, *suyðe* 17, *suilċe* 61). The MS also has *uu* for *w* (*uuenden* 2, *uuæren* 23, *uureċċe* 17). Use of *i* for [j], written *ġe* in OE (*iafen* 10, *iærd* 52, *ieden* 48; *y* for *i* is still infrequent (*ċyrċe* concurrent with *ċirċe* 52, *sylver* 22, *myhtes* 45, *yvele* 19, *fylden* 18). And the letters *æ, a* and *e* are used rather interchangeably.

The former digraphs of OE are replaced by single letters. Instead of *ea* one finds *a* (*nareu* 30, *-wardes* 36, *alle* 13, *hals* 36) or *æ* (*sċærp* 35, *iærd* 52, *ælle* 10), instead of *ie* we find *e* (*werse* 50), instead of *eo*, either *e* (*clepeden* 43), or *y* = [ɪ] (*sythen* 53, *sylver* 22), or *u* (*sċulde* 2), or *o* (*sċort* 30).

Phonology. OE *ā* remains *ā* (*þa* 7, *athes* 13, *bathe* 20, *nan* 14, *stanes* 31, *mare* 50, 62), *y* = [ü] becomes *i* = [ɪ] *diden* 21, *sinnes* 63).

OE diphthongs are reduced: *ēa* > *ē* (*hefed* 25) or *æ* (*ræveden* 54, *ræveres* 57); *ēo* > *ē* (*ben* 3, *undep* 30, *ieden* 48) or *æ* (*ġæde* 27). There is, however, a sporadic survival of *eo*, either as a digraph (*weorces* 18) or as representing an historical diphthong (*heolden* 16, *deovles* 19, *preostes* 54), or even representing an OE *ēa* (*beom* 34, *eom* 3).

Some new diphthongs appear: *æ + ġ* > *æi* (*dæies* 20), *e + ġ* > *æi* (*sæin* 62, *læiden* 42), *a + w* > *au* (*saule* 5), *o + w* > *ou* (*nouther* 51), *eo + w* > *eu*, *eo* (*treuthe* 14, *treothes* 15).

Unstressed vowels are recorded quite irregularly: *æ* occurs for OE *e* (*hungær* 38, *forcursæd* 59), *e* for OE *o* (*tegædre* 53). The pret pl ending *-on* (*brendon* 44, *bæron* 37) is also written *-an* (*coman* 56) and, as early as this, *-en* (*hadden* 43, *ræveden* 44).

Inflexions. *Substantive.* — The dat sg sometimes survives (*throte* 35, *ċæste* 30), sometimes is without flexion (*hus* 29, *beom* 34).

The *-(e)s* form tends to be generalized in the plural for all classes of nouns and all cases. One finds *tunes* 42, 44, *castles* 16, 17, *martyrs* 23 (but *wunder*, pl 13), likewise the neuter *weorces* 18; this is also carried over into consonantal declensions (*nadres* 28, *þumbes* 25, *neves* 10), but *halechen* 62, *fet* 26, *wimmen* 21 occur.

337

The gen sg is in -(e)s (*mannes* 35), perhaps also the pl (*bisċopes* ? 54), cf. however *wintre* 41.

Adjective. — No more distinction between wk and str flexions. In the sg, adjs like *ful* 24, *an* 30, *sċort* 30, *al* 52, 59, have already become invariable. In the plural besides invariable forms like *cnotted* 26, *hethen* 50, some str forms survive, such as *alle* 13, 39, *yvele* 19, *sċærpe* 30, *swilce* 61.

Personal pronoun. — Note the forms 1 sg *I* 39, 3 pl *hi* 10, *her* 26 (*here* 11, 15), *heom* 21, etc.
The relative is still *þe* 19, 48, but more frequently *þat* 30, 31, 32, 33, etc.

Verb. — The pres tense is rare in this selection (3 sg *is* 34, pl *cunnen* 62). Wk pret sg in -*e* (or sometimes without ending: *todeld, scatered* 4), pl. in -*en* (*forsuoren, forloren* 59). The preverb *i*- (*ġe*-) never appears. Pres participle in -*end*(*e*) (*sittende* 46, *ridend* 56).

In str vbs of class IV and V the *a* in the pret pl is no doubt due to Scandinavian influence: *iafen* 10, *waren* 18, 48, *namen* 52, *drapen* 37, *forbaren* 51, see § 85.

Syntax is still close to that of OE. Note the abundance of locutions for 'put' (10, 21, 28), 'place' (26, 30), 'commit' (13) formed with *don* which bear witness to the poverty of style.

Use of the definite article in place of the possessive: *the eom* 'his uncle,' *the hefed* 'his head,' 25 is possibly due to Scandinavian influence (cf. § 123.3).

Vocabulary. French loan-words: *prisun* 10, 21, *justise* 12, *castle* 11, 16, etc., *martyrs* 23, *tenserie* 43. For words of Scandinavian origin see the following notes.

---

1. Although the following selection is in the MS dated 1137, it cannot have been written before the end of the reign of Stephen ca. 1154 (cp. 1. 40 *ðat lastede þa* xix *wintre* and 1. 63 *we þoleden* xix *wintre*). The truth of the facts reported here is confirmed by the historians of the time, the *Gesta Stephani* and the *Historia Novella* of William of Malmesbury (both published in the Rolls Series); see further, K. Norgate, *England under the Angevin Kings* (London, 1887), A. L. Poole, *From Domesday Book to Magna Carta*, Oxford, 1951, Chapter V and J. H. Round, *Geoffrey de Mandeville* (London, 1892).

1. King Stephne: Stephen, count of Blois, had come over to have himself crowned King of England in 1135. — **ofer sæ** 'from the other side of the English Channel.'

2. underfangen etc. 'accepted (as leader) because they thought he would be quite like his uncle (Henry I) and that he still [*ġet*] had his treasure.' According to William of Malmesbury this 'treasure' accumulated by Henry I was estimated at £100,000.

4. Henri King preserves the OE word-order, while *King Stephne* (ll. 1 and 7) shows the new one. The English language in the middle of the 12th cent. was changing rapidly.

5. me 'one, they (impersonal).' The form *men, me*, replaces in ME the OE *man, mon*, cp. ll. 23, 24, 26, 60. Here, as is sometimes the case, *me* followed by an active vb (*dide*) has a completely passive sense. Translate 'no good was done for his soul with it.'

7. þa...þa lit. 'then...when'; correlative constr as in OE, see § 162 and *HOE* § 191.

8. his gadering: the Assembly of Oxford which took place in June 1139. The arrests of the bishops, which Stephen had carried out, paralyzed the administration of the realm and were the signal for the civil war and the anarchy into which the country was plunged. — **Roger of Serberi:** Roger of Salisbury had been named regent in 1123; *Serberi* represents OE *Searobyrig*. The modern form *Salisbury* with medial *s* and dissimilation ($r - r > l - r$) is greatly altered.

9. te: a form frequently assumed by the article *þe* after a *-t* (the MS *ampersand* [7] which is transcribed *and* was probably pronounced *ant* before *þ-, t-*).

10. hise neves: Alexander, bishop of London, was indeed the nephew of Roger, bishop of Salisbury, but Roger, the Chancellor, was in reality his son. — **til:** the first known example of this word used as conjunction 'until' (in place of OE *oþ-þæt*). As a preposition *til* is rare in OE where it only appears in Northumbrian (Ruthwell Cross, Lindisfarne Glosses); it is a loan from ON.

11. here castles: the abandoned castles were those of Devizes, Malmesbury, Newark, Sherborne and Sleaford.

11. milde: Wm. of Malmesbury says of him 'lenis et exorabilis hostibus, affabilis omnibus.'

12. na justise ne did: this is the OF locution *faire justise* 'punish, inflict a punishment.' On this trait of Stephen's character, cp. the anecdote reported by Bruce DICKINS *RES* 2, 343 taken from the *Histoire de Guillaume le Maréchal.*

13. wunder 'terrible crimes.' cp. J. S. P. TATLOCK, *Amer. Hist. Review*, 41 (1935-36), 703. According to J. H. ROUND, *Geoffrey de Mandeville* (London, 1892) p. 214 ff., the well-known scene which follows was probably inspired by the terror sown in the Fen country in 1144 by Geoffrey de Mandeville.

14. hi nan 'not one of them.' — **alle hi** 'all of them.'

16 f. The castles in question here are those called by historians " adulterine castles," built without authorization of the Crown. According to the Treaty of Wallingford, 1115 of these illegal castles were to be razed.

19 f. þe...hefden 'who thought they possessed some wealth'; the subject of *hefden* is not expressed.

20. bathe...and: first known example of this expression borrowed from ON and which replaces OE *ægþer ġe...ġe.* — **be nihtes and be dæies** 'night and day'; OE had the simple adverbial genitive *dæġes and nihtes.*

21. carlmen 'men' (as opposed to women) is an ON term that is already to be found in pre-Conquest English. — **efter gold and sylver** 'in order to get gold and silver.' This use of *æfter* is not unknown in OE. cp. EINENKEL, *Historische Syntax*, 3rd ed., 24 and KLAEBER, *Anglia* 50, 213 (*Beowulf* l. 2179).

22. pined...pining 'inflicted unspeakable tortures on them'; an example of the so-called " cognate accusative ", cp. *HOE* § 156.

24. After *henged* the object *heom* is omitted.

25. hengen 'they strung (them) up' with the pret pl of the str vb *hange(n)* 'suspend'; *henged* is the pret sg of the wk vb 'to hang.' — **bryniġes**

'coats of chain mail,' because of their weight. The word was borrowed from
ON *brynja.*

27. wrythen to ðat etc. 'twisted to the point that (the cords) went (*gæde*)
into the brains (through the skull) '; *hærnes* is another ON loan (*hjarni*).

29. drapen 'killed'; from ON *drepa.*— **crucet-hus** 'torture-cage' is explained by what follows. This is probably the Latin *cruciatus*, with -*hus*
due to popular etymology.

31 f. him bræcon alle þe limes 'broke all his limbs' poss dat cp. § 109.

32. lof and grin: text possibly corrupt. Although the word *engin*(*e*) is not
attested before 1300, J. HALL proposes to read *loþ engins* 'frightful engines'
(of torture). The scribe may have misunderstood what was being dictated to
him. However it is not impossible that the expression *lof and grin* is an
authentic locution (technical, familiar or humorous) to designate the 'halter'
or 'rope' that is placed over the neck of the victim; *grin* 'snare, collar'
causes no difficulty: the word is still recorded in the King James Bible. As
for *lof*, a gloss gives it the sense of Latin *redimiculum* which is used at least
by Plautus with the meaning 'cords, fetter.' cp. F. P. MAGOUN Jr., *MLN*, 40,
411-12, O. F. EMERSON, *ibid.* 41, 170-2 and Bruce DICKINS, *RES* 2, 342.

33 f. ðat ... onne ' (so heavy) that two or three men would have difficulty
carrying a single one.'

34. The construction is awkward: we interpret *ðat is* 'that is to say'
(as in l. 29).

36. After **myhte** the verb of motion 'turn himself' is omitted.

40 f. XIX wintre: *wintre* is here, as in l. 63, the gen pl (OE *wintra*).

42. ævre um wile 'at regularly recurring intervals', cp. *æfre embe stunde*
Maldon 271.

43. tenserie 'tax exacted by lords from their vassals for protection and
defense' (from Med. Latin *tensare* 'to protect').

44. The burning of Worcester 1139, Nottingham 1140 and 1153, Winchester
1141, Oxford 1142, Cambridge 1144.

44 ff. ðat wel etc. 'in such a fashion that you might well travel a whole
day's journey, you wouldn't find etc.'

48. ieden on ælmes 'lived on charity, alms.'

50. hethen men 'The Danes.'

51. oversithon 'too frequently.' There are many diverse interpretations
proposed for this difficult nonce-word; Plummer's seems the most plausible.
He sees an adverbial dat of **ofer-sið* 'a time that recurs too frequently'
just as we have *oft-sið* 'a time that often recurs.' But the MS *ouer sithon*
might also be read *ower* (cp. the following note) *sithon* 'everywhere afterwards' (EMERSON). Another interpretation of *over sithon* 'contrary to
custom' (from OE **ofer siðum*) was suggested by J. HALL.

55. ævriç ... myhte 'everyman (robbed) another anywhere he could.' *ower*
(MS *ouer*) for *o-wher* OE *ā-hwǽr*. For another interpretation see Bruce
DICKINS, *RES* 2, 342.

56. tun is the village, **tunscipe** the inhabitants (hence the pl vb that
follows).

58. was heom naht þarof 'they cared nothing for it.'

59. forloren ' damned ' — **warsæ me tilede** ' wherever men tilled the soil ';
warsæ = wher-so.
61. hi sæden ' they said (impersonal).'

II

Text from Lambeth MS 487 (*L*), copied towards the end of the 12th c;
some readings are borrowed from Egerton MS 613 (*E*) in the British Museum,
and from MS Trinity College, Cambridge, B. 14.52 (*T*). Four other MSS
of this text are in existence.

Dialect. MS *L* is a copy of an original in the Southern dialect (the author
lived in Hampshire) made by a scribe from the southern part of the Midlands
area. This scribe at times introduces into the text the sounds of his own
dialect.

Spelling. Like the preceding text, a mixture of OE traditions and innovations partly due to Norman French influences.

I. *OE traditions.* — Use of *sc* (marked *sċ*) for the sound [š]: *sċal* 24, 35
etc. *sċulen* 20, 47, etc. In exceptional cases we find the new spelling
schal (19).

ð for the interdental spirant (*kuðe, soððen, i-queðen* 9, *fulieð* 12) except
initially, and sometimes finally, where there is þ (*þingþ* 5).

ea (as in *befealt* 7) has become exceptional; *eo* is rare (*beoð* 17, *beo* 29,
eow 25, *seon* 16) because the digraphs (and diphthongs) of OE are dis-
appearing.

II. *Norman-French innovations.* — Use of *o* for the sound [ö] long and
short (*bon* 2, *bo* 4; 21 *boð* 26, *fole* 9, *frond* 30, *solf* 12, *hom* 18, *hovene* 25,
soððen 9, *sovene* 26, *doð* 53, *þove* 43, *love* 44, *lovre* 29).

Use of *u* for the sound [ü] long and short (*muchel* 12, 22, *ufele* 17, *lutel* 46,
fure 43, *i-gult* 27, *i-hud* 28, *stude* 42).

Use of *qu* for *cw* (*i-queðen* 9), of *w* for *hw* or *wh* (*wenne* 35) and sometimes
t for þ, ð (*ofþinchet* 10, *bifealt* 7).

Phonology. OE ā remains ā (*lare* 1, *mare* 2, *an* 26 etc.); æ > *e* (*wes* 1, *ent* 1)
or *a* (*habbe* 3, 5); OE *y* = [ü] long and short generally remains and is
written *u* (see above), but sometimes unrounds to [i], written *i* (*first* 37,
king 50, *litel* 28) or *e* (*dede* 2, *unnet* 5).

The diphthongs were reduced: *eo* > [ö] written *o* (see above).

Inflexions. Masc and neuter sbs which were str in OE still have their
dat sg in *-e* (*werke* 27, *fure* 43, but *God* 49).

Personal pronoun. — 1 sg *ich* (except *I* 5);
3 sg M *he* 21, acc *es* 55, *hes* 56, dat *hom* 18.

Article. — þe 44, Nt þet.
The *relative* is still þe (10, 33 etc. þa 12).

Verb. — Pres 3 sg in -(*e*)ð (*fulieð* 12); contract forms *sent* 42, 46, *þench*
33; 3 pl in -(*e*)ð (*weneð* 41, *boð* 26).

The past participle is regularly preceded by *i-*, and for str vbs ends in *-en*.
The infinitive is mostly in *-en*.

Vocabulary predominantly Germanic. The only loan-words in the passage
quoted here are *sot* 30 (French) and *wrang* (*wise*) 48 (ON).

Versification. Here for the first time in English is found the seven beat line (septenary, ballad meter or common meter of modern times) in rimed couplets with caesura after the fourth beat.

Ich 'em | nu 'ald | er 'þenę | ich 'wes || a 'win | trë 'ent | a 'larë
Ich 'wel | dë 'ma | rë 'þenę | ich 'dede || mi 'wit | 'ahtë | bon 'marë   1-2
'þah ich | 'bo a | 'wintrë | 'ald || to '3ung | ich 'em | on 'redë.   4

Elision and syncope of *e* are frequent: *þennę* 6, *sarę* 6, *habbę* 7, *hovęne* 25, *sovęne* 26.

Certain feet are trisyllabic: | *'God me nu* | 8, | *'solf he bi-* | 12, | *'cumen in* | 24, | *-erę is an* | 26.

The poem is probably original. About the same time, Guiscart de Beaulieu wrote a verse-sermon in Anglo-Norman which shows striking analogies with the *Poema Morale*; cp. the edition by A. GABRIELSON (Uppsala, 1909) and *Archiv* 128, pp. 309-28.

---

2. 'I have more experience than I had.'

6. 'When I reflect carefully, I am much afraid.'

8. bute 'unless'; similarly l. 24.

10. þe me ofþinchet nuþe 'of which I now repent'; *þe*, invariable relative particle, the vb *ofþinchen* is generally impersonal.

12. þa 'whoever.'

13. hefde ich þen i-selðe 'if I then had better (sense).'

18. 'More do men stand in awe of men than they do of Christ.'

20. 'When they must mow and reap what they previously had sown.'

23. þe 'whoever'; same in ll. 33, 35, 42.

24. bute etc. 'unless God be merciful to him.' A current formula.

26. þenne boð, etc. 'than seven (will) be afterwards.'

27-28. These two lines, as other MSS show, should come after l. 10.

33. þe hwile þe he mot: we add *he* following the sense, rhythm and other MSS.

36. 'Many a man's hard work often profits his enemies.' cp. Psalm CVIII. 11: Scrutetur foenerator omnem substantiam eius: et diripiant alieni labores eius.

37. Ne sċal namon don a first 'let no man put off doing'; *sċal* has here its OE adhortative sense.

45. of 3eve ne of 3elde 'bribes or taxes.'

47. dra3en en don 'carry there our (goods) and (there) put (them) down.'

48. me 'they' (impersonal); cp. 1/5 note.

50. ou 'from you.'

51. hefden: the other MSS have the present.

53. for habben 'in order to have.' MS *E* has *for to habben*.

55 f. 'whoever wishes to keep or manage [*halden*] his property well, while he has the power [*muʒe*] to keep it in his possession [*welden*], let him give of his (store) for the love of God, then does he keep it well'; *echte* (OE *æhte*) is a feminine plural and agrees with the personal pronoun *es* (l. 55) which is an accusative plural (cp. *OED*, s. v. *es*). In verse 56 *hies*, *hes* are undoubtedly to be interpreted as contractions of *he es*. This pronoun *es* (see again *OED*, s. v. *his*, *hise*) is of obscure origin but recalls the enclitic *se*, with a similar meaning that is found in Old Frisian and in Middle Dutch (cp. MORSBACH, *Beiblatt zur Anglia*, 7, (1897), 331 ff.). Essentially these lines are a paradox like 'to save your life you must lose it,' with *halden* used in both its possible senses of 'hold' and 'manage.'

III-IV

Although they appear in different MSS ANCRENE WISSE (*III*) *and* SAWLES WARDE (*IV*) *are written in an absolutely identical dialect. From a grammatical point of view they can be treated together.*

Text. *Ancrene Wisse* (III). — Text from MS 402, Corpus Christi College, Cambridge, still largely unedited (a few extracts from it have been published by Joseph HALL, *Selections from Early Middle English* 1130-1250, Oxford, 1920, pp. 54-74). There are several other MSS of the same work, in particular MS Cotton Nero A. 14 from the British Museum published by J. MORTON under the title *Ancren Riwle*; Mabel Day ed. 1952 (*EETS* 225). The French text is that of MS Cotton Vitellius F. 7, the Latin text of MS C. 1.5 Merton College, Oxford, and, for the last extract, that of MS Cotton Vitellius E. 7.

Sawles Warde (IV). — Text from Bodleian MS 34, Oxford. The lacunae of this MS have been filled in from Royal MS 17 in the British Museum.

Dialect: West Midland (Herefordshire?). On this dialect consult especially: J. R. R. TOLKIEN, '*Ancrene Wisse*' and '*Hali Meiðhad*' in *Essays and Studies by Members of the English Association*, Vol. 14 (1929), pp. 104 ff. [cp. also J. R. HULBERT, *JEGP*, 45 (1946), 411-414].

Mary R. SERJEANTSON, "The Dialect of the Corpus Christi MS of the *Ancrene Riwle*" in *London Mediæval Studies*, I (1938), pp. 225-248.

An edition of þe Liflade and te Passiun of Seinte Iulienne by S. T. R. O. d'ARDENNE (Bibl. de la Fac. de Phil. et Lettres de l'Univ. de Liège, Fasc. LXIV), Liège and Paris, 1936 [by far the best edition of a text from this group, with a detailed grammatical introduction].

Spelling very regular and consistent, in general still close to that of OE: use of *þ*, *ð*, *hw-*, *cw-*; *ea* indicates the sound [ę], *eo* the sound [ö]; note the ambiguousness of *u* which indicates both [u] (*sunne* 'sun' 4/2) and [ü] (*sunne* 'sin' 3/17); The letter *y* is only a variant of *i* and it is found almost exclusively in loan-words or foreign proper names (*Ysaias* 3/104); as in OE *h* indicates the breath sound [h]. as well as the spirant [x] in a medial or final position (*seh* 3/11, *mahte* 3/106, *bohte* 3/109, *cnihtes* 3/115), but, besides, the sound [j] between palatal vowels (*hehe* 3/42, *ehelid* 4/42); *f* and, more rarely, *v* indicates the voiced sound [v] (*fan* 3/55 alongside *van* 3/72, *underfeng* 3/61 alongside *underuon* 4/31); after *sch*, *ch* and *ȝ* before *a*, *o*, *u* appears an *e*, conforming to an OE tradition (cp. *HOE* § 12) (*scheome* 3/74, *scheot* 4/42, perhaps *cheorl* 3/52, *ȝeoi* 3/106) which is purely graphic; to indicate [ts], before *e* and *i*, the letter *c* is used (*deciples* 3/95, *milce* 4/18) and as a final the letter *z* (*vestemenz* 3/141), following French usage; of course *c* and *k* normally have the value of the sound [k]; in French words before a palatal vowel *g* indicates [dž] (*messagers* 3/87); note that the letter *w* regularly indicates *u* in diphthongs (*nawt* 3/1, *fowr* 3/30); oppositely in *euch* 3/107, *euchon* 4/18 the *eu* spelling possibly indicates a disyllabic pronunciation (OE *eǵhwylč*). In *Sawles Warde d* for *ð* is only a scribal negligence which we have corrected (MS: *sol* 7, *i-wurden* 14, *deorewurde* 18, *odres* 23, *beod* 25, *odre* 28).

Phonology. OE *ā* is *o* (*mon* 3/17, *lond* 3/55, *honden* 3/74); OE (Mercian) *e* remains *e* (*hwet* 3/1, *þet*, *wes* 3/2); OE *ea* becomes [ę] long or short but is still written *ea* (*leapen* 3/31), OE *eo* becomes [ö] but is still written *eo* (*beo* 3/1, *deovel* 3/6, *leop* 3/28, *eorðe* 3/29, *seoð* 4/12); OE *y* remains [ü], written *u* (*uvel* 3/1, *prude* 3/5, *lust* 3/12, *moncun* 3/15, *lutel* 3/33, *muchel* 3/34, *wurse* 3/36, *murie* 3/65, *dude* 3/66, *swuch*, *stude* 3/117, *suster* 3/126, *murhðe* 4/23, *wule* 4/43, 45, *munne* 4/21, *lutlin*, *wursin* 4/48, *þulli* 4/47); OE *ā* remains *ā* (*an* 3/1, *twa*, *wa* 3/2, *mare* 3/63).

OE *f* becomes [v] in all positions, even where it is still written *f*, as at the initial; *þ* becomes *t* after *t*, *d* (*bihaldest te mon* 3/17, *went te* 3/19, *chalengest tu* 3/21) and the form *ant* for *and* is regular.

Note the unstressed forms *o* 3/10, 18, 20 (for *on*), *i* 3/11 (for *in*), *me* 3/52 (for *men* 'they' indefinite pronoun), *se* 3/43, 4/10 (for *so*, *swa*), *te* 3/118 (for *to*); also the syncope of *e* in composite adverbs with *þer* (*þrof* 3/12, 4/47, *þrefter* 3/15, *þron* 3/19, 119, *þrin* 4/36).

Inflexions. *Substantive.* — Numerous plurals in *-en*, either inherited from OE or formed by analogy (*sustren* 3/24, *dehtren* 139, *ehnen* 3/28, *feren* 3/48, *sonden* 3/50, *fan* 3/55, *honden* 3/74, *deoflen* 3/86, *deden* 3/87, *siden* 3/96, *scoren* 3/140). The gen pl of *man* is *monne* 3/139.

Adjectives. — Final *-e* is used for the vocative (*leove suster* 3/16), the weak form after the possessive adjective (*ure alde moder* 3/6), the plural (*monie feren* 3/48, *alle men* 3/64), the pl of adjs used as sbs (*deade* 'the dead' pl 3/66) or as pronouns (*monie* 3/59, *alle* 3/97), hence a clear contrast between *uvel lust* 3/15 and *his uvele dede* 3/51, for example. The strong adj has a genitive in *-es* in *uveles cunnes* 3/83 or when it is used substantively (*his leoves luve* 'the love of his darling' 3/94). Note the genitive pl *alre* in *on alre earst* 'first of all' 3/6.

Personal pronouns. — 1 sg *ich* 3/26; 3 sg M: note the old form of the acc *hine* 3/11, 54 alongside the current form for all oblique cases *him*; 3 sg F: nom *ha* 3/19, 84, 4/32 and *heo* 3/30, 56; poss *hire* 3/12; dat *hire* 3/57, 4/31; 3 sg Nt: *hit* 3/13; 3 pl: nom *ha* 3/65, 4/1, 3; poss *hare* 3/25, 4/6; dat-acc *ham* 3/76, 4/17.

Definite article. — Normally invariable *þe*; but there are some survivals of the old flexion like acc M sg *þene* 3/32, dat F sg in the expression *to þer eorðe* 3/29 and the neuter *þet* (*þet leðer* 3/113).

Relative pronouns. — *þe* 'who, that,' *þe þe* 'he who' 3/51 and *þet* 3/79.

Verb. — Pres. 3 sg: *-eð* (*spekeð* 3/13, *lureð* 4/18), contracted forms *schilt* 3/100, *scheot* 4/42; pl: *-(e)ð*, *-ieð* (*luvieð* 4/16, *beoð* 4/10). Infinitive in *-en* (*habben* 3/23), rarely in *-e* (*habbe* 3/124, *makie* 4/45), gerund: *to donne* 3/89, *to eotenne* 3/22. The pres participle, not to be found in our selections, is in *-inde*, *-iende*. The past part is always preceded by *i-*; in weak vbs it ends in *-t* (*i-cwemet* 4/34), rarely in *-d* (*i-seid* 3/18).

In the 2nd class of wk vbs a clear distinction is established between long and short stems. Long stems have the infinitive in *-in* (*delitin* 3/11, *þeolkin* 3/53, *openin* 3/120); pres 2 sg has *-st* (*lokest* 3/18), imperative 2 sg has *-i* (*loki* 3/131) as does the pres subj sg (*loki* 3/26). Short stems have infinitive in -*ien* (*makien* 3/68, *pilien* 3/53, *herien* 4/40, *cwakien* 4/45), pres pl in -*ieð* (*ondswerieð* 3/25, *luvieð* 4/1) and the pres subj sg in -*ie* (*makie* 3/142, *luvie* 3/80).

Style. In *Sawles Warde* (IV) note the marked preference for alliterative prose: *þe derne beoþ ant deopre þen eni sea dingle* 4/11, *ne mei hit munne na muð ne spealie na speche* 4/21.

On recluses cp. the recent work of Francis D. DARWIN, *The English Mediaeval Recluse*, London, 1944.

3-4. lo her 'here'; the F text has *veez ci la pruve.*

6-7. on alre earst, lit. ' in first of all '; *alre* gen pl of *al.*

11. hine, M acc sg, agrees with *eappel* which was M in OE; cp. similar use of *him* in ll. 25 and 26.

13. inwardliche: the F text has *parfitement.*

16-17. lust and delit of sunne are the subjects of *falleð to.*

18. in Eve point ' in Eve's situation.'

20. Me 'why, but,' a word characteristic of *Ancrene Wisse* and the 'St. Catherine Group' (cp. no. IV), part conjunction, part interjection as the French *mais* can be (OF *meis*, Anglo-Norman *mes*) from which this may be derived. In OE the glosses in the Vespasian Psalter render Latin *magis* (from which F *mais*) by *mæ, me.* The word is found again farther on, ll. 25 and 105.

23. i-noh reaðe 'quickly,' lit. ' soon enough ' (ME ' enough ' often means ' very ' and cp. ModE phrases like *sure enough, readily enough*).

24. as Eve haveð monie dehtren: cp. the F text: *Come Eve ad mult des filles* and the Latin text: *O quot filias ... habet haec mater.*

29. to þer eorðe: *þer* dat F sg, *eorðe* is F here as in OE.

31. were 'husband,' the Latin has *vir eius.*

33. ase me seið ' as people say '; on *me* ' they ' (indefinite) cp. 1/5 note.

43. deð se muche mis ' does so many wrong things.'

45. þah ' however ' (cp. the F text's *nepurquant*).

48. let i-wurðe ' let be.' — **Ne geast tu nawt te ane** ' you are not alone in this ' (l. 47 *nart tu nawt te ane i þis þing*).

51. as þe þe seið ' as the one who says.'

52. as þu dest wel! ' how right you do there ' (cp. the F text *come vous fetes bien*). MS Cotton Nero A XIV has *hwat* instead of *as.*

52 f. þe betere ' the better '; cp. l. 62 *þe neorre.*

61. as on unrecheles ' like an indifferent person.'

71. swa þet ' to such a point that.'

79. þe luve þet ich cuðe þe ' the love that I made known to thee.'

80. hwen þu naldest lives ' when you would not (do so) while (I was) alive '; *lives* adv genitive of *lif* ' life.'

83 f. of uveles cunnes cunde ' of a nature (*cunde*) of an evil kind (*cunnes*). The adj *uvel* retains strong flexion (gen *uveles*) in locutions of this type.

89 ff. ' The passage in which Christ is described as a Norman knight in homeliest English phrase is alone enough to give a vivid idea of that fusion of English and French traditions and sentiments which—in spite of *Ivanhoe*—was almost completely carried out by the beginning of the thirteenth century (H. SWEET).

91. on euche half ' on every side.'

94. as þe an fot, etc.: Down to the end of the 12th century, crucifixes showed the two feet nailed separately rather than one on top of the other as here (cp. B. WHITE, *MLR*, 40 (1945), pp. 206-7).

100. nawt ane ' not only.' — **ne** is superfluous.

102. Daviˇ is in apposition with the preceding pronoun *he.* Cp. the French text for the sense.

104. willes adv gen ' voluntarily ' cp. ModE periphrastic ' *of* his own free *will.*'

110. wiˇ his heorte blod ' with his heart's blood '; *heorte* is gen neut consonantal stem.

119. His leofmon bihalde ' let his dearly beloved behold.'

125. ancre ' recluse ' from OE *ancra* which no doubt had become *āncra* by popular etymology and the influence of *ān* ' one, alone ' (otherwise the form in this dialect would have been **oncre*). — **þuncheˇ bet husewif** ' seems rather (to be) a housewife.'

128. olhnin ' ingratiate oneself ' a word peculiar to *Ancrene Wisse* and the *St. Catherine Group*. — **heiward:** cattle-tender in the communal meadow; the *hayward* kept the beasts from breaking through the hedges into the plowed land. Cp. 21₃/16. The word has survived as a family name *Hayward, Haward.* — **wearien hwen he punt hire,** ' curse when he impounds them.'

130. man ' moan, complain,' ' when someone complains, in the locality, of the recluse's cattle.'

131. loki þet etc. ' see to it that it harms no one.'

138. sumhwile. The author, to whom the *Vitae Patrum* are familiar, is undoubtedly thinking of the eremites, Fathers of the Desert, or early Christian solitaries who used to weave mats of palm. The remark has a general significance; it is hardly applicable to the sisters for whom *Ancrene Wisse* was written. Their social condition put them above such need (J. HALL).

139. nawt ... ne wite ȝe ' keep back nothing '.

140. boistes: here, undoubtedly ' jewel caskets '.

141. calices: because it was forbidden for women to touch a chalice.

IV

5. hearmin oˇer eilin ' harm or trouble ', cp. 3/138 *loki þet hit namon ne eili ne ne hearmi.*

10. nebbe to nebbe ' face to face ', *facie ad faciem* (I COR. XIII. 12).

12. sea dingle here ' abyss of the sea '. The word *dingle* survives in a modern Yorkshire dialect with the meaning of ' deep, narrow cleft between hills '. Attested for the first time in this passage it does not reappear until 1630 in Drayton (a native of Warwickshire), then in Milton (*Comus* l. 311). It is also found in place-names, once in Worcestershire, once near Liverpool.

The etymology is unknown. It seems to be peculiar to the West Midland vocabulary.

17. bi ham i-don ' (what He) has done for them '.

17 f. hwet . . . ȝelden ' what they have to repay his precious mercy '.

21. spealie ' pronounce, articulate ' rather from F *espeler* than from OE *spellian*.

24 ff. þet euchan, etc. ' that each one has, separately, as many joys as there are numerous saints (in heaven) ; and each one of the said joys is for each one in particular a joy as great as his (the saint's) own; however, above all this, since each one loves God more than all the others, he rejoices more in God, beyond all measure, than in his own blessedness and that of all the others '.

27. hwen ' since '; cp. 3/81.

30 ff. Neomeð, etc. ' Take heed, then, (that) [pick up ' that ' below]—if no heart, of itself alone [*anes* adv gen], is able [*mei*] to receive and contain in itself [*in hire*] its own gladness, separately,—so immensely great is the individual bliss, that it [*ha*, ' she ' = *hcorte*] does take into itself [*hire*] thus many and thus much (joy)'. *Hcorte* is still feminine as in OE, hence the F pronouns *hire* (31, 33) and *ha* (32).

37. in is needlessly repeated from the preceding line.

V

Text. Of the two MSS of the *Brut,* our extracts follow the oldest, Cotton Caligula A 9 (about 1250).

Dialect of the South West Midlands (Worcestershire), rather mixed, with considerable wavering in indication of sounds and forms, no doubt due in part to the scribe(s) and to the conservative tendencies of the author.

Spelling rather conservative. The MS shows a preference for þ initially and ð in other positions. The letter *y* is unknown; ȝ is frequent for the palatal spirant or semi-vowel [j]. *c* is found for [tš] and *sc* for [š], *gg* for [dž] (*seȝȝe* 31), *qu* for *cw*. The letter *u* indicates [u] (*þuhte* 4, *funde* 11, along with *ou*: (*coupe* 21) as well as [ü] (*putte* 14027, *guldene* 14033); *o* also indicates [u] (*wonede* 3, alongside *wunede* 13996) ; OE *hw-* is regularly *wh-*, sometimes *w-* (*wat, wonene* 8) ; *co,* which is retained, indicates [ö] long or short (*heort* 13, *sweord* 14013, *corðe* 14023, *seoc* 14041, *feond* 14059, *weorld* 14066).

Phonology. OE *æ* is rather frequently preserved (*æðelen* 3, *æfter* 10, *sæ* 14036) but *a* is also found (*fader* 32, *habbe* 14045, *hafde* 104056) and *e* (*wes* 1, 2) ; OE -*ân*- is -*on*- (*longe* 14062, *gon* 14022, *lond, hond* 14054, *mon* 14050, *atstonden* 14030). On the other hand OE *ea, ëa* are reduced and represented by *a* (*halle* 14010, -*sah* 14012, *alle* 14060) and *æ* (*ærmes* 14023, *i-sæh* 14037, *ært* 14050, *slæn* 14060) ; OE *y* remains (written *u*) or becomes *i* [I] (*king* 14070).

f voices to *v* initially (*væir, i-varen* 14006, *volke* 14014, *veol, valle* 14022, *vlode* 14038) but is still also written *f* (*fader* 32, *fingren* 25, *feire* 18, *feol* 14023, *fallen* 14059).

Inflexions. A curious aspect of Lawman's language is a parasitical (also called ' paragogic ') final -*n*, as in the sgs of vbs like *wcoren* 14029, *fereden* 14040, *bilaven* 14060, *cumen* 14072, or sbs like *lcoden* 1, *feðeren* 25.

Substantives. — Strong: gen sg in *-es* (*kinges* 12); dat in *-e* (*mode* 6, *flode* 10, *Arðure* 13999), pl in *-es* (*ærmes* 14004, *wives* 13, *fuȝeles* 14032). Weak: sg in *-e*, pl in *-en* (*boden* 14000); cp. the gen pl in *-ene* of *Englene* 9.

Adjectives. — Rather numerous traces of the strong declension persist: Sg acc M *þisne* 14073, *alcne* 29, *ane* 14027; gen *heȝes* 22; dat F *aȝere* 14054, *mire* 14024, *þire* 14075, *are* 3, 13997, 14010. Pl acc *gode* 14000, gen *alre* 13991, 14061.

But, in a general way, it is the weak flexion which is dominant in all positions: Sg subject - (*e*), object *-en*, *-e*, pl *-en*.

And occasionally the adj is invariable in the sg: *mid mire* leoft *hand* 14024.

Definite article. — Still inflected.

Sg M nom *þe* 14048; gen *þes* 22; dat *þan* 10, *þene* 29. — F acc *þe* 19, *þa* 16; dat *þare* 21, *þere* 14023. — Pl acc *þa* 7, 23, 27.

Personal pronouns. — 1 sg *ich*; 3 M nom *he*, acc *hine* 31, 32; poss *his*, dat *him*; F nom *heo* 14071, acc *heo* 14027, poss *hire* 14019, dat *hire* 34; pl 3 nom *heo* 8, poss *heore* 13, dat *heom* 13; dual 1 nom *wit* 14039.

The relative is *þe* 13, 14051, *þa* 15, 16, 14012 etc.

Verb. — 3 sg in - (*e*)ð (*hafeð* 3, *rixleoð* 14050, *wuneð* 14051, *bið* 14062). 3 pl in *-eð* (*nulleþ* 14066, *weneð* 14072).

Infinitive in *-en* (*tellen* 7, *liðen* 14, etc.) or in *-ien* (*quakien* 14042), exceptionally in *-e* (*valle* 14022, *liðe* 14040).

Gerund: *to suggen* 14074, *to hewene* 14016.

Past participle is preceded by *i-*; in str vbs it ends in *-e*(*n*) (*i-hoten* 1, *i-don* 14069, *i-do* 14056, *i-limpe* 14052, *i-nume* 14053).

Note that the preposition *on* (1) is often *an* (14015) or even *a* (14008, 14023).

Syntax. The locution *þa com a man riden* 'a man came riding' is frequent in Lawman.

Vocabulary. Almost solely Germanic; aside from *Latin* 17, *Frenchis* 20, and other proper names, there are hardly any French words (*preost* 1, *archen* 13, *seint* 15 were already current in OE).

Versification. Lawman's verse is midway between OE alliterative verse (cp. *HOE*, appendix II) and the isosyllabic and rimed verse borrowed from French. We find in Lawman:

1st. Verses in which the half lines are linked solely by alliteration:
Uppen 'Sevarne 'staþe 'sel þar him 'þuhte	4
Þa 'Englene 'londe 'ærest 'ahten	9
And þe 'alre 'wiseste þe 'wuneð under 'weolcne	14051

2nd. Verses in which rime (or assonance) appears with the alliteration:
He is 'king and heo is 'quene ‚of þine 'kume nis na 'wene	14071
'Alle þa 'lond þa ich 'ah 'alle ich þer 'over'sah	14012
And 'seoð-ðen ich heo adune 'sette in ane 'swarte 'putte	14027
Þen ȝet þu 'mihtest þe a'wreken 'wurðliche mid 'wepnen	14057

3rd. But the stress pattern could also be:
'He is 'king and 'heo is 'quene	
Of 'þinë 'kumë 'nis na 'wene	14071

4th. And thus we come to an isosyllabic verse with rime (or assonance) and no longer any alliteration, a verse with four beats:

'Arður 'lay alle 'longë 'niht
and 'spac wið 'þenë 'ʒeongë 'cniht   14001

(similarly in 14044, 14053) or with three beats:

'Longë 'bið 'æverę
'þat no 'wenę ich 'naverę   14062

The rime can be perfect, either masculine (*lond: hond* 14070) or feminine (*bistrídèn : rídèn* 14011, *i-wíssè : blíssè* 14045); but is is often only approximate *sune : i-nume* 14053, *atstónden : wólden* 14030, *live : driʒe* 14046, *fállèn : únnèn* 14059.

---

1. on leoden ' (living) amidst the people ' — a secular priest, not a monk. — **Laʒamon wes i-hoten** ' (who) was called L.'; zero relative, the same in l. 20.

3. Ernleʒe is the present village of King's Areley, near Bewdley, Worcestershire, PNWo (EPN Soc 5) 29: *earn-leah*. **at æðelen are chirchen** ' in a splendid church '; *are* dat F sg of *an*, source of ModE indefinite article. On this word-order cp. 14026 *deore mine sweorde* ' my dear sword ', 14076 *leoven þire quene* ' thy dear queen ', and the Elizabethan expressions *dear my lord, good my lord*.

5. Radestone, steep red sandstone cliff which dominates the Severn at the crossing (Redstone Ferry) between Astley and Areley, PNWo (EPN Soc V) 35. — **þer he bock radde** ' there he said mass ' lit. ' read the (mass) book ' if we adopt the interpretation of J. HALL, *bock* ' missal ' (OE *mæsse-bōc*), although this meaning is unparalleled in OE or ME. DICKINS-WILSON, suggest the not infrequent sense of ' Bible ' and interpret ' where he read his Bible '.

6. him on mode ' into his mind ' poss dat.

6. mern þonke ' as a bright idea ' or ' into his distinguished mind ' (OE *mǣre*).

7. þa æðelæn ' the noble deeds '.

9. þa relative particle (same in ll. 15, 16, 21, etc.), here ' those who '. — **ærest ahten** ' first (conquered and) ruled '.

11. which (deluge) killed all here (below) that it [*he*] found alive [*quic*].

**14. gon l
yourname**...

14. gon liðen ' traveled '; *gon* sometimes means ' begin ', often is equivalent to ModE *do* ' did travel '. As such it serves frequently as a metrical expletive in ME verse; see § 134.

16. This no doubt refers to Bede's *Ecclesiastical History* in its OE translation (cp. *HOE* nos. VII and VIII). In fact Lawman may not have consulted Bede, whom he contradicts on many points.

17 f. Albinus (who was never canonized) was the abbot of Saint Augustine at Canterbury, and died in 732. He was one of Bede's chief sources of information, but we do not have any of his own work. Albinus certainly could not have collaborated with St. Augustine († 604). Lawman, who has just made the error of attributing the OE version of the *Ecclesiastical History* to Bede himself, has perhaps made the mistake of thinking that the Latin text of the *History* was by Albinus and Augustine (Augustine's nine *Quaestiones* to Gregory figure in Bede's first book, cp. 29.) Actually Lawman gives these Latin sources because it is the thing to do. But he has not consulted them. See J. L. P. TATLOCK, *The Legendary History of Britain,* (Berkeley, 1950), pp. 487-490.

20. Wace, Anglo-Norman *trouvère,* author of the *Brut,* a verse-chronicle completed in 1155 from Geoffrey of Monmouth's *Historia Regum Britanniae.* It tells the mythical history of Britain from the destruction of Troy and the coming of Brutus to Britain to the death of Cadwalader (689). Wace is the principal source of Lawman's poem. On this question consult R. IMMELMANN, *Laʒamon, Versuch über seine Quellen* (Berlin 1906) and G. J. VISSER, *Laʒamon, An Attempt at Vindication* (Assen, 1935).

21 f. Lawman is our only source for this presentation of the *Brut* to Eleanor of Aquitaine, wife of Henry II.

22. þes heʒes kinges, this apposition with *Henries* is put in the same case (§ 146).

23. þa leaf ' the pages, leaves '.

26. þa soþe word ' the true, authentic words '.

27. þrumde to are OE *þrymman,* ' compressed into one '. *Boc* is feminine, therefore *are* dat F sg of *an.*

28. The verse is incomplete. No gap in MS.

30. runan (plural) here has the sense of ' learning ', ' histories '.

32. his fader saule ' his father's soul '. Nouns for close family relationships still show zero flexion in the genitive, as in OE, cp. 1. 33 *his moder saule,* 1. 13999, 14053 *suster sune* and the same in 16/66, 28/3948 etc.

34. þat hire þe selre beo ' that (it) be the better for it (*hire* refers to *saule* OE *sawle* f.).

13995 ff. Arthur's dream does not appear in Wace and seems to be an invention of Lawman's, like many other episodes in his *Brut.* It may be recalled that the dream is a commonplace and very fashionable device in medieval romance (cp. the French *chansons de geste*). After having conquered Ireland, France, and a good part of the Scandinavian countries, Arthur declares war on the emperor of Rome. Leaving his realm in charge of Moddred, his sister's son, he proceeds as far as Burgundy and sees Rome about in his grasp. A messenger arrives from home but does not tell Arthur the truth. Arthur then dreams the following dream about Moddred. Upon awakening and telling the dream the messenger admits the truth.

13999. his suster sune ' his sister's son ', cp. above l. 32 note. Besides, OE as well as ON had compounds of the type *swuster-sunu* (ON *systursonr*) *broðordohtor,* etc. The relationship between a man and his sister's son was very close in the whole Germanic culture-complex (cp. Tacitus, *Germania,* ch. 20).

14003. dæi a marʒen cp. ModE dialect ' great day in the morning '.

14005. swulč he weore swiðe seoc ' as if he was very sick '.

14006. to-niht ' last night '.

14007. a mode him wes uneðe ' his spirit was ill at ease '. *him* poss dat.

14013. Walwain: Gawain, brother of Moddred, and consequently also Arthur's nephew, is the faithful companion-at-arms of the king.

14018. Wenhever: Guenevere, Arthur's wife (Welsh *Gwenhwyvar*). — **wimmonen leofvest me** ' the dearest of women to me '.

14020. to hælden 'to heel, lean over on one side'; 'heel over' for a boat, in ModE with redundant 'over' due to loss of feeling for meaning of 'heel' by itself. This is a frequent word in Lawman.

14024. mi sweord leove 'my dear sword', the magic weapon called *Calibeorne* by Lawman and *Caliburn* by Geoffrey of Monmouth. (*Excalibur* in Tennyson's *Idylls of the King*).

14025. smæt of 'smote off'. — **Modred his hafd** 'Moddred's head' for *Modredes hafd*: from a very early time the genitive flexion was detached from the sb and written as the poss pronoun; also 26/23. — **hit wond** 'it rolled'.

14026. ich al tosnadde 'I cut her all to pieces'. The OE intensive prefixes for verbs of mayhem *for- to-* etc. were further re-enforced by *al* in ME. These intensive prefixes are lost in ModE; *all* remains.

14029. under Criste has the vague sense of ModE 'at all'; cp. 14051 *under weolcne* 'anywhere' with the same force.

14031. agon 'did' rather than 'began' — the metrical expletive as in the preceding verse and like *gun* in l. 14036; see note l. 14.

14034. Deoren swiðe hende 'very gracious and graceful beasts'.

14035. me orn foren to 'ran towards me'.

14036. gun hire ȝeongen lit. 'began to go herself'. Personal pronouns in the dat accompany intransitive verbs of motion as pseudo-reflexives. They survive as archaisms in ModE, 'he wends him on his way' etc.

14039. wit 'we two' is one of the rare survivals in ME of the OE dual (eleven examples in Lawman, a few in the *Ormulum* cp. 7/7); they are no longer found after 1250.

14043. swulc ich al fur burne 'as if I was all burning with fever [*fur*]'. The *OED* does not record this meaning of *fire* 'fever' (s. v. 12) until 1386. If this is evidence, the use is much older. But J. HALL suggests we have the intensive *for-* and *fur burne = forburne* 'completely burning'.

14045. Agan is al mi blisse 'gone is all my joy (in life)'.

14046. For a 'forever'. — **to mine live** 'during (all) my life'.

14049. me 'they' indefinite impersonal cp. 1/5 note.

14052. swa nulle hit ure Drihte 'God forbid', lit. 'may our Lord not will it so'.

14054. an his aȝere hond 'in his own hand'; *aȝere* dat F sg of *aȝen* 'own'.

14056. And he hafde 'if he had'.

14062. Longe bið ævere, etc. 'it would have been a long time before I would have ever thought'.

14065. wakien on þonke 'weaken in thought', i. e. 'give way to low thoughts'.

14066. 'Nor (that they) would desire to begin [possibly 'do'] (such a thing) for no man in the world'.

14067. Æfne þan worde 'directly with these words'.

14078. þa sæt hit al stille 'Then it was all still', 'there was a great silence'.

VI

Text from MS Cotton Caligula A 9 called *C* (ca. 1250), written by two scribes, (the second begins at l. 911) with readings from MS Jesus College, Oxford, E 29 (designated *O*).

Dialect of the South, localization varying between Dorsetshire and Surrey (Western Surrey according to the recent study of B. SUNDBY, *Lund Studies in Engl.* 18, 1950).

Spelling much influenced by practices of Anglo-Norman scribes. The letter *u* indicates [u] as well as [ü]. The sound [ö] is sometimes written *eo* by scribe II (*heovene* 916, *heorte* 946, *þeode* 905, *neode* 906) but most often [ö] is shown in the Anglo-Norman manner by *o* (*bo* 860, 866, 879, *bon* 883, *soþ* 'they see' 884, *bor* 'beer', *dor* 'animals' 1012, *hoven* 862, *honne* 864, *hom* 868, *hore* 880, *horte* 945).

The sound [v] is written *v* (*vor* 863, *venne* 962, *velle* 1013, *vrom* 1029) or *f* (*fundeþ* 862, *for* 886, *farest* 917, etc.); *hw-* is written *hw-* and also (French influence) *w-* (*war* 1031, *ware* 892, *wane* 894, *wi* 905, 913, 995, *weþer* 991, *wat* 997, 1010, *wei* 'whey' 1009, *wile* 1016, 1020), but this may represent actual loss of *h*. The sound [š] is written *sh*, *sch* and even *s* (*fleses* 895, *solde* 975, 977, *sold* 1025); [w] is sometimes written *u* (*suich* 1008) or *v* (*visest* 973, *vise* 961). The scribes do not yet use the letter *y*; on the other hand they use *þ*, and, from l. 911 on (the second scribe), *ð* as well as *p* 'wynn' which is here transcribed as *w*.

Phonology. The OE diphthongs have completely disappeared. OE *ā* is most often *ō* (*wot* 867, *wonunge* 870, *nowiȝt* 884, *sore* 885, *ore* 886, *wo* 892, *wonie* 975), sometimes *ā* (*laverd* 959, *overgan* 952). OE *ă* before nasal is *o* (*mon* 871, *monne* 887, *const* 972, *vrom* 1029) or *a* in *an*(*d*). As in all the South and in the West Midlands, the most striking feature is the sound [ö] for which the spellings have been indicated above; as the rimes show clearly, this sound is unstable and in process of unrounding, that is, it is already tending to become [e] (cp. the rimes *hovene : stevene* 897-8, *stevene : heovene* 915-6, *wede : neode* 937-8, *bore : spere* 1021-2, *dest : prost* 'priest' 977-8).

Inflexions. *Substantives.* — Gen sg is in *-es* (*fleses* 895, *monnes* 941), dat sg in *-e* (*monne* 887, *hovene* 897); *deovlene* 932 is a trace of a weak gen pl (extended to an older strong substantive).

For the *adjective* note dative *þire* 914, 915 and the gen pl *tweire* 888.

The definite article þe still has a flexion: M sg acc *þan* 889, 891, dat *þan* 862, gen *þes* 882.

Personal pronouns. — 1 sg *ich* 860 etc., *ih* 868 or *I* 903, 924, 929.

3 sg M *he*, acc *hine* 871, 873, *hin* 890, dat *him*; F *heo* 934, poss *hire* 940, dat *hire* 935.

1 dual gen *unker* 993.

3 pl nom *hi* 884, 885, *heo* 926, 931, poss *hore* 880, *here* 978, dat *hom* 868, 881, etc., and *heom* 931.

Verbs. — Pres indicative 2 sg in *-st* (*gest* 875, *draȝst* 895, *sittest* 894, *nevestu* 898, etc.); 3 sg in *-(e)þ* (*goþ* 877, *longeþ* 881, *haveþ* 888); 3 pl also in *-(e)þ* (*fundeþ* 'aspire' 862, *boþ* 882, *wepeþ* 885, *biddeþ* 886).

Pres subjunctive in *-(e)* (2 sg *singe* 876, 3 sg *biþenche* 871, *groni* 872, *bo* 866), pl in *-(n)* (*bo* 860, *bon* 883, *beon* 932, *wepen* 931).

The infinitive is in -*e*(*n*) (*overgan* 952, *speken* 953, *erien* 1039; but *forlete* 961, *ȝolle* 972, *sowe* 1039).
Past participle always preceded by *i-* (*i-mend* 870, *i-borȝe* 883).
Vocabulary almost purely Germanic. The rare French words in this extract are *foliot* 868 (?), (*di*)*sputinge* 875, *plaideþ* 944.
Versification. Octosyllabic rimed couplets with masculine or feminine rime (after the French pattern).

x x́ | x x́ | x   x́ | x   x́
þarto ich helpë God it wot

or

867

x   x́ | x   x́ | x   x́ | x   x́|(x)
Ich redë þi þat men bo ȝarë

860

but the stress might often fall on the first syllable of the first foot:

x́   x | x   x́ | x   x́ | x x́|(x)
Wenstu þat wisë men forletë

961

or the two first:

x́   x | x́ x | x   x́ | x x́
For hit seidë þe king Alfred

942

and sometimes the unstressed syllable is lacking:

Λ x́ | x   x́ | x x́ | x   x́
þat boþ her, wo is hom þes

882

Λ x́ | x   x́ | Λ x́ | x   x́
East and west feor and neor

923

x́Λ |x́ x | x   x́ | x   x́|(x)
Ne sunnë þe later shinë

963

---

860 ff. " Here the Owl pleads that the kingdom of heaven is better won by weeping than by singing, and boasts his own frequent tears (l. 876). Is not this one of the many medieval echoes of that sentence of Jerome's, so dear to St. Bernard, ' Monachus non docentis sed plangentis habet officium '? " (G. C. COULTON).

860. þi ' therefore' instrumental Nt sg of demonstrative article þe whose use with this meaning was no doubt influenced by ON *þui, þy, þi* (already found in OE, for example in Wulfstan, cp. *HOE* 12/2, 51, 144).

862. þat fundeþ ' who aspire towards heaven's king ' and by synechdoche, ' heaven '; *men* (l. 860) is antecedent to *þat*.

868. foliot ' foolishness.' There is here, perhaps, a satiric reference to Foliot, bishop of London (1163-87), Thomas à Becket's adversary. This allusion would have more force if the poem was written before 1187.

881. ' they long nevertheless (to depart) from this place (to heaven) '.

882. ' (The fact) that (they) are here is shameful to them because of that [*þes* adv gen] '. Pronoun subject omitted.

888. tweire kunne salve ' two kinds of salve ', lit. ' a salve or remedy of two kinds '.

889. þan gode ' the good '... 891 *þan sunfulle* ' the bad ' accusatives preceding the verb.

890. hin is either a scribal error for *him* or a form of *hine*. In OE *langian* takes the accusative (but cp. l. 881 where MS *C* reads *hon longeþ* for *hom longeþ*).

892. ware = where.

896. þat 'who', antecedent *men* (l. 895).

897 f. The rime (feminine) is *'hovęnë : 'stevęnë* (similarly ll. 915-16).

901 f. 'Nobody takes your piping for the singing of a priest in church'.

903. an oðer 'another thing'.

907 ff. According to Atkins this passage is based on information probably drawn from Neckham, *De naturis rerum*, to the effect that the nightingale avoids cold countries (Ireland, Scotland, Norway); if she gets lost in one of these she is unable to sing. Cp. also R. CHAPMAN, *MLR* 41 (1946), 408-9.

910. Galeweie 'Galloway', petty kingdom of southwest Scotland which preserved its independence almost to the end of Henry II's reign. This seems to show that the author of this poem knew well the political situation in Great Britain under this king.

925. bere 'cries', 'carrying-on'.

929 f. 'I bid them cease deceiving themselves'.

930. heo subject of *biswike* is not expressed after *þat*.

932. deovlene wk gen pl of *devel*: in OE *deovel* was a str sb: the older morphological system is here decaying.

941. þe wraþþe. This use of the definite article before an abstract sb is exceptional (French influence?). GRATTAN-SYKES propose to read *þat* (conjunction) instead of *þe*.

943 f. 'Seldom do the hateful grind well and seldom do the wrathful plead (argue) well'. The MS text is corrupt here. The exact proverb (which does not appear in the ME poem *The Proverbs of Alfred*) is restored here from British Museum MS Add 35116, f. 24*d*, pointed out by Bruce DICKINS in the (London) *Times Literary Supplement* 1927, pp. 250-1.

946. so wilde flod 'like a wild flood'.

948. breþ 'passion, fury' (late OE *bræð*).

951. hi 'these things', 'this'.

952. 'And (she) let her (angry) mood pass away'; despite the spelling, *lette* here is certainly the preterit of *lete* 'let, allow'.

953. a sele 'in a good (humor)'.

955. þ'ule heo seide 'she said to the owl'.

959. liggeþ 'dwell' (cp. Eliz. English, 'The Queen lies today at Westminster').

961 ff. 'Do you think that sensible people leave the high road on account of a foul ditch? Neither does the sun slow down though (because) it is dirty in your nest (and the sun must shine on it on the way)?'

965. one hole brede 'hollowed board' = 'a seat in an out-house', cp. ll. 937-8 and BRETT, *MLR*, 14. 8 (OE. ME *bred* 'board, tablet', cp. ModGerm *Brett*).

976. Riȝt suich 'just as if'.

981 f. þar ... þar 'where ... there'.

983 f. 'Church song, at the proper time, can be neither too loud nor too long'.

987. Ever mote þu 'May you ever ...'

987 f. wépen : forléten: assonance instead of rime.

990. bo þin eʒe 'both your eyes'.

991. 'which is better of the two?' *twere twom* < OE *twēġra twām*, possibly a pleonastic expression (cp. *bām twām*). ATKINS reads *twene* and proposes here the gen pl of OE *twēo* 'doubtful matter', but this latter is unrecorded in ME.

996. oþer londe, cp. ll. 907-18. — To be scanned

Intó 'oþer 'londę and 'singë 'þarë

x x́ | x x̌ | x x̌ | x x̌|(x)

999-1014. There is a striking resemblance between this description of Norway and that found in the famous account of voyages added by Alfred to his translation of Orosius' *Historia adversum Paganos* (cp. *HOE* no. V). There also, (ll. 4-5) the land is said to be almost deserted (l. 999-1000), very rocky (*clūdig*, l. 1001: *cludes*), and not at all peaceful l. 23; l. 1004-5), etc.

1001. cludes 'rocks' (the older meaning of Mod E *cloud*). — hovene-tinge 'which touches the sky', 'heaven-touching', cp. OE *heofone ġetenġe* and *Beowulf* 2758 *grunde-ġetenġe*. ATKINS recalls *a heaven-kissing hill* (Shakespeare *Hamlet* III, iv, 59).

1007. fihs, flehs are possibly scribal errors for *fish, flesh*, possibly an index of dialectal pronunciation (cp. OE *fix* and ME [Wyclif] *flehs*).

1016. 'As recently someone came from Rome'; an evident allusion to some mission sent from the Holy See, but which one? It is tempting to agree with ATKINS on the embassy of Cardinal Vivian, in 1176, to Scotland, Ireland and Norway.

1018. leten here has the form of the verb 'to permit, let' but the meaning of *lette* 'hinder' (OE *lettan*).

1021. bore (MS *O*: *beore* 'bear'. — For this rime *bore : spere* cp. the grammatical introduction to this text.

1026. 'No matter how long I sang to them'.

1028 f. The rhythm would be better if *hom* was put in line 1029.

> For ne mai halter ne bridel
> Bringe hom vrom hore wode wise

The stress shift in *bri'del* to rime with *del* is a poetic licence much indulged in this poem and in ME in general.

VII

Text from the unique holograph Bodleian MS Junius 1, written about 1200. This MS was reviewed and corrected by Orm.

Dialect of the Northeast Midlands (north of Lincolnshire), probably Orm's original home.

Spelling: The orthographic system invented by Orm provides the originality of this poem. Besides the extensive and rigorous general normalization, the system uses the innovation of doubling consonants after short vowels, except in open syllables. Thus all the vowels in the following words are short: *unnderrstanndenn* 50, *goddspell* 50, *hellpenn* 47, *twiȝȝess* 104, *enngell* 3336, etc. In open syllables, when there is any risk of ambiguity, the short vowel has a superscribed breve ˘, thus the past participles *wrĭtenn* 106, *tăkenn* 7, the long vowel a superscribed acute accent mark ´, thus *wrítenn* 109 (infinitive) and *tákenn* 'token' 3363; but this is used much less regularly than the doubling of consonants.

When a long vowel is followed by *t*, the author doubles the acute accent ″, or even triples it ‴, to assure the reader's attention, thus *ȝȅt* 6, *mȍt* 55, 57, *ȕt* 99, 3371, *hȅ't* 97, 107, *ȝȅ't* 3367 (perhaps also because in Latin vowels followed by *t* are always short: *at, et, ut, caput*, etc.). Thus the first four lines of the dedication should be read:

> Nū brōþer Walter, brōþer mīn
> After þe flæshes kīnde
> And brōþer mīn ī Cristendōm
> Þurh fulluht and þurh trowþe

The conjectures are quite various as to what purpose Orm had in mind in doubling these consonants. It has been suggested that:

a) Orm thus wished to mark the quantity of the preceding vowel (Ellis, Sweet, Morsbach; see Norman Eliason, *MLN* 69, 137 and Jordan § 15);

b) he wanted to show consonant length (Trautmann);

c) even if the point of departure was to show consonant length, the final result was a marking of vowel quantity (Björkman, Luick, Jordan);

d) Orm invented the whole procedure to underline the division into syllables to aid the preacher in reading the sermon more clearly, distinctly and correctly (as Orm saw correctness) (Sisam);

e) finally it has been thought (Glunz) that Orm wanted to give to each of the syllables of his verse — which is perfectly regular — the same quantitative value. To this end he *makes each syllable equally long* in lengthening, by reduplication of the consonant, all syllables with short vowels.

In order not to overload the glossary, the words used by Orm are listed there without the redoubled consonants; for example the reader will find the words in line 4 under *þurh, fulluht, and, trowþe* and those from l. 3336 under *engel, com, of* and *hefnes*.

Other spelling particulars. — Use of þ in preference to ð; of ȝ for the semivowel [j] and ȝh for the voiced velar spirant [g] thus *follȝhenn* 8, *hallȝhe* 14, *sæȝhenn* 3342; use of *aȝȝ* for the diphthong [ai], of *eȝȝ* for the diphthong [ei]. In the first two-thirds of the MS Orm hesitates between *eo* for [ö] and *e*. From l. 13853, as well as in the dedication written after the rest of the work, there is no longer any trace of *eo*; further, in revising his work, Orm struck out the *o* in *eo* up to line 13852. Thus in our extract he first wrote *heoffness* 3336, 3341, 3350, *leome* 3341 and *beo* 3349 (cp. the MS, plate 2). But these *o*'s have often been restored by a later hand in a different ink; however they were not added where they were originally lacking, in the last third of the work. We can deduce from this that Orm's dialect hesitated between [ö] and [e], or, more exactly, that [ö] was losing its lip-rounding and passing over to

[e]. After a long period of hesitation Orm seems to have chosen exclusively [e].

Phonology. The orthographic precautions taken by Orm give us the phonological facts of his dialect with great clarity. Particularly to be noted is the complete disappearance of all the OE diphthongs. For the rest, OE *ā* remains *ā* (*hād* 9, *lāre* 14, *ān* 3336, *tākenn* 3363), OE *ǎ* is *a* (*mann* 3382, *annd* 3344), OE *y* becomes *i* (*birrþ* 35, *mikell* 3353, *drihhtin* 3375, *kiþenn* 3351, *birde* 3364); [g] is retained and written *ȝh* (see above), OE *ċ* before a palatal vowel is written *ch* (*child* 3364, *chesstre* 3359) except in words showing Scandinavian influence like *swillc* 101, *i-whillc* 3382, *mikell* 3370.

After *d*, *t* and sometimes *s*, *þ* becomes *t* (*annd tær* 3367 for *þær*, *þatt tatt* 3656 for *þatt*). Note elided forms *he't* for *he itt* 97, 107, *ȝe't* for *ȝe itt* 3367, *t'* for *to* 48 and the unemphatic form *te* 12.

Inflexions. In principle *substantives* already have reached the state of ModE; thus we find nom sg *goddspell* 34, gen *goddspelles* 14, dat *goddspell* 33, 56, pl *goddspelles* 30. A few forms remain with dat sg in -*e* like *leme* 3341 (nom *lem*) and a few gen sgs in -*e* like *sawle* 36(?), 3653. In the wk declension -*e* appears in all cases.

The definite article is the invariable *þe*; an indefinite article *an* 3336 appears, also *a* 3370, acc *ænne*, gen *aness* 3337.

Personal pronouns. — 1 sg *icc* 11; 3 sg M *he* 107, *hiss* 3610, *himm* 3342; Nt *itt* 46, 47; F *ȝho* 3624; 1 dual *witt* 7; 2 pl nom *ȝe* 3349, poss *ȝure* 3355, dat-acc *ȝuw* 3352; 3 pl nom *þeȝȝ*, poss *þeȝȝre* 36, dat-acc *þeȝȝm* 49 and also *hemm* 3344, 3346.

The relative pronoun is *þatt*.

Verb. — Pres indicative 3 sg in -(*e*)*þ* (*hafeþþ* 16, *birrþ* 35, contracted *stannt* 33), pl in -*en* (*hafenn* 7, *redenn* 47). Infinitive in -*en* (*habben* 5382, *writenn* 109), gerund in -*en* (*follȝhen* 8). The strong past participle is in -*en* (*cumenn* 3353, *borenn* 3354) without preverb (single exception: *ȝe-hatenn* 3360). The past part may be inflected (*offdredde* 3343, *fordredde* 3348). For the vb ' to be ' note pres 3 pl *sinndenn* 31, subjunctive 3 sg *si* 3378.

Versification. The *Ormulum* is written in absolutely regular septenary verse of 15 syllables, with cæsura after the eighth syllable (for typographical convenience this is usually printed in two lines):

$$x \acute{x} \mid x \acute{x} \mid x \acute{x} \mid x \acute{x} \mid\mid$$
$$x \acute{x} \mid x \acute{x} \mid x \acute{x} \mid x$$

At the beginning of the second half-line there is someitmes *x́x* instead of *x*x́ (*goddspelles* 14, *affterr* 2, 15, *unnderr* 9, *Hælennde* 3355, *drihhtin* 3375, *summ þing* 3363); it is useless in such cases to suppose any displacement of the word stress.

Final -*e* is regularly elided before a following vowel or *h-* (*soṇe anan* 3368, *herrtẹ annd* 3383).

Orm's septenary is not rimed like that of the *Poema Morale* (II), but assonanced. In fact the last syllable of every second half line invariably contains the vowel *e*.

---

5. **i Godess huse:** that is, in the convent where they were both canons.

7. **witt** ' we two '; its use is hardly found after the middle of the 13th

century; it will be noticed that here it is already followed by the reinforcing form *ba* 'both'.

9. kanunnkess had 'rank of canonry'. Already in OE *hād* was used to denote rank in the ecclesiastical hierarchy.

10. Sannt Awwsten: Augustine established a monastic rule (*reʒhellboc*) based on that of Benedict.

29 ff. These collections of sermons (homilies) for Sundays and feast days of the liturgical year were common in the Middle Ages. Ælfric had already composed two such collections (cp. *HOE* Nos. IX and X).

31. sinndenn 'are' a form still very close to OE *sindon* and which disappeared after the 12th century.

33 f. The method followed by Orm consisted in telling in English the gospel for the day (as the following extract shows), then commenting on its significance and meaning.

34. þatt tatt that is to say *þatt þatt* 'that which'. Cp. the grammatical introd. above.

35. mann birþ 'it behoves one'; impersonal verb with dat pronoun (here *mann* which no longer has a dat flexion, but see l. 49 *þeʒʒm birrþ*).

44. ríme 'meter, rhythm' actually 'the count', similarly in l. 101.

49. te bettre 'the better', *te* for *þe* cp. 34 note.

55. wha-se 'whosoever' (*whoso*).

95. wilenn shall 'will [*shall*] desire [*wilenn*]', rare future of *wilenn* 'desire'.

97. hĕ't contraction for *he itt*.

98. swa summ 'just as'; *summ* as used here corresponds to ON *sem*.

3337. 'in the form of a man'.

3342. forrþriht summ 'as soon as'; cp. 98 note.

3352. all follc 'to all people', a dative.

3355. Hælennde 'the Savior'; this term is peculiar to West Germanic (OE *hǣlend*, OHG *heilant*, OSax *hēliand*). It was no longer used in English after the beginning of the 13th century. In origin it is the substantivized pres part of the OE vb *hǣlan* 'to heal, help, make well'.

3363. to witerr tákenn 'as a clear token'.

3368. sone anan se 'as soon as'.

3380. griþþ annd friþþ, a frequent expression in Orm; both words mean 'peace', the first is Old Norse, the second English.

3603 ff. This passage is part of the commentary on LUKE II. 4-7: And Joseph also went up from Galilee, out of the city of Nazareth, into Judæa, unto the city of David, which is called Bethlehem; (because he was of the house and lineage of David:) to be taxed with Mary his espoused wife, being great with child. And so it was, that, while they were there, the days were accomplished that she should be delivered. And she brought forth her first born son, and wrapped him in swaddling clothes, and laid him in a manger; because there was no room for them in the inn.

3630-5. Orm here follows his custom and gives an allegorical interpretation of the proper names; Nazareth 'flower', Galilee 'wheel', Bethlehem 'house of bread ' (only the last is etymologically exact). Then in the following lines he draws from these their mystical significance.

3633. soþ boc: this 'true book' which Orm refers to may be any one of the lists of proper names which, from the 12th century appeared as an appendix to the Vulgate MSS with the title *Interpretatio hebraicorum nominum*, or may be a contemporary encyclopedic work like the *Excerptiones allegoricae* (MIGNE, *Patrologie latine*, CLXXV, 635 – CLXXVII, 193), or the *Distinctiones dictionum theologicalium* by Alain de Lille (MIGNE, *ibid*, CCX, 685) which give the allegorical sense of biblical proper names, or again any other similar work.

3649. Gastlike 'mystically'.

3652 f. þatt . . . inne 'in which'.

3661. 'two natures in one person *(had)* '. Cp. (Anglican) *Book of Common Prayer*, Articles of Faith, No. II.

VIII

Text from University Library, Cambridge, MS Gg IV 27. 2 (*C*) with readings from British Museum MS Harleian 2253 (*L*) and Bodleian, Oxford, *Laud Misc.* 108 (*O*). *C* dates from about 1260; it was copied by a rather negligent scribe and is often faulty.

Dialect of the Southeast (Surrey?) with Midland traits.

Spelling. The letter *u* denotes both [u] (*adun* 455, *ure* 549, *sume* 498) and [ü] (*luþere* 498, *furst* 544, *duntes* 573, *murie* 521; perhaps also *wulle* 542, *wurþ* 460); *eo* denotes the sound [ö] (*beon* 446, *heo* 561). The letter ʒ represents the velar spirant [x] (*swoʒning* 444, *soʒte* 465) as well as the palatal spirant [ç] (*kniʒt* 446, *ariʒte* 457) and the semi-vowel [j] (*i-ʒolde* 460, *ʒaf* 466). Note the spelling *ihc* 542, 546, etc. for *ich*.

Phonology. OE *y* formed by *i*-umlaut of *u* is often *e* (*kesse* 'kiss' 583, *leste* 'list' 473); final *-n* is sometimes lost (*seve* 448 for *seven*, *bifore* for *biforen*). Many *e*'s are silent: *makede* 520 was probably pronounced [ma·d].

Inflexions. *Personal pronouns.* — 1 sg *ihc* 453 and *I* 544, 3 sg F *heo* 445, 3 pl nom *hi* 498, dat *hem* 520.

Verb. — Pres 2 sg in *-st* (*hast* 539) but cp. *sedes* (: *dedes*) 538, 3 sg *haþ* 513, *stondeþ* 554, 1 pl *beþ* 547 (alongside *stonde* 512), 3 pl *beoþ* 571. The present participle (no examples in the extract printed here) is in *-inde*. Past participle preceded by *i-*; final *-n* is often lost in strong verbs (*i-ʒolde* 460, *i-fare* 468, *i-sprunge* 548) but cp. *i-done* 446, *forloren* 479.

Versification. The original was most probably written in rimed couplets with three accents; cp. the beginning of the selection:

> 'Rymęnhild þat 'swetë 'þing
> 'Wakedę of 'hirę swoʒ'ning
> ' 'Horn ', quaþ 'heo, ' wel 'sone
> 'Þat schal 'beon i-'done
> Þu 'schalt beo 'dubbed 'kniʒt
> Are 'comë 'sevë 'niʒt.

But in the corrupt condition in which the text survives the verse sometimes has four accents:

And 'se he 'holde 'forë'ward   452

or two

Þe 'king sedę 'sone   483

---

448. 'within a week', lit. 'ere (before) seven nights have come'. On this use of the subjunctive cp. *OED* s. v. *come* 35*b*.

449. Have 'take, carry'.

450. þer-uppe ' in addition '.

451. Aylbrus or (v. 471) Aþelbrus, steward or major-domo for king Aylmar.

452. se 'and see (to it that) '.

455. adun falle: one kneeled to address the king.

461. 'May Christ lend him success'. It was not until the 14th century that *lend* succeeded the older *lene* (OE *lǣnan*) for 'lend, grant'.

466. þat 'what' (similarly farther on l. 518).

471. also swiþe 'as fast (as possible)', 'very fast'.

473. þu leste imperative 'listen'.

474. mid þe beste 'among the best'.

478. geste is not clear; the meaning 'guests' does not fit the context. HALL proposes '(symbolic) gesture', as, for example, that of dubbing Horn knight. Farther on (l. 522) *gestes* means 'games'.

479. 'it would not be out of place'.

482. 'he will turn out (to be) a good knight'.

484. The MS reading is evidently defective. HALL has proposed the correction *He is wel i-done* 'he is perfect' and FRENCH *þat is wel to done* 'that will be very good' following respectively the readings of *L* and *O*.

486. 'he gives promise of being a good knight'. Cp. the readings of the other MSS; *L: knyht him wel bysemeþ* 'knight-(hood would) well become him', and *O: to be knict him byseme*. The original must have had something like these.

498. 'Certain ones of them were wicked'. *sume* in apposition with *hi.*

499-504. This description conforms to what is known from other sources about this ceremony.

505. Aþulf: the best of Horn's twelve companions.

510. Suddenne is the unexplained name of Horn's native country. Some have read into it the country of the South Danes (*Suðdene*) mentioned in *Beowulf*, others the Isle of Man (called *Suðrey* by the Vikings). The word appears in Gaimar's *L'estorie des Engleis*, v. 955-6:

Edelbrit fu feit reis de Kent
E de Sudeine ensement

where other MSS have *Surrie* or *Suthreie.* It is not impossible that *Suddenne* designates the south coast of England.

527. one 'alone'.

530. Hornes come 'Horn's coming'.

532. þe biforn = *biforn þe.*

535. 'Do now what you previously [*er*] spoke about.'

541. beo stille 'calm yourself'.

554. 'Therefore it is up to me [*standeþ me*] (to be) the more in a hurry.' The sense is not entirely satisfactory, anymore than the divergent readings from the other two MSS: *L: oþer wyþ wymmon forewart make, O: þerfore ne have ich þe forsake.*

563. gold ring: medieval metrical romances abound in magic rings.

564. The reading of MS *C* could be defended: 'it is beautifully cut or engraved' taking *dubbing* as 'ornament' and *him ... þe* as equivalent to a possessive, as was frequent in OE (cp. *HOE* § 158.2). But the other two MSS have a different meaning: *L: Hit is ful god to þi dobbyng, O: He his god to þi dubbing.* FRENCH proposes the reading *Hit is god to þi dubbing.*

571 ff. Belief in the magical power of certain stones to avert injury was widespread.

581. erndinge 'success'; it is true that elsewhere (besides being rare) this word only has the meaning 'intercession'. The other two MSS have *endyng(e)*.

IX

Text from Bodleian MS Laud Misc. 471: French original from MS Douce 270 from the same library.

Dialect: Kentish, but in a text copied by a scribe apparently from the South Midlands.

Spelling. Note *ss* or *s* for [š] (*ssipe* 'ship' 2, 5, 11, *sal* 'shall' 14) and *sc* for [ss] (*blisce* 'bliss' 30); *þ* is sometimes written *t* (*perisset* 7, *to* 'þo' 10) or *dh* (*clepiedh* 21); *hic* 20, 22 represents *ich*; the *ȝ* is unknown in this MS which uses either *y* (*yede* 2, *yef* 23) or *gh* (*i-seghe* 11) or *ch* (*þurch* 24).

Phonology. OE *hw-* is reduced to *w-* (*wat* 9, *wanne* 21); OE *ēo* is *ie* [je] (*bie* 14, *nyede* 16, *niedes* 22, *yede* 2), OE *ēa* is *ia* [ja] (*believe* 9, *diadliche* 25; with the exceptions *great* 3 and *beleave* 8); OE *ȳ* is *ē* (*senne* 'sin' 24, *prede* 'pride' 24, *evel* 27); OE *ǣ* has become *ē* (*hedde* 5, *þet* 8, etc., *wreþe* 25); OE *f* is voiced to [v] (*vaire* 'fair' 13).

Inflexions. The pl of *substantives* is in *-en* (beside *-es*) even when it is a case of old strong sbs (*sorghen* 21, *saulen* 29).

Definite article. — Alongside the current invariable *þe* (1, 3,ˑ19 etc.) there was still an extensive flexion marred by uncertainty about gender of sbs. M nom sg *se devel* 23, acc *þane wynd* 10, dat *þa peril*; F nom *si miracle*, acc *þo miracle* 12, dat *þo blisce* 29, Nt nom *þet godspell* 13, dat *þo ssipe* 3, 5, 11; pl *þo men* 11, *þo saulen* 28. There was also a *demonstrative* use in *se þet* 'he who' 16.

Personal pronouns. — Nom 1 sg *hic* (for *ich*) 20, 22; nom M 3 sg *he* 15, *ha* 7, acc *hine* 6, poss *hise* 5, dat *him* 8; neuter *hit* 10; 2 pl dat *yw* 9; nom 3 pl *hi* 8, acc *hi* 22, poss *hure* 14, *hire* 21, *here* 22, dat *hem* 9.

Verb. — Present 3 sg in *-(e)þ* (*telþ* 13, *doþ* 15, *seith* 19, with contracted form *dret* for *dredeþ* 9); pl in *-eþ* (*redeth* 1, *bisecheth* 18, *clepiedh* 21, *perisset* 7).

Imperative (or hortative) 1 pl *grede we* 23, *sigge we* 26; subjunctive in -(*e*) (*clepie, helpe* 17, *mote* 29; *yef* 28, *perissi, delivri* 29); infinitive in -(*n*) (*bie* 14, *bien* 29, *do* 15, 18, *gon* 29, *acumbri* 24); gerund *to done* 28, *to slepe* 4 (?).
Preterit pl in -*e*(*n*) (*seiden* 6, *weren* 11, *hadde* 8, *hedde* 5, 11, *awakede* 6). Past part preceded by *i*- (*i-leid* 4, *i-seghe* 11).

Syntax still close to OE. Note the impersonal verb forms like *wat dret yw* 9, *awondrede hem* 12 and the conjunction *er þane* 'before' 5.

Vocabulary. Numerous French loans: *deciples* 2, 5, *tempeste* 4, 5, *miracle* 13, 14, *peril* 16, *sucuri* 16, 17, 22, *merci* 18, *acumbri* 24, *anvie* 24, *manere* 25, *sauve* 26, 29, *perissi, delivri* 27.

---

1. **þe holi godspelle of to-dai:** that for the fourth Sunday after Epiphany, MATTHEW VIII, 23 ff.

3. **so ... so** 'when ... then'.

4. **was i-leid him don** 'had laid (himself) down [*don*]' with *him* as reflexive pronoun.

6. **so awakede hine** 'therefore they waked him'; *hine* is acc of 3 sg M personal pronoun.

9. **wat dret yw** 'what frightens you', if we consider that *dret* is contracted form of 3 sg *dredeþ* and that *drede* can mean 'frighten' as well as 'fear'.

10. **tok** 'scolded'. — **also raþe** 'at once'.

16. **se þet** 'he who' in correlation with the following *þet* (cp. the F text *cil qui ... qu*').

19. **Salus populi ego sum:** this is the introit of the mass for the Thursday after the third Sunday of Lent: 'Salus populi ego sum, dicit Dominus: de quacumque tribulatione clamaverint ad me, exaudiam eos: et ero illorum Dominus in perpetuum'.

X

Text from the unique Bodleian MS Digby 86 (ca. 1272-1283) which contains another fabliau, *Dame Siriz.*

Dialect of the South but probably copied by a West-Midland scribe trained in Anglo-Norman writing tradition.

Spelling is quite peculiar. *ou* is written for [u] not only in *grounde* 91, *founde* 92, *adoun* 85, *mouþe* 100, but also in *soum* 104, *hounger* 145 etc. On the other hand the cluster [oxt] is written either *out* (in which *ou* is a true diphthong: *nout* 77, *biþout* 81, *i-brout* 82, *þoute* 94, 125, *route* 260) or *ohut* (*brohute* 70, *nohut* 220, *þohut* 223) to avoid confusion with *ou* [u]; cp. similarly *sehid* for *seid* 210. This can indicate the total vocalization of [x]. Cp. for instance at the end of a word *lou* 148, *inou* 197, *dou* 256 and *i-kaut* 86, 103 for *i-caȝt.*

Attention is called to excrescent *h* (which has been marked *ḥ*) in this MS: (*overḥede* 90, *ḥertou* for *ertou = ert þou* 120, *ḥounderstod* 77, *ḥoup* 'up' 126, *ḥete* 'ete' 156, *ḥiis* 'is' (106); in contrast *h* is omitted in *ou* 'how' 230. Note *ihc* for *ich* 159, *goed* for *god* 161, 173 *luitel* for *lüttel* 260, *srive* 184 and *srift* 186 for *shrive* and *shrift*. Finally, the doubling of vowels (*liif* 187, *wiis* 105, *reed* 192, *meel* 247) does not necessarily mark a long vowel, since we find *wiit* 'wit' 105, *ḫiis* 'is' 106.

Phonology. OE *y* remains and is written *u* = [ü]: *putte* 71, *muchel* 98, *lust* 96, *sunne* 165, *fulþe* 165, *bruche* 233, etc.

OE *æ* has become *e* (*wes* 71, *hedde* 135).

OE *ả* before nasals is *o* (*hongi* 88, *dronk* 93, *stonk* 94, *shome* 99, *londe* 101, *honde* 102).

f- voices to *v* (*vox* 81 etc. *vind* 253, *vroggen* 'frogs' 256) but is still often written *f* (*for* 125 etc. *founde* 214).

OE *hw-* is reduced to *w-* (*wen* 75, *wat* 89, *wo* 122, *won* 181, *weder* 244, 245) unless this is the mark of an Anglo-Norman scribe who could not distinguish between [w] and [hw] or [ʍ].

Inflexions. *The definite article* is generally the invariable *þe*; but there are some traces of flexion: M sg acc *þene* 113, 126, 242, neuter *þat* 74, 75, 76, 78, 94.

Personal pronouns. — 1 sg *ich* exceptionally *I* 105; M nom 3 sg *he* 77, acc *hine* 123, dat *him* 94; dat-acc 2 pl *ou* 214, 215, 216; nom 3 pl *hy* 204, dat *hem* 162.

Verb. — Present 3 sg in -(*e*)*þ* (*haveþ* 121, *beþ* 153, *beginneþ* 80), 3 pl in -(*e*)*þ* (*haveþ* 256, *beþ* 166, 167, *doþ* 217). Past participle preceded by *i-* (*i-ben* 87, *i-maked* 72, *i-brout* 82, *i-writen* 204).

Versification. Octosyllabic rimed couplets, with occasional imperfect rimes (*blive : swiþe* 109-10, *kun : him* 123-4, *putte : mette* 241-2, *meel : smal* 247-8, etc.).

---

74 ff. 'The first [*þat oþer*] went to the bottom (in such a way) that when a person [*me = men*] would wind that one up, the second would wind down'. This contrivance (a well with double bucket) which is stressed by every medieval writer who tells the tale must have been, at the time, a novelty.

85. adoun he moste (go): verb of motion omitted after modals. Similarly in l. 244, 246.

89 f. 'What with sorrow and with fear (to worry about), his thirst disappeared completely.'

96 f. 'May pleasure [*lust*] and joy turn [*worþe*] to woe for the man who knows no measure in his food'.

106. 'But now I'm finished'.

108. þer com a wolf gon 'a wolf came walking (by)'. Verbs of motion are often pleonastically linked, but there was a distinction between *gon* and *ride* 'walk' and 'ride'. See .13₃/25 note.

113. In the French text (MS *A* ed. by E. Martin ll. 209-28) Ysengrin leaning into the well thinks he sees his wife Hersent down there with Renart and he bursts into invective. This feature must have been lost in the MS or oral form used by the English writer. One may note that it is also absent from another French MS called *H*.

116. gossip. Besides the usual meaning (OE *godsibb*) 'one who has contracted spiritual affinity with another by acting as a sponsor at a baptism' (*OED*) the ME word had already acquired the sense of 'a familiar acquaintance, a friend, chum' which is possibly that of the present usage. — **of children bore** 'from the time we were children'.

128. Sigrim: popular form taken in English oral tradition by the Wolf's name in the F *Roman de Renart* where the Fox bears the name of *Renart,* cp. below *Reneuard,* l. 133. (In Caxton Isegrym and Reynard are forms borrowed into English from Holland Dutch).

133. þi frend 'your kinsman' (sense due to ON *frændi*); cp. 14/4136 and note.

134. þine come 'your coming'.

151. storve 'died', the old meaning of the vb 'to starve'.

159 f. 'Thanks be to God that it is now thus, that I have gone to Christ — none of my friends know it yet—' or, as amended ⟨*seþ*⟩ 'Since I have gone to Christ I no longer know [*not*] any of my friends'.

167. shep and get 'sheep•and goats' old umlauted pl of *got* which survived until the 16th cent.

169. ȝare 'for a long time'.

181 f. 'To whom ... should I confess my sins?' The amusing scene 181-225 in which Sigrim confesses to Reneward is not known in any of the French originals of the *Roman de Renart.* It can be seen in the French text (l. 312-328) that Ysengrin has already confessed to the rabbit and the goat, and he polishes off the last part to Renart in a rather earthy fashion.

189. þin ore 'your mercy', 'have mercy'.

191. ich worþe ded 'I shall be dead'. The old verb for 'become' is used as in OE as the future of the verb 'to be'. Similarly in l. 248.

192. 'unless you give me some advice'.

197-199. " Tell your sins one by one, (so) that there is left never (a) one? " " At once," said the wolf, " very gladly."

201. widewene kors 'widows' curse' for all the 'husbands' he had eaten; *widewene* old wk gen pl.

208. elleswer i. e. 'in Hell'.

214. ou = *you*; similarly in following lines.

217 ff. 'I thought, as others do, (that) what [*þat*] I saw was true, and therefore you were hateful to me'.

230. ou for *hou* 'how'.

233. a bruche 'an opening into the bliss of heaven'. This is probably the oldest record of the meaning.

237. way sumdel 'weighed some little' litotes for 'quite a lot'.

241. amidde þe putte 'half-way down the well'.

244. 'What are you going to do? Where are you going?'

246. wiþ þi meel 'towards your meal'. This meaning of *wiþ* 'towards' is recorded in OE.

254. bind 'render helpless'.

260. In the English fabliau, a friar from the convent comes to draw water from the well, sees the wolf and thinks it is the devil (which he knew he would see because he was out when he should have been at prayers). He rouses the others and they beat Sigrim before he gets away.

XI

Text from the MS preserved in the Public Record Office, London.

Dialect of London, 1258, which is South-east with East-Midland influence.

Spelling. Note the use of *eo* for [ö], of *oa* for [ǫ] (*Yrloande* 2 etc.) and of *lh* in *lhoaverd* 1. The letter *u* represents [u] and [ü].

Phonology. OE *ā* has become [ǫ] written sometimes *oa* (*lhoaverd* 1, *moare* 5, 14, *hoaten* 10, *noan* 17, *i-foan* 20, and, as a result of lengthening, *loandes* 6, *foangen* 17) sometimes *o* (*oʒen* 11, *þo* 36, *alswo* 15, *oþe* 16, *two* 25); OE *ǣ* is still written *æ* (*þæt* 4, etc. *ætforen* 35, *stedefæst* 9) or *e* (*wes* 27), similarly OE *ǣ* is still written *æ* (*i-lærde* 3, *dæl* 5, 14, *rædesmen* 5) or *e* (*redesmen* 9, *i-lestinde* 10), OE *y* remains *u* (*kuneriche* 7, *Kanteburi* 28) with possible [e] from *i-wersed* 18.

Inflexions. *Substantives.* — Plurals in *-en*: *i-foan* 20, *worden* 36, gen pl in *-ene*: *Englene loande* 1, 37.

Definite article. — Inflected forms are found alongside invariable *þe*: M sg acc *þane* 24, dat *þan* 16, F dat *þære* 37, neuter nom *þæt* 6; nom pl *þo* 36, dat *þan* 9, 13.

Personal pronoun. — 3 pl nom *heo* 11, dat *heom* 6, 14, 20.

Verb. — Present pl in *-eþ* (*beop, habbeþ* 7 — Southern forms) alongside forms in *-en* (*beon* 13, *senden* 22, *willen* 4, *unnen* 5, *hoaten* 10 — Midland forms).
Infinitive in *-en* (*healden* 12, *don* 7) and *-ien* (*makien* 13, *werien* 12). Present participle in *-inde* (*i-lestinde*, Southern form), str past part in *-n* (*i-chosen* 6, *i-don* 7, *i-sworene* 27).
Retention of prefix *i-* (<OE *ʒe-*) in the past participle as well as in the sbs (*i-gretinge* 3, *i-lærde* 3, *i-setnesse* 13, *i-foan* 20).
Generally declensional endings still have full forms. In particular note the distinction between sg *oni* and pl *onie* in l. 19.

Vocabulary. Outside of proper nouns (*Octobre* 25) and numerous surnames (*Henri, Boniface, Walter, Simon, Richard* etc.) words of French origin are rare (*duk* 2, *i-seined* 22, *seel* 22, *cruninge* 26, *marescal* 31).

---

1. **on** ' of '; cp. also l. 7.

3. **send:** contracted form of 3 sg pres *sendeþ*.

4. **þæt witen ʒe wel alle þæt:** correlative *þæt ... þæt*: ' This let all of you know (namely) that '. While the French text has simply *sachez ke*.

5. **þæt þæt ure rædesmen** ' that what our counsellors ... have done '. This seems to be a direct reference to the Council of Twenty-four who had drawn up the Provisions of Oxford.

6 f. **þæt loandes folk on ure kuneriche.** Cp. the French text *le commun de reaume.*

15 f. **alswo alse** ' so as ', ' just as '. — ' and that each should help the other to act by the same oath, towards all men, to do right and to receive it '.

22. **writ open** ' letters patent ' (as compared with letters *close*), a document setting up certain legal powers.

24. **usselven:** plural of majesty in contrast to French sg *meismeismes.*

27 ff. Note that the English text is signed by thirteen witnesses, the French copy by sixteen.

36 ff. and al on, etc.: The corresponding phrase is missing from the French text and from the English text now at Oxford.

37. þære kuneriche: notice the use of the feminine dat *þære* before an originally neuter sb.

XII

Text from Bodleian MS Laud Misc. 108 (ca. 1300-20). Fragments from the Cambridge MS cited in the notes were published by W. W. SKEAT, *MLR*, 1911, pp. 455 ff.

Dialect. The original was composed about 1270 in a Northeast Midland dialect (Lincolnshire), at the southern limit of the Northern dialect where Scandinavian influence was very strong. But before coming to us it evidently passed through scribes of Southern origin; thus the dialect is very mixed: in it are found forms from the North, the Midlands and the South.

Spelling. The MS is very faulty which explains the great number of corrections introduced here, just as other editors have done. These corrections are of two kinds: 1st, words added, removed, or displaced by reason of either sense or meter; 2nd, restored spellings: the last copyist was undoubtedly Anglo-Norman; he introduced practices from his own language which can only confuse the student. I have not hesitated to adopt spellings more conformable to general ME practice. In particular the MS has the following variants for *ht: th, ct, cht, c* and *w* for *hw, s* for *sh.* The absence of ʒ, replaced by *y* is striking (*yede, yere, yunge*). As a vowel, *i* is much more frequent than *y*. The sounds [ö] and [ü] no longer appear in this dialect. [u] is indicated by *u* (*clutes* 547, *ful* 539) and [u·] by *ou* (*nou* 483, *you* 484, *þou* 527, *doumbe* 543, *bounden* 545); but this digraph *ou* also indicates the diphthong [ou], alongside the spelling *ow* (*slou : drow* 501-2, *brouht* 513 etc.).

Phonology OE *ā* is generally *ō* (*sō*<OE *swā* 714, *wo* 611, *mo* 511) and occasionally *ā* (*blawe* 587, but *blou* 585); OE *ǎ* is *ǫ* (*Engelond* 725, *hond* 726, *sond* 735) and *a* (*Engeland* 610, *hand* 611); OE *ȳ* is *ī* (*sinne* 536, *fir* 585); open and close *ē* have a tendency to be merged, at least from such rimes as *sē* (<OE *sǣ*) with *bē* 519, *hē* 554, *frē* 561). Flexional final *-e* seems most often to be pronounced, thus:

> 'Loverd we 'arën 'boþë 'þinë,
> 'þinë 'cherlës, 'þinë 'hinë   619-20

Inflexions. *Substantives.* — A few wk pls (*eyne* 680) and invariables (*hine* 620, *swin, hors* 701) otherwise always in -(*e*)*s*.

Personal pronouns. — 1 sg *I, y;* F 3 sg *she* 566 alongside *sho* 649; 3 pl *he* 516, 554, 599, 741; poss 3 pl *here* 742, dat *hem.*

Verb. — Present 2 sg in -*es* (*wenes* 598, *haves* 688) but *sest* 534; 3 sg in -*es* (*behoves* 582, *menes* 597) and in -(*e*)*þ* (*swereþ* 647, *dereþ* 648, *eteth* 672, *liþ* 673).

Most often the infinitive has lost final -*n*, especially as a rime-word (*yeve* 485, *live* 486, *swere* 487, *þrive* 514, etc.; but *wirchen* 510, *taken* 518, *casten* 519, *ben* 517 in the middle of the line). Present participle: *starinde* 508 (a Southern form!); past participle without *i*-.

Vocabulary. Numerous words of Scandinavian origin: *krike* 708, *þral* 527, 684, *kevel* 547, *serk* 603, *hend* ' hands ' 505 (<ON *hendr*) ; *late* 486, *taken* 518, *greyþe* 714, *slo* 512, *flo* 612, *heþen* 683, 690, *or* 728, *fro* 721, *þrinne* 716, 761.

Versification. Octosyllabic rimed couplets.

---

474. bi þe wawe ' along the wall ' semantically empty metrical expletive.

484. bidd'I for *bidde I* ' I offer '. There is constant confusion in ME between OE *bēodan* ' command, announce ' (ME *bede*) and OE *biddan* ' ask, pray, offer ' (ME *bidde*) the latter often taking the form and meaning of the former.

487. on boke ' on the bible ' (cp. 5/5).

494. Bircabein is, according to Stefán EINARSSON, a name possibly formed on the ON model *Birkibeinar*, a name given to King Eysteinn Haraldsson's men, who wrapped their legs in birch bark as a cold weather measure. (*Heimskringla, Saga Magnús Erlingssonar*, chapt. 36 and f.).

497. bigan him for to rewe is impersonal ' he began to have pity '.

498. The pronoun subject of *withdrow* is omitted.

503. Havelok here counts for three syllables; elsewhere the word can be two, accented on either the first (l. 544) or the last (l. 632).

505 f. ' But only that he, with his (own) hands, did not kill him, the foul fiend '. *on* ' only '; *hend* ON pl. (*hendr*). Cp. this corrected passage with 2227 ff.

> He havede reunesse of þe knave
> So þat ⟨þanne⟩ he with his hend
> Ne drop him nouht, þat sori fend!

524 f. ' a fisherman that he thought would do all he wanted '.

538. ' As long as there was rope to bind with '.

544. ' O Havelok, may (Jesus Christ) avenge you on Godard '; MS *wreken* is irregular form for *wreke*.

546. This sentence is obscure; something is undoubtedly missing in the MS. The line which follows in the Cambridge MS supplies this deficiency but violates the couplet rime scheme established by the whole poem.

547. kevel of clutes ' bundle of rags ' as a gag.

549. Hwere undoubtedly ' wherever ' (Cambr. MS has *quider so*).

566. The order of events is reversed following the rhetorical formula called *hysteron-proteron* ' the cart before the horse '.

572. ' (what a pity) that a griffon or an eagle (*ern*) had not seized him '.

586. Als she shulde ' As she was about to '.

591. ' from his mouth there issued a ray of light '. OE use of *stōd* as in *Beowulf* 726-7 *him of ēagum stōd ... leoht unfæger* ' a horrible light came from his eyes ' and as in ModE ' the ship stands into the harbor ', ' stand Navy down the field '. Kingly lights appear in the French version 71 ff.

> Totes les houres q'il dormoit
> Une flambe de lui issoit
> Par la bouche li venoit fors,

Si grant chalur avoit el cors.
La flambe rendoit tiel odour,
Onc ne sentit nul home meillour.

Livy reports a similar fact about Servius Tullius (book I, ch. 39).

600. ' A man should have good will ' — gnomic author-intrusion.

606. þis ure eir: *þis* = *þis is* (a frequent contraction).

641. wel is me ' things are good for me '. — mayht a blending of *may* and *miht,* similarly in l. 689.

644. The pastries were meat pies; the custards (*flaunes*) were made with cream or cheese as today. See FURNIVALL, *Early English Meals and Manners* (EETS 32), p. 287.

677. bihete't = *bihete it.* Same elision in l. 714.

681. wiltu ben erl: hypothetical inversion ' if you want to be (an) earl '.

686 f. ' for (very) little, I would have [*do*] you led to the gallows '.

691. Lit. ' it seemed to him to be too long (no matter how fast he got out) until he ran '.

693. Hwat shal me to raþe ' what shall I (take) as counsel? ' The rimes *rede : beþe* have been corrected according to 2542-3:

And seyde: ' Hwat shal me to raþe
Goddot! I shal do slon hem baþe '.

The forms *boþe* and *rede* are also found in the poem; but *raþ* is most likely an ON loan from *rāð.* The bad rime *beþe : rede* must be due to a Southern copyist.

694. wite he him live ' does he know he (is) alive ' = ' if '.

698. children gen pl, just as *wives* is gen sg of *wif* ' my children's and my wife's lives '.

702. yerd ' farm-yard '.

705. ' he converted all into cash '.

709. dide as in OE ' put or place '.

715 ff. Cp. the French version, 97 ff.

Quant sa nief fut apparaillee
Dedenz fist entrer sa meisnee,
Ses chevalers et ses serganz,
Sa femme demeine et ses enfanz:
La reyne mist el batel,
Haveloc tint souz son mantel.

But in this version the ship runs into pirates, not a storm. The pirates kill all but Grim and his family.

718. leyde in an ore ' put out (a sailing?) oar (as a rudder?) '.

733. Humber: The Humber estuary.

733 ff. Cp. the French version, 122 ff.:

Tant ont nagé et tant siglé
Q'en une havene ont parvenu

Et de la nief a terre issu.
Ceo fut el North, a Grimesbi.
A icel tens qe jeo vus di
Ni out onques home habité
Ne cele havene n'ert pas haunté.
Il i adresca primes maison,
De lui ad Grimesbi a non.
Quant Grim primes i ariva
En .ii. moitez sa nief trencha
Les chiefs en ad amont dresté,
lloec dedenz s'est herbergé.

735. sat his ship '(he) landed his ship'.

739. þere for to erde 'in order to live there'.

741. he ... were 'they were'.

745. Grimesbi: As a second element *-by* from ON *búr* (Old Danish *by*) 'town, village' is common in English place-names of Scandinavian origin, especially in the old Danelaw area.

746. þat 'those who'.

XIII

1a

Text from British Museum MS Harley 978 (end of 13th century). See facsimile, plate III.

Dialect of the South.

Spelling. Note *lh-* in *lhude* 3, *lhouþ* 9.

Phonology. OE *f* has become *v* (*verteþ* 'farts' 10).

Inflexions. *Verb.* — Pres 2 sg in *-es* (*singes* 13); 3 sg in ꞉(*e*)*þ* (*groweþ* 5, *springþ* 6). Str past participle: *i-cumen* 3.

Versification. Stanza $a^4b^3c^4b^3b^2 \parallel d^4b^3e^4b^3b^2 \parallel b^3b^3$ (*c* and *e* with interior rime).

From the point of view of music, see H. E. WOOLRIDGE, *The Oxford History of Music*, 1901, I, 326-38 and M. F. BUKOFZER, *Univ. of Calif. Publ. in Music* II, 2 (1944) who dates the *music* at about 1310, though the *text* may be much earlier. "The Latin text (see facsimile) does not fit the time very well and overlooks the *Pes* or burden altogether; it is probably the result of an unskillful attempt to convert the lyric to religious uses. The careful instructions in the MS for the rendering of the song suggest that it was of a type unusual at the time" (G. L. BROOK). For a record the student is referred to the *Columbia Hist. of Music*, vol. I, part 12.

---

3. somer here means 'spring'. ME *lenten* had long been understood to mean the original fast and gradually lost its specific meaning of 'spring'. Because of this ME writers were compelled to use *somer* in this sense since the adoption of spring dates only from the 16th century (A. K. MOORE in *Notes and Queries*, 19 Feb. 1949).

1b

Text from MS Digby 20 (2nd half of 13th cent.).

---

1 ff. " The picture suggested in these four lines — the sinking of the sun behind some lonely forest, the shadows of evening and then darkness — makes a beautiful and appropriate figure to represent the death of the Son of Man and the grief of the heart-broken Mother " (C. BROWN).

2. rode ' face, complexion '. (OE *rudu*) and not *rōde* ' cross ' (as the rime with *wode* shows).

2

Text from Jesus College (Oxford) MS 29 (ca. 1275).

Dialect of the South-west.

Spelling. Note *hw-* (*hwer* 65, *hwat* 77). *eo* indicates [ö], *u* [ü] (*prute* ' pride ', OE *prȳte*) as well as [u] (*lufsum* 93, *muþ* 98, *suþ* 100).

Phonology. OE *æ* > *e* (*glede* 92, *eny* 113, *enne* 88; OE *ā* > *o* (*mon, londe* 97, *honde* 99 etc., except *man* 108; OE *f* > *v* (*veyr* 83 alongside *feyr* 91, *vouh* 106, *volde* 117).

Inflexions. *Pronouns.* — 1 sg *ich* 88, 118; 3 pl *heo* 71 (*hi* 76), poss *heore* 78, dat *heom* 73; the indefinite is *me* [mə] 74.

Relative particle: þe 80.

Verb. — 2 sg in -(e)st (*wilnest* 87, *bist* 120); 3 sg in -eþ (*haveþ* 74, *speketh* 98), contracted forms *halt* 102, *byt* 105; 3 pl in -þ (*beoþ* 71). Past participle with prefix *i-*.

Versification. Stanza of eight 4-beat lines, riming *abab`abab*.

---

67. There is an Old French metrical romance from the early 13th cent., with *Amadas* and *Ydoine* as hero and heroine. The original of this must have been written in Anglo-Norman (cp. G. PARIS in *An English Miscellany presented to Dr. Furnivall*, London, 1901, 386-392). Allusions to these adventures are rather frequent in English literature. In both *Sir Degrevant* and *Emare* there is a reference to the story of *Amadas* and *Ydoine* being embroidered on a tapestry.

73. al so ' as if '.

74. me [mə] ' people ', ' they ' indefinite.

82. This allusion (and that in l. 101) to Henry III (1216-72) gives a *terminus ad quem* for the composition of the poem, cp. also l. 101.

83. Absalon, 3rd son of David, reputed for his great beauty; cp. II SAMUEL XIV. 25-6.

84. ' who had on earth no equal '.

86. ' in the end it would not be worth a herring '.

94. of wisdom wilde ' of great wisdom '.

96. ' if you could put yourself under his protection '.

102. '(king Henry) holds (England) as His vassal and to Him bows '.

105. Ne byt he wiþ þe 'he does not ask of you'.

111. þe to = *to þe* 'to you'. — **suche** .... **þat** 'such ... as'.

117. 'It is fairer by many times'.

3

Text from Trinity College, Cambridge, MS 323, folio 34 a (ca. 1300).

Dialect of the Southwest.

Spelling. Not a careful MS; in it *þ* is written *y*, *-ȝt(e)* is written *-st(e)*; There is *wid* for *wiþ* 7, etc., *foret* for *forþ* 19, *wou* for *how* 26. The scribe has forgotten to repeat lines 9, 27 and 33 (which we have supplied), but he has written *ii* (i. e. 'repeat twice') at the end of the preceding verse. The letter *u* indicates [u] (*ure* 1) and [ü] (*bugge* 3).

Phonology. OE *y* survives and is written *u* [ü] (*rugge* 4, *cunesman* 6, *sulle* 20, *cunnes* 21, 23, *stude* 30), OE *æ* > *e* (*wes* 1, *fer* 5, *stret* 5; the original most likely had *þet* and not *þat* in v. 29).

Versification. Rimed couplets of six to seven beats to a line; rimes sometimes defective or approximate (*aros : Judas* 1-2, *þat* [*þet*] *: spec* 29-30, *miȝte : cniȝtes* [originally *cniȝte*] *: fiȝte* 31-4).

---

1. Scere Þorsday 'Holy Thursday' lit. 'Thursday of purification' alluding to confession and cleaning of altars on this day. This term, in opposition to Maundy Thursday is of Scandinavian origin (ON *Skiri þōrsdagr*, Danish *Skærtorsdag*).

1. aros riming with *Judas*; it is tempting to correct to *aras* as consonant with the original, but approximate rimes with proper names are rather frequent.

3. þou most to Jurselem: verb of motion omitted after modal, cp § 150. — **oure** here and in l. 28 is a form of 2 sg 'your'.

4. þritti platen of selver. 'thirty pieces of silver'. Note the wk pl *platen*. The Wyclifte translation of the Bible has *plates* (MATTH. XXVI. 15).

8. 'Judas you were worthy (that) people stoned you with stones'.

12. 'If my Lord Christ knew it'.

14. Slep þou þe 'go to sleep'. The reflexive with verbs is quite current in ME. Cp. farther on, *hym com* 19, 25, 33, *stod him* 29, *him stod* 31, *him crowe* 36.

17. 'He pulled out his hair till (his head) was bathed in blood'. Ballad style is very free with exaggeration.

20. Wolte for *wolt þou* 'do you want to'.

25. 'Our Lord came walking in', see § 129.1a.

26. Wou = *how*.

29. am I þat 'is this me?' To rime with *spec* C. F. CHILD supposes an omitted *frec, am I þat frec,* 'am I that man?'

30. 'I was never in [o] a place where people spoke evil of you'.

32. cniȝtes: the original must have had *cniȝte* (OE gen pl. *cnihta*) to rime with *miȝte, fiȝte.*

4

Text from Harley MS 2253 (ca. 1310).

Spelling. Note *ant* for *and* (3, 7, 14 etc.), *u* for *w* (*suete* 15, etc. and *bituene* 33).

Phonology. OE *y* survives, written *u* [ü] (*muchel* 31, *nulle* 20). Palatalized *k* > *ch* is abundant: *þench* 15 (concurrent with *þenke* 31), *seche* 20, *speche* 18, *eche* 22, *leche* 24, *muchel* 31.

Inflexions. *Verb.* — Pres 2 sg *mihtes* 22 alongside *lovest* 27; 3 sg in *-s* (*singes* 1, *springes* 3, *drynkes* 7, *says* 27) alongside *-þ* (*reweþ* 14, *deþ* 8); 3 pl in *-en* (*waxen* 2).

Versification. Stanza of four verses with four plus three beats (printed on separate lines) and a single rime (*aaaa*). The last stanza is irregular (*aaab*).

4. **Averyl** is the French form (OF *avril*).

8. **deþ me tene** 'causes me grief' (if *tene* is a noun) or 'does trouble me' (if *tene* is a vb).

18. 'a speech of love'.

25. The vb *preȝe* was formerly constructed with *of* followed by the thing desired where today we should use 'for', cp. *OED*, s.v. *pray* 1 *c* (G. L. BROOK).

30. **þou loke þat it be sene** 'see to it that it is apparent'.

32. **grene** 'pale' cp. 'green-sickness'.

33 f. Another of the 'Harley Lyrics', *Advice to Women*, l. 30 has also *from Leycestre to Lounde* and it has been supposed that Lounde refers to a place now called *Lound* in Lincs, Notts or Suffolk (from ON *lundr* 'grove'); but Lounde is also a possible 14th cent. form of London (recorded for instance in *Beves of Hamptoun* l. 3490) and if London is 57 miles from Northampton, Lindsey is 100 miles from Lincoln, so that it cannot be argued that the distance is too great.

36. **as I go fore y-bounde** 'for whom I go in slavery'; the preposition *fore* is postpositional.

40. 'to one who it belongs to'.

5

Text from same MS as preceding selection.

Same remarks.

Versification. Stanza of eight verses *aaa⁴b³ccc⁴b³*, with alliteration and assonance.

9. **wurhliche won** 'the world', a current ME alliterative phrase.

15. 'She must mingle with (i. e. be compared to) many merry things'.

29. **smal** 'slender', a sense common in OE and ME.

43. Böddeker's emendation of *fiele* to *fiþele* 'fiddle' is not absolutely necessary; *fiele* might be the form (unrecorded in English before the 18th cent.) of OF *viele* (ModF *vielle*) influenced in its initial consonant by OE *fiþele* (G. L. Brook). *crouþ* is a Celtic word for an early, six-stringed fiddle (Welsh *crwth*).

45 ff. A comparison of the lady's virtues with precious stones was a frequent feature in French metrical romances (and their ME counterparts).

48. 'the banner of beauty'.

52. The qualities and virtues praised in the 'lady' answer to the chivalric ideal of the time; cp. G. L. Brook, *The Harley Lyrics*, pp. 11-12.

55-78 contain an allegory in which the poet complains that his lady has taken possession of his heart.

XIV

Text from British Museum MS Harley 1701, called *H* (ca. 1360) with readings from Bodleian MS 415, called *O* (ca. 1400). Anglo-Norman original from MS Harley 273.

Dialect of the Northeast Midlands (south of Lincolnshire) at the beginning of the 14th century.

Spelling. The MS prefers *u* to *o* before nasals and *r* (*sunne* 57, *cumpanye* 66, *tunge* 78, *cumþ* 4154, *turnede* 77, *wurlde* 4139, *wurþy* 4134); note *noun* for *none* 4050 etc.; the letter *y* is preferred to *i* in all positions. The MS, being late, has *gh(t)* instead of *ȝ(t)*. It also shows the current Northern practice of using *y* to mark the length of a preceding *e* (thus *weyl* 87, 4053, 4076 alongside *wele* 4066, *beyn* for *bēn* 85).

Inflexions. *Personal pronouns.* — 3 sg nom *þey* 4020, poss *here* 4014, dat *hem*.

Verb. — Present 3 sg in -(*e*)*þ* (*greteþ* 61, *seyþ* 4162, *clepyþ* 82, *doþ* 4137) exceptionally in -(*e*)*s* (*sees* 81 : *pecches*) 3 pl in -(*e*)*n* (*clepyn* 80, *seyn* 4164, *beyn* 85) or in -*e* (*calle* 4005, *be* 4026, *are* 4133, *make* 4135, *synne* 4151, *have* *be* 4140).

Present part in -*yng* (*stynkyng* 4127, *consentyng* 4128); past part without preverb *i-*; -*n* is often lost in strong vbs (*slayn* 4096, 4102 but *do* 4097, 4106, *be* 4140).

Syntax rather loose; many sentences badly constructed.

Versification. Octosyllabic rimed couplets. The last *MS* suppresses a certain number of -*e*'s which the meter shows were pronounced:

A 'gode 'clerk⟨ë⟩ 'was þe 'toon	4007
For 'þat he 'shuld⟨ë⟩ 'dwel a'lonë	4024
Þus 'prey⟨ë⟩d 'Florens 'yn hys 'bedë	4031
Yn 'God 'truly y 'tryst⟨ë⟩ 'so	4110

---

57 ff. Robert of Brunne " addresses himself rather particularly to the souls close to whom he lives and in whose midst he perhaps served his ministry, that is to the good people of Bourne, and especially the parish of Sempring-ham. And it is this care to offer his readers a spiritual nourishment quite appropriate to their needs which presides over his task and which explains the manner in which he conceives and carries out his role of translator." (E. J. Arnould).

62. þat may to prow 'that may (be) to good advantage'.

63. Brunnewake yn Kestevene is nothing (according to John W. HALES, *Academy* 31, 27) but the village of Bourne, the author's birthplace, and probably surnamed *Wake* from the name of some important family in the district.

65. þe pryorye: that of Sempringham. According to what is known about the priors Jone of Cameltoun (1. 68) and Jone of Clyntoun (1. 71) mentioned by the author, it is probable that Robert of Brunne was there from 1302 to 1317 (cp. Ruth CROSBY, "Robert Mannyng of Brunne: A new Biography" in *PMLA* 57 (1942), 15 ff.), that he was a canon and that he possibly was master of the novices.

73. Dane Felyp: Philip of Burton who was master of the order of Gilbertines from 1298 to 1332.

74. ryme 'poem in rimed verse'.

76. Very useful information. The poem must have been started in 1303; but the best MS dates no earlier than ca. 1360.

79. 'from a book where [as] I found (it) in'.

88. Note that this *Manuel de Pechiez* attributed to William of Wadington and the direct source of *Handlyng Synne* was the object of two other English translations. One in prose, about 1350, still in MS (cp. H. E. ALLEN, "An English Prose Version of the *Manuel des Pechiez*" in *Modern Philology* XIII, 743 ff., and E. J. ARNOULD, *l. c.*, 319 ff.); the other is an adaptation in verse made in the 15th century by a certain Peter Idle (cp. *Peter Idley's Instructions to his Son* ed. by Ch. d'EVELYN, Boston and London, 1935, and E. J. ARNOULD, *l. c.*, 335 ff.) based on *Handlyng Synne*.

4001 ff. The story that follows is taken from St. Gregory, *Dialogues* III, xv (*Patrologie Latine*, LXXVII c. 249) and is also found in the medieval English fabulist Odo of Cheriton. It was frequently retold in England in the Middle Ages.

4014. 'in their time the abbot did die'.

4015. þys yche 'this same'; yche is a Midland form which corresponds to *ilk(e)* in the North. Similarly in 1. 4837, 4043, 4065 etc.

4031. yn hys bede 'in his prayers'.

4037-8. Note the clear distinction between the Northern dialect loan-word *gate* (ON *gata*) 'way, road' and Southern ȝate 'gate, doorway' (OE ȝeat); *gate* survives in Standard English but with the Southern meaning.

4041. Piece of humor added to the original by Robert of Brunne.

4047. For a myracle 'For it was a miracle'.

4058. twyys 'for the second time'.

4059. at hygh undurne 'at terce,' the third hour of the canonical day ending about nine in the morning.

4062. þe noun 'the hour of nones', a daily office said at the ninth hour of the day (about 3 p.m.) but in later use sometimes earlier; hence ModE *noon*.

4068. At hys bere 'from his bear'.

4074. he ȝafe to hem kepe 'he gave them protection'.

4078. shepe to were 'to tend sheep'.

4089. þey dyd þat woghte 'they did that wrongful thing'.

4099 ff. 'yet he lamented more the unfortunate fact that vengeance must certainly [*shulde*] fall on them, than he lamented his own loss [*dere*] (in) that they had slain his good bear'.

4106. was do adawe 'had been put [*do*] to death'.

4114. þat hylpe me 'the one who helped me'; *hylpe* is the str pret of *helpe.*

4116. he ded no man folye, cp. the French text 'il ne lur fesoit mal ne ennui'.

4119. þat 'since'.

4126. 'Their limbs rotted under their eyes', (*yne* pl. of *eye*) or perhaps 'before their eyes did rot', cp. French text, l. 4009.

4127 f. Note these two uses of the expanded form and cp. § 133. From the 14th to the 16th cent. the verb *consent* was widely used in the form *to be consenting.* (F. MOSSÉ, *Histoire de la Forme périphrastique*, Paris, 1938, II § 72).

4130 f. resun why þat 'because'.

4136. 'or (make it so that) relatives [*frendys*] are not avenged'. This meaning of *friend* is current in OE, but its currency here in ME is due to Scandinavian influence (cp. 10/133), as is the term *unsaght* (ON *ūsáttr*).

4147 ff. These touching international reflections on the French leanings towards lechery and the English towards envy are Robert of Brunne's personal additions to his French original.

4158. hym shryve 'confess himself and be pardoned'.

4159 f. 'Though every day a man practises it (confession for the sin of envy), it (absolution) will not be granted him'.

4162. He seyþ aȝen 'he replies'; *aȝen* here is 'again' or 'back'.

4166. 'so that envy may not blind us (to ourselves)'.

XV

Text from the holograph and unique British Museum MS Arundel 57; the original French from MS Cotton Cleopatra A 5. *Book of Vices and Virtues* from Huntington Library MS HM 147 (after the edition of Nelson FRANCIS, London, 1942); Caxton's text from the edition of 1486.

Dialect: pure Kentish of about 1340.

Spelling. *u* is frequently used for *w* after *z* (*zuych* 3, *zuyn* 5, *zuo* 8, *zuelz* 37), after *h, hu-* equals OE *hw-* (*huanne* 10, *huet* 24, *huer* 61, *huader* 25, *huo* 42) also apparently after *g* (*guo* 5, *guod* 27) and *k* (*kueade* 31); *ss* seems to represent [š] (*ssepe* 'sheep' 13, *viss* 'fish' 15, *ssame* 'shame' 17, *sselt* 'shalt' etc.). *y* is used, concurrently with *i*, as well for the vowel [i] (*wyn* 29, *matyns* 23, *hy* 40) as for the semi-vowel [j] (*yaf* 4, *yesteneven* 27, *yelde* 64, *voryet* 'forget' 48); *y* and *i* have the value [j] before a vowel in the same syllable (*þyef* 34, *þieves* 77, *dyad* 29, *sostyeni* 68); *ȝ* indicates [ç] after front vowels (*liȝte, riȝte* 64) and [g] (*oȝene* 61, *zuelȝ* 49) or [x] after back vowels (*þaȝ* 50, *maȝt* 51).

Phonology. West Saxon *ȳ* is represented by *ē* (already present in Old Kentish): *verst* 'first' 1, *zenne* 'sin' 1, *cherche* 'church' 22, *dede* 'did' 14, *nelle* ' nill ' 51, *velþe* ' filth ' 72; similarly West Saxon *ǽ>ē* (*veste* ' fast ' 19, *hedde* 27, *wes* 29, *þet* 1, *efter* 51, *hest* 56); Old Kentish *ĭō* (West Saxon *ēo*) >*ye* (*dyevel* ' devil ' 2, *yernþ* 12, *þyef* 34) similarly Old Kentish *ē* (West Saxon *ĭe*) >*ye* (*y-hyerþ* 56, *hierþe* 65); OE *ēa>ya* after *d* (*dyad* 29, *dyave* 65) elsewhere reduced to *a* (*grat* 3), sometimes written *ea* (*heaved* 30, *cheastes* 75); after *g* there is *no* (<OE *ā, ō*): *guo* 5, *guod* 27.

Initially and before *l* and *r*, *f>v* (*velaȝe* ' fellow ' 10, *vynde* ' find ' 25, *volke* ' folk ' 39, *vot* ' foot ' 68); before a vowel or *w*, *s>z* (though with much less regularity): *zigge, zenne* 1, *zuyn* ' swine ' 5, *ze* ' sea ' 6, *zeche* ' seek ' 17, *zayþ* ' saith ' 19.

Inflexions. *Substantives.* — Alongside normal forms (gen sg -(e)*s*, pl. -(e)*s*) there is dat sg in -*e* (*manne* 3, *dyevle* 60); pl. in -*en* : *nykken* 53, *blyssen* 4$_A$/12, 13, *dyevlen* 4) .

Definite article. — Alongside invariable *þe* there is acc sg *þane* 15, dat sg *þan, þa*, neuter *þet* 29, 30, 4$_A$/23, acc pl *þo* 4$_A$/21.

Personal pronouns. — 1 sg *ich;* 3 sg M nom *he* 33, *ha* 67, acc *hine* 35, dat *him* 13, F *hy* 22; ;3 pl nom *hi* 5, *hy* 9, acc *hise* 5, 7, *his* 4$_A$/18, poss *hyre* 4$_A$/2, *hare* 37, dat *ham* 5, 7.

Verb. — Present 3 sg in -(*e*)*þ* (*makeþ* 16, *loveþ* 18, *heþ* 3, *nymþ* 15) and numerous contracted forms in -*t* (*halt* 10, *arist* 11, *abyt* 22, *let* 32, *voryet* 48, *gret* 48, *onderstant* 69, *ret* 72); pl in -*eþ* (*we redeþ* 4, *hi habbeþ* 42).

Infinitive without -*n* (*ete* 8, *telle* 42, *bere* 68), often in -*i* or -*ye* for OE. second class wk vbs (*maki* 44, *hongi* 76, *herye* 4$_A$/22, *zuerie* 73) and for French loans (*porchaci* 40, *werri* 77, *askapie* 51). Present participle in -*inde* (*onzyginde* 4$_A$/9). Past participle almost always preceded by *y*- (*y-by* 29, *y-herd* 56); loss of -*n* in str vbs (*y-dronke* 31, *y-come* 46, *y-do* 59'*).

Verb ' to be ': infinitive *by* 4$_A$/23; pres 3 sg *ys* 60, 3 pl *byeþ* 37; subjunctive pres 3 pl *by* 43; past part *y-by* 29.

Vocabulary. Large number of French loan-words.

---

1 f. *þet þe dyevel is moche myde y-payd* lit. ' which the devil is very well satisfied with [*myde*] '.

4. *þe dyevlen* ' to the devils '.

5. *hise adreynten* '(they) drowned them [*hise*] '; *hise*, acc pl of 3rd personal (cp. 2/55 note). Same construction l. **7.**

18 f. *in him y-lefth* ' believe in him '. Dan Michel has read French *croit* instead of *crient*.

22. *þe cherche nys non hare, hy abyt me wel* ' the church is not a hare, it [*hy*, fem = ' church '] will surely wait for me '.

30. *t'eve* ' yesterday evening '. — *by an ese* ' be at ease '. — *alhuet* ' until '.

31. *þous to þe kueade zayþ* ' Thus he says to the evil ', does not render the French *Ci a malvais dit* ' This is a bad speech '.

32. *let = ledeþ* ' leads '.

35. The author now explains that the sin of gluttony is divided into five branches according to whether one eats and drinks before the appointed time or too greedily, or without moderation, or with too much ardor, or, finally, in too great abundance. This last point is the subject of the ' fifth branch ' (*vifte boȝ*) that follows.

36. bysihede here and l. 39, like *bysinesse*, l. 43, means 'deep concern about', almost 'research in' food and drink (OF *curiosité*).

37. zuelȝ renders the French *palais* 'palate' and ll. 38, 49, the F *goule* vulgar for 'mouth'.

43. to þan þet 'so that'.

50. þe tonge þe lyckestre: Dan Michel has misunderstood the French text, *la langue la lecheresse* 'the tongue of the voluptuary woman'.

52. recorder: we would expect *recordinge;* Dan Michel has negligently reproduced the French *recorder*.

54. mosseles 'morsels' pl in spite of the sg vb *blefte*. Dan Michel has taken the French *morsiaus* 'morsel' for a pl, but has neglected concord.

72. ret = *redeþ* 'reads'.

XVI

Text. 1. Thornton MS (Lincoln Cathedral, before 1450) with readings from Durham MS (Cosin Library). — 2. Cambridge Univ. Library MS Dd. v. 64 (ca. 1400) with readings from MS Rawlinson A 389 (called *R*).

Dialect of Yorkshire (Northern English).

Spelling. These late MSS use *gh* instead of ȝ (*noghte* 1, *lyghtly* 5); *y* often replaces *i* (*lyf* 54, *fyre* 94 etc.); final *-es* is often *-ys*, sometimes *-ez* (*wyngez* 6).

Phonology. OE *ā* remains *ā* (*gaa* 41, *sary* 61, *gaste* 79, *swa* passim and *sa* alongside *so*, *twa* 14, *fra* 10); OE *ō>ū* or [ü] (*gude* 15); OE *ȳ̆>ī̆* (*miry*-85<OE *myrġe*, *syn* 88); in final position or before *i*, *k* is not palatalized and remains *k* (*wyrke* 2, *swylke* 24, *mekill* 22, *whylke* 29 'which').

Inflexions. The pl of sbs is always in -(e)s.

Personal pronouns. — 3 sg F *scho* (1, 2, etc.); 3 pl nom *þay* 8, *þey* 24, poss *þaire* 18, *þeire* 28, dat *þam* 19, *thaym* 3.

Verb. — Present 3 sg in -(e)s (*has* 1, *castys* 3, *puttes* 3, etc.); 3 pl. equally in -(e)s (*has* 37, *lufes* 7, *afforces* 19, *passes* 32) but in -(e) when the pronoun subject immediately precedes, or follows (*þay take* 11, *we luf* 86 etc.).

The infinitive is without *-n*; when it is a verb complement it may be preceded by *at* (*at cleth* 92) instead of *to* (*to reve* 19, etc.).

Present participle in *-and* (*prayand*, *thynkande*, *redande* 8), past part without *-i*; str vbs in *-n* (*blawen* 12).

Verb 'to be': pres indicative 3 sg *es*, pl *are* (*ere* 8), pres subjunctive *be*, infinitive *be*.

Note the forms *dose* 63, 92, 93 for 'does', *thou will* 74, *sal(l)* 91, 98 for 'shall', *sulde* 18 for 'should'.

---

1. thre kyndis 'three (distinctive) features'.

4. scho takes erthe: these first lines are an adaptation, undoubtedly through some intermediate Latin source, of the *Historia Animalium*, ix, 40 usually attributed to Aristotle (which accounts for the use of his name in l. 17 and 31).

5. 'so that she is easily carried too high in the windy air'.

17. þe bees are feghtande: cp. *Hist. Anim.*, ix, 27; the expanded forms are quite current in 14th cent. Northern English, but the exact meaning and use are still very uncertain. That Rolle delighted in series of present participles and made them a stylistic feature of his prose is shown by ll. 9-10 above.

21. The MS *ynesche* has been emended by K. Sisam to *ynence* 'towards'. The Durham MS reads *anempts* which has the same meaning.

39. in þe waye 'on the way'.

45. strucyo or storke is an error. Latin *struthio* can mean either 'ostrich' or 'stork', but here it is 'ostrich' that fits most naturally.

51 ff. The passage is taken from *The Form of Living*, chap. x. In lines 51-91 "much is taken from Hugo of Strasbourg's *Compendium theologicae veritatis* (v, cap. 23) which is here quoting *De Vita Contemplativa* of Julianus Pomerius. St. Augustine *De Ecclesiasticis Moribus* (1. 11) is also drawn on. It was also the fashion to define secular love with much eloquence (cp. *Romania* 4, p. 382, where examples are cited in French, English and Latin" H. E. ALLEN and cp. also 13/5 above).

67. trowthe here 'faith' (similarly in l. 69).

72. til beggar-staf: perhaps 'even to the beggar-staff' — **if we kan** 'if we know'.

73. Construe *es ordande noght bot sorow and torment*.

76. þat nane etc. 'which none but God knows'.

91-96. Imitated from St. Bernard, *De dilig. Deo*, cap. x, *Sermo xix in cant.*, 5 (MIGNE *Patr. Lat.* CLXXXII, cc. 991, 183, 865).

98. als it war 'as it were'.

<h2 style="text-align:center">XVII</h2>

Text from the unique British Museum MS Cotton Galba E IX (ca. 1400-20). **Dialect:** Northern with Midland traits.

Spelling very modern; *y* is avoided except as a final, *ʒ* is transcribed *gh*; note *cum* 42, *gude* 47.

Phonology. OE *ā* remains *ā* (*gaste* 8, *hame* 89), but *o* also appears (*fro* 20, *no* 57 etc.); OE *ǟ* is *a* (*langer* 16, 65 alongside *lenger* 35, an umlauted form), OE *ǣ* is often *ā* (*whare* 14, *þare* 65, *war* 54, 71 etc.).

Inflexions. Note the demonstrative pl *þo* 32, and 3 pl personal pronoun *þai* 85, *þaire* 15, *þam* 34.

Verb. — Pres 3 sg in -(*e*)*s*, *-is* (*has* 2, *ordanis* 5). Imperative 2 pl in *-es* (*leves* 73). Note *suld* 86 for 'should'.

Vocabulary. Note Scandinavian *ger* 'do, make', *so-gat* 'thus' 93.

Versification. Stanza $a^4a^4b^3c^4c^4b^3$ with a loose and frequent use of alliteration, cp. v. 10.

And Mari moder of mercy fre.

---

1 ff. For this poem the reader is referred to the passage in Froissart's *Chronicles* dealing with these events, ed. S. LUCE Bk I, §§ 85-88. COVILLE describes the situation thus (in LAVISSE, *Histoire de France*, IV, 1, 43-4): "At the end of September 1339 the King of England finally brought an army of various forces to besiege Cambrai, defended by a French garrison. On his part, the King of France had given orders for his knights and vassals to gather at Péronne, Bapaume and Arras for the summer of 1339, but he, as well as they, was late getting into the field. The operations, started in the autumn, could not last long. Edward III, in spite of the fine displays of prowess of his knights, had to give up the difficult siege of Cambrai. Having advanced into Picardy as far as Buironfosse during a three weeks' ravaging of the countryside, he found himself opposed by the French army about half a league off. A formal battle was requested for the 21st or 22nd of October; but on the 21st the French troops were too tired by their march. The 22nd was a Friday and King Robert of Sicily, 'grand astrologer', had written Philip to dissuade him from battle. The King of France made no attack and finally departed. This was a check to Edward III who had prepared this formidable appearing expeditionary force over a long period of time."

6. 'until [*to*] (the) time he thinks (it best) for fighting'.

7. of mightes maste 'most of might', 'the most powerful'.

18. grapes 'wine' as is possible also in ModE.

22. The Duke of Brabant was actually allied with Edward III against the French; this alliance may have determined Philip's refusal to fight.

25. þe riche floure-de-lice i. e. Philip of Valois (similarly *þe lely flowre*, l. 91).

28. þe right aire: allusion to Edward III's pretensions to the French throne.

31. Sir Philip þe Valayse is Philip of Valois or Philip VI, King of France (1293-1350), under whom the Hundred Years War started. This poem refers to one of the first episodes of the war.

40. ascry: according to J. HALL 'report by spies'.

43-48. Detail perhaps invented by the poet (Froissart does not report it) to exalt the king and his power. Edward prays to God and the weather clears.

51. The subject of *thoght* is *oure king*.

53. bydene is a frequent metrical expletive adding nothing appreciable to the verse meaning.

56. dwell 'await battle'.

57. gayned him no gle 'this availed him no sport'; this locution is not rare, cp *OED*, s. v. *glee* 3*b*.

62 f. Philip had 'great oaks felled' to slow the English pursuit; but it was his pride that was beat down (*abated*, l. 64).

67. The King of Bohemia, John of Luxembourg, and the King of Navarre (l. 70) as well as the King of Scotland, allies of Philip, were with him in Flanders.

71. The MS text is corrupt; we adopt J. HALL's emendation 'they were happy [*fain*] for fear, to hide their heads in the ferns'.

73. 'and believe (it) well—it is no lie'; *leves* is 2 pl imperative.

77. 'and dukes who were held to be [*tolde*] valiant'.

80. Froissart too shows Edward penetrating into Berwick in 1333 'a grant solennité de trompes et de nakaires' (Bk I, § 52).

91. Cp. above l. 25.

95. him till = *till him* 'to him'.

96. keped him in þe berde ' opposed him resolutely, bearded him '; although the sense is clear, the form of this idiom is obscure.

XVIII

Text from unique British Museum MS Cotton Nero A 10.

Dialect of the Northwest Midlands (South Lancashire or Northwest of Derby).

Spelling. The letter ȝ is used with different phonetic and graphic values.

a) Voiceless palatal spirant [ç] (German *ich*): *knyȝt* 734, *nyȝtes* 730;

b) Semi-vowel [j] which was most generally written *y* in London and Southern dialects: *ȝelde* ' yield ' 1263, *ȝere* ' year ' 1382, *ȝonge* ' young ' 1317;

c) Owing probably to a tradition going back to OE scribes ȝ was still used wherever OE had had a voiced velar spirant [g] (cp. *HOE* § 14). For instance what was pronounced [au] is written either -*aȝ*- or -*aw*-: *haȝþorne* ' hawthorn ' 744, *saȝe* ' saw ' 1202 (<OE *sagu*), but *drawen* 1233; what was pronounced [u] was sometimes written -*oȝ*- and sometimes -*ow*-, -*ou*-; *roȝe* ' rough ' 745, *droȝ* ' drew ' 1188, *boȝed* ' bowed ' 1189, *unnoȝe* ' enough ' 1251 (also *innoghe* 730), but *innowe* 1401, *douthe* 1365 (< OE *duguð*);

d) Further, in this MS the letter ȝ is used *at the end of words* to represent the letter *z* borrowed by English scribes from French, which indicates either [s] or [z] according to phonetic environment (ModE writing uses *s* for this: cp. *bugs/bucks*). In this case to avoid confusion this ȝ has been transcribed *z* and we print *frendez* 714, *rydez* 714, *watz* ' was ' 741, *gotz* ' goes ' 1293 where the MS has *frendeȝ*, *rydeȝ*, *watȝ*, *gotȝ*. But this last use was not obligatory in the MS where we also find -*s* (*wolves* 720, *rydes* 740, *twyges* 746).

qu- is used alongside *wh-* and apparently with the same phonetic value [hw], [xw] or [ʍ]. We find *quyl* 1180, *quat* 1186, *quen* 1194, etc. alongside ·*whyle* 720, *what* 1163.

There is occasional confusion of *v* and *w* (*wowche* ' vouch ' 1391, *awyse* ' advise ' 1389); note also the use of *w* with the value of [u] in *blw(e)* ' blew ' 1141, 1362, *nwe* ' new '. The sound [u] besides has other various but more usual spellings, *ow* (*yowre* 1279, *now* 1292), *ou* (*foule* 717, *goud* 1213, *mounte* 740) and finally *u* (*hunt* 1320, *bullez* 722) not to mention *o* before *m, n, v* (*wondered* 1201, *slomeryng* 1182, *gome* 748, *loved* 1281).

Phonology. OE *ā* before nasals is sometimes *a* (*game* 1314, *hande* 1203, but most often *o* (*gomen* 1376, *honde* 1270, *bonkkez* 1163, *þonk* 1380, *fongen* 1265).

OE *y* is generally represented by *i* (written *i* or *y*) *hillez* 742, *dyn* 1183, *kysse* 1303, *myry* 1263) but remains [ü] in *lur* (OE *lyre*) 1284, *burde* (OE **byrde*) 752, *dunte* (OE *dynt*) 1286 and even occasionally appears as *e* (*meryly* 740).

OE *eo* before *r* becomes either [ü] (*burne*<OE *beorn*, 1189; *rurde*<OE *reord* 1149) or most often *e* [ɛ] (*erthe* 728, *herttez* 1154).

Inflexions. *Personal pronouns.* — 3 sg F *ho* 738 (also, but infrequently, *scho* 1259); 3 pl nom *þay* 1127, poss *hor* 1127, 1252, *her* 1129, 1232, exceptionally *þayr* 1363, dat *hem* 748, 1130.

Verb. — Pres 3 sg in -*(e)s*, -*ez* (*rennez* 731, *glydez* 748 etc.), pl in -*en* (*brayen, bleden, deʒen* 1163, *folden* 1363), sometimes in *-e* (*fonge* 1363, *bere* 1229, *crave* 1384), sometimes with zero flexion (*haf* 1396) and also in *-es, -ez* (*folʒes* 1164, *lykez* 1234).

Present participle in *-ande* (*crakkande* 1166, *claterande* 731, *laʒande* 1207), exceptionally in *-ing* (*sykyng* 753). Past participle without preverb *i-*, in *-en* for str vbs (*knowen* 1272).

Vocabulary. As in all alliterative poetry (cp. *HOE* § 205), there are many synonyms for frequently used notions. Thus for 'man, men' or 'knight(s)' there is *burne* 1189, 1232, 1325, *frekes* 1172, 1275, *hapel* 1138, *gome* 748, *knyʒt* 736, *ledes* 1170, 1195, 1231, 1306, *mon* 718, *renk* 1134, *segge* 1385, *wyʒe* 715, 1132, 1276; similarly 'move (rapidly) towards' appears, according to alliterative needs, as *busk* 1136, *boʒe* 1189, 1220, *kever* 1221, *meve* 1312, *steppe* 1191.

This great richness of vocabulary forms one of the difficulties with this poem. Many words are Scandinavian loan-words, for example *cost* 'observance' 750, *boun* 'ready' 1311, *layke* 'play' 1178, *trayst* 'assured' 1211, *stor* 'strong' 1291, *frayst* 'ask' 1395, *wayth* '(spoils won by) hunting' 1381. Some words otherwise familiar in ME are found here in a phonetic form influenced by Scandinavian, thus *lig* 'lie' 1179, *gef* 'give' 1290, *skere* 'sheer, pure' 1261 (beside *schyre* 1378).

But the French loan-words are still more numerous. We cite *plytes* 'plight' 733, *baret* 'trouble' 752, *cacheres* 'dog-grooms' 1139, *mote* 'moot' 1141, *braches* 'hounds' 1142, *vewter* 'keepers of deer-hounds' 1146, *abloy* 'carried away' 1174, *aspye* 'discover' 1199, *bourdez* 'jests' 1212, *daynté* 'courtesy' 1250, *louve* 'to praise' 1256, *barayne* 'barren' 1320, *querré* 'quarry' 1324, *chevicaunce* 'gain' 1390, *beau sir* 1222, *grant mercy* 'many thanks' 1392, *pure joye* 1247.

Versification. Alliterative stanza with indefinite number of lines (from 12 to 38) without rime, terminated by a 'bob and wheel' of five short rimed verses of type $a^1b^3a^3b^3a^3$.

Note on Middle English Alliterative Verse.

Between 1340 and 1450 in the West-Midlands and the North there was what is known as the Alliterative Revival, a movement which produced verse comparable to OE forms: the most notable works being *Sir Gawain*, *Morte Arthure* and *Piers Plowman*. This requires a long line divided by a caesura into two half-lines linked to each other by alliteration. For the fundamental structure of this verse the reader is referred to the first part of this series (*HOE* § 208 ff.). The present note will be confined to the differences and alterations which appear in Middle English, basing these remarks chiefly on *Sir Gawain and the Green Knight*.

In the following sketch, I designate by •*A* the first stressed syllable of the second half-line which commands the alliteration of the whole line, by *a* or *b* other stressed syllables which bear the alliteration and finally by *x* a stressed syllable that plays no part in the alliteration. In OE, where many variations were possible, the normal pattern for an alliterative long line was *aa Ax*.

1. Instead of the first, it is sometimes the second strong stress in the 2nd half-line that carries the alliteration (pattern *aa xA* instead of *aa Ax*):

   And 'set hir ful 'softly   on þe 'bed-'syde   1193

2. Not infrequently both strongly stressed syllables in the 2nd half-line alliterate (pattern *aa Aa*):

ᵓRichen hem þe ᵓrychest   to ᵓryde alle aᵓrayde   1130
In a ᵓsomer ᵓsesun,   whon ᵓsofte was þe ᵓsonne   21₁/1

3. The alliteration in the whole line may be reduced to two stressed syllables, one in each half-line (patterns *ax Ax, xa Ax*):

Bi þay were ᵓtened at þe ᵓhyȝe   and ᵓtaysed to þe ᵓwattrez 1169
Þen ᵓmuch of þe ᵓgarysoun   oþer ᵓgolde þat þay ᵓhaven   1255

4. The alliteration may be double (patterns *ab Ab* or *bb Aa*):

Bot hit ar ᵓlaydes inᵓnoȝe   þat ᵓlever wer ᵓnowþe   1251
Bot þe ᵓburde hym ᵓblessed   and bi þis ᵓskyl ᵓsayde   1296

5. Three stressed alliterating syllables are often found in the first half-line (*aaa Ax*):

He ᵓfonde a ᵓfoo hym byᵓfore   bot ᵓferly hit ᵓwere   716

and thus possibly five alliterating syllables in the same verse (pattern *aaa Aa*):

ᵓDer ᵓdrof in þe ᵓdale   ᵓdoted for ᵓdrede   1151

6. On the other hand some verses have no alliteration at all:

Hit is þe ᵓworchyp of yourᵓself,   þat ᵓnoȝt bot wel ᵓconnez 1267

7. Words starting with *h* may alliterate with words starting with a vowel,

And he ᵓhevez up his ᵓhed   ᵓout of þe ᵓcloþes   1184

w, wh, qu alliterate,

I schal ᵓware my ᵓwhyle ᵓwel   ᵓquyl hit ᵓlastez   1235

and voiced with the corresponding voiceless sound (especially *f* and *v*):

ᵓVerayly his ᵓvenysoun   to ᵓfetch hym byᵓforne   1375

Similarly 21₂/194, 21₃/49, 53.

8. Contrary to OE practice the rhythm is purely accentual and the stressed syllable is not necessarily long.

9. With this reservation there are, in the 2nd half-line, structures analogous to Sievers' types A, B, C and E:

A	ᵓglydez hem ᵓunder 748	x́ x x́ x
B	watz ᵓnot þe ᵓlast 1133	x x́ x x́
C	and ᵓyow ᵓgod þoȝt 1245	x x́ x́ x
E	ᵓmon all hym ᵓone 749	x́ x x x́

10. But this four syllable structure has become the exception. What has become the rule in ME is the large number of unstressed syllables, especially in the first half-line, either before the stressed syllable (anacrusis) or after.

A	ᵓRichen hem þe ᵓrychest 1130	x́ x x x x́ x
E	ᵓDouteles he hade ben ᵓded 725	x́ x x x x x x́
A	Nade he ben ᵓduȝty and ᵓdryse 724	x x x | x́ x x x́ x
E	Into a ᵓforest ful ᵓdep 741	x x x | x́ x x x́

Therefore the distinction into types A, B, C, E becomes sometimes difficult if not artificial. Thus the last two examples cited might equally be interpreted as an elongated B-type. Often the impression made on the reader is only that of a falling (A) or rising (B) rhythm or of a combination of both.

On the whole question see the very careful study by J. P. OAKDEN, *Alliterative Poetry in Middle English*, I. *The Dialectal and Metrical Survey* (Manchester, 1930).

---

716. bot ferly hit were ' unless he found ... it was something extraordinary '.

717. foule ' ugly, frightful ' (meaning still current in dialectal British English, and standard American in *a foul day*).

718. bi mount ' in the mountains '.

724. and Dryȝten had served ' and (if he) had (not) served the Lord '.

726. þat ' but that '.

731. þer as ' there where '.

745. raged probably ' hoar-frosted '; according to Mrs. E. WRIGHT, *Englische Studien* 36.217, who compares the English dialect *rag* ' hoar-frost '.

748. Gryngolet: Gawain's horse.

749. al hym one ' all alone '. To reinforce *one* ' alone ' the personal pronoun is added in the dative *hym one, us one*, etc., or *al* (from which *al one* for example l. 736) or both as here. The poss adj could also be used, for ex. *oure one* ' us alone ' l. 1230. Note the pleonasm in ModE *all *al-one* (*a-lone*).

750. carande for his costes: the interpretations of this passage vary. It can be read ' anxious about his difficult situation ' (cp. l. 2495 *costes of care* ' difficult trials ') or, with TOLKIEN-GORDON ' concerned about his (religious) duties ' — **kever** ' get to '.

762. Cros Kryst me spede ' Christ's cross help me succeed ', current formula (generally in the order *Kryst Cros*; but this is possibly a trace of OF *crois Christ*). It was used at school before saying the alphabet which was arranged on the hornbook in the form of a cross, and was called *croscrist* or *Christ cross* (cp. ModE *criss-cross row*).

1126 ff. The author's uncommonly detailed information about deer-hunting has been admired in this description. Cp. another hunting-scene in 27₁/344 ff.

1137. ' At the moment when [*by þat*] the last [*any*] ray of daylight gleamed on earth '.

1141. þre bare mote ' three plain notes '. The *mot* was a long note. The 14th cent. hunting horn had only one note and the calls were like modern Morse code—long, half-long, short. Three longs, *mots*, were sounded to unleash the pack.

1142. braches ' hunting dogs '; the same kind of hounds as *rachchez* (1362), scenting hounds hunting in a pack. They were small hounds, in build resembling the beagles of today (T-G).

1143. chastysed ' checked or curbed ' and not ' chastised '. — **on chasyng þat went:** inversion imposed by alliteration; the antecedent of *þat* is *þay* ' those who left for the chase ', the *cacheres* (1139), picked up by *a hundreth of hunteres* in the following line. An alternative interpretation reads " they whipped in and turned back (the hounds) that strayed away on other scents " (TOLKIEN-GORDON).

1161. wende is ambiguous: either ' at each turning, if a sb, or (but less probably) ' at each one that passed ', if *wende* is a vb.

1165. with hyȝe horne ' with loud blowing horn '.

1167 ff. "'Whatever animal escaped the men who were shooting was pulled down and slain at the receiving stations, by the time they had been driven from the high ground and down to the waters; the men at the lower hunting-stations were so skilled, the greyhounds so huge which seized them at once and pulled them down right there, as fast as men might look'." (Tolkien-Gordon)

1174. for blys abloy. Mrs. E. Wright, *MLR* 18. 86 has *abloy* = *esbloi*, past part of OF *esbloir*, with Anglo-Norman change from *es-* to *a-*: 'The lord, carried away (lit. dazzled) with joy, did often dash forward and light...'.

1183. upon: 'open' an infinitive dependent on *herde* in preceding line. *upon*, adj 'open' appears in *The Pearl* etc. (Tolkien-Gordon)

1199. in space 'at once'; *in* which is not in the MS is added by analogy with other passages in the poem, for ex. l. 1503.

1200. to hir warde 'towards her'.

1202. as bi his saȝe þe saver to worthe "and opened his eyelids and let on as if it surprised him and signed himself (with the sign of the cross) as though by this pious ejaculation [*saȝe*] (= *Cros-Kryst me spede*, 762) to become the safer".

1219. prysoun 'prisoner'.

1224. 'I will fasten you here (and on) that other side also'.

1230. we bot oure one 'we (are) but ourselves alone', cp. l. 749, note.

1239-40. 'It behoves of very necessity that I be your servant, and I must be'. On syntax and *schale* see Tolkien-Gordon, p. 102. This declaration is hardly cautious, a witness of the haste or inexperience of the lady. Gawain's reply (l. 1276 ff.) is much more in conformity with the rules of courtly love.

1246. At saȝe oþer at servyce 'in words or deeds'.

1247. To þe plesaunce of your prys 'at the pleasure of your excellence' = 'at your pleasure'.

1250. 'If I found fault with it [*lakked*] or set (it) at little (value) it were (= would show) little good breeding'.

1251. hit ar 'there are' (cp. German *es sind*). — **þat lever wer** 'who would rather'; in correlation with *þen* 'than' of l. 1255.

1255. þe garysoun oþer golde: This phrase is a variation of *gold and gersum* 'gold and treasure', a common alliterative phrase (of Scandinavian origin) in ME. In this text the Scandinavian loan-word *gersum* has been replaced by the French *garysoun*. (Tolkien-Gordon)

1256-7. 'And I praise [*louve*] that very Lord who reigns over [*haldez*] heaven (that) I have it wholly in my hands, what all desire'; *louve* is OF *louver* variant of *louer*.

1262. to uche a cace 'to each thing (she said)'.

1264 ff. Morris takes *nysen* in l. 1266 as a verb 'make foolish by over-refinement', so do Tolkien-Gordon [amended] "for I have found in good faith, your generosity (to be) noble; and people very commonly take their line of action from others (i. e. they are showing honor to Gawain because of what they have heard from others), but the honor they apportion to me they exaggerate above my desert".

1281. 'And always the lady behaved as if (she) loved him greatly'.

1283 ff. We adopt here the corrections if not the punctuation of Morris. " Even if I were the fairest of ladies ", the lady thought, " the less love would there be in his manner " — by reason of the harm he sought without delay, the blow which would strike him down, and needs must be done (Tolkien-Gordon).

1295. in fourme of his costes ' in the decorum of his manners '.

1296. hym blessed ' reassured him, smiled on him '.

1297 ff. ' So good as Gawain excellently is held (to be), and (all) courtesy is so much contained in him, (that he) would not know how [*couth not*] (to have so) lightly lingered so long with a lady, but (that) he would have craved a kiss, according to his (and all proper) courtesy '.

1308. Ho dos hir forth at þe dore ' she puts herself out at the door '.

1316. two so dyngne dame: this unexpected *s*-less plural can only be explained as poetic licence meeting the needs of the rime.

1317. þe alder: this refers to the old lady, described l. 950-69, who accompanies the lady of the castle.

1319 ff. A clever return to the description of the chase. Verses 1325-61, omitted here, give a detailed account of the hunting ritual for cutting up deer.

1362. þay blw prys ' they blew for the capture '; contrary to French practice ' the capture ' is blown in England at the end of the chase, just before leashing the hounds and returning to the castle.

1377. þe tayles ' notches (on a piece of wood), tally of deer slain ' (from OF *taille*). Another interpretation is ' tails ' used here in the sense of ' hind-quarters ', the whole line being ·parallel to the one which follows: ' points out to him the hind-quarters ... shows him the fair flesh ' (E. Wright).

1382. þis seven ȝere ' for a long time '.

1384. by accorde of covenaunt: the master of the castle and Gawain had agreed to exchange whatever they got each day.

1391. ' I would grant it to you quite completely, even if it was more '.

1393. ' It may be that it is the better of the two '. — **and** ' if '.

XIX

Text, dialect and grammatical remarks: see no. XVIII.

Versification. The *Pearl* is written in stanzas of twelve verses using only three rimes in a pattern *abababababbcbc*; each verse has four beats, with a great deal of freedom in dealing with unstressed syllables, both as to their number and position. Alliteration is interspersed in this pattern only as ornament and may fall on two, three, or four stressed syllables; there may also be a double alliteration (*aabb*) in the same line; and finally there may be none (which is the case in 33 out of 100 verses). This stanzaic form is not infrequent in English religious poetry in the 14th cent. (for instance in most of the poems to be found in the Vernon MS, cp. C. Brown, *Religious Lyrics of the 14th Century*, nos. 95, 100, 103, 106, 110, 118, 120). But in the *Pearl* each stanza is linked to the next, the last word of a stanza appearing in the first line of the next. This is the medieval rhetorical device of ' concatenation ' (thus the word *John* for the first five stanzas of this selection, then the expression *sunne ne mone* and finally *mone* alone). This is not all. The poem is divided into groups of five stanzas each having the same final refrain. These refrains are not always absolutely identical, but the last word is always the same, and consequently so is the third rime of the stanza (c). Thus in this illustrative passage,

In (þe) Appocalyppez þe apostel John

which is repeated four times, then with a variation:

For meten hit sy3 þe apostel John.

The refrain of the next group of five stanzas is less regular, but uniformly ends in *mone*.

The price of this rigorous and intricate form is that the rimes are not always perfect (this is not, however, the case in the passage selected here), and, as well, the author was constrained to use rare and unusual words, whence the great richness of his vocabulary. Cp. for example the terms in this passage which express the idea of 'brilliant', 'gleaming': *glemande* 990, *glente* 1001, 1026, *lemed* 1043, *blysned* 1048, *schynez* 1075, *schym* 1077, *glymme* 1088.

---

985 ff. This description is directly inspired by *Revelation*, ch. xxi and xxii. Spenser's evocation in *Faerie Queene* I. x. 55-8 may be compared with this.

980. REV. XXI. 10: "... and showed me that great city, the holy Jerusalem, descending out of heaven from God."

989 f. REV. XXI. 18: "... and the city was of pure gold, like unto clear glass."

991 ff. REV. XXI. 19: "And the foundations of the wall of the city were garnished with all manner of precious stones."

992. bantelez: An architectural term difficult to gloss precisely. The word is only attested here and in *Cleanness* 1458 (which is undoubtedly by the same author). GOLLANCZ uses 'pillars', OSGOOD 'steps' (cp. l. 1022) which appears more likely. It can be seen that the terms *bantel* 992, 1017, *foundement*, 993 and 1010, *tabelment* 994, *basse* 1000, *stale* 1002, *table* 1004 are more or less synonyms, and the richness of the author's vocabulary is due in part to the requirements of alliteration.

997-1016. REV. XXI. 19-20: "The first foundation was jasper; the second sapphire; the third a chalcedony; the fourth, an emerald; (20) the fifth, sardony; the sixth sardius; the seventh, chrysolite; the eighth beryl; the ninth, topaz; the tenth, a chrysoprasus; the eleventh, a jacinth; the twelfth, an amethyst."

1002. stale 'step (as of stairs)'.

1013. ty3t rimes here, it will be noted, with the words in [it] *quyt*, *plyt*. This can be explained by the spelling *i3*, *y3* often representing [i]. But it is also true that *ty3t* 'described' is not a very satisfactory meaning and EMERSON has proposed the reading *tyt* 'well spoken of', a Scandinavian loan (ON *tiðr*, neuter *tit* 'usual, often spoken of, famous') which is attested elsewhere.

1017 f. REV. XXI. 18: "And the building of the wall of it was of jasper." The vb *watz* is understood before *bent*.

1023 f. REV. XXI. 16: "And the city lieth four-square, and the length is as large as the breadth."

1026 repeats verses 1017-8.

1029-32. REV. XXI. 15: "And he that talked with me had a golden reed to measure ... (16) And he measured the city with the reed, twelve thousand furlongs. The length and the breadth and the height of it are equal."

1030. er ever hit fon 'before ever it ended' is a metrical expletive; *fon* is an analogous str pret from the French loan *fine* (<OF *finer*).

1031. cayre 'to square, give the form of a square' satisfies the context. If the altered spelling of the word could not be simply attributed to the needs of the rime (instead of *quare* < OF *quarer*) a loan could be supposed from Provençal *cairar* 'to square'. Other editors assume ON *keyra* 'lash, prick on, drive, etc.'>ME *kayre* 'go, move, take oneself', as often in the Alliterative Poems and other works, e. g. 21₄/305.

1034 f. REV. XXI. 12-3: "And had a great wall and high, and had twelve gates ... (13) On the east three gates; on the north three gates; and on the west three gates."

1037 f. REV. XXI. 21: "every several gate was of one pearl."

1038. fatez for *fadez*; the unvoicing of a voiced stop is not unusual in this MS.

1039 f. REV. XXI. 12: "... and had twelve gates ... and names written theron which are the names of the twelve tribes of the children of Israel."

1041. as her byrþ-whatez 'according to the order of their birth' (EMERSON).

1043. stratez 'streets' in opposition to the form *stretes*, current in this dialect; used for rime.

1045 ff. REV. XXII. 23: "And the city had no need of the sun, neither of the moon, to shine in it: for the glory of God did lighten it, and the Lamb is the light thereof."

1055 f. REV. XXII. 1: "And he shewed me a pure river of water of life, clear as crystal, proceeding out of the throne of God and of the Lamb."

1058. 'as this swelling flood flowed out of the ground'; *flode* is here the pret of a verb 'to flow', cp. ON *flōa.*

1061 ff. REV. XXI. 22: "And I saw no temple therein: for the lord God Almighty and the Lamb are the temple of it."

1063. mynyster is ambiguous; it could be *minster* 'monastery' or *minister.* The latter seems to me more plausible: in the New Jerusalem the All-Powerful is his own minister.

1064. This difficult verse in the MS version is easily cleared up by adopting *refet* as proposed by E. WRIGHT (*JEGP* 38, 21). The vb *refete* 'to satiate' is attested in this poem (l. 88). Here *refete* is the sb 'nourishment' (from OF *refet*), recorded in the *OED* but only in the 15th century. The Lamb, at the banquet of the elect, is at once the symbolic sacrifice of the mass and the nourishment of the blessed. This line refers to the celebration of the Mass in heaven as Osgood points out in citing ALBERT LE GRAND, *De Eucharistica* (*Opera*, ed. Borgnet, 30. 328): Haec (eucharistia) enim erit coena nuptiarum Agni (APOC. XIX. 9) ... In deliciis paradisi dei nostri sumitur corpus Domini. Ibi enim Patre aeterno nos honorante per suum consensum ad mensam sedemus. Ibi Filius praecinctus decore et lumine se nobis ministrat.

1065. REV. XXI. 25: "And the gates of it shall not be shut at all by day ..."

1066. 'but always open at every road'; this undoubtedly refers to roads outside which lead towards the city.

1067 f. Rev. xxi. 27: "And there shall in no wise enter into it anything that defileth . . ."

1071. Rev. xxi. 25: ". . . for there shall be no night there."

1077-80. Rev. xxii. 2: ". . . and on either side of the river, was there the tree of life, which bare twelve manner of fruits, and yielded her fruit every month."

1087. Lit. 'so that I felt neither rest nor fatigue', which is 'I had lost all feeling'.

XX

Text from Lincoln Cathedral's unique MS A 1, 17. This MS, which contains many other poems, was in great part copied in 1440 by a certain Robert Thornton, a native of Oswaldkirk (Yorkshire) who was archdeacon of Bedford in the diocese of Lincoln.

Dialect. Northern English transcript from a text written originally in Northwest Midland (cp. S. O. Andrew, *RES* 4 (1928), 418-423).

Spelling. As in the two preceding texts the letter ʒ is used in this MS in the final position for [s/z]: it is transcribed z. As often happened in the North w alternates with v (*hewen* 705 alongside *heven* 'heaven' 795, *ewen* 762, *ewyn* 774 alongside *even* 799; the same in *abwen* 775, *abowen* 823 for 'above'). There is *ch* for *sch* [š] (*wyrchippe* 700). The scribe makes a practice of using y [ɪ] or [ə] in finals, both in sb pls (*maylys* 769) and wk preterits (*semyde* 773, *rappyd* 785); similarly there is *wandyrs* 798, *mekyll* 711, *betakyns* 822.

Phonology. OE ă remains a (*landez* 762, *thane* 713); OE ā remains, generally, ā (*rarede* 'roared' 784) but is sometimes ō (*lordez* 694, *one* 704).

Inflexions. *Personal pronoun.* — 3 sg F *cho* 715, 716, 720; 3 pl nom *þey* 814, dat *þam* 777, *þem* 810.

Verb. — The infinitive in *-n* is rare (*drenchen* 761). Pres indicative 2 sg in *-s* (*þow has* 711), 3 sg in *-es*, *-ez*, *-iz* (*takez* 693, *lenges* 696), pl in *-es*, *-ez* (*leves* 694, *saillez* 831). Present part in *-a(u)nde* (*wepande* 697, *walkande* 762) quite distinct from the verbal sb in *-yng(e)* (*wepynge* 707). The past participle never has the preverb *y-*.

Note the forms of 'shall': Present 1, 2, 3 *sall* (706, 827), pret *sulde* 704. There was another future auxiliary characteristic of the Northern dialect, *mon* 813.

Versification. See above under XVIII.

---

694. at 'from'; similarly l. 713.

697-704. This portrait of Guenevere's grief seems to be original.

697. Waynour: another form of *Gaynour* (l. 705), name of Arthur's wife. Similarly in *Sir Gawain* the name of the hero is *Wowen* or *Wawen* alongside *Gawayn* following the demands of alliteration.

699. thatt this werre movede 'who started this war', cp. Latin *bellum movere*.

704. by myne one 'by myself'. cp. 18/749 note.

716. swelte as cho walde 'as (if) she would die'.

720. Sandwyche: as a port of embarkation for the army, Sandwich is rather unusual. The chronicles have Southampton (*Hamo* in G. of Monmouth).

756 ff. As can be seen, Thomas Malory has copied this famous passage from the poem practically word for word. In Malory's text (from Vinaver's edition), which is printed as a note, his additions are italicized.

760. a dragon: that of Mont Saint-Michel.

767. schrympe: this word, which was applied to various crustaceans, appears here (cp. *OED* s.v. *shrimp* 1b) to mean 'monster covered with scales'.

772. flayre: as BJÖRKMAN has rightly pointed out, *flayre* cannot mean 'stench' here but 'flame'; see Malory's paraphrase.

796. He hade weryede 'he would have worn out'.

808. the sevyn scyence 'the seven liberal arts'; *scyence*, pl without -*s* ending due to final sibilant.

812 13. as wysse me oure Loverd 'by our Lord who guides me, I will die at once unless you interpret me my dream'. This use of *ore* is exceptional; on *mon* cp. § 139, REM. II.

XXI

Text. *A-Version:* that of the Bodleian MS Vernon (called *V*) with readings taken from Trinity College, Cambridge MS R. 3, 14 (called *T*).

B-Version: that of the Bodleian MS Laud Misc. 581 (called *L*) with readings taken from University Library, Cambridge, MS Dd 1. 17 (called *C*) and from MS Rawl. Poet 38 (called *R*).

C-Version: that of the Huntington Library, MS HM 137 [formerly MS Phillipps 8231] (called *P*) with readings taken from MS Ilchester (called *I*) and from MS Cotton Vespasian B. 16 (called *M*).

Dialect of the Southwest Midlands but rather mixed. Cp. R. W. CHAMBERS, "The Three Texts of 'Piers Plowman' and their Grammatical Forms," *MLR*, 14 (1919). 129-51.

Spelling. In the C-version the scribe of MS *P* used French writing practices that have been corrected, like the reduction of *wh-* to *w-* (*wanne* 3/1, *wyle* 3/25, *wat* 3/38, etc.), the omission of *h-* (*eggen* 3/20 for *heggen*), *wit* 3/6 or *whit* 3/43 for *with*, or, on the contrary, the addition of a superfluous *h* (*hyf* 3/42 for *yf*, *his* 3/99 for *is*).

Unaccented vowels in declensional endings are usually written *u* (*mannus* 1/197 alongside *cattes* and *cattis* 1/178, *clerkus* 3/61), also those in the short grammatical words (*hus* 3/58, *thuse* 3/61).

Phonology. OE *y* often remains [ü], written *u* (*hulles* 1/5, *murie* 1/10, *cullen* 'kill' 2/185, *Cornehulle* 3/1) or *ui* when long (*pruide* 1/23).

OE *å* before nasal + consonant is generally *o* (*fond* 1/17, *wombes* 1/56, *longe* 2/195, *londes* 3/26); before a simple nasal there is hesitation between *a* (*whan* 4/356, *many* 2/197) and *o* (*whon* 1/1, *monie* 1/22).

OE *eo* becomes *e* (*cherle* 4/360, *selver* 3/72 alongside *sylver* 2/168).

The velar consonants *g, k* are well preserved, without palatalization (*bugge* 2/168, *geven* 4/326, *rigge* 4/349, *segges* 2/160, *liggen* 3/16, *heggen* 3/19, *seggynge* 3/107, *kirke* 4/305, *dykere* 4/320). The form *cherche* 4/308, 319 must be due to a scribe who spoke a different dialect, as the alliteration shows in 3/60, 104, 105.

Inflexions. *Substantives.* — The C-version has gen pl sb forms like *menne* 3/29, 70, *lollarene* 3/31, *knavene* 3/54.

Personal pronoun. — 1 sg *I* in A and B, *ich* in C; 3 pl, A-version has the form *heo* 1/43, B and C the form *þei, they* 2/206; besides, there is the possessive *here* 1/34, 2/148, 3/72 (*hure* 3/48) and the dat *hem* 1/20, 2/147 (*heom* 1/25).

Verb. — Present 2 sg in *-st* (*havest* 3/26), 3 sg in *-(e)þ* (*askeþ* 1/19, *caccheþ* 2/193, *telleth* 3/38); in the pl the A-version has *-eþ* (*habbeþ* 1/37, *holdeþ* 1/28, *ryseth* 1/44), B and C have forms in *-e* or *-en* (*aren* 2/164, 3/56, *ben* 3/59, *han* 3/71).

The infinitive is in *-en* (*knitten* 2/169) or in *-e* (*cacche* 2/206), the present part is in *-yng(e)* (*worchinge* 1/19, *wailinge* 3/108). The past part is almost always preceded by *y-*. In the A-version, note the wk past participles in *-et* (*i-maket* 1/14, *degyset* 1/24, *i-crommet* 1/41).

1

2. schroud 'cloak'. — **a scheep as I were** 'as (if) I was a shepherd' (the C-version MSS read *shepherde*), but this meaning of the work *sheep* is quite uncommon; see SKEAT'S long note on this word.

3. unholy of werkes, that is, living outside the cloister as vagabonds; the opposite of those anchorites who 'keep themselves in their cells and don't want to go roaming about the country' (l. 28 f.).

5. Malverne Hulles in Worcestershire, bordering on Herefordshire. Here the dreamer goes to sleep, but as SKEAT justly remarks, it is of London that he dreams, and it is the London social milieu that fills the poem.

7. wente me: use of reflexive pronoun with intransitive vbs of motion is frequent.

11. gon I meeten 'I began to dream' (*gon* for *gan, bigan*). — **a mervelous swevene:** this 'marvellous dream' that follows constitutes, actually, the first 'vision' of the dreamer about Piers the Plowman (cp. the dreamer's awakening, B-version, passus VII, l. 139 ff.).

14. a tour: this tower, as is explained in passus I, is the abode of Truth.

15. This deep valley is the domain of Death and evil spirits. The dungeon is the castle of Care, dwelling-place of Falsehood.

17 ff. The social categories that the author is going to consider are the following: farm laborers (20-23), fops (24-25), devout people (25-30), merchants (31-32), entertainers, good (33-34) and bad (35-39), beggars and vagabonds (40-45), pilgrims and palmers (46-51), false hermits (52-54), mendicant orders (55-64).

17. This 'fair field full of folk' symbolizes the world. The scenery imagined by the poet recalls that of the Morality plays, in which scaffolds were erected to represent the world and heaven and the abodes of vices and virtues in the four corners around an open space. A. H. BRIGHT, however, thinks he sees here a real countryside near Malvern. — **þer bitwene** 'between them', i. e. between the castle of Truth and the dungeon with its ditches.

19. as þe world askeþ 'as the world requires', 'as this life demands (of people)'.

20. putten hem to þe plou3 'some put themselves (to work) at plow(ing)', reflexive, cp. *OED*, s. v. *put* V¹, 27b.

22. þat 'that which, what'.

23. putten hem to pruide 'took up prideful ways' (see 1. 20 above).

24. cuntinaunce of cloþinge 'display of (fancy) clothing'; on this meaning for *countenance* cp. *OED* s. v. 2. — **degyset** 'decked out strangely'.

29. in cuntré 'in the country', namely, England. — **cairen** 'run around', 'be on the bum' (Scandinavian loan, ON *keyra*) cp. further, selection 4, 1. 305.

30. (coveite not) for non likerous lyflode 'do not seek after a fancy and fast living'.

32. As hit semeþ to ure siht etc. 'as it appears to us that such men ought to'; *to ure siht* is only a periphrasis for 'to us'.

33. And summe: *chosen* is understood.

35. Alongside these harmless (*giltles* 1. 34) minstrels, there are the 'children of Judas' who are the *japers and jangelers* ('jesters and tellers of slanderous—and often obscene—stories'). On the latter cp. what we learn from Chaucer's *Parson's Tale*: 'Janglynge is whan men speken to muche biforn folk and clappen as a mille, and taken no keep what they seye'.

36. founden hem: 'invented (for) themselves'. — **fantasyes** perhaps 'fabliau', 'broad stories' (cp. *turpiloquium* farther on). — **hem** is reflexive.

37. to worchen 3if hem luste 'and yet had good intelligence to use whenever they wanted to'.

38. þat 'what'.

42. feyned hem 'pretended to be (sick, lame etc.) to get their living'. **atte alle** 'at the tavern'; also found is *atten ale; atten, atte* = OE *æt ðæm*.

44. This Roberdes knaves 'vagabonds, marauders'; a statute of Edward III in 1331 prescribed the arrest of any individual suspected of being one of a band of 'Roberdesmen, Wastours [marauders] and Draghlacce [draw-latches, housebreakers]'; the term bears some not very clear relation to the proper name *Roberd* 'Robert' (cp. *OED* s. v. *Roberdsmen*).

46. palmeres: originally pilgrims to the Holy Land whose badge was a palm; later on, 'one who made it his sole business to visit different shrines, travelling incessantly and living by charity' (SKEAT), a sort of professional pilgrim.

47. to seche 'to go venerate the relics of a saint (cp. *OED* s. v. *seek* 4).— **Seint Jeme:** saint James of Compostella in Galicia (Spain), a famous pilgrim resort in the Middle Ages. — **Seintes at Roome:** the churches at Rome and the relics therein.

51. Walsyngham: Our Lady of Walsingham, another pilgrim resort in Norfolk. — **wenchis** 'mistresses'.

53. copes: the *cope* is here considered to be the mark of the medicant friar (*breþeren*).

55. þe foure ordres: Carmelites (white friars), Augustines (Austin friars), Jacobins or Dominicans (black friars), and Minorites (gray friars, Franciscans), all violently attacked by Wyclif.

59. at lyking ' as they liked '.

61. seþþe charité haþ be chapmon ' since Christian Love has turned pedlar ', allusion to the Franciscans. Chaucer describing one of them in the *Gen. Prol.* (ll. 233-4) says, " His typet [hooded cloak] was ay farsed [stuffed] ful of knyves / And pynnes, for to yeven [give] faire wyves." — **cheef** ' and (interested) chiefly (in)'.

63. But ' unless '. Allusion to the quarrel between the secular clergy and the Friars over the right to hear confession.

64. mounteþ up faste ' will mount up fast '; present = future.

2

This fine piece, which is not in the A-version, must have been written after the death of the Black Prince (June 1376) and that of Edward III (June 1377). For more details see J. J. JUSSERAND, *Piers Plowman* p. 39 ff.

In 1376, outraged by the Court's high-handedness, Parliament instituted a vigilance committee (the collar to put on the cat's neck), composed of a dozen Lords half of whom were to be present at all of the King's business. Parliament was then dissolved on the orders of John of Gaunt, Duke of Lancaster; its acts declared null and void and its committee dismissed. The speaker of the House of Commons, Peter de la Mare, the ' rat of renown, most runnable (and/or reasonable) of tongue ', was put in prison. The wise mouse (l. 182) (the poet himself) — was right to caution Parliament against too strict a limitation of the royal powers and to tremble at the anarchy that would come if the palace cat should disappear (l. 195 ff.).

This fable of ' belling the cat ' is known at least as early as the 13th century (in the Latin fables of Odo of Cheriton). It is later found in the Anglo-Norman writer Nicole Bozon's *Contes Moralisés* (about 1320). It seems to have been current in the 14th century and, by a curious coincidence, Thomas Brunton, bishop of Rochester, applied it in one of his sermons to the events of 1376, just like our poet (cp. G. R. OWST, *MLR*, 20. 270-9, E. KELLOG, *PMLA*, 50. 57-67 and M. A. DEVLIN, *PMLA*, 51. 300-302. On the folklore motif see Stith THOMPSON, *Motif-Index of Folk Literature* (Bloomington 1932-6) J. 671. 1.

150. overlepe hem ' jumped over them ' (similarly farther on l. 199).

152. For doute of ' for fear of '.

155. '(so) that we loathe life before [*or*] he lets us die (or, possibly, ' before he lets us go ')'.

157. aloft ' of high rank, powerful ' (cp. *OED* s. v. 8).

158. renable of tonge ' glib-tongued ', ' eloquent ' (Norfolk dialect has still *runnable*).

159. ' announced what was, in his eyes (*to hymselve*), the sovereign remedy '.

160. segges: here ' official people '.

163. wareine ' hunting preserves '. — **waste** ' uncultivated land '. — **where hem leve liketh** ' wherever they pleased '.

167. me sheweth ' shows me, tells me ' (cp. *OED* s. v. 22*d*).

169. Pronoun object not expressed after *knitten*. Cp. the variants in l. 179.

171. where ' whether '. — **ritt, rest** contract forms for *rideþ, resteþ*.

173. þer-while 'as long as' (OE *on þære hwīle*).

174. 'and if he gets angry, be wary and stay out of his way'.

175. reson 'speech, advice'.

176. Ac þo 'but when'.

177. for alle þe rewme of Fraunce: allusion to the Hundred Years War (then current).

180. 'And admitted themselves to be weak'.

181. leten here laboure lost 'and allowed their labor was lost'.

182. þat moche good couþe 'who had much commonsense', lit. 'who knew much of many things'.

183. stroke forth sternly 'came out resolutely'.

184. reherced 'repeated'.

185. 'Even if we killed [*culled*] the cat, another (i. e. John of Gaunt) would appear'.

187. alle þe comune 'all the people'. "The reference seems to be to the entire community — or possibly to the common people en masse — rather than to any political estate represented in the royal council." (E. T. DONALDSON, *Piers Plowman, the C-Text and its Poet*, p. 100). — **to lat þe catte worthe** 'to let the cat be'.

189. is sevene ȝere y-passed 'it was seven years ago', that is, in 1368. "The remark was, at that time, a pertinent one: for in 1368-9 ... the Black Prince's disease had suddenly increased ... and it had become evident he would never reach old age. Wise men could therefore say with anguish: 'Vae terrae ubi puer rex est'." (J. J. JUSSERAND, *Piers Pl.*, 47). But the phrase 'sevene ȝere y-passed' was also commonly used in the vague meaning of 'a long time ago'.

190. a kitoun: this kitten was Richard II, 10 years old, heir to the throne after the death of the Black Prince. — **elyng** 'unhappy'.

193. owre caroyne 'our (dead) bodies'.

194. fet hym al with venesoun 'feed him completely on venison [the *conynges* of the preceding line]: *fet* contract for *fedeþ*, the verb is reflexive (*hym*). — **defame we:** hypothetical inversion, 'if we do not calumniate him'.

196. 'the anarchy which would ensue, even though we get rid of a tyrant' (or 'even if we should miss a shrew[-mouse]').

199. Nere þat cat of þat courte 'if it were not for that court-cat (i. e. John of Gaunt)'.

201. 'I speak for myself, I see far in the future'.

203. 'nor by talking about this collar, which cost me nothing' (because the wise mouse would not have contributed to the purchase).

204. catel 'money'.

3

This autobiographical piece appears only in the C-version of the poem. Here the author describes his life in London, where he lived in Cornhill (l. 1) with his wife Kit and his daughter (as passus XXI tells us). The tone with which he talks of his life as a poet and Bohemian (*lollere* l. 2) has a quite individual charm. This is, for its time, a unique page. Cp. J. J. JUS-

SERAND, *Piers Pl.* p. 95 f. and E. T. DONALDSON, *Piers Plowman*, ch. IV, which is the most elaborate study of the biographical elements.

3. lytel y-lete by 'and not considered to be much'.

5. ich made of þo men: either 'I judged these men' (K. SISAM) or 'I wrote poems about these men' (W. W. SKEAT).

6. as ich cam by Conscience 'as I met Conscience', allusion to a previous vision.

8. lovede wel fare 'I loved good living'.

10. in hele and in unité 'healthy in body and mind'. — **on me aposede** 'someone [*on*] questioned me'.

14. mowe oþer mowen 'mow or put grain in shocks' despite their homonymy, etymologically these two words have no relation to each other.

16. haywarde see 3/128 note. — **a nyghtes** 'at night', 'nights'.

24. to long 'too tall'. Cp. B-version, passus XV, l. 148 *my name is Longe Wille*. This comment corroborates the autobiographical nature of the passage.

29. at menne hacches 'at the doors of houses', *hacche* ModE *hatch*, lit. 'half-door'; *menne* is genitive plural of *man*.

36. founden me to scole 'boarded me at school'.

39. by so ich wolle continue 'provided I persevere'.

41. longe clothes 'cassock', the long garment marking the secular clergy.

44. 'I live in London and on London'. For the many possible employments for a clerk in London see J. J. JUSSERAND, *Piers Plowman* p. 89 ff.

46. prymer: elementary book of religious instruction containing the principal prayers, a few psalms and a few hymns in Latin and English. — **placebo et dirige:** synonym for the Office of the Dead; following the first two antiphons of this office; *dirige* used in this way is the origin of ModE *dirge*.

47. sevene psalmes: the seven penitential psalms.

48. The antecedent of *suche as* is *hure*.

52. 'without a knapsack (to carry away food) or a gourd (for drink) but only my stomach'.

54. knavene werkes 'menial work'; *knavene* is the genitive pl of *knave* (cp. *lollarene* l. 31 above).

56. crouned 'tonsured' (cp. *uncrouned* l. 62). — **of kynde understondyng** probably refers to *clerkes* and means 'with native intelligence' (cp. *OED* s. v. 1*b*).

58. hus fo 'their enemy'; *hus*, by-form of *his*, can be used for *here* 'their'.

59. it ben aires of hevene 'they [*it*] are heirs of heaven'; this is a normal ME construction.

63. That is *no clerk shold be crouned bote yf* . . .

66. Thuse bylongeþ to labour 'these are suited to labor'.

69. rede 'advise'. — **þat** 'those who'.

73. leid here rentes to wedde 'put up their incomes as pledges'.

79. Symondes sone 'son of Simon Magus', that is, some one guilty of simony or who has no other quality but money.

88. fynt ous alle þynges 'provides us all we need'; *fynt* contract form of *fyndeþ*.

89. ich can nat see this lyeþ 'I cannot see what this applies to '.

91. he has an indefinite meaning ' one, they '. — **obediencer:** a religious in a convent who has been requested to carry out a charge under his superior's orders.

96. he was þe bet evere ' he was ever after the better (for it) '.

97. sette hus los at a lef ' set all that loss at very little ', lit. ' at the value of a leaf '.

4

304 ff. ' Glutton ' is the personification of the sin of overindulgence in food and drink (*gula*). The scene takes place in a London tavern not far from ill-famed Cock Lane (l. 319). The personification of the deadly sins — here gluttony — was not a novelty. It is worth while to compare the scene painted here by Langland with an analogous passage from Frère Lorens' *Somme* as translated by *Dan Michel of Northgate* in his *Ayenbite of Inwyt* (no. XV).

305. kaires hym ' turns and goes '. — **to-kirke-ward** for *toward kirke* ' towards church '. — **his coupe to shewe** ' to confess his sins '.

307. whiderward he wolde: verbs of motion (here *go*) are often not expressed after modals.

311. auȝte ' anything '.

312. piones ' peony seeds ' generally used in medicine but also, as here, as a kind of spice.

313. fastyng-dayes: from what is said farther on, l. 367, it can be assumed the scene takes place on Friday, a day of fasting and abstinence.

314. Grete-Othes, another personification: blasphemous false swearing usually accompanies drunkenness.

315. Cesse diminutive of ' Cecily '. — **souteresse** feminine of *souter* ' shoemaker '. This feminine is not attested anywhere else. The A-version has *souters wyf* and C has *sywestere* ' seamstress '.

316. Watte: diminutive of Walter. — **warner** ' gamekeeper '; survives as a family name.

317. Tymme: diminutive of Timothy.

319. Cokkes-Lane: Cock Lane, West Smithfield. According to the *Liber Albus* women of easy virtue after being put in the pillory were taken by way of Cheapside and Newgate to live in Cokkes-Lane. — **the cherche:** either the church of Bow-Lane, or Saint Peter's in Cornhill.

320. Dawe ' David '.

321. Sir Piers of Pridie: SKEAT conjectures that this refers to a monk, ' Dan Pierre de Prie-Dieu ', *prie-dieu* being French for ' kneeling desk ' (unless it refers to Priddy in Somersetshire whose spelling in 13th century documents is *Pridie*); *sire* at this time was the usual title for a monk. Chaucer writes:

> Wherefore, sire Monk, or daun Piers by youre name (*C. T.*, B. 3982)

As for *Peronelle of Flaunders*, she, like Clarice of Cokkes-Lane, is a woman of easy virtue. At this time *Flemish woman* was a synonym for prostitute.

322. Chepe: Cheapside.

323. redyngkyng: an obscure word; one MS reads *rydyngkyng* and it has been conjectured that it was a form of *radknight* 'cavalier'; here perhaps with the meaning of 'groom, ostler'?

324. Garleke hithe near Wintry Ward. John STOW, *Survey of London* ed. 1842, p. 93 says, "There is the parish church of St. James, called at Garlick-hithe or Garlick-hive; for that of old time, on the bank of the river Thames, near to this church, garlick was usually sold."

328. atte New Faire: this is a reference to an ancient game which the *OED* describes: A kind of sport having an element of chance in it, in which one person challenges some article belonging to another for which he offered something of his own in exchange. On the challenge being entertained, an umpire was chosen to decree the difference of value between the two articles, and all three parties deposited forfeit money in a cap or hat. The umpire then pronounced his award as to the 'boot', or odds, to be given with the inferior article, on hearing which the two other parties drew out full or empty hands to denote their acceptance or nonacceptance of the match in terms of the award. If the two were found to agree in holding the match, either 'in' or 'off', the whole of the money deposited was taken by the umpire; but, if not, by the party who was willing that the match should stand.

Here Clement puts up his cloak. Hikke then throws in [*hitte*] his cap and demands that Bette the butcher represent him [*ben on-his side* l. 330]. Someone else seems to represent Clement and these two try to evaluate [*preise* l. 331] the articles [*chaffere* l. 331] and the odds, but cannot agree (l. 335) and Robyn is appointed umpire: Hikke gets the cloak, Clement gets the cap but Hikke must buy Clement a drink to boot [*fille þe cuppe*, i. e. Clement's] and acknowledge that he agrees to this deal [*holde hym y-served* l. 341]. The first one who disagrees must buy Glutton a gallon of beer.

334. penyworthes 'goods', 'second hand articles'.

336. arose bi þe souþe: this phrase, found in all B MSS gives a very poor sense 'arose forsooth, indeed'. The C reading *aryse þey bysouhte* 'they besought (him) to get up' seems much better.

337. debate 'dispute'.

338. hem þre, that is, Robyn and the two handicappers.

351. wexed with a wispe of ferses 'stopped up with straw stopper'.

353. liche a glewmannes bicche 'like a wandering minstrel's dog' (probably a blind minstrel).

355. 'Like a man putting out lines to snare birds'.

357. and threwe to þe erthe 'and fell to the ground'.

359. leyde him on his knowes 'got him to his knees'.

361. coughed up a caudel. A caudle was 'a warm drink consisting of thin gruel, mixed with wine or ale, sweetened and spiced, given chiefly to sick people' (*OED*).

363. durst lape for *þat durst lape* with zero subordinating relative.

364. with al þe wo of þis worlde 'with all the trouble in the world'.

366. accidie lit. 'laziness, indolence (< Latin *accidia*)'; here 'access of laziness' possibly by influence of French *access* 'attack'.

XXII

Text. The *Bruce* is preserved in two late MSS, both copied by John Ramsay; the first (called *C*) is at St. John's College, Cambridge, MS G 23, and dates from 1487; the second (called *E*) is now at the Advocates' Library, Edinburgh and dates from 1489. Our first selection follows *E*, the second *C*. A few readings are taken from Hart's edition, 1616 (called *H*) and from Andrew Anderson's, 1670 (called *A*). The MSS use two abbreviations which make reading difficult: *y* for *þ*, *th*, which we transcribe by *th* (thus l. 413 *that thai* in MS is *y*ᵗ *yai*); and this superior *t* is also used for *cht* (thus *no*ᵗ which we transcribe *nocht*).

Dialect: Northern English (Lowlands Scots).

Spelling. We have preserved the letter ß of the MSS which represents *ss*, but it should be noted that this letter is transcribed *ss* in the glossary. Occasionally, after a vowel, *i* or *y* serves only as a diacritical mark to indicate the length of the preceding vowel, thus *weill* 235, *deid* 269, *may*ß 226, *maid* 457, *haiff* 226, *soyn* 467 must be read *wēll*, *dĕd*, *mǎss*, *mād*, *hāff*, *sōn*.

-is, *-ys* represent the plural flexion (*thingis* 241, *clerkis* 249) and the genitive of substantives (*lordis* 256), and the ending of 3 sg present of verbs (*levys* 228); *-it*, *-yt* the preterit flexion (*assayit* 237, *hapnyt* 400, *lufit* 413, *persavit* 411) and that of the past participle of weak verbs (*levyt* 233, *wrechyt* 235.)

ch is used where other dialects have *ʒ* or *gh*: *nocht* 230, *awcht* 255, *mycht* 429, for *noght*, *aught*, *might*; one finds *quh-* for *wh-* (*quhat* 245, *quhen* 250, *quhyll* 270, *quhethir* 254 for *what*, *when*, *while*, *whether*). Note also *ʒh* and *yh* for *ʒ* (*failʒhe* 231, *ʒharnyt* 232, *yheyt* 246 for *failʒe* 'fail', *ʒarned* 'yearned', *ʒete* 'yet').

v and *w* are often interchangeable; one finds, thus, *discoweryngis* 242, for 'discoverings' and especially *vent* 401, *vode* 404, *vith* 405, *vachit* 421 for *went*, *wode*, *with*, *wachit*.

Finally, consonants are often doubled, in particular *f* (*wyff* 253, *gyff* 231, *lyff* 270, *off* 243, 262) to note unmistakably that this was the unvoiced sound [f].

Phonology. OE *ā* remains *ā* (*nane* 'none' 229, *banys* 'bones' 271, *stane* 'stone' 471, *smat* 'smote' 449); OE *ō* becomes *u* [ü?] (*tuk* 463); *-ed* > *-it* in the preterit and past participle of weak verbs (*prisit* 442, *followit* 464); [š] > *s* in *sall*, *suld* 239.

Inflexions. *Personal Pronoun.* — 3 pl nom *thai* 250, poss *thar* 409, *thair* 434, dat *thaim* 260, *thame* 435.

Verb — Pres 3 sg and pl in *-s* (3 sg *giffis* 227, *has* 243, *drawis* 248, pl *may*ß 249, *has* 485); but the pl has no ending when preceded by a personal pronoun *thai fall* 250, *thai mak* 261). Present participle in *-and* (*cumand* 409), past participle without preverb *y-*.

Vocabulary. Note terms or forms characteristic of the North and of Scots: *till* 'to ' 245, etc., *syne* 255, *sen* 261 'since ', *sic* 'such ' 261, *but* 447, *forouten* 462 'without ', *gang* 'go ' 415, *at* as a relative particle.

1

232. our all othir thing 'above everything else'; **our** 'over'.

233. na 'nor'.

243. has nocht his 'has nothing that is his own'.

247 f. 'the free choice not to do (*leyve*) or to do that which his heart urges him to'.

248. That at 'that which'; *at* is here a relative particle.

254. let 'let go, neglect'.

256. do furth 'go on and do'.

272. And dede anoyis him bot anys 'and death annoys him only once'.

273. is nane can tell 'there is no one who can tell' with zero relative for 'who', cp. § 152 REM. II.

2

401. he: Bruce; the scene takes place in 1307.

413. na kyn þyng 'in no manner whatsoever'.

423. Johne Cwmynys: Bruce had stabbed John Comyn before the high altar of the Franciscans at Dumfries a little before 1306, as is related in Book II, l. 25 ff.

439. Haf ʒhe 'if you have'.

447. but langar frest 'without more delay'.

455. top our taill 'head over tail'; **our** 'over'.

471. he draf 'he fell'.

XXIII

Text from MS Cotton Titus C 16 in the British Museum c. 1410-20 (there are about 300 MSS of these *Voyages*); French text from MS Harley 4383. **Dialect** of the South-east Midlands.

Phonology. OE *ā* > *ō* (*ston* 28, *on* 'one' 31), OE *ǎ* before nasal + consonant is *o* (*lond* 1, *longe* 5, *strong* 7) but *a* (*man* 12, *many* 15) before simple nasal.

Inflexions: *Demonstrative pronoun.* — *þo* 27, *þeise* 35.

Personal pronoun. — 3 pl nom *þei* 25, poss *hire* 48, dat *hem* 45, *hemself* 56, 62.

Verb. — Present indicative 3 pl in -*en* (*clepen* 2, *beren* 14, *ben* 70). Pres participle in -*inge*, -*enge* (*beryŋge* 12, *rennynge* 38, *seyenge* 43). Past participle without preverb *i*-, and in -*e(n)* for strong verbs (*dronken* 45, *sene* 70, *founde* 24, *slayn* 63).

---

1. the yle of Pentexoire: in Odoric de Pordenone's French text *Pentexoire* is located near the Yellow River; for Mandeville most oriental countries are 'islands'. — On the 'old man of the mountain' see Ch. E. NOWELL, *Speculum* 22 (1947), 497-519. — **Prestre John:** Prester John was supposed to have been the Christian leader of a great oriental realm, but he seems to belong in the domain of legend.

5. Gatholonabes: unexplained name not found elsewhere.

40. see the craft: the translator has probably taken the word *menistriers* 'minstrels' in the French text for *mystère,* hence his translation 'craft'.

XXIV

Text: 1. Bodleian MS 788; 2. MS 296 from Corpus Christi College, Cambridge.

Dialect of the South-east Midlands.

Phonology. The use of *u* instead of *e* in *foundun* 26 (alongside *founden* 42) is an East-Midland feature.

Inflexions. *Substantives.* — Plural almost always in *-is* (*goodis* 3, 5, 6, *servantis* 22, *þingis* 30, but *chirches* 56). Note the weak plurals *shoon* 23, *hynen* 12.

Personal pronoun. — 3 pl nam *þei* 67, poss *here* 46, 47, dat *hem* 1.
þes 30, 65 is the form of the demonstrative plural.

Verb. — Pres 3 sg in *-iþ* (*falliþ* 2, *writiþ* 57) or in *-eþ* (*witnesseþ* 52), pl. in *-en* (*eten* 11, *usen* 64, *ben* 12, 66, *doun* 67).

Weak pret in *-ide* (*departide* 3, *wastide* 5, *axide* 30, *clepide* 29); cp. however, *clevede* 8).

Present part in *-ing*(*e*) (*turninge* 11, *renning* 18, *havyng* 65). Past part without preverb *i-*, weak vbs generally in *-id* (*endid* 6, *killid* 38) or in *-ed* (*quykened* 25, *cursed* 66), str vbs in *-e*(*n*) (*founden* 42, *comen* 31, *come* 38).

---

1 ff. Taken from the *Sermons* (*Þe Saturday Gospel in þe Secunde Weke in Lente*). The text is from LUKE xv. 11-32. The student will derive great profit from a comparison between this translation by Wyclif and those of the 11th cent. OE (*HOE* no. I, 4) and the Gothic version.

9. toun 'enclosure, (enclosed) field'.

13. loves, pl of *lof* 'loaf'.

18. aȝens 'to meet'.

22. þe firste stoole 'the best garment'.

25. fede us 'feast ourselves'.

43 ff. The following passage is an extract from *Þe Grete Sentence of Curs Expouned.*

52. as Petir witnesseþ: cp. ACTS III. 2-6.

55. wakyng of gret þouȝt 'care for high and serious thought'.

57. Seynt Bernard writiþ: in his treatise *De consideratione* addressed to pope Eugene III, book IV, chap. III.

67. þei doun 'they act'.

XXV

Text from the unique MS in the Public Record Office, Ancient Petitions File 20, no. 997.

Dialect of London (Middlesex).

Spelling. No use of either *þ* or *ȝ* (except as equivalent of *z* which, following the principle adopted in this book, we transcribe *z* (in *emprisonementz* 19 and *busshmentz* 30). The letter *u* stands for both [u] as in *puttyng* 40 and [ü] in *lust* 43.

Phonology. OE *å* before nasal + consonant is *o* (*long* 5, *londe* 34, *honde* 13, *stonden* 57; but *hanged* 62), before a simple nasal *a* (*many* 4, *man* 38); OE *å* is *ō* (*moost* 1, *oon* 7). The adverbial suffix is always palatalized in *-lich* (*frelich* 9, *openlich* 23, *oonlich* 65, *outerliche* 71).

Inflexions. *Personal pronoun.* — 3 pl *they* 69, poss *her* 24, dat *hem* 5.

Verb. — Pres 3 sg *hath* 36, pl *compleynen* 2, *ben* 36, *stonden* 57. Present part *grocchyng* 39, *displesyng* 41. Past participle generally without preverb *y-*; str vbs in *-e(n)* (*knowen* 13, 20, *holden* 36, *drawen* 61 and *y-do* 5, *be* 55, 66, *knowe* 49).

Syntax very cumbersome and awkward. The amanuensis knows what he wants to say, but has considerable difficulty in putting it clearly. In several cases (cp. 38 ff. and 59 ff.) interpretation depends on guess-work.

On the historical circumstances and the rivalry of the gilds at the time when Northampton and Brembre were mayors of London, see G. M. TREVELYAN, *England in the Age of Wycliffe* (1909), pp. 278 ff.

2. compleynen has *the folk of Mercerye* as subject. For the agreement see § 146. 2.

4. as a membre: the Mercers constituted one of the twelve Livery Companies of the City which played an important role in the City's administration.

5. wronges subtiles: Here, as in French, the adjective is placed after the substantive and given a plural mark.

5. by longe tyme ' during ' or ' for a long time '.

7. is to be to ' belongs to '.

9. at o day: cp. the text of the Cordwainers' petition: *que la Election du Maire de la dite Citee deusse estre franchement fait chescun an le jour de Seint Edward le Roy*, that is, 13 October.

10. Nichol Bembre: a member of the Grocers' Company and declared partisan of Richard II, Nicholas Brembre had himself elected mayor for 1383-4 using considerable pressure, as is recounted here. He later became a counsellor of the king, was accused of treason (1387), fled to Wales, was arrested and hung in London in 1388.

11. purposed hym ' proposed himself ' (as a candidate); a rather rare meaning.

12. John Northampton: leader of the Wyclifite faction supported by John of Gaunt; elected mayor in 1381, he was put in prison by Brembre in 1384.
Cp. the petition of the Cordwainers: *ove forte main, debat et graunt multitude des gentz encontre la peas par avisement purvoiez.*

23. did crye openlich ' caused to be publicly proclaimed '; same construction l. 26, cp. § 136.

24. her Mair: the plural *her* agrees with the collective (morphologically sg) *noman* (l. 23).

25. of his ordynaunce ' of his party '.

26 ff. Cp. the petition of the Cordwainers: *Lequel Mons Nicholl, la noct* *ensivant, fict carier a la dite Gyhall graunt quantité d'armure, ove quele si bien foreins come autres feurent armeez.*

28. of withinne *the city of London* understood.

34. hidynges: cp. the petition of the Cordwainers: *en mesons et autres liewes secretz.*

35. in comune ' all together '.

37. of conquest or maistrye ' by conquest or main force '. Petition of the Cordwainers: *Et issint la Mairaltee du dite Citee depuis le dit temps tant que en cea ad estee tenuz par conquest et maistrie.*

38 ff. This sentence with its anacolutha is rather obscure. The sense appears to be as follows: " If Bembre knew [*wyte*] that any complained [*pleyned*] about any of his wrongs, in private or in public, and if this person displeased him [*and it were displesing to hym*], he had him put in prison by the accusation of somebody [*bi puttyng forth of whom so it were*], however untenable the charge might be [*were it never so unprevable*].

40. of whom so it were: MORSBACH and EMERSON take *whom-so* as the object case of *what-so* ' whatever '. We prefer, with CHAMBERS *London English*, p. 244, to interpret ' whoever '; cp. the corresponding passage in the Cordwainers' petition: *ils les fesoient enditer de felonie, et lour enditours feurent de l'affinité et assent le dit Mons Nicholl et gentz de male fame (Rot. Parl., III, p. 226).*

41. unprevable ' unprovable, untenable ' is the reading proposed by CHAM-BERS, *l. c.* where his predecessors read *unprenable* which is not satisfactory. — **and it were** ' if it was '; *and* for *and an.*

43. that hym lust meynteigne ' that he liked to support ' (with *lüst* for *list*).

52. of us ' by us '.

53. or ony: that is *or yif ony.*

55. wolden has *ony conseille* as subject (l. 53).

56. were anon apeched: that is *thei were.*

61. drawen ' quartered '.

62. the which thyng lyke to yowre worthy lordship, etc. ' may it please your lordship to have the aforesaid thing proved or not proved before an impartial judge '.

63. the whether that trowthe may shewe ' that truth may show which of the two [*the whether*] is (right).

67. poyntes of trewe governaunce: allusion to the *Jubilee Book* compiled in 1376, Edward III's jubilee year, by a committee on which was found Northampton and other adversaries of Brembre's party. Revised by the latter in 1384, this collection of City ordinances was burned in 1387 under Nicholas Exton, as is said in l. 71. Cp. the corresponding but more detailed passage in the Cordwainers' petition: *Item les avant ditz supliantz se pleignont ... de ceo que la ou feust compris en une livre que feust appellé le Jubilee, touz les bones articles appurtinantz al bone governaille du dite Citee, feurent jurrez de les tenir et sustenir as touz jours, a l'honour de Dieu, et profit de comune poeple, lequel livre le dit Nicholl Exton et ses accomplises ount ars sanz con-sent de a bone comune du dite Citee, a graunt destruccion et anientissement des plousours bones libertees, franchises et custumes de mesme la Citee.*

69-70. for thei sholde nought be knowen 'so that they (the laws) should not be known'.

XXVI

Text from MS Cotton Tiberius D 7 in the British Museum (called *C*) with readings taken from MS Harley 1900 (called *H*).

Dialect of the South-west with Midland features.

Phonology. John of Trevisa's language does not show the expected voicing of initial *f*. On the other hand OE *y* is regularly represented by [ü] written *u* (*buþ* 1, *furste* 4, 20, *burþ* 16, *supthe* 19, *lurnede* 30, etc.); note however *i* (in *bysynes* 24 and *lift* 'left' 39) and *e* (in *septhe* 27).

Inflexions. *Substantive.* — Note the appearance of the double plural *chyldern* 16, 34, 37, *children* 21.

Personal pronoun. — 3 pl nom *hy* 9, 11 (and the unstressed form *a* 21, 36, 39), poss *here* 4, 19, dat *ham* 23, 39.

Verb. — Pres 3 sg in -*e*(*þ*) (*haþ* 46), pl in -*e*(*þ*) (*buþ* 1, 2, 3, etc., *woneþ* 7, *habbeþ* 7, 19, *spekeþ* 8, etc.).

Pres part in -*ing* (*slyttyng, frotyng* 60). Past part always preceded by *y-*.

Adverbs in -*lych* (*scarslych* 51, *specialych* 59).

From a grammatical point of view the student will profit greatly by comparing Trevisa's translation with Caxton's 'modernisation' into 1485 London dialect.

---

5. bote ȝef 'except that' translates *nisi forsan*.

7. þe Flemmynges: Flemish had been settled in Pembrokeshire from the beginning of the 12th cent. In 1154, Henry II favored the immigration of new Flemish settlers.

9. þre maner speche: Bede, in his *Historia ecclesiastica* is the first to speak of the three continental tribes who participated in the invasion of Celtic Britain. But his information is less summary than Higden's. According to Bede the Jutes occupied Kent, the Saxons the rest of Southern England, and the Angles the Midlands and North. From a linguistic point of view it is true that the Midlands and North formed one dialect area, Anglian (subdivided into Mercian and Northumbrian). — For the construction *þre maner speche*, cp. § 167, REM. 1.

11. come is here a preterit plural (similarly in l. 20).

12. Danes: allusion to Viking invasions in the 9th cent.

14. ys apeyred 'has deteriorated'. It is a widely spread but quite mistaken idea that a mixture of languages produces 'corruption'.

17 ff. Allusion to the well-known fact that French, or rather Anglo-Norman, was for a long time the language of the Norman invaders and their descendants. On this point see K. LAMBLEY, *The French Language in England*, Manchester, 1920.

23. a child hys brouch 'a child's toy'. Construction which results, in part, from a false analysis of genitives in -*is*, -*es*; cp. § 109 REM.

25. more y-told of. A knowledge of French was considered a necessary upper class accomplishment at this time.

26-40. This passage, of great interest for the history of English, is a personal addition by Trevisa, as can be readily seen by comparing it with the original. Cp. W. H. STEVENSON in *An English Miscellany presented to Dr. Furnivall*, p. 421 ff.

26. þe furste moreyn: refers to the great plague of 1348-9.

27. Johann Cornwall, a mayster of gramere: his name is mentioned in the archives of Merton College, Oxford, in 1347-8. Like John of Trevisa, John of Cornwall and Richard Pencrych probably came from Cornwall.

39-40. and a scholle passe þe se ' if they are to cross the Channel '.

40. caas ' circumstances '.

47-49. Interpolation by Trevisa.

50. a þre ' into three (parts) '; *a* is the unstressed form of *in*.

51. ys abyd ' has survived '.

59-66. This passage in Higden is borrowed from the *Gesta Pontificum* by Wm. of Malmesbury, a work dated from 1125. It can hardly be considered as evidence in the 14th century.

XXVII

Text. 1. *Book of the Duchess*: MS Fairfax 16, Bodleian, Oxford (called *F*) with most of the normalizations proposed by F. N. ROBINSON. — 2. *Troilus and Criseyde*: MS 61, Corpus Christi College, Cambridge (called *Cp*) with readings from a MS of the same family, L. I, of Saint John's College, Cambridge (called *J*). — 3. *Legend of Good Women*: text of *F* with readings from MS Gg. IV, 27, University Library, Cambridge (called *G*). — 4. *Canterbury Tales*: text from Ellesmere MS, Huntington Library, California (called *El*), with readings or variants taken from MSS Hengwrt 154, National Library, Aberystwyth (called *He*), 198, Corpus Christi College, Cambridge (called *Cp*), Landsdowne 851 in the British Museum (called *Ld*).

Dialect of London.

Spelling. The best MSS do not use *ʒ* but *y* or *gh*; on the other hand *þ* alternates with *th*. — *i* and *y* are interchangeable (*arys* 4b/827: *arise* 2/1190, *right* 4b/962: *ryght* 1/356, *bitide* 4b/900: *bityde* 4b/934); similarly *ey* (*ei*) and *ay* (*ai*) (*agayn* 4b/766, *maister* 4b/680, *slayn* 4b/686, *abaysed* 2/1233 and *streight* 4b/671, *peyned* 1/318, *wey* 4b/761, *seye* 2/1191). — The long vowels *ē*, and *ō* are often written *ee* (*cleer* 4b/914, *deeth* 4b/728, *heeng* 4a/676, *deere* 2/1210) and *oo* (*goon* 1/355, *doon* 1/374, *smoot* 4b/677, *wroot* 4b/890); [ū] is written *ou*, *ow* before a consonant (*foules* 1/295, *trouthe* 3/267, *pardoun* 4b/917, *clowde* 1/343).

Phonology. Before nasal + consonant *o* appears in *hond* 4a/702, *honge* 4b/868, *lond* 4b/790, etc. (alongside *a: hand* 4b/697).

OE *y* is represented by *i* [I] (*me thynketh* 4b/681, *dide* 4b/691, *synne* 4b/905, *myrie* 4b/963, *stirte* 4b/705), but the West Midland [ü] is also found (*murie* 4b/843, *murierly* 4a/714) as well as the South East *e* [ɛ] (*merie* 4b/883, *mery* 1/319, *ken* ' kin ' 1/438).

Inflexions. *Substantives.* — Note the plurals *yer* 1/455 and *eyen* 4a/684, *bretheren* 4b/777.

Personal pronoun. — 1 sg *I* or *y*, exceptionally *ich* in *so thee'ch* (riming with *breech*) 4b/947; 3 pl nom *they* 4b/467, poss *hir* 4b/468, 472, etc., dat *hem* 1/304, 2/1233, 4b/473.

Verb. — Pres indicative 3 sg in -(*e*)*th* (*hereth* 2/1235, *rolleth* 4b/838, *comth* 2/1221, *seth* 2/1240). Cp. the contract forms *bytrent*, *writhe* 2/1231.

3 pl in -*e*(*n*) (*bryngen* 2/1204, *make* 1/463, *bee* 4b/409). Pres part in -*yng* (*hangyng* 3/264, *dwellyng* 4a/702). Str pret 2 sg *toke* 1/483, *spak* 4b/753.

Past part with or without preverb *i-*, *y-*; examples of str vbs *y-founde* 1/378, *goon* 1/396, *ben* 2/1211, *i-take* 2/1197, *taken* 4b/482.

Versification. In the selections printed here Chaucer uses octosyllabic rimed couplets in *The Book of the Duchess*, heroic couplets in the *CT*, and rime royal (*ababbcc*) in the *Troilus* and the *Ballad of Good Women*. For details of the versification the reader is referred to the treatise by B. TEN BRINK.

It should be noted, however, that final -*e* is generally silent in sandhi situations, except for substantives and adjectives preceding a word starting with a consonant (*justë cause* 2/1227, *bothë two* 2/1223, 4b/888, *fairë body* 3/256, *falsë traytour* 4b/699.

In final syllables before a consonant, *e* is usually pronounced in -*ëd* (*avysëd* 4b/690, *walkëd* 4b/722), -*ës* (*Of founës, sowrës, bukkës, doës* 1/429, but *relikęs* 4b/920, 944, *siręs* 4b/915), -*ëth* (*passëth* 4b/668, *clepëth* 4b/675, but *makęth* 3/267, *comęth* 3/255 also written *comth* 4b/781), -*ën* (*comën* 4a/671, but *comęn* 4a/687). According to the requirements of the meter an unaccented -*e*- in the middle of a trisyllable might be pronounced (*trewëly* 4b/788, *evërich* 4b/768) or syncopated (*evęrich* 4b/931, *brethęren* 4b/777, *develës* 4b/470, *owęnë* 4b/790, *seurętee* 4b/937). The same is sometimes the case with other vowels (*parąventure* 4b/935). There is often diæresis in long words (*ha-bi-ta-ci-oun* 4b/689, *ec-cle-si-as-te* 4a/708). On the other hand, before a word beginning with a vowel, it frequently happens that final -*ie*, -*y* merges with the following syllable (and is then pronounced [j] before the vowel), thus '*any of* 'you* 4b/923, '*erly and* 'late* 4b/730, the '*pothe*'*carie and*'*swerde* 4b/859.

lu'*xurie and* '*hasar*'*drye* 4b/897, '*myrie of* '*cheere* 4b/963; finally, feminine rimes are not unusual in Chaucer ('*tarie : *'*carie* 4b/799-80, '*oother : *'*brother* 4b/807-8, '*merie : *'*berie* 4b/884-5, '*neces*'*sarie : *'*adver*'*sarie* 4b/681-2, '*storie : *'*offer*'*torie* 4a/709-10.

1

291. " Like most poetic dream visions at the time [cp. for example the vision of William Langland, no. XXI, 1] Chaucer's starts with a dream of a beautiful morning in May. What is lacking in originality in his theme, Chaucer always makes up for by the richness and charm of his details. Beyond Machaut and Guillaume de Lorris, he matches Chrestien de Troyes, whom he does not know, in his prettiest decorative tableaux." (E. LEGOUIS, *Chaucer*, p. 67. Pages 65 to 74 of this book are the most judicious to have been devoted to *The Book of the Duchess*, and the reader should look at this discussion).

302. the mooste solempne servise by noote ' the most marvellous concert of voices '.

304-5. som . . . som ' one . . . another '; *som* is singular here.

308. but ' unless '.

310 11. ' that, certainly, not for the town of Tunis would I have missed their singing '. Tunis [*Tewnes*] seems wrung in for the rime as well as the exotic effect.

326 ff. Echoes of the Troy legend which Chaucer could have read in Benoît de Sainte-More or Guido delle Colonne.

343. ne in: pronounced *nin*, eliding the vowel of *ne*.

344 ff. As EMERSON has shown so well ("Chaucer and Medieval Hunting" in *Romanic Review* 13, 115-50 or *Chaucer Essays and Studies*, 320-77) Chaucer shows that he is a connoisseur in matters of venery. In the office of valet to Edward III, the poet must often have participated in a royal hunt such as he describes here. This description may be compared with the one in *Sir Gawain* (no. XVIII, 2, ll. 1126-77).

344. wonder lowde ' very loud '.

347. Whether, pronounced *wher* (and often so written, for ex. farther on 4b/748) counts for only one syllable.

351. slee the hert with strengthe ' slay the deer by main force ' that is, using horses and dogs.

352. upon lengthe: after a long chase.

353. embosed: ' worn out with running ' lit. ' covered with foam ' (cp. O. F. EMERSON, *Chaucer Essays and Studies*, 323-30).

361. foresteres ' game-keepers '. ' A forester is an officer of the King (or any other man) that is sworn to preserve the Vert and Venison of the forest, and attend upon the wild beasts within his Bailiwick' (MANWOOD, *Lawes Forest*, XXI, § 4).

362. relayes ' relays ', fresh horses and dogs to replace those tired out in the stag hunt.

368. th'emperour Octovyen: probably this refers to the Roman emperor Octavian who, in the stories of Charlemagne, marries Florence, daughter of Dagobert, king of France. He here symbolizes the king of England, Edward III, who at 57 or 58 was still young enough to engage in his favorite sport.

370. in good tyme ' right away '.

375-386, 419-433. " Here the lines give a picture that has all the formality and all the freedom of manners made perfect, a style which may be seen exactly if unconsciously repeated in the loveliest of the paintings ascribed to Paolo Uccello that hangs in the Ashmolean Museum at Oxford, and is called *The Hunt at Night*.

" In this picture, under a sky of deep night-blue where there floats a feathery edge of moon, a great grove of regularly spaced and slender trees stretches into a far and dusky perspective. The slender boles are branchless until they burst forth into leafy umbrellas, high above the forest floor. Against the stillness and the darkness there is a splendid rout of riders, hounds, and servants of the hunt; men are for the most part in brightest gules; every figure has animation and a variety of stance proper to a view-halloa, somehow combined with the static formality of heraldic imagination as in other of his paintings, and as in Chaucer's poem." Nevill COGHILL, *The Poet Chaucer*, p. 32.

376. thre mot: cp. 18/1141 note.

377. the uncouplynge ' unleashing ' the dogs to take after the deer.

378. y-founde: discovered by the dogs when he starts to run.

379. y-halowed: 'shouted' or perhaps 'blown a horn', cp. 'Quant tu aras trouvé [*y-founde*] du limier, tu dois corner [*halowe*] pour chiens et dois corner un lonc mot [*mot* 376] bien lonc. Et (se) les chiens sont bien loings de toy de que tu aies haste de les avoir, tu dois corner un lonc mot et pues un court ensuiant'. (*Le livre des deduis du rey Modus*, ed. G. TILANDER, p. 48.)

381. rused 'used ruses' the word is used here in its primary OF meaning when applied to game 'using all sorts of turns and expedients to escape the dogs' (LITTRÉ).

384. on a defaute y-falle: dogs were said to have 'fallen on a default' at the very moment when, the scent being lost, the pursuit was checked.

386. a forloyn: a recall from the hunt, sound of the horn indicating the dogs were far off from the game (OF *forlonge*).

387. I was go walked 'I had gone walking'. OE had the construction *feran on huntaᵭ* 'go on a hunt', in which *huntaᵭ* was a substantive. In the 14th cent. the final of these sbs in *-aᵭ* became *eᵭ*, and was confused with *-ed* of the past participle; *on* remained under the reduced form *a* (*goon a-begged* 'go begging') or, as here, disappeared completely. — **my tree:** The poet is represented in the guise of an observer who follows the chase (ll. 357-64) without taking part in it. He imagines here that he had stopped — the slot of the deer having been lost — and rested under a tree.

390. koude no good 'had no training'.

395. I wolde have kaught hyt: a hunting dog, even a young one, was too valuable to risk its getting lost.

408. swiche seven: 'seven times as many'.

435. Argus or rather *Algus* (alongside *algorithme*) was in OF the adaptation of *al-khọrizmi*, the Persian pronunciation of *Al-Khwārizmī* 'the (native) of Khwārizm', a name given to the Arabian mathematician Abū 'Abdallāh Muhammad ibn Mūsā (9th cent.). The form *Argus* is found in the *Roman de la Rose*, l. 13731, where Chaucer may have read it.

437. his figures ten: the ten arabic numerals 0 to 9. These arabic numerals came into Europe following a translation of a treatise on algebra by the mathematician mentioned above.

438. ken, South-eastern form for *kin* (but current in London dialect), is probably used here for the rime.

445. a man in blak: probably John of Gaunt, but he was 29 (not 24 as mentioned in l. 455) when his wife died. — From this point on the hunt disappears from the story; it does not come back until the last lines, 1311-23.

479. After this line an edition by Thynne (1532) adds:

And thus in sorwe lefte me alone

which all modern editors except Koch consider apocryphal because of its rhythm and rime.

2

1192. The comparison is a recall from Boccaccio's *Filocolo* 2, 165-6: 'dove Filocolo timido, come la grù sotto il falcone, o la colomba sotto il rapace sparviere, dimorava'.

1194. The bitterness of soot was proverbial at the time.

1203. *the blisful goddess sevene* are the seven planets that govern the destiny of men. Other MSS, like MS L 1 of Saint John's College, Cambridge read *bryghte* instead of *blisful.*

1231. Bytrent and writhe, etc. ' as the sweet woodbine rolls around and enwraps '. 3rd sg vbs with *-eth* completely assimilated to the preceding dental. The loverlike tree and woodbine twining, could be found by Chaucer in Ovid, Dante, Boccaccio or Petrarch.

1235. ' when she hears some shepherd speak '.

1241. dyen mot ' must die '; other MSS have here the preterit *moste* which weakens the sense of obligation.

1242. rescous doth hym escapen ' rescue causes him to escape (death)'. *doth* is a causative.

3

249. Absolon: Absalom was remarkable for the beauty of his hair, cp. 2 Sam. XIV 26.

251. Jonathas: Jonathan had a great friendship for David, cp. 1 Sam. XIX 2.

252. Penalopee: Penelope who waited for Ulysses. — **Marcia Catoun,** Marcia, daughter of M. Cato Uticensis accepted being ' lent ' to Hortensius, a friend of her husband's.

254. Isoude: Iseult; the Tristan legend was known in England through many poems.

257. Lavyne: Lavinia, cp. $27_1/33$.

258. Polixene: according to OVID, *Met.* XII 448, Polyxena, daughter of Priam, was sacrificed on the tomb of Achilles; but according to Guido delle Colonne she was killed by Pyrrhus.

263. Herro: Hero of Sestos, beloved by Leander, cp. OVID, *Her.* XVIII, XIX. — **Laudomia** is Laodamia, wife of Protesilaus, cp. OVID, *Her.* XIII.

265. Canace: Canacee, daughter of Æolus, who loved her brother, and killed herself.

266. Ysiphile is Hypsipyle, daughter of Thoas, king of Lemnos; she saved her father when the women of Lemnos killed all the men on the island; cp. OVID, *Her.* VI.

268. Ypermystre: Hypermnestra, the only one of the Danaids who saved her husband, Lynceus; cp. OVID, *Her.* XIV. — **Adriane:** Ariadne, daughter of Minos.

4

A

669. hym: the Summoner (cp. l. 673). **Pardoner:** on the pardoner, or seller of papal indulgences, see J. J. JUSSERAND, *Chaucer's Pardoner and the Pope's Pardoners* in Chaucer Society Essays, Part V, no. 13 and J. M. MANLY, *Some New Light on Chaucer,* 122-30.

670. Rouncivale: not the distant Spanish convent of Nuestra Señora de Roncesvalles, but one of its dependencies, the hospice founded in 1229 by William Marshall, count of Pembroke, near Charing Cross just at the entrance to London. The Pardoners of Rouncivalle were, in Chaucer's time, the object of satires.

672. '**Com hider**', etc.: refrain of some popular love song. — **to me:** note the rime with *Romë*.

673. Somonour: the Summoner was a petty officer who cited persons to appear before the ecclesiastical court. — **burdoun:** the bass accompaniment.

680. for jolitee: 'free and easy manner ', 'bravado '.

684. glarynge eyen: according to the physiognomy of the day, this (and the other traits) reveal a debauched and drunken libertine (cp. Walter C. Curry, *Chaucer and the Medieval Sciences*, New York, 1926, pp. 57, 61-64).

685. vernycle: diminutive of *veronica*; an insignia representing the veil of St. Veronica with the Holy Image; this insignia was worn by those who had made the pilgrimage to Rome.

692. fro Berwyck into Ware: that is from the North of England (Berwick) to the South (Ware, in Hertfordshire); the expression is probably used for the rime.

707-14. On the interpretation of this passage see F. Mossé, ' Chaucer et la liturgie ', in *Revue germanique*, 1923, 283-9.

708. a noble ecclesiaste, perhaps ' an excellent preacher '; the word *ecclesiaste* as a common noun seems very rare. The *OED* recognizes only this example from Chaucer and defines ' one who performs public functions in church '. Has Chaucer taken the word in its etymological sense of ' preacher ', a function in which the Pardoner excelled?

709. a lessoun or a storie ' a lesson (*lectio*) or even all the lessons (*historia*) of the office for the day from the breviary ' (cp. C. Young, *MLN* 30 (1915), 97-9).

710. alderbest ' best of all ' with the gen pl of *al* as the first element. — **an offertorie:** the offertory is the antiphon, psalm or response chanted during the ceremony of offering. As a melody it is one of the richest parts of the Gregorian chant. The offertory comes after the *Credo*, at the beginning of the second part of the Mass.

711. whan þat song was songe, either ' once those songs were finished ' (taking *whan þat* as a subordinant, and *song* as a collective) or ' once this offertory was sung ' (with demonstrative *þat*). The sermon, which today comes between the Gospel and the Creed, could come after the Offertory, cp. G. R. Owst, *Preaching in Medieval England* (Cambridge, 1926), p. 235.

712. He moste preche: not all pardoners were authorized to preach. That Chaucer's pardoner was an able preacher is demonstrated by his Tale. The prologue to the Tale, not reproduced here, gives a fair sample of his sermons (all based on the one text *Radix malorum est cupiditas*) and of his cleverness in his profession.

714. the murierly and loude ' the more merrily and loud ', an irregular addition of the adverb suffix -*ly* to a comparative form, *murier* (cp. *formerly, nearly* etc.).

B

466. where as ' where ' cp. § 161.

471. abhomynable ' monstrous '.

476. The Tale is interrupted by a long digression (ll. 477-600) which is really a homily on sins of the tavern. H. B. Hinckley, *Notes on Chaucer*

(Northampton, Mass. 1907), p. 157 suggests quite plausibly that this homily was orginally designed for a *Parson's Tale* in verse.

472-5. Cp. similarly l. 709. Chaucer says, further, in the *Parson's Tale*: ' For Cristes sake ne swereth nat so synfully in dismembrynge of Crist by soule, herte, bones and body. For certes, it semeth that ye thynke that the cursede Jewes ne dismembred nat y-nough the preciouse persone of Crist, but ye dismembre hym moore '. Thus in l. 692 the low wretch swears ' by God's arms ' and in l. 695 ' by God's holy bones '.

661. Thise riotoures thre of whiche I telle: actually Chaucer has not yet mentioned these three wretches who are going to be the heroes of the Tale itself. In the meanwhile he has changed his subject.

It is not known from what direct source Chaucer was inspired to write the story of the ' three thieves and the treasure '. The theme was widespread in the East as well as the West where it is found in numerous collections of *exempla* and Italian *novelle*. On this subject see Bryan-Dempster, *Sources and Analogues of Chaucer's Canterbury Tales* (Chicago, 1941), 415-38.

665. a cors, was with zero-relative pronoun, cp. § 152, Rem II.

667. Go bet ' go faster '; the expression was often used for dogs in the chase.

673. to-nyght ' last night '.

675. men is here the indefinite pronoun ' they, someone, one ' and is followed by the sg form *clepeth*. The same in l. 746.

677. his spere: many medieval MSS represent death as a skeleton bearing a spear.

679. this pestilence: under Edward III's reign alone there were four plague epidemics in England.

684. my dame ' my mother '.

690. ' It would be very wise to be on one's guard '.

696. al ones ' all one ', ' all in agreement '.

697-8. Allusion to the medieval institution of ' sworn brothers '.

702. plight ' sworn ' contract past participle of *plighte(n)*.

710. shall be deed ' shall die '.

715. God you see ' God look out for you, protect you ', salutation formula.

716. proudeste ' the most arrogant '.

717. with sory grace: stereotyped curse ' the devil take you ' (lit 'may you encounter misfortune ').

722. Ynde i. e. ' to the end of the world ', cp. Kittredge, *Harvard Studies and Notes*, I, 21 ff.

727. ne[1] at the head of the sentence and followed by a second negative (here *ne*[2]) is the equivalent of ' and ' (cp. ModE *nor*).

734. cheste: Chaucer plays on the two senses of ' clothes-press ' and ' coffin '.

739. to yow ' on your part '.

741. but ' unless '.

743. agayns ' in presence of ' Levit. xix, 32.

745 ff. cp. Eccles. viii. 6.

748. God be with yow polite formula whose contraction gave ModE *good* *bye.* — where ye go or ryde typical Chaucerian metrical filler (*where* 'whether').

755-6. 'By my faith, just as sure as you are one of his spies, tell where he is, or you shall pay for it'.

761. leef 'desirous'.

770. floryns: the florin, minted in England from 1339 on was valued at six shillings eight pence.

775. doun they sette hem 'they set themselves down', 'they sat down'.

782. wende 'who would have supposed'. (from vb *wenen*).

792. As wisely and as slyly: another filler; in older English *slyly* and *wisely* were practically synonymous.

803. bad 'ordered' (from *bidde*).

819. Shal it be conseil 'will you keep it secret'.

826-7. that ryght anoon Arys: *thou* is not expressed here before the subjunctive *arys* '(see to it that) you get up'.

858. destroyed 'pestered'.

885. par cas 'by chance'.

889. Avycen: celebrated Arab physician and philosopher († 1037). His principal work is entitled *Kitāb-al-Qānūn fi'l-Tibb* or 'Book of the Canon of Medicine'.

890. fen 'subdivision, section' (from the Arabic *fann*).

904. goode men is not addressed to the fellow pilgrims, but to his standard audience to which he returns, once the tale itself is finished, to dwell on the sin of avarice.

907. nobles: gold pieces minted from 1340 on, which were worth one third of a pound.

915. And lo, sires, thus I preche: Here the Pardoner's sermon ends. What follows is addressed to his fellow-pilgrims to whom he has just revealed, rather cynically, his professional secrets. W. C. CURRY, *l. c.* p. 67 proposes this ingenious explanation of the following verses: " to hypnotize the Pilgrims into buying relics after he has declared their worthlessness and his own perfidy would constitute the crowning success of his career. He says, in effect: 'Lo, sirs, this is the way I preach to *ignorant* people. But *you* are my friends; may God grant that *you* may receive the pardon of Jesus Christ; I would never deceive *you*'! " Kittredge has a quite different interpretation.

929. so þat 'provided that'.

935. Paraventure is trisyllabic here; it is often found written *paraunter*.

939. bothe moore and lasse 'high and low'.

941. oure Hoost, namely, Harry Bailly, who in this group imagined by Chaucer is the controller of the sequence of the tales and master of ceremonies on the trip.

947. so thee'ch 'as I hope to prosper'.

951. Seint Eleyne, St. Helen, mother of Constantine who was the finder of the true Cross.

952. coillons OF for 'testicles'.

953. Seintuarie: here 'Sacred object or relic'.

961. al the peple lough: *peple* has sg concord (as here) or pl; *folk,* by contrast takes a pl (*e. g.* 18/1126).

962. it is right y-nough ' that is certainly enough '.

967. as we diden ' as we did before '.

XXVIII

Text from Bodleian MS Fairfax 3.

Dialect of London (South-east Midland) with some Kentish features.

Spelling. Initial *sch-* for *sh-* (*schuldres* 4082, *sche* 3947 and passim); *-ht* (*riht, liht, nyht, wyht*) and *-h* (*sih* 3945, *styh* 3991) appear before *i* (alongside *-ght*).

ie indicates close *ẹ̄* (*hiere* 3954, *hield* 3980, *hiewh* 4072). Also notable are the spellings *freissh* 3969, etc. and *fleissh* 4072, and the letter *u* to indicate [ü].

Phonology. OE *ạ̄* > *o* before nasal plus consonant (*sond, lond, hond, onde*); OE *y* > *i* normally, but [ü] sometimes remains (*puttes* ' pits ' 4047, *hulles* ' hills ' 3995) as in West Midland, or becomes *e* as in the South-east (*pettes* ' pits ' 4047, *dede* ' did ' 3953). Note the palatalization in *lich* ' like ' 4170, *behovelich* 4012.

Inflexions. *Personal pronoun.* — 3 pl nom þei 4062, dat *hem* 4007.

Verb. — Pres 3 sg in -(*e*)þ (*spekeþ* 4101), pl in -*e*(*n*) (*finde* 4110, *longen* 4055). Pres participle in *-inge* (*drecchinge* 3975). Past part not preceded by preverb *y-* and ending in *-e*(*n*) for str vbs (*writen* 4096, *falle* 4150).

Versification. Octosyllabic rimed couplets.

3945 ff. The reader might profitably compare Gower's text with Ovid whom he uses as rather close inspiration.

3946 f. ' Jason ... did not hesitate to call on Medea's magic arts '; the construction is a little obscure.

3963. wiþ open hed ' bare-headed '.

3965. ' she wore a girdle around her clothes ' (cp. OVID: *vestes induta recinctas*).

3970. sche wiþstod ' stood stock still '.

3976. ' and when she was once more master of her speech '.

3994. The lond of Crete: the Latin text of Ovid that Gower was using, very probably had the reading *Cretis* (instead of *certis*). The poet deduced from this that Medea traversed Crete where he seems to place Othrys and Olympus.

4010. whiche as = *whiche* cp. § 161.

4011. the Rede See: G. C. MACAULAY suggests that Gower might have had *rubrum mare* instead of *refluum mare* in l. 267 of his Ovid.

4034. ' Of which an alter was made there '.

4039. field-wode is perhaps the same word as OE *feld-wyrt* ' gentian '; cp. *OED* s. v. *field,* 20. But the reader may notice that Ovid speaks of *silva agrestis* which Gower has possibly taken for a plant-name and for which he has coined an English equivalent.

4064-114. As G. C. MACAULAY remarks, this picturesque passage is mostly original.

4084. 'changed into a different nature'.

4107. as who seiþ 'as one would say'.

4110. 'what is beyond human nature'.

4119. 'of which the remedy was made'.

4127 ff. Ovid says 'she did not at all forget the scaly skin of a small chelydre (= venomous snake) from the Cinyps (stream in Lybia)'; Gower misreads this and makes *Cimpheius* and *Chelidre* the proper names of two helpful snakes.

4134. nyne hundred wynter: survival of the Gmc custom of reckoning by **w**inters instead of years; similarly in 1. 4170. Note the invariable pl *wynter*.

4138. seewolf 'a voracious sea-fish, the wolf-fish (*Anarrhicas lupus*)'; Ovid (1. 270-1) speaks of the entrails of a werewolf or lycanthrope.

4143. hem wiþ to stere 'to stir them with'.

4172-4. lich ... Riht so 'just as ... exactly so'.

XXIX

Text from the unique MS formerly at Townely Hall, now in the Huntington Library, San Marino, Calif. It dates from the second half of the 15th century. The *Second Shepherds' Play* is from the end of the 14th century, perhaps about 1380-90, but it is not later than 1410.

Dialect of the North (Yorkshire).

Spelling. As in no. XXII the vowel *i*, *y* serves as a diacritical mark to indicate the length of the preceding vowel (*haytt* 227, *waytt* 226, *naymes* 190, *goyth* 204, *moyn* 190 (alongside *mone* 662), *soyne* 478, *noyse* 612, *steyll* 226). Reciprocally *i*, *y* as second elements of diphthongs are not indicated, thus *fare* 'fair' 220, 560, 569, *lade* 'laid' 520, *brane* 'brain' 540, *wate* 'wait' 586.

There is *w* for *v* in *dewill* 'devil' 217, 585, 604, *wh*- for *qu*- in *whik* 'quick' 548; *qw*- for *qu*- is frequent (*qwantt* 593). There is also frequent doubling of final consonants (*greatt* 202, *outt* 215, *itt* 497, *fott* 517, etc.).

Inflexions. *Personal pronoun.* 1 sg in general *I*, sometimes *ich* 201, 207; 3 sg fem *sho* 235 alongside *she* 246; 3 pl nom *thay* 287, poss *thare* 560, 621, dat *thaym* 561, 621.

Verb. — Present 2 sg in -(*y*)*s* (*has* 199, *goys* 222, *dos* 576, *spyllys* 540) 3 sg in -(*y*)*s* (*walkys* 197, *has* 198, *haldys* 227), pl in -*ys* (*commys* 532, *trowes* 510, *trowys* 512), exception: *doth* 213; pl without ending after a personal pronoun (*thay slepe* 287, *ye do* 208) or before (*say we* 513).

Imperative 2 pl in -*es*, -*ys* (*drawes* 290, *spekys* 484, *drynkys* 507); exception: *goyth* 204.

Past participle without preverb *y*-; in -*n* for str vbs (*gon* 199, *commen* 200, *sene* 219, *eten* 245).

Vocabulary. Note Northern lexical items and forms: *ilk* 'each' 241. *sich* 'such' 203, *gyf* 'give' 250 (*gaf* 571), *lyg* 'lie' 258, 634, *syn* 'since' 520, *gar* 'to do, make, cause' 610, 651, *fang* 'receive' 667, *gang* 'go', *till* 'to'.

Versification. The *Second Shepherds' Play* is regularly written in stanzas of thirteen verses with four rimes of the type:

$$abababab^2c^1ddd^2c^2$$

with rather frequent alliteration (in the text *ab* is printed on a single line).

The Latin stage directions are in the MS; those in ModE have been added following A. S. Cook, *Middle English Literary Reader*, also the division into scenes.

191. thi will, Lorde, of me tharnys 'reason (which comes from Thee), Lord, is lacking to me'. This same meaning of 'reason, intelligence' for *will* is found again in l. 198.

192. all uneven 'all confused, topsy turvy'.

196. I foore 'I fared'.

200. Then ylkon, etc. 'Then let every man look out for his things'.

201. a yoman: the word which dates from the second half of the 14th century designates 'a servant or attendant in a royal or noble household, usually of a superior grade, ranking between a sergeant and a groom or between a squire and a page' (*OED*).

203. And sich 'and so on'.

208. Why make ye it so qwaynt 'Why do you behave so strangely'.

209. lyst ye saynt 'do you want to play the saint'. First example of this word as a vb in this sense; later the bound phrase *saint it* is used, for example.

> Let mistress nice go saint it where she list   *Faire Em.* III, 1280.
> Whether the charmer sinner it or saint it   Pope, *Ep. Lady*, 15.

210. the shrew can paynt 'the rascal knows how to deceive people'.

215 f. Mak who is passing himself off as a royal officer has probably imitated the tone and pronunciation of people of the court. Thus the first shepherd advises him to drop the Southern (London) pronunciation (*sothren tothe*) and speak Yorkshire.

219. God looke you 'God bless you'.

220. fare = *faire* 'fine, fair'. — **Can ye now mene you** lit. 'are you able to remember yourself now', 'have you come back to your senses' (Mak seems to have lost his mind, cp. l. 191, 198).

224. an yll noys 'a bad reputation'.

233. an nedyll 'a mouthful'.

236. full of brude 'full of children'.

242. a lakan 'a baby' (lit. toy).

244. gracyus 'prosperous'. — **be far** 'than that, by far'.

247 f. 'There is no person to be believed who knows a worse (woman than my wife)'. Trowse is 3 sg of *trow* used with a passive meaning found in 14th century Northern usage (*Cursor Mundi*, Rolle of Hampole).

250 ff. Mak means that he is ready to give all he owns, immediately [*to-morne at next*], for a mass for her soul [*offer hed-maspenny*]; he wishes he was rid of her.

253. forwakyd 'weary with waking'.

256. wery forrakyd 'weary with walking too much'.

261. There are probably two lines missing after this one, the following stanza being incomplete.

263 f. 'Then I would soon prevent you (saying those things) that you'd like to whisper together, for sure'.

265-8. With Mak's prayer compare what another shepherd says in the *First Shepherds' Play:*

Cryst-crosse, benedyght eest and west,
Ffor drede.
Jesus onazorus,
Crucyefixus
Marcus, Andreus,
God be oure spede!

278 ff. Mak draws a magic circle [*a serkyll*] around the shepherds so that they will sleep till he gets away with the sheep and sets up his alibi.

279. To 'until the time'; similarly *to that* in the next line.

286. And 'if'.

485. at maylleasse 'still in child bed' (OF *malaise* 'disease').

496. thynk ye on yit 'do you know one?'

497. my dreme this is itt 'my dream, this is it'; my dream has come true.

498. 'for a while'.

504. 'Neither food nor drink will help us, the way we feel'.

505. alys you oght bot goode lit. 'ails you anything but good', 'is there anything wrong'.

509. 'someone would have sorely paid for it'.

510. that ye wore 'that you were (the thief)'.

516. hir: that is, the sheep.

523. as have I ceyll '(as true) as I (hope to) have happiness [*ceyll*] (in heaven)' cp. 549; *ceyll* is an aberrant spelling for *sele.* — avyse the 'reflect, take heed'; *the* is 'thee'.

531. farne 'what I have gone through, suffered (in childbirth), travailed' see *OED* s.v. *fare vb¹,* 7.

534. my medyll 'my middle'.

549. 'No live cattle [*whik catell*] ever smelled so strongly [*lowde*] after sheep as he does'.

551. 'We are mistaken, I think we're deceived' (dramatic irony).

552. don 'completely'. This word reenforces what the first Shepherd just said.

554. 'Is it a boy? the second Shepherd means to say, but *knave* by this time has already moved on to its ModE meaning of 'low-life', hence Mak's response in the following lines.

557. that joy is to se '(such) that it is a joy to see'.

560. fare (= *fair*) fall 'may they have happiness', cp. *OED* s.v. *fall* 46 *d.*

568. all glad were ye gone '(I would be) quite happy if you were gone'.

580. do way 'leave him alone'.

586. 'He is unfortunately birthmarked; we (are wasting our time [*ill*] to) wait around here'. The shepherds have not yet found out Mak's trick.

587. ' An ill spun weft produces only bad cloth ', a proverb.

591 f. Another proverb: ' Human nature creeps in where it can't walk in ';
cp. § 135.

596. ' A false scold will hang at last ', probably another proverb.

603. ' I am he who begot him, yonder woman bore him ', that is, we know
our child better than anyone, and if there is a sheep in the cradle, a changeling
has been thrust upon us.

617. takyn with ' bewitched by '.

623. with you will I be left ' I put it up to you '. — **Do my reede** ' take
my advice '.

627. have done as tyte ' finish it as quickly as possible '.

628. Cl. CHIDAMIAN, *Speculum* 22 (1947), 186-90, recalls, concerning this
incident, the popular belief that tossing a woman in a blanket helps her
delivery; this detail, if it was known to the audience would have added to
the humor of the passage.

629. what I am sore ' man, am I tired '.

631. VII skore ' 140 pounds '.

632. ' I want to sleep and I don't care where '.

635. yit I mene ' I am still thinking '.

639. that Adam had lorne ' what Adam had lost '.

640. warloo to sheynd ' to destroy that wizard (*i. e.* the Devil) '.

649. upward ' from above '.

654. yond starne is the subject.

657. thre brefis to a long: " The relation of *longa* to *brevis* (usually *modus
perfectus*: one to three) had been settled by Franco of Cologne in the 13th
century and the *ars nova* (14th and 15th centuries) was chiefly concerned with
the mensuration of smaller note values: only the tenors in masses and motets
of the 15th century used the *modus perfectus* in their *cantus firmi* of slow-
moving, long-held notes over which elaborate polyphonic structures were
erected. The words of the *Tercius Pastor* ' was no crochett wrong ' show that
his ear, at least, is attuned to quicker notes. At any rate, the shepherds are
overwhelmed by the angel's music, because it represents a type of artistic,
learned music more recherché than the simple polyphony in discant style
which probably constituted their own performances." N. C. CARPENTER,
" Music in the Secunda Pastorum " *Speculum* 26, (1951), p. 698. — **he hakt it:**
POLLARD proposes ' chopped away at it ', and so ' had his will of, mastered '.

INDEX OF PROPER NAMES

A

Absalon, Absolon Absalom 13_2/83, 27_3/251.

Achilles 27_1/329.

Adam 15/14, 29/639.

Adriāne Ariadne 27_3/268.

Ælienor Eleanor (1122?-1204) wife of Henry II, 5/22.

Aylbrus see **Aþelbrus.**

Ailmar, Aylmar 8/494, 506, 517.

Albin (seinte) 5/17.

Aldithel Audley 11/35 (<OE *Aldġȳþs leāh*).

Alexander, bishop of Lincoln († 1148) 1/9.

Alfrę̄d (king) 6/942.

Amadās Amadis 13_2/67.

Amphrisos river of Thessaly 28/4005.

Anjōw Anjou 11/2.

Aquitaine 11/2.

Arestotill, Arystotill Aristotle 16/17, 31.

Argus Arab mathematician, see note 27_1/435.

Arðūr (king) Arthur 5/13995, 13998, 13999, etc.

Aþelbrus, Aylbrus 8/451, 465, 471.

Aþūlf 8/505, 532, 577.

Aubemarle Albemarle 11/33 (< F *Aubemarle*).

Austin, Awsten (saint) Augustine of Canterbury 5/18, 7/10.

Avycēn Avicenna 27_{4B}/889.

B

Bę̄da (seint) the Venerable Bede 5/16.

Bedlem, Beþleæm Bethlehem 7/3360, 3625, 3634, 3650, 29/643, 665.

Bēme Bohemia 17/67 (<OE *Bēme*).

Bernard (seynt) of Clairvaux 24/57.

Berwyk Berwick 27_{4A}/692.

Beton 21_4/306.

Bette 21_4/330.

Bircabein, king of Denmark and father of Havelok 12/494.

Bonefāce Boniface, archbishop of Canterbury 11/27.

Braband Brabant 17/2, 13.

Brembre (Nichol) 25/10.

Brunne, Brunnewāke Bourne (Lincolnshire) 14/Introd, 14_1/58, 61, 63.

Brütlǫnd Britain 5/14077.

Burguine Burgundy 5/13995.

C

Canacē Canace, daughter of Æolus 27_3/205.

Cantelōw Cantlop (Shropshire) 11/28.

Cēsar Cæsar 13_2/70.

Cesse diminutive of Cecily 21_4/315.

Cham Ham 5/12.

Chę̄pe Cheapside (London) 21_4/322.

Cimpheius Cinyps, stream in Lybia (taken 28/4127 for the name of a serpent).

Clarice Clarissa 21_4/319.

Clement 21_4/427, 340, 358, 361.

Cleopatre Cleopatra 27_3/259.

Cokkes-lāne Cockslane, London alley 21_4/319.

Constantyn Constantine 24/59.

Cornehülle Cornhill, district of London 21_3/1.

Cornwal (Johan) 26/27.

Crēte 28/3994, 4018.

Criseyde Cressida 27_2/1198, 1209, 1226, 1238.

Crīst(e), Krīst Christ 1/61, 2/18, 3/130, 5/14029, 6/887, 981, 7/3644, 3651, 3660, 8/461, 555, 579, 581, 13_3/12, 23, 18/1307, 20/714, 27_{4B}/898.

Cwmyn (Johne) John Comyn 22_2/423.

Horn name of a legendary king 8/445,
463 etc.
Horne (John) name of a shepherd
29/563.
Hughe 21₄/318.
Humber estuary 12/733.
Huntendoneschīre Huntingdonshire
11/4.
Hurtford Hertford 11/30.

I

Idoine, Ideyne woman's name 13₂/67.
Īrelǫnde, Īrlǫnde, Irloande Ireland
6/907, 11/2, 38.
Israēl 19/1040.

J

James of Aldithel James Audley
11/35.
Japhet 5/12.
Jasoūn, Jason Jason 27₁/330, 27₃/266,
28/3945, etc.
Jēme Saint James of Compostella
21₁/47.
Jeremīe Jeremiah 3/99.
Jerusalem, Jurselem 13₃/3, 18, 19/987.
Jēsu, Jēsus, Jhēsu 3/85, 4₄/4, 13₃/20,
21₂/165.
Jēsu Crȳst, Jhēsu Crīst, Jēsu Crīst
Jesus Christ 3/118, 4/8, 4₄/5, 7/
3356, 3608, 3666, 3669, 9/1, 12/542,
545, 14/4112, 16/29, 27₄ᵦ/698.
Jeu, Jew; pl Jewes 13₃/18, 19.
Jhēsu see Jēsu.
Jǫhan John 11/33.
Jǫhan of Plesseiz Jean de Plessis,
nobleman 11/33.
Jǫhn (Prestre) Prester John 23/1.
Jǫhn (seint) 27₄ᵦ/752.
Jǫhn þe apostel the apostle John 19/
985, 996, 997, 1008 etc.
Jǫhnathas Jonathan 27₃/251.
Jǫne of Camelton prior of Sempring-
ham 14₁/67.
Jǫne of Clyntone prior of Sempring-
ham 14₁/71.
Jūdas 12/482, 13₃/2, 3, 8 etc., 21₁/35.
Juvente Hebe, goddess of youth, 28/
4038.
Jurselem see Jerusalem.

K

Kantebüry Canterbury 11/28.
Kent 15/Introd.
Kytte woman's name 21₃/2.
Krȳst see Crīst.

L

Laȝamon Lawman 5/1, 14, 23, 28.
Lamedon Laomedon, king of Troy
27₁/329.
Laudomia Laodamia, wife of Prote-
silaus 27₃/263.
Lavyne Lavinia, wife of Æneas 27₁/
331, 27₃/257.
Leirchestre Leicester (England)
11/29.
Lēovenaǒ father of Lawman 5/2
(< OE Lēof-nōǒ).
Lēve Grim's wife 12/558, 565, 576,
595, 618, 642.
Lyncolne, Lincol Lincoln 1/9, 13₄/33.
1. Lindeseye Lindsey (NE of Lin-
colnshire) 12/734.
2. Lyndeseye Lindsey (Suffolk) 13₄/
33.
Lǫndon(e), Lōunde, Lūndene London
11/24, 13₄/34, 21₃/4, 44.
Lūcifer, Lūcyfer 3/4, 14/4141, 21₁/39.
Lūcresse Lucrece 27₃/257.
Lūndene see Lǫndon(e).

M

Mak the thieving shepherd 29/199,
208, 209, 214 etc.; gen Makys 29/
604.
Malverne Malvern 21₁/5.
Mannyng (Robert) 14/Introd.
Marcia Catōun Marcia, Cato's daugh-
ter 27₃/252.
Mārȳ, Mārī, Mārīe, Marȝe the virgin
Mary 3/126, 7/3622, 17/10, 18/754,
1263, 27₄ᵦ/685.
Marthe Martha 3/125, 126.
Medēa 27₁/330, 28/3946, etc.
Mercii Mercians 26/55.
Milstorak 23/2.
Moddrẹd, Mǫdrẹd, Mordrẹde nephew
of Arthur 5/13999, 14014, 14021
etc., 20/711 (< Welsh Medrawt).

GLOSSARY

TO BE READ BEFORE USING THE GLOSSARY

I. **Alphabetical order of words:** *a, b, c, d, e, f, g, ʒ, h, i, j, k, l, m, n, o, p, q, r, s, t, þ (th), u, v, w, y-, z.*
æ comes after *ad-, ʒ* after *g*. *þ-* (or *th-*) words are listed separately following all words in *t-*; it should be noted particularly that *y* and *i* are alphabetized under *i* except initially: *yle* is found under *y-*, *ilke* under *i*, but *dyen = dien*, *lay = lai*, etc.
Proper names are listed in a separate Index which precedes the glossary.

II. **Abbreviations** frequently used are *adj* adjective, *adv* adverb, *pers* personal, *pp* past participle, *prep* preposition, *pron* pronoun, *sb* substantive, *str* strong, *vb* verb, *wk* weak. For the remainder see list of abbreviations on p. xix.

III. **OED references** (see preface, p. x and note, p. x). Several cases are to be carefully distinguished:
1. The word considered is entered in the following glossary and in the *Oxford English Dictionary* (*OED*, also called *New English Dictionary*) under the same form. In this case, as a rule, *no reference is given*, even if the word is obsolete. For instance, when the student finds in the glossary an entry such as:

> amad *pp adj* mad, foolish.

he should look up the word in the *OED* under **amad,** *ppl a.*
2. The word considered is entered in the glossary under a form which differs, even slightly, from that of the *OED*:
(*a*) If *form and sense* are still in common use, the *OED* reference appears in SMALL CAPITALS as the meaning of our entry (generally the first when there are several), thus:

> dȯr *sb* DOOR.
> ferien *wk vb* FERRY, transport.

(*b*) If the ME *meaning* is now obsolete, the *OED* reference is printed in small capitals between square brackets following the period which ends the gloss, for instance:

> angyr *sb* unhappiness 22₁/235. [ANGER].

(*c*) If the *word* is marked by the *OED* as obsolete or dialectal, the *OED* reference is bracketed and *italicized* at the end of the gloss, for instance:

> pade *sb* toad. [*Pad¹*].

Often such forms appear in the *OED* after the vocable has been printed several times previously with more common modern semantic equivalents. *This is not always the case.* There is a considerable variety of practice on these matters from volume to volume. When the part of speech to search for is not given along with the small capital *OED* indicator, it is the same as that attributed to the ME entry in the glossary, e. g.

> run *sb* RUN, brook

should be looked up under RUN *sb* not under RUN *vb*.

IV. **Diacritical marks:** for the phonetic value of these signs see §§ 8-12. In the glossary open *ē* is marked *ẹ̄* to distinguish it from close *ē*. (marked simply *ē*) ; *ę* indicates final silent *e*.
The student must not forget that there is considerable uncertainty about the pronunciation of Middle English, and that these indications of length, quality and degree of aperture for vowels are well informed and probable reconstructions.

422

GLOSSARY

A

1. a *3 pl pers pron* they 26/21, 36, 39, 62, 65, 66. (Unstressed form of *hi²*).
2. a *adv* AY, always 4/1, 37.
3. a *prep*, in, at, of, *a lare* in wisdom 2/1, *a blode* with blood 13₃/17, *a nyht* 13₅/22, *a knees* on (his) knees 8/505. [*A¹*]. (Unstressed form of OE *an, on, of*).

abaysed *pp adj* ABASHED, intimidated.
abak *adv* 6/877 ABACK.
aby see abȳ(e).
abīde, abȳde *str vb 1* ABIDE, stand up under; *pres 3 sg* abȳt 15/22; *pp* abyde in *ys* ⁓ has survived 26/51; abiden.
abȳ(e), abüg̈g̈e *wk vb 2* BUY, expiate, pay (for); *þou shalt it* ⁓ you will smart for it; *pret* aboūhte; *pp* aboū3t. [*Aby*].
abȳt see abīde.
abīte *str vb 1* taste. *pp* abiten.
abloy *adj* carried away (with joy) 18/1174. (OF *e(s)bloi* 'dazzled').
abof, abowen, abwen *prep* and *adv* ABOVE.
aboū3t, aboūhte see *abȳe*.
aboūte(n), oboūt, abūton, abūten 1. *adv* here and there.—2. *prep* ABOUT, around.
abowen see abof.
abüg̈g̈e see abȳe.
1. abūten *prep* without 11/10.
2. abūten, abuton see aboūte(n).
abwen see abof.
ac, ah, auh, oc *conj* but; and 7/3644.
accidīe *sb* access of laziness 21₄/366.
accordandly *adv* ACCORDINGLY.
1. acord(e) *sb* agreement; *al of oon* ⁓ in complete agreement 27₁/305; ACCORD.
2. acord(e) *wk vb* be in accord, fall into an agreement, ACCORD.
acroche *wk vb* acquire. [ACCROACH].
acumbri *wk vb* encumber 9/24. [*Accumber*].
adawe *adv* *do* ⁓ kill, put to death 14/4106. [*Adaw²*].

adoūn, adown, adūn(e) *adv* ADOWN.
adradde see adrede(n).
adrēde(n) *wk vb* be frightened, DREAD, *pp* adrad. [*Adread*].
adreynten see adrenche.
adrenche *wk vb* drown, (reflexive) drown oneself; *pret pl* adreynten 15/5. [*Adrench*].
adūne see adoūn.
adversārie *sb* ADVERSARY.
ǣch see ę̄ch(e).
ǣfne see ę̄ven².
ǣft see eft.
æhc = ǣch see ę̄ch.
ælle see al.
ælmes see almes.
æm see bē(n).
ǣnde see ēnde.
ǣnne see an¹.
ǣrd *sb* region 7/3336. [*Erd*].
ǣrest see erst.
ærm see arm.
ært see bē(n).
ætfǭren *prep* before 11/27. [*Atfore*].
ǣðele *adj* noble 5/3, *þa æðelæn* the noble (deeds) 5/7. [*Athel*].
ǣvere, ǣvre see ę̄ver.
ǣvrič, ǣvrich see everich.
affeccyon, affeccion *sb* AFFECTION.
affīle *wk vb* sharpen.
afflyciōn *sb* AFFLICTION.
afforce *wk vb* force, try.
affraye(n) *wk vb* frighten. [*Affray*].
afingret *pp adj* very hungry 10/110, 190, 258. [*Afingered*] (<OE *of-hyngred*).
after, efter 1. *adv* far, in the future 21₂/201; 2. *prep* on account of, for 1/21, AFTER.
ag̈ǣns see agayns.
agayn, a3ain, ageyn, a3ēn, a3ein, ayēn, agāne 1. *adv* AGAIN 2. *prep* AGAINST.
agayn(e)s, agaynez, ogānis, a3ēn(e)s, a3eines, ayein(s), ag̈ǣnes, on3ēnes 1. *prep* towards, AGAINST; in the presence of 27₄ᴮ/743.—2. *adv* in opposition to, AGAINST.
agan see agōn².
agāne, ageyn see agayn.

423

424

aght, auhte, echte *sb* goods, property
[*Aught¹*].

1. **agon** *str pret* I began 5/14031.
[*Aginne*].

2. **agǫn, agǫǫn, agän, agǭ** *pp* gone,
passed, AGO. [AGONE].

agraiþi *wk vb* get ready 15/40.
[*Agraith*].

agraunte *wk vb* promise, grant; *pp*
agraunt 14/4160.

agrīse *str vb 1* become frightened
10/240.

aȝ see **ay**.

aȝain see **agayn**.

aȝaynez see **agayns**.

1. **aȝein** see **agayn**.

2. **āȝein** *wk vb* conquer, rule 5/13994,
[OWN].

aȝeines see **agayns**.

aȝeinward, ayēnward *adv* in the opposite 15/66, once more 28/3949.
[*Againward*].

aȝen see **agayn, owen²**.

aȝēn(e)s see **agayns**.

aȝere see **owen²**.

aȝtþe *adj* EIGHTH.

ah see **ac, owen¹**.

āhen, āhne see **owen¹, ²**.

āhte see **eiȝte, owen¹**.

āhten see **owen¹**.

ay, aȝ *adv* AYE, ever; ~ *oc* ~ forever
and ever 7/3644. (OE *ā*, ON *ei*).

ayein(s) see **agayns**.

ayein-say *wk vb* oppose, refuse.
[*Again-say*].

ayein-stande *st vb 6* resist. [*Again-
stand*].

ayēn see **agayn**.

ayēnward see **aȝeinward**.

ayer(e), ayre *sb* AIR.

ayle(n) *wk vb impersonal* AIL, cause
to suffer. Cp. *eilin*.

aire, ayre *sb* HEIR, son.

ayre see **ayer(e)**.

aisheist see **aske**.

ayþer, aythor see **eyþer**.

aywhere, aywhore, eȝwhær *adv* everywhere, somewhere, anywhere.

āke *wk vb* ACHE; **ākþ** 15/30.

al, all 1. *adj* ALL; *pl* alle, ælle; *gen pl*
alder, alre 3/6, 5/13995; *alderbest,
alþerbeste* 12/720 best of all; *alre-*

wīseste wisest of all 5/14051; *alþerverst* first of all 15/32. — 2. *adv*
very; ~ *glad* very glad.

alblast *sb* ARBALEST, cross bow.

alcne see **ęch**.

āld, älder see **ǫld**.

alderbest see **al**.

āldest see **ǫld**.

ale, alle *sb* ALE, tavern.

alēsnesse *sb* redemption 4/9. [*Alese-
ness*].

alhuet *conj* until 15/30. [*Allwhat*].

ālien, älyen *sb* ALIEN, stranger.

alyhte *wk vb;* *pret* alyhte ALIGHT¹.

ālys see **ayle(n)**.

allāne see **allǫne**.

alle see **al, ale**.

allǫne, allāne *adj* ALONE.

allunge *adv* entirely 3/44. [ALLINGE].

almes, ælmes, elmesse *sb* ALMS.

almyȝty, almiht *adj* and *sb* ALMIGHTY.

aloft *adv* ALOFT; *lordes* ~ powerful
lords 21₂/157.

alpi see **ānlēpi**.

alre see **al**.

alrewīseste see **al**.

als see **also**.

alsǭ, alswǭ, alsuǭ, alswā, alse, als

1. *adv* ALSO, equally, similarly. —
2. *conj* AS, as if, *als if* as if 7/3631;
also soon as soon as.

alsuǭ, alswā, alswǭ see **alsǭ**.

alswilĉ, alsuiĉ *adj* just like; ~ *alse*
just as 1/3. [ALL + SUCH].

alter, auter *sb* ALTAR.

alþerbeste see **al**.

alþerverst see **al**.

alwey *adv* ALWAYS. [ALWAY].

amad *pp adj* mad, foolish.

amāng, amānges see **amǫng**.

amatyst *sb* AMETHYST.

amende(n) *wk vb* AMEND.

amendes *sb pl* AMENDS.

amidde(n) 1. *prep* AMID 10/241. —
2. in the middle 5/19.

amǫng, emǫng, amāng, amānges 1.
prep AMONG. — 2. *adv* during this
time 27₁/298.

1. **ān, ā** *indef article* A, AN; *gen* ānes
4/30, 7/3337; *acc* ænne 7/3364,
3374, ēnne 13₂/88; *dat F* āre < *anre
5/3. Cp. *on(e)*.

2. **an** *prep* IN 5/14013, 26/34. [ON].
3. **an** see **and**.
anān, anānriht see **anǫne**.
ancre *sb* recluse 3/125, 21₁/28. [*Anchor²*].
and, ande, ant, an, ent *conj* 1. AND —
2. if.
andswarede see **ondswerien**.
āne see **ǫn(e)**.
anēle *wk vb* pursue 18/723. [*Anhele*].
angyr *sb* unhappiness 22₁/235. [ANGER].
angwys *sb* ANGUISH.
anhei3 *adv* ON-HIGH. [*An-high*].
an-honge *st vb* 7 HANG. [*Anhang*].
any, ani *adj* and *pron* ANY. Cp. *eny*.
ānys see **ǫnes**.
anker *sb* ANCHOR¹ for a ship.
ānlēpi, alpi *adj* alone, one single;
(with negative) not one 10/132.
[*Onelepy*].
anóy *wk vb* ANNOY.
anónder see **anunder**.
anǫn(e), anǫǫn, anān *adv* at once;
sōne ~ id; ~ *ryght*, ~ *riht* 4/13
immediately, right away. [ANON].
anóþer, anōthire *adj* and *pron* ANOTHER.
ansuereþ see **ondswerien**.
ant see **and**.
anunder, anónder 1. *adv* below 2. *prep*
under.
anvie see **envie**.
apẹche *wk vb* accuse. [*Appeach*].
apeyre, appayre *wk vb* deteriorate
26/14. [*Appair*].
apeyring, appayring *sb* deterioration.
[*Appairing*].
aperseive *wk vb* perceive. [*Apperceive*].
apert *adj* APERT, open.
apertly *adv* clearly.
apocalyppez, apocalyppce *sb* APOCALYPSE, book of Revelation.
apointen *wk vb* APPOINT.
apōse *wk vb* question, interrogate.
[*Appose¹*].
apostle, ap(p)ostel *sb* APOSTLE.
appayre see **apeyre**.
appayring see **apeyring**.
apparayle *wk vb* attire, adorn. [APPAREL].

apparaylmente *sb* APPARELMENT, clothes.
appẹre *wk vb* APPEAR.
appon see **upon**.
a-quelle(n) *wk vb* kill, destroy; *pret*
a-quelde 5/11; *pp* a-quold 13₂/76,
[*Aquell*].
a-quenche *wk vb* calm. [*Aquench*].
a-quold see **a-quelle(n)**.
ār see **bē(n), ẹr**.
aray *sb* rank, station; display ~ *of
vanyté* 24/66, ARRAY.
arās see **arīse**.
arayed(e), arayde *pp adj* ARRAYED.
a-rāte *wk vb* chide, scold 21₃/11.
arche *sb* ARCH.
archidekene *sb* ARCHDEACON.
ār(e) see **ẹr**.
āre see **ān¹, ǫn(e), ǫre¹**.
a-recchan *wk vb* interpret 5/14049.
[*Arecche*].
āren see **bē(n)**.
a rẹren, arearen *wk vb* raise (the
dead). [*Arear*].
aright, ariht, ary3t, ari3te *adv* ARIGHT,
all right, well, as it should be.
arīse, arīze *st vb* 1 ARISE; *pres 3 sg*
arīst 15/11; *pret* arǫs, arǫǫs, arās.
arm, ærm, earm *sb* ARM.
armonȳe *sb* HARMONY.
armure *sb* ARMOUR, armor.
arn see **bē(n)**.
arǫs, arǫǫs, see **arīse**.
arow, arwe *sb* ARROW.
arrēre *adv* ARREAR.
arrȳser *sb* riser, rebel, [*Ariser*].
artow = *art thou* see **bē(n)**.
arüdden *wk vb* save 3/76; *pret* arüdde
3/81; *pp* arüd 3/106. [*Aredde*].
arwe see **arow**.
as, asẹ 1. *conj* like, AS; *as . . . monie*
how many 3/24; *as þū dẹst wel!*
My, you are doing well; as if;
(frequently an expletive before an
imperative or subjunctive) *as ẹvere
mōt I gōn* as I hope to go on forever! 27₂/1206; 20/812, 29/523,
549. — 2. *rel adv* where *thider as*
there where 27₄ᴮ/749.
asche see **aske**.
ascrȳ(e) *wk vb* cry out 18/1153, report 17/40. [*Ascry*].

aşę see as.
askápie see escápe(n).
aske, asche, axe *wk vb* ASK; *pres 2 sg*
  aisheist 6/995.
asonder *adv* ASUNDER, apart.
aspe *sb* aspen-tree. [ASP¹].
aspȳe, asspȳe *wk vb* find out 18/1199,
  spy, perceive. [*Aspy*].
assay *sb* ASSAY, trial; *of assay* of
  good quality.
assay(e) *wk vb* try; attack 22₂/440.
  [ASSAY, ESSAY].
assále, assálȝe *wk vb* ASSAIL, attack.
assent *sb* opinion, accord, ASSENT;
  by oon⁓ by common agreement.
assoille *wk vb* grant absolution,
  ASSOIL.
asspȳe see aspȳe.
as-swȳþe *adv* directly 18/1400, right
  away 20/813, 14/4097. [*Aswithe*].
astáte *sb* order 29/228, state. [ES-
  TATE].
as-tȳt *adv* at once 18/1210 [*Astite*].
astrangli *wk vb* strangle 15/13. [*As-
  trangle*].
astrengþe *wk vb* affirm. [*Astrength*].
1. at, att, ate *prep* AT, from.
2. at *relative particle* that; *that* ⁓
  that which 22₁/248.
atelich, eatelich *adj* horrible 3/6.
atír *sb* preparation, mixture. [AT-
  TIRE].
atrayt *adv* continually 15/20. [*Atreet*].
at-stonden *st vb 6* take up fighting
  position 5/14030. [*Atstand*].
att see at¹.
atte = at the; *atte laste* finally; *atte
  alle* at the tavern 21₁/42.
attempre *adj* soft, moderate, luke-
  warm.
at-wape *wk vb* escape 18/1167.
a-twinne, otwynne *adv* in two, apart
  [*A-twin*].
at-wíte *st vb 1* reproach; *pp* atwiten
  6/935.
a-twō *adv* in two.
áthe see ōthe.
aucht see owen¹.
auȝte *pron* anything at all 21₄/311.
  [AUGHT²].
aughte see aght, owen¹.

aunǧel(e), enǧel *sb* ANGEL.
auter see alter.
autóur *sb* AUTHOR.
avay see awei.
aventúre *sb* ADVENTURE; *on* ⁓ by
  chance 10/70.
averil *sb* APRIL.
avȳs *sb* opinion, vote. ADVICE.
avȳse, awȳse *wk vb* devise, consider,
  notice, ADVISE oneself.
avȳsed *pp* resolved, decided, on one's
  guard, ADVISED.
avōw *sb* VOW.
awcht see owen¹.
awe *sb* EWE.
awei, awaye, avay *adv* AWAY, far.
awen see owen².
awēne *wk vb* believe, think 13₃/18;
  pret pl awēnden.
awȳse see avȳse.
a-wòndre *impers wk vb* astonish 9/12.
  [*Awonder*].
a-wrȩken *st vb 4* avenge 5/14057.
  [*Awreak*].
axe see aske.

B

bā see bō¹.
bachelēre *sb* young man; BACHELOR.
bad(de) see bidde.
bǣron see bȩre(n).
bagge *sb* BAG.
baye *wk vb* BAY¹, bark 18/1142,
  1362.
bayly *sb* domain 19/1083. [*Baillie*].
bak, bac *sb* BACK.
báldely *adv* BOLDLY.
bále *sb* calamity, grief, unhappiness,
  BALE¹.
bálefull *adj* dangerous, evil, BALEFUL.
balie see beli.
baltyre *wk vb* leap 20/782. [*Balter*].
1. bān *sb* BONE: *pl* bānys.
2. ban *wk vb* curse 29/625, BAN.
bānd see bǫnd¹.
banēr *sb* BANNER¹.
bantel *sb* step, pillar? 19/992 see
  note, 1017.
bar, bare, bāren see bȩre(n).
barayne *adj* BARREN, sterile.
baret *sb* strife, grief. [*Barrat*].
bargān *sb* BARGAIN¹.

barm *sb* bosom, lap. [*Barm*¹].
barn(e), bern *sb* child, BAIRN.
bāsyng *sb* base 19/992. [*Basing*].
basse *sb* BASE¹.
bataile, batell *sb* BATTLE.
batale *wk vb* BATTLE¹.
batell see bataile.
bāþe, bāðe, bāthe see bǫth(e).
bawde *sb* procuress, BAWD¹.
1. be *prep* BY.
2. be- see also bi-.
3. bē see bē(n).
bead see bēde.
bealté see bewté.
bēast see bẹ̄st(e).
beawbelex *sb pl* baubles, finery 3/59.
 [*Beaubelet*].
bed see bedde¹, bidde.
1. bẹ̄de *sb* prayer. [BEAD].
2. bēde, beōde *st vb 2* order, offer,
 bid, announce: *pret 2 sg* bẹ̄de
 12/668, *3 sg* bead 3/68. (West
 Saxon *beōdan*).
1. bedde, bede, bed *sb* BED.
2. bedde see bidde.
bedēne, bydēne, bidēne *adv* completely
 12/730, 29/263; as well (metrical
 filler without exact meaning)
 17/53.
bed-reden *adj* BED-RIDDEN.
been see bē(n).
befǫren see byforn(e).
beggar-staf *sb* BEGGAR-STAFF.
begger *sb* BEGGAR.
begȳle *wk vb* deceive, BEGUILE.
behẹ̄ste *wk vb* order, promise. [BE-
 HEST].
behight, behihte see bihǫte.
behōve see bihōve.
behōvelich *adj* necessary. [*Behovely*].
bey see bō3e.
beye see bȳe(n).
bei3 *sb* collar 21₂/161, 165; *pl* bī3es.
 [BEE²].
beyn see bē(n).
beine see bǫ.
bēlden *wk vb* encourage 7/3345.
 [BIELD].
beleave, beliave *sb* BELIEF.
beli, balie, belly *sb* 1. bags, knapsacks
 21₁/41. — 2. BELLY.
belle *sb* BELL.

bẹ̄me, beōm *sb* BEAM¹ of wood, or
 light.
bemẹ̄ne *wk vb* signify. [*Bemean*¹].
bē(n), bee(n), beō(n), bie(n), bön
 2/2, 39, bö 6/979 *irreg vb* BE: *pres
 indic 1 sg* am, æm 5/14009, em 2/1,
 bē 29/201; *2 sg* art, ært 5/14050,
 artow, hertou 10/120; *3 sg* is, es
 16/1, etc. hiis 10/106, bið 5/14062,
 beō 3/1; *pl* ār(e), āren, arn, ẹ̄re
 14/Introd, bē, bee, bēþ, büþ, beōþ
 2/17, 6/911, 11/6, 13₂/71, böþ 6/882,
 1004, byeþ 15/37, beyn 14/85, sinden 7/31; *pret sg* was, watz, wes;
 2 sg wǫre 12/684; *pl* wēr(e)n,
 wēr(e), wār(e), weōre, weōren 5/8,
 wǫre 12/503, 717, wǫren 12/721,
 wǣron 1/14, wǣren 1/23, wāren
 1/18. — *pres subj sg* bē, bö 2/4,
 6/866, beō 3/3, bȳ 15/25, sī 7/3378;
 pl bē, bö 6/860, bön 6/883; *pret*
 wēr(e), weōre 5/14052, wǣre
 7/3655. — *imper 2 pl* bē(3ē) 7/3348.
 — *pp* bē, bēne, i-bēn, i-bön 2/3,
 i-beōn 3/96, y-bȳ 15/29. — *contracted negative forms: pres 2 sg*
 nart 3/47; *3 sg* nis 3/46, 13₄/13;
 pret sg nas, nes 13₅/35; *pret subj*
 nēre.
bēnd *wk vb* BEND in an arc 19/1017;
 pret bēnd; *pp* bent.
1. bēne *sb* prayer, favor, BOON¹.
2. bēne see bē(n).
beneme see benime.
benime, bineomen, beneme *st vb 4* deprive, take away: *pp* binome 10/
 173, binume 5/14077. [*Benim*].
bent-felde *sb* hunting-field 18/1136.
 [tautologous form from OE *beonet*
 'meadow' etc., see BENT¹].
beō see bē(n).
beōde see bēde².
beohēold see bihǫlde.
beōn see bē(n).
beōm see bẹ̄me.
beōþ, beōð see bē(n).
bẹ̄rd *sb* BEARD; *kepe in þe* ∼ oppose
 17/96.
1. bẹ̄re *sb* clamour, outcry (or behavior, bearing) 6/925.
2. bẹ̄re, bōre (6/1021) *sb* BEAR¹.
 (Ursus).

bẹre(n), bǣron *st vb 4* BEAR[1], carry,
sustain; accompany 27₄ₐ/673, give
birth; *pret* bar(e), bāren, bēren;
pp y-bǫre, born(e), i-bǫren, bǫre,
bǫren.
berȝe(n), berwen *st vb 3b* protect,
save 12/697; *pp* i-borȝe 6/883.
[*Bergh*].
berie *wk vb* BURY.
beryl *sb* BERYL.
bern see barn(e).
bɘrnen *st vb 3a* BURN[1]; *pret* burne.
berste see breste.
berwen see berȝe(n).
besaly *adv* BUSILY.
besēche, bisēche *wk vb* BESEECH; *pret*
besoght.
besy see bysy.
besiȝte *sb* precaution, provision 11/9,
18. [*Besight*].
bẹst(e), bēast *sb* BEAST.
bet 1. *comp adv* better; *go ⁓* hurry
up. [*Bet²*]. — 2. *compar adv* better.
[*Bet*].
betākne, betākyn, bitācne(n) *wk vb*
signify, BETOKEN 7/3632.
bēte *wk vb* 1. expiate, do penance
6/865. — 2. stir up or light (a
fire) ; *pp* bette 18/1368. [*Beet*].
betẹche(n) *wk vb* entrust 5/14055,
12/558, 13₃/22, hand over to 20/
714; *pret* bitauhte, bitaiȝte, *2 sg*
bitahtest 5/14055. [BETEACH].
beter, betre *compar* adj and adv
BETTER.
betre see beter.
bette see bēte.
betwyx, betwix, bitwixen *prep* between, BETWIX. [*Betwixen*].
bẹþ see bē(n).
beþenke see biþenche.
bewēpe see biwēpe.
bewté, bealté *sb* BEAUTY.
1. by̆, bĭ 1. *prep* BY, thanks to 6/871.
— 2. *adv bi þat* at that moment —
3. *conj* at the moment when 18/
1169; *bi þat* id 18/1321, 1365; *by
so* provided that 21₃/39.
2. bi- see also be-.
3. by see bē(n).
bicche *sb* BITCH[1], female canine.
bicômen, bycumen *st vb* BECOME; *pret*
bicom 3/6.

bidde(n), bedde *st vb 5* 1. command,
order, offer. — 2. ask 6/886. — 3.
pray 5/28, *pres 1 sg* bidd 12/484,
3 sg byt 13₂/105, biddeð 5/28; *pret*
bad, badde, bit, bed; *pp* i-bede. BID.
(< OE *biddan*, but *bēodan* and *biddan* are confused in ME).
bīde *st vb 1* wait for, BIDE.
bydēne, bidēne see bedēne.
bie(n) see bē(n).
by̆e(n), beye, bü̆ǧǧe(n) *wk vb* BUY;
pres 3 sg bü̆ð 3/109; *pret* boghte,
boghten, bohte, bouhte; *pp* y-bouȝt,
i-bouȝt.
byeþ see bē(n).
bifalle, bifealle *st vb 7* BEFALL, happen (*impers*) ; *pres 3 sg* bifealt
2/7; *pret* bifel.
bifōr see following.
byforn(e), biforn, bifǫren, befǫren,
bivǫre(n), bifōr *prep* and *adv* BE-
FORE.
bigynne(n), bigin, beginne *st vb 3a*
BEGIN; *pret sg* bigan, bigon 5/14016,
pl bigunne; *pret subj sg* bigunne
4/15.
bygynnyng, biginnunge *sb* BEGINNING.
bygly *adv* BIGLY, loud 18/1141.
bigon see bigynne(n).
bigotten *pp* inundated, penetrated
4/36. [*Bigeten*].
bigunne see begynne.
bīȝes see beiȝ.
biȝete *sb* profit 3/135, 10/248.
[*Beget*].
bihalde(n) see bihǫlde(n).
bihaldunge *sb* BEHOLDING, contemplation.
bihāte(n), bihēt(e) see bihōte.
bihēold see bihǫlde(n).
behȳnden *prep* BEHIND.
byhōde see bihōve(n).
bihǫlde(n), bihālde(n) *st vb 7* BEHOLD,
contemplate; *pret* beohēold 21₁/13,
bihēold 3/4, 5/24.
bihōte, bihāten *st vb 7* promise; *pret*
behihte, bihēt, *2 sg* bihēte; *pp* behight, behǫte 13₂/119, bihōten 12/
564. [*Behight*].
bihōve(n), by-, be- *impers wk vb* BE-
HOVE, be fitting; *pret* byhōde 18/
717.

bikenne *wk vb* declare, commend, commit, entrust [*Beken*].
biknowen *st vb* 7 recognize. [*Beknow*].
bilāven see bilẹ̄ve(n)².
bile *sb* beak, BILL².
bileg̈g̈e *wk vb* explain, gloss, resolve 6/904. [BELAY].
1. bilẹ̄ve *wk vb* BELIEVE.
2. bilẹ̄ve(n), bilẹ̄fen, bilāven, blẹ̄ve *wk vb* (be)LEAVE, let, remain, survive; *pret 3 pl* blefte; *pres subj* bilaven 5/14060. [*Beleave*].
1. bylyve *sb* subsistance 21₃/21. [*Bylive*].
2. bilȳve, blīve, blȳve *adv* quickly, fast, right away. [*Belive*].
bȳnde(n), bīnd *st vb 3a* BIND; render helpless 10/254; *pret* bọ̄nd 12/537; *pp* y-bōunde(n), bōunden.
bineomen see benime.
binēþ(e), binēōþ, binēōðe(n) *adv* BENEATH.
bynne, binne 1. *prep* within, inside of 20/804. — 2. *adv* inside 12/584. [*Bin, Binne*].
binôme, binụme see benime.
birde *sb* nation, tribe 7/3361.
byre(n) *impers wk vb* be convenient or fitting, birþ it is proper 7/35, ʒow birþ you ought 7/3616; happened, befell 14/4071. [*Bir*].
byrne *wk vb* BURN.
byrnyng *sb* BURNING.
bȳrþ-whate *sb* succession of births 19/1401 (cp. ON *hvata* 'hasten').
bischop, bisċop *sb* BISHOP.
bisēche see besēche.
bisēme *wk vb* BESEEM.
bisetten *wk vb* besiege, BESET; *pp* biset.
bysy, besy *adj* BUSY.
bysihēde *sb* research, application 15/36, 39. [*Busyhede*].
bysynes, bysinesse, besynes *sb* occupation, application, BUSINESS 15/43, 26/24, preoccupation 16/27.
bisne *sb* model 5/15, 7/100. [*Bysen*].
bist see bē(n).
bistẹ̄le(n) *st vb 4* STEAL towards, surprise 2/15; *pp* bistolen. [*Besteal*].
bistrīden *st vb 1* BESTRIDE 5/14011.
biswīke(n) *st vb 1* deceive 2/12, 5/14064, 6/930. [*Beswike*].

byt, bit see bidde.
bitācnen see betākne.
bitācnunge *sb* BETOKENING.
bitahtest, bitaiʒte, bitauhte see betẹ̄che(n).
bȳte(n) *st vb 1* BITE; *pret sg* bọ̄te.
bitellunge *sb* excuse 3/108 cp. [*Betell*].
bitīde, bitȳde *wk vb* happen, BETIDE.
bitiʒt *pp* covered, clothed 6/1013. [*Bitight*].
bytrende(n) *wk vb* surround, encircle; *pres 3 sg* bytrent. [*Betrend*].
bitter, bittre *adj* BITTER.
betuēne, bituhēn see bitwēne.
biturne(n) *wk vb* (*upon*) turn towards 3/57. [*Beturn*].
bitwēne, bituēne, bituhēn 3/77 *prep* BETWEEN.
bitwixen see betwyx.
bið see bē(n).
biþenche, beþenke *wk vb* reflect, BETHINK, concern oneself (refl) 6/871, 939; *pret* biþohte 6/939, beþoght; *pp* biþout 10/81, biþocht 2/8.
biþocht, biþout see biþenche.
bivien *wk vb* shake violently 5/14043. [*Bive*].
bivọ̄re(n) see byforn(e).
biwāken *st vb 6* guard, watch; *pret 3 pl* biwōken 7/3339. [*Bewake*].
biwēpe, be- *wk vb* BEWEEP, mourn 6/974, 15/28.
bewinne(n) *st vb 3a* get, acquire; *pret* biwon 5/15. [*Bewin*].
biwōken see biwāken.
biwreye(n) *wk vb* betray. [BEWRAY].
blak, blac *adj* BLACK.
blande *sb* BLEND, mixture; *in* ⌒ all together 18/1205. [*Bland*¹].
blāse *sb* BLAZE¹.
blasphemọ̄ur *sb* BLASPHEMER.
blast *sb* BLAST, noise.
blaw, blawe(n) see blowe(n)¹.
blēd *sb* flower 6/1042. [*Blede*].
blēde *wk vb* BLEED.
blefte see bilẹ̄ven.
blende *wk vb* BLEND², mix together; *pret* blente.
blēo *sb* hue, tint, color 13₁/66, 13₅/23. [BLEE].
blēre *wk vb* hang out the tongue 20/782. [*Blear*²].

blēte *wk vb* BLEAT.
blēþelīche see blȳþely.
blēve see bilēve(n)².
blew *adj* BLUE.
blykyen *wk vb* shine, glisten 13₅/23.
   [*Blik*].
blynke *wk vb* deceive 14/4166. [BLINK].
1. blys *wk vb* BLESS¹. [*Bliss*].
2. blys, blis, blisce, blisse *sb* joy,
   BLISS; *pl* blissen 4ₐ/12, 13.
blysfol *adj* BLISSFUL.
blysne *wk vb* shine 19/1048.
blisse see blys².
blissed, y-blyssed *pp adj* BLESSED.
blȳþe, blīþe *adj* BLITHE, joyous.
blȳþely, blīþeli₃, blēþelīche *adv* joyously, BLITHELY 7/3617; willingly
   10/171, 15/12.
blīve, blȳve, see bilȳve².
blōd(e) *sb* BLOOD.
blōmen *wk vb* BLOOM¹ 7/3636.
blonk *sb* horse, mount; *pl* blonkkez.
blosme, blostme *sb* BLOSSOM.
1. blowe(n), blow, blaw(e) *st vb* 7
   BLOW¹, sound a horn; *pret pl* blwe
   18/1141, blw 18/1362; *pp* blawen
   16/12.
2. blowe(n) *wk vb* BLOW², blossom.
blusche *wk vb* look at 19/1083.
   [BLUSH¹].
blw(e) see blowe(n)¹.
1. bọ̄, bā *adj* BOTH 3/31, 4/46, 6/990,
   7/7; beine 5/14023.
2. bö̈ see bē(n).
bōc see bōk(e).
bōc-felle *sb* parchment 5/25. [*Book-
   fell*].
bochēre *sb* BUTCHER.
bōck see bōk(e).
bōc-staf *sb* letter 7/104. [*Bocstaff*].
bọ̄d *sb* message 5/14000; *pl* bọ̄den.
   [BODE²].
bodi, body *sb* BODY.
bodyly *adj* BODILY, corporeal 19/1090.
bōgh, bōwgh, bō₃ *sb* BOUGH.
boghte(n) see bȳe(n).
bō₃ see bōgh.
bō₃e *st vb* 2 BOW¹ 10/194; turn oneself 18/1189; ~ *of* leave 18/1220,
   direct oneself 18/1311; *pres 3 sg*
   būhþ 13₂/102; *pret* bey 10/194.

bohte see bȳe(n).
boiste *sb* box, coffer 3/140. [*Boist*].
bōke, bōck, bōc *sb* BOOK; *pl* bōc 5/27.
bōket *sb* BUCKET.
bōld(e) *sb* dwelling. [*Bold*].
bolle *sb* BOWL.
bön see bē(n).
1. bọ̄nd, bānd *sb* BOND¹, BAND¹, liga-
   ture.
2. bọ̄nd see bȳnde(n).
bōne *sb* BOON¹, prayer 17/46; favor
   19/1090. See bēne.
bonk *sb* BANK¹; *pl* bonkkez.
bọ̄ost see bọ̄ste.
bör *sb* BEER 6/1011.
1. bọ̄rẹ *sb* BOAR.
2. bȫre see bēre².
bọ̄re(n) see bēre(n).
bor₃ *sb* BOROUGH, town.
borne *sb* BOURN¹, small stream.
   [BURN¹].
borwe(n) *wk vb* BORROW¹; save; be
   security for; *pp* borwen.
bọ̄ste, bọ̄ost *sb* BOAST.
1. bōt(e), bṳ̈t(e), būton, būten, boūte
   1. *conj* BUT, and, unless 2/8, 24;
   27₁/308, 27₄ᴮ/741; *but þat* except
   12/505, 12/690, nowi₃t bōte nothing
   but 6/884. — 2. *prep* except, ~ ₃ef
   unless 3/123, except 26/5, without
   2/52, 4/2, 22₂/447. — 3. *adv* only;
   ~ ōure ọ̄ne only us alone 18/1230.
2. bōte *sb* remedy. [BOOT¹].
3. bọ̄te see bȳte(n).
botel(le) *sb* BOTTLE.
bọ̄þ see bē(n).
bọ̄th(e), bọ̄þen, bāþe, bāðe 1. *adj* and
   pronoun BOTH. — 2. *adv* at the
   same time.
boūele *sb* BOWEL¹, guts.
bouhte see bȳe(n).
boūn *pp adj* ready; built 19/992.
   [BOUND¹].
boūnne *wk vb* get ready 20/783.
   [*Boun*].
1. boūrde *wk vb* joke. [*Bourd¹*].
2. boūrde, būrde *sb* joke. [*Bourd*].
boūre, būr(e) *sb* bedroom, dwelling,
   BOWER¹.
boūrne see būrne².
boūte see bōt(e).

bōwgh see bōgh.

brache *sb* hound 18/1142 [BRACH].

brād see brǫd.

bræcon see bręke.

bræd see brēd(e)[1].

branche *sb* BRANCH.

bray *wk vb* BRAY[1] 18/1163.

brayell *sb* waist, stomach 20/793. [BRAIL[1]] (<OF *braiel,* L *brācale* 'belt').

brayn, brāne *sb* BRAIN.

bratful see bretful.

braundysche *wk vb* BRANDISH 20/782.

brēche, breech *sb* BREECH, hose.

bręd *sb* plank, (out-house) seat, *dat sg* bręde 6/965 see note.

1. brēd(e), breed, bræd *sb* BREAD.

2. bręde *sb* breadth. [BREDE[2]].

breed see brēd(e)[1].

bręfe *sb* BREVE (musical note).

bręke *st vb* 4 BREAK; *pret pl* bræcon 1/31, brēken 25/32, 5/14023, brǫke lame, maimed 21₃/33.

brēme *adj* strong, fierce 18/1142, 1155; merry 13₅/16.

bren see brenne.

brende *pp adj* burnt (gold) 19/989. cp. BURN *vb*[2].

brenne, bren *wk vb* BURN[1], *pret pl* brenden, brendon; *pp* brent.

brent see brenne.

brest *sb* BREAST.

breste, briste, bryst, berste *st vb* 3b BURST; *pp* brusten.

bretful, bratful *adj* BRET-FULL, full to the very top.

breþ *sb* BREATH; passion 6/948.

brētheren see brōther.

brēve *wk vb* reveal 18/1393.

brewestere *sb* tavern keeper [BREW-STER].

briche, brüche *sb* BREACH, opening 10/233.

bryd(de), brid(de) *sb* BIRD.

brydel, bridel *sb* BRIDLE.

bry3t, bri3tte, bryht, briht *adj* BRIGHT; *compar* brihtre 4/1.

brym *sb* BRIM[2].

brynge(n) *wk vb* BRING; ~ *aboute* accomplish 27₄ᴮ/821; *pret* bro3te, brouhte, brohute; *pp* broght, i-brout, y-bro3t.

bryniġe *sb* coat of chain mail armor 1/25. [BRINIE].

briste, bryst see breste.

britten *wk vb* break in pieces 20/802.

broche, brouch *sb* BROOCH; child's toy 26/23.

brǫd, brād *adj* BROAD.

broght, bro3te, brohute see brynge(n).

1. brōke *sb* BROOK.

2. brōke see bręke.

brōnd *sb* BRAND.

brōþer, brōther, brōþir *sb* BROTHER; *pl* brētheren.

brouhte see brynge(n).

1. brōun *adj* BROWN.

2. brōun *sb* hide (of deer) 18/1162. [BROWN].

broute see brynge(n).

brōw *sb* BROW[1]; *pl* brōwen 13₅/18.

brüche see briche.

brüde *sb* BROOD.

brusten see breste.

Brüttisc *adj* BRITISH 5/14080.

buffet *sb* BUFFET[1].

büġġen see bȳe(n).

būhþ see bō3e.

builen *wk vb* BOIL.

bukke, bucke *sb* BUCK[1].

bulle *sb* BULL[2] (papal).

bulluc *sb* BULLOCK.

1. bürde *sb* virgin, young girl 18/752, 13₅/5, 25. [*Burd* (<OE **byrde* 'embroiderer')].

2. bürde see bōurde[2].

burdōun *sb* bass accompaniment. [BOURDON[2]].

būre see bōure.

burne see bernen.

1. bürn(e) *sb* knight, warrior, man 18/1189, 19/1090. [*Berne*].

2. bürn(e), bōurn(e) *sb* BURN[1], run, branch, rivulet. [BOURN[1]].

burnist *pp adj* BURNISHED.

bürþ-tónge *sb* BIRTH-TONGUE.

buske *wk vb* get ready, dressed; hurry. [BUSK[1]].

busshel *sb* BUSHEL[1].

busshment *sb* ambush. [*Bushment*].

bustōus *adj* savage, brutal 20/775, 783. [*Boistous*].

bŭt(e), būten, būton see bōt(e)[1].

butere *sb* BUTTER[1].
büþ see bē(n).
büð see bȳe(n).
buven *prep* above. [BOVE].

C

caas see cǎs.
caban(e) *sb* CABIN 20/757.
cace see cǎs.
cache, cacche *wk vb* CATCH; *pret*
cauhte, caȝt, cauȝte; *pp* i-kaut 10/
86, 103.
cacheres *sb pl* dog-handlers 18/1139.
[CATCHER] (cp. OF *chacechien?*).
ćǣse see chēse.
ćǣst see cheste.
caȝt see cache.
1. cayre *wk vb* square, give the form
of a square 19/1031. (< Provençal
cairar ' to square '). [Cp. *Quare*].
2. cayre, cairen, kaire *wk vb* go, ride;
~ *aboute* roam at will 21₁/29.
[*Cair*].
calf *sb* CALF[1]; *dat* calve 13₁ₐ/9.
calīce *sb* CHALICE.
calle(n) *wk vb* CALL.
calsydoyne *sb* CHALCEDONY 19/1003.
cam see cóme(n).
1. can, con, kan(e) *perf pres vb* CAN[1],
know how, be able, know; *pres 2 sg*
canstow, const 6/904; *pl* cónneþ,
cunne(n), kunne 6/911; *pret* kōude,
kōuþe, küðe, cōwde, cōuþe, cōuth;
pres subj 2 sg cónne 12/622, 623;
pp cūþ.
2. can see ginne.
cancelēr *sb* CHANCELLOR.
canōn *sb* CANON[1], rule, the canon of
Avicenna 27₄ᴮ/890 see note.
canstow = *canst þou* see can[1].
capōun *sb* CAPON.
cappe *sb* CAP[1].
1. cāre, kāre *sb* CARE.
2. cāre, kāre *wk vb* CARE.
carie(n) *wk vb* CARRY.
carke *wk vb* annoy. [*Cark*].
carl *sb* rustic, villain, churl. CARL[1].
carlman *sb* man 1/21. CARL + MAN.
caroyne *sb* CARRION.
carpyng *sb* babbling, talking. [CAR-
PING[1]].

cart *wk vb* use a car, CART.
cǎs, cass, caas, cace, kas *sb* CASE[1],
chance, *par* ~ by chance.
1. cast *sb* fraud.
2. cast, casten, kest *wk vb* CAST,
throw; *pres 3 sg* castys 16/3; *pret*
kest; *pp* castyn 20/819.
castel(l) *sb* CASTLE; *pl* castles.
castelweorc *sb* CASTLEWORK 1/18.
casten, castyn see cast[2].
cat *sb* CAT[1]; *gen* cattes, cattis.
catel *sb* CATTLE, money.
caudel *sb* CAUDLE, warm wine, etc.
cauȝte, cauhte see cache.
cautele, cawtele *sb* ruse. [*Cautel*].
ceyll, cēle, see sēle.
cercle, serkyll *sb* CIRCLE.
cerǧe *sb* CIERGE, wax taper.
certayn(e) *adj* CERTAIN; *adv* 20/817.
certes *adv* certainly.
1. chaffare, chaffere *sb* 1. commerce.
2. merchandise. [CHAFFER[1]].
2. chaffare *wk vb* do business, specu-
late, [CHAFFER[1]].
chaynǧe see chaunǧe.
chalenǧe(n) *wk vb* accuse 3/21.
[CHALLENGE].
chämberlayn *sb* CHAMBERLAIN, servant.
chämbyre *sb* CHAMBER.
chapmon *sb* merchant, pedlar. [CHAP-
MAN].
char *sb* chariot, car. [*Char*[2]].
charme *sb* magic, CHARM[1].
charre *wk vb* force back. [*Chare*].
chartre *sb* CHARTER[1], act 3/140.
chāse *wk vb* CHASE.
chastyse *wk vb* reprimand, CHASTISE.
chaunǧe, chaynǧe *wk vb* CHANGE,
modify.
chēaste *sb* dispute 15/75. [*Chest*[2]].
cheef *sb* CHIEF.
cheeven see chēve.
chēke *sb* CHEEK.
cheorl see cherl.
chȩpen *wk vb* sell, deal in. [*Cheap*].
chȩpilt *sb* (female) trafficker 3/135.
[*Cheapild*].
cherche see chirche.
chēre, cheere *sb* demeanor, appearance.
[CHEER].

cherl(e), cheorl *sb* rustic, CHURL;
slave.
chę̄s see chēse².
1. chēse, ćǣse *sb* CHEESE¹.
2. chēse, chǭse *st vb 2* CHOOSE; *pret*
chę̄s, chēse; *pp* chǭsen, y-chǭse,
i-chǭsen.
cheste, ćæste *sb* CHEST¹, cage 1/30.
chestre *sb* town 7/3359. [*Chester*¹].
chēve, cheeven *wk vb* obtain; ACHIEVE.
[*Cheve*].
chēvicaunce *sb* gain(s) 18/1390.
[*Chevisance*¹].
chēviss *wk vb* succeed. [*Chevise*].
chīld *sb* CHILD; young knight 8/480;
pl chyldern, children, childeren.
chīlden *wk vb* bear, give birth to
7/3627. [*Child*].
chīldhād *sb* CHILDHOOD.
chinne, chynn *sb* CHIN.
chirche, chürche, cherche, ćirće *sb*
CHURCH.
chirche-ȝērd, ćirće-iærd *sb* CHURCH-
YARD.
chirche-sǫng *sb* religious, church
music.
chireche see chirche.
chȳte *wk vb* reprimand, CHIDE.
chyteryng *sb* chattering 26/14. [CHIT-
TERING].
cho *personal pron 3 sg F* SHE 20/715,
716, 720.
chǭse see chę̄se².
chülle = *ich wolle* see wille.
ćirće(-) see chirche(-).
cyrograffe *sb* contract 3/141. [CHIRO-
GRAPH].
citee, cyté, cyty *sb* CITY, town .
clāne see clę̄ne.
clannesse *sb* spiritual purity, CLEAN-
NESS.
clatere *wk vb* CLATTER.
clāðes see clōþes.
clēne, klę̄ne, clāne 1. *adj* CLEAN. — 2.
adv completely 18/1298, 5/14060.
clenlȳche *adv* sumptuously 20/757.
[CLEANLY].
clense *wk vb* CLEANSE.
cleo *sb* hillside 13₂/72 [*Cleo*, cp.
CLEVE¹].
clę̄pen, clę̄pyn, clę̄pie *wk vb* call, name.
[*Clepe*].

clēr(e), cleer *adj* CLEAR.
clerǧye *sb* learning, knowledge 20/809.
[CLERGY (II)].
clerk(e), clereke, clerc *sb* educated
person, CLERK, cleric.
clę̄th *wk vb* get dressed. [*Clead*].
clę̄ve *sb* room, dwelling, cottage 12/
557, 596. [*Cleve*²].
clę̄ven *wk vb* cling to, CLEAVE².
clym *st vb 3a* CLIMB.
clynke *wk vb* CLINK¹.
clóche, klók *sb* CLUTCH¹ 20/792, 21₂/
154.
clok *sb* CLOCK.
clōke *sb* CLOAK.
clǭse *wk vb* CLOSE; contain 18/1298.
clōþes, clāðes *sb pl* CLOTHES.
clōwde, clōwdde, clūde *sb* 1. rock. —
2. CLOUD.
1. clowe *sb* CLAW.
2. clowe *wk vb* CLAW.
clōwt, clūte *sb* cloth; rag 12/547.
[CLOUT¹].
clūde see clōwde.
cnawen see knowe(n).
cnawlechunge see knaulechynge.
cniȝt, cniht see knyght.
cnihtschipe *sb* KNIGHTSHIP.
cnotted *adj* KNOTTED.
cobelēre *sb* COBBLER.
coc *sb* COCK¹.
cogge *sb* ship 20/756. [*Cog*¹].
coillons *sb pl* testicles. [CULLION].
coyne(n) *wk vb* COIN¹, make money.
cōk *sb* COOK.
coke *wk vb* put hay into cocks 21₃/13.
[COCK⁴].
coker *sb* harvest-hand. [COCKER³].
cǭle *sb* COAL.
cǭlen *wk vb* COOL.
colēre *sb* COLLAR.
cólpon *sb* strand, shred. [CULPON].
colure *sb* COLOUR.
cóman see cóme(n).
cóme, küme *sb* coming 5/14071, 8/530.
[COME¹].
cóme(n), cómme, cumen, cum *st vb 4*
COME; *pres 3 sg* cumþ; *pret sg* cōm,
cōme, cam, *pl* cōme 26/11, cōmen
21₂/148, cōman 1/56; *pp* cómen,
cómmen, cumen, y-cóme, y-cumen.

comforth, comfurthe see confort².
comyn, comune *adj* COMMON.
cómly, cumly *adj* and *adv* beautiful,
COMELY; noble, nobly.
cómlyly *adv* fitting, seemly. [COME-
LILY].
cómlyng *sb* stranger. [COMELING].
commandyne *sb* order, COMMANDING.
cómme(n) see cóme(n).
commyxstion *sb* mixture. [*Commix-
tion*].
communliche *adv* COMMONLY.
cómpaignȳe, cómpané, cumpanȳe *sb*
COMPANY, band.
cómpanȳe *wk vb* unite in a group.
[COMPANY].
comparysoun *sb* COMPARISON.
1. compas *sb* circle, COMPASS¹.
2. compas *wk vb* keep inside a circle;
meditate 18/1196, COMPASS¹.
compeer *sb* comrade, COMPEER.
compēryng *sb* COMPARING.
comūne *sb* people, community. [COM-
MON].
1. con *pret function word* (synonym
to *gan*) = ModE did 18/1175, 19/
997, 1000, 1078.
2. con see can¹.
concyens *sb* understanding, mind 18/
1196. [CONSCIENCE].
conduyt *sb* CONDUIT.
confiture *sb* mixture. [COMFITURE].
1. confort, cumfort *sb* COMFORT.
2. confort, comforth, comfurthe *wk vb*
COMFORT, re-assure.
1. cónyng *adj* CUNNING.
2. cónyng *sb* knowledge, learning,
CUNNING.
3. conyng *sb* CONY, rabbit.
cónne, cónneþ, cónnez see can¹.
cónseil(le) *sb* 1. COUNSEL. — 2. secret
counsel.
cónseille *wk vb* COUNSEL.
constreyne *wk vb* CONSTRAIN.
construcciōn *sb* interpretation, CON-
STRUCTION.
construe, constrēwe *wk vb* interpret,
CONSTRUE.
contacky *wk vb* fight 15/74. [*Con-
teck*].
contrār *adj* CONTRARY.

cóntrē(e), cóntray(e), cuntré, cǒuntrey
sb COUNTRY.
copuland *adj* uniting.
cornlond *sb* wheat-land. [CORNLAND].
cors *sb* CORPSE.
córtaysȳe, cǒurtaysȳe, curteysīe *sb*
COURTESY.
córtyn *sb* CURTAIN.
córtyned *pp adj* CURTAINED 18/1181.
cosse, cos *sb* KISS.
cost *sb* quality 18/1272, (pl) manners 18/1295, observance (of religious duties) 18/750. [*Cost¹*].
costnin *wk vb* COST.
cǫte *sb* hut, cottage. [COT¹].
cǒu see cū.
cǒunterfēte *wk vb* imitate, COUNTER-
FEIT.
cǒuntǒur *sb* 1. arithmetician 27₁/436.
[COUNTER²]. — 2. abacus, COUNTER³.
cǒuntrey see cóntré(e).
cǒupe *sb* sin. [*Culpe*].
cǒuth(e), cǒuþe see can¹.
covayties, coveitise *sb* greed, desire
16/54. [*Covetise*].
covenaunt(e) *sb* pact, agreement,
COVENANT; *in ∼ þat* on condition
that.
coveite(n), coveyte *wk vb* desire,
want, COVET.
covertǒur *sb* cover. [COVERTURE].
cǒwde see can¹.
cǒwpe *wk vb* strike 20/799. [*Coup³*].
cǒwple, cǒuple, *wk vb* COUPLE, leash
18/1139, 21₂/206, tie 22₁/236.
crache, cracchy *wk vb* scratch.
[*Cratch*].
crādel, crēdyll *sb* CRADLE.
craft *sb* artifice, cleverness, trade,
CRAFT.
crafty *adj* skillful.
crak, crake(n) *wk vb* 1 bawl; sing at
top of voice 29/656. — 2. CRACK,
break.
crakkande *pres part adj* resounding
18/1166, CRACKING.
crāse *wk vb* crack, CRAZE.
crāve *wk vb* CRAVE, ask for.
crēde *sb* CREED.
crēdyll see crādel.
crēpe *st vb* 2 CREEP; *pret* crǫpe.
crest *sb* CREST.

cribbe *sb* CRIB, manger 7/3366.
crȳe *wk vb* CRY; weep 18/760; proclaim 25/23.
crysolȳt *sb* CHRYSOLITE 19/1009.
crysopāse *sb* CHRYSOPRASE 19/1013.
christendom *sb* CHRISTENDOM 7/3.
crystyn, cristine *adj* CHRISTIAN.
croft *sb* CROFT, enclosed field.
croyne see crōne.
croys, crois see cros.
crōked, crōkid *adj* CROOKED 27₄ᴮ/761; deformed 15/64, 24/52.
crōne, croyne *wk vb* CROON, moan.
crōpe see crēpe.
croppe *sb* CROP of a bird, top, comb.
croppen *wk vb* CROP, cut 3/54.
cros, croys, crois *sb* CROSS.
crōune, crūne *sb* 1. CROWN. — 2. top of head 12/568.
crōuned *pp* tonsured 21₃/56 [CROWNED].
crōuþ *sb* violin 13₅/43. [*Crowd*[1]].
crūċet-hūs *sb* torture-cage 1/29.
crūne see crōune.
crūnen *wk vb* CROWN; *pp* i-crūnet 3/103.
crūninge *sb* CROWNING.
cū, kū, cōu *sb* COW; *pl* kȳn.
cuccu *sb* CUCKOO.
cülle see kille.
cum, cumen, cumest see cóme(n).
cumforte see confort[1].
cumly see cómly.
cummer *wk vb* bother, annoy; *pret* cumrit 22/486. [CUMBER].
cumpanye see cómpaignye.
cumrit see cummer.
cumþ see cóme(n).
cünde see kinde.
cünesmen *sb pl* KINSMEN 13₃/6.
cünne see kin.
cünne see can[1].
cuntinance *sb* display 21₁/24. [COUNTENANCE].
cuntré see cóntre(e).
cuppe *sb* CUP.
curs, kórs *sb* CURSE.
curse *wk vb* CURSE.
curteysīe see córtaysȳe.
cut *sb* 1. straw. — 2. lot, chance, CUT[1], ~ *drawen* draw straws.
cūþ, cuuþ see can[1].
cüðen see kiðen.

cwākien see quākien.
cwēn see quēne.

D

dǣde see dēde[1].
dæi see dai.
dæl see dẹl.
dǣre see dēre[4].
daggere *sb* DAGGER.
dai, dæi, day(e) *sb* DAY; *pl* daies, dæies.
daynté 1. *sb* courtesy 18/1250, favor 18/1266, DAINTY, delicate food 18/1401. — 2. *adj* charming 16/1253. [DAINTY].
day-starne *sb* DAY-STAR.
daly *wk vb* DALLY, flirt 18/1253.
damysele *sb* DAMSEL.
dampnable *adj* DAMNABLE.
dan(e), danz sir, etc.; title especially placed before the name of a male religious 14/71. [*Dan*[1]].
1. dar(e) *perf pres vb* DARE[1]; *pret* dórst.
2. dāre *wk vb* be disconsolate 13₅/54. [*Dare*[2]].
dāsed *adj* DAZED.
daunce *wk vb* DANCE.
dawenynge *sb* DAWNING.
dẹ̄ad see dẹd.
dẹ̄adlīche see dẹdly.
dẹ̄ale see dẹle.
dẹ̄að see dẹþ[2].
debāte *sb* dispute 21₄/337, DEBATE[1].
deboneirté *sb* gentleness. [*Debonairty*].
decīple *sb* DISCIPLE.
dẹd, dẹẹd, dẹ̄ad, dyad 15/29 *adj* DEAD.
1. dēd(e) dǣde *sb* DEED; *pl* dēden 3/87.
2. dẹde, deid *sb* death. [*Dead*[2]].
3. dēde see dō(n).
dedeyn *sb* DISDAIN.
dẹdly, dẹdely, diadlīche, dẹ̄adlīche *adj* DEADLY.
dẹẹd see dẹd.
deer(e) see dēre.
dẹf, dyaf *adj* DEAF; *pl* dyave.
defāme *wk vb* DEFAME.
defaute *sb* DEFAULT 27₁/384 see note.
dēfel see dēvel.
degȳse see desgȳse.

dēȝe see dȳe(n).

dehtren see douhter.

deid see dẹ̄de².

deye see dȳe(n).

dẹl, dǣl *sb* part, share. [DEAL¹].

dẹle, dēale *wk vb* divide, share, DEAL; exchange (words) 6/954.

delectābely *adv* DELECTABLY.

delȳt, delīt(e) *sb* DELIGHT.

delītin *wk vb* DELIGHT.

delivere, delivrie *wk vb* DELIVER¹; *subj pres 3 sg* delivri 9/27.

dēme(n) *wk vb* judge, DEEM.

dēoflen see dēvel.

dēop, dēopre see dēp.

dēōr see dēr(e)¹.

dēōre, deorre see dēre⁴.

dēōvel, dēōvlene see dēvel.

dēp, dēōp *adj* DEEP; *sb* the DEEP.

departe(n) *wk vb* divide, share. [DE-PART].

depeint *pp adj* dirtied. [*Depaint*].

depeynte *wk vb* paint pictures. [*Depaint*].

deprēce *wk vb* release 18/1219. (< OF *de(s)presser* 'cease to oppress' / *de(s)priser* 'release from prison').

1. dēr(e), dēōr *sb* wild animal, stag; *pl* dēōren 5/14034, dör 6/1012. [DEER].

2. dẹ̄re *sb* wrong, evil.

3. dẹ̄re *wk vb* do wrong, harm 14/4053.

4. dēre, deere, dǣre, dēōre 1. *adj* DEAR; *comp* deorre 3/110. — 2. *adv* DEAR.

dērely *adv* pleasantly 18/1253, magnificently 19/995, DEARLY, costly.

dērewórþe, dēōrewurðe *adj* precious. [*Dearworth*].

derf *adj* solid 18/1233, powerful 20/811.

derfly *adv* quickly 18/1183.

derk *adj* DARK.

derling *sb* DARLING.

derne *adj* hidden, secret 4/12. [*Dern*].

dernly *adv* secretly 18/1188.

dēs see dees.

desclǫse *wk vb* DISCLOSE.

deserven *wk vb* win (one's life). [DE-SERVE].

desgȳse, degȳse *wk vb* DISGUISE, dress up.

desport see disport.

dēst see dō(n).

destanye *sb* DESTINY.

destróye(n), destruy(e), destrūe(n), distrūe *wk vb* torture, consume, pillage, DESTROY.

det *sb* DEBT.

1. dēþ see dō(n).

2. dēþ, dẹþth, dēāð *sb* DEATH; *grĕte* ~ plague.

dẹve *wk vb* knock down 18/1286. [*Deave*].

dĕvel, dēvell, dēfel, dēōvel, dyēvel, dēwyll *sb* DEVIL, demon; *pl* dēōflen 3/86, dyēvlen 15/4, *gen pl* dēōvlene 6/932.

devīne *wk vb* DIVINE, guess.

devȳse *wk vb* describe. [DEVISE].

devȳsement *sb* description. [DEVISE-MENT].

dēwyll see dēvel.

dȳ see dȳe(n).

dyad see dẹd.

diadlīche see dẹ̄dly.

dyave see dẹf.

dyapred *adj* ornamented in fret work pattern, DIAPERED.

dich *sb* DITCH¹.

dictōur *sb* executive officer 20/712.

did(e) see dō(n).

dȳe(n), deye, dēȝe, dȳ *wk vb* DIE¹.

dyēvel see dēvel.

dyȝt *pp adj* ornamented. [*Dight*].

dykere *sb* care-taker of ditches 21/320. [DIKER].

dyllydōwne *sb* charming child 29/609. [*Dillydown*].

dym *adj* DIM.

dyn *sb* DIN, noise; merrymaking 18/1308.

dȳne *wk vb* DINE.

dingle *sb* abyss; *sea* ~ bottom of the sea 4/12, DINGLE.

dyngne *adj* worthy. [*Digne*].

dynt, dintte, dünte *sb* blow. [DINT].

disceyte *sb* DECEIT.

dischevelee *pp adj* with straggling hair. [*Dishevely*].

disclaundre *wk vb* calumniate. [*Disclander*].

discoweryngis *sb* *pl* manifestations 22₁/242.

disert *sb* what one deserves, DESERT¹.

dishonour *sb* *do a ⁓* harm.

disour *sb* professional story-teller.

dispīsyng *sb* contempt, DESPISING.

disport, dysport, desport *sb* pleasure, (di) SPORT, leisure.

dissheres *sb* female seller of dishes 21₄/323. [*Disheress*].

disteyne *wk* *vb* make pale, tarnish, STAIN. [DISTAIN].

distrūe see destrōye(n).

dit *pp* closed, locked 18/1233.

dō see dō(n).

dǫe *sb* DOE.

dǫgh, dou *sb* DOUGH.

dóghty, du₃ty *adj* brave, valiant, DOUGHTY.

doyne = dōne see dō(n).

dǫle *sb* part 18/719, DOLE¹.

dómb, dōumb *adj* DUMB, mute.

dōmę *sb* DOOM, destiny, 2/48, 4/11, 18/1216, 22₁/235.

domesdai, domesday *sb* DOOMSDAY, day of last judgment.

dō(n), doo *irreg* *vb* 1. DO, make. — 2. put or place: *⁓ in quarterne* put in dungeons 1/28, *⁓ in prisun* put in prison 1/10, 21, *⁓ strenges* put cords 1/26, *⁓ stānes* put stones, *⁓ a mast* set a mast 12/709, *⁓ justise* inflict punishment 1/12, *⁓ wunder* sow terror 1/13. — 3. causative *I shal dō casten* I will have him thrown 12/519, *to dō ęte* cause to eat 15/8. — 4. metrical expletive *he dēde sende* he sent 12/523, etc. — 5. *dōn on* put on (clothes) 12/578. — *pres 2 sg* dōs 29/576, dēst 3/51, 6/977, 10/152, *3 sg* dōth, dōþ(e), dooth, dōs, dēþ 2/35, 13₄/8, 15/6, *3 pl* dōun, dōþ 2/19, 10/217; *subj pres 3 sg* dō 2/21; *pret sg* did(e) dūde 3/66, 6/1016, dēde 15/14, *pl* diden; *imp* dooth; *pp* doon, doyne, idō, y-dō, i-dōn(e); *gerund* tō dōne 2/17, 9/28, 10/236, tō dōnne 3/89.

1. dȯn see dȯūn(e).

2. don *adv* completely 29/552. [*Done*].

dȯng *sb* DUNG 15/17.

doo, dooth see dō(n).

1. dȯr *sb* DOOR.

2. dör see dēr(e).

dȯrst see dar(e).

dōs, dōse see dō(n).

dōte *wk* *vb* be out of one's wits, DOTE¹, be a fool.

dōth, dōþ(e) see dō(n).

dou see dǫgh.

douhte see dowe.

douhter *sb* DAUGHTER; *pl* douhtres, dehtren 3/24, 139.

dōumb see dómb.

dōun see dō(n).

dōun(e), dūn, dȯn 9/4 *adv* DOWN.

dȯut(e) *sb* fear, DOUBT.

dȯute *wk* *vb* fear, DOUBT.

dȯuteles *adv* DOUBTLESS.

dȯuthe, dū₃eðe *sb* assemblage, company 18/1365, men (in an army) 5/14003. [*Douth*].

dowe *perf* *pres* *vb* be of worth, avail; *pret* douhte 12/703. [*Dow*¹].

dȯwse *sb* bawd, bitch 29/246. [*Douse*²].

dózeine *sb* DOZEN.

dradde see drēde.

drāf(e) see drȳve.

drā₃e(n), drāhe see drawe(n).

drāpen see drępe(n).

drauhte *sb* DRAUGHT, mouthful, gulp.

drawe(n), drā₃e(n) *st* *vb* 6 DRAW; entice 6/895; *cut ⁓* draw straws; *to þe peni ⁓* turn into money 12/705; *pres 2 sg* dra₃st 6/895; *pres subj* drāhe 3/134; *pret sg* drou(h), drō₃, drowgh, dreuch, *pl* drowe; *pp* drawe(n).

drecchinge *adj* disturbing 28/810. [*Dretch* *v*¹].

dreche *wk* *vb* afflict, trouble in sleep. [*Dretch*¹].

1. drēde *sb* DREAD, danger; *no ⁓ no* doubt, indeed.

2. drēde, dreid, *wk/str* *vb* DREAD; *pres 3 sg* drēt (for *drēdeth*) 9/9, *pret* drēd, dradde.

drēdfull *adj* DREADFUL.

dreghte *sb* distance; *on ⁓* afar, 20/786, 787. [*Dreigh*].

dreid see drēde².

dreinchen see drenchen.

drēme *wk vb* DREAM (*impers* 20/760).

drenchen, drynchen, dreinchen *wk vb* drown, DRENCH.

drēpe(n) *st vb 4* kill 18/725; *pret* drop* 12/506, drāpen 1/29. [*Drepe*].

drēry *adj* DREARY.

drēt see drēde.

dreuch sec drawe(n).

drȳe, drī3e *wk vb* suffer, put up with. [*Dree*].

drȳ3e *adj* full of endurance. [*Dree*].

dry3tyn see drihte(n).

drihte(n), drihtin, dry3tyn *sb* lord, GOD. [*Drightin*].

drinchen, drynchen, see drenchen.

drynke(n) *str vb 3a* DRINK[1]; *pret* drank, dronk, *pp* y-drónke 15/31, *as adj* drónken.

drit-cherl *sb* DIRT + CHURL 12/682.

drȳve(n) *st vb 1* DRIVE; flee 18/1151, pass (time) 18/1176; *pret* drǫf, drāf(e).

drǫf see drȳve(n).

drō3 see drawe(n).

dronk, drónken see drynke(n).

drop see drēpe(n).

drou(h) see drawe(n).

drūupne *wk vb* languish, decline, DROOP. [*Droopen*].

drowe, drowgh see drawe(n).

dubbe *wk vb* ⁓ *to kni3te* arm as a knight and raise to that rank, DUB[1].

dubbing *sb* 1. the arming of a knight, DUBBING 8/407. — 2. ornamentation 8/564.

dūc see dūk(e).

düde see dō(n).

dü3eðe see dǒuthe.

du3ty see dóghty.

dūk(e), dūc *sb* DUKE.

dūle *sb* grief, misery. [DOLE[2]].

dūn see dǒun(e).

dūne *sb* DOWN[1], hill, slope.

dunǧun *sb* DUNGEON.

dünte see dynt.

dūre *wk vb* endURE.

dwell *wk vb* wait for battle 17/56, DWELL.

dweóle-sǫng *sb* deceitful song 6/926. [Cp. *Dwele sb*].

E

eādi *adj* blessed 4/39.

eany see eny.

eappel *sb* APPLE 3/10, 16, 22.

earm see arm.

earst see erst.

eāst see ēst.

eatelich see atelich.

eāver see ēver.

eavereuch see everych.

ēc see ēk(e).

ecclēsiaste *sb* preacher, ECCLESIAST 27₄ₐ/709.

ęch, ǣch, üche, euch. 1. *adj* EACH; (with *one*) ęchon, üchon, euchan; (indefinite) any 4/2; *acc M sg* alcne 5/29. — 2. *pron* EACH. Cp. *ilke*.

1. ēche *adj* eternal.

2. ēche *wk vb* augment, eke.

ęchon see ęch.

echte see aght.

ed-fleǒn *st vb 2* escape 3/74. [*Atflee*]

ee, een, see eye.

eek see ēke.

ęęre-marke *sb* EARMARK on sheep as owner's mark.

effeir *sb* behavior, attitude 22₂/412.

eft, ǣft *adv* again, once more; *now and* ⁓ now and again.

efter see after.

efterþan *adv* after which 15/28.

efterward *adv* AFTERWARD.

eftwhȳte *wk vb* repay, make restitution. [*Eft-white*].

ē3e see eye.

e3te see ei3te.

e3tetenþe *numeral* EIGHTEENTH.

e3whær see aywhere.

ēhe, ęhnen see eye.

ēhelid see ȳ3e-lyd(de).

ēhsihðe *sb* EYESIGHT 3/7, 66.

ei *indef adj* ANY 4/29.

eie *sb* fear 2/18, 3/142, AWE.

eye, eie, ē3e, ēhe, ee *sb* EYE; *pl* eyen, eien, eyghen, een, eyne, ȳne, ęhnen.

ei3te, e3te, ahte *sb* property, goods, money 13₃/21, 11/17, cattle 3/125, 140, AUGHT.

eilin *wk vb* harm, interfere with 3/132, 4/5. AIL. Cp. *ayle(n)*.

eir *sb* HEIR, prince 12/606.
eyse see ēse.
eyþer, ayþer *adj* and *pron* EITHER; ⁓
ōþer each other 26/58, 18/1307.
ēk(e), eek, ēc *adv* also. [EKE].
ēke(n) *wk vb* augment, add to, EKE
out.
ēlde *sb* old age. [*Eld²*].
elder(e) see ọ̄ld.
ēlyng *adj* miserable, sad 21₂/190.
[*Elenge*].
elles, ellys, ellis 1. *adv* ELSE, otherwise. — 2. *pron* other thing(s).
elleswher, elleswer, elleshwar *adv*
ELSEWHERE.
elmesse see almes.
em see bē(n).
embọ̄se(n) *wk vb* get covered with
foam, be tired out. [EMBOSS¹].
emerāde *sb* EMERALD 19/1005.
emọ̄ng see amọ̄ng.
empoysonēre *sb* EMPOISONER.
empoisonyng *sb* EMPOISONING.
enarmynge *sb* attack by main army.
[Cp. *Enarm*].
enbandownyt *pp* given over to 22₁/
244, ABANDONED.
enclọ̄se(n) *wk vb* hide in, ENCLOSE.
ēnde, ǣnde *sb* END, on ⁓ at last, in
(the) end 3/63.
endent *wk vb* set in 19/1012, INDENT.
endeure *wk vb* ENDURE.
endīte *wk vb*, accuse, INDICT¹.
enes see eny.
e-neuch, e-newe see y-nọ̄ugh.
enǧel see aunǧel(e).
enǧle-þēd *sb* band of angels 7/3370.
[ANGEL + *Thede*].
English, englisċ, englysh, englyssh,
englysch, engliss, englys, inglis(s)
adj and *sb* ENGLISH.
eny, eni, eani *indef adj* ANY; ⁓ kyns
any kinds 21₃/20, enes cünnes any
kind 13₃/23. Cp. *any*.
enlevenþe *numeral* ELEVENTH.
ēnne see ān¹.
enqueste *sb* INQUEST.
ent see and.
entent(e) *sb* INTENT, resolution.
entewne *sb* melody, tune 27₁/309.
[*Entune*].
entremēs *sb* dish coming between
roast and final dish, entremets.
[*Entremẹss*].
enurne *wk vb* ornament 19/1027.
[*Enorn*].
envȳ, anvīe *sb* ENVY.
envyrọ̄un(e) *wk vb* surround, EN-
VIRON.
envyūs *adj* ENVIOUS.
envolüped *pp adj* plunged, ENVELOPED.
ēode, ēoden *pret* went 3/14, 21₁/40.
[*Yode*].
eom *sb* uncle 1/3. [*Eme*].
ēorl, ērl *sb* EARL.
ēorþe, ēorðe see ērthe.
ēorðene *adj* EARTHEN.
eoten see ete(n).
ēow see 3ē².
ẹ̄r, ār(e), ọr(e) 1. *prep* before. — 2.
adv before; ẹ̄rest superlative. — 3.
conj at first; ẹ̄r þane before 9/5,
ERE.
ērd *sb* country, land.
ērde *wk vb* dwell, establish oneself
12/739*.
1. ẹ̄re *sb* EAR¹.
2. ẹ̄re see bē(n).
ẹ̄rende *sb* request, ERRAND.
ẹ̄rest see ẹ̄r, erst.
er3 lazy 2/17. [*Argh*].
ẹ̄rien *wk vb* to plow 6/1039. [*Ear*¹].
ẹ̄ringe *sb* plowing. [*Earing*].
ērl see ēorl.
erly, erliche *adv* EARLY.
ẹ̄rn *sb* eagle 12/572. [ERNE].
erndinge *sb* success (?) 8/581 (see
note). [*Ernding*].
ẹ̄roust see erst.
erst, ẹ̄roust, ẹ̄rest, ǣrest, earst *adv*
previously; at first; *on alre* ⁓ first
of all 3/6. Cp *ẹ̄r*.
ert see bē(n).
ērthe, ērþe, ēorþe, ēorðe *sb* EARTH.
ērthely, ērtly *adj* EARTHLY, terrestrial.
es see bē(n), hī².
escāpe(n), askāpie *wk vb* ESCAPE.
ēse, ess, eyse *sb* EASE.
1. espȳe *sb* spy. [*Espy*].
2. espȳe *wk vb* discover, unmask,
ESPY.
ess see ēse.
ẹ̄st, ēast *sb* EAST.

estāt *sb* ESTATE, condition.
ēste *adj* pleasant 6/999, 1031.
ēt see ẹ̄te(n).
etayn *sb* ogre, monster 18/723. [*Eten*].
ẹ̄te(n), ēōte(n) *st vb 5* EAT; *gerund* to ēotene 3/22; *pret* ēte, hẹ̄te 10/156, ēt 3/12; ẹ̄ten, i-ẹ̄te 10/98.
etlunge *sb* proportion, measure 4/29. [*Evening*²].
etstonden *st vb 6* resist 4/44. [*At-stand*].
eu see ȝē².
euchan, euch(e) see ẹ̄ch.
ēve see ēven¹.
ēvel, ȳvel, üfel, üvel *sb, adj, adv* EVIL.
1. ēven, ēve *sb* evening, EVE (night before), EVEN¹.
2. ẹ̄ven, ẹ̄vyn, ẹ̄wen, ēwyn, ǣfne, *adv* EVEN, exactly, same.
ẹ̄venyng *sb* the same, the equal. [*Evening*²].
ẹ̄ver, ǣvre, ǣvere, ēaver *adv* EVER.
everemoore, eavermāre see evermọ̄re.
everych, everich, evrych, evreich, ǣvric̆, ǣvrich, eavereuch *adj* and *pron* each, EVERY.
everychon *pron* EVERYONE.
evermọ̄re, everemọọre, evirmār, eavermāre *adv* never again; now and always, EVERMORE.
ẹ̄vez *sb* EAVES.
evreich, evrych see everych.
ẹ̄wen, ẹ̄wyn see ẹ̄ven².

F

fǎder, fǎdir, vǎder *sb* FATHER; *gen sg* fǎder.
fadme *sb* FATHOM.
fæstnen *wk vb* FASTEN.
1. fay, fey *sb* faith. [*Fay*¹].
2. fay see fọ̄¹.
faie *sb* fairy, FAY².
fayis see fọ̄¹.
fayle *sb* FAIL², *withoute* ⁓ without slackening 14/4069.
failȝhe *wk vb* FAIL.
fain, fayn 1. *adj* glad, satisfied. — 2. *adv* willingly.
fair(e), fār(e), feir, feyre, feier, veir(e), veyr, vaire, væir 1. *adj*

FAIR, beautiful; *comp* feyrure 13₂/117; *super* feherest 3/64. — 2. *adv* beautifully, distinctly.
fayrhẹ̄de *sb* beauty 16/57. [FAIR-HEAD].
fairness, feiernesse *sb* beauty, FAIR-NESS.
faiten *wk vb* beg 21₃/30. [*Fait*¹].
fǎlde *sb* (sheep) FOLD² 7/3339.
fale *adj* FALLOW¹, faded, yellow.
falle(n), valle *st vb 7* FALL, happen etc.; as an inheritance 24/2; to fell 5/14059, trip 6/955; *pret* fīl, fēl, fēll, vēōl 5/14022, fēōl 5/14023; *pp* y-falle, falle.
fallinge, vallynge *sb* FALLING; ⁓ *doun* diminishing 4ₐ/26.
fallow see felawe.
falshōd, falshẹ̄d *sb* FALSEHOOD.
fān see fọ̄¹.
fang, foangen, fọ̄nge, fōn *st vb 7* take, get; received 18/1315; *pret* fēng 3/11; *pp* i fōn 5/14669. [*Fang*¹].
fantasȳe *sb* FANTASY 21₁/36.
fǎrd *adj* afraid, FEARED.
fār(e) see fair(e).
1. fāre *sb* voyage; *a dæis* ⁓ one day's journey 1/45; action 29/602. [*Fare*¹].
2. fāre *st vb 6* go, FARE¹; behave; suffer, travail 29/531, 533; *wel* ⁓ to live well; *pret* foore, fōr 1/1; *pp* fāren, fārne, i-fāre, i-vāren.
fārne see fāre².
fast *adj* firm, FAST.
1. faste *adv* firmly, FAST 12/537, in a hurry, FAST 21₁/40.
2. faste, veste 15/19 *wk vb* abstain from food, FAST².
fasūre *sb* appearance.
fāte *wk vb* FADE¹ 19/1038.
faune(n) *wk vb* FAWN¹, flatter.
fē, fēō *sb* wealth, goods 12/563, 13₂/70 [*Fee*¹].
feaw, few *pl adj* FEW.
fēble, frēble *adj* FEEBLE.
fech *wk vb* FETCH.
fēde, feede *wk vb* FEED; *pres 3 sg* fet 21₂/194; *pp* fed.
feeld see fēld.
feend see fēnd.

feere see fēre².
feete see fōt(e).
feff *wk vb* endow; *pp* feft. [*Feoff*].
feght(te) see fighte(n).
feghtyng *sb* FIGHTING.
fegüre *sb* FIGURE.
feȝt see fighte(n).
feherest see fair(e).
feht see fiht.
fey see fay¹.
feier see faire.
feiernesse see fairness.
feiȝen, fīe *wk vb* write 5/25. [FAY¹].
feyll see fēle².
feynd see fēnd.
feyne(n) *wk vb* FEIGN, pretend; *re-flexive* disguise oneself 21₁/42.
feir, feyre see fair(e).
feyrīe *sb* a fairy-like thing, FAIRY.
feyrure *comparative* see fair(e).
feytt = *fēte* see fōt(e).
feyþ *sb* FAITH.
1. fel, vel *sb* animal skin, FELL¹.
2. fel see felle(n).
felaurede *sb* company, companionship. [*Fellowred*].
felawe, felowe, fellow, velaȝe 15/10 *sb* FELLOW, comrade; *pl* felowse.
felaweshipe, felaushepe, felyschip *sb* company, society, community (religious). [FELLOWSHIP].
fēld, feeld, vēld *sb* FIELD.
felde see fēle².
1. fēle, fōle, feōle, vēle *adj* much, many *comparative* fēler 18/1391.
2. fēle, feyll *wk vb* FEEL; *pret* felde 19/1087.
felyschip see felaweshipe.
1. fell *adj* cruel, terrible, FELL.
2. fell see falle(n).
felle(n) *wk vb* strike down, FELL; *pp* y-veld 15/10.
felónly, felunlȳche *adv* cruelly, wickedly.
1. fen *sb* chapter, section 27₄ᵦ/890 (see note). [*Fen³*].
2. fen, ven *sb* marsh, (muddy) sewer 6/962, ditch, FEN¹ (2).
fēnd, feend, feynd, feōnd *sb* FIEND.
fēnel-seed *sb* FENNEL-SEED.
feng see fang.
feō see fē.

feōl see falle(n).
feōle see fēle¹.
feolevolde *adj* manifold, multiple; *of* ∼ by many times 13₂/117. [*Fele-fold*].
feōnd see fēnd.
fer, feor, ferre *adj* and *adv* FAR; ∼ tō far too; *on* ∼ AFAR.
1. fērd(e) *sb* fear. [*Ferd²*].
2. fērd(e) see fēre⁴.
1. fēre *sb* companion; *pl* fēren 3/48, 8/489. [*Fere¹*].
2. fęre, fęęre *sb* FEAR.
3. fēre *sb* power, capacity 13₂/79. [*Fere³*].
4. fēre *wk vb* go, journey; *pret* ferd(e). [*Fere¹*].
5. fęre *wk vb* FEAR; *pp* fērde fearful 18/1295, fērd afraid 17/61.
ferene see ferne.
ferien *wk vb* FERRY, transport; *pret* fereden 5/14040.
fērly 1. *adj* marvellous, extraordinary, exceptional 18/716.—2. *adv* strange and wonderfully. — 3. *sb* fantastic and magical experience 21₁/6.
fermysoūn *sb* closed season for game 18/1156. [*Fermison*].
ferne, ferene *sb* FERN.
ferre see fer.
fērsly *adv* FIERCELY with great pomp 18/1323.
ferst see first.
ferte, verte *wk vb* FART 13₁ₐ/10.
ferthermōre *adv* FURTHERMORE.
ferthyng-worth *sb* quarter-penny's worth, FARTHINGSWORTH.
fest *sb* FIST¹.
fęste *sb* FEAST.
1. fet, fete *wk vb* fetch, take, look for; *pret* fott.
2. fet see fēde.
fēt(e) see fōt(e).
1. fęte *wk vb* conduct o.s. 18/1282. [*Feat*].
2. fete see fet¹.
fētte see fōt(e).
feþer *sb* FEATHER.
fēvre *sb* FEVER.
few see feaw.
fīeble see fēble.
fiede see feiȝen.

fīeld-wòde *sb* gentian? 28/4039 (note). [*Fieldwood*].

fȳere see fȳr.

fyftēne *number* FIFTEEN.

fyfþe, vifte *number* FIFTH.

fighte(n), fiȝte, feȝt, feght(te) *str vb* *3c* FIGHT.

fihs see fish.

fiht, feht *sb* FIGHT.

fikelere *sb* flatterer 3/35. [*Fickler*].

fīl, fȳl see falle(n).

fylden see fille(n).

fȳlyng *sb* defilement. [FILING²].

fille(n) *wk vb* FILL; fulfill 7/3628; *pret* fylden.

filtyrde *pp adj* shaggy 20/780. [*Feltered*].

fylþe, fylthe, fülþe, velþe *sb* FILTH.

fȳnde(n), fīnden, vȳnde, vīnd *str vb* *3a* FIND, also, provide board and lodging [see FOUND *sb*]; *pres 3 sg* fynt 21₃/88, vīnd 10/253; *pret* fǫnd(e), fǫnt, fǒunde, fūnde, *pl* fǒundun, fǫnden, fūnden; *pp* fǒunden, y-fǒunde.

1. fȳne *str vb 1* finish 19/1030; *pret* fǫn [*Fine¹*].

2. fȳne *adj* beautiful, FINE; pure, sheer 18/1239.

finger *sb* FINGER; *dat pl* fingren 5/25.

fȳnly *adv* completely 18/1391. [FINELY].

fynt see fȳnde(n).

fȳr, fīr, fyère, für *sb* FIRE.

fȳri *adj* FIERY.

firse *sb* FURZE, *a wisp of firses* a stopper made of straw 21₄/351.

1. first, fyrst, ferst, fürst, fryst, verst 15/1. 1. *number* FIRST, best 24/22. — 2. *adv.*

2. first see frest.

fish, fisċ, fihs, viss 15/15 *sb* FISH.

fishere, vissere *sb* FISHER 15/14.

fiþele *sb* FIDDLE.

fȳve *number* FIVE.

flæsch see flesch(e).

flayre *sb* flame 20/772, FLARE.

flaune *sb* custard. [*Flawn*].

flawe *sb* spark 20/773. [FLAW¹].

flē, fledde see flē(n).

flees, flēse *sb* FLEECE.

fleet(e) see flēte(n).

flehs, fleissh see flesch(e).

flēme *sb* flight. [*Fleme²*].

flē(n), flēo *str vb 2* FLEE; *pret* fledde.

fles see flesch(e).

flesch(e), flesċ, flæsh, fleissh, fles, flehs *sb* FLESH.

fleschly, fleschely, flesshly *adj* FLESH-LY, carnal.

flēse see flees.

flet see flet(te).

flēte(n), fleete *str vb 2* float, flow; wander; *pp* flǫten 18/714. [FLEET¹].

flet(te) *sb* ground 19/1058, floor; *on þe* ~ in the great hall 18/1374. [*Flet¹*].

flex *sb* FLAX.

flȳe, flyghte *str vb 2* FLY¹; *pret* flǒwe, *pl* flugen, flugæn, fluhen.

fly(e)ghyng *sb* FLYING 16/32, 33, 35.

flȳte *wk vb* scold, reprove 29/625. [*Flite*].

flǫ *str vb 6* FLAY, *quic* ~ flay alive 12/544a, 612.

flōd, vlōd *sb* FLOOD, river, water; deluge 5/10.

flōde see flǒwe¹.

flok *sb* FLOCK.

flokke *wk vb* flock.

flǫne *sb* arrow 18/1161. [*Flane*].

flōr(e) *sb* FLOOR.

floresche *wk vb* splendidly clothed 20/771. [FLOURISH].

flǫte *sb* company, following 12/738. [*Flote²*].

flǫten see flēte(n).

flōþ see flǒwe¹.

flōur, flǒwre *sb* FLOWER.

flōure *wk vb* FLOWER.

flōure-de-lice *sb* FLEUR-DE-LIS.

flōury *adj* FLOWERY.

1. flǒwe *wk vb* FLOW 6/920, 947, *pres 3 sg* flōþ, flǒweþ; *pret* flōde 19/1058.

2. flǒwe see flȳe.

flǒwre see flōur.

flugen, flugæn, fluhen see flȳe.

fnaste *wk vb* breathe 12/548. [*Fnast*].

1. fǫ, fǫǫ, fay *sb* FOE; *pl* fān 3/55, vān 3/72, 81.

2. fǫ, fǫne, foyne *indef adj* some, cp. FEW.

foangen see fang.

fodder *sb* FODDER.

fōde *sb* FOOD.
foyne = fǫne see fǭ².
foysoūn *sb* abundance 19/1058. [FOI-
SON].
fōl *sb* FOOL.
1. folde *sb* earth 18/1275. [*Fold*¹].
2. fǫlde *wk vb* FOLD¹ 13₅/27, turn
towards 18/1363.
fōle see fēle¹.
folewe, folʒe, folʒhen, folhið see
folwe(n).
folȳe *sb* FOLLY¹; harm 14/4116.
foliot *sb* foolishness 6/868.
folk, volk *sb* FOLK, *in* ⁓ in a group
18/1323.
folwe(n), folowe(n), folewe, folʒe,
fulien, folʒhen, folhin *wk vb* FOL-
LOW; imitate 3/24.
fǭm(e) *sb* and *wk vb* FOAM.
fǫn see fang, fȳne.
fǫnde see fȳnde(n).
fǫnd(e) *wk vb* try, test, examine.
[*Fand*].
fǫnden see fȳnde(n).
fǫne see fǭ².
fǫnge see fang.
fǫnt see fȳnde(n).
fǫǫ see fǭ².
foore see fāre².
foot see fōte.
1. for, fore, vor 1. *prep* FOR, ⁓ *tō* id,
⁓ *þat* because 12/743, 14/4024. —
2. *conj* FOR, on account of 1/57,
21₂/192.
2. fōr see fāre².
forbēde *str vb 2* FORBID; *pp* forbǫden
3/10, forbǫde 3/22.
forbēre(n) *str vb 4* FORBEAR; *pret*
forbāren 1/51, 53.
forbȳ *adv* by, near.
forbyseyn *sb* example, proverb 14/
4149. [*Forbysen*].
forbǫde(n) see forbēde.
forcursæd *pp adj* cursed 1/59. [*For-
curse*].
fordō(n) *irreg vb* destroy, spoil; *pp*
fordōn. [FORDO].
fordrēden *wk vb* terrify; *pp* fordrēd
7/3348. [*Fordread*].
fordrónke *pp adj* completely drunk.
[*Fordrunken*].
fordrüe *wk vb* dry up 6/919. [*Fordry*].

fore see for¹.
foren *adv* before; ⁓ *tō* towards 5/
14035. [*Forne*].
forestēr *sb* FORESTER, game-keeper.
foret see forþ.
foretravaillede *pp adj* worn out 20/
806. [*Fortravail*].
foreward see forward².
forfaite *wk vb* FORFEIT.
forgaa *irreg vb* FORGO 16/30.
forgat, forʒat see forgete(n).
forgete(n), forʒeten, voryete *str vb 5*
FORGET; *pres 3 sg* forʒet 2/23,
voryet 15/48; *pret* forgat, forʒat;
pp forgete, forgeten.
forʒelde *wk vb* repay, give back. [*For-
yield*].
forʒet, forʒeten see forgete(n).
forʒēve, foryēve *str vb 5* FORGIVE, *imperative* forʒef.
forhewen *str vb 7* cut down; *pret*
forhēou 5/14017. [*Forhew*].
forhoʒhen *wk vb* despise 7/3645.
[*Forhow*].
for-hwī see for-whȳ.
forlēre *wk vb* seduce 6/926.
forlēse *str vb 2* [for] LOSE; *pres 3 sg*
forlēost 6/949; *pret 2 sg* forlost;
pp forlǫren, vorlǫre 15/70.
forlēte(n) *str vb 7* give up, abandon.
[FORLET].
forlóyn *sb* lost, gone away 27/386
(see note). [*Forloin*].
fórlonge *sb* FURLONG.
forlǫren, forlost see forlēse.
forme *adj* first 3/35.
forōuten *prep* without. [*Forout*].
forrākyd *adj* run out, tired 29/256.
[*For-raked*].
forsāke, fursāke *str vb 6* FORSAKE;
pp forsāke 10/177.
forseyde, forsayd *pp adj* FORESAID.
forshāpyn *pp adj* magically and
pejoratively changed in shape 29/
619. [*Forshape*].
forspǫkyn *pp adj* bewitched [FOR-
SPEAK].
forswēre(n), vorzuērie *st vb 6* perjure
oneself. [FORSWEAR].
forswōren, forsuōren *pp adj* falsely
sworn 1/15, 59. [FORSWEAR, FOR-
SWORN].

forþ, furth, vorþ, foret 13₃/19 adv onwards, ahead, FORTH.
forþen wk vb carry out, accomplish 7/12. [Forth].
for-þī, for-thȳ, vor-þī conj because, therefore, thus; ~ ðat because 1/2. [For-thy].
forthynk wk vb impers misthink, dislike, suspect 29/511. [Forthink].
forþriht, forðriht adv right away, immediately, ~ sum as soon as 7/3342. [FORTHRIGHT].
forthward adv farther on 12/731.
forwāked adj worn out by staying up all night 29/253. [FORWAKED].
1. forward adv right away.
2. forward, foreward sb agreement; þat watz not ~ that was not agreed upon 18/1395, tō þat ~ on condition that 12/486.
forwerpen str vb 3b reject 7/3645. [Forwerpe].
for-whȳ, for-hwī conj why, because.
forwrapped pp adj all wrapped up. [Forwrap].
foryet(e) see forgete(n).
foryēve see forȝēve.
fōt(e), foot sb FOOT; pl fēte, feete, feytt, fētte; fōte (old genitive pl) 20/801.
fōt-hǫt adv swiftly, FOOT-HOT.
fott see fet.
1. fōul(e), fōwll, fōull, fūl, vōul 1. adj FOUL, vile, ugly 18/717, dirty (weather), excrementally filthy 6/962. — 2. adv. in an ugly manner, disgracefully.
2. fōul(e), fōwhele, fōwle, fuȝele sb FOWL, bird.
fōundement, fūndament, fūndement sb foundation for a wall 19/993, 1010; the buttocks 27₄ᴮ/950. [FUNDAMENT].
fōunden, fōundun see fȳnde(n).
fōune sb FAWN¹.
fōur, fōwr number FOUR.
1. fōurme sb FORM.
2. fōurme vb FORM¹, create.
fōwertiȝþe number FORTIETH.
fōwhele, fōwle see fōul(e)².
fōwll see fōul(e)¹.
fōwr see fōur.

fox, vox sb FOX.
frā see frǫ.
frayst wk vb ask. [Fraist].
fram, vram, vrom prep FROM.
frankys see frenshe.
fraunchis sb generosity 18/1264. [FRANCHISE].
frawd sb FRAUD.
frē, free, frēo 1. adj noble, generous, FREE. — 2. sb noble being 29/644.
frēdom(e), frēdam sb FREEDOM.
freend, freynd see frēnde.
freynsch see frenshe.
freissh, fressh see fresch.
frek adj hardy, bold. [Freck].
frēke, frēc sb man.
frēkly adv boldly. [Freckly].
frēlich adv FREELY.
frēman sb FREEMAN.
frȩme sb advantage 11/8.
fremede, fremmede adj foreign 2/34, 3/97, 16/21. [Fremd].
fremedly adv as an exile. [Fremdly].
fremmede see fremede.
frenchype sb FRIENDSHIP.
frenchis see frenshe.
frēnd, freend, freynd, frönd sb FRIEND; relative 14/4136.
frēndly adj FRIENDLY.
frenshe, frensch, fren(s)sh, freynsch, frenchis, frankys adj FRENCH.
frēo see frē(e).
frȩre sb FRIAR.
fresch, fresh, freissh, fressh adj FRESH.
freschly adv FRESHLY.
frēse str vb 2 FREEZE; pret frȩs.
frest, first sb delay; but langar ~ with no more delay 22₂/447; dōn a ~ put off doing 2/37. [Frist].
freuch adj frail 19/1086. [Frough].
frym adv in abundance 19/1079. [Frim].
fryst see ferst.
frȳt see frūte.
friþ sb peace 7/3380. [Frith¹].
frǫ, frā prep FRO, from.
frōfren wk vb encourage, comfort 7/3345. [Frover].
frogge, vrogge sb FROG; pl vroggen.
frönd see frēnde.
frotyng adj grinding, rubbing. [Frotting].

frōunt *sb* FRONT.
frūte, frȳt *sb* FRUIT.
fuȝele, fūl see fōul(e).
ful, vol 15/17, 1. *adj* FULL 2. *adv*
   very; ~ *wel* very well, completely.
fulien see folwe(n).
fully *adv* FULLY.
fulluht *sb* baptism 5/18. [*Fullought*].
fülste *wk vb* aid, encourage 6/889.
   [*Filst*].
fultume *sb* help, grace. [*Fultum*].
fülþe see fylþe.
fündament see fōundement.
1. fünde *wk vb* seek out, aspire to.
   [*Found*¹].
2. fünde see fȳnde(n).
fündement see fōundement.
fünden see fȳnde(n).
für(e) see fȳr.
fursāke see forsāke.
fürst see first¹.
furþ see forþ.
furþe *number* FOURTH.

G

gaa see gō(n).
gabbe *wk vb* GAB¹, lie, boast.
gadere(n), gadre, gedere *wk vb*
   GATHER.
gadering *sb* GATHERING, parliament
   1/8.
ġǣde see ȝēde.
ġǣld see ȝēld.
ġǣre see ȝēr.
ġǣt see ȝēt(e).
gaf see gif.
1. gayn *sb* GAIN², favor 18/1241.
   [*Gain*¹].
2. gayn *wk vb* GAIN¹; got him no
   good cheer 17/57.
gaynly *adj* courteous, polite, GAINLY.
galle *sb* mud 19/1060. [GALL²].
galoūn *sb* GALLON.
galwe-trē *sb* GALLOWS-TREE.
galwes *sb pl* GALLOWS.
gāme, gāmen, gomen, gammyn *sb* 1.
   GAME; — 2. *in* ~ gaily 18/1376. —
   2. venison; *pl* gamnez.
gammyn see gāme.
gan see ginne.
gāne see gō(n).
gang, gangen, gōngen *str vb* 7 go;

subj *pres* 2 *sg* gōnge 12/690.
   [*Gang*¹].
ganggynge *sb* departure. [*Ganging*¹].
gar see gēr.
garysoūn *sb* treasure 18/1255 (< OF
   gariso(u)n, infl. by ON *gersumi*).
   [GARRISON (1 *obs*)].
garray *sb* fuss, row 29/564.
garryng *adj* grating 26/15. [cp.
   Garre v].
gāste, gōst *sb* GHOST, spirit, soul.
gāstlīke *adv* piously 7/3649. [GHOSTLY].
gat, gatt see gete(n).
gāte *sb* road, way 14/4037. [*Gate*²].
gawde *sb* trick, fraud. [GAUD²].
gēast see gō(n).
gedere see gadere(n).
gees see goos.
gef see gif.
geldyng *sb* GELDING.
ġemme *sb* GEM.
genge *adj* normal, expected 6/1002.
ġent *adj* refined, noble 19/1014.
ġentil, ġentyl *adj* noble, distinguished,
   GENTLE, kind; precious (stone) 19/
   991, 1015.
gēr, gar *wk vb* do or make (ON);
   pret gert. [*Gar*].
1. gert *pp* belted, GIRDED = GIRT,
   GIRD¹.
2. gert see gēr.
gesse(n) *wk vb* GUESS, be of opinion,
   expect.
gessynge *sb* appreciation, evaluation;
   wiþoute ~ no doubt, without GUESS-
   ING 4ₐ/15.
gest *sb* GUEST.
1. ġeste *sb* deeds [*Gest*³] 8/478.
2. ġeste *sb* game, JEST 8/522.
gēt see gōot.
ġēt see ȝēt(e).
gete(n), gett *str vb* 5 GET; *pret*
   gat(t), *pl* geten.
gēþ see gō(n).
geven see gif.
ġyaunt, ġeant *sb* GIANT.
1. gif *str vb* 5 GIVE *pres* 3 *sg* giffis;
   pret sg gef, gaf, *pl* geven. Cp. ȝeve¹.
2. gif, gyff *conj* if. [*Gif*]. Cp. ȝef.
gild see gilt.
gilt, gild *adj* GILT.
gylt, gült *sb* GUILT.

gilte(n) *wk vb* sin; *pp* i-gült 2/27.
[*Guilt*].
giltless *adj* GUILTLESS, innocent.
1. g̈inne *sb* cleverness 10/72, ruse 10/
125, snare, trap 10/86, 103, mech-
anism 10/77, 87. [GIN¹].
2. ginne *str vb 3a* BEGIN (*to*); *pret
sg* gan, gon, can, gun *pl* gunne.
Also used as empty word indicating
tense, cp. ModE *do*. [*Gin¹*].
gyrd *wk vb* strike; ⁓ *of* cut off.
[GIRD²].
gistninge *sb* hospitality, banquet,
feast 10/255. [*Gestening*].
gyterne *sb* kind of guitar, cithern.
[GITTERN].
g̈yven see ʒeve.
1. glad *sb* GLADness, joy 29/668.
2. glad, gled, glead *adj* happy, bright
27₁/338, GLAD.
glayre *sb* amber (< OE *glær*).
glāse(n) *wk vb* GLAZE¹.
glāsynge *sb* GLAZING, stained glass.
glē *sb* GLEE, gaiety.
gleade see glad².
gleadien *wk vb* ⁓ (*of*) take joy in
4/29. [GLAD].
gleadschipe *sb* joy 4/25, 26. [GLAD-
SHIP].
gleadunge *sb* gladness. [*Gladding*].
gled(e) see glad².
glēmande *adj* GLEAMING.
glent *sb* glance 18/1290.
glente *wk vb* GLINT, shine; *pret* glente.
[*Glent*].
glet *sb* slime, filthy ooze 19/1060.
[GLEET].
glewman *sb* GLEEMAN, wandering
minstrel.
glīde(n) *str vb 1* GLIDE, move across,
disappear; *pret* glǫd; *pp* i glyden.
glymme *sb* light. [GLIM].
glysnande *adj* GLISTENING.
glǭd see glīde(n).
glǭse *wk vb* GLOSS. [GLOZE¹].
glótonȳe, glótou̅nȳe *sb* GLUTTONY.
glótou̅n, glótow̅n *sb* GLUTTON.
gǭ see gǭ(n).
gobet *sb* fragment, GOBBET.
1. God, Godd *sb* GOD; *gen* Goddys,
Goddes.
2. gōd, good, gou̅d, goed, gud, guod

1. *adj* GOOD. — 2. *sb* GOODS, wealth,
pl 23/4.
goddhead *sb* GODHEAD.
goddot *interjection* by GOD 12/606
(< *God wǭt* 'God knows').
gōdlec *sb* bounty, goodness. [*Good-
laik*].
gōdly *adv* GOODLY, graciously.
gōdnesse *sb* GOODNESS.
godspel(le) *sb* GOSPEL.
goed see gōd².
gǭys, gǭyth see gǭ(n).
gōld *sb* GOLD.
gǭlnesse *sb* wantonness, lasciviousness
6/899. [*Goleness*].
gǭme *sb* man. [*Gome¹*].
gomen see gāme.
gǭ(n), gǫǫ(n), gaa, guo 15/5 *irreg vb*
GO; *pres 2 sg* gǭys 29/222, ge̅ast
3/48, 6/875, *3 sg* gǭtz, gǭys 29/488,
ge̅þ 15/47; *imp 2 pl* gǭyth 29/204;
pp gǭ, gǫǫn, gǭn, gāne.
gon see ginne.
gǭne *wk vb* open mouth wide 28/4064,
yawn. [*Gane*].
gǭnge see gang.
good, goodis see gōd².
goos *sb* GOOSE; *pl* gees.
gǫǫt *sb* GOAT; *pl* gēt 10/167.
gossib, gossip, gossyppe *sb* god-par-
ent; *pl* god-father and god-mother;
close friend. [GOSSIP].
gǭst see gāst(e).
gǭstly *adj* spiritual [GHOSTLY].
gǭtz see gǭ(n).
gothely *wk vb* rumble, gargle.
[*Gothele*].
gou̅d see gōd².
góvernaunce *sb* GOVERNANCE, administration.
grāce *sb* favor, GRACE, *sory* ⁓ disfavor.
gradde see grēde.
gramēre *sb* GRAMMAR.
grant *adj* GRAND, big.
grante see graunte.
grāpes *sb pl* wine, the GRAPE¹ 17/18.
gras *sb* GRASS.
grāt see grēt.
graunte, grant *wk vb* promise, GRANT.
grāve *wk vb* bury. [GRAVE¹].
gre̅at(t) see grēt¹.

grēde *wk vb* cry out 9/23, 26; *pret* gradde 6/936.

grēdy *adj* greedy.

grēet see grēt¹.

grēf(e) *sb* GRIEF, sorrow.

grēfe, grēve *wk vb* GRIEVE; torture, harm 21₂/153.

greyn see grēne.

greyþe *wk vb* get ready, fit out 12/706, 14. [*Graith*].

grendeð see grīnde(n).

grēne, greyn 1. *adj* GREEN; pale 13₄/32. — 2. *sb* the GREEN, (grass, etc).

1. gręt, gręet, grēat(t), grāt 15/3 *adj* GREAT, big, tall.

2. grēt see grēte(n)².

1. grēte(n) *wk vb* GREET¹; drink a health 21₄/343; *pret* grette.

2. grēte(n) *str vb 2* weep, cry; *pres 3 sg* grēt 15/48; *pret* grēt 12/615. [*Greet²*].

grētely *adv* GREATLY.

grette see grēte(n).

1. grēve *sb* thicket, copse. [*Greave¹*].

2. grēve see grēfe.

grym, grim *adj* savage, GRIM; heavy 21₄/360.

grin *sb* hangman's noose, collar 1/32 (see note). [GRIN¹].

grīnde(n) *str vb 3a* GRIND¹; *pres 3 sg* grendeþ 6/943.

grīp(e) *sb* griffon 5/14032, 12/572. [*Gripe³*].

grisbit(t)yng *sb* grinding of teeth 26/15. [*Gristbiting*].

grisly, grislich *adj* horrible, GRISLY.

grith *sb* peace 6/1005, 7/3380, 12/511.

griðfullnesse *sb* peacefulness 3/127. [*Grithfulness*].

grócche see gruche.

gróm *adj* irritated 6/992. [GRUM].

gróme *sb* GROOM¹, servant.

gróne, grónie *wk vb* GROAN; *subj pres 3 sg* gróni 6/872, 874.

gróte *sb* GROAT.

growe(n) *str vb 7* GROW.

gruche, grucche, grócche *wk vb* GROUCH, grudge, complain. [*Grutch*]. (OED supplement lists ModE *grouch* (U. S.), see MATHEWS, *Dict. of Americanisms*).

grūnd *sb* GROUND, bottom of sea.

grūndlike *adv* heartily, with appetite 12/653. [*Groundly*].

gud(e) see gōd².

gülden *adj* golden. [*Gilden*].

gült see gylt.

gun, gunne see ginne.

guo see gǫ(n).

guod see gǫd².

gutte *sb* GUT; *pl* guttis.

3

ʒaf see ʒeve¹.

1. ʒāre *adj* ready 6/860. [YARE].

2. ʒāre *adv* quick; for some time 10/169. [*Yare*]. Cp. *ʒǫre*.

ʒarne, ʒharne *wk vb* YEARN¹ for, desire, covet; *pp* ʒharnyt.

ʒāte *sb* GATE¹.

ʒāvest see ʒeve¹.

1. ʒę̄, yę̄, yęę *adv* YEA, yes.

2. ʒē, ʒhē *2 pl pers pron* YE, YOU, *dat-acc* ʒōw, yōw, ʒuw 7/3352 ʒōu, ʒew, eu, yw, ōu, eow 2/25, ōw 3/129; *poss* ʒūre YOUR.

ʒēar(e) see ʒēr.

ʒēde, yēde, ʒōd, ʒeid, yōde, ġæde *pret* went 18/1146, 1400, 19/1050, 21₄/367; *pl* īēden 1/48 (OE *ġe-ēode*). [*Yode*].

ʒę̄derly *adv* right away 18/1215 (< OE *ġe-ǣdre* 'id.'). [*Yederly*].

ʒeer see ʒēr.

1. ʒef, yef, ʒif, yif *conj* IF. Cp. *gif²*.

2. ʒef see ʒeve¹.

ʒę̄ʒe *wk vb* ~ *after* ask for 18/1215. [*Yeie*].

ʒe-hāten see hǫte(n).

ʒeid see ʒēde.

ʒēld, ġæld *sb* taxes 2/45. [YIELD].

ʒēlde(n), yēlde *str vb 4* YIELD, pay; *refl* give in; *pp* ʒǫld, i-ʒǫlde.

ʒelpe *wk vb* boast 6/971, YELP.

ʒēme *sb* heed 3/1, 4/30. [*Yeme*].

ʒēmen, ·yēmen *wk vb* take care, heed. [*Yeme*].

ʒēne *wk vb* reply, refute 6/893 (?< OE *gegnian*, cp. ON *gegna* 'id.').

ʒeoi *interjection* yes, certainly 3/106, cp. YEA.

ʒeond see ʒond.

ʒeóng see ʒóng.

ʒeóngen *st vb 7* go 5/14036. [*Yong*].

ȝēr, ȝeer, ġear, yēr, yeer *sb* YEAR; *þis seven* ⁓ for a long time 18/1382.

ȝērne, ȝorne, yorne *adv* willingly; eagerly. [*Yerne*].

ȝērnyng *sb* YEARNING.

ȝēt(e), yheyt, ȝit, ȝüt, ġēt, ġæt 1. *conj* YET; *bot* ⁓ and yet. — 2. *adv* YET, still.

1. ȝeve, yeve, ȝyve, ġyven *str vb 5* GIVE; ⁓ *up* id; *pret* yaf, ȝef 3/12, *2 sg* ȝāvest, *pl* iāfen 1/10; *pres subj 3 sg* yef; *pp* yeven, i-ȝeven 3/99. Cp. *gif²*.

2. ȝeve *sb* gift 2/45. [*Give¹*].

ȝew, ȝhē see ȝē².

ȝharn *wk vb* YEARN; ȝharnyt 22/232.

ȝhō see schē.

ȝif see ȝef¹.

ȝynge see ȝóng.

ȝit see ȝēt(e).

ȝyve see ȝeve¹.

ȝōd see ȝēde.

ȝǫld see ȝelde(n).

ȝolle *wk vb* yell 6/972; *2 sg* ȝolst 6/985. [*Yoll*].

ȝoman, yoman *sb* royal officer. [YEO-MAN].

ȝond, ȝeond *prep* through, across 5/14, 14031. [*Yond*].

ȝóng, ȝeóng, yóng, ȝung, yunge, ȝynge *adj* YOUNG.

ȝóngthe, yǫngthe *sb* youth. [*Youngth*].

ȝǫre *adv* in past time, of YORE. Cp. *ȝāre*.

ȝorne seę ȝerne.

ȝórselven *2 pl intensive pron* YOUR-SELF/SELVES.

ȝōu see ȝē².

ȝōuþe *sb* YOUTH.

ȝōw see ȝē².

ȝung see ȝóng.

ȝūre *2 pl poss adj* YOUR.

ȝüt see ȝet(e).

ȝuw see ȝē².

H

ha see hē, heō¹, hī².

habbe(n) see hāve(n).

habbe(þ), habbeð see hāve(n).

habetācioūn *sb* HABITATION.

hacche *sb* (half) door, HATCH¹.

hād *sb* rank 7/9, species of existence 7/3661. [*Had*].

hælden *wk vb* fall 5/14020, pret hæld 5/14020, HEEL². [*Hield*]. Cp. *hĕlde*.

hælende *sb* savior, healer 7/3355. [*Healend*].

hærne see harn.

hæved see hęd.

haf see hāve(n).

hafd see hęd.

hafde, hāfe(n), hāfeð, hāfeþ see hāve(n).

hafved see hęd.

hafveð see hāve(n).

haȝel *sb* HAIL¹.

haȝþorne *sb* HAWTHORN.

hay *interj* HEY!

haiff see hāve(n).

haytt see hǫt.

haywarde, heiward *sb* parish-officer in charge of the fences and enclosures, herdsman of the cattle feeding on the common, HAYWARD 3/128, 21₃/16.

hak *wk vb* jangle 29/477; warble? but see note 29/657. [HACK v¹ (6)].

hakeneyman *sb* HACKNEY-MAN, man who keeps hackney-horses for hire 21₄/318.

hālde(n) see hǫlde(n).

halechen, halȝen *sb pl* saints 1/62, 15/78. [HALLOW¹].

hālely *adv* wholly, entirely 17/92, 20/764. [*Halely*].

half *sb* side, hand (direction), HALF; *a Goddes* ⁓ on God's behalf, in God's name 7/3346, *on eiþer halve* on both sides (the good and bad) 6/887.

halȝen see halechen.

halȝhe see hāli.

hāli, hāly, halȝhe, hǫly, hǫǫly *adj* WHOLE; HOLY; *sacred* 7/14.

1. halle *sb* HALL, palace.

2. halle *adj* WHOLE. [HALE].

halle-rōf *sb* HALL + ROOF.

halowe(n) *wk vb* sound a horn. [HAL-LOW²].

halp see helpe(n).

hals *sb* neck. [*Halse*].

1. halt *adj* lame, HALT.

2. halt see hǫlde(n).

halve see half.

ham see hī².

hāme see hǫm(e).

hamsylf, hamzelve see hemself.

han see hāve(n).

hand(e) see hǫnd.

handel *wk vb* HANDLE[1].

handlyng *sb* handbook 14/80, cp. HANDLING.

hange(n), hǫnge, hǫngi *str vb* 7 (and *wk pp*) HANG, cause to hang, suspend; *pret* hēng, heeng, hyng, hēngen; *pp* hanged.

hansel *sb* New Year's or Christmas gift. [HANDSEL].

hapnyt see happe[1].

1. happe, happen, happyn *impersonal wk vb* HAPPEN. [*Hap*[1]].

2. happe *wk vb* enclose 18/1224. [*Hap*[2]].

3. happe *sb* chance, fortune. [HAP[1]].

happen, happyn see happe[1].

harbar, herber, herboru *sb* dwelling, shelter. [HARBOUR[1]].

1. hārd, hēard *adv* HARD.

2. hard see hēre(n).

hārdely, hārdlīche *adv* boldly, strong. [HARDLY].

hārdy *adj* HARDY.

hardyment *sb* courage, boldness. [HARDIMENT].

hārdlīche see hārdely.

1. hāre *sb* HARE 15/22.

2. hare see hī[2].

harled *pp adj* entangled 18/744. [cp. *Harl v*[2]].

harn, hærne *sb* brain. [*Harn*[1]].

harpōur *sb* minstrel, HARPER[1] 14/ Introd.

harryng *sb* snarling 26/15. [cp. *Harr v*].

hart see hert(e).

harwen *wk vb* HARROW.[1]

hasard *sb* game of HAZARD 27₄ᴮ/465.

hasardōur *sb* gambler, HAZARDER.

hasardrȳe *sb* gambling. [*Hazardry*].

hasel *sb* HAZEL[1].

haspe *sb* HASP.

hasppe *wk vb* secure with hasps, HASP.

hass, hastōw see hāve(n).

hāt, hatt, hǫt see hǫte.

hatters *interj* by the garments (of Christ). [*Hatters, Hater sb*[2]].

haþel *sb* knight, companion, man 18/1138 (<OE *hæleþ* 'warrior' with infl of *æþele* 'noble'). [*Hathel*].

haunte(n) *wk vb* hang around, be addicted to, HAUNT.

hāve(n), habbe(n), hān, haf, haiff *wk vb* HAVE; *hāve þat* take that 5/14021. *pres 1 sg* habbe, haf, hāfe 7/11, *2 sg* hast, hest 15/56, hāvest 21₃/26, 10/222, hāves 12/688, hastōw 21₄/311, *3 sg* hāth, hēþ 15/3, 68 hāfeþ 7/16, hāveþ 4/17, 10/122, 12/564, hafveð 5/14077, has 20/711, hass 22₁/233, *pl* hān, habbeþ, hāven, hāfen 7/7. *pret* hadde, had, hafde 5/14053, hedde 9/5, 10/135, hevede 10/134, hefde 2/13, *pl* hedden. *pret subj 3 sg* hefde 3/20, *pl* hefden 1/20. *Contracted negative forms:* *pres 1 sg* nabbe 5/14047, *2 sg* nevestu 6/898, *3 sg* nāveþ 13₂/107; *pret* nedde 10/100, neddi 10/99, nade, nevede.

hāven(e) *sb* port, HAVEN.

hāvyng *sb* demeanor, behavior 22₂/412. [HAVING].

hawe *sb* hedge, enclosure, court. [*Haw*[1]].

haweke *sb* HAWK[1], falcon.

1. hē, hee, ha *3 sg M pers pronoun* HE, *acc* hine 5/32, 33, 9/6, hin 6/890; *dat-acc* him, hym; *poss* his, hys, hüs 21₃/58, hies 2/56. [*Hin*], HIM, HIS.

2. hē see hī[2].

hēalden see hǫlde(n).

hēard see hārd[1].

hēard-i-heortet *adj* HARD-HEARTED 3/61.

hearm *sb* HARM.

hearmin *wk vb* HARM 3/132, 4/5.

hēaved see hēd.

hēd, hēde, hēed, heyd, hēfed, hēved, hēvid, hæved, hafd, hafved, hēaved 15/30 *sb* HEAD.

hedde(n) see hāve(n).

1. hēde *sb* HEED.

2. hēde *wk vb* HEED.

heder, hederward see hider, hiderward.

hēd-maspenny *sb* to offer ∼ have masses said for repose of s. o.'s

soul 29/252. [*Head Mass Penny*],
s. v. HEAD *sb* (66).
1. hee *interj* hey! *or* alas! [*He¹*].
2. hee sée heigh.
hēed see hēd.
heeng see hange(n).
heer(e) see hēr(e).
hefde(n) see hāve(n).
hēfed see hēd.
hefne, hefnes see heven.
heğğe *sb* HEDGE.
heğğen *wk vb* trim hedges. [HEDGE].
hēgh see heigh.
heghtte see heʒt.
hēʒ see heigh.
hēʒe see heighe.
hēʒly *adv* devotedly, HIGHLY 18/755.
heʒt, heghhte, hight *sb* HEIGHT.
heh(e) see heigh, heighe.
heyd see hēd.
heie, heye see heigh, heighe.
heigh, hei, hēgh, hēh, hēʒ, hee, hīʒ,
hȳʒ, hȳ, hȳh *adj* HIGH, mighty, loud
18/1165, celestial; *superl* heste 13₅/
36, hexste 6/970.
heighe, hēʒe, hēhe, heie, heye *adv*
HIGH, loud.
heiʒte see hōte.
heynd see hende.
heyre-clōwt *sb* hair-shirt. [*Haire* +
Clout¹].
heite see hōte.
heiward see haywarde.
hēlde *wk vb* bend, sink (of the sun)
18/1321; *pret* hēldet. [*Hield*]. Cp.
hælden.
hēlde(n) see hōlde(n).
1. hēle *sb* healing; health, prosperity.
[*Heal*].
2. hēle, heele *sb* HEEL.
3. hēle *str vb 4* hide. [*Hele²*].
hēle(n) *wk vb* HEAL.
hēlere *sb* salvation. [HEALER¹ (2)].
helle *sb* HELL.
helpe(n) *str vb 3b* HELP; *pret* hylpe
14/4114, halp 10/84.
hem see hī².
hemme *sb* HEM¹; first row of foundation stones 19/1001.
hemself, hemselve, hamsylf, hamzelve
4ₐ/9, homsölve 6/883, heomseolve

6/930 *3 pl intensive pron* THEM-
SELVES. Cp. *hī²*.
hēnde, see hōnd(e).
hēnde, heynd *adj* gracious, courteous,
nice. [*Hend*].
hēndelayk *sb* courtesy. [*Hendelaik*].
hēndely *adv* graciously. [*Hendly*].
hēnge, hēngen see hange(n).
hēnge *wk vb* HANG.
1. henne *sb* HEN.
2. henne, hönne *adv* hence. [*Hen*].
hennes *adv* HENCE; *many ʒér* ~ many
years ago.
hente(n) *wk vb* catch, seize, get; *pret*
hente; *pp* y-hent. [*Hent*].
1. hēo, hue, hŏ; hǐ; ha *3 sg F pers
pron* SHE; *dat-acc* hir, hire 5/34
hüre; *acc* hēo 5/21 [*Heo*]*; poss*
hir(e), her(e) HER.
2. hēo see hī².
hēold(en) see hōlde(n).
heom see hī².
heordemon(n) see hȳrdman.
heore see hī².
heorte see hert(e).
heortelīche *adv* HEARTILY.
heoven(e) see heven.
heowe see hewe.
heowin *wk vb* HUE¹, color.
hēp(e) *sb* HEAP; *an* ~ in a heap.
1. her, hir *3 pl poss pron and adj*
THEIR. [*Her*]. Cp. *hī²*.
2. her see hir¹.
herber, herboru, see harbar.
herbifōre *adv* up to now [*Herebefore*].
herborwe *wk vb* house 12/742. [HAR-
BOUR].
herd see hēre(n).
hērde, hȳrde, hīrde *sb* shepherd.
[HERD²].
1. hēr(e), heer *sb* HAIR.
2. hēr(e), heer(e) *adv* HERE; ~ *efter*
hereafter 3/86.
3. her(e) see hēre(n), hi², hir¹.
hēre *sb* army 7/3370. [*Here*].
hēre(n), hīere *wk vb* HEAR; *pret* hard
29/978; *pp* herd, y-hyerd 15/56.
heremȳte *sb* HERMIT.
hērien, hēryre *wk vb* praise 4/37, 4ₐ/
22; *pp* y-hēried. [*Hery*].
hēriinge, hēryinge *sb* praise 6/981,
4ₐ/25. [*Herying*].

heryng *sb* HERRING.

herkken, herkne(n) *wk vb* HEARKEN.

herof *adv* from this 6/875. [HEREOF].

hert, hertte *sb* HART, deer.

hert(e), hart, heorte, hörte *sb* HEART.

hertŏu 10/120 = *art pŏu* see bē(n).

hervest *sb* HARVEST, fall season.

hes see hī².

hest see hāve(n).

heste *superl* see heigh.

1. hẹte *sb* HEAT.

2. hẹ̄te see ẹ̄te(n).

heterly *adv* violently.

hette see họte(n).

heþ see hāve(n).

hẹ̄þe *sb* HEATH, country.

1. hẹ̄þen *adj* HEATHEN.

2. heþen *adv* hence. [*Hethen*].

hẹved, hẹvid see hẹd.

hevede see hāve(n).

hẹve(n) *str vb 6* lift, HEAVE; *pret* hōf 5/14010.

heven, hewen, hefne, höven, heoven(e) *sb* HEAVEN.

heveneriche *sb* heavenly kingdom. [*Heavenric*].

heven-king, höven-king *sb* king of heaven. [*Heaven-king*].

hēvy *adj* HEAVY, loaded (with *in*) 16/28.

heviddes see hẹd.

hevynes(se) *sb* HEAVINESS.

hewe, heowe *sb* form, appearance 7/3337, HUE¹ 16/93.

hewe(n) *str vb 7* cut, HEW; *pret* hīewh; *gerund* tō hewene 5/14016.

hewen see heven.

hexste see heigh.

1. hȳ *sb* haste. [*Hie*].

2. hĭ, hȳ, heŏ, hŏ, hē̆, ha, a 4/1, 3, 10 etc. *3 pl pers pron* they. acc hī 9/22, hise 15/5, his 4ₐ/8, hes, hies 2/56, es 2/55; *dat-acc* hem, ham, heom, höm 6/868; *poss* her, here, hire, hör, heore, hüre, höre, hare 3/25, 4/6, 20, höre 6/880, 1018. [see *Hi, His, Es, Hem,* 'EM, *Her*].

3. hȳ, hī see heŏ¹, hȳe¹, heigh.

hic see ich¹.

hyd, hidde see hȳde.

hȳde *wk vb* HIDE; *pp* hid, hyd, i-hüd 2/28.

hider, heder *adv* HITHER.

hiderward, hederward *adv* HITHER-WARD, up to now.

1. hȳe, hī3e, hȳ, hīe *wk vb* hasten, HIE.

2. hȳe see heigh.

hīeld see họlde(n).

hīere see hēre(n).

hȳere see hīre.

hies see hē, his(e).

hīerþe *sb* hearing 15/65. [*Hearth*²].

hīewh see hewe(n).

hight, hyght see he3t, họte.

hī3, hȳ3e see heigh.

hī3e see hȳe¹.

hȳ3e *sb* height. [HIGH *sb*²].

hy3t see họte.

hȳh see heigh.

hiis 10/106 = *is* see bē(n).

hil, hülle *sb* HILL.

hylde *sb* protection, keeping 13₂/96. [HELD].

hylpe see helpe(n).

himself, himselven, himsölve, hinesölf 2/12, himseolf 3/4, himseolven 4/19, himzelve 4ₐ/11 *3 sg M intensive pron* HIMSELF.

hin see hē¹.

hȳnde *sb* HIND¹, female of the red deer.

hine see hē¹.

hȳne, hīne *sb* slave, servant, HIND²; *pl* hīne 12/620, hȳnen 24/12.

hinesölf see himself.

hyng see hange(n).

hyppe *sb* HIP¹.

1. hir, hire, her, here *3 sg F poss pron and adj* HER.

2. hir see her¹, heŏ¹.

hīrd *sb* followers, court 3/60.

hīrde, hȳrde see hērde.

hīrde-floc *sb* group of shepherds 7/3372. [*Herd-flock*].

hȳrdman, heordemon(n) *sb* shepherd. [*Herdman*].

1. hīre, hȳere, hüre *sb* HIRE, wages.

2. hire see heŏ¹, hī², hir¹.

hirself, hirselven *3 F intensive pers pron* HERSELF.

his, hise see hē¹, hī².

his(e), hys, hüs, hies *possessive M*

and Nt 3 sg HIS (spelling equivalent for genitive *s*? 26/23).
hit, hyt, yt, it *3 sg neuter pers pron*
IT; *hit ar* there are 18/1251; *it ben*
they are 21₃/59.
hitte *wk vb* throw to the ground 21₄/
239; *pret* hitte. [HIT].
hō see heō¹, hī².
hoaten see hǫte.
hōde, hood(e) *sb* HOOD, parka.
hoere see hī².
hōf see hęve(n).
hog *sb* HOG, *gen* hogges.
hoǧe *adj* HUGE, enormous 18/743.
hōker *sb* scorn, disdain 3/69.
hōkid *pp adj* HOOKED, crooked.
1. hǫl, hǫǫl *adj* WHOLE; ⁓ *of* in the
shelter of.
2. hol *adj* hollow, with a hole 6/965.
[*Holl*].
hōld *adj* faithful. [*Hold* (2)].
hǫlde *sb* power, possession, HOLD¹
(over s. o.).
hǫlde(n), hālde(n), heālden *str vb* 7
HOLD; *pres 3 sg* halt 13₂/102, 15/
10; *pret* hīeld, hēo¹d 3/69, helde;
pl hēlden, heōlden 1/14; *pp* hǫlden,
hālden, i-hālden.
hōle, hoole *sb* HOLE
hǫly see hāli.
hólyer *sb* whoremaster 15/34. [*Holour*].
holinesse, holynesse *sb* HOLINESS.
holly *adv* WHOLLY.
holt *sb* woods. [HOLT¹].
holt-wóde *sb* forest, wood. [HOLT-
WOOD].
hom see hī².
hǫm(e), hǫǫm, hāme *adv* (at, to, etc.)
HOME.
homsölve see hemself.
hǫnd(e), hand(e) *sb* HAND; *pl* hēnd
12/505, hǫnden 3/74.
hōne *sb* delay. [*Hone²*].
hǫnge, hǫngi see hange(n).
hónger see hunger.
hōny *sb* HONEY.
hönne see henne².
honoūrie *wk vb* HONOUR.
honōwre *sb* HONOUR.
hool(e) see hǫl¹, hōle.
hǫǫly see hāli.

hǫǫm see hǫm(e).
hǫǫr see hǫr¹.
hoord see hōrd.
hoore, hooris see hōre¹.
hoost *sb* HOST², inn-keeper.
hǫǫt see hǫt.
hǫpe *wk vb* HOPE; *pret* hǫpede.
1. hǫr, hǫǫr *adj* gray, HOAR.
2. hör see hi².
hōrd, hoord *sb* HOARD, treasure.
1. hōre, hoore *sb* WHORE.
2. höre see hī².
1. hors *sb* HORSE; *pl* hors 12/701, 27₁/
349.
2. hors *adj* HOARSE.
hörte see hert(e).
hostellēre *sb* tavern-keeper. [HOS-
TELER].
hǫt, hǫǫt, hayt 1. *adj* HOT; 2. *sb* heat.
hǫte(n), hatt, hoaten *str vb* 7 1. command, order 2. call, be named; *pret
3 sg* hāt 15/19; *pret* hyʒt, heiʒte,
heite, hette; *pp* i-hǫten 5/1, 20, ʒe-
hāten 7/3360. [*Hight¹*].
hōule *wk vb* HOWL.
hǫunderstōd see understande.
hōunger see hunger.
hǫup 10/126 = ōup see ŭp.
hóuse, hówse, hūs *sb* HOUSE.
höven(e) see heven.
hövene-tinge *adj* heaven-touching 6/
1001 (<OE *heofone ġetenge* 'id').
hōw, hōu, hōuʒ, hū, hw, wōu, ōu *adv*
HOW, *how that* id.
hū see hōw.
huader see whether.
huanne see whan.
huam see whō.
hue 13₅/28 see heō¹.
huere see whēr(e)¹.
huerof see whērof.
huertō see whērtō.
huet see what.
huyche see which.
hülle see hil.
hundredfald 1. *adj* HUNDREDFOLD. —
2. *adv* id.
hundreth *sb* HUNDRED.
hunger, hungre, hungær, hónger,
hōunger *sb* HUNGER.
hunt *sb* hunter. [*Hunt¹*].
huō see whō.

hüre see heŏ¹, hī², hire.
hus see hē, his(e), hŏūs(e).
hūsewīf *sb* HOUSEWIFE.· [HUSSY].
hw see hŏw.
hwan see whan.
hwarof see whērof.
hwārtō see whērtō.
hwa-se see whō-sǫ.
hwat see what.
hwen see when.
hwēr(e) see whēr(e)¹.
hwērof see whērof.
hwērseeaver see whēr-sǫ.
hwērtō see whērtō.
hwet see what.
hwī see whī.
hwīl(e) see whīl(e).
hwnt *sb* the HUNT².
hwon see whan.
hwō-sǫ see whō-sǫ.
hwücche see which.

I

I see ich¹.
i see in.
iāfen see ȝeve¹.
i-bede see bidde.
i-bēn, i-beŏn, i-bŏn, see bē(n).
i-bȩre(n) *str vb 4* BEAR, carry, bring
　　into the world 5/33; *pret* i-ber.
　　[*I-bere*¹].
i-bǫren see bȩre(n).
i-borȝe see berȝe(n).
i-bouȝt see bȳe(n).
i-bringe *wk vb* BRING.
i brout see brynge(n).
1. ich, ihc, ih, ic, hic, Ī, ȳ *1 sg pers
　　pron* I; *dat-acc* mē. ME; *poss*
　　mȳ(n), mī MINE, MY.
2. ich, yche see ilk¹˒².
i-chǫsen see chēse.
ichot = *ich wōt* see wite(n).
i-crommet *pp* loaded, crammed 21₁/41,
　　cp. CRAM.
i-crūnet see crūnen.
i-cumen see cŏme(n).
i-cwēmet see i-quēme.
īdel see ȳdel.
i-dō, i-dōn(e) see dō(n).
iēden see ȝēde.
i-ȩte see ȩte(n).

i-faie *adv* willingly 10/199　(< OE
　　ȝefæȝen).　Cp. FAIN.
i-fāre see fāre².
i-fēlen *wk vb* FEEL 3/16.　[*Y-fcle*].
i-festnet *pp* FASTENED.　[*Yfastned*].
i-fǫ *sb* FOE; *pl* i-foan 11/20.
i-fŏn see fang.
i-glȳden see glīde(n).
i-grāmed *pp adj* angry 6/933, cp.
　　GREME.
i-grāve *pp* GRAVEN.　[*Y-graven*].
i-grētinge *sb* GREETING.
i-grīpen *str vb 1* seize GRIPE; *pret*
　　i-grāp.　[*I-gripe*].
i-gült see gilte(n).
i-ȝeven see ȝeve¹.
i-ȝǫlde see ȝēlde(n).
i-kaut see cache.
i-knēde see knēde.
ih see ich¹.
i-hālden see hǫlde(n).
ihc see ich¹.
i-herde see hēre(n).
i-hēren, y-hēre, *wk vb* hear.　[*Yhere*].
i-hǫten see hǫte(n).
i-hüd see hȳde.
i-knowe(n) *str vb 7* make known,
　　KNOW; confess 10/182; *pret* iknen,
　　2 sg i-knowe; *pp* i-knowe.　[*Yknow*].
i-lærd *pp adj* learned, educated.
　　[*Ylered*].
i-last see i-lȩste.
ilche see ilk(e)¹.
i-leawed *adj* ignorant, untaught, LAY,
　　[cp. LEWD].
i-lȩd see lȩde(n).
i-leid see leye(n).
i-lȩste *wk vb* LAST, endure; *3 sg* i-last
　　6/1038; *pres part* i-lȩstinde 11/10.
　　[*Ylaste*].
i-let see lette¹.
i-lȩve see y-lȩve.
i-līch, y-lȳch 1. *prep* LIKE — 2. adj
　　ALIKE.
i-limpen *str vb 3a* happen, come
　　about; *pret* i-lomp 3/27; *pp* i-lum-
　　pen 3/143; i-limpe 5/14052.　[*I-
　　limp*].
1. ilk(e), ylk, ilche, yche *adj* same,
　　very (reinforces a preceding demon-
　　strative) *thise ⁓tweye* these same
　　two 27₂/1193, *þat ⁓ lorde* that very

same lord 18/1256, *þys yche abbot
this same abbot* 14/4015; ~ *on
each one* 29/200. [ILK¹]. Cp.
þilke.

2. ilk(e), ych, ich *adj* each; (*indef*)
someone, all. Cp. *ęch.*

ill-spón *pp adj* badly spun, ILL-SPUN.

i-lōme *adv* often. [*Ylome*].

i-lomp, i-lumpen see i-limpen.

i-mǽn *adv* together 7/3376. [*I-mene*].

i-māked, i-māket see māke(n).

i-mend see menǧe.

i męte *wk vb* meet; *pret* i-mette.
[*Y-mete*].

i-męte(n) *wk vb impers* dream, appear in a dream; *pret* i-mette,
i-mætte. [cp. *Mete* v²].

imprēvāble *adj* unprovable. [IMPROV-
ABLE].

i-münt *pp* decided 10/244. [*Mint* v¹].

in, yn, ine, inne, i *prep* IN, on 15/3.

infernal *adj þe god* ~ god of the
lower regions, (of the) INFERNAL
(areas) 28/4052.

Inglis see English.

inȝǫng *sb* entrance 3/7. [*Ingang*].

1. inne *adv* within.

2. inne see in.

innoghe, innōwe, i-nōȝe, i-nōh, i-nōu(h)
see y-nōugh.

intel see intill.

intill, intel *prep* in, into, up to; *wend*
~ *English* translate into English
7/13.

i-nume see nyme.

inwardlīche *adv* completely, perfectly
3/13; profoundly 3/121. [IN-
WARDLY].

inwyt *sb* conscience 15/intr. [*Inwit*].

inwið *prep* in, within 3/56. [*Inwith*].

i-ondsweret see ondswerien.

i-quēme *wk vb* please 8/485; *pp*
i-cwēmet 4/34.

i-quēðen see quęthe(n).

īren see ȳren.

i-sǽid see seye(n).

i-sǽt see sette.

i-sauved see sāve¹.

is see bē(n).

īse* *sb* ICE.

i-segh see sē(n).

i-seid see seye(n).

i seie, i-seih see sē(n).

i-seined see sayn.

i-selðe *sb* happiness, prosperity; good
sense 2/13. [*I-selth*].

i-sēn, y-zȳ *str vb* 5 perceive, SEE;
pres 3 sg y-zȳcþ 15/69; *pret* i-seh,
i-sæh. [*I-see*].

i-send see sende.

i-set see sette.

i-setnesse *sb* ordinance 11/13.

i-siist see sē(n).

i-slein see slę̄(n).

i-sǫld see selle.

i-spent see spende(n).

i-spild see spille(n).

i-spread see sprę̄de(n).

i-sprunge see sprynge(n).

i-srīve see schrīven.

i-straht *pp adj* STRETCHED. [*I-
stretche*].

i-swīke *wk vb* stop, cease 6/929.

i-swinc *sb* work, labor 2/36. [*I-
swinch*].

i-swǫrene see swę̄re(n).

it see hit.

i-tāke see tāke(n).

i-tǫld see telle(n).

i-tuket *pp* mistreated 3/82. [cp.
TUKE].

i-turnd see tórne.

i-þoht see thenke(n).

i-þurlet see þurlin.

i-vāren see fāre².

i-veng *str pret* seized, grabbed.
[*I-fang*].

i-wākien *wk vb* WAKE UP. [*I-wake*].

i-wēnd see wę̄ne(n).

i-wersed see werse(n).

i-wende *wk vb* wend, go, plunge 5/
14038.

i-weorret *pp* attacked 3/72. Cp. WAR,
v¹.

i-whilc *adj* EACH 7/3382.

i-wille *sb* WILL. [*I-will*].

i-wys(se), i-wiss, i wisse, y-wis 1. *adv*
for sure, for certain. — 2. *sb* cer-
tainty [*Iwis*].

i-wrīten see wrīte(n).

i-wunet see wóne(n).

i-wurðen *str vb* 3b become 3/3, 4/14;
let ~ be calm 3/48. [*I-worth*].

J

jacyngh *sb* JACINTH (probably sapphire).
jangelēr *sb* clown, loud-mouth 21₁/35. [JANGLER].
1. jāpe *sb* JAPE, joke, trick.
2. jāpe *wk vb* joke.
jāpēr *sb* showman, professional jester.
jaspe, jasper, jasporye *sb* JASPER 13₂/ 115, 19/999, 1018, 1026. [*Jasp*].
jet *sb* fashion. [*Jet²*].
jille *sb* GILL³, ¼ pint.
1. joie *sb* JOY.
2. joye *wk vb* rejoice. [JOY].
jóyn *wk vb* JOIN¹, add.
jolyf *adj* JOLLY 13₅/39.
joliftee, jolitee *sb* JOLLITY; bravado 27₄ₐ/680.
jöurnee *sb* JOURNEY, battle 20/825.
Jūdisk *adj* JEWISH 7/3361.
jūs *sb* JUICE.
justīse *sb* ~ *don* inflict punishment; JUSTICE.

K

k- see also c-.
kable *sb* CABLE.
kacle *wk vb* CACKLE¹.
kaǧe *sb* CAGE.
kaȝt see cache.
kaire see cayre².
kayser *sb* KAISER, emperor.
kaityf *sb* wretch. [*Caitiff*].
kan(e) see can¹.
kandel *sb* CANDLE.
kanunk *sb* CANON², cathedral prelate.
kāre see cāre.
karp *wk vb* talk, chatter. [CARP¹].
kas see cãs.
kempe *sb* champion 15/10. [*Kemp¹*].
1. ken *wk vb* know, recognize, KEN.
2. ken see kin.
kĕnde see kīnde.
kēne *adj* pointed, sharp, KEEN; hardy, bold.
kenel-dóre *sb* KENNEL² + DOOR 18/1140.
kĕpare *sb* KEEPER.
kēpe *sb* care, attention, KEEP, ȝeve ~ give protection 14/4074.
kēpe(n) *wk vb* KEEP, guard; insult, ~ *in þe berde* oppose 17/96; *pret* kēped.

kesse see kisse.
kest see cast².
kevel *sb* gag. [*Kevel¹*].
kever *wk vb* succeed 18/750; obtain 18/1221. [*Cover²*, RECOVER].
kide *sb* KID, young goat.
kyde see kīþen.
kille, cülle *wk vb* KILL.
kin, kyn(ne), ken, cünne, kün(ne) *sb* 1. KIN¹ — 2. kind, sort 19/1028, *tweire* ~ of two kinds 6/888; species; *nā* ~ *thyng* in no manner 22₂/413.
kȳn see cū.
kinde, kȳnde, cünde, kēnde *sb* KIND, nature, species; *þurgh* ~ by very nature 14/4073.
kyndel *wk vb* KINDLE.
kyndlȳche *adv* KINDLY, graciously.
kinedom *sb* KINGDOM.
kinelich *adj* royal [cp. *Kine-*].
kynemerk *sb* royal mark 12/604. [cp. *Kine-*].
kyng-ryke, küne-riche *sb* realm [*Kinrick*].
kyn(ne) see kin.
kyppe *wk vb* seize. [*Kip*].
kyrk, kirke *sb* church, KIRK 7/3651.
kisse, kysse, kesse *wk vb* KISS; *pret* kiste.
kitōun *sb* KITTEN.
kīþen, cüðen *wk vb* make known, announce 7/3352, 3377, show, manifest 3/79; *pp* kyd known, recognized. [*Kithe*].
klóke see clóche.
klyffe *sb* CLIFF.
knakke *wk vb* knock; carried it (the tune) 29/659. [KNACK].
knarre *sb* rock 6/1001, 18/721. [KNAR].
knaulechynge, cnawlechunge *sb* knowledge 4ₐ/3. [*Knowledging*].
knāve *sb* domestic, slave; boy (as opposed to girl); *gen pl* knāvene 21₃/54. [KNAVE¹,²].
knaw, knawe see knowe(n).
knē, knowe (21₄/359) *sb* KNEE; *a knēs* on (his) knees 8/505.
knēde *wk vb* KNEAD; *pp* i-knede 10/256.
knēle(n) *wk vb* KNEEL.
kneu see knowe(n).

knīf *sb* KNIFE.

knyght, kny3t, kniht, cni3t, cniht *sb* KNIGHT.

knyght-fee *sb* knight's revenue [KNIGHT'S FEE].

kni3te(n), kni3ti *wk vb* arm and create a knight, KNIGHT 8/480, 490, 491.

kni3thǫde *sb* KNIGHTHOOD.

knitten *wk vb* KNIT, attach 21₂/168.

knokke *wk vb* KNOCK.

knowe see knē.

knowe(n), knaw, cnawen *str vb* 7 KNOW; *pret* kneu; *pp* (y-)knowe, knowen.

kórs see curs.

koūde see can.

krīke *sb* arm of the sea 12/708, CREEK¹.

kū see cū.

kueād see quēd.

küme see còme.

künde see kīnde.

küne-riche see kyng-ryke.

kün(ne) see kin.

kunne, küðe see can¹.

L

lābōre *wk vb* LABOUR.

la(c)che *wk vb* catch, seize, LATCH¹ (on); take (name) 12/744; *pret* lau3te, lauhte.

ladde(n) see lēde(n).

lāde see leye(n)¹.

lādy, lafdi3, lavedi, lẹvedi, leafdi, lẹdy *sb* LADY.

lādlich see lǫthely.

læi see li̧g̑g̑e(n).

læiden see leye(n).

læwed see lewede.

lafdi3 see lādy.

lāferd see lǫrd.

laft(e) see lẹve(n).

laghe see laughe(n).

1. la3e *sb* LAW¹.

2. la3e see laughe(n).

la3ter *sb* LAUGHTER.

lai, lay see li̧g̑g̑e(n).

lay, layd(e) see leye(n).

layke, laike *wk vb* to sport, to play. [*Lake¹*].

lākan *sb* plaything, doll 29/242. [*Lakin¹*].

lakk(e) *wk vb* to find fault with 14/4082, 18/1250. [LACK¹ (6)].

lance see launce.

lānde see lǫnd(e).

1. lang *wk vb* LONG¹ for, want to be (an officer of the king) 29/209.

2. lāng see lǫng.

langāg̑e, longāg̑e *sb* LANGUAGE.

langar, langer(e) see lǫng.

lanhüre *adv* at least, in any case 3/80.

lantyrne *sb* LANTERN.

lap see lẹpe(n).

lape *wk vb* LAP¹.

lappe *sb* LAP¹.

lāre see lǫre.

larg̑esse *sb* generosity. [LARGESS].

lārspell *sb* sermon 7/56. [*Lorespell*].

lasēr *sb* LEISURE 22₂/424.

lasse see lesse.

lāst(e), lēast(e) *superl adj* LAST.

lāste(n), lẹste(n) *wk vb* LAST¹; *pres part* lẹstinde 11-21.

lāsteles *adj* perfect. [*Lastless*].

lāt(e) see let(e).

lāte *adv* LATE, recently; *compar* lāter.

latoūn *sb* brass. [LATTEN].

lāþe see lǫþ.

laudes *sb pl* LAUD(S)¹ (2), first of the day-hours of the Church.

laughe(n), la3e, laghe *str vb* LAUGH; *pret* loūgh, loū.

lau3te, lauhte see la(c)che.

launce, lance *wk vb* move, ride at a gallop 18/1175. [LANCE(2)].

lāve *wk vb* flow. [LAVE¹].

lavedi see lādy.

lāverd see lǫrd.

laverock *sb* LARK¹.

lẹ see lȳe.

lēaf see lẹf.

leafden see lẹve(n).

leafdi see lādy.

lealté *sb* loyalty. [*Lealty¹*].

leāpen see lẹpe(n).

leasse see lesse.

leāst(e) see lāst(e).

lēche *sb* medical doctor; healing remedy 13₄/24. [LEECH¹].

lecherīe, lecherȳe *sb* LECHERY, debauchery.

lechur *sb* LECHER 15/37.

lēde see leude.

lẹ̄de(n), leid *wk vb* LEAD; *pres 3 sg* lẹ̄t 15/32; *pret* ladde, ladden; *pp* i-led.

lẹ̄dy see lādy.

lẹẹf see lẹ̄f¹.

leel, lēle *adj* loyal. [LEAL].

lẹẹst see lẹ̄ste.

leet see lēt(e).

leeve see lēf².

1. lēf, lẹẹf *sb* LEAF; *pl* lēaf 5/23, lẹ̄ves.

2. lēf, lēof, lōf 1. *adj* dear; *þat lēver wẹ̄r* who would rather 18/1251; *inflected forms* lēve, lȫve; *vocative* leeve, leove; *compar* lēver, lȫvre 2/29; *superl* lēofvest 5/14018. — 2. *sb* loved one. [LIEF].

1. lēflīch(e) *adj* gracious. [*Liefly*].

2. lēflīche, lēoflīche *adv* kindly, graciously 5/24 [*Liefly*].

left, lift, leoft *adj* LEFT.

leften see lẹ̄ve(n).

lēġe-man *sb* vassal. [LIEGE MAN].

legge *sb* LEG.

le₃d see leye(n).

lei see liġġen.

leid see lẹ̄de(n).

leid(e), leyde, leidest see leye(n)¹.

1. leye(n), lei, lay *wk vb* LAY, put, place, stretch out, go to bed; *pret* leyde, leid(e), layde, lāde, *2 sg* leidest; *pl* læiden 1/42; *pp* layd, i-leid, le₃d.

2. leyen see liġġe(n).

leyf see lēve¹.

leyfe see lẹ̄ve².

leyne see lēne².

leysche *sb* LEASH.

leit see lēt(e).

leyve see lēve¹, lẹ̄ve(n).

lēle see leel.

lelȳ see lilīe.

lēm *sb* ray, light 7/3341. [*Leam¹*].

1. lēme, lūme *wk vb* gleam, shine 18/1137, 1180, 19/1043. [*Leam¹*].

2. leme see lyme.

lemman, lemmon see lēofmon.

1. lēnde *wk vb* debark, land 12/733; *is lent on* is occupied with 18/1319. [*Lend¹*].

2. lēnde see lēne².

1. lẹ̄ne, lēone *wk vb* LEAN¹.

2. lēne, leyne, lēnde *wk vb* grant, LEND².

lenge *wk vb* remain, linger. [*Leng*].

lenger see lọng, lọnge.

lengþe, lenþe *sb* LENGTH; *on ⌐* far away 18/1231.

lent see lēnde¹.

lenþe see lengþe.

lēō *sb* lion.

lēōde(n) see leude.

lēof see lēf.

lēoflīche see lēflīche².

lēofmon, lēovemon, lemmon, lemman *sb* lover, mistress, lady. [LEMAN].

leoft see left.

lēofvest see lēf².

lēone see lẹ̄ne¹.

lēop see lẹ̄pe(n).

leornia see lerne.

lēōun *sb* LION 12/573.

lēōve see lēf².

lẹ̄pe(n), lēapen *str vb* 7 LEAP, bound, run; *pret* lap, lēp, lēōp 3/5, 28.

lẹ̄re *wk vb* teach.

lẹ̄redman *sb* cleric, priest 1/58. [*Lered* + MAN].

lẹ̄rne, lūrne, lēornien *wk vb* LEARN; *3 sg pres subj* lēornia 5/30.

lēs *sb* lie. [*Lease²*].

lēse *str vb* 2 LOSE. [*Leese¹*].

lesse, lasse, leasse 1. *compar adv* LESS. — 2. *compar adj* LESS.

lessinge *sb* lessening, diminution 4ₐ/2. [LESSING].

lessōun *sb* LESSON; lesson (from the breviary) 27₄ₐ/709.

1. lẹ̄ste, lẹẹst *superl adj* LEAST.

2. leste see liste².

lẹ̄ste(n) see lāste(n).

1. let *sb* delay; *wiþoute let* without delay 28/4041. [LET¹].

2. lẹ̄t see lẹ̄de(n).

lēt(e), lāt(e), leet *str vb* 7 LET¹, permit; neglect 22₁/254; (in periphrastic adhortative) *God lat ūs*

nevere mĕte may God never let us
meet ... 27₂/1246; ~ *as* let on, pretend 18/1190; behave 18/1206; ~
by regard, estimate 21₃/3; *pret* leit
22₂/415, lette 3/125.
leten see lette¹.
1. **lette, lett, leten** *wk vb* stop, im-
pede; *pret* lette; *pp* i-let 11/8.
[LET²].
2. **lette** see let(e).
leðer *sb* LEATHER.
lettunge *sb* obstacle 4/44. [LETTING²].
leude, lēde, lēode *sb* man 18/1170,
knight 18/1306; (collective) people;
on leoden among the people, secular
5/1. [*Lede*].
1. **lēve, leyve, leyf** *wk vb* believe 20/
702; *imper 2 pl* lēves 17/73.
[*Leve²*].
2. **lęve, leyfe** *sb* LEAVE, permission.
3. **lēve** *adj* see lēf².
4. **leve** *wk vb* see live(n).
lęvedi see lādy.
lęveful *adj* permissive 25/48. [*Lee-
ful*].
lęve(n), leyve *wk vb* LEAVE¹, cease;
remain 20/694; *pret* lafte; *pl* leften,
leafden; *pp* laft, y-left, left.
lēver see lēf².
lęves see lęf¹.
lēvyn *sb* lightening. [LEVIN].
lęvynges *sb pl* LEAVINGS, vomit.
lewe *adj* warm 12/498. [LEW¹].
lewede, lewde, læwed *adj* ignorant,
simple, lay (as opposed to cleric).
[LEWD].
lhoaverd see lǫrd.
lhouþ see lōwe².
lhūd(e) see lōwd.
lȳ see liǧǧe(n).
libbe(n), lybbeþ see live(n).
līcam, līcome *sb* fleshly body, corpse.
[*Licham*].
līch(e) see lȳk(e).
lyckestre *sb* female who licks, greedy
woman 15/50. [*Lickster*].
līcome see līcam.
lȳe, lę *sb* LIE¹.
lȳȝe see lȳȝen.
līen see liǧǧe(n).
lif see live(n).
lȳf(e), lyff, liif *sb* LIFE; *brouht of*

live killed 12/513; *adverbial gen sg*
līves alive 3/80, 12/509.
līfdaie *sb* life, life-time. [*Life-day*].
lȳf-holynesse *sb* holiness of life.
[*Life-holiness*].
līflǫde, lȳflǫde *sb* LIVELIHOOD, manner
of living.
lift see left.
lyfte *sb* heaven 18/1256. [*Lift¹*].
lȳf tȳme *sb* LIFETIME.
liǧe, lȳǧe 1. loyal. — 2. *sb* subject 25/
18. [LIEGE].
liǧǧen, lyg, lȳȝe, lȳ, līen *str vb 5* LIE¹,
lie down; reside, be 6/959; *pres 3
sg* lyys 29/229, līþ 12/673, 15/38;
pret lay, lai, læi, lai 3/30, *pl* leyen
12/475.
light see liȝt².
lȳȝe see liǧǧe.
lȳȝen, lȳȝeȝe *wk vb* LIE², tell a lie
15/73.
1. **liȝt, liht** *sb* LIGHT.
2. **liȝt, lyȝt, light, liht** *adj* LIGHT¹,
easy; *set at* ~ set at nought, take
lightly 18/1250.
3. **lyȝt** *wk vb* LIGHT¹, get down; *pret*
liȝte; *pp* lyȝt.
lihten see liȝte¹.
1. **liȝte, lihten** *wk vb* LIGHT², light up,
cause to see 16/64.
2. **liȝte, lyhte, liht** *adj* and *adv* LIGHT²,
illuminated.
3. **liȝte** see lyȝt³.
lyȝtly, lyȝtlich, lihtlīche, lyghtly *adv*
LIGHTLY, easily.
liht see liȝt¹, ², liȝte².
lyhte see liȝte².
lyys see liǧǧe(n).
lȳk(e), līch(e) 1 *adj* LIKE (often followed by *to*); *conj let* ~ let on
like, pretend 18/1281. — 2. *adv*
LIKE, as.
likeroūs *adj* tempting to the palate,
dainty 21₁/30. [*Lickerous*].
līking, lȳkynge *sb* pleasure, desire
20/701; LIKING¹, free choice 22/226.
likne, lykne, likene *wk vb* LIKEN.
lilīe, lelȳ *sb* LILY.
lime, lyme, leme *sb* LIMB.
lymēre *sb* scent-hunting stag-hound
27₁/362. [*Limer¹*].
lȳnāǧe *sb* LINEAGE, family.

lynde-wóde *sb* wood 18/1178. [*Lind*
+ WOOD].
līne, lȳne *sb* LINE[2], rope 12/539; net,
snare.
lipnien *wk vb* have confidence 2/21.
[LIPPEN].
lyppe *sb* LIP.
list *sb* wish, desire. [LIST[4]].
1. list(e), lüst(e), lyst *wk vb* (*impers*)
please, desire, wish; *as hir* ~ *as* it
pleased her; (*pers*) want, wish;
pret liste, lüst. [LIST[1]].
2. liste, lüste, leste *wk vb* listen.
[*List*[2]].
lystyly *adv* by trickery. Cp. *List* sb[2].
lī(t)tel, ly(t)tel, littyl, lüitel, lite
adj adv and *sb* LITTLE.
litunge *sb* color, tint. [*Litting*].
līþ see liǧǧe(n).
līþe, līðe *adj* gracious, merciful 5/2,
24, LITHE.
līþe(n) *str vb* go, travel 5/14. [*Lithe*[1]].
līve, līves see lȳf(e).
live(n), libben, lybbe, leve, lif, livie(n)
wk vb LIVE.
liveneð *sb* food, means of living 3/60.
[*Livenath*].
lǫ, low *interjection* ~ *her* here is 3/3.
loand see lǫnd(e).
lóbre *sb* LUBBER, big clumsy oaf
21₁/52.
lǫde *sb* LOAD; *in his* ~ on his way
18/1284.
1. lof *sb* collar, halter 1/32 (cp.
note) ; < OE *lof* cord, filet?.
2. lǫf *sb* praise 7/3375, 3379 [*Lof*].
3. lǫf *sb* LOAF; *pl* lǫves 24/13.
4. lǫf see lēf[2].
lófly see lóvely.
loft *sb* air; *on* ~ ALOFT.
loftsǫng *sb* song of praise 4/38.
[*Lof-song*].
logh(e), loʒ(e) see low[1], lowe[1].
lōke(n), looke, lōkien, lōkin *wk vb*
LOOK; take care, see to; look with
favor, look after, protect 29/219,
look about 21₂/152.
lokerde *adj* shaggy 20/779. [*Locke,
Red*].
lōkyng *sb* LOOKING 19/1049.
lokke *sb* LOCK.
lollēre, lollare *sb* vagabond, bum

21₃/2 ; *gen pl* lollarene 21₃/31.
[*Loller*[1]].
lǫmb *sb* LAMB.
1. lōme *adv* frequently, often 2/27.
2. lōme *sb* LOOM[1].
lompe-lyʒt *sb* lamp, LAMP-LIGHT.
lǫnd(e), lǎnde, loand *sb* LAND.
lǫne *sb* lane, by-road. [*Loan*[2]].
longǎǧe see langǎǧe.
lǫng, lǎng *adj* LONG; tall 21₁/52.
compar lenger, langere, langar.
lǫnge *adv* LONG.
lǫnge(n) *wk vb* belong. [*Long*[2]].
lǫnges *adv* for a long time. [*Longs*].
lǫnginge *sb* LONGING.
looke see lōke(n).
lǫrd, lhǫrd, lǫverd, lhoāverd, lāverd
4/6, lāferd *sb* LORD; *gen pl* lǫrdene.
lǫrdyng, lǫverding *sb* master, lord.
[LORDING].
lordischipe *sb* LORDSHIP, power.
lǫre, lāre *sb* (method of) instruction
26/28, *yn* ~ in learning, educated
14/4011; LORE[1], learning, knowledge
2/1, 7/14, 3657.
lǫrne *pp adj* lost, abandoned, LORN.
lóssom see lufsum.
1. lost *sb* loss 21₃/97. [*Lost*].
2. lóst see lust(e).
lǫte *sb* speech 18/1399 [*Late*[1]].
lǫþ, lāþ *adj* LOATH.
lǫthe *wk vb* (*impers*) LOATHE 21₂/155.
lǫþely, lādlich *adj* LOATHLY, repul-
sive; ugly, odious 3/129.
lothen *adj* shaggy 20/778.
lōu, lōugh see laughe(n).
lóuryng *sb* LOURING, threat(s).
lōute *wk vb* bow [LOUT[1]].
lóuve, lowe *wk vb* praise 18/1256; *to*
~ worthy of praise 18/1399 (< OF
louver, var. of *louer*). [*Low*[3]].
1. lóve, luf(e), luve *sb* LOVE, loved
one.
2. lóve, lufe, luvien, lóvie *wk vb* LOVE.
3. lóve see lēf[2].
lóve-bēne *sb* request, favor (required
by love) 13₄/26. [LOVE + *bene*].
lóvely, lóvelich, lófly, lufly, lufly(ch)
adj and *adv* LOVELY, graciously.
lǫverd see lǫrd.
lǫverding see lǫrdyng.

lǫves see lǫf³.
lóvie see lóve².
lö̈vre see lēf².
1. low, loȝ, logh adj LOW.
2. low see lǫ.
lōwable adj praiseworthy. [Lowable].
lōwd, lōud, lhūd, lūd adj LOUD; won-
　der ～ very loud 27₁/344.
lōwde, lōude, lhūde adv LOUD, loudly.
1. lowe, loȝe, loghe adv LOW; on ～
　below.
2. lōwe, lhōwe wk vb LOW₄, moo; 3 sg
　lhōuþ 13₁ₐ/9.
3. lowe see lōuve.
lūd(e) see lōwd, lōwde.
luf(e) see lóve¹, ².
lufar sb LOVER.
lufly(ch) see lóvely.
lufsum, lussom, lóssom adj LOVESOME.
lüitel see lit(t)el.
lüme see lēme¹.
lūr sb disaster 18/1284. [Lure¹].
lüre sb visage. [Leer¹].
lurk(k)e wk vb LURK, lie hidden.
lūrne see lērne.
lussomore see lufsum.
1. luste, lóst sb pleasure, desire 10/
　96, 13₂/93, 15/38, taste-desire 15/45.
　[LUST].
2. lüste see list(e)¹, ².
lusty, lusti adj 1. lively, joyous 4/38.
　— 2. vigorous. [LUSTY].
lütlin wk vb diminish 4/48. [Little].
lutterd adj bandy-legged 20/779.
　[Luttered].
lüþere adj evil, wicked, bad. [LITHER].
luve, luvie(n) see lóve².
luve-wurðe adj worthy of love. [Love-
　worth].
luxurīe sb LUXURY, lechery.

M

maaden, mācod, mād, māde(n) see
　māke(n).
mæi see mei¹.
maȝ see may².
1. maȝe see mei¹.
2. maȝe sb stomach, MAW 15/48.
mahe(n), maht, mahte(n) see may².
1. may sb maiden, virgin 13₄/35.
　[May¹].

2. mai, mai, maȝ, mei perf pres vb I
　have the physical capacity to do, I
　can, I may (possibility) MAY¹; pres
　2 sg maht 3/73, pl muȝen 2/19,
　muȝhen 7/3367, moȝe 15/44, mahen
　4/24, mōw, mōwe(n); pret myght,
　mycht, myȝt, meiȝt, mihte, miȝtte,
　moȝt, moohte, mahte 3/106, mouhte
　12/478, 704, 2 sg mihtes, myhtestu,
　pl mahten 3/66; pres subj mahe
　3/44, 4/4, muȝe 2/23, 11/18, moȝe
　15/68, mōwe 12/675, 2 sg mayht,
　mote 6/987.
maid see māke(n).
mayde(n), maiden sb MAID, MAIDEN.
mayht see may².
mayle, maylle sb (in the pl) coat of
　MAIL¹ 20/769.
maylleasse see malēse.
mair sb MAYOR.
mairaltee sb MAYORALTY, mandate of
　the mayor.
mais, mayss see māke(n).
maister, mayster, meistre sb MASTER¹,
　teacher.
mayster-hunte sb master of the hunt
　21₁/375. [MASTER-HUNT].
maistresse sb MISTRESS, miss.
maistrȳe, meistrīe sb 1. power, force,
　MASTERY. — 2. masterpiece, marvel.
māke(n), mākien, māki wk vb MAKE¹;
　compose, write 21₃/5; manrēd ～ do
　feudal hommage 1/13; pres 3 sg
　makeð 3/40, 45, 130, mayss, mais;
　pret mād, maid, mākede, mācod
　1/17, pl māden, maaden; pres subj
　3 sg mākie 3/142; pp mād, y-mād,
　māket, i-māket, māked, i-māked.
māle sb pack, luggage. [MAIL³].
malēse, maylleasse sb sickness, harm
　[Malease].
1. man, mon sb MAN¹; (used as indef
　personal pronoun) one, they 5/
　14010. gen sg mannes, monnes,
　mannus 21₂/197, pl men, mene 16/9,
　menne 21₃/29, gen pl mennes.
2. mān see mǫne².
manayre sb MANOR, (fortified) town
　19/1029.
mandement sb command, order 24/36.
　[Mandment].

manēr(e), maneir, manyēre *sb* MAN-
NER[1], fashion, kind (complement
not preceded by *of*) *a ~ sǭng* a
kind (of) song.
many, maniȝ, mony, monie, meny *adj*
MANY; *~ on pronoun* many a one;
as . . . monie how many 3/23.
mankin, mankünne, moncün *sb* MAN-
KIND 3/15, 6/973. [*Mankin*][1].
mannus see man[1].
manrēd(e) *sb* feudal homage 1/13,
12/484. [*Manred*].
manslaȝþe *sb* homicide 15/75. [*Man-
slaught*].
manteyn see meynteigne.
mār see mǭre[2].
marchaundīe *sb* merchandise. [*Mer-
chandy*].
māre see mǭre[2].
marescal *sb* MARSHAL.
marǧyrȳe *sb* pearl 19/1037. [*Mar-
gery*].
māry *interjection* (*oath*) by the
Virgin Mary 29/510, 657.
marȝen see morne.
māse *sb* confusion 21/196. [MAZE].
masse, messe *sb* MASS[1], church service.
mast *sb* MAST[1].
māste see mǭst(e)[1].
matynez, matyns *sb pl* MATIN(S),
church service.
mawen see mowe(n)[1].
1. me *interjection* why, now 3/21 (cp.
note), 25, 105. [*Me*].
2. me see ich, men.
mechel see mykel.
mēcnesse see mēknesse.
mēd *sb* meadow, MEAD[2].
mēde *sb* wages, recompense, bribe.
[MEED].
medecine *sb* medicine 28/4135.
medyll see myddel.
medle *wk vb* mix, mingle. [MEDDLE].
Cp. *melle*.
medlyng *sb* mixture. [MEDDLING].
medwe-grēne *adj* MEADOW GREEN.
meel see mēl(e).
meete see mēte(n)[1].
meeten see mēte(n)[2].
1. mei, mæi, maȝe *sb* kinsman, relative 5/14063, female relative 2/29.
[*May*[2]]. Cp. *may*[1].

2. mei, meiȝt, meiht see may[2].
meynd see menǧe.
meyne *sb* MAIN[1], force, power, 13₂/69.
meynteigne, maynteigne, manteyn *wk
vb* MAINTAIN, sustain.
meistre see maister.
meistrīe see maistrȳe.
mēk *adj* MEEK.
mekel see mykel.
mēkely *adv* MEEKLY.
mekyll, mekill see mykel.
mēknesse, mēcnesse, mēkenes *sb*
MEEKNESS.
mēl(e), meel *sb* MEAL[2], repast.
męle *wk vb* speak, talk.
melk see milc.
melle *wk vb* mix, mingle. [*Mell*[2]].
Cp. *medle*.
mellynge *sb* 1. mixture. — 2. meeting,
fight, melee 22₂/401. [*Melling*].
men, me *indefinite pers pronoun* one,
they 1/23, 24, 26, 60, 2/48, 3/52, 54,
115, 117, 130; *as me seið* as people
say, as they say 3/33. Note lack
of logical concord.
mendinaunt *sb* beggar, mendicant.
[*Mendinant*].
mendys *sb pl* amends, compensation
29/567. [MEND].
1. męne *adj* MEAN[1], *~ and rich* poor
and rich, or, humble and powerful
21₁/18.
2. mene see man[1].
męne(n) *wk vb* MEAN[1], have the intention, etc.; gather one's wits 29/
220; think 29/635; *pret* mente.
menǧe *wk vb* agitate 6/945, mix 6/
870, 28/4049; *pres 3 sg* meinþ
6/945; *pp* meynd 28/4049, i-mend
6/870. [*Meng*].
menȝé see menȳ.
menȳ, menȝe *sb* 1. household. — 2.
following, army. [*Meinie*].
meny(e) see many.
menne, mennes see man[1].
menskful 1. *adj* courteous, gracious,
worthy of adoration. — 2. *adv*
adorably, gracefully.
menskly *adv* in a dignified fashion.
mente see męne(n).
meoster see mestere.

mercerȳe *sb* company of cloth merchants, [MERCERY].

merci *sb* MERCY.

mēre *adj* splendid; luminous (idea)
5/6; *dat M sg* mern. [*Mere*¹].

mered *pp adj* purified [Cp. *Mere* v¹].

mery, mürye, myrie, myry, mirie 1.
adj MERRY; *superl* mürġest 13₅/41.
— 2. *adv* joyously.

meryly *adv* MERRILY.

meryness, mirynes *sb* MERRINESS.

merke *wk vb* MARK, aim.

mern see mēre.

merre *wk vb* MAR, spoil; *pres 3 sg*
merrys 22₁/271.

merrys see merre.

merveille, merveyle, mervayl(e), mer-
wayle, mervell *sb* MARVEL.

mervaylous, merveyllous, mervelous,
merveylus *adj* MARVELLOUS.

mes *sb* MESS (dish, course) way of
serving food 15/45.

mesel *sb* leper.

mēselfen see mȳself.

messaġer *sb* MESSENGER.

messe see masse.

messe-bōc *sb* MASS-BOOK, missal.

mǫst see mǫst(e)¹.

mestere, meoster *sb* occupation, craft,
trade. [*Mister*¹].

met *sb* measure, moderation 4/16.

1. męte, mette *sb* food, nourishment.
[MEAT].

2. mēte 1. *adj* MEET and right, fitting. — 2. *sb* equal, duplicate.

męteles *sb* dream. [*Metels*].

1. mēte(n), meete *wk vb* MEET; *pret*
mette.

2. męte(n), meeten *impers wk vb*
dream; *me mette* I dreamed 27₁/
293. [*Mete*²].

3. męte(n) *str vb 5* measure 19/1032;
pp męten. [METE¹].

mette see męte, mēte(n)¹,².

meþ *sb* measure, moderation. [*Methe*].

mēve, mōve *wk vb* MOVE; lead (to)
18/1197: start 20/699.

mǐ see mȳ(n).

miċel see mykel.

mych see much.

michel see mykel.

1. mycht, michte see may².

2. mycht see my₃te.

mid, myde 15/2 *prep* with, among
8/474, in 15/40.

mid(d)el, myddel, medyll 1. *adj* MID-
DLE, mid-, 2. *sb* MIDDLE, belly, groin
29/534, waist 5/14035, 13₅/29.

middelærd *sb* earth, world 7/3638,
3640. [MIDDLE-ERD].

myd-morn *sb* MID MORN (about 9
o'clock) 18/1280.

mydnyht, middelniht *sb* MIDNIGHT.

myght, my₃te see may².

my₃t, myhte, mycht *sb* MIGHT, power.

my₃tvòl *adj* mighty 4ₐ/23. [MIGHT-
FUL].

mi₃tte, myhte, mihte, mihtes see
may².

mihte see my₃te.

myhtestu see may².

mihti *adj* MIGHTY.

mikel, mykel, mekyll, mekill, mekel,
miċel, michel, mechel, muchel,
môchel 1. *adj* big. — 2. *adv* a lot,
MUCH. — 3. *sb* size, stature 27₁/454.
[*Mickle*].

milc, mylk, melk *sb* MILK.

milce *sb* mercy, compassion 4/18.

milde *adj* MILD 1/11.

mildhertnesse *sb* mercy 7/3381. [*Mild-
heartness*].

mȳle *sb* MILE¹.

mylk see milc.

mȳn, mǐ *1 sg pron and poss adj* MY,
MINE (anaphoric form) *dat F* mīre
5/14024; *pl* mīne 3/24.

1. mynyster, mynestre *sb* MINISTER,
priest.

2. mynyster, mynstre *sb* MINSTER¹,
monastery.

mynystralcȳe *sb* merry-making, MIN-
STRELSY.

mynstre see mynyster.

mīre see mȳ(n).

mȳre *sb* MIRE¹, mud, muck.

mirie, myrie, müry see mery.

myrke *sb adj* dark, murky 16/100
[MURK].

mis *sb* MISS¹, error, evil 3/43.

mȳs see mōūs.

myschaunce *sb* MISCHANCE, bad luck.

mischeef *sb* MISCHIEF, evil deed,
trouble.

mysdẹde, misdẹde *sb* MISDEED, sin.
mȳself, mēself *1 sg intensive pron*
MYSELF.
misfēren *wk vb* go wrong. [*Misfare*].
misy *sb* marsh, bog, swamp 18/479.
[MIZZY].
mislīke(n) *wk vb* displease (impers
subject, personal object). 2/11.
[MISLIKE].
mispaye *wk vb* displease 15/16. [MIS-
PAY].
mysse *wk vb* MISS¹, be lacking, be
rid of.
mysspende *wk vb* use badly. [MIS-
SPEND].
miste *sb* MIST¹, fog.
miszigge *wk vb* MISSAY, slander
15/74.
mīþe *wk vb* avoid, conceal. [*Mithe*].
mọ̄, mọọ *adj* and *adv* more. [MO].
moare see mọ̄re².
móche see muche.
móchel see mykel.
mōd(e) *sb* MOOD¹, mind, heart.
mōder, mooder *sb* MOTHER; *gen sg*
moodres 27₄ᴮ/729, mōder 5/33.
moghte, moȝe, moȝt see may¹.
moyn see mōne³.
molde *sb* earth, ground. [MOULD¹].
1. món *perf pres vb* intend, shall,
must (used as future indicator or
auxiliary); 20/813. [*Mun*]. Cp.
móne.
2. mon see man¹.
moncün see mankin.
1. mọ̄ne *sb* companion 8/528. [*Mone*¹].
2. mọ̄ne, mān *sb* MOAN, complaint.
3. mōne, moyn *sb* MOON.
4. móne, munne *perf pres vb* 1. remember 4/21. — 2. mention 13₄/
39. [*Mone*]. Cp. *mòn*.
mōne-liht *sb* MOONLIGHT.
monge *wk vb* mix, mingle 13₅/15.
[*Mong*²].
mony, monie see many.
monne, monnes see man¹.
móntance *sb* AMOUNT. [*Mountance*].
mooder see mōder.
mọọre see mọ̄re².
moot(e) see mōt(e)².
1. mōre *sb* MOOR¹, upland plain.
2. mọ̄re, moore, mār(e), moare 1.

compar adv MORE. — 2. *compar adj*
MORE, bigger.
móreyn *sb* plague. [MURRAIN].
morȝen see morne.
morne, morōun, morȝen, marȝen *sb*
tomorrow MORNING, MORN; *gōd* ⁓
good morning; *a marȝen* in the
morning 5/14003. Cp. *morwe*.
morsel, mossel *sb* MORSEL.
morwe *sb* morning, MORROW, tomorrow; *good* ⁓ good morning. Cp.
morn.
morwnynge *sb* MORNING.
mosseles see morsel.
1. mọ̄st(e), māste, mẹst 1. *superl adj*
MOST, biggest. — 2. *superl adv* MOST.
2. mọ̆ste see mōt(e)².
1. mōt(e) *sb* long single note (on
hunting horn) 18/1141, 1364; 27₄ᴮ/
376. [*Mote*³].
2. mōt(e), moot(e) *perf pres vb* I can,
I may, I must; *pres 2 sg* mōst 10/
207, 208; *pret* mọ̆st(e). [*Mote*¹].
3. mote, mouhte see may².
mōunt *sb* MOUNT, mountain 28/4052.
mōunte *wk vb* MOUNT, get up, fly
20/769.
mōus *sb* MOUSE; *pl* mȳs.
mōve see mēve.
mōw, mōwe see may².
1. mowe(n), mawen *str vb* 7 MOW¹,
cut down 2/20, reap a harvest
6/1040; put in shocks 21₃/14.
2. mōwe(n) see may².
muche, móche, myche 1. *adv* MUCH;
so ⁓ as much. — 2. *adj* big 5/14019.
muchel(e) see mykel.
much-quat *sb* many things 18/1280.
[*Muchwhat*].
muȝe(n), muȝhen, muhte(n) see may¹.
müngunge *sb* memory, remembrance,
commemoration 3/116. [*Minging*].
munke, muneke *sb* MONK.
munne see móne⁴.
münstral *sb* MINSTREL.
mūren *wk vb* wall in. [MURE].
mürġest *superl*, mürye, mürie see
mery.
mürȝþe see mürþe.
mürierly *compar adv* more merrily,
'merrierly.' Cp. MERRILY.

murþere(n) *wk vb* MURDER 24/38.

mürþe, mürþhe, mürhŏe, mürȝþe *sb*
MIRTH, joy, good time.

mūþ, mūŏ, mūth, mŏuth(e) *sb* MOUTH.

N

nǎ see ne, nǫ.

nabbe *contracted negative form* see
hāve(n).

nacht see naȝt.

nade *contracted negative form* see
hāve(n).

nadre *sb* viper, ADDER 1/28.

nǣvre see nẹ̄ver(e).

naȝt, naht, nacht, nawt, naut, nawiht
adv NAUGHT, NOT, not at all. Cp.
nat, noght(e), not.

nay *adv* NAY[1], no.

nayl *sb* NAIL.

nayme see nāme.

nāked, nākit *adj* NAKED; unarmed
22₂/434.

nakẹ̄r *sb* kettle-drum. [NAKER[1]].

nākit see nāked.

nam see nyme.

nāme, nayme *sb* NAME.

nāmelīche *adv* NAMELY.

nāmen see nyme.

nāmon see nǫman.

namo(o)re *adv* NO MORE, nevermore.

nān(e) see nǫn(e).

nānes-weis see nǫnes weis.

nar see ner(e).

nareu see narwe.

narwe, nareu, nearow *adj* NARROW.

nas *contracted negative form* see
bē(n).

nat *adv* not. [*Nat*]. Cp. *naȝt, not,
noghte.*

nāthelẹ̄s, nathelẹ̄es *adv* NEVERTHELESS.
[*Natheless*]. Cp. *nẹ̄þelẹ̄s, nǭþelẹ̄s.*

naut see naȝt.

naver(e) see nẹ̄ver(e).

nāveþ, nāveŏ *contracted negative
form* see hāve(n).

nawiht, nawt see naȝt.

nawþer *conj* (followed by *ne* or *no*)
neither. [*Nauther*]. Cp. *neythir,
nouther.*

ne, na 1. *adv* not (before the vb and
generally followed by a second

negative like *not* etc.). — 2. *conj*
(after *neyther* or *ne*) nor; (foll by
another neg) and 27₄B/727. [*Ne,
Na*].

nearow see narwe.

nēaver see nẹ̄ver.

neb, nebbe *sb* face, visage 3/64, 4/10.
[*Neb*(4)].

necessarīe *adj* NECESSARY.

nedde, neddi see nēde(n), *ne hadde*
(*I*) see hāve(n).

1. nēde, neid, nēod(e), nıēde, nȳede *sb*
NEED.

2. nēde, nēdez *adv* and *adverbial genitive* NEEDS, necessarily. [*Need*].

nẹ̄delēr *sb* seller of needles. [NEEDLER].

nēde(n) *wk vb* NEED; *pret* nedde.

nēdez see nēde[2].

nẹ̄dy *adj* NEEDY.

nẹ̄dyll *sb* 1. NEEDLE — 2. mouthful
29/33.

nēdlunge *adv* necessarily, absolutely
3/31. [NEEDLING].

neemly *adv* NIMBLY.

nēgh *wk vb* approach. [NIGH].

nēȝ, nēh, ney see nȳȝ.

neid see nēde[1].

neygh see nȳȝ.

neiȝebŏre *sb* NEIGHBOUR.

neir see ner(e).

neythir *conj* NEITHER (followed by *ne*
or *nor*). Cp. *nawþer, nouther.*

nekke, nykke *sb* NECK; *pl* nykken.

nelle, neltŏū, *contracted forms* see
wille[1].

nemme, nempne *wk vb* NAME, call.
[*Nemn*]. Cp. *neven.*

nente *adj* NINTH 19/1012.

nēod(e) see nēde[1].

neome, neomeŏ see nyme.

neorre see ner(e).

neowe see newe.

nēr(e), nēor, neir, nār *adv* NEAR[1,2];
compar nerre, neorre 3/62, ner.

nēre, nes *contracted negative forms*,
see bē(n).

nẹ̄se *sb* NOSE. [*Nese*].

nesh *adj* tender. [*Nesh*].

nest *sb* NEST.

nẹ̄t *sb* farm animal, bovine 12/700.
[NEAT].

neþelēs *adv* NEVERTHELESS. [*Netheless*]. Cp. *nápelēs, nōpelēs.*

nēve *sb* NEPHEW 1/10. [*Neve*¹].

nevede *contracted negative form*, see hāve(n).

neven(e), nevyn *wk vb* NAME. [*Neven*]. Cp. *nemme.*

nēver(e), nēvre, nǣvre, naver(e), neāver *adv* NEVER; *nēver a dęęl* not one bit.

newe, neowe, nwe 1. *adj* NEW. — 2. *adv* NEW, once again.

nevestu *contracted negative form* see hāve(n).

nīede, nȳēde see nēde¹.

nieȝ see nȳȝ.

nyght, nyȝt, niȝt, nyht *sb* NIGHT; *adverbial gen* nyghtes *a* ⁓ at night, NIGHTS (considered as a pl in ModE *He works nights*).

nyghtyngāle, niȝtingāle, nyhtegāle *sb* NIGHTINGALE.

nȳȝ, nȳ, neygh, nēȝ, nēh, ney, nyeȝ 15/29 *adv* NIGH, near.

nyht see nyght.

nykken see nekke.

nil *contracted negative form*, see wille¹.

nyme, nime(n), neomen *str vb* 4 take, grab, betake oneself, go, be taken 4/37; *imp* nim 3/1, neomeð 4/30; *pret* nōm, nam *pl* nāmen; *pp* nómen 10/250, i-nume 5/14053 [NIM].

nyp *wk vb* pilfer, steal, lift. [NIP¹].

nis *contracted negative form*, see bē(n).

nȳsen *wk vb* make foolish; (they) foolishly exaggerate 18/1266. [based on NICE ' foolish,' see also *Niced*].

nǫ, nā *negative adv* NO¹·², not; nor 5/14065.

noan see nōne.

1. nǫble, nǫbele, nǫbill *adj* NOBLE, great.

2. nǫble *sb* gold coin, first minted by Edward III, then currently worth 6 s. 8 d. [NOBLE¹ (B 2)].

nǫbletee *sb* splendor. [*Noblety*].

nocht see noght(e).

noght(e), noȝt, nocht, nought, nowht,

nohut, nout, nōwiht *adv* NOUGHT, NOT, not at all. Cp. *not, naȝt, nat.*

nohut see noght(e).

noyne see nǫn.

1. nóise, nóys *sb* NOISE, rumor; reputation 29/224.

2. noyse see nǫse.

noldes *contracted negative form*, see wille¹.

nōm see nyme.

nǫman, nāmon *indef pron* NO MAN, no one.

nómen see nyme.

nōn, nōun, noyn(e) *sb* NOON.

nǫn(e), nǫǫn, noan, nān(e), nōun *indefinite pron* NONE (before a comparative) ; ⁓ *mǫre* no more.

nǫnes, nǫnys in *for þe nǫnes* for this occasion, for now 28/4010, 29/527. [NONCE].

nǫnes-weis, nānes-weis *adv* NOWAYS, not at all 3/44, 4/36.

nǫǫn see nǫn(e).

nǫǫt *contracted negative form*, see wite(n).

nǫǫte see nǫte².

nóres *sb* NURSE¹.

norþeron *adj* NORTHERN.

nǫse, noyse *sb* NOSE.

1. nǫt *contracted negative form* see wite(n).

2. not, nott *adv* NOT. Cp. *noght(e), naȝt, nat.*

1. nǫte *sb* service 6/1034. [*Note*¹].

2. nǫte, nǫǫte *sb* music; musical NOTE² ; *by* ⁓ in chorus 27₁/303.

nǫti *wk vb* use 6/1033. [*Note*¹].

nott see not¹.

nǫþelēs *adv* NEVERTHELESS. [*Netheless*]. Cp. *náthelēs, nēþelēs.*

nǫther see nouther.

nǫthing *adv* NOTHING, not at all.

nōu see nōw.

nought see noght.

noughtwithstondyng *prep* NOTWITHSTANDING.

1. nōumbre *sb* NUMBER.

2. nōumbre *wk vb* NUMBER, count, calculate.

nōumpēre *sb* UMPIRE.

nōun see nōn, nǫne.

nout see noght(e).

nōuþe see nōwþe.

nouther, nǫther *conj* NEITHER (followed by *ne* or *nor*). [*Nouther*]. Cp. *nawþer, neythir.*

nóvellerīe *sb* NOVELTY 28/3955. [*Novelry*].

nōw, nōwe, nōu, nū *adv* NOW; ~ *and eft* now and then; ~ *þenne* (introducing an important point in an argument) then 4/30, see NOW (10).

nowht see noght(e).

nǫwiderwardes *adv* in no single direction 1/36 [*Nowitherwards*].

nōwi3t see noght(e).

nōwþe, nōuþe, nūðe *adv* now. [*Nowthe*].

nū see nōw.

nül(e), nülde, nülle, nülleþ, nültu *contracted negative forms* see wille[1].

nüste, nüte *contracted negative forms*, see wite(n).

nūðe see nōwþe.

nwe see newe.

O

ō̆ see of[1], on[1], ōn(e).

obediencēr *sb* OBEDIENCER, one who obeys, a Church officer.

oblyst *pp adj* OBLIGED 16/79.

obōut see abōut.

oc see ac.

1. of, off, o *prep* OF; concerning 5/14076; with 27₁/334.

2. of *adv* OFF, afar; (idea of separation) *smæt* ~ *his hafd* cut off his head 5/14025.

ofdrāhen *str vb 6* draw (from) 3/110, 122. [*Ofdraw*].

ofdrēde *wk vb* frighten, terrify (*trans*); be afraid (*intrans*); *pp* ofdrad, ofdrēd.

ofēren *wk vb* frighten 6/978. [*Afear*].

off see of[1].

offertōrie *sb* OFFERTORY.

offre(n) *wk vb* OFFER.

ofgān *str vb 7* gain, obtain 3/78. [*Ofgo*].

ofkest *wk vb* reject, OFFCAST; *couples* ~ uncouple, unleash 18/1146.

ofschāmed *pp adj* ASHAMED 6/934. [*Ofshamed*].

ofsprüng *sb* lineage [cp. *Ofspring, vb.*]

ofte *adv* often, OFT.

oftentȳme *adv* OFTENTIME.

oftesȳthes, oftesīðen *adv* OFTEN. [*Oftsithe(s)*].

ofþinken, ofþinchen *impersonal wk vb* *mē ofþinkeþ* I repent 2/10, 10/205. [*Ofthink*].

ogānis see agayne(s).

oght(e), ought, owcht, ouht *indef pron* something, anything, AUGHT *sb*[2].

ǫ3en see owen[1,2].

oht *adj* brave, valorous 5/13997. [AUGHT *sb*[2] (B)].

ǫk(e), ǫǫk *sb* OAK.

ǫld, ǫǫld, āld *adj* OLD. *compar* elder(e), ālder; *superl* āldest.

olhnin *wk vb* cajole, flatter, ingratiate o. s. with 3/128. [*Oluhnen*].

1. on, o, onne. 1. prep ON, in 3/4, 7/29, of 11/2, 7. — 2. *adv* ON, upon.

2. ǫn see ǫn(e).

ǫnde *sb* breath, sigh. [*Onde* (4)].

ónderstant, see understande(n).

ónderstondinge *sb* UNDERSTANDING, judgment.

ondswerien, ansuerie, andswarien *wk vb* ANSWER; *pret* andswarede 5/14007; *pp* i-ondsweret 3/20, 23.

ǫn(e), ǫǫn(e), āne, ǫǫ, ǭ 1. *adj* ONE; *that* ~ the one; *te āne* 3/49, *al* ~, *al hym* ~ 18/749, *by mȳne* ~ 20/704 ALONE, *ōure* ~ we alone 18/1230. — 2. *indef pronoun* someone, ONE. *acc sg* ǫnne 1/34, *dat F sg* āre 5/27. — 3. *adv* only 3/100.

ǫnes, ānys *adv* in agreement 27₄ᴮ/696; *at* ~ at ONCE (at the same time) 20/789, at ONCE (immediately) 21₂/146, ONCE 22₁/272.

onfest, onfast *prep* nearby, not far from 5/5, 7/3358. [*Onfast*].

on3ēnes see agayns.

ony, oni *adj* and *pron* ANY; *dat sg* onie 11/18; *pl* onie 11/19.

onne see on, ǫn(e).

ónneaþe see un-ēðe.

onōh see y-nōugh.

ónpaye *wk vb* displease 15/2. [*Unpay*[1]].

ónpayit *pp adj* UNPAID.

ónzyğinde *pres part adj* UNSAYING, ineffable 4ᴀ/9.

ǫǫ see ǫn(e).

ǫǫld see ǭld(e).
ǫǫn(e) see ǭn(e).
ǫǫnlich *adv* ONLY.
oother see ōther.
ǭpen, upen *adj* OPEN; uncovered 28/
3963; evident 3/44.
ǭpenen, ōpenin, upon *wk vb* OPEN.
ǭpenlĭch(e) *adv* OPENLY, publicly.
óplondysch see uplondysch.
ópon see upon.
ópriȝt *adv* UPRIGHT, standing up
straight 15/67.
ópward see upward.
ópwīnde *st vb 3a* wind up(wards)
10/75. [*Upwind*].
or *conj* than (after comparative).
[OR].
ordayn, ordāni *wk vb* ORDAIN, order;
pres 3 sg ordānis 17/5; *pp* ordaynde, ordānd.
ordyre *sb* ORDER.
ǭr(e) see ēr.
1. ǭre, āre *sb* grace, mercy 6/886;
þin ~ if you please 10/189. [ORE¹].
2. ǭre *sb* OAR.
3. ore *conj* OR, unless 20/813 (see
note). [*Or*¹].
orysūn, orysōwn, oreysón *sb* ORISON,
prayer.
orn *strong pret* ran 5/14035. [RUN].
Cp. *renne*.
otwynne see atwinne.
ǭthe, ǭþe, āthe *sb* OATH.
1. ōther, oother, ōþer, ōðer, ōthir,
ōthyr *adj* OTHER; second 3/36; inflected forms ōthre; *gen* ōtheres 10/
224; ōðers 2/30; *pl* ōthre, ōþren
4ₐ/9.
2. ǭþer, ǭðer, ōuthire, ōwthyre *conj* or
[*Other*].
ōþer-whȳle, ōþer-quȳle *adv* sometimes,
on occasion; at other times 18/722.
[OTHERWHILE].
ōu see ȝe², hōw.
ought, ouht see oght.
ouhte see owen¹.
ōule see ūle.
ōunce *sb* OUNCE; tuft 27₄ₐ/677.
ōunderfonge *str vb 7* receive. [*Under-
fang*].
ōundyd *pp adj* wavy 20/765. [*Oundy*].

oune see owen².
ōunwiis see unwys.
ōup see up.
our see ǭver.
ōur(e), ōwre, ūre *1 and 2 pl pron* and
poss adj 1. OUR. — 2. YOUR 13₃/3,
28.
ōure *sb* HOUR.
ōus see wē.
ōut(e), ōwt(e), ōutt, ūt *prep* and *adv*
OUT.
ōuterlīche, ōutrely, ūtrely *adv* UT-
TERLY.
ōutryȝte *adv* OUTRIGHT, directly out
of.
ōutrynge(n) *str vb 3a* sing at full
voice. [OUTRING].
ōuthire seě ǭþer².
ǭver, our 1. *prep* OVER, on. — 2. *adv*
(before *adj*) very, too much 3/46.
ǭveral *adv* everywhere. [*Overall*].
ǭverclīmbe *str vb 3a* climb up, over.
[OVERCLIMB].
ǭvercóme(n) *str vb 4* OVERCOME, conquer; *pp* ǭvercumen.
ǭvergān *irreg vb* invade, dominate 6/
947, pass away, go away 6/952.
[OVERGO].
ǭverhēde *pret* passed, disappeared 10/
90. [OVERHEAVE].
ǭverheghede *pp* carried too high up
16/5. [*Overhigh vb*].
ǭverhērunge *sb* exaggerated praise
3/42. [OVER + *herying*].
ǭverlēpe *str vb 7* leap or spring upon,
OVERLEAP 21₂/150, 199; *pret* ǭverlēpe.
ǭverlynge *sb* governor 20/710. [*Over-
ling*].
ǭversēn *str vb 5* look out over, en-
compass with the eyes; *pret*
ǭversah 5/14012. [OVERSEE].
ǭvershēten *str vb 2* OVERSHOOT the
scent ǒr track; *pp* ǭvershette.
ǭversithon *adv* too frequently? 1/51
note.
ǭverspredde(n) *wk vb* OVERSPREAD;
pret ōverspradde.
ǭvertāke *str vb 6* OVERTAKE, meet.
ōw see ȝē².
owcht see oght.

1. **owen,** ǫȝen *perf pres vb* possess,
OWN 12/743; *3 sg pres* āh 3/133,
3 *pl* āhen 4/18; *pret* ouhte, awcht,
aucht, auhte, āhte OUGHT 2/2, 3/69.
[OWE].

2. **owen, oune, awen,** āȝen, āhne, ǫȝen
15/34 *adj* OWN; *dat F sg* āȝere
5/14054.

1. **ōwer** *poss* OUR.

2. **ǫwer** *adv* anywhere 1/55. [*Owhere*].

ōwr(e) see **ōur(e)**.

ōwte see **ōute**.

ōwthyre see **ǫþer²**.

P

paas *sb* PACE¹, step; *goon a* ~ go on
foot, walk 27₄ᴮ/866.

pade *sb* toad. [*Pad¹*].

paye *wk vb* 1. please 18/1379, 15/2. —
2. PAY¹ 15/35; *pp* y-paid 15/2.

paynt, peynte *wk vb* PAINT¹; deceive.

pāle *wk vb* appear pale 19/1004,
PALE².

palez *sb* PALACE¹.

palfray *sb* PALFREY.

palmer *sb* professional pilgrim, PAL-
MER¹.

pāne *sb* section (of wall) 19/1034.
[PANE¹].

par *prep* by, through.

paradīs, paradȳs, paradiis, parais (3/
29) *sb* PARADISE.

paraventüre *adv* PERADVENTURE, by
chance.

parcenel *sb* partaker 16/91.

pardee, perdé *interj* truly, indeed.
[PARDIE].

pardonēr, pardoneer *sb* PARDONER, seller of indulgences (cp. 27₄ᴀ/669 n.).

pardoūn *sb* forgiveness of sin 27₄ᴮ/
917; indulgence, document convey-
ing a PARDON¹ 27₄ᴀ/687, 27₄ᴮ/906,
etc.

parfyt *adj* PERFECT.

parfytnesse *sb* PERFECTNESS.

parishe see **perishe**.

parte(n) *wk vb* divide up, PART.

partenēr(e), partynēr *sb* PARTNER,
partaker in 26/56.

partȳ, partīe *sb* PARTY, person, part,
company.

parvenke *sb* PERIWINKLE¹, evergreen
trailing shrub with blue or white
flowers.

passe(n) *wk vb* PASS, surpass, trans-
gress, disobey 24/35; die.

passyoūn *sb* PASSION.

pastee *sb* PASTY.

paume *sb* PALM², *pl* antlers, 'flat
expanded part of the horn in some
deer, from which finger-like points
project' 18/1155.

pavilyoūne *sb* PAVILION; standard.

pęęs *sb* PEACE.

peyne *sb* PAIN.

peyne(n) *reflexive wk vb* hym peyned
took pains 27₁/318. PAIN (III. 4).

peynte see **paynt.**

penaunce *sb* PENANCE.

peny, peni *sb* PENNY; *to þe peni drou*
turned into money 12/705; *pl* pens,
pence.

penywórthe *sb* PENNYWORTH; bargain
21₄/334.

pens, pence see **peny.**

peolkin *wk vb* pluck, rob 3/53. [*Pilch*].

1. **pēpe** *wk vb* PEEP¹, cry 29/581.

2. **pēpe** *wk vb* PEEP², look cautiously.

pēple, pēople, pöple *sb* PEOPLE.

perdé see **pardee.**

pēre *sb* PEER, equal.

pēren *wk vb* APPEAR. [*Pear*].

perfay *adv* by (my) faith.

perilouslych *adv* PERILOUSLY.

perishe, perisse, parishe *wk vb* PER-
ISH; *pres 1 pl* perisset (for per-
isseþ) 9/7; *pres subj 1 pl* perissi
9/27.

perquer *adv* by heart, completely 22₁/
238.

perré *sb* (precious) stone 19/1028.
[*Perrie*].

persāve *wk vb* PERCEIVE 22₂/411.

persōn *sb* PARSON, curate.

pēse-hóle *sb* PEASE-HULL, pea-pod.

pestilence *sb* plague, PESTILENCE.

pette see **pyt.**

picche *wk vb* 1. PITCH¹. — 2. ornament, set (with jewels); *pp* pyȝt
19/991, pyked ornamented 19/1036.
[*Pight*].

pigge *sb* PIG¹.

pyȝt see **picche.**

pike *wk vb* PITCH [2] (the seams)
12/707.

pȳke *sb* prickle, spine, quill 20/777.
[PIKE[1]].

pyked see picche.

pyker *sb* thief. [*Piker*[1]].

pilien *wk vb* rob, pillage 3/53 [PILL[1]].

pilwe-beer *sb* pillow-case, PILLOW-BERE
(and -*Bear*[4]).

1. pȳne, pīne *sb* torture, pain. [PINE[1]].

2. pȳne *wk vb* suffer, PINE; torture
1/22.

pīning *sb* torture, suffering.

piones *pl sb* PEONY seeds.

pȳpe *wk vb* squeak 29/195. [PIPE[1]].

pīpinge *sb* PIPING[1].

pyt, pette, pütte *sb* hole, well, PIT[1].

pitee *sb* PITY.

pitósly *adv* PITEOUSLY.

pitóŭs 1. *adv* pitiable. — 2. *adv* piti-
ably. PITEOUS.

plaide, plḙde *wk vb* PLEAD.

plāte *sb* PLATE of precious metal
19/1036; piece (of money) 13₃/4;
pl plāten.

plḙde see plaide.

pleye(n), pleie, playe, plaie *wk vb*
PLAY.

pleyne *wk vb* complain; recite a complaint about unrequited love etc.
[*Plain*].

plentevóŭs *adj* PLENTEOUS.

plesaunce *sb* pleasure. [PLEASANCE[1]].

plḙse, pless *wk vb* PLEASE.

plȳe *wk vb* show 19/1039; bend 20/
777. [PLY[1]].

plighte(n), plihte *wk vb* promise,
swear, PLIGHT[1]; *pret* plehten 21₁/
46; *pp* plight 27₄ᴮ/702.

ply3t, plīt, plȳt *sb* manner; circum-
stance, PLIGHT, condition; *pl* perilous situation.

plóŭ3 *sb* plow, PLOUGH[1].

poysóŭn, poysón *sb* POISON.

pǫke *sb* bag, sack, POKE[1].

pol-cat *sb* skunk, POLE-CAT.

poore see póŭre.

pṏple see pḙple.

porchaci *wk vb* PURCHASE 15/40.

porcióŭn *sb* PORTION.

pōre see póŭre.

portal *sb* PORTAL.

possed see posshen.

posshen *wk vb* PUSH; pushed them
around 21₂/151; *pret* possed.

pǫst *sb* POST[1], pillar.

postle *sb* APOSTLE; *pl* postlis.

potel *sb* half-gallon. [POTTLE[1]].

pothecārīe *sb* druggist, APOTHECARY.
[*Pothecary*].

póŭre, pōre, poore, povre, pover *adj*
POOR; powerless.

póŭrseut *sb* PURSUIT, *in* ～ following
suit, the same one after another
19/1035.

póŭrvei see purvay.

povert *sb* POVERTY.

povre, pover see póŭre.

prayse see preyse.

prangle *wk vb* press tightly, pinch
12/639.

pratty *adj* PRETTY.

prḙche *wk vb* PREACH.

prēde see prȳde.

preie, preye, pre3e, prye *wk vb* PRAY,
supplicate, ask.

preyēre, preyóŭr *sb* PRAYER, petition.

preise(n), preyse, prayse *wk vb*
PRAISE; appraise, evaluate.

preke *wk vb* PRICK, spur, ～ *of* spur
forward and away (on horseback)
20/718.

prentis *sb* apprentice. [*Prentice*].

preóst see prēst.

preōven see prōve.

preōve *sb* PROOF 3/4.

press *sb* peril, danger 22₂/418.
[PRESS[1]].

prēst, preōst, prȫst *sb* PRIEST.

prestly *adv* quickly, promptly.

prēve see prōve.

prevely see prively.

prȳde, prēde, prüde, pruide, prüte *sb*
PRIDE.

pyre see preie.

prȳorȳe *sb* PRIORY.

prȳóŭr *sb* PRIOR.

1. prȳs, prīse *sb* PRICE, valor, glory;
your ～ your grace, excellency etc.
18/1247; praise 18/1379.

2. prȳs *adj* noble, valorous. [*Price*].

3. prȳs *sb* PRIZE[3], capture 18/1363.

prīsit *pp* praised, highly PRIZED.

prysoūn, prisun *sb* 1. PRISON. — 2. PRISONER 18/1219 [PRISON (c. 2)].

pryss *wk vb* PRIZE[1], appreciate.

privé see privy.

prively, prevely *adv* PRIVILY, secretly.

privy, privee, privé *adj* secret, mysterious, PRIVY.

propyrtē *sb* PROPERTY.

proprelīche *adv* PROPERLY.

prŏst see prēst.

proūd *adv* PROUD, hardy, fierce.

prŏve, prūvien, prēve, prēoven *wk vb* PROVE, put to the test (of battle) 17/15; demonstrate 3/87.

prŏw *sb* advantage, goodness, good things 14/62. [*Prow* sb[2]].

prŏwes, prūesse *sb* PROWESS.

prüde see prȳde.

prüesse see prŏwes.

pruide, prüte see prȳde.

prūvien see prŏve.

pülte *wk vb* impel, drive, force 6/873. [*Pilt*].

pünden *wk vb* enclose, IMPOUND 3/129; *pres 3 sg* pünt. [*Pind*].

pürly *adv* PURELY, with purity 19/1004.

purpre *adj* violet, PURPLE. [*Purpur*].

purs *sb* PURSE.

purvay, poūrvei *wk vb* prepare, PROVIDE, make provision or get provisions ready, PURVEY.

pütte see pyt.

Q

quayle *sb* QUAIL.

quākien, cwākien *wk vb* QUAKE[1], tremble.

quarterne *sb* cellar-hole, prison-cell 1/28. [*Quartern*[1]].

quat see what.

quath, quaþ see quēthen.

quēd, kuēad *adj* bad, evil, guilty. — 2. evil, sin.

queer *sb* CHOIR.

queynt, qwantt *adj* clever, tricky [QUAINT].

queintelīche *adv* elaborately, curiously, [QUAINTLY].

quelle(n) *wk vb* kill; put an end to, QUELL[1] 18/752.

quen see when.

quēne, qwēne, cwēn *sb* QUEEN 3/68, 5/22.

quêre see where[1].

quêr-fǫre see whêr-fǫre.

querré *sb* QUARRY[1] of deer, entrails; pile of dead game.

quēthe *sb* utterance 18/1150.

quēthe(n) *str vb 5* say, announce; *pret* quod, quoþ, quaþ; *pp* i-quēðen. [*Quethe*].

quhat see what.

quhen see when.

quhethir see whether.

quhyll see whīle.

quyk, quik, quic, whik *adj* alive, living, QUICK.

quyken *wk vb* bring to life 24/25, QUICKEN.

quȳl(e) see whīle.

1. quyt *adj* free, QUIT.

2. quyt *vb* (well) paid 29/497. QUIT (II, 10).

3. quit, quyȳt see whīte.

quod, quoþ see quēthe(n).

qwantt see queynt.

qweasse *wk vb* breathe? 29/487. [*Quease*[2]].

qwēne see quēne.

qwytt see quyt.

R

rachche *sb* hunting dog 18/1164, 1362. [*Rache*[1]].

rachentēģe *sb* chain 1/33. [*Rakenteie*].

radde see rēde[3].

radly *adv* rapidly.

rēdesman see rēdesman.

rēve(n) see rēve(n).

rēvere *sb* robber, marauder 1/57. [REAVER].

raged *adj* white with frost 10/745. (Cp. Anglian *rag* 'hoar-frost'.)

rayled, railed *pp* arranged, arrayed 18/745, placed 17/83. [*Rail* vb[1]].

raiss see rīse.

rākyer *sb* scavenger, street-cleaner, garbage collector, RAKER[1].

ran see renne(n).

1. rāpe *sb* haste. [*Rape*[1]].

2. rāpe *wk vb* hasten 18/1309, 21₃/102. [*Rape*[1]].

rappe *wk vb* RAP¹.
rāre see rǫre.
rāse *wk vb* rush, run. [*Rase*⁴].
ratōn *sb* rat. [*Ratton*].
ratónēre *sb* rat-catcher. [*Rattoner*].
raþ *sb* counsel, advice 12/693*.
  [*Rathe*¹].
rāthe, rāþe, rēaðe, rēðe *adv* quick, at
  once.
ravyst *pp* RAVISHED 19/1088.
raw see row.
rawmpe *wk vb* advance by leaps and
  bounds. [RAMP¹].
read see rẹ̄d(e)¹.
rēade see rēde²,³.
reall *adj* regal, royal, magnificent.
  [*Real*¹].
reame, rewme, rēm *sb* REALM.
rēaðe see rāthe.
recche *wk vb* be important, matter;
  care about, RECK; *pret* route 10/260.
rechāse *wk vb* pursue (game). [*Re-
  chase*¹].
rẹ̄che *wk vb* REACH¹; get to (with a
  blow).
recordēr *sb* remembering 15/52 (see
  note). [*Recorder*¹].
recordinge *sb* remembering, RECORDING.
rēd see rēde.
1. rẹ̄d(e), rẹẹ̄d, rēad *adj* RED.
2. rẹ̄d(e), reede, rēad *sb* advice, counsel; common sense, reason 6/941.
  [REDE¹].
3. rēde *wk vb* 1. READ, *bock* ~ say
  Mass 5/5. — 2. advise. — 3. ask 14/
  4097; *pres 3 sg* rēt 15/72; *pres
  subj* rēd, rēade; *pret* radde 5/5.
rẹ̄desman, rǣdesman *sb* counsellor,
  steward. [*Redesman*].
rẹ̄dy, rẹ̄de *adj* READY.
rẹ̄dily *adv* READILY, fast.
rẹ̄dyngkyng *sb* groom, hostler? 21₄/
  323. [*Reding-king*].
reed(e) see rēd(e)¹,².
refet *sb* food, nourishment 19/1064.
  [*Refete*].
reȝhel-bōc *sb* monastic RULE 7/8.
  [*Regle* + BOOK].
reherce, reherse *wk vb* describe 18/
  1243: pronounce, repeat, REHEARSE.
reyll *wk vb* REEL¹.

1. reyne *sb* REIGN, royal power, sov-
  ereignty; realm 13₂/71.
2. reyne *wk vb* REIGN.
reisūn see rẹ̄són.
rekene *wk vb* RECKON, count.
relay *sb* RELAY station 27₁/362 (see
  note).
relike *sb* RELIC.
rēm see reame.
rẹ̄nāble *adj* eloquent, ~ *of tonge*
  ready of speech, loquacious 21₂/158.
  [*Renable*].
rencyān *sb* kind of cloth 13₂/106.
  [*Rencian*].
rēnde(n) *wk vb* REND¹, tear; *pret*
  rente; *pp* rent.
reneye *wk vb* abjure one's faith etc.
  15/74. [*Renay*].
renk(e) *sb* man, knight; *pl* renkkez.
  [*Rink*¹].
renne(n), ryn(ne) *str vb 3a* RUN;
  pret ran; *pp* ryn.
renón, renōun *sb* RENOWN, fame.
renōwle *wk vb* renew. [*Renovel*].
1. rente *sb* RENT¹, income.
2. rente see rēnde(n).
reowe see rewe.
reowðe see rōwthe.
repayre *wk vb* assemble, get together.
  [REPAIR¹].
rẹ̄pe(n) *wk vb* REAP¹.
rẹ̄pe-reyve *sb* farm foreman 21₃/15.
  [*Reap-reeve*].
reprēfe *sb* REPROOF, shame, reproach.
rerd, rürd *sb* tumult 18/1149; voice
  10/114. [*Rerd*].
rēs *sb* rush, run. [*Rese*].
resayt *sb* receiving station, hunting
  blind? 18/1168, refuge, reception?
  19/1067. [RECEIPT].
resceyve *wk vb* RECEIVE.
rescōūs *sb* RESCUE, assistance, aid.
reset see resayt.
rẹ̄són, rẹ̄sun, reisun *sb* REASON; reasoning, argument 21₂/175; ~ *whȳ
  þat* because 14/4130.
1. rest, ryste *sb* REST¹, repose.
2. rest, reste(n), ryst(e) *wk vb* REST¹,
  repose; *pres 3 sg* rest; *pret* reste.
restaye *wk vb* turn back 18/1135.
  [*Restay*].

restelees *adj* RESTLESS.
rẹsun see rẹsón.
rēt see rēde³.
rēðe see rāðe.
reule *wk vb* RULE, govern.
reulīche *adv* pitifully. [*Ruly*].
reuþe see rowthe.
rēve *sb* bailiff, farm official. [REEVE¹].
rẹve(n), rǣven *wk vb* rob, pillage,
    RAVAGE. [REAVE¹].
rever *sb* RIVER 19/1055.
reverence *sb* reverence, honor.
rewe, reowe, röwen *wk vb* RUE¹, re-
    gret; (impersonal) repent, have
    pity 12/497, 13₁ᵦ/2.
rewme see reame.
rewnesse *sb* pity 12/502. [*Rueness*].
ryally *adv* royally, majestically.
    [*Rially*].
rialtee *sb* realm, domain. [*Rialty*].
ribaud *sb* bawd, lecher 15/34. [RIBALD].
ribaudȳe *sb* lechery. [*Ribaldy*].
rybbe *sb* RIB¹.
rybé see rubie.
ribibóūr *sb* female player of a fiddle-
    like instrument 21₄/322.
1. riche, riče *adj* powerful, RICH.
2. riche, rych(e) *wk vb* decide 18/
    1223, get ready 18/1130, 1309.
    [*Rich²*].
3. ryche, riche *sb* realm. [*Riche*].
richesse, rytches *sb* riches.
richt see right.
rȳde(n) *str vb 1* RIDE; run here and
    there 21₂/171. *pres 3 sg* ritt; *pret
    sg* rọọd, *pl* ryden; *pres part* rīdend.
rȳfe see rȳve.
riǧǧe, rydge, rüǧǧe *sb* RIDGE, back.
riǧǧe-bọn *sb* back-bone. [*Rig-bone*].
1. right, riht *adj* RIGHT, just.
2. right, ryght, riht, richt *adv* RIGHT,
    exact, just, very well; *right as . . . ,
    right sọ* just . . . thus (reinforcing
    function word); *right anọn* right
    away; *riht y-nóūgh* just enough.
righte, ri3t(e) *sb* RIGHT¹, privilege
    8/516.
rightful, ri3tful *adj* RIGHTFUL, just.
rightfulnesse, ryht- *sb* RIGHTFULNESS,
    justice.
ryghtwȳse, ryghtwis *adj* RIGHTEOUS,
    just, equitable.

rigorusly *adv* RIGOROUSLY.
ri3t, riht see right¹, ².
1. ri3te *wk vb* set straight 15/64,
    RIGHT.
2. ri3te see righte.
rīme, rȳm(e) *sb* RIME¹, poetry, rimed
    poem 14/Introd; rhythm, meter,
    count 7/44.
ryn see renne(n).
rȳnde *sb* RIND¹.
rynge(n) *str vb 3a* RING²; resound;
    pret rọ̄ng.
rynne see renne(n).
rīot *sb* wild party.
rȳot *wk vb* amuse oneself 20/785.
    [RIOT].
rīotóūre *sb* reveller, loose-living per-
    son. [RIOTER].
rype *wk vb* RIP², tear.
rīs *sb* twigs, small branches, rise *dat
    sg* 6/894. [*Rice¹*].
rīse, ryss *str vb 1* RISE. *imperative 2
    sg* ris; *pret* rọ̄s, rọọs, raiss 22₂/414,
    rȳsed 18/1313; *pl* risen.
ryste see rest¹, ².
rytches see richesse.
ritt see rȳde(n).
rȳve(n), rȳfe *str vb 1* pull or tear or
    split apart, RIVE¹.
rixlien *wk vb* reign; *pres 3 sg* rixleoð
    5/14050. [*Rixle*].
robbe(n) *wk vb* ROB.
roc see rokke¹.
1. róde *sb* tint, color, visage 13₁ᵦ/2.
    [*Rud*].
2. rōde, rood(e) *sb* cross. [ROOD].
rogge *wk vb* tremble 20/784. [*Rog*].
ro3, ru3 *adj* ROUGH; hairy, shaggy
    6/1013, 18/745.
1. rokke, roc *sb* ROCK¹, boulder.
2. rokke *wk vb* ROCK¹ a cradle, etc.
rōme *wk vb* roar 20/784. [*Romy*].
rōme(n) *wk vb* ROAM, wander about.
rón *sb* song. [*Ron¹*].
rọ̄ng see rynge(n).
rood see rȳde(n).
rood(e) see rōde².
ropere *sb* rope-maker or seller.
    [ROPER].
rọre, rāre *wk vb* ROAR 20/784.
rọọs, rọ̄s, see rīse.
rōte *sb* ROOT¹.

rōunde *adv* easily. [ROUND].
rŏune, rŏwne *wk vb* whisper. [ROUND²].
1. rōut(e), rōwte *sb* troop, assemblage. [ROUT¹, 18th cent. poet. usage].
2. route see recche.
row, raw *sb* ROW, (battle) line 17/79, 83.
rowen see rewe.
rŏwt *sb* heavy blow or stroke. [*Rout³*].
rŏwte see rōut(e)¹.
rŏwthe, reuþe, reowðe *sb* compassion, pity, RUTH¹; misfortune, calamity 3/33; lamentation.
rūbie, rȳbé *sb* RUBY.
rüğğe see riğğe.
ruȝe see roȝ.
ruydly *adv* RUDELY, violently 20/785.
rūne *sb* secret 4/11 (pl) writings; lore, learning 5/30. [*Roun*].
rürd see rerde.
rūse *wk vb* make a detour or other movement to escape hunting dogs 27₁/381 note. [*Ruse¹* (2)].
ruwet *sb* small horn or trumpet. [*Ruet*].

S

sa see sǫ̆.
saaf see sāf.
sābyll *sb* SABLE¹ 20/771.
sacrifīse, sakerfȳse *sb* SACRIFICE.
sadel *wk vb* SADDLE.
sǣ see sę̄¹.
sǣden see seye(n).
sæȝhen see sē(n).
sǣin see seye(n).
sǣrinesse *sb* SORRINESS, sadness 5/14079.
sæt see sitte(n).
sāf, saaf, sāve *adj* SAFE; *I wŏwche it* ⁓ I would freely grant it 18/1391; *compar* sāver.
saffer see saphīr.
sağğe *adj* SAGE, wise.
sagh, saȝ see sē(n).
saȝe *sb* word *or* prayer 18/1202; *at* ⁓ *ǭþer at servyce* in word or deed 18/1246. [SAW²].
sah see sē(n).
say see seye(n).
saille *wk vb* SAIL¹, set sail.
sayn, seine(n) *wk vb* SIGN (o. s. with

sign of the cross) 18/761, 1202; seal; *pp* i-seined. [*Sain*].
saynt *wk vb* play the saint 20/209, SAINT.
sakerfȳse see sacrifīse.
sale *sb* hall. [*Sale¹*].
sall see shal.
salve *sb* SALVE, ointment 6/888.
1. sāme(n), sam *adv* together; *al* ⁓ all together. [*Samen*].
2. sāmen, samnen *wk vb* gather, assemble. [*Sam¹*].
sāmyn *adj* SAME.
samnen see sāmen².
sang *sb* SONG 7/3374.
sant see seint.
saphīr, saffer *sb* SAPPHIRE 13₂/115, 19/1002.
sardonyse *sb* SARDONYX 19/1006.
sāre see sǭre.
sāri, sāry see sǭry.
saugh, sauh see sē(n).
saule see soule.
sauter *sb* PSALTER.
sauve see sāve¹.
1. sāve, sauve *wk vb* SAVE; *pp* i-sauved 9/29.
2. sāve, sāver see sāf.
sāwe, sawh see sē(n).
sawle see soule.
Saxon, Saxonlych *adj* SAXON 26/8.
scærpe see scharp.
scāle *sb* surface 19/1005. [SCALE²].
scārslych *adv* SCARCELY.
scater *wk vb* SCATTER 1/4. [SHATTER].
scele see skyl(e).
scęre see skęre.
sch- see also sh-.
schac *str vb* 6 SHAKE.
schadde see schęde.
schālyd *pp adj* covered with scales, SCALED 20/766. [*Shaled* 'shell-covered' is possible].
1. schāme, shǫme, shāme, ssāme 15/17 *sb* SHAME.
2. schāme *wk vb* feel shame, become ashamed. [SHAME].
scharp, scærp *adj* SHARP 1/30, violent, impetuous 13₂/69.
schawde, schawin see schewe(n).
schĕ, schō, shō, ȝhō 7/3624 *3 sg F pers pron* SHE.

scheawen see schewe(n).
schęde *wk vb* fall, tumble; *pret*
schadde 18/727. [SHED¹].
scheep *sb* shepherd 21₁/2. [*Shep*].
schęf see shęf.
scheft *sb* SHAFT², arrow.
scheld(e), sheld *sb* SHIELD.
schēn *adj* shining, resplendent 4/1;
compar schēnre. [SHEEN].
schēnde, sheynd *wk vb* destroy, con-
found, disgrace; *pp* schent(e).
[*Shend*¹].
schēome *adj* ASHAMED 3/74. Cp.
SHAME *sb*.
schēomefule *adj* SHAMEFUL.
scheot see schōte.
schȩre *str vb* 4 SHEAR; *pp* schorne.
schewen, shæwen, schawin, shew,
sseawy *wk vb* SHOW; instruct 21₂/
167; confess 21₄/305; *pret* schawde
3/63, 67, 89.
schilden *wk vb* SHIELD; *pres 3 sg*
schilt 3/100.
schym *adj* shining, bright 19/1077.
[*Shim*].
schȳne, shīne *str vb* SHINE; *pret*
schǫn.
schyp(pe), ssipe *sb* SHIP¹.
schippe-burde *sb* bynne þe ⌒ aboard
ship 20/804; SHIPBOARD.
schīr, shīr, schȳree *adj* beautiful,
white 18/1378, shining 20/766.
[SHEER (4) *Shire*].
schīre *sb* SHIRE, county.
schō see schē.
scholde(n), scholle see shal.
schǫn see schȳne.
schop see shape(n).
schorne see schȩre.
schort, sćort *adj* SHORT.
schōte, schūt *str vb* 2 SHOOT 4/42;
throw (o. s.) 22₂/467; *pret sg* schǫt.
schēot 4/42, *pl* schǫtten.
schōure *sb* SHOWER¹.
schrȩęde *wk vb* SHRED.
schrewe, shrew(e) *sb* rascal, villain,
jerk; tyrant 21₂/196. [SHREW²].
schrifte, srift *sb* SHRIFT, confession
and absolution; *go to* ⌒ go to confession.
schrympe *sb* monster, scaly dragon
20/767. [SHRIMP].

schrinke *str vb* 3a frighten 20/767.
[SHRINK].
schrīven, shrȳve, srīve *str vb* 1 hear
confession etc.; confess successfully
and be forgiven 14/4158; *pp*
shryven, i-srive 10/176. [SHRIVE].
schroūd *sb* mantle, cloak 21₁/2.
[SHROUD¹].
schulde, schullen, schuln see shal.
schūt see schōte.
scōle *sb* SCHOOL.¹.
scǫre *sb* account, record of possessions
and income 3/140; SCORE, set of
twenty; *pl* scoren.
sċort see schort.
scot *sb* tavern bill, reckoning 15/35.
[SCOT²].
sċulde, sċuldest, sċulen see shal.
1. sę, sęę, sæ, sēa, zē 15/6 *sb* SEA.
2. sē see sē(n), sō, þe.
sēche see sēke².
secoūnde *adj* SECOND.
1. sēd(e) *sb* SEED.
2. sęde see seye(n).
sęę see sę¹.
sęęl *sb* SEAL² 11/22.
sęę-wolf *sb* SEA-WOLF, a voracious
fish.
1. sęǧǧe *sb* man, knight 18/1385.
[*Segge*¹].
2. sęǧǧe see seye(n).
sęǧǧer *sb* professional story-teller
14/Introd. [SAYER¹].
se3, sey see sē(n).
se3d, se3de, sehid, seyde, seide(n) see
seye(n).
seye(n), seyn, sæin, sei(e), say, sęǧǧe,
siǧǧe, süǧǧe, ziǧǧe *wk vb* SAY. *pres*
2 sg seist, *3 sg* zayþ 15/19, *3 pl*
seyn; *imperative 2 sg* seie; *pret sg*
seyde, seide, sęde, se3de 7/3346, *pl*
seiden, sæden 1/61; *pp* i-seid,
i-sæid, y-zed 4ₐ/18, se3d 7/3366,
sehid 10/210.
seyl *sb* SAIL.
sein, seyn see sē(n).
seyn see seye(n).
seyne see sen.
seine(n) see sayn.
seint, sant *sb* and *adj* SAINT.
seyntewarie, seintuarie *sb* SANCTUARY,
holy reliquary.

seist see seye(n).
1. sēk(e), sēoc *adj* SICK.
2. sēke, sēche, zēche *wk vb* SEEK;
   journey 20/720; visit and reverence
   a shrine 21,/47; *pret* soughte,
   so3te.
sēkenes *sb* SICKNESS.
sekyre see siker.
sēl *adj* good, agreeable 5/4; *compar*
   selre 5/34. [*Sele*].
sēlde, sēldene, sēldom *adv* SELDOM.
sēle, ceyll, cēle *sb* bliss (of paradise);
   a ~ with good humor 6/953.
self, sölf, sülf *adj* SELF.
sēly, sēli *adj* innocent, blessed, simple,
   poor. [*Seely*, SILLY].
selle, sülle(n), zelle *wk vb* SELL; *pret*
   sǫlde; *pp* i-sǫld.
selly *adv* very 18/1194.
selver see sylver.
semblant, semblaunt *sb* appearance,
   look 14/4055, way.
sēme *wk vb* SEEM.
sēmly *adj* SEEMLY, fitting.
sē(n), sēon, see *str vb 5* SEE; protect,
   look after: *God yow see* 27₄ᴮ/715;
   see to, take care 8/452. *pres 2 sg*
   sēst 12/534, *3 sg* sēth, siþ 6/950,
   pl söþ 6/884; *imperative 2 sg* sē;
   pret sāw(e), saugh, sawh, sauh, sa3,
   sagh, sah 7/3372, sey, se3, si3(e),
   sih, *pl* sæ3hen 7/3342; *pp* seene,
   sēne, sein, y-sein, i-seghe.
sen, seyne 1. *adv* then, after that. —
   2. since. [*Sen, Sene*]. Cp. *siþen, syn*.
sēnde(n), zēnde *wk vb* SEND (for).
   pres 3 sg send 11/3, sent 2/42; *imperative 2 pl* sēndeð 2/25; *pret*
   sente; *pp* i-send 11/36, send 7/3350.
1. sēne *adj* SEEN, visible, evident.
2. sēne see sē(n).
senne see synne¹.
sēoc see sēk(e)¹.
seolf, seolve(n)¹ see self.
sēon see sē(n).
seoðöen see siþen.
seovevald *adv* SEVENFOLD, seven times
   4/1.
sēr *adj* separate, particular 16/40; *pl*
   several. [*Sere*].
serewe see sorwe.
serk *sb* shirt 12/603. [SARK].

serkyll see cercle.
serlypez *adj* separate, distinct. [*Sere-
   lepes*].
sermone *wk vb* preach. [SERMON].
serve *wk vb* deserve 18/1380. [SERVE²].
servise, servyce, servese *sb* concert
   27,/302, deed, SERVICE¹ 18/1246.
sēsón, sēsoūn, sēsun *sb* SEASON.
sēst see sē(n).
sēsun see sēsón.
sete see sette.
seten, set(te), see sitte(n).
sette, sett *wk vb* SET, place; wait
   (for game) 22₂/240; *sett abo̅ute*
   decorate 28/4042; ~ *by* set store
   by, value; *pret* sette, sete; *pp* i-set,
   i-sæt.
sēth see sē(n).
seþen, seþthe, seþþe see siþen.
seuretee *sb* SURETY.
sevyn, seve, sövene *number* SEVEN.
sexte *number* SIXTH.
sh- see also sch-.
shadewe *sb* SHADOW.
shæwen see schewe(n).
shal, schall, sall *perf pres vb* I must,
   I am obliged, I am to, I shall, will;
   am about to 12/586; future aux. in
   all persons; *pres 1 sg* ssel 15/30,
   2 sg shalt, sselt 15/20, *3 sg* ssolle
   15/25, *pl* shole, scholle, shul, shul-
   (l)en, ssolle 15/24, sćulen 2/20.
   pret sholde, sholden, shuld(e),
   schulde, suld(e), solde 2/51, 6/975.
shāme see schāme¹.
shāpe(n), schāpe, shappe *str vb 6*
   SHAPE, create, form; (*refl*) arrange
   18/1210, clothe, dress 21,/2; *pret*
   shǫǫpe, schǫp; *pp* y-shapen.
shāve *str vb 6* SHAVE; *pp* shāve.
shēf, schēf *sb* SHEAF; *pl* shēves.
sheynd see schēnde.
shēp(e), ssēp 15/13 *sb* SHEEP.
shepard *sb* SHEPHERD.
shette(n) *wk vb* SHUT.
chew see schewe(n).
shir see schir.
1. shō *sb* SHOE; *pl* sho(o)n 21₃/18,
   24/23.
2. shō see schē.
sholde, shole see shal.

shǫme see schāme.
shön see shō[1].
shónye *wk vb* SHUN.
shoon see shō[1].
shǫǫpe see shāpe(n).
shortly *adv* SHORTLY, in brief.
shrew(e) see schrewe.
shryne *wk vb* enclose (relics) in a
 shrine. SHRINE.
shul, shuld see shal.
shulder, schoͧulder, shólder *sb* SHOUL-
 DER; *pl* shuldres, shuldre 13₅/26.
shulen see shal.
sī see bē(n), þe[1].
sibbe, sybbe *sb* 1. family 2/34, 16/21.
 — 2. peace 6/1005. [*Sib*[1]].
sic, syche, sich(e) see swich.
siǧǧe see seye(n).
sīde *sb* SIDE; *pl* sīden 3/95.
si₃(e) see sē(n).
sy₃t, siht, sihðe, zy₃þe *sb* SIGHT[1];
 looking 3/3, 33, 4/6.
sih see sē(n).
siht, syht see sy₃t.
sihðe see sy₃t.
sȳk *sb* SIGH.
sykel *sb* SICKLE.
sȳke(n), sīke(n) *wk vb* SIGH.
siker, sekyre, zyker *adj* sure, faithful,
 SECURE; *by* ⁓ assuredly 4ᴀ/12.
 [*Sicker*].
sikerlīche *adv* surely, SECURELY.
 [*Sickerly*].
sykernes(se) *sb* SECURENESS, cer-
 tainty. [*Sickerness*].
siknesse *sb* SICKNESS.
sylver, selver *sb* SILVER.
symphonīe *sb* music. [SYMPHONY].
syn, syne *conj* since. [*Sin*]. Cp. *sen,
 siþen.*
sinden see bē(n).
syne see syn, synne[1].
singe(n), synge(n), singin *str vb 3a*
 SING; *pret sg* sǫng, sǫǫng, sunge, *pl*
 sóngen, sungen; *pp* sónge.
sinke *str vb 3a* SINK.
1. synne, sinne, syne, senne, sünne,
 zenne, zen *sb* SIN; *pl* sünnen 10/177.
2. synne, sünegi *wk vb* SIN.
sīre, sȳre *sb* SIRE, SIR, mister, father.
sitte(n), syt *str vb 5* SIT; beach (a
 ship) 12/735; be situated; *pret*

sot, sæt, sette, set, *pl* sēten; *pres
 part* sittende 1/46; *pp* sitte, set,
 sittyn.
siþ see sē(n).
1. sȳthe *sb* SCYTHE.
2. sīþe, sȳþe *sb* time, occasion. [*Sithe*[1]].
siþen, syþen, sytthen, syþyn, sith(e),
 seþthe, seþþe, seþþen, seoððen,
 süþthe 1. *adv* then, after that. —
 2. *conj* since, since then. [*Sithen*]
 Cp. *sen, syn.*
syxe *number* SIX.
skärd *pp adj* SCARED.
skawde *sb* foul-mouthed woman,
 SCOLD 29/596.
skentinge *sb* entertainment 6/986.
 [*Skenting*].
skēre, scēre *adj* purified, clean; in ⁓
 þorsday SHEER THURSDAY, Maundy
 Thursday in Holy Week 13₃/1.
 [SHEER, *Skere*].
skyl(e), skyll, scele *sb* reason, intelligence, SKILL, cause; *bi þis* ⁓ in
 this fashion 18/1296, *for þys* ⁓ for
 this reason 14/87.
slā see slę̄(n).
slad(e) *sb* valley, SLADE[1] 18/1159.
slæn, slayn see slę̄(n).
slake *wk vb* grow weak 13₅/83, SLACK.
slane, slast see slę̄(n).
slāwen *wk vb* neglect, be slow in 2/37
 (cp. OE *slāwian* 'id'). [SLOW].
slę̄(n), slę̄ę(n), slæn, slā, slǫ *str
 vb 6* SLAY[1], strike down, ⁓ *with
 strenythe* kill by violence 27ᴀ/351.
 pres 2 sg slāst 15/49; *pret* slouh,
 slough, slou, slowe, *pl* slowen; *pp*
 y-slayn, y-slawe, i-slein 3/82, slayn,
 slāne.
sle₃ly see slȳly.
slentyng *sb* oblique flight 18/1160.
 [*Slent* v[1]].
1. slēp(e), sleep *sb* SLEEP; *a* ⁓ ASLEEP.
2. slēpe *str vb 7* (*but mostly wk in
 these texts*) SLEEP; *pret* slepte,
 slēped, slēp(e).
slēper *sb* SLEEPER.
slēte *sb* SLEET.
sleu₃þe *sb* sloth. [*Sleuth*[1]].
slȳde *str vb 1* SLIDE; *pret* slǭde.
slider *adj* slippery 6/956, [*Slidder*].

slȳly, sleȝly *adv* SLYLY, skilfully, carefully.
slypę *wk vb* SLIP¹.
slyttyng, slyting *adj* piercing 26/60
[SLITTING].
slǫ see slę̄(n).
slǫde see slȳde.
slómeryng(e) *sb* SLUMBERING.
slou, slough, slouh, slowe(n) see
slę̄(n).
smac *sb* taste 15/44. [SMACK¹].
smacky *wk vb* taste, savor 4ᴀ/6.
[SMACK¹, *Smake*]. Cp. *smake*.
smæt see smȳte(n).
smāke *wk vb* taste, give off flavor,
pret pl smauȝte. [SMACK¹, *Smatch*].
Cp. *smacky*.
smal *adj* SMALL.
smāt see smȳte(n).
smauȝte see smāke.
smertly *adv* SMARTLY, with force.
smīke *sb* smoke. [*Smitch*¹].
smylle *wk vb* SMELL 29/549.
smȳte(n) *str vb 1* SMITE; *pret* smǫǫt,
smǫt, smāt, smæt.
smǫke *sb* SMOKE. Cp. *smike*.
smǫǫt, smǫt see smȳte(n).
smōth *adj* SMOOTH, soft.
snel *adj* quick, fast 6/918 [*Snell*].
snou *sb* SNOW.
snōwte *sb* SNOUT¹.
sǫ̇, sǭ, să, se *adv* so, thus, also; *sone*
⁓ as soon as; (in wishes) as 10/
130, 149; as if 12/589; like, as
6/946. Cp. *swā*.
sōberly *adv* sincerely, SOBERLY 18/
1278.
sódeynly *adv* SUDDENLY.
sófforyng *sb* SUFFERING, putting up
with.
softe *adj* SOFT.
sǭ-gat *adv* thus, in this manner 17/93.
[*So-gate*].
soȝte see sēke².
soyn(e) see sōne.
sojūrne *wk vb* SOJOURN, remain.
solace, solas *sb* pleasure ⁓ *sette* have,
find pleasure 18/1318, ⁓ *māke*
have some fun 14/Introd.
solde see shal, selle.
solempne *adj* ceremonial, dignified,
splendid. [SOLEMN].

sölf see self.
solsecle *sb* marigold.
sómdę̄l(e), sumdę̄l *adv* somewhat.
[*Somedeal*].
sóm(e), sómme, sum, summe, sǭum,
sǭumme 1. *adj* and *indefinite pron*
SOME, some one, certain one, they;
som . . . som this/that . . . these/
those. — 2. *conj* as, *forþriht* ⁓ as
soon as 7/3342.
sómer *sb* SUMMER¹.
somet *adv* together 3/59. [*Samed*].
sómonōur *sb* officer who cites persons
to appear in ecclesiastical courts,
SUMMONER 27₄ᴀ/673.
sómpne *wk vb* summon. [*Sompne,
Somne²*].
sómtȳme *adv* SOMETIME ago.
1. sǫnd *sb* SAND².
2. sōnd *sb* SOUND¹, branch of the sea
12/708.
sǫnd(e) *sb* envoy, messenger; *pl*
sǫnden 3/58. [*Sand¹*].
sóndry, sóndri *adj* various, SUNDRY.
sōn(e), soyn *adv* SOON, right away,
immediately; ⁓ *so* as soon as;
compar sōnner.
sōne, sónn, sune *sb* SON.
1. sǫng *sb* SONG.
2. sǫ̇ng, sónge, sóngen see singe(n).
sonn see sōne, sónne.
sónne, són(n), sunne *sb* SUN.
sōnner *compar* see sōn(e).
sǫǫng see singe(n).
soot *sb* SOOT¹.
sooth see sōth³.
soothly see sōthly.
sop *sb* light meal, a bit 18/1135.
[SUP].
1. sǫper *sb* soap-merchant or maker.
[SOAPER].
2. sóper *sb* SUPPER.
sorcerie *sb* SORCERY.
sǫre, sāre *adv* SORE¹, sorely, a lot,
bitterly; much 3/111.
sorghe, sorȝe see sorwe.
sǫry, sǫri, sāry, sāri *adj* SORRY, sad;
bad, unfortunate.
sorwe, sorow, sorghe, sorȝe, serewe
sb SORROW.
sorwful *adj* SORROWFUL.

soster, süster *sb* SISTER: *pl* süster 3/16, süstren 3/24.

sóstyeni *wk vb* SUSTAIN 15/68.

sot *adj* stupid, foolish [*Sot* (3B)].

sótyle, sótyll see subtil.

sotlíče *adv* foolishly 1/4. [*Sotly*].

1. sōþ, sōð, sōuthe, zōþ *sb* truth, SOOTH; *tō sōðe* in truth, for sure 5/13995, *vor zōþe* in truth 4ₐ/23, *bi þe sōuthe* id. 21₄/336.

2. sōþ see sē(n).

3. sōth, sōþ, sōð, sooth, sōuth, zōþ *adj* true 4/7, 5/26; ~ *tō seyn* to tell the truth, *for* ~ indeed, in truth. [SOOTH].

sōðfest *adj* sincerely true 5/31. [*Soothfast*].

sōthly, soothly, sōthely *adv* truly. [*Soothly*].

sōþ-saʒe *sb* true saying, proverb 6/1038. [*Soothsay*].

sóthren, sōuþeron *adj* SOUTHERN; deceitful, fancy court (speech)? 29/215. [*Southron*].

sōðð en see siþen.

soule, saule, sawle *sb* SOUL.

soule-cnül *sb* passing bell, death knell 10/251. [*Soul-knell*].

sōum, sōumme see sóm(e).

sōun *sb* SOUND³, tone.

sōunyng *sb* SOUNDING¹, replete with.

sōure *adv* SOUR.

sōuteresse *sb* female shoemaker? or shoemaker's wife. [*Souter*, -ESS¹].

sōuthe see sōþ¹, ³.

sōuþeron see sóthren.

sövene see sevyn.

sóvereygne *adj* SOVEREIGN, good anywhere and for anything.

sowe *wk vb* SEW.

sowe(n) *str vb* 7 SOW¹; *pret pl* sowen 2/20.

sowynge *sb* SOWING¹.

sōwme *sb* SUM¹, number.

sōwnen *wk vb* SOUND¹, resound.

sōwre *sb* four year old deer. [SORE²].

spāce *sb* moment, time; *in* ~ right away 18/1199.

spǣche see spēche.

spak̃, spac, spakk see spēke(n).

spāre *wk vb* show mercy, forbearance 17/16. [SPARE¹ (2)].

spealie *wk vb* SPELL² 4/21.

spec, spek see spēke(n).

spēche, spǣche *sb* SPEECH¹.

sped see spēde².

1. spēde *sb* success. [SPEED].

2. spēde *wk vb* succeed; make succeed, benefit; (reflexive) hasten, SPEED; *pret* sped.

spēdely *adv* SPEEDILY, fast.

spēke(n) *str vb* 4 SPEAK; *pret* spak(k), spek, spec, spac; *pp* spōke, spēken.

spēkyng *sb* SPEAKING, discourse.

spell(e) *sb* word, instruction 7/3657. [SPELL¹].

spelle(n) *wk vb* explain, recite, tell. [SPELL¹].

spellinge *sb* story, enumeration. [*Spelling*¹].

spēnde(n) *wk vb* SPEND¹, dispense; *pp* i-spent 2/28.

spēnding *sb* money to spend. [SPENDING].

spēndōur *sb* big SPENDER², spendthrift 21₃/28.

spēre *sb* SPEAR¹.

sperhauk *sb* sparrow-hawk. [*Sparhawk*].

spylle, spille *wk vb* destroy; *pp* i-spild [SPILL].

spille-tӯme *sb* time waster, loafer. [SPILL-TIME].

spōke see spēke(n).

spotty *adj* SPOTTY, stained.

spraule(n) *wk vb* SPRAWL.

sprēden *wk vb* SPREAD; *pp* i-spread.

sprynge(n), springe *str vb* 3a SPRING¹; ~ *up* grow; *pret* sprōng, sprāng; *pp* i-sprunge.

sprōng see sprynge(n).

sprüten *wk vb* sprout 3/153. [*Sprit*].

spūme *sb* SPUME, foam.

spure *sb* SPUR¹.

sputing* *sb* disputing 6/875. [*Spute*¹].

srift see schrifte.

srīve see schrīven.

ssāme see schāme¹.

sseawy see schewe(n).

ssel, sselt see shal.

ssēp see shēpe.

ssipe see schyp(pe).

ssolle, ssoldest see shal.

staal see stẹ̄le(n).

stābylnes *sb* STABLENESS, stability 16/44.

stablye *sb* group of beaters 18/1135. [*Stably*].

stablyng *sb* STABILISATION. [*Stabling*[1]].

stad *pp* in an exposed position 22₂/425. [STEAD *v*].

staf(fe) *sb* STAFF[1]; *pl* stāves.

stayr *adj* steep 19/1022. [*Stair*].

stāle *sb* rung, row, step 19/1022. [*Stale*[2]].

stalke(n) *wk vb* STALK[1].

stalwȯrtly *adv* valiantly. [*Stalworthly*].

stāne-dẹ̄d *adj* STONE-DEAD, cp. STONE *sb* (19).

stant see stonde(n).

stārinde *pres part* STARING 12/508.

stark *adj* STARK, strong, powerful.

starne *sb* star. [*Stern*[2]].

stāþe *sb* river-bank 5/4. [STAITHE].

stāves see staf.

steal *sb* place, state 4/3. [STALL[1]].

1. stēde *sb* STEED, battle-horse.

2. stẹde, stide, stüde *sb* place. [STEAD].

stẹ̄defæst *adj* STEADFAST.

stẹ̄defæstlīche *adv* STEADFASTLY.

steyll, stel see stēle, stẹ̄le(n).

stēle, steyll *sb* STEEL[1]; *trew as* ~ true as steel 29/226.

stẹ̄le(n), steyll *str vb 4* STEAL[1]; ~ *away* escape; *pret* staal, stel; *pp* stọllyn.

stem *sb* stalk, ray, burst? of light 12/591.

stēne *wk vb* stone a person 13₃/8; *pret* stēnde. [STEEN].

stente(n), stynte(n) *wk vb* stop, cease. [STINT].

stēre, stürien *wk vb* STIR.

sterlynge *sb* STERLING.

sterre *sb* STAR[1].

sterre-liht *sb* STAR-LIGHT.

sterte, stirte *wk vb* START, leap, jump, leave; *pret* stirte 12/566.

sterve(n) *str vb 3b* die; *pret 2 sg* storve 10/151; *pl* storven, sturven 1/48. [STARVE].

steven(e), stevyn *sb* voice. [*Steven*[1]].

stide see stẹde.

stīe *str vb 1* climb; *pret* styh [*Sty*[1]].

stif *adj* strong. [STIFF].

styh see stīe.

stikke *sb* STICK[1], branch.

styll, still *adj* STILL.

stilly *adv* silently 18/1191. [STILLY].

stynke *str vb 3a* STINK; *pret* stonk.

stynte(n) see stente(n).

stirte see sterte.

stiward, stuard *sb* STEWARD, regent 12/666.

stywe *sb* brothel, STEW[2].

stōd(e) see stonde(n).

stọken *pp* barricaded, closed 19/1065. [Cp. *Steek* v[1]].

stọllyn see stẹ̄le(n).

stọn *sb* STONE.

stonde(n) *str vb 6* STAND; exist 2/18; go (out of) 12/591. *pres 3 sg* stant 7/33; *pret sg* stōd(e), *pl* stonden.

stọnye *wk vb* ASTONISH. [*Stony*].

stonk see stynke.

stoole *sb* STOLE, church vestment.

stȯr *adj* severe 18/1291. [*Stour*].

stȯrie *sb* legend of a saint, set of lessons from the breviary 27₄ₐ/709 note. [STORY[1]].

storke *sb* STORK.

storve(n) see sterve(n).

stott *sb* young steer, bullock 29/518. [*Stot*].

stọ̄unde *sb* moment. [STOUND[1]].

stọ̄upe *wk vb* STOOP.

stọ̄ut *adj* majestic, noble 13₅/38.

strāk see strȳke(n).

strākande *pres part* sounding (on the horn) 18/1364. [Cp. *Strake* v[2]].

strang see strọng.

1. strānǧe *adj* STRANGE; foreign 26/8.

2. strānǧe *wk vb* become strange 28/4103.

strāte see strēt(e).

strecche(n) *wk vb* STRETCH; *pret* strehte.

strehte see strecche(n).

streyne *wk vb* STRAIN[1].

strẹme *sb* STREAM of light.

streng *sb* STRING, cord.

strenger see strong.

strenghe *sb* force. [*Strength*].

strengðe *sb* force, STRENGTH.

strēt(e), strāte *sb* STREET.
strīf *sb* fight 15/75, STRIFE.
strīke *sb* STRIKE (2) of hair, skein.
strȳke(n) *str vb* 1. STRIKE. — 2. ⁓
　forth move forward; *pret* strāk,
　strǭke.
striplynge *sb* STRIPLING, youth.
strógele(n) *wk vb* STRUGGLE.
strǭke see strȳke(n).
strǫng, strang 1. *adj* STRONG; *compar*
　strenger. 2. *adv* STRONG.
strūcyō *sb* ostrich (explained by error
　as stork) 16/45. [*Strucion*].
stuard see stiward.
stǖde see stę̄de².
stūrien see stēre.
sturven see sterve(n).
subtil, sótyll, sótyle, sutel *adj* SUBTLE,
　tricky.
subtilly *adv* SUBTLY, with skill, clever-
　ness.
such(e) see swich.
sǖcre *sb* SUGAR.
sucūre, sucūrīe *wk vb* SUCCOUR; *pres
　subj 3 sg* sucuri 9/17.
sucūrs *sb* SUCCOUR.
suddandly *adv* SUDDENLY.
suenćten see swenche(n).
suēte, suētyng, suētly, suētnesse see
　swēte², swēting, swētly, swētnesse.
suffisant *adj* SUFFICIENT, competent.
suffre *wk vb* SUFFER, put up with,
　allow.
sü̆ǧǧe see seye(n).
suich, suilć see swich.
suīke see swīke².
suȳre see swȳre.
suȳ̆e see swīthe.
suld(e) see shal.
sülf see self.
sülle(n) see selle.
sulphre *sb* SULPHUR.
sumdę̄l see sómdę̄l(e).
sum(me) see sóm(e).
sumwhȳle, sumewhüle *adv* sometime.
　[SOMEWHILE].
sunderlę̄pes *adv* separately 4/24.
sunderlīche *adv* separately 4/27.
　[*Sunderly*].
sune see sóne.
sünegi see synne².

sünfull *adj* SINFUL (used as *sb*)
　6/891.
sunge(n) see singe(n).
1. sunne see sónne.
2. sünne see synne¹.
sunnebę̄m *sb* SUNBEAM.
sunneglēam *sb* SUNGLEAM 4/41.
sünnen see synne¹.
suǫren see swę̄re(n).
suōte see swēte².
supprīse(n) *wk vb* SURPRISE.
sūr *adj* SOUR.
suspówse *sb* SUSPICION, supposition.
　[*Suspose*].
süster, süstren see soster.
sutel see subtil.
sūþ *sb* SOUTH.
süþthe see siþen.
suwen *wk vb* follow, accompany, pur-
　sue. [SUE].
swā, zuǭ 15/18 *adv* so, thus, also.
　Cp. sǭ.
swange see swinge.
swāre *adj* SQUARE 19/1023, 1029.
swart *adj* SWART, black.
swā-sum *conj* as 7/10. [Cp. *Sum* rel
　adj].
swedyll *wk vb* SWADDLE.
swefnynge *sb* dream. [*Swevening*].
sweye *wk vb* SWAY and fall 20/716.
swelt(e) *wk vb* die 20/716, 29/525.
　[SWELT].
swenche(n) *wk vb* oppress (by forced
　labor) 1/17.
swērd(e), swēōrd *sb* SWORD.
swę̄re(n), swę̄rien, zuę̄rie *str vb* 6
　SWEAR; *pp* swōr(e)n, i-swōren,
　suōren.
1. swę̄te *wk vb* SWEAT.
2. swēte, suēte, swōte, suōte *adj*
　SWEET.
swētelīche, swōtelīche *adv* SWEETLY.
swēting, suēting *sb* sweet-heart.
　[SWEETING¹].
swētly, suētly, swētelīche *adj* SWEET-
　LY, SWEET.
swētnesse, suētnesse, swēttnes *sb*
　SWEETNESS.
sweven(e) *sb* dream. [*Sweven*].
swich, swych, suich, zuych, swylk,
　suilć, swilc, swilk, sich, sych, sic,
　swüch, swulc, such 1. *adj* and *pron*

SUCH; ᴖ *seven* seven times as much 27₁/408. — 2. *conj* as if 5/14005, 14011, 6/976.

swift, zuyft *adj* SWIFT.

1. swīke *wk vb* stop, cease.

2. swīke, suīke *sb* traitor 1/11, 12/ 551, 626. [*Swike*¹].

swīkedom *sb* treason.

swikele *adj* false, perfidious. [*Swikel*].

swilk, swylk see swich.

swȳn, swīn, zuȳn 15/5 *sb pl* SWINE 12/701.

swinc see swinke¹.

swynge *str vb 3a* SWING, flow 19/ 1059; *pret* swange.

1. swinke, swinc *sb* work, trouble, pain. [*Swink*].

2. swynke, swink *str vb 3a* labor, work; *pret pl* swȯnken. [*Swink*].

swȳre, suȳre *sb* neck and shoulders. [SWIRE].

swīthe, swīŏe, swȳþe, swīþe, suȳŏe 1. *adj* big, strong. — 2. *adv* fast; very. [*Swith*].

swoghe, swough *sb* rustle, murmur. [*Swough*].

swoȝning see swȯūnyng.

swȯnken see swynke².

swȯr(e)n see swẹre(n).

swȯte see swẹte².

swȯtelīche see swẹtelīche.

swȯūne(n) *wk vb* SWOON.

swȯūnyng, swoȝning *sb* SWOONING.

swüch, swulc see swich.

T

t' elided form of tō before vowel.

tā, taak(e) see tāke(n).

tābelment *sb* foundation stone, TABLE-MENT 19/994.

tāble *sb* horizontal course of stone, apparently 'rise' and 'step' in 19/ 1004. [TABLE (12a)].

tācnen *wk vb* mean, stand for 7/3634. [TOKEN].

tæchen see tẹche(n).

tær see þer¹.

taght see tẹche(n).

tayl, taile *sb* TAIL¹.

tayles *sb pl* notches (on stick), TALLY of deer slain 18/1377.

tayse *wk vb* hunt, force, tease 18/ 1169. [*Teise²*].

tayt *adj* in good state 18/1377. [*Tait*].

tāke(n), taak(e), tā *str vb 6* TAKE; touch 15/59; rebuke 9/10; *imperative* tās; *pret* tōc, tōk(e), tūk, tākyd; *pp* i-tāke, tān, tāken 7/7.

tāken see tọkyn.

takles *sb pl* TACKLE, equipment, lines.

tālde see telle(n).

1. tāle *sb* TALE (1), story; count, enumeration 19/998, TALE (2).

2. tāle *wk vb* speak, tell.

talȯūn *sb* TALON, claw 20/800.

tān see tāke(n).

tarie(n) *wk vb* TARRY.

tās see tāke(n).

tauhte see tẹche(n).

tat see þat¹.

taughte see tẹche(n).

tavernēr, tavernyer *sb* TAVERNER, tavern-keeper.

te see tō, þe¹, thȯu.

tẹche(n), tæchen *wk vb* TEACH, show; learn 15/76; *pres 3 sg* tekþ 15/73, 76; *pret* taughte, tauhte, taght; *pp* y-tauȝt.

tegædre see tōgedre.

teȝ see þei.

teyn see tēne².

tekþ see tẹche(n).

telle(n) *wk vb* 1. TELL. — 2. count 28/4133. — 3. be taken account of 26/25, be thought of (+ *of*) 20/813; *pp* estimated 17/77; *pret* tọlde, tālde; *pp* tọọld, tọ̄ld, y-tọ̄ld.

temptatiūn *sb* TEMPTATION.

tẹ̈n *number* TEN.

1. tēne, tyẹne *sb* distress; suffering 12/729, 13₄/8, spite 14/4084, disquiet 4ₐ/2. [*Teen*¹].

2. tēne, teyn *wk vb* pursue 18/1169, trouble 29/218, bother 29/636. [*TEEN*¹].

tenȯūn *sb* TENON which fits a mortise to make a firm joint 19/993.

tenserīe *sb* land tax paid for feudal protection 1/43. [*Tenser, -ie*].

1. tẹre *str vb 4* TEAR¹, rip.

2. tẹre *wk vb* TAR¹ 12/707.

3. tẹre *sb* TEAR¹.

terestre *adj* TERRESTRIAL 15/14. [*Ter-restre*].

t'ēve *adv* yesterday evening (OE *tō ēfen*) [TO + EVE¹].

1. **tȳde** *impersonal wk vb* return; fall to one's share 18/1396. [TIDE¹].

2. **tȳde, tīde** *sb* time, hour, TIDE, *atte mydnyht* ∼ at midnight 28/3961; *þat* ∼ then 18/736; *dat sg* **tīden** 5/13997.

tīdinge *sb* TIDING(s), news 5/13998.

tyēne see **tēne¹**.

tyffe *wk vb* put in order, get ready. [*Tiff¹*].

ty3t *wk vb* describe 19/1013, 1053; *pret* **ty3te**; *pp* **ty3t**. [*Tight²*].

til, till 1. *prep* to, TILL — 2. *conj* UNTIL.

tile(n) *wk vb* TILL¹, cultivate 1/46.

tȳm(e), tīme *sb* TIME; *þat* ∼ *þat* at the moment when 7/3610, 3626, while 20/810; *to* ∼ until 17/6.

tȳmely *adv* TIMELY.

tȳne *wk vb* lose; suffer deprivation of; infect, ruin 20/770; *pp* **tynt**. [*Tine²*].

tynkere *sb* TINKER.

tynt see **tȳne**.

tirven *wk vb* pull off (a shirt) 12/603. [*Tirve¹*].

tȳte *adv* fast, rapidly. [*Tite*].

tȳthyng, tīþinge *sb* TIDING(s) 6/1035, 29/199. (<ON *tiðindi*).

1. **tǫ̆, te** 1. *prep* TO, during 5/14046; *for* ∼ in order to (before infin or gerund). — 2. *conj* until 29/279; ∼ *that* id. 29/280, as 7/3363.

2. **tō** *adv* TOO.

3. **tō** see **þe¹**.

4. **tō-** as prefix 'apart' or intensifier. TO-.

tō-brēke *str vb 4* BREAK up 13₃/11; *pret* **tō-brac** 5/14021. [*To-break*].

tō-brǫde *pp* pulled apart 6/1008. [Cp. *To-braid*].

tōc see **tāke(n)**.

tō-clēve *str vb 2* split apart 15/8. [*To-cleave*].

tō-dai, tō-day, tō-da3, te-day *adv* TODAY.

tō-dēle(n) *wk vb* split up; *pret* **tōdēld** 1/4. [*To-deal*].

tō-drawe(n) *str vb 6* pull apart; *pret* **tōdrōh** 5/14019. [TO-DRAW].

tō-ę̄ven *wk vb* equal 19/1073.

tō-fylche *wk vb* throw down, seize fiercely 18/1172. [?].

tōfǫre, tofǫren *prep* and *adv* before.

toft *sb* height 21₁/14.

tōgedre, tōgedyr, tōgederes, tōgidre(s), tōgedyr, tegædere, tōgadere *adv* TO-GETHER.

tō-3eines *prep* against. [*To-gains*].

tō-hir-warde *adv* towards her 18/1200. [Cp. -WARD *suffix* (4 ff.)].

toyne see **tǫne**.

tǫk(e) see **tāke(n)**.

tǫkyn, tāken *sb* sign, miracle 7/3363. [TOKEN].

tō-kirke-ward *adv* towards church 21₄/305. [Cp. -WARD *suffix* (4 ff)].

tǫkninge *sb* sign, proof, TOKENING 15/6.

tǫlde see **telle(n)**.

tōm *adj* empty [*Toom*].

tō-morne, tō-more3e, tō-morwen *adv* tomorrow. [*To-morn*].

tǫne, toyne *sb* TONE, tune; *out of* ∼ out of tune.

tǫnge, tunge *sb* TONGUE; stinging appendages 20/821.

tō-niht *adv* last night 5/14006. [TO-NIGHT].

tǫǫ *sb* TOE.

tǫǫld see **telle(n)**.

tǫǫn *adj* and *pron* one, in *þe tǫǫn* the one, this one. [*Tone*].

tóórd see **tórde**.

topasye *sb* TOPAZ 19/1012.

toppe *sb* TOP¹ of the head 20/801.

tor *adj* difficult 18/719.

tō-rāce *wk vb* pull down or tear apart 18/1168.

tórde, tóórde *sb* TURD.

tō-renden *wk vb* tear up, REND apart; *pret* **tō-rente**. [*To-rend*].

tórn *sb* TURN, service.

tórne, turne *wk vb* TURN; translate; *pp* **i-turnd** transformed.

tō-snǣden *wk vb* cut to pieces 5/14026; *pret* **tō-snadde**. [Cp. *Snath*].

tō-spredde *wk vb* stretch, undo; *pp* **tō-sprad**. [TO-SPREAD].

tō-sumne *adv* together 5/31. [Cp. *To-same*].

tō-tęre *str vb 4* tear to pieces. [*To-tear*].

tōtunge *sb* looking 3/1. [Cp. *Toot* v¹].

tōthere, tōthir, tōuþer *adj* and *pron* OTHER in *the tōthere* the other, that one. [*Tother*].

tōu see thōu.

tōun, tōwne, tūne *sb* TOWN, village, farm, farmyard 24/9, 29/492.

tōur *sb* TOWER, castle.

tōuþer see tōthere.

tōwardes, tōwart *adv* TOWARD, TO-WARDS.

tōwch *sb* allusion, hint 18/1301. [TOUCH].

tōwche *wk vb* TOUCH.

1. traist *wk vb* expect (*of*) 17/58.

2. trayst *adj þat be ȝe* ~ be sure of that 18/1211. [*Traist*].

traytōur, traitur *sb* TRAITOR.

1. travaile, traveile, travayle *sb* trouble, pain, TRAVAIL¹.

2. travaile, traveile, travayle *wk vb* 1. labor, TRAVAIL. — 2. TRAVEL.

trawe see trowe.

trē, tree, treo *sb* TREE.

tręde(n) *str vb 4* TREAD, walk; trample; *pp* trǫden.

treo see trē.

treothe see treuthe.

treowe see trew(e).

treowþe see treuthe.

tręsōr *sb* TREASURE.

tręsōun *sb* TREASON.

trespas *sb* TRESPASS, sin, fault.

trespasse *wk vb* TRESPASS, commit sin.

tresse *sb* TRESS.

tressōur *sb* coiffure. [TRESSURE].

treuthe, treuþe, treowþe, treothe, trowth(e), trouthe *sb* TRUTH, faith, *by my* ~ by my faith; fidelity, allegiance.

trewe, trwee, treowe *adj* TRUE, sincere, faithful.

trewely, trewly *adv* TRULY; ~ *to tell* to tell the truth 17/4.

trȳe *wk vb* TRY (a case) 21₄/338.

trȳfle, trüfle *sb* TRIFLE.

trȳȝely *adv* perfectly 21₁/14. [Cp. *Triedly*].

trinytē *sb* TRINITY.

trīste(n), trȳst *wk vb* trust. [TRYST].

trystor, tryster *sb* hunting station 18/1146, 1170. [*Tristre*].

trǫden see tręde(n).

trómpe see trumpe.

trǫne *sb* THRONE.

trowe, trawe *wk vb* believe: be worthy of faith 29/247. [TROW].

trowth(e), trouthe see treuthe.

trüe *sb* TRUCE.

trüfle see trȳfle.

trumpe, trómpe *sb* TRUMP¹, horn.

trusse *wk vb* TRUSS; ~ *up* tie up, pack.

trwee see trewe.

tū see þōu.

tuk see tāke(n).

tūne see tōun.

tūnen *wk vb* close 4/42. [*Tine*¹].

tunge see tónge.

tuǫ see twǫ.

tūnsċipe *sb* population, villagers 1/56. [TOWNSHIP].

turf *sb* TURF; *pl* turves.

turne see tórne.

turneiment *sb* TOURNAMENT.

turnyng *sb* TURNING (*fra*) from 16/77.

tus see þus.

twā see twǫ.

tweye, tweyne, tueyne *numer adj* two, TWAIN; *gen* tweire 6/888, twere 6/991. [TWAY].

twȳes, twyys, twiȝes *numer adv* TWICE; the second time 14/4058.

twinne, twynne *adj* TWIN, double 7/3661, ~ *-how* id. 19/1012.

twǫ, tuǫ, twā *number* TWO; *dat* twǫm 6/991.

þ, TH

th', þ' *clided form of def article* the, þe.

þā, see þe¹,², thǫ.

þær see þēr¹.

þære see þe¹.

þæt see þat¹.

þæw see þewe.

þaȝ, þah see thogh.

þay, thai see þei.

thaim, thaym, thair, þeire see þei.

thāme see þei.

þāmselve *3 pl intensive pron* THEM-
SELVES.

1. þan, þanne, than(ne), thane,
þen(e), þenne *adv* and *conj* THEN;
er ⁓before 9/5; THAN 1/51, 62 etc.

2. þan, þane see þe¹.

thār see þei.

þārbȳ see þērbī.

þār(e) see thēr¹.

þāre see þe¹.

tharn *wk vb* lack, need 29/191.
[*Tharn*].

thārof see þērof.

þārtō see thēr-tō.

þās see þes¹.

1. that, þat, ðat, thatt, þæt, þet, þyt,
tat A. *demons adj* 1. THAT 12/565.
— 2. used as article; *that ǫǫn* the
one, *that ǫǫther* the other. — B. *rel
pron* THAT, who, what, which 3/2,
etc. *þat tat = þat þat* what, that
which 7/34. — C. *conj* THAT (function word introducing noun clause
3/3, etc.) so that, in order that,
since 14/4119, until 12/576, introducing exclamatory proposition 12/
571, *tō* ⁓ to the point that 1/27,
þurh ⁓ because 3/4. *þat* is added
to *when, while* etc. in ME where
ModE uses the plain form, e. g.
27₄ₐ/701, 704.

2. þat see þe¹.

þau, þauh see thogh.

1. þe, the *def article* THE; *M sg nom*
te 1/9, si 9/13, se 9/23, *acc* þane
9/10, þene 3/52, 10/113, 126 *gen*
þes 5/22, *dat* þō 9/3, 12, þā 9/16,
þan 5/10, þēne 5/29; *F acc* þā 5/15,
16, tō 9/10, *dat* þǣre 11/37, þāre
5/21, þer 3/29; *neuter nom* þat 10/
74, 76, 94, þet 3/113, *adv gen* þes
because of this 6/882, *instrumental*
þi therefore, thus, by this 6/860
[*Thy*]; *nom pl* þō 9/11, þā 1/19,
5/23, *dat* þan 11/9, 13.

2. þe, þa *relative particle* that, who
1/48, 13₂/80, 3/6, that 1/19, the
one who 2/23, 33, those who 2/19,
5/9, *þe þe* he who 3/51, 64.

3. þe, the *adv* (ModE instrumental
case) ; *the murierly* the more merrily 27₄ₐ/714, *þe bet* the better off
21₃/96, *þe ner* the nearer 13₄/13,
þe betere the better 3/53. In general this *the* = ' by so much ' in
ME and ModE.

4. thē̆, þē̆, thee, þee see thōu.

thee'ch *thee ich* see thee(n).

thee(n) *str vb 2* prosper, succeed, get
along in this world; *so thee'ch* as I
hope to prosper 27₄ᵦ/947. [*Thee¹*].

þēf, theef, þōf, þȳef *sb* THIEF; *pl*
thēves, þeeves, thēfys, þīeves.

þeȝ see þey, thogh.

þēȝe *sb* THIGH.

þeȝre see þei, þeire.

þei, þeȝ, teȝ, þay, thai *3 pl pers pron*
THEY, *poss* þeȝre 7/36, thār 22₂/409,
thair 22₂/412, þayr 18/1363, *dat-acc*
thaim 22₁/260, thāme 22₂/435,
thaym 16/2, þeȝm 7/49 THEM.

þeyȝ, þeih, þeyh see thogh.

þeire, þeȝre, thair, þayr, thār *3 pl
poss pron* and *adj* THEIR.

þeise *demons pl* THESE.

þen see þan¹.

þenche(n) see thenke(n).

þen(e) see þan¹, þe¹.

thenke(n), þenke(n), þenche(n) *wk vb*
THINK² (often reflexive) ; *pres 2 sg*
(with enclitic *te* for *þu*) þenkeste
12/578; *pret* thoght(e), thoucht,
þuȝte; *pp* i-þoht.

þen(ne), þenn, þeonne 1. *adv* THEN. —
2. *conj* THEN, when; (after compar)
THAN.

þenne see þan¹.

þēo see þō.

þēode *sb pl* nations, peoples 6/905.
[*Thede*].

þeonne see þen(ne).

þēos see þes¹.

1. thēr, þēr, þār(e), thore, þǣr, tǣr
1. *adv* THERE. — 2. *rel adv* THERE,
where 3/30, *þǣr þǣr* there where
7/3338; ⁓ *as* there where 18/731;
when 14/81.

2. þer see þe¹.

þēran see þēron(e).

þērbī, þarbȳ *adv* nearby, THEREBY.

þērbiforn *adv* before then 12/655. [*Therebefore*].

þērefter, þrefter *adv* after that, THEREAFTER.

þerf see þurfen.

þērfǫre, þārfǫre, þērvǫre *adv, conj* for that reason, THEREFORE.

þērinne, þērin, þrin *adv* in there, THEREIN.

þērof, þēroffe, thārof, þrof *adv* of, THEREOF.

þēron, þēran, þron *adv* on; from this, THEREON.

þēröute *adv* out of there, this. [THEREOUT].

þērtyll(e) *adv* there, up to there, on there. [*Theretill*].

thērtō, þārtō *adv* in addition, besides; in this, to this. [THERETO].

þērtōward *adv* towards that 3/12. [THERETOWARD].

þērvǫre see þērfǫre.

þēruppe *adv* in addition, into the bargain 8/450. [*Thereup*].

þērwhīle *conj* while 21₂/173. [*Therewhile*].

1. þes, thes, þis, this *adj* and *dem pron* THIS, THESE; *masc sg acc* þisne 5/14073, *fem acc* þeos 5/30; *dat* þisse 3/85; *pl* thise, þās 5/14, þēos 5/24, 21₂/22, þēs, 2/41, 24/30, thies 29/814, þis 21₁/44, þēse 21₂/184, þuse 21₃/66.

2. þes see þe¹.

þēsölf see þīself.

þet see that¹, þe¹.

thēves see þēf.

þew *sb* servant 7/3629, 3636, 3644, 3656. [*Theow*].

þewdom *sb* slavery, servitude. [*Theowdom*].

þewe, þæw *sb* quality, custom, excellence 6/1017, 7/3647. [THEW¹].

1. þī, þȳ, thȳ see þīn(e).

2. þi *conj* thus 6/860. [*Thy*].

3. þi see þe¹.

thider *adv* to there, THITHER, ~ *as* there where.

þiderwarde *adv* in that direction. [THITHERWARD].

þyēf see þēf.

thies see þes¹.

þīeves see þēf.

thikke 1. *adj* THICK (with *of* 27₁/418).— 2. *sb* THICKET.

thilke *demons* this 6/1038. [*Thilk*].

þīn(e), þī, þȳ, thȳ *2 sg pron* and *poss adj* THY, THINE: *gen F sg* þīre 5/14053, *dat* þīre 5/14076, 6/914.

þing *sb* affairs, business. [THING].

thinke(n), thynke(n), þinge, þünchen *wk vb* seem, appear (impers) *me þingþ* 2/5, *mē thynk* 29/503 ME-THINKS, it seems to me, *ūs thynketh* id. us 27₄ᴮ/801, *mē thoght(e)* it seemed to me 27₁/291, 345, *hym thoughte* 27₄ᴀ/682, *him þuhte* 5/4 it seemed to him. [*Think¹*].

thynne *adj* THIN.

thir *pl demons pron* these 22₂/482.

thyrde see thridde.

þīre see þīn(e).

thyrldome, threldome *sb* slavery, THRALDOM.

thirst, þürst *sb* THIRST.

þys *adv* in this way 14/4149. [THIS].

this, thise see þes¹.

þīself, þēsölf *2 sg intensive pron* THYSELF.

þisne, þisse see þes¹.

þyt see þat¹.

1. þō, thō, þeo 1. *dem pl* these, those. — 2. *3 pl pers pron* they. [*Tho*].

2. thǫ, þǫ, þā 1. *adv* then.— 2. *conj* when; þā . . . þā when . . . then 1/7. [*Tho*].

3. þō see þē¹, thōu.

thogh, þogh, thoucht, þaʒ, þau, þah, þeyʒ, þeyh, þeih, þeʒ 1. *adv* still, even 3/36.— 2. *conj* THOUGH, just because 3/26, 6/964, if.

1. þoghte *sb* THOUGHT.

2. thoght(e), thoucht, thoughte see thinke(n), thenke(n).

þǫle(n), þǫlien *wk vb* suffer. [THOLE].

þonk *sb* 1. thought, mind 5/6.— 2. THANK(S).

thore see ther¹.

thorgh, throgh, thorugh, thōurgh, þurʒ(e), þorw, thorow, þoru, þurch, þurh, þuruh *prep* THROUGH, by, by means of, because of; ~ *þat* because.

þoruhlīke *adv* THOROUGHLY, search-
ingly 12/680.

thōu, þōu, þow, þŭ, þó 15/21, tōu, tŭ
3/21, 25 2 *sg pers pron* THOU; *dat-
acc* þē, thē, þee, thee, tě 3/19.

thoucht see thogh.

þouȝt *sb* THOUGHT[1].

thōurgh see thorgh.

þōus see þus.

þōusynd, þōusent, þūsen(t) *sb* THOU-
SAND.

þóve see þēf.

þral *sb* slave, THRALL. Cp. *thryll*.

thrē, three, þrēo *number* THREE.

þrefter see þērefter.

threldome see thyrldome.

threll see thryll.

þrenǧen *wk vb* press with stones 1/31.
[*Threng*].

þrēo see þrē.

thresshewolde *sb* THRESHOLD.

threwe see throwe[2].

thrid(de), þridde, þryd, third, thyrde
number THIRD.

þrien *adv* three times 13₃/36. [*Thrie*].

þrīes, thrīes *adv* THRICE.

thryll, threll *sb* slave. [*Thrill*[2]] Cp.
þral.

þrin see þērinne.

þrinne *number* three 12/716.

þriste *adj* bold, ready 2/17. [*Thriste*].

þriste(n) *wk vb* THRUST; *pp* þrist.

þritte, þritti *number* THIRTY.

þrȳvandely *adv* in abundance, THRIV-
INGLY (based on *þrīve*).

þrīve *str vb 1* THRIVE.

þrof see þērof.

throgh see thorgh.

þron see þēron.

thrōte, þrǫte *sb* THROAT.

1. throwe *sb* moment, *a* ⁓ for a certain time 14/Introd. [*Throw*[1]].

2. throwe, threwe *str vb 7* THROW;
fall 21₄/357.

þrumme(n) *wk vb* condense, push together 5/27; *pret* þrumde. [*Thrum*[1]].

þŭ see thōu.

þuften *sb* servant, slave 3/70.
[*Thuften*].

þuȝte, þuhte see thenken, thinken.

þŭlli *indef adj* such 4/47, 48. [*Thel-
lich*].

þumbe *sb* THUMB.

þünchen see þinke(n).

þurch see thorgh.

þurfen *perf pres vb* need; *pres* þerf
2/43; *pret* þurfte 13₂/95. [*Tharf*].

þurfte see þurfen.

þurȝ(e), þurh see thorgh.

þurȝ-ūt *adv* THROUGHOUT, entirely
6/879, 880.

þürlin *wk vb* pierce 3/120; *pp* i-þürlet
3/91. [*Thirl*[1]].

þürst see thirst.

þuruh see thorgh.

þus, thus, þōus, tus *adv* THUS.

thuse see þes[1].

þūsen(t) see þōusynd.

þus-gāte *adv* in this manner, thusly.
[*Thusgate*].

thwang *wk vb* be whipped 29/211.
[THONG].

þwert-ūt *adv* entirely 7/99. [*Thwert-
out*].

U

üche, üchon see ēch.

üfel see ēvel.

ūle, ōule *sb* OWL: *dat* þ'üle to the owl
6/955.

umbepyȝt *pp* ornamented. [UMBE-
PITCH].

umstrīde *str vb 1* mount, BESTRIDE.
[*Umstride*].

umwhīle, umwīle *adv* awhile, mo-
mently. [*Umquhile*].

unbāld *adj* beaten, discouraged 5/
14080. [*Unbold*].

unbīnden *str vb 3a* UNBIND; *pret*
unbōunden.

unblendyd *pp adj* unmixed (with)
16/15. [UNBLENDED].

unblȳþe *adj* unhappy, distressed.
[*Unblithe*].

unbókele *wk vb* UNBUCKLE.

unclęne *adj* UNCLEAN.

unclǫþen *wk vb* UNCLOTHE, undress.

uncōupylynge *sb* UNCOUPLING 27₁/
377 note.

uncōupled *pp adj* not on a leash 21₂/
162, UNCOUPLED.

uncrōuned *adj* not tonsured. [UN-
CROWNED].

undēp *adj* shallow, not deep. [UN-
DEEP].

under, undur, undyre *prep* UNDER.

underfangen see underfǫ(n).

underfǫ(n), undervǫn, undervongen
str vb 7 receive, accept; *pret* underfeng 3/61; *pp* underfangen 1/2.
[*Underfo, Underfong*].

underġete(n) *str vb* 5 perceive, understand; *pret pl* underġæton 1/11.
[*Underyete*].

underling *sb* UNDERLING, subject 5/
14068.

understande(n) *str vb* 6 UNDERSTAND;
pres 3 sg ónderstant 15/69. *pret*
hǫunderstōd 10/77.

undervǫn, undervongen see under-
fǫ(n).

undirtāk(e) *str vb* 6 UNDERTAKE, take
12/644; *pret* undyrtōke, undertōk.

undur see under.

undurne *sb* third hour of day (nine
o'clock); *at hygh* ～ noon or mid-
afternoon 14/4059 [*Undern*].

un-ēðe, unnēþe, unnēth, ónnēaþe *adv*
with difficulty 15/11, 26/61; uneasy
5/14007. [*Uneath*].

unfrēly *adv* hideously 20/780. [*Un-
freely*].

unhardy *adj* fearful, UNHARDY.

unhelðe *sb* sickness 2/14. [UNHEALTH].

unhōld *adj* as *sb* enemy 2/36.

unimēte 1. *adv* immeasurably 3/57,
4/32. — 2. *adj* enormous 5/14014.

unisēle *adj* miserable 6/1004. [*Unsele*].

unitē *sb* sanctity (of spirit) 21₃/10.
[UNITY].

unker *poss 1 dual* ours (to us two)
6/993.

unkevelen *wk vb* take out a gag 12/
601. [*Unkevel*].

unlēde *adj* unhappy, miserable 6/976.

unlōuke *wk vb* UNLOCK, open 18/1201.
[*Unlouk*].

unnen *perf pres vb* grant; wish, desire, *ufel* ～ wish evil; *pret pl*
unnen. [*Unne*].

unnet *adj* vain, useless 2/5. [UNNUT].

unnēth, unnēþe see un-ēðe.

unrecheles *adj* careless, indifferent.

unryghtwȳsely *adv* UNRIGHTEOUSLY,
unjustly.

unriht *sb* legal wrong, wrong. [*Un-
right*].

unsaght *adj* unrevenged 14/4136.
[*Unsaught*].

unschāpe, unshāpe *adj* UNSHAPEN, un-
formed.

unseȝendliȝ *adj* ineffable 7/3613. [Cp.
Unsaying].

unsly *adj* unwary 18/1209. [*Unsly*].

unsode *adj* uncooked, unboiled, raw.
[UNSOD].

untellendliċ *adj* inexpressible 1/22.
[Cp. *Untelling*].

unto *prep* UNTO, towards.

unþewe *sb* evil behavior, customs 6/
1018. [*Unthew*].

unvēle *adj* horrible 6/1003. [*Unfele*].

unwerġet *adj* UNWEARIED 4/37.

unwȳs, ounwiis *adj* UNWISE, foolish.

unwrast *adj* of vile quality; ('very
wickedly' if *adv*) 12/547. [*Unwrast, Unwraste*].

unwrench *sb* sin, fault 6/872.

ŭp, ōup, hōup *adv* and *prep* (possible
adj, sb) UP.

ūpbērer *sb* supporter. [*Upbearer*].

upen see open.

upholdere *sb* second hand clothes
merchant 21₄/325. [UPHOLDER].

uplǫndysch, óplǫndysch *adj* countri-
fied, rustic 26/23, 51. [UPLANDISH].

1. upon, upo, uppen 5/4, appon, ópon
prep UPON.

2. upon see openen.

uppen see upon[1].

uprȳse *str vb 1* get up; *pret pl* uprysen. [UPRISE].

upward, ópward *adv* UPWARD.

ūr(e) see ōur(e).

1. ŭs *sb* USE.

2. ŭs see wē.

ūse(n) *wk vb* USE.

ūsselven *1 pl intensive pron* ourselves
(in an oblique case,—no longer
used in ModE), used as pl of
majesty 11/24. [Cp. SELF (A 3, 4)].

ūt see ōut(e).

ūtlēsen *wk vb* release, deliver 7/3619.
[Cp. *Outloose sb*?].

ūtrely see ōuterlīche.

ūtward *adv* OUTWARD.

ŭðe, üðen see ȳthe.

üvel see ēvel.

V

vach see wacche.
văder see făder.
væir see fair(e).
vay see wey(e)².
vaire see fair(e).
valle see falle(n).
vallynge see fallinge.
vān see fǫ¹.
vanysshe *wk vb* VANISH, fall away, decay.
vār = *wār* see bē(n).
vauntwarde *sb* vanguard. [*Vantwarde*].
veyr see fair(e).
vel see fel¹.
velaȝe see felawe.
vēld see fēld.
vẹ̄le see fẹ̄le¹.
velþe see fylþe.
ven see fen².
veng see fang.
venysōun, venesōun *sb* VENISON.
venjaunce *sb* VENGEANCE.
venymōus *adj* VENOMOUS.
vent see wēnde(n)¹.
vẹ̄ol see falle(n).
verayly *adv* VERILY, actually, truly.
vernycle *sb* VERNICLE, insignia of pilgrims who have been to Rome.
verray *adj* absolutely, really truly, VERY.
verst see first¹.
verte see ferte.
vertü *sb* VIRTUE, excellence.
verveine *sb* VERVAIN.
ves = *wes*, *was* see bē(n).
veste see faste².
vestement *sb* VESTMENT¹.
vewter *sb* keeper of deer-hounds 18/1146. [FEWTERER].
vicht see wight.
vifte see fyfþe.
vileynye *sb* VILLAINY; impropriety: *tō spẹ̄ken* ⁓ speak in a foul-mouthed manner.
vyn see wynne.
vīnd, vȳnde see fȳnde(n).
visāge *sb* face, VISAGE 28/4169.
visibely *adv* VISIBLY.
viss see fish, wȳse.
vissere see fishere.
vith see with.
vithōuten see withōute(n).

vlōd see flōd.
vǒde see wǒde.
voyded *pp adj* VOIDED, empty.
vois, voys *sb* VOICE.
vol see ful.
volk, volc see folk.
vor see for.
vorlǫre see forlēse.
vorþ see forþ.
vor-þǣn *adv* on account of this 5/14080. [*Forthon*].
vor-þī see for-þī.
voryet see forgete(n).
vorzuelȝe *wk vb* swallow up 15/55. [*Forswallow*].
vorzuẹ̄rie see forswẹ̄re(n).
vǒuche, wǒwche *wk vb* VOUCH, grant 18/1391; ⁓ *saf* guarantee, VOUCHSAFE 21₃/49.
vouh *sb* ermine 13₂/106. [*Faw*].
vǒul see fǒul(e)¹.
vox see fox.
vram see fram.
vroggen see frogge.
vrom see fram.

W

wā see wǫ¹.
wacche, vach *wk vb* WATCH, stay awake.
wẹ̄re(n), wǣron see bē(n).
way see wey(e).
way *adv* = *away*; *do* ⁓ stop, leave alone 29/580.
waik *adj* WEAK.
waykly *adv* WEAKLY, softly 20/697.
wayte, waiten, wāte *wk vb* WAIT 29/586; spy on 12/512; look 18/1186.
waytt see wite(n).
wayth *sb* venison 18/1381. [*Waith*¹].
wāke(n) *str vb 6* WAKE; look after 12/630.
wākien *wk vb* WEAKEN 5/14065.
wākyn see wākne.
wākyng *sb* WAKING, care 24/25.
wākne, wākyn *wk vb* WAKEN.
wal *sb* WALL.
walde see wille.
walden see welden.
1. wāle *adj* great, swelling, splendid 20/763.
2. wāle *wk vb* choose 18/1276, take 18/1238, discern 19/1000. [*Wale*¹].

3. wāle *interj* alas 5/14047.

walet *sb* knapsack, pack. [WALLET].

walkyn see welken.

walld see wille[1].

walle see wal.

walshe *adj* WELSH.

walter *wk vb* welter.

wan see wynne[2].

wande *sb* branch; *under* ⁓ in the woods 18/1161. [WAND].

wandren, wǫndre, wǫndrien *wk vb* WANDER.

wane, wanne see whan.

wante *wk vb* WANT.

wapnid *pp* WEAPONED, armed.

wappe *wk vb* rush, whistle 18/1161. [WAP[1]].

1. war 1. *adj* AWARE, warned. — 2. *interj* WARE! look out! (hunting cry) 18/1158.

2. war, wer *adj* worse.

wār(e) see bē(n).

1. wāre *wk vb* spend, pass (time) 18/1235. [*Ware*[2]].

2. wāre *wk vb* guard, protect. [WARE[1]].

3. wāre see whēr(e)[1].

wareine *sb* game preserve 21₂/163. [WARREN].

wāren see bē(n).

warice *wk vb* heal. [*Warish*].

wark see werk.

warld see world.

warly *adv* WARILY.

warloo *sb* impostor, traitor. [WAR-LOCK[1]].

warne *wk vb* deprive of 20/700. [*Warn*[2]].

warner *sb* game-keeper 21₄/316. [WAR-RENER].

warni *wk vb* WARN[1] 6/925.

warpe(n) *str vb 3b* throw; *pres 2 sg* warpest 3/20; *pret* weorp 3/19, warpe threw out 21₄/369. [WARP].

wārsǣ see whērsǫ.

wār-tō see whērtō.

warth, warþ see wórþe.

warþe *sb* river bank, shore 18/715. [*Warth*].

wāste *sb* uncultivated, open territory 21₂/163.

wāstūr *sb* WASTER.

wat see what, wite(n).

wate see wayte, wite(n).

water *sb* WATER; *pl* wattrez.

wattrez see water.

watz = *was* see bē(n).

wāwe see wōӡe[2].

waxe(n) *str vb 6* WAX[1], grow, become; *pret* wox, waxe, wēx; *pp* waxen.

wē *1 pl pers pron* WE; *dat-acc* ŭs, ōus US.

wēane *sb* misery, WOE. [*Wane*[3]].

wearien *wk vb* swear, curse 3/128. [*Wary*].

wēd *sb* WEED[1] 6/937.

1. wedde *sb* pledge. [WED].

2. wedde *wk vb* WED; *my wedde lorde* my wedded (legal) husband 20/700; *pp* y-wedded.

wēde *sb* clothes. [WEED[2]].

1. weder *sb* WEATHER.

2. weder see wheder.

weel see wēl[1].

weӡe, wey(e) *str vb 5* 1. lift 6/1022 — 2. WEIGH[1]; *pret* way.

wei *sb* WHEY 6/1009.

1. wey(e) see weӡe.

2. wey(e), wei, way *sb* WAY[1], road; room 3/15.

weilawei *interj* alas! [WELLAWAY].

weill, weyl(l) see wēl[1].

weytt see wet.

1. wēl, weel, weill, weyl(l) *adv* WELL.

2. wel see wēle, welle.

welcum, wilcume *adj* WELCOME.

wēlde(n), walden *str vb 3b* rule over, possess 2/2, 55, govern 5/14058. [WIELD].

wēle, wēl, *sb* WEAL[1], wealth, riches 18/1270, goods 18/1394, joy 18/1371; ⁓ *is me* happily for me 12/641.

wel-fārynge *adj* of beautiful appearance (modeled on ON cp. *bezt-farandi* 'very handsome'). [*Well-faring*].

wēli *adj* wealthy. [WEALY].

welked *adj* withered, faded, dried up.

welken, weolcen, walkyn *sb* heaven, cloud. [WELKIN].

welle, wel *sb* WELL[1], spring 6/917, 15/58.

wemme *sb* spot, blemish 19/1003. [*Wem*].

wen see wene, when.

wenche *sb* WENCH, girl.

wenchel *sb* child, baby 7/3356.
wēnde *sb* turn 18/1161 (OE *wend*),
    possibly ' path, passage ', see *wente*.
    [*Went*].
1. wēnde(n) *wk vb* go, turn and go,
    WEND, ∼ *awei* turn 3/19; translate
    7/13. *imperative* went 3/19; *pret
    sg* went, wende 5/23, vent, *pl* wen-
    ten; *pp* wend 7/13, 10/74, y-went.
2. wēnde(n) see wēne(n).
wēne, wēn *sb* hope, expectation;
    opinion 3/94, doubt? desire? 15/
    Introd. [*Ween*].
wēne(n) *wk vb* expect, believe; take
    for (*for*) 6/901; *pres 2 sg* wēnestu
    6/961; *pret sg* wēnde 5/13994, *pl*
    wēnden; *pp* i-wend. [*Ween*].
wēnestu see wēne(n).
wenge see wynge.
wenne see when.
went see wēnde(n)¹.
wente *sb* path 27₁/398. [*Went*].
weōlcne see welken.
weōre(n) see bē(n).
weōri see wēry¹.
weorld-mon *sb* man in the world, no
    one! 5/14066. [WORLD-MAN].
weorp see warpe(n).
wēpe *str vb* 7 WEEP, *pret* wēp.
wēpyn, wepne *sb* WEAPON.
wēpynge *sb* WEEPING.
wer see war².
werche(n), wirchen, wyrk(e), wòrche,
    wurche *wk vb* WORK; create, com-
    pose, do, make. *pret* wroghte,
    wrahte 3/66; *pp* y-wroght, y-wraht.
wēr(e), wēr(e)n see bē(n).
1. were *sb* man 7/3337; husband
    2/31; *in ānes weres hewe* in human
    form 7/3337. [*Were*¹].
2. wēre, wērien *wk vb* guard, protect.
3. wēre see whēr(e).
wereldshipe *sb* worldly thoughts 7/
    3646. [WORLDSHIP].
wēre(n) *wk vb* WEAR.
1. wēry, wēori *adj* WEARY; as *adv*
    20/806.
2. wery *wk vb* curse 20/699. [*Wary*].
wērye *wk vb* tire, wear out, WEARY.
wērien see wēre².
wērynesse *sb* WEARINESS.
werk, wark *sb* WORK.

werlde see world.
wēr-mid see whēr-mid.
1. werre *sb* WAR.
2. werre, werri *wk vb* WAR¹, make
    war.
werse, wurse, wòrs *compar adj* and
    adv WORSE.
werse(n), wursin *wk vb* weaken;
    WORSEN; *pp* i-wersed 11/18.
    [*Worse*].
werste, wurste *superl adj* and *adv*
    WORST.
wes = *was* see bē(n).
wesseþ see wisshe.
1. węste *sb* desert 6/1000, WASTE.
2. weste see wite(n).
wet, weytt *adj* WET.
wēte *wk vb* WET; *pret* wette.
wette see wēte.
weþer see whether.
1. wex *sb* WAX¹.
2. wēx see waxe(n).
wexe *wk vb* stuff 21₄/351. [WAX²].
whaym, whām see whō.
whan, whanne, hwan, huanne, hwon,
    wanne, wane *conj* WHEN. Cp. *when*.
whāre see whēr(e).
whārefǫre see whēr-fǫre.
wharfen *wk vb* turn out, happen, re-
    volve 7/3641. [*Wharve*].
whā-se see whō-sǫ.
what, whatt, wat, hwat, hwet, huet,
    quat, quhat 1. *interrogative* and *rel
    pron* WHAT, *what . . .* so whatever.
    — 2. *adv* like, as ∼ *for* partly on ac-
    count of . . . and of 12/635. — 3.
    interj what!
wheder, weder *adv* WHITHER.
whēl *sb* WHEEL.
whelp *sb.* puppy, WHELP.
when, whon, hwen, wen(ne), quhen,
    quen *conj* WHEN; since 3/79, 4/27.
    Cp. *whan*.
1. whēr(e), whāre, wēre, wāre,
    hwēr(e), huēr(e), quēre *adv* WHERE,
    there where, wherever 12/549, ∼ *so*
    wherever.
2. wher(e) see whether.
whēreas *rel adv* where. [WHEREAS
    (1)].
whērfǫre, whārefǫre, quērfǫre *adv*
    WHEREFORE, why.

whērmid, wērmid *rel adv* with which 10/112.

whērof, hwārof, hwērof, huērof *rel adv* concerning what 3/21, concerning which 15/3. [WHEREOF].

whēron *rel adv* on which, in which 28/4119. [WHEREON].

whērsǭ, hwerseeaver, wārsǣ *adv* and *conj* everywhere, WHERESOEVER. [WHERESO].

whērtō, wārtō, hwārtō, hwērtō, huērtō *interrogative adv* for what? why? 3/105, 4/14, 10/137, to what end 4_A/8, [WHERETO].

whērthōūrgh, whērþurʒ *rel adv* whereby 11/17. [WHERETHROUGH].

whēte *sb* WHEAT.

whether, wheþer, wher(e), huader, quhethir 1. *conj* WHETHER — 2. *interrogative adj* which.

whȳ, whī, wī, hwī *interrogative adv* WHY.

which, hwücche, huyche, whilk, wylke 1. *rel pron* who, that, WHICH. — 2. *rel adj* WHICH, *the* ~ id.

whiderward *adv* WHITHER, to where. [WHITHERWARD].

whik see quyk.

1. whīle, whȳle, wīle, quȳle, quhīll *sb* WHILE, time, moment; *sum* ~ previously 1/49-50, *ǣvre um* ~ at regular intervals 1/42, *þe* ~ *þet* during the time that 2/21, 25, *þe* ~ *þe* id 2/33, *þe* ~ id 2/35.
2. whīl(e), wīle, hwīl, quhȳll, quȳl 1. *conj* WHILE; *þe* ~ , ~ *þet* during, while. — 2. *adv* recently, a little while ago 6/1017.

whilk see which.

whīlōm *adv* in time gone by, once upon a time.

whȳls *conj* during, meanwhile. [WHILES].

whīte, whīt, quīt, quȳt *adj* WHITE.

whō, wō, huō 1. *interrogative pronoun* WHO. — 2. *indef pron* whoever 25/44; *gen* whoos; *dat-acc* huām 4_A/5, wōm 10/181, whaym 20/770, whām 13_4/40. (Not used as relative in ME, see §§ 71, 72).

whon see when.

whōsǭ, hwōsǭ, whāse, hwāse *indef pron* WHOSO(ever).

wī see whȳ.

wī-ax *sb* battle axe 6/14015. [*Wi* + AXE].

wicke *adj* WICKED, evil. [*Wick*].

wid see with.

wȳdene *adv* far and WIDE. [*Widen*].

widewe *sb* WIDOW; *gen pl* widewene 10/201.

wȳ(e) see wȳʒe.

wīes see wȳs.

wīf, wȳf, wȳff *sb* WIFE, woman; *dat sg* wȳve, *pl* wȳves.

wīfhōd *sb* womanness. [WIFEHOOD].

wight, vicht *adj* vigorous 17/87.

wyght, wyht, wiʒt(e) *sb* being, creature, person; bit, *a litel* ~ a little bit 8/503. [*Wight*].

wyghtnesse *sb* vigor [WIGHTNESS].

wȳʒe, wȳ(e) *sb* man, warrior. [*Wye*[1]].

wyht, wiʒt(e) see wyght.

wiis see wȳs.

wiit see wit[1].

wilcume see wēlcum.

wild see wille.

wilde *adj* strong, powerful 13_2/94. [*Wield*].

wȳlde 1. *adj* WILD, savage. — 2. *sb* wild animal 18/1150, 1167.

wildernisse *sb* WILDERNESS.

wile(n) see whīl(e), wille.

wylke see which.

1. wille, wilen *irreg vb* 1. desire, want to, mean to, intend to (merging into meaning 2), WILL[1]. — 2. function word "future auxiliary" in all persons. *pres* will, wil, wyle, wȯl, wȯle, wȯlle, wülle 3/26, wüle 2/34, chülle 3/75, *2 sg* wȯlt 10/244, 13_3/36 (with pronoun suffix) wiltōw, wilte 12/529, wȯltōū 10/186, wȯlte, *pl* wilen 12/732; *pret* wolde, walde 3/23, walld, wulde, *2 sg* woldest 13_2/109, *pl* wilt 14/Introd.
— Contracted negative forms: *pres* nül, nüle, nülle, nelle, *2 sg* neltōū 10/189, nülltu 6/905, *pl* nülleþ 5/14066; *pret* nalde 3/107, nulde 5/14002, *2 sg* naldest 3/80. (ModE vocable *will* is seldom a gloss for ME vocable *will*, see *OED*).

2. **wille, wyl(le)** *sb* desire (voluptuary), pleasure 10/96, (good) will, WILL¹, *at* ∼ AT WILL 18/1371, *at your* ∼ at your pleasure 18/1214, *with gōd* ∼ with good will 18/1387; tendency, disposition, *of hǫly* ∼ 14/4001.

willes *adverbial gen* voluntarily, of his own will 3/104. [Cp. WILL sb¹ (10)].

wilne *wk vb* desire.

wilte, wiltōw see wille¹.

wimmen, wymmen, wimon see wómman.

wīn, wȳn *sb* WINE.

wīnde(n) *str vb 3a* WIND¹, go, turn, roll 5/14025, *adoun* ∼ descend 10/76; wrap up 12/546, 7/3365. *pret* wǫnd; 5/14025; *pp* wōunden, wünden.

wīndeclūt *sb* swaddling clothes 7/3365. [Cp. WIND¹].

wynge, wenge *sb* WING.

wynkyng *sb* WINKING, closing the eyes.

1. **winne** *sb* joy 12/660. [*Win²*].

2. **wynne, wyn** *str vb* WIN¹; fight 22₂/441, gather, come 18/1365; *pret* wan; *pp* wónen, wónnen, wónnyn.

wyntyr *sb* WINTER.

wirchen see werche.

wyrchippe see worchyp².

wyrk(e) see werche.

wȳs, wiis, wȳss, wīes, vīss *adj* WISE, prudent.

wysdom *sb* WISDOM.

wīse, wȳse, vīss *sb* manner, WISE¹.

wysse, wisi *wk vb* guide, direct 18/739, 208/12, show 6/915, 927, 973. [*Wis¹*].

wisshe *wk vb* WISH; *pres 3 sg* wesseþ 15/33.

wiste, wyst see wite(n).

1. **wit, wiit** (10/70, 124) **wytte, witt** *sb* WIT, intelligence, cleverness, ingenious plan, ability 18/1394.

2. **wit** *1 dual pers pron* we too; I and you 5/14039, 7/7; *gen* unker 6/993. [*Wit*].

3. **wit** see with.

wite *wk vb* protect, guard. [*Wite²*].

wite(n), wyt(e) *perf pres vb* know; keep 3/138. *pres sg* wǫt, wǫǫt, wāt, *2 sg* wǫǫst, *pl* wāte 14/Introd, waytt 29/226; *pret* wiste, wyst, wüste, weste 10/238; *pres subj sg* wite 12/694, *pl* witen 11/4; *imperative 2 pl* wite 3/139. Contracted forms: ichǫt 13₅/5; negative *pres sg* nǫt, *pl* nüte 6/1010. [WIT¹].

witer *adj* clear, evident, certain 7/3363. [*Witter²*].

wyterlīche, witerlīke *adv* surely. [*Witterly*].

witnesse *sb* WITNESS, evidence.

witnien *wk vb* WITNESS, bear witness 3/99. [*Witne*].

wytte, witt see wit¹.

witunge *sb* care 3/142.

with, wyth, wiþ, wið, wid, wit, vith *prep* WITH.

wiþal *adv* besides, in addition; *forþ* ∼ right away. [WITHAL].

withdrawen *str vb 6* WITHDRAW; *pret* withdrow 12/498, 502.

wiðin *sb* soul 3/53. [*Withen*].

withinne *prep* in, WITHIN.

withōute(n), wiþōute, withōwten, withūte, wiðūte(n) 1. *adv* outside 27₁/299. — 2. *prep* WITHOUT; beyond, ∼ *ei etlunge* beyond any measure 4/29.

wiðseǧǧen *wk vb* WITHSAY, deny 3/45.

wiþstande, withstonde *str vb* stand in front of 28/3970; *pret* wiþstōd. [WITHSTAND].

wiþstōd see wiþstande.

wyþstondinge *sb* resistance. [*Withstanding*].

withtāke *str vb 6* reproach 16/9. [WITHTAKE].

with-þan *conj* on condition that 12/532 (OE *wið þam þe*). [Cp. WITH (16*b*)].

withūte, wiðūten see withōute(n).

wīve, wȳve see wīf.

wlaffyng *sb* stammering, indistinct speech 26/14. [*Wlaffe*].

wlite *sb* beauty, splendor 4/1, 9.

1. **wǫ, wǫǫ, wā** 1. *sb* WOE, misfortune. — 2. *adj* bad.

2. **wō** see whō.

1. wōd *adj* crazy. [*Wood*].
2. wǭd *sb* blue color 29/650. [WOAD¹].
wóde, wude, vóde *sb* WOOD¹, forest.
wódebȳnde *sb* WOODBINE.
wódwos *sb* *pl* forest trolls 18/721. [*Woodwose*].
woghte *sb* evil deed, wrong 14/4089. [*Wough²*].
1. wōȝe, wōwen, wōhin *wk vb* WOO, court 3/85, 8/546; *pret* wǭheđe.
2. wōȝe, wōwe, wāwe *sb* WALL 12/474, 18/1180, 19/1049. [*Wough¹*].
woh *sb* wrong 3/21. [*Wough²*].
wōheđe see wōȝe¹.
wǭhere *sb* WOOER 3/86.
wōhin see wōȝe¹.
wōhlech *sb* courting 3/58. [*Wouhleche*].
wolde see wille¹.
wǭlde(n) *sb* forest 5/14030. [WOLD].
wól(e) see wille¹.
wolf, wulf *sb* WOLF; *pl* wólves, wulves.
wóll(e) *sb* WOOL.
wólle, wólt(e), wóltōu see wille¹.
wólves see wólf.
wōm see whō.
wǭmbe *sb* belly. [WOMB].
wómman, wimon 13₂/7 *sb* WOMAN; *pl* wymmen, wimmen, *gen pl* wimmonen 5/14018.
1. won *adj* WAN, pale.
2. wǒn *sb* habitual action. [*Wone¹*].
wǭnd see wīnde(n).
1. wónder *impers wk vb* be astonished, surprised 18/1201.
2. wónder, wóndur, wunder *sb* WONDER, marvel, miracle, horror; ~ dōn do frightful things, sow terror 1/13; tō wundre cruelly, horribly; *pl* wóndres.
3. wónder, woonder, wunder 1. *adv* wonderfully, very 27₁/344, 385 etc. — 2. *adj* astonishing, marvellous 3/70.
wóndyrfull *adj* WONDERFUL.
wǭndrien, wǭndringe see wandren.
1. wón(e) *sb* dwelling, lodging(s); (same sense in *pl* wónes, wónys 18/1386, 29/526). [*Wone²*].
2. wón(e) *sb* pleasure 18/1238, multitude, host 17/37, 18/1269. [*Wone³*].

wónen, wónye, wunien *wk vb* inhabit. *pp* wóned, i-wunet accustomed. [*Won*, WONT, *Wone* adj].
wónen, wónnen, wónnyn see wynne².
wonene *adv* whence 5/8. [*Whenne*].
wónes, wónys see wón(e)¹.
wǭnie *wk vb* lament, weep aloud 6/975; *2 sg* wǭnest 6/985. [*Wone²*].
wónyeþ see wóne(n).
1. wǭning *sb* lamentation, loud weeping 6/870. [*Wone* vb²].
2. wóning *sb* dwelling-place. [*Wonning¹*].
wǭnryde *sb* pain, distress 20/707. [*Wandreth*].
wǭnunge *sb* WANING, diminution 4/4.
wǫǫ see wǭ.
woonder see wónder²,³.
wǫ(ǫ)st, wǫǫt see wite(n).
wōp *sb* WEEPING 6/865, 878, lamentation 6/986.
wórche see werche.
1. wórchip *wk vb* respect, revere, WORSHIP.
2. wórchyp, wyrchippe, wórshep *sb* honor, WORSHIP, generosity 18/1267.
wōrd, wurd *sb* WORD, message; *pl* wurdys, wōrden 11/36.
wórdle see wórld.
wǭre = were see bē(n).
wórld, wurld, werlde, wórdle *sb* WORLD.
wórldly, wurldly *adv* WORLDLY, terrestrial.
wórm(e) *sb* great serpent, dragon 18/720, 20/796. [WORM].
wórmōde *sb* WORMWOOD, (fig) bitterness 16/26.
wórpest see warpe(n).
wórs see werse.
wórshep see wórchyp².
wórþ, wurþ *adj* WORTH.
wórþe, wórthe, wurþ *str vb 3b* become; future for 'to be'; *me schal* ~ it will be with me 18/1214, ~ *as yōw lȳkez* let it be as it pleases you 18/1302, ~ *wiþ chílde* be pregnant 7/3622; *pret* warth, wurth 8/460, *pl* wurden 7/3343. [*Worth¹*].
wórthilȳche, wórhlīche, wurhlīche, wórþly *adj* noble. [*Worthily*].
wórþnesse *sb* honor. [*Worthness*].

wǭt(e) see wite(n).
wou see hō̄w.
wōūnden see wīnde.
wōwche see vōuche.
wōwe see wō3e.[2]
wōwen see wō3e.[1]
wox see waxe(n).
wrahte see werche(n).
wrang adj and adv WRONG; do ‿ be
wrong.
wrangwīse adj unjust, iniquitous 2/
48. [Wrongous].
wrappe wk vb WRAP.
wrāthe, wrātthe wb vb afflicted 18/
726; (impersonal) become angry
21₂/174. [Wrath].
wrāþþe sb WRATH 6/941, 945. Cp.
wreþe.
wreah see wrīen.
wrecche, wreche, wrecce sb and adj
WRETCH, WRETCHED, poor.
wrecched sb misery 1/50. [Wretched-
hede].
wrechidnes sb WRETCHEDNESS 16/28.
wrechyt pp adj WRETCHED, miserable.
wrẹ̄ke(n) str vb 4 avenge; pp wrǭkyn
29/615, wrẹ̄ke 13₃/12. [WREAK].
wrenche sb ruse, trick. [Wrench¹].
wrẹ̄þe sb wrath, anger. [Wrethe].
wrīen str vb 1 cover, hide 3/92; pret
wreah. [Wry¹].
writ(e), writt sb WRIT, writing, Holy
Scripture, hǭly ‿ id.
wrīte(n), wrȳte str vb 1 WRITE; pret
wrǭt, wrǭte; pp writen, i-writen,
y-write 15/Introd.
writelinge sb trilling, warbling 6/914.
[Writeling].
writt see writ(e).
wrīþe str vb 1 WRITHE¹, twist;
stretched himself 18/1200; pret
wrǭth; pp wrythen 1/27.
wroghte, wrohte see werche(n).
wrokyn see wreke(n).
wrǭng sb WRONG² 6/887.
wrǭt see wrīte(n).
1. wrǭþ, wrǭth adj WROTH, angry.
2. wrǭth see wrīþe.
wrǭþe adv angrily 6/972. [Wrothe].
wude see wȯde.
wulde see wille¹.
wulder sb glory 7/3379.

wüle see wille¹.
wulf, wulves see wȯlf.
wülle see wille¹.
wulvine sb she-wolf 12/573. [Wolfen].
wünde sb WOUND
wünden see wīnden.
wunder see wȯnder²,³.
wundyrly adv very. [Wonderly].
wunieð see wȯne(n).
wünlich adj beautiful, superb.
[Winly].
wurche see werche(n).
wurden see wȯrþe.
wurd(ys) see wȯrd.
wurhlīche see wȯrthilȳche.
wurld, wurldly see wȯrld, wȯrldly.
wurse, wurste see werse, werste.
wursin see werse(n).
wurþ see wȯrþ, wȯrþe.
wurþe sb honor 7/3375, WORTH.
wurþy adj WORTHY.
wurǭlīche adv honorably, with dignity
[Worthly].
wurþmint sb adoration 7/3379.
[WORTHMINT].
wüste see wite(n).

Y

y see ich¹.
yaf see 3eve¹.
y-by see bē(n).
y-blyssed see blissed.
y-bǭre see bẹ̄re(n).
y-bou3t see bȳe(n).
y-bōunde(n) see bȳnde(n).
y-bro3t see brynge(n).
y-chaunǧed see chaunǧe.
ych(e) see ilk¹,².
y-chǭse see chēse.
y-coyned see coyne(n).
y-cȯme see cȯme(n).
ȳdel, ȳdill, īdel adj IDLE, on ‿ use-
lessly 6/920.
ȳdyllnes sb IDLENESS.
y-dǭ see dǭ(n).
y-drȯnke see drynke(n).
yẹ̄, yẹ̄ see 3ẹ̄¹.
yēde see 3ēde.
yeer see 3ēr.
yef see 3ef¹, 3eve¹.
yēlde see 3elde.
yelowe adj YELLOW.

yēmen see ȝēmen.
yēr see ȝēr.
yẹ̄rd *sb* YARD[1], farm-yard.
y-erne *str vb 3a* run 15/12. [*Yern*].
yestenēven *adv* last night 15/27.
   [*Yesterneven*].
yeve(n) see ȝeve[1].
y-falle see falle.
1. y-fēre *sb* companion.
2. y-fēre *adv* together.
y-folowed see folwe(n).
y-foūnde see fȳnde(n).
y-globbed *pp* swallowed, gobbled.
   [*Globbe*].
ȳȝe-lyd(de), ēhelid *sb* EYELID.
y-halowed see halowe(n).
y-heyt see ȝēt(e).
y-hent see hente(n).
y-hēre see i-hēre(n).
y-hẹ̄ryed see hẹ̄rien.
y-hyerd see hēre(n).
yif see ȝef[1], yeve.
y-knowe see knowe(n).
yl *sb* ILL, harm.
ȳle sb ISLE.
y-lēave *sb* LEAVE, permission 15/4.
y-left see lẹ̄ve(n).
y-lefth see y-lẹ̄ve.
y-lēte see lēte.
y-lẹ̄ve, i-lẹ̄ve *wk vb* believe; *pres 3 sg*
   y lefth 15/19.
y-lych see i-lich.
ylk see ilk(e).
y-long *adj* belonging, due 13₄/40
   [*Along*[1], *Ylong*].
ȳlond, īlond *sb* ISLAND.
y-mād see māke(n).
y-maymed *pp* MAIMED.
y-melled see melle.
ynde *sb* indigo 19/1016. [*Inde*].
ȳne see eye.
ynence *prep* towards, in regard to
   16/21.
y-newe see y-noūgh.
y-noūgh, i-noū(h), y-nōw, innōghe,
   innōwe, y-newe, i-nōȝe, i-nōh,
   e-neuch, e-newe, onōh *adv* ENOUGH,
   ENOW.
yōde see ȝēde.
yoman see ȝoman.
yȯng see ȝȯng.

yȯngthe see ȝȯngthe.
yorne see ȝērne.
yōw see ȝē[2].
y-paid see paye.
y-passed *pp adj* PAST.
ȳren, ȳrn, īren *sb* IRON; (in *pl*)
   armor 18/729.
y-sein see sē(n).
y-served *pp adj* satisfied, content.
   [SERVE].
y-shāpen see shāpe(n).
y-slawe, y-slayn see slẹ̄(n).
ysse-ikkle *sb* ICICLE.
yt see hit.
y-tauȝt see tẹ̄che(n).
ȳthe, üðe *sb* WAVE; *pl* üðen 5/14037.
yunge see ȝȯng.
ȳvel see ēvel.
y-veld see felle(n).
yw see ȝē[2].
y-wār *adj* AWARE, warned, on guard.
y-weddide see wedde[2].
y-went see wende(n)[1].
y-wis see i-wysse.
y-wite *pret pres vb* know 15/Introd.
   [*I-Wite*].
y-wraht, y-wroght see werche(n).
y-wrīte, y-wrȳte see wrīte(n).
y-zed see seye(n).
z-zycþ, y-zyeþ see i-sēn.

Z

zayþ see seye(n).
zē see sẹ̄[1].
zech *sb* SACK[1], bag 15/17.
zecheþ see sēke[2].
zelþ see selle(n).
zen(ne) see synne[1].
zentest see sēnde(n).
ziǧǧe see seye(n).
zyȝþe see syȝt.
zyker see siker.
zōþ see sōþ[1, 3].
zuelȝ *sb* taste 15/37, gullet 15/49.
   [SWALLOW[2]].
zuẹ̄rie see swẹ̄re(n).
zuyft see swift.
zuȳn see swȳn.
zwych see swich.
zwǭ see swā.